REGIONAL APPROACHES TO THE PROTECTION OF ASYLUM SEEKERS

Law and Migration

Series Editor
Satvinder S. Juss, King's College London, UK

Migration and its subsets of refugee and asylum policy are rising up the policy agenda at national and international level. Current controversies underline the need for rational and informed debate of this widely misrepresented and little understood area.

Law and Migration contributes to this debate by establishing a monograph series to encourage discussion and help to inform policy in this area. The series provides a forum for leading new research principally from the Law and Legal Studies area but also from related social sciences. The series is broad in scope, covering a wide range of subjects and perspectives.

Other titles in this series:

Immigration, Integration and the Law
The Intersection of Domestic, EU and International Legal Regimes
Clíodhna Murphy
978-1-4094-6251-4

Migrants and the Courts
A Century of Trial and Error?
Geoffrey Care
978-1-4094-5196-9

Migration, Work and Citizenship in the Enlarged European Union
Samantha Currie
978-0-7546-7351-4

Refugee Law and Practice in Japan
Osamu Arakaki
978-0-7546-7009-4

International Migration and Global Justice
Satvinder Juss
978-0-7546-4671-6 (hbk)
978-0-7546-7289-0 (pbk)

Regional Approaches to the Protection of Asylum Seekers

An International Legal Perspective

Edited by

ADEMOLA ABASS
United Nations University, Belgium

FRANCESCA IPPOLITO
Cagliari University, Italy

ASHGATE

Published by
Ashgate Publishing Limited
Wey Court East
Union Road
Farnham
Surrey, GU9 7PT
England

Ashgate Publishing Company
110 Cherry Street
Suite 3-1
Burlington, VT 05401-3818
USA

www.ashgate.com

British Library Cataloguing in Publication Data
A catalogue record for this book is available from the British Library

The Library of Congress has cataloged the printed edition as follows:
Regional approaches to the protection of asylum seekers : an international legal perspective / edited by Ademola Abass and Francesca Ippolito.
pages cm.—(Law and migration)
Includes bibliographical references and index.
ISBN 978-1-4094-4297-4 (hardback)—ISBN 978-1-4094-4298-1 (ebook)—ISBN 978-1-4094-7458-6 (epub) 1. Refugees—Legal status, laws, etc. 2. Asylum, Right of. I. Abass, Ademola, editor of compilation. II. Ippolito, Francesca, editor of compilation.
K3230.R45R45 2014
342.08'3—dc23

2013041509

ISBN 9781409442974 (hbk)
ISBN 9781409442981 (ebk – PDF)
ISBN 9781409474586 (ebk – ePUB)

MIX
Paper from responsible sources
FSC® C013985

Printed in the United Kingdom by Henry Ling Limited,
at the Dorset Press, Dorchester, DT1 1HD

Contents

Notes on Contributors		*vii*
Preface		*xi*
List of Abbreviations		*xiii*
1	Introduction – Regional Approaches to the Protection of Asylum Seekers: an International Legal Perspective *Ademola Abass and Francesca Ippolito*	1
2	The African Union Legal Framework for Protecting Asylum Seekers *Ademola Abass and Dominique Mystris*	19
3	The Role of the African Human Rights System with Reference to Asylum Seekers *Gino J. Naldi and Cristiano d'Orsi*	45
4	Sub-regional Frameworks for the Protection of Asylum Seekers and Refugees in Africa: Bringing Relief Closer to Trouble Zones *Solomon T. Ebobrah*	67
5	The African National Human Rights Institutions and the Protection of Asylum Seekers: Existing Practices and Opportunities Through the Optional Protocol to the UN Convention Against Torture *Elina Steinerte*	87
6	Establishing the Common European Asylum System: 'it's a long long way to Tipperary' *Francesca Ippolito*	113
7	External Aspects of EU Asylum Law and Policy – 'New' Ways to Address 'Old' Woes *Samantha Velluti*	145

8 The International Protection of Refugees and Asylum Seekers: the Role of Article 3 of the European Convention on Human Rights 171
Colin Harvey

9 'The Right to have Rights': the European Convention on Human Rights and the Procedural Rights of Asylum Seekers 191
Gina Clayton

10 The Protection of Asylum Seekers with Particular Reference to African Women: the Contribution to the Contemporary Jurisprudence 213
Rebecca Wallace

11 Fora and Programmes for Refugees in Latin America 245
Liliana Lyra Jubilut

12 Protection of Asylum Seekers under the Inter-American Human Rights System 267
David James Cantor and Stefania Barichello

13 ASEAN and the Conceptualization of Refugee Protection in Southeastern Asian States 295
Susan Kneebone

14 The 1989 Comprehensive Plan of Action (CPA) and Refugee Policy in Southeast Asia: Twenty Years Forward What Has Changed? 325
Sara E. Davies

15 The Protection of Asylum Seekers in East Asian State Parties to the 1951 Convention Relating to the Status of Refugees and its 1967 Protocol 347
Kelley Loper

16 Conclusions: the Future of the Regional Protection of Asylum Seekers 377
Ademola Abass and Francesca Ippolito

Index *381*

Notes on Contributors

Ademola Abass is Head of the Peace & Security Programme and Research Fellow at the United Nations University, Belgium. He was formerly Professor of International Law and International Organizations at Brunel University, London, and was the African Union's first Expert on Regional Mechanisms. He regularly consults for states and international organizations, and is currently a visiting professor to several universities in Europe and Africa. Professor Abass researches in public international law and peace and security. He is a Fellow of Cambridge Commonwealth, and a member of the Academic Council on the United Nations System (ACUNS).

Stefania Barichello is a Doctoral Candidate at the School of Advanced Study, University of London. Her research focuses on refugee protection and responsibility-sharing in Latin America, primarily the origins, development and implementation of the Mexico Plan of Action. She has previously worked in the fields of Refugee Law, Human Rights and Public International Law. She was an intern with the Brazilian Mission.

Dr David James Cantor is Director of the Refugee Law Initiative and Reader in Human Rights at the School of Advanced Study, University of London. He researches on the protection of refugees and persons displaced by armed conflict and generalized violence in the Andes, Central America and Mexico. His chapter results from the ESRC-funded project *Pushing the Boundaries: New Dynamics of Forced Migration and Transnational Responses in Latin America* (ES/K001051/1).

Gina Clayton has taught and written about immigration and asylum law since 1997. She is the author of the main student textbook on the subject in the UK and a former editor of the *Journal of Immigration Asylum and Nationality Law*. She has a special interest in the human rights of refugees, and is currently involved in grassroots refugee organizations in South Yorkshire and research into the use of internal relocation.

Sara E. Davies is Senior Research Fellow at the Griffith Asia Institute, Griffith University, Australia. She is Convenor of the Prevention of Genocide and Mass Atrocities Program, Asia Pacific Centre for the Responsibility to Protect. Sara's research interests are in global health governance, international refugee law and the responsibility to protect. Sara has authored two books: *Global Politics of*

Health (Polity 2010) and *Legitmiizing Rejection: International Refugee Law in Asia* (Martinus Nijhoff 2008).

Solomon T. Ebobrah, LLB (Rivers State University) and LLM, LLD (University of Pretoria), is Senior Lecturer and Acting Head of the Department of Jurisprudence and Public Law at the Faculty of Law, Niger Delta University, Nigeria and an Extra-Ordinary Lecturer with the Centre for Human Rights, University of Pretoria. He is an editor of the *African Human Rights Law Journal*. Dr Ebobrah has worked as a Senior Legal Officer at the African Commission on Human and Peoples' Rights.

Colin Harvey is Professor of Human Rights Law at Queen's University, Belfast, and served as Head of School 2007–12. He was Professor of Constitutional and Human Rights Law, School of Law, University of Leeds 2000–04 and has held visiting positions at: University of Michigan, Fordham University and the London School of Economics and Political Science. He publishes on human rights law and politics. He is the General Editor of *Human Rights Law in Perspective* (a new series published by Hart Publishing which he founded). He is on the editorial board of *Human Rights Law Review*, *Northern Ireland Legal Quarterly* and *European Human Rights Law Review* and is the Case Editor for the *International Journal of Refugee Law*.

Francesca Ippolito JD (Bologna), PhD (Milan) is currently Assistant Professor of International Law and the European Union at the University of Cagliari, Italy. She served as Consultant in European Union Law at the Foreign Affairs Ministry in Rome and she is currently the project leader of two international research projects on Cooperation Agreements in the Mediterranean and on asylum seekers in Mare Nostrum: a French and Italian appraisal of judicial practice. She was chosen to be a member of the Research Center of the Hague Academy of International Law on International Migrations in 2010 (directors G. Goodwin-Gill and P. Weckel) and has been Visiting Fellow at the School of Law, University of Glasgow as well as Visiting Professor in European Union law in France at the University Montesquieu-Bordeaux IV. Dr Ippolito has written extensively in the area of EU migration and asylum law and non-discrimination.

Liliana Lyra Jubilut, PhD and Masters in International Law (Universidade de São Paulo, Brazil) and LLM in International Legal Studies (NYU School of Law, New York), is Visiting Scholar at the Columbia Law School, Professor of the Post-Graduate Program *Stricto Sensu* in Law at Universidade Católica de Santos, Brazil and has been working with refugee issues in Brazil for 14 years.

Susan Kneebone is a Professor of Law at Monash University. She has published widely on issues of forced migration, human trafficking and refugee law. Since 2003, Kneebone has been a member of the International Association for the Study of Forced Migration (IASFM) and is currently Secretary for IASFM. Professor Kneebone teaches Forced Migration and Human Rights, International Refugee Law and Practice, and Citizenship and Migration Law. Professor Kneebone is the leader of the Asia Pacific Forced Migration Connection (APFMC), established as an Institutional Partner with the Refugee Research Network (RRN – see http://www.refugeeresearch.net/), Refugee Studies Centre Canada.

Kelley Loper is Assistant Professor in the Faculty of Law at the University of Hong Kong. She also serves as the Director of the LLM in Human Rights Programme, Deputy Director of the Centre for Comparative and Public Law, and Co-Editor in Chief of the Asia-Pacific Journal on Human Rights and the Law.

Dominique Mystris is Visiting Lecturer, Bedford University, United Kingdom. She has served both in the United Kingdom and in international research institutions and organizations, including the United Nations University-Institute of Comparative and Regional Integration Studies in Bruges, Belgium; the International Refugee Rights Initiative in Kampala, Uganda; and REDRESS in London. She has consulted for a number of non-profit organizations on human rights issues and developed policy and advocacy approaches. Her research interests lie in the areas of international law, peace and security policy; frameworks for regional organizations; as well as issues pertaining to conflict and post-conflict situations.

Gino J. Naldi, LLM, PhD, spent 30 years in higher education but is presently an independent scholar, specializing in Public International Law and International Human Rights. He has published widely on these subjects with special reference to Africa. He is author, with Professor Konstantin Magliveras, of *The African Union* (Kluwer 2009).

Cristiano d'Orsi is a post-doctoral research scholar at the University of Michigan Law School, affiliated to the Program in Refugee and Asylum Law. He holds a PhD in International Relations (International Law) from the Graduate Institute of International and Development Studies in Geneva and a two-year DEA (Masters equivalent) from the same institution. He also holds a one-year certificate in diplomatic studies from the Italian Society for International Organization in Rome.

Dr Elina Steinerte is Research Associate at the Human Rights Implementation Centre, Law School, University of Bristol. Elina joined the School in June 2006 on a significant AHRC-funded research project examining the implementation of the Optional Protocol to the UN Convention against Torture (OPCAT). Thus Elina has been involved in OPCAT-related processes in over 30 countries and has worked closely with the OHCHR and the Subcommittee on Prevention of Torture. She is the co-author of *The Optional Protocol to the UN Convention against Torture* (OUP 2011).

Samantha Velluti, LLB, LLM, PhD, is currently Reader in EU Law at Lincoln Law School, UK. Previously, she was Lecturer in Law at the School of Law of the University of Manchester and the University of Liverpool. Dr Velluti has researched European Governance extensively, with a particular focus on the relationship between New Governance, law and constitutionalism, including the role of the ECJ, in the policy areas of EU sex equality, employment and migration. Her future research interests are in the promotion of human rights and ILO standards in the EU's Common Commercial Policy. Her forthcoming publication is entitled *Reforming the Common European Asylum System – Legislative Developments and Judicial Activism of the European Courts* (Springer 2013).

Rebecca Wallace, MA, LLB, PhD, is Research Professor of International Human Rights and Justice at Robert Gordon University, Aberdeen. In academia for 37 years she has specialized in international human rights law and has conducted research and written extensively on a wide range of issues including the international protection afforded to marginal groups, corporate social responsibility, sustainable development and migration and human trafficking.

Preface

In bringing this volume together, we hope to address how various regions tackle the asylum crisis through regulatory and institutional frameworks. There is an extensive literature on the asylum crisis but the regional focus of this volume is under-researched. The aim is not to compare one region to another, but to study how individual regions deal with the asylum crisis and whether there are crosscutting issues across the board.

We were very fortunate to work with a very renowned and diverse group of legal scholars who grappled with the varied challenges of asylum in the major regions of the world: Africa, Europe, the Americas, Asia and the Pacific. We hope that readers will benefit considerably from their knowledge and insights about the various themes of their engagement. For their enthusiasm, cooperation and patience we profoundly thank all of them.

At Bruges we were assisted by interns and visiting researchers, whose dedication was critical to bringing the volume to fruition. Special thanks to Silvia Bottega and to Susan Phillips Clavarino for editorial assistance.

We also want to thank the trio of Professor Parvati Nair, Dr Sara Iglesias Sanchez and Dr Thomas Gammeltoft-Hansen, who found time to read several chapters of the book and so kindly offered their words of appreciation.

Our gratitude is also for the Ashgate team who worked with great proficiency, and understanding. Alison Kirk, Sadie Copley-May and Alex Papworth all deserve a big thank you for their excellent work.

Ademola Abass and Francesca Ippolito

A special thanks to my colleague and friend Ademola for his friendship and the guidance. All my love goes to Francesco for his enduring love and for helping me to keep things in perspective. While we were working at this book Sofia was born: this book is dedicated to her, my precious ducky.

F.I.

List of Abbreviations

AALCO	Asian African Legal Consultative Organization
ACDEG	African Charter on Democracy, Elections and Governance
ACHPR	African Commission on Human and Peoples' Rights
ACHR	American Convention on Human Rights
AEC	ASEAN Economic Community
AFSJ	Area of Freedom, Security and Justice
AHRD	ASEAN Human Rights Declarations
AICHR	ASEAN Intergovernmental Commission on Human Rights
AMMTC	ASEAN Ministerial Meeting on Transnational Crime
APC	Inter-governmental Asia-Pacific Consultations on Refugees, Displaced Persons and Migrants
APD	Asylum Procedures Directive
APSA	African Peace and Security Architecture
APSC	ASEAN Political-Security Community
ASCC	ASEAN Socio-Cultural Community
ASEAN	Association of the Southeast Asian Nations
AU	African Union
BIA	United States Board of Immigration Appeals
BPEAR	Bureau for the Placement and Education of African Refugees
CCAR	Coordinating Committee on Assistance and Protection to Refugees and Internally Displaced Persons in Africa
CEAS	Common European Asylum System
CEDAW	The Convention on the Elimination of all Forms of Discrimination Against Women
CHRAJ	Commission on Human Rights Administrative Justice in Ghana
CJEU	Court of Justice of the European Union
COPAX	Council for Peace and Security in Central Africa
CPA	Comprehensive Plan of Action
CPP	Comprehensive Peace Plan
DAR	Development Assistance for Refugees
DRC	Democratic Republic of Congo
EAC	East African Community

EASO	European Asylum Support Office
EC	European Community
ECCAS	Economic Community of Central African States
ECHR	European Court of Human Rights
ECOWAS	Economic Community of West African States
ERF III	European Refugee Fund
EU	European Union
EUCFR	EU Charter of Fundamental Rights of the European Union
FGM	Female Genital Mutilation
GAM	Global Approach to Migration
GFC	Global Financial Crisis
HARDP	Humanitarian Affairs, Refugee and Displaced Persons Division
HLWG	HighLevel Working Group
HPA	Hanoi Plan of Action
IACHR	Inter-American Commission on Human Rights
IACrtHR	Inter-American Court of Human Rights
IBM	Integrated Border Management
ICARA	International Conference on Assistance to Refugees in Africa
ICC	International Criminal Court
ICCom	International Coordinating Committee of National Institutions
ICCom Sub-committee	Sub-committee on Accreditation
ICCPR	International Covenant on Civil and Political Rights
ICEM	Inter-governmental Committee for European Migration (now International Organization for Migration)
ICGLR	International Conference on the Great Lakes Region
ICTR	International Criminal Tribunal Rwanda
IDP	Internally Displaced Persons
IGAD	Intergovernmental Authority for Development
IGADD	Intergovernmental Authority on Drought and Development
JHA	Justice and Home Affairs
KNHRC	Kenya National Human Rights Commission
MEDA	Mésures D'Accompagnement
NGO	Non-governmental Organization
NHRC	International Human Rights Commissions
NHRI	National Human Rights Institutes/Institutitutions
NPM	National Preventive Mechanisms
OAS	Organization of American States
OAU	Organization of African Unity

ODP	Orderly Departure Program
OHCHR	Office of the High Commissioner for Human Rights
OPCAT	Optional Protocol to the Convention Against Torture
ORP	Orderly Return Programme
PCC	Public Complaints Commission
PEP	Protected Entry Procedure
PHARE	Poland and Hungary Assistance for Restructuring their Economies
PRC	Permanent Representatives' Committee
PSC	Peace and Security Council
PSG	Particular Social Group
R2P	Responsibility to Protect
RABIT	RAPID Border Intervention Teams
RCM	Regional Conference on Migration
REC	Regional Economic Community
RPP	Regional Protection Programmes
RWLG	Refugee Women's Legal Group
SADC	Southern African Development Community
SADCC	Southern African Development Coordination Conference
SAHRC	South African Human Rights Commission
SPT	Sub-committee on Prevention of Torture and other Cruel, Inhuman or Degrading Treatment or Punishment
TACIS	Technical Assistance to the Commonwealth of Independent States
TFEU	Treaty on the Functioning of the European Union
ToA	Treaty of Amsterdam
ToL	Treaty of Lisbon
UN	United Nations
UNCHR	United Nations High Commissioner for Refugees
UNDP	United Nations Development Programme
VAP	Vientiane Action Plan
Western NIS	Western Newly Independent States

Chapter 1
Introduction – Regional Approaches to the Protection of Asylum Seekers: an International Legal Perspective

Ademola Abass and Francesca Ippolito

An Overview

Few issues have proved to be more contentious in academic and policy discourse than the protection of asylum seekers. Although the vast majority of States accept, as a matter of principle, that people fleeing persecutions in their own countries for various reasons deserve refuge in foreign lands, deciding who amongst the needy millions should be catered for, and according to whose regulations and for how long, has proved to be more daunting than rocket science.

Many domestic laws governing the protection of asylum seekers often clash with those emanating from such multilateral bodies as regional organizations to which almost every single State in the world belongs. For their own, regional organizations often adopt asylum-specific and general human rights treaties which regional adjudicatory bodies apply in a way that frequently create tension between the organizations and their Member States. International reactions to the asylum protection crisis have suffered as much from truculent politicization of facts and figures as they have from the absence of a genuine desire by States to establish coherent, systematized and standardized legal regimes for protecting asylum seekers. While some States regard the asylum issue as one which deserves a systematic and coherent development, the majority of States view the asylum *problematique* through the lens of security. Not only does such 'securitization' of the asylum theme routinely downgrade the humanitarian essence of asylum concerns, but also it renders policy consideration of asylum issues as a handmaid of more egregious security concerns of States.

Perhaps the politicization of the asylum crisis by States is only surpassed by the polarization of academic views on the crisis. Discussions and discourses on the asylum crisis, on whatever fora such are expressed, are often characterized by a perfunctory adumbration of the issues in bland, binary terms: developing countries are mainly responsible for generating asylum seekers while developed countries provide refuge to the greatest numbers of the world's refugees; Western and rich States are at the forefront of developing effective legal and institutional frameworks for the protection of asylum seekers while developing and poor countries eternally grope for what to do; asylum is mostly a consequence of Third World countries' interminable conflicts; the list of such entrenched commonalities is endless.

Not only have some conflicts, such as the one in Eritrea in the 1990s, punctured the assumed correlation between conflicts and refugee outflows, it will also be seen later that there is currently irrefutable evidence that the majority of the world's refugees are catered for not by Western countries, but by their developing counterparts which, admittedly, generate the largest numbers of the world's asylum seekers.

Academic treatment of the asylum subject is extensive, and whole libraries have been written on various issues concerning asylum. The vast majority of writers agree that the attitude of most States towards the asylum crisis has more been driven by security considerations rather than by any altruistic desire to pursue a genuine development of the subject matter. Even then the majority of existing studies on the asylum theme address their subject matter from a rather restrictive perspective, focusing principally on the causes and consequences of asylum or on the examination of States' compliance with the various obligations they assume under international or regional regimes. Often, writers focus mainly on issues affecting asylum seekers within specific geographic areas. Some of the more recent works on the subject matter have tended to focus on the weaknesses and unintended consequences of the international and Europe-specific legal and policy frameworks on refugees and asylum, such as the 1951 UN Convention and the 1967 Geneva Protocol, the Dublin (I, II and III) Regulation and the ECHR (European Court of Human Rights) strategies *inter alia*.

While existing literature makes valuable contributions to our understanding of the asylum crisis, the issue of how different regions of the world deal with this crisis through regulatory frameworks remains grossly understudied. The asylum protection crisis is complex and multidimensional. While there are incontrovertible similarities in the problems affecting asylum seekers worldwide, multiple differences arising from cultural, regional and institutional idiosyncrasies also abound. This book provides an analysis of the asylum crisis with particular focus on the regional legal regimes for protecting asylum seekers in Africa, Europe, Latin America and the South Asia.

This book does not cover the problems faced by individual countries in these regions *per se*, except insofar as such a remit is indispensable to the study of the particular region. The book's principal objective is to seek an understanding of what legal regime exists, at the level of regional organizations in each region, for the protection of asylum seekers, and how regional institutions such as human rights commissions and regional courts enforce and adjudicate the laws. Particular attention is thus paid to the African Union, the European Union, the Inter-American Organization, and the Association of the South East Asian (ASEAN) among others. This continental approach, it should be noted, is sometimes complemented by an examination of what happens at the sub-regional level where, for instance, sub-regional organizations are found to develop parallel legal regimes of their own even if such are complementary to the continental structures.

Defining 'Asylum Crisis'

The phrase 'asylum protection crisis' or 'asylum crisis', which is the subject of this book, has come to represent different things to different users. Sometimes it is used to depict the state of confusion and uncertainty that characterize the processes and procedures through which governments decide to accept or reject foreigners who seek refuge in their countries. Often, the term is used to describe disastrous humanitarianism, implying, *inter alia*, the shabby and unpalatable treatment of asylum seekers by their host States, governmental entities or even by ordinary citizens. The phrase has also been used sometimes to refer to the absence of appropriate legal and policy instruments to anchor a decisive and effective asylum regime. In this book, we use 'asylum protection crisis' or 'asylum crisis' interchangeably as connoting the crisis affecting the legal protection of asylum seekers.

The real crisis with asylum protection is not necessarily due to the absence of the relevant laws or policies, or the lack of international and national regulatory mechanisms for ensuring that the passage of those genuinely fleeing death and other life-threatening situations is not made any more excoriating than is absolutely necessary. The heart of the matter, so to speak, lies squarely in the interplay of several variables – laws, cultures and norms – that shape how the fate of asylum seekers is determined by their host States. By the law and policies of most States, asylum seekers are expected to convince their putative host State of their plights through stories expected to be told with brutal consistency and accuracy, and with solid conformity to the dialectics and cultural imperatives of that State, regardless, in most times, of the peculiarities of the applicant's own experiences or cultural existence which might make such expectations unrealistic.

Both at the international and the national level, States assume various obligations towards asylum seekers. However, the performance of these obligations, almost invariably, is a function of how sensitive and aware the host States are of the circumstances of asylum seekers, as well as of the situations in the countries that produce them. Although these conditions might appear rather simplistic and banal, and come across as the minimum qualities that host States should expectedly possess in dealing with asylum seekers, the reality is different and humbling. With disturbing alacrity, many host States continue to make dangerous assumptions both about the asylum seekers and their States of origin with devastating consequences. From the moment an asylum seeker steps onto the shore of a potential host country, a game of cat-and-mouse ensues between the asylum seeker and the myriad governmental agencies assembled to 'process' him/her into a potential 'refugee'. However, unlike the mouse in the familiar anecdote – where the chase is enacted in a level playing ground – the mouse in the asylum game is often blindfolded by different layers of disorientating laws and documentations, and many convoluted interview processes largely designed to catch it out, often on the most trivial slip-up that inevitably lands it on the wrong side of the eagle-eyed cat – the host State.

Thus, the notion of 'asylum crisis' as used in this book is much wider than the generalized issues of confusion and uncertainty – which are, in any case, incontrovertible. It encompasses the consistent misunderstanding of the asylum seeker's cultural and personal idiosyncrasies, which often directly impact on their attitude and response to the process that aims at transposing them from their countries of origin to their new States. These idiosyncrasies are many and, as will be seen later, range from the personal to the cultural, from the social to the political. But regardless of the varied dynamics of these factors, an acute understanding of them will go a long way in enhancing how regional systems deal with refugees and asylum seekers in particular which, in turn, should substantially address the various deficits in the asylum process.

The Asylum Crisis: Facts, Figures and Myths

The polarized nature of the academic and policy discourse of the asylum-crisis theme is incorrigibly conducive to the distillation of myths and the bandying of 'facts' and 'figures' that are more products of exuberant imagination than being evidences of veritable research. It is commonplace, for instance, to read, especially in the media, that the sub-Saharan Africa generates the highest number of refugees worldwide, and that Western States, especially in Europe, play host to the largest portions of refugees at any given time. Moreover, the picture is perpetually painted of continuous and unabating outflows of refugees from Africa and other developing parts of the world to the West with little or no recognition of efforts made by such regions towards alleviating or sharing the asylum burden.

Apart from implicitly correcting pervasive erroneous assumptions about facts and figures concerning the current state of asylum and refugee in the world today, available statistics also controvert some of the most eagerly promoted myths about the origin of refugees and responsibility bearing for asylum: that Europe, for instance, produces fewer refugees but shoulders a disproportionate responsibility for refugees and asylum seekers than other regions of the world. As will be seen later, the hosting of refugees generated in Africa within Africa is important to the examination of how Africa, as a region (rather than the African Union or African regional organizations), deals and copes with the scourge of asylum seekers and refugees compared to Europe. Also noticeable in the statistics is the rarely acknowledged fact that the poorest countries of the world do actually shoulder a heavier financial burden for refugees per capita compared to their Western counterparts. For instance,

> At the end of 2009, Pakistan was hosting the highest number of refugees compared to its national economy. As such, it hosted 745 refugees per 1 USD GDP (PPP) per capita. The Democratic Republic of Congo was second with 592 refugees per 1 USD GDP (PPP) per capita, followed by Zimbabwe (527), the Syrian Arab Republic (244), and Kenya (237). The first developed country was Germany at 26th place with 17 refugees per USD GDP (PPP) per capita.[1]

One of the consequences of ventilating myths about refugees and asylum, aside from pandering to Far-rightism in Europe and elsewhere, is feeding the citizens' frenzy and imagination that bedlam is the inevitable consequence of asylum-friendly policies. Precipitously, many European countries have devised methods and processes, which are arguably deliberately geared towards ensuring that asylum seekers are prevented from setting their foot within their shores, at which point it may be a little too late for such States to prevent the application of international legal and policy frameworks. So draconian have some of these processes and treatments of asylum seekers become in Europe that the United Nations High Commissioner for Refugees (UNHCR) observes that

> The conditions for asylum-seekers in Greece, which is among the principal entry points to the EU, are notoriously difficult. Most asylum-seekers receive no assistance. Many live on streets, including women and children. The refugee status determination system does not operate properly and as a result, persons needing international protection are not identified as such. This is a humanitarian crisis situation which should not exist in the European Union.[2]

Such debilitating developments have also been condemned by two principal judicial bodies: the European Court of Human Rights and the Court of Justice of the European Union respectively in *M.S.S. v Belgium and Greece*[3] and *N.S. and M.E.*[4]

Irrefutable evidence also reveals that Latin American countries host a total of more than 400,000 refugees, asylum seekers and others in need of international protection. Since the adoption of the Mexico Plan of Action in 2004 (see below), the legal framework for the protection of refugees in the region has improved. With the addition of Colombia and Chile, a total of 14 Latin American countries

---

1 UNHCR Global Trend 2011, available at http://www.unhcr.org/4fd6f87f9.pdf [last accessed 04/6/2013].

2 UNHCR spokesperson Adrian Edwards at the press briefing on 21 September 2010 at the Palais des Nations in Geneva, available at http://www.unhcr.org/4c98a0ac9.html [last accessed 04/6/2013]. See also Commissioner for Human Rights of the Council of Europe, CommDH (2009) 6 February 2009, available at http://cmr.jur.ru.nl/cmr/docs/CHR.2009.greece.pdf [last accessed 04/6/2013].

3 ECtHR, *M.S.S. v Belgium and Greece* (App no 30696/09) 21 January 2011.

4 CJEU, Joined cases C-411/10 e C-493/10, *N.S. and M.E.*, judgment of 21 December 2011, not yet reported.

have now included the broader definition of refugee, contained in the 1984 Cartagena Declaration on Refugees, in their domestic legal systems. One of the aims of this work is therefore not only to recognize the important contribution of Latin America and the Inter-American System to the international protection of asylum seekers through the Cartagena Declaration, but to also seek to understand such progress through the compendium of principles, norms and jurisprudence of the Inter-American Commission and the Inter-American Court of Human Rights, as well as consider the impact of the Brasilia Declaration on the protection of asylum seekers.

The population movements in the Asia-Pacific region are no less complex and multi-layered with people coming into, as well as moving within, the region for a variety of reasons. Therefore, an exploration of how regionally consistent and coherent processes and practices have been established in the Asia-Pacific is crucial in order for States to better determine, in practical ways, where the responsibility for the processing of individual cases under these arrangements lie. Thus the book considers the role ASEAN plays in promoting 'neighbourliness' and human rights in Southeast Asia, especially considering that it is currently developing a Charter on Human Rights. This development follows on from the enshrining of refugee rights in the Southeast Asia Final Text of the Asian African Legal Consultative Organization (AALCO) and the 1966 Bangkok Principles on Status and Treatment of Refugees (2001).

The Scope of this Book

This book has two main remits. First, it inquires into the various factors that make the objectives sought by both asylum-producing and asylum-receiving States, such as speedy and fair processing of asylum seekers' applications, among others, almost impossible to achieve. In particular the book considers cogent issues undermining an effective asylum process in Europe, Africa, Asia and Latin America. The book tackles why most European asylum-receiving States have difficulties dealing with the various circumstances concerning African asylum seekers. The book probes into the relatively unexplored but fundamental challenges that constantly undermine international efforts at dealing with the asylum crisis. Such issues include, but are not limited to, the evolution and implications of the 'push-back' strategy adopted by certain European States to curtail international legal obligations; the impact of State/society interrelation on asylum-seeking; and the hindrance constituted by importunate and flawed assumptions about asylum seekers and their States of origin by the receiving States.

Secondly, the book discusses the nature of the regional protection of asylum seekers within the existing regional systems and asks what shapes individual regional experiences and how regional institutions deal with the crisis. European institutions – in particular, the European Court of Human Rights and the European Court of Justice – play a crucial role in developing the international legal jurisprudence on asylum and refugees and, to a reasonable extent, in setting standards that are often reflected in policy-making on the subject matter. The African and Inter-American counterparts – the African Commission on Human and Peoples' Rights (ACHPR, hereafter African Commission) and the Inter-American Commission and Court of Human Rights (hereafter IACHR) – have not traditionally dealt with such issues as asylum-seeking. This is primarily because unlike the EU system, under which the European Community exercises jurisdiction on asylum, such issues have largely remained under individual States' competence in Africa. However, the recent inauguration of the African Court of Human and Peoples' Rights and Justice is certain to alter this picture. Also, more recently, the African Commission has been playing a more visible and active role in the protection of human rights of Africans. It will therefore be useful to discuss the protection of asylum seekers within the African human rights system. In Latin America, States have greatly contributed to the development of safeguards for the care and protection of refugees through regional consultative migration *fora*. But a significant role in this regard has been increasingly played by the IACHR, and may be played in the future also by the Inter-American Court of Human Rights (IACt).

It is worth mentioning that while the primary focus of this book is to study how regional integration processes, such as the Europe Union and African Union, deal with the asylum crisis, the book is not so confined. Thus discussions often include the roles played by national institutions and practices of individual States where such contributions are so vital as to justify their inclusions. The chapters by Elina Steinerte and Rebecca Wallace are examples of such contributions.

Structure

In addition to this introduction, the book consists of 15 other chapters, including the conclusion, divided into four parts. In Chapter 2, Ademola Abass and Dominique Mystris examine the development of Africa's legal and policy frameworks on asylum protection. However, rather than repeat the extensively remarked pivotal and standard-setting legal regimes developed by the Organization of African Unity (OAU), this chapter briefly outlines the major contributions of the OAU legal regimes and moves swiftly to consider whether the advent of the African Union (AU) engenders any significant development in African regional law on the protection of asylum seekers. It also considers whether the emergence of such organs and institutions of the AU as the Peace and Security Council (PSC) has altered the landscape of asylum protection in Africa.

The emergence of the AU coincided with the exacerbation of conflicts in Africa. From the Democratic Republic of Congo (DRC) to Darfur, from Niger to Chad, African countries have witnessed if not an increase in the cases of armed conflicts, definitely a resuscitation of some of the old. One of the (unavoidable?) consequences of these conflicts is the extensive displacing of people either within their countries (thus constituting them as internally displaced persons or IDPs) or refugees.

Ingeniously, the OAU Convention on asylum extends the definition of asylum – and the conditions warranting the grant of asylum – beyond the one offered by the UN in 1951, and has accordingly been credited with being the first truly universal instrument of this nature. Several commentators on asylum (Grahl-Madsen, Rifaat and so on) have written considerably on the innovations of the OAU Convention on asylum. Such works, however, deal more with hypothetical situations especially since they were published in the early 1980s, a period when the asylum and refugee crisis in Africa was not as challenging as today, and when there was virtually no interaction between Africa and Europe on this issue. It was a period when Africa had to deal more with IDPs than refugees, at least on a scale that inspired the present work.

Before the inauguration of the African Court, protecting the rights of asylum seekers, as with other more generic human rights issues in Africa, fell on the African Commission. Gino J. Naldi and Cristiano d'Orsi's chapter reviews the work of the Commission from its inception until the period when the African Court went operational. Since the Court now has the adjudicatory role over the protection of asylum seekers, its functions displace the role previously played by the Commission in this regard although the latter remains the institution with oversight responsibility for human rights in Africa. Naldi and d'Orsi also consider the role of the African Court in protecting the rights of the asylum seekers.

The African Court went through a long period of gestation for many reasons but principally because most African States were reluctant to concede to the Court any serious human rights jurisdiction. Human rights were one of the most jealously guarded subjects by many African States and a turning point in this attitude only came when the AU jettisoned the notorious non-interference principle of the OAU (the shield with which the defunct organization prevented international scrutiny of its activities) for the principle of non-indifference. The endorsement by several African States of the principle of Responsibility to Protect (R2P) adopted by the General Assembly in 2005, a few months after the AU adopted a similar principle at Ezulwini in Swaziland, proved to be the final nail in the coffin of the non-interference principle. The mellowing of African States' adherence to absolute sovereignty and non-interference doctrines has enabled the installation of institutions, such as the African Court, that will hopefully play a more robust and decisive role in the protection of human rights in Africa.[5] Thus, Naldi and

5 For analysis of potential challenges to the role of the African Court of Human and Peoples' Rights and Justice in dispensing its criminal jurisdiction, see Ademola Abass, 'Prosecuting International Crimes in Africa: Rationale, Prospects and Challenges' (2013) 24(3) European Journal of International Law 933–46); Ademola Abass, 'The Proposed International Criminal Jurisdiction for the African Court: Some Problematic Aspects' (2013) Netherlands International Law Review LX 27–50; Frans Viljoen, 'AU Assembly should consider human rights implications before adopting the Amending Merged African

d'Orsi's chapter is an early assessment of whether the constitutive aspirations of the African Union legal regimes on the matter of human rights protection are being realized through an independent and astute regional judicial body.

The examination of the African regional frameworks for dealing with asylum-seeking is further strengthened by Solomon T. Ebobrah who, in Chapter 4, investigates the approach of the Regional Economic Communities (RECs) in Africa to the asylum crisis. These sub-regional groupings are famous for developing parallel mechanisms to the continent-wide system in Africa. Although RECs are envisaged by the African Peace and Security Architecture (APSA) to be the building blocks of regional peace and security in Africa,[6] and are expected to coordinate their activities with the AU, the truth remains that some RECs have better developed regulatory and institutional mechanisms than the AU itself. It is accepted by many commentators on African affairs that RECs, especially the Economic Community of West African States) (ECOWAS) outpace the AU in most areas covered by APSA, particularly on themes concerning the protection of human security, such that the issue of asylum undoubtedly is.[7] Therefore, this chapter offers an analysis of the implications of APSA for asylum-seeking in Africa.

The ability of regional systems to effectively and robustly protect legal norms, as the rights of asylum seekers, is often a reflection of the national institutions of the States that make up the concerned regional system. National institutions thus play a critical role in articulating and defending national (and international) law and policies and this will be crucial to how individual States support law and policies when they become regional norms. The role played by national human rights institutions (NHRIs) is prescient in the universal desire to achieve a more efficient and sane asylum system. Elina Steinerte's chapter examines how NHRIs and national courts in particular deal with the asylum crisis. NHRIs play a different role to the courts.

Whereas NHRIs engage mainly in the protection and promotion of asylum seekers' rights, as Steinerte demonstrates in Chapter 5, courts play the last-resort role when all else has failed. That does not mean that there is a given understanding of what NHRIs do. Typologies vary between those that are more traditional, such as Public Complaint Commissions (PCCs) (also known as Ombudsman) and those that are more modern. Ombudsmen are usually one-man/one-woman bodies established by States to receive complaints from aggrieved citizens and conduct inspections in respect of such claims. But there are also the national human rights

Court Protocol', African Law 23/12/2012, available at http://africlaw.com/2012/05/23/au-assembly-should-consider-human-rights-implications-before-adopting-the-amending-merged-african-court-protocol/ [last accessed 04/6/2013].

6 Art 16 Protocol Establishing the Peace and Security Council of the African Union, available at http://www.au.int/en/sites/default/files/Protocol_peace_and_security.pdf [last accessed on 04/6/2013].

7 See A Abass (ed.), *Protecting Human Security in Africa* (Oxford University Press, 2010).

commissions (NHRCs) which are more common nowadays, and which undertake much wider tasks than ombudsmen and are, at least theoretically, more independent of the governments. Steinerte discusses the premise of the various instruments concerning NHRIs, such as the Paris Principles and the Kigali Declaration, and examines some of the challenges faced by such institutions in the implementation of their mandates.

More often than not, the decisions of NHRIs (whether NHRCs or PCCs) do not bind the States that set them up. Since most decisions made by these bodies are recommendatory in nature, States are largely at liberty to either implement them or not. On the contrary, decisions of regional human rights commissions and courts or tribunals are binding on States even if, as is common in Africa, States regularly disobey and ignore court orders in unfortunate acts of executive lawlessness.

The second section of the book deals with the approach of the European region towards protecting asylum seekers. While available statistics on refugee and asylum-seeking grossly undermine the assertion that European countries are the biggest host of refugees or the highest recipient of asylum applications, the fact still remains that Europe remains a destination of choice for thousands of those who decide to seek asylum outside their country of origin. Arguably, the EU has the most comprehensive and perhaps the most sophisticated frameworks for dealing with asylum seekers. Indeed, in no other region has the complex relation between a regional organization's asylum framework and its Member States' legislation on asylum on the one hand, and the views of States on the laws and the regional court's jurisprudence on the other come under such intense scrutiny as in Europe. The chapters in this section engage with these varied, enthralling and often intriguing contours.

Francesca Ippolito's chapter and Samantha Velluti's chapter (6 and 7) both tackle Europe's approach towards protecting asylum seekers since the emergence of the Amsterdam Treaty. Ippolito examines the State of play of the Common European Asylum System (CEAS), particularly in light of the EU's salutary effort to recast most of its existing legislation governing asylum and other forms of international protection. The dynamics relating to identifying which State is responsible for determining an asylum application lodged by a Member State by a national of a third State is as complex as ensuring that the various procedures for securing the rights and entitlements of an asylum seeker conform to requisite international human rights standards. The intersection between the obligations set out in the Dublin Directive, which applies to the former situation, and the Procedure and Reception Directives, concerning the latter situation, receive a deft analysis in Ippolito's chapter.

The aims of Velluti's chapter are at one and the same time tantalizing and refreshing. In recognition of Europe's peculiar status as the region with the strongest magnet for asylum seekers, Velluti inquires into the double-pronged strategy of the EU towards dealing with the asylum crisis. She engages variously with the EU's new approach, which focuses on cooperation with refugee sending and transit countries. The EU's nascent approach, on the one hand, attempts to restrict access to asylum systems by externalizing traditional domestic or EU migration control measures while, on the other hand, it addresses the root causes of migration and refugee flows thereby providing refugees with access to protection in regions of their origin. Within the context of the external and internal dimensions of the EU strategy, Velluti analyses the content of such unfolding EU asylum and migration policy as 'external governance', 'externalization' or 'extra-territorialization'.

Aside from the collective role that the EU plays in protecting the rights of asylum seekers, such European institutions as the ECHR have also emerged as veritable bodies for vindicating the rights of asylum seekers. Although the ECHR itself does not provide for asylum-based rights, the ECtHR has pronounced that

> … in exercising their right to expel such aliens, Contracting States must have regard to Article 3 of the Convention which enshrines one of the fundamental values of democratic societies and prohibits in absolute terms torture or inhuman or degrading treatment or punishment, irrespective of the victim's conduct, however undesirable or dangerous. The expulsion of an alien may give rise to an issue under this provision, and hence engage the responsibility of the expelling State under the Convention, where substantial grounds have been shown for believing that the person in question, if expelled, would face a real risk of being subjected to treatment contrary to Article 3 in the receiving country. In such circumstances, Article 3 implies an obligation not to expel the individual to that country.[8]

Indeed, it is in the framework of Article 3 of the ECHR that asylum applications have mostly been brought before the ECtHR, despite the fact that, as already noted, the ECHR does not contain asylum-specific provisions. Colin Harvey's contribution in Chapter 8 grapples with the various contours of the application of Article 3 to asylum cases and the attempts by many EU States to roll back on the remarkable advancement made by the ECHR in creatively accommodating asylum cases under Article 3. While the Court, on its own, requires that certain conditions must exist before it could successfully apply Article 3 to asylum cases, EU States have stepped up their efforts to circumvent Article 3 by securitizing the provision. Most States now claim that national security considerations justify the curtailing of Article 3 despite the fact that conditions inimical to the asylum seekers await them in their countries upon deportation.

8 *Salah Sheekh v the Netherlands* (App no 1948/04), judgment of 11 January 2007, para 135. The application of Article 3 to asylum issues had already been specifically admitted by the Court in *Cruz Varas and others v Sweden* (App no 15576/89), judgment of 20 March 1991; *Vilvarajah and others v the United Kingdom* (App nos 13163/87, 13164/87 and 13165/87), judgment of 30 October 1991; *Chahal v the United Kingdom* (App no 22414/93), judgment of 15 November 1996; and *Amuur v France* (App no 19776/92), judgment of 25 June 1996. It has also been reaffirmed in *Saadi v Italy* (App no 37201/06), judgment [GC] of 28 February 2008 and in subsequent case law.

The manner in which the European Court of Human Rights has consistently adverted the 'spirit' of the ECHR (European Convention of Human Rights) towards protecting asylum seekers, despite the absence of any specific provisions in the Convention covering that category of people, deserves a special mention. The wide array of cases surveyed by Gina Clayton reveals the spirited attempts by the States Parties to the ECHR to either narrowly interpret or altogether truncate the application of the ECHR to asylum seekers through what one commentator has poignantly referred to as procedural sophistications.

In testimony to the increasing vigilance of the Court to the weight given by States to the asylum seekers' evidence, and to its paying greater attention to the substantive evidence given by the asylum seeker, the ECrtHR robustly applies the various provisions of the Convention in situations where less ambitious judicial bodies would have been remiss. The Court applies Article 4 of Protocol Nos 4, 6, 13, amongst others, in such a way that while preserving the sovereign right of the Convention Parties to determine who to allow or not allow on their territory, it prevents such decisions from being based on processes that disregard States' overarching obligation under the Convention.

Arguably, nowhere is the Court's robust approach to protecting asylum seekers' rights more compelling than in its dealing with the effect of the Grand Chamber's explicit exclusion of Article 6 (fair trial in criminal matter) from applying to immigration and asylum seekers. What the Court has done, as Clayton's chapter shows, is not to pursue the 'fair trial' jurisprudence route, but rather to develop, within Article 13, the concept of 'fairness' that focuses on whether the procedure adopted by States provides protection against *refoulement.* In this way, the Court has repeatedly been able to roll back on States' recourse to such processes as 'accelerated procedures' and 'push back' on the sea, amongst others, to trump asylum seekers' rights.

In Chapter 10 Rebecca Wallace offers an insightful analysis of how African asylum cases, especially concerning women, have influenced the international legal jurisprudence on the protection of women asylum seekers. Certain cultural idiosyncrasies of female African asylum seekers (for example silences) are routinely treated as evidence of dubiety by several refugee-receiving European States. But the travail of African women asylum seekers does not stop at that. If their situations do make it to the court, they confront a different kind of challenge: the applicability of the concept 'particular social group' (PSG) to female African asylum seekers in particular. There is no doubt that the rationale behind this concept is to ensure that only those who constitute a particular group (and really desire protection) are accorded the status of refugee. Comparable international concepts include the concept of 'protected group', found in the 1948 Genocide Convention, which is aimed at assisting a court to determine whether those who are targeted by genocidaires fall within the 'protected group' for the purpose of establishing the culpability of the perpetrators.

However, the fact that the evolution of international refugee law and policies are male-dominated and orientated means that the such laws, policies, as well as judicial interpretation of the 'particular social group' concept was, for a long time, disastrously insensitive to the plights of women in general, and of African women in particular, given the already referred cultural predilections of the latter category. The lethargic legislative and policy attitude towards female refugees began with the ignominious absence of women and gender-specific issues in both the UN 1951 Refugee Convention and the 1967 New York Protocol. This rather costly omission was partly due to the UN's hope, in the 1950s, that the 'refugee situation' would be short-lived, a hope that was reflected in the fact that the UNHCR was originally given a three-year mandate period to help settle the Second World War refugees. Also, whereas the 1951 Convention, as with most others, concerned itself mainly with refugee-generating conditions occasioned or perpetrated by the State, it is beyond doubt that the situations that cause harm to women often originate from non-State actors. Indeed, it was not until 1993 that the international asylum system provided for the first wave of skilled female interviewers in refugee-status determination procedures.

Wallace surveys a cavalcade of important cases and portrays the characteristically inconsistent manner in which the courts have dealt with such principles as the PSG. What these cases demonstrate is precisely how more developed legal traditions, such as in the UK, have applied such human rights terms and standards as Gino Naldi discusses in relation to the African Human Rights Commission. Wallace's chapter therefore completes the picture about the judicial attitude towards applying 'universal' terms to the particularized world of asylum seekers and refugees.

The experience of the Latin American region in dealing with asylum seekers is rich and varied. Not only is Latin America a pioneer, of some sort, in developing a systematic regional agenda for dealing with asylum seekers, it is also the region where the academics have taken the leadership in propelling States towards establishing a comprehensive approach to the subject through the creation of what Liliana Lyra Jubilut has called 'fora and programs' in Chapter 11. The Specialized Migratory Forum of MERCOSUR and the Regional Conference on Migration (RCM) are examples of such fora and programs which serve as the regional platform in the Americas for the exchange of information and good practices with regard to refugee and migrant protection. The organic mapping of the regional path by the Cartagena Declaration is sustained and strengthened by a variety of such other constitutive efforts as the 2004 Mexican Plan of Action. Liliana Lyra Jubilut and Cantor and Barichello's chapters (that form the third section of the book) provide a comprehensive analysis of the Latin American regime from divergent perspectives.

The Inter-American Court of Human Rights and the Inter-American Commission on Human Rights have, as with their African and European counterparts discussed above, had to shoulder a heavy responsibility with regards to the application of the various legal regimes governing asylum protection in Latin America as discussed in Jubilut's chapter. Cantor and Barichello's contribution analyses the new 'complementary' human rights framework for refugees and asylum seekers developed by the Inter-American human rights system. The authors especially inquire how 'the recent distinctive and progressive "jurisprudence" on point from the system's main institutions – the Inter-American Commission of Human Rights and the Court – advances the frontiers of international legal protection for such persons'. The crux of the contribution is to demonstrate that the Inter-American human rights system thus provides complementary protection to asylum seekers.[9]

The subtle and often open tension between States Parties to various international and regional legal frameworks, and regional enforcement and adjudicatory mechanisms are all very well witnessed in the literature and jurisprudence on asylum/refugee protection in Africa, Europe and Latin America. Although States parties in these regions continue to find ways to minimize some of their international obligations, with regional courts doing their best to keep them in check, this 'game' is made possible because the majority of the States in these regions accept their core obligations towards asylum seekers under international and regional instruments in the first place. The reality, which is often taken for granted, makes all the difference between the State of asylum protection in these three regions and the experience in the Asia-Pacific region. Not only have the majority of States in this region not acceded to either or both of the 1951 Refugee Convention of the 1967 Protocol, but there are also no corresponding legal regimes or systematic and effective processes of asylum protection in the region.

The tragedy of the pallid state of asylum protection in the Asia-Pacific region is made more complex by the fact that this region, on its own, is accountable for nearly one-third of the world's population. Asia Pacific is also a the third largest host region of the people living in 'protracted situations', that is those who have lived for more than five years in detention camps without the prospect of either being formally accepted as refugees by their host States, or being treated fairly under the international refugee law minimum standards. As seen in Susan Kneebone's opening chapter in this section (Chapter 13), the region has 10 million people (including internationally displaced persons) who are of interest to the UNHCR. This number represents a third of the global refugee output.

Kneebone's chapter discusses the conceptual problems of asylum protection in the Asia-Pacific region. By focusing on the regional organization ASEAN, she reveals that the foundation of this region's asylum crisis lies in the conceptualization of the refugee/asylum/migration issue in security terms. Thus, the regional approach is one that essentially sees the problem as an 'irregular migration' issue.

---

9 KW Yundt, 'The Organization of American States and Legal Protection to Political Refugees in Central America' (1989) 23 International Migration Review 201; MC Pulido and M Blanchard, 'La Comisión Interamericana de Derechos Humanos y sus mecanismos de protección aplicados a la situación de los refugiados, apátridas y solicitantes de asilo' in L Franco (ed.), *El asilo y la protección internacional de los refugiados en América Latina* (Editorama, 2004).

Yet, this is a region that strongly recognizes the need to develop a strong normative foundation for refugees and asylum seekers by building a bridge across different regions. Through the (1966) AALCO and Bangkok Principles on Status and Treatment of Refugees (2001), the Asia-Pacific region pioneered the recognition of a regional solution to the refugee/asylum crisis as well as recognizing the imperative of South-South cooperation in dealing with the problem.

Sara E. Davies and Kelley Loper's contributions approach the Asia-Pacific asylum crisis in different but complementary ways. Davies provides an in-depth analysis of the paradoxical consequences of the adoption by the Southeast Asian States, the majority of which are non-signatories to the 1951 Convention and the 1967 Protocol of the Comprehensive Peace Plan (CPA). The CPA became a necessity, in 1988, to enable these countries to deal with the influx of asylum seekers to such States as Australia, Malaysia, Indonesia and Thailand. The CPA was, in a sentence, a vacuum-filling strategy to give the most basic protection to those who otherwise would be left without protection from the States where they seek asylum during a particularly daunting phase in their existence. Ironically, while the CPA ensured the repatriation and resettlement of asylum seekers, it also enabled the concerned Southeast Asia States to strengthen their rejection of asylum and their non-compliance with the minimum international human rights standard for dealing with asylum seekers. Davies's chapter reviews more than two decades of CPA and returns a verdict that is both apt and accurate in its varied observations.

That is not to say, however, that the Asia-Pacific region is not making efforts towards developing a more effective regime of asylum protection. Not only are the key States in the East Asia sub-region parties to the 1951 Convention and 1967 Protocol, but they also have, to varying degrees, made efforts towards complying with their obligations under these regimes. Even States in this region, such as Hong Kong which is not party to the 1951 Convention and the 1967 Protocol, have been able to use their strong rule of law culture at their domestic level to offer protection to asylum seekers and comply with international human rights obligations. Loper's chapter considers the extent to which such key countries in the East Asia sub-region as Japan, China and South Korea, all of which are signatories to the 1951 Convention and the 1967 Protocol, have attempted to implement the regime's obligations internally, as well as measure their varied level of compliance with their international obligations. The importance of this analysis is strongly underscored by the fact that not only is China the world's most populous country, but it is also the largest refugee-generating (as well as being a significant receiving country) country in Asia. The economic and political importance of Japan and South Korea, in addition to China, in that region certainly affects the balance of the region's asylum scale.

Conceptual Clarification of the Terms 'Asylum Seekers' and 'Refugees'

Although this book focuses on asylum seekers and not refugees, it is impossible not to refer to the term 'refugee' when discussing the protection of asylum seekers.

At the national, regional or international level, the legal frameworks for dealing with asylum seekers are often the same for dealing with refugees. This is not surprising since whether one who seeks asylum in another country is regarded an asylum seeker or a refugee depends mainly on whether his or her application for refuge succeeds. Until a successful determination of an asylum application by the State in which a person seeks refuge, he or she is regarded as an 'asylum seeker' since, indeed, all s/he has done up to that point is to seek asylum. Thus, once the application succeeds, s/he becomes a refugee. The law often does not change, only the application of it since a refugee enjoys certain rights and privileges not accorded to an asylum seeker. States and regional organizations therefore adopt the same body of laws to deal with the two distinct but interlinked stages of asylum-seeking and refuge, although more specialized agencies, such as the UNHCR, are often more precise in their usage.

Often, the use of the term refugee becomes indispensable when it is adopted in a discourse as a term of art to refer to a generic act rather than to a legally specific characterization. Hence, in some of the chapters in this book, the term 'refugee' is used when in actual fact the purpose is to describe a development that applies to both asylum seekers and refugees. For instance, some chapters refer to legal instruments defining 'refugee'. In such a usage, the term 'refugee' logically subsumes 'asylum seeker' since one may not become a refugee without first seeking asylum. Most legal instruments do not refer to the definition of 'asylum seeker' but to that of a 'refugee' even though that definition applies to both categories and, in fact, more so to an asylum seeker. Thus, it is impossible to avoid a perfunctory conflation or interchangeable use of the two terms despite this book focusing mainly on asylum seekers.

The impression must be avoided, at all cost, that this book undertakes a comparison of how different regions deal with the protection of asylum seekers. What the book does not do is compare one region to another – each regional experience is unique and informs its legal framework and system – but it does critically examine how each region, on its own, tackles the problem of asylum seekers. This aim is to appreciate what informs each region's approach to the subject matter and determine whether there are crosscutting issues common to every region.

References

Abass A (ed.), *Protecting Human Security in Africa* (Oxford University Press, 2010).

Abass A, 'The Proposed International Criminal Jurisdiction for the African Court: Some Problematic Aspects' (2013) Netherlands International Law Review LX 27–50.

Abass A, 'Prosecuting International Crimes in Africa: Rationale, Prospects and Challenges' (2013) 24(3) European Journal of International Law 933–46.

Barbou des Places S, *Burden Sharing in the Field of Asylum Legal Motivations and Implications of a Regional Approach* (European University Institute, 2002).

Beyani C, *Protection of the Right to Seek and Obtain Asylum under African Human Rights System* (Martinus Nijhoff, 2013).

Clayton G, *Textbook on Immigration and Asylum Law*, 5th edn [rev. and updated] (Oxford University Press, 2012).

Goodwin Gill GS, *The Refugee in International Law* (Oxford University Press, 2007).

Gortázar Rotaeche CJ, Parra M-C, Segaert B and Timmerman C (eds), *European Migration and Asylum Policies: Coherence or Contradiction?: An interdisciplinary evaluation of the EU programmes of Tampere* (Bruylant, 2012).

Grahl-Madsen, *Commentary on the Refugee Convention 1951*, reprinted by UNHCR, Geneva, 1997.

Hathaway JC, *The Rights of Refugees under International Law* (Cambridge University Press, 2005).

Kneebone S (ed.), *Refugees, Asylum Seekers and the Rule of Law: Comparative Perspectives* (Cambridge University Press, 2009).

McAdam J (ed.), *Forced Migration, Human Rights and Security* (Hart Publishing, 2008).

Peers S, *EU Immigration and Asylum Law: (text and commentary)*, 2nd rev edn (Martinus Nijhoff, 2012).

Pulido MC and Blanchard M, 'La Comisión Interamericana de Derechos Humanos y sus mecanismos de protección aplicados a la situación de los refugiados, apátridas y solicitantes de asilo' in L Franco (ed.), *El asilo y la protección internacional de los refugiados en América Latina* (Editorama, 2004).

Taylor S, 'Sharing Responsibility for Asylum Seekers and Refugees in the Asia Pacific Region' in SS Juss (ed.), *The Ashgate Companian to Migration Law, Theory and Policy* (Ashgate, 2013).

Viljoen F, 'AU Assembly should consider human rights implications before adopting the Amending Merged African Court Protocol' African Law 23/12/2012, available at http://africlaw.com/2012/05/23/au-assembly-should-consider-human-rights-implications-before-adopting-the-amending-merged-african-court-protocol/ [last visited 04/06/2013].

Yundt KW, 'The Organization of American States and Legal Protection to Political Refugees in Central America' (1989) 23 International Migration Review 201.

Documents

Article 16 Protocol Establishing the Peace and Security Council of the African Union, available at http://www.au.int/en/sites/default/files/Protocol_peace_and_security.pdf [last visited on 04/6/2013].

CJEU, Joined cases C-411/10 e C-493/10, *N.S. and M.E.*, judgment of 21 December 2011, not yet reported.

ECtHR, *M.S.S. v Belgium and Greece* (App no 30696/09) 21 January 2011.

UNHCR Global Trend 2011, available at http://www.unhcr.org/4fd6f87f9.pdf [last accessed 04/6/2013].

UNHCR spokesperson Adrian Edwards at the press briefing, on 21 September 2010, at the Palais des Nations in Geneva, available at http://www.unhcr.org/4c98a0ac9.html [last accessed 04/6/2013]. See also Commissioner for Human Rights of the Council of Europe, CommDH (2009) 6 February 2009, available at http://cmr.jur.ru.nl/cmr/docs/CHR.2009.greece.pdf [last accessed 04/6/2013].

Chapter 2
The African Union Legal Framework for Protecting Asylum Seekers

Ademola Abass and Dominique Mystris

Introduction

Ranked by its legacy of armed conflicts and undemocratic governments, it comes as no surprise that Africa has one of the highest numbers of people living either as internally displaced or as refugees in foreign lands.[1] Africa's chronic legacy of brutal civil wars and violent uprooting of its people from their homesteads is matched only by the continent's noted primacy in prospecting for, and adopting ground-breaking multilateral instruments adapted to tackling the egregious humanitarian consequences of its multiple wars. The Refugee Charter, adopted by the Organization of African Unity (OAU) in 1969, blazed the trail of an endless repertoire of precocious regional instruments that span the entire legal orbit of the continent.[2]

The 1969 Convention remarkably set new international standards for defining who a refugee is.[3] Rather than just piggybacking on the pioneering definition offered by the UN 1951 Refugee Convention, the OAU Charter drew weightily on Africans' experience with colonialism and its harrowing effects on its people,

1 Africa has the second largest refugee population outside of Asia and the Pacific region in 2011; see UNHCR statistics available in UNHCR Global Trends 2011, available at http://www.unhcr.org/4fd6f87f9.html.

2 Some of these pioneering instruments include: the African Charter on Human and Peoples' Rights (Banjul Charter) which introduced the concept of collective (peoples') rights in a regional human right instrument; the African Union Constitutive Act (2000) which, in Art 4(h) embodies the right of humanitarian intervention, arguably the first time an international legal instrument has explicitly done so; the African Union Convention for the Protection and Assistance of Internally Displaced Persons in Africa – also known as the Kampala Convention (2012), the first ever binding regional instrument on internal displacement; the ECOWAS Protocol Relating to the Mechanism for Conflict Prevention, Management, Resolution, Peace-Keeping and Security (1999), being the first instrument of a regional organization to dispense with the consent of the Member States of that organization before undertaking an enforcement action in their territory; (2012), amongst others.

3 It is important that the distinction that exists between individuals classified as asylum seekers and refugees is understood as the terminology is often used interchangeably. For an explanation of this distinction and the usage of the two terms in this chapter, see Chapter 1 of this book.

especially those it regarded as 'freedom fighters'. Asylum seeking during the anti-colonial struggle in Africa was thus inspired by reasons not countenanced by the 1951 UN Refugee Convention – the latter having been solely motivated by the devastation of the Second World War.

The peculiar context and the *raison d'être* for asylum seeking during Africa's struggle for political emancipation underwrote the generous attitude of many African States in offering refuge to thousands of those fleeing colonial powers' retribution. However, the attitude of most African States towards asylum seeking began to change during the late 1960s and early 1970s. Concomitantly with the majority of African States obtaining political independence during this time, the numbers of Africans who sought refuge from colonial governments' reprisals waned considerably. This was rapidly replaced by those fleeing repression by the emergent, arguably often more brutal, African ruling elites who saddled the governments of newly independent African States.

The plight of this new class of asylum seekers elicited less sympathy from newly independent African States most of which, in the immediate post-colonial period, were dominated by autocratic, and sometimes maximum rulers. The fear that accommodating foreign dissidents and activist-asylum seekers fleeing authoritarianism in their own countries might sow disaffection, where none yet existed, in their prospective countries of refuge consternated many African States. Only in the isolated cases where ideological differences existed between the asylum-generating State and the potential receiving State, or where commonly regarded repugnant practices, such as Apartheid in South Africa and the Supremacist regime in South Rhodesia, inspired asylum-seeking, was refuge still generously offered from the late 1970s Africa. Otherwise, Africa quickly slipped from an asylum-friendly continent to one where Ghana, which embodied the hope of an African Unity in 1957, become the first to expel foreigners from its soil in 1969, provoking a retaliation by Nigeria in 1983 that would define much of Africa's future on the asylum issue.

Aside from the transformed political climate of the 1960s occasioning an attitudinal change by many African States towards asylum seekers, economic realities also played a crucial role in retarding the legal protection of asylum in the early post-independence Africa, and in the shaping of most African States' policies in the later years. Most asylum-granting African States had originally assumed, as had the United Nations with its 1951 Convention, that the refuge problem would be short term and that granting asylum would be a solution for what was largely considered to be a transient malaise. On the contrary, the seemingly endless flow of asylum seekers, with its formidable strain on the economic resources of many receiving States, had not only compelled many African States to rethink asylum granting; it also triggered a search for a continent-wide protection regime of asylum seekers, starting, as already noted, with the OAU Refugee Charter in 1969.[4]

4 G Okoth-Obbo, 'Thirty Years On: a Legal Review of the 1969 OAU Refugee Convention Governing the Specific Aspects of Refugee Problems in Africa' (2001) 20(1) Refugee Survey Quarterly 79, 90.

The establishment of the AU in 2000 somewhat transformed the way in which the African region deals with the issue of asylum seekers and refugees. Not only has the poor treatment of asylum seekers exacerbated in Africa since the end of colonialism due to weak and ill-suited legal instruments, but the regional institutions meant to enforce the rights of the asylum seekers, and the means by which to vindicate breaches of those rights, are endemically weak and grossly under-resourced. The African Union's efforts to address these problems have led to a change in the thinking of Africa's premier organization. Consequently, the AU has set up regional institutions that could play a vital role in enforcing the rights of asylum seekers.

This contribution reflects on the AU's approach to the protection of asylum seekers in Africa, specifically in terms of its nascent normative developments. The chapter seeks to understand whether the AU's efforts so far demonstrate a better commitment to the protection of asylum seekers than that obtained under the OAU regime. In pursuing its remit, this chapter does not attempt to compare the OAU regime to the AU's or delve substantially into a discussion of the legal instruments adopted under the OAU (although some discussion is inevitable), of which libraries have already been written, but the modest task here is to shine the spotlight on what improvements, if any, the AU has brought to the protection of asylum seekers in Africa as far as the law governing the subject is concerned. Thus our attention is mostly paid to the legal frameworks adopted under the AU auspices. It should also be noted that this contribution does not cover the legal protection of asylum and refugees by individual African States, except where such may be incidental to the remit of the chapter. And whereas regional human rights systems, such as the African Commission on Human and Peoples' Rights (ACHPR), the similarly named African court and sub-regional organizations, play crucial roles in asylum protection in Africa, those important issues are dealt with in Chapters 3 and 4 of this book respectively.

OAU/AU Convention Governing the Specific Aspects of Refugee Problems in Africa 1969[5]

The OAU Convention Governing the Specific Aspects of Refugee Problems in Africa (1969 OAU Convention)[6] is considered by many to have been a great achievement for refugees and asylum seekers within Africa.[7] A result of a consultation process of what was known as the Commission of Ten on Refugees

5 45 States have signed and ratified, 4 have signed but not yet ratified and 5 States have not signed nor ratified.

6 The OAU Convention Governing the Specific Aspects of Refugee Problems in Africa, 1001 U.N.T.S. 45 (adopted 10 September 1969, entered into force 20 June 1974).

7 See Okoth-Obbo, 'Thirty Years On' 79.

in 1964,[8] the 1969 OAU Convention achieved numerous legal advancements, but there are many misconceptions over these achievements and the reasoning lying behind them.[9]

The 1969 Convention reflects a shift in Africa's approach to asylum-seeking from that of a protective nature to one focused more on containment.[10] Given that the 1969 Convention was motivated by political reasons as opposed to legal ones,[11] it is not surprising that the legal approach taken reflects the concerns of the African States at the time. Despite the numerous legal and political achievements, the 1969 OAU Convention does not take a strong human rights approach and therefore cannot claim to expand human rights applicable to refugees and asylum.[12]

The preamble to the 1969 Convention makes clear the OAU Member States recognized the problems faced by refugees and asylum seekers and the impact the decolonization process had. The 1969 OAU Convention further seeks to place itself as a complementary instrument to that of the UN's 1951 Convention. It does this through encouraging those African States that have not acceded to the Convention to take such steps as well as calling on the OAU Members to apply the provisions within Africa.[13] The result was a clear indication, from the OAU, that the 1951 UN Convention is applicable to refugees within Africa, and that international standards were to be met as a minimum, while the 1969 OAU Convention develops the standards further and in an African-specific context.

Regarding the actual provisions of the Convention it is without a doubt that there exists a solid legal protection framework in terms of granting rights and seeking to address the conditions for them within the receiving State. One of the most commonly cited achievements of the 1969 Convention is that it expanded the definition of a refugee offered by to the 1951 UN Convention.[14] The need to extend protection to those involved in the decolonization process and the so-called freedom fighters is thought to have promoted this expansion.[15] The 1969 Convention also potentially applies to individuals and groups fleeing natural

8 See AHG/Res. 26(II). See also CM/Res. 36(III) which detail the mandate of the Commission of Ten on Refugees.

9 See Okoth-Obbo, 'Thirty Years On' 79.

10 See Okoth-Obbo, 'Thirty Years On' 79, 83 and R Murray, *Human Rights in Africa: From the OAU to the African Union* (Cambridge University Press, 2004).

11 Okoth-Obbo, 'Thirty Years On' 79, 90.

12 Murray, *Human Rights in Africa*.

13 See preamble para 10, 'calling upon Member States of the Organization who had not already done so to accede to the United Nations Convention of 1951 and to the Protocol of 1967 relating to the Status of Refugees, and meanwhile to apply their provisions to refugees in Africa'.

14 It is claimed that the 1951 UN Convention definition of a refugee was problematic when applying it to situations which had not been contemplated at the time of drafting as well as to Third World situations. See SA Aiboni, *Protection of Refugees in Africa* (Volume 3 of Studies in International Law, Svenska institutet för internationell rätt 1978) 30.

15 Okoth-Obbo, 'Thirty Years On' 79, 116.

disasters, people that were not contemplated in the 1951 UN Convention.[16] While the undeniably broader definition in the 1969 OAU Convention which opens up protection to those who may have fallen outside the UN protection framework is commendable, concerns remain over the lack of commentary on the determination of refugee status, which is left solely to States' discretion.[17]

Furthermore, the comparative commodiousness of the OAU definition of refugee seems to be shackled by rampant exclusions and cessation clauses.[18] The provision in Article 2, which relates to asylum, is generally viewed to be 'amongst [OAU's] most important contributions to refugee jurisprudence in general'[19] Many have argued that one of the key improvements to protection established by the 1969 OAU Convention is that is has created a *right* of asylum.[20] According to Article 2(1):

> Member States of the OAU shall use their best endeavours consistent with their respective legislations to receive refugees and to secure the settlement of those refugees who, for well-founded reasons, are unable or unwilling to return to their country of origin or nationality.

The language of this provision is more recommendatory than mandatory, thus making it much easier for OAU/AU Member States to adopt overtly subjective and overbearing domestic legislation to trump or side-step any notion of a right to asylum that the provision might be believed to enshrine. It is also questionable, considering the wording of the provision and the political mood at the time of the drafting of the OAU Convention, whether African States could be confidently presumed to be agreeing to the creation of a right to asylum at a time when most of them were struggling with and trying to contain what they viewed as a continual flow of asylum seekers and a drain on their overstretched resources. Nevertheless the 1969 OAU Convention goes further than the 1951 UN Convention in this respect, *de minimis*, by providing for a *quasi* right to asylum and in placing a greater level of protection on the ability to claim asylum.

---

16 There are some concerns over the extent to which this is true given the intention of the 1969 OAU Convention drafters. See R Murray's discussion in Murray, *Human Rights in Africa* 188.

17 See Murray, *Human Rights in Africa*, citing AC. Helton, *The Price of Indifference. Refugees and Humanitarian Action in the New Century* (Oxford University Press, 2002) 164.

18 EO Awuku, 'Refugee Movements in Africa and the OAU Convention on Refugees' (1995) 39 J Africa L 79.

19 See Okoth-Obbo, 'Thirty Years On' 79, 88 citing J Oloka Onyango, 'Plugging the Holes: Refugees, OAU Policy and the Practices of Member States', USC Issue Brief (Washington DC, October 1986).

20 J Oloka Onyango, 'Plugging the Holes' 7 as cited in G Okoth-Obbo, 'Thirty Years On' 79.

A particularly strong protection provided for is the principle of *non-refoulement* under Article 2(3),[21] an issue that is covered in more depth by Naldi and d'Orsi's chapter in this volume. By canvassing protection for asylum seekers at one of the points they are most vulnerable, that being when they first flee their country, the OAU explicitly expresses its desire for Member States to provide protection and to ensure those seeking it are afforded the opportunity to claim asylum and the consequential rights and protections international and African regional laws afford. Also, unlike the provision in Article 2(1) referred above, the language used in the present is mandatory and of utmost applicability by OAU/AU Member States.[22]

African States have not however always complied with Article 2(3) of the 1969 Convention. Egregious instances of violations include Tanzania's and Zaïre's closing of their respective borders to asylum seekers, as well as incidents of mass deportations to countries of asylum origin.[23] The principle of *non-refoulement* has also been argued to give way 'if [the] individual acts contrary to the principles of the Convention'.[24] On the basis of Article 1(4)(g) it is possible to exclude the application of the Convention from an individual where 'he has seriously infringed the purposes and objectives of this Convention'. The exclusionary criteria provided for in Article 1(4) and 1(5) constitute a hurdle to implementing any of the OAU Convention's provisions and appear to give with one hand while taking with another. This calls into question the true extent of protection available and the political will available to deliver on the 1969 OAU Convention's promises.

Linked to the principle of *non-refoulement* is the concept of voluntary repatriation governed by Article 5. This can be considered a further protection against forcible expulsion by/from a receiving State, which strengthens the principle of *non-refoulement*, while at the same time going further. Article 5(4) stipulates that '[r]efugees who voluntarily return to their country shall in no way be penalised for having left it for any of the reasons giving rise to refugee situations'. While many may not contemplate their safety once the situation that caused them to seek refuge elsewhere ends, this provision enables those who left their country to return without fear of repercussions. It is this thoroughly thought-out scope of protection that helps place the 1969 OAU Convention in the admirable position it occupies amongst comparable instruments.

---

21 'No person shall be subjected by a Member State to measures such as rejection at the frontier, return or expulsion, which would compel him to return to or remain in a territory where his life, physical integrity or liberty would be threatened for the reasons set out in Art I, paragraphs 1 and 2'. Similarly Arts 1(5)(c) and (d) enable the receiving State not to allow someone who they have serious reason to believe has acted contrary to the purposes of the OAU and the UN respectively to benefit from the provisions.

22 See Gino J. Naldi and Cristiano d'Orsi's chapter in this volume for a more elaborate discussion of the principle of *non-refoulement* of the OAU Charter.

23 See J Hathaway, *The Rights of Refugees Under International Law* (Cambridge University Press, 2005) 281.

24 Murray, *Human Rights in Africa* 189 and see Art 1(4)(g).

As to be expected, there is a non-discriminatory clause (Article 4) preventing States from not applying the OAU Convention's provisions based upon 'race, religion, nationality, membership of a particular social group or political opinions'. This is vital for asylum seekers and refugees who, in many African conflicts, have been fleeing ethnic or politically motivated violence. Despite this non-discrimination clause, concession was made to alleviate the fear of many African States over self-determination struggles. Article 3 prohibits refugees and asylum seekers from subversive activities, which is linked to political beliefs and social groups, thus asylum and refugee protection can be limited based upon Article 3. This provision takes the idea of the granting of asylum and refugee status and tries to reinforce the notion that such an act is a friendly one and should not create hostility between States, as receiving States will not be allowing asylum seekers and refugees to undertake acts which undermine their State of origin. Article 3 can be seen as drawing a distinction between those who seek genuine refuge and are seeking protection in the receiving State, and those with ulterior motives who can cause conflicts to spill over into the receiving State.

While the OAU has gone to some lengths to protect asylum and refugee rights, it is actually limited in its scope and these limitations and exclusions undermine many of its achievements. As already noted Articles 1(4) and 1(5) contain potentials for limiting the application of the 1969 OAU Convention. Many of these provisions do appear logical limitations and exclusions, such as gaining a new nationality and thus receiving protection as a citizen from another State (Article 1(4)(c)), or voluntarily going back to their country (Article 1(4)(d)). The areas of concern centre around the potential abuse by the receiving State which may easily preclude the 1969 OAU Convention on the sole basis that an individual, who is otherwise protected by the Convention, has acted contrary to the purposes and objectives of the OAU Convention,[25] the purposes and principles of the OAU/AU itself,[26] as well as those of the United Nations.[27] While these purposes, objectives and principles are clearly set out in the relevant instruments, there are no criteria for determining when an act violates these principles. This leaves the door wide open to those receiving States that are so inclined to determine violations without any set criteria or specifications as to the manner of determination. While it is hard to argue that individuals who engage in subversive activities, which the OAU Convention specifically prohibits, shall be availed of the OAU Convention protections and rights, the lack of determination criteria to guide States is worrying as this leaves it up to States themselves to determine. Given the recognized concerns of African States, the desire to contain asylum and refugees and the lack of a human rights approach, this provision can lead to States selectively applying the OAU Convention, thereby weakening the level of protection within the African system.

25 Art 1(4)(g).
26 Art 1(5)(c).
27 Art 1(5)(d).

Comparable regional human rights systems, such as the European Union (EU), often permit their Member States to derogate from human rights obligations when noxious activities of beneficiaries of such rights, or other inimical situations, undermine the security or welfare of the concerned State. But here is where the comparison ends. The big difference lies essentially in the European system ensuring that the process by which its Member States may invoke their domestic legislation, in order to curtail or altogether suspend the application of human rights regimes, is tightly controlled and more often than not subject to transparent and objective verification. On the contrary, African States are notorious for the inscrutability of their actions and processes, and it is thus regrettable that the provisions of such a fundamental treaty as the 1969 OAU Refugee Convention can be subject to unregulated departures and derogations.

Of even greater concern is the ability of African States to denounce the provisions under Article 13 altogether. All that is required is a written notification to the Administrative Secretary-General, and the denunciation will be effective within a year of notification. The ability of a State to opt out of the OAU Convention will undermine the regional protection and create further hurdles for an already under-utilized and not-often-understood system by those the OAU Convention seeks to protect.

Overall, the OAU Refugee Convention recorded a great advancement for protecting asylum and refugees, at least in so far as enumerating such rights and protections are concerned. It was the first regional instrument to specifically address asylum and turn this somewhat political minefield into a legally enforceable regime. Yet the impact of this has not been significantly felt by those it is meant to protect.

Nonetheless, the OAU Refugee Convention has largely remained stagnant with little to no revision or debate over its content.[28] There was originally no regional mechanism tasked with implementation and enforcement, albeit this has changed with the ACHPR mandate being extended to cover the 1969 OAU Convention. What is more, the level of rights granted by the OAU Convention is very limited in applicability. As will be seen later in other chapters in this volume, the OAU Convention is not being utilized by the regional mechanisms in place, however all the while it is routinely called upon to glorify the work being done for asylum and refugees in Africa and is presented as a model for the international community as a whole.[29] Certainly the true test of such a Convention should not be merely in its ability to depoliticize the issue and apply a coherent approach,[30] which the OAU Convention does achieve. Instead, the Convention's true values should lie in its ability to achieve actual change and protection, demonstrated by its continual use and development within the case law of the African system, and to continue to inspire debates amongst the African institutions which oversee the asylum

28 Okoth-Obbo, 'Thirty Years On' 79.

29 Okoth-Obbo, 'Thirty Years On' 79, 82.

30 Okoth-Obbo, 'Thirty Years On' 79.

and refugee issues, as well as amongst those States in which asylum seekers and refugees are to be found.

African Charter on Human and Peoples' Rights 1981 (Banjul Charter)[31]

The OAU Charter on Human and Peoples' Rights, otherwise known as the Banjul Charter (so named after the capital of The Gambia where it was adopted), is the prescient regional human rights instrument for Africa and remains the corner stone of the AU's human rights efforts. The Charter is innovative in terms not only of recognizing the rights of individual's but also for pioneering the recognition of group rights. The Banjul Charter has been the subject of much discussion but an in-depth analysis of the human rights system and its subsequent protection is beyond the scope of this chapter and can be found in Naldi and d'Orsi's chapter in this book.

However, it is important to make a few observations regarding the weaknesses of the OAU Human Rights Charter especially since, with the 1969 Refugee Convention, it forms the bridge between the efforts of the OAU and those of the AU in the specific field of asylum seekers/refugee protection and the broader human rights issues.

As part of the AU's legal framework, the Banjul Charter has not been improved upon in any way by the AU and as such the problems associated with its effectiveness of the Charter, which the AU inherited, remain: for instance, the provisions of the Charter which base asylum application on the laws of the receiving State State is worrying.[32] Many African States do not have national laws that meet the requirements set out in international let alone regional instruments, such as the OAU Convention. This provision is devastating to the futuristic ambition of the 1969 Refugee Convention, and its continuous existence makes a high mockery of the AU's clarion call to its Member States, in the Kigali Declaration, to treat refugee and asylum issues as a grave crime. It certainly makes no sense to regard States whose activities necessitate their citizens' flight for asylum to kindly grant asylum requests by other nationals. If this provision was motivated by the need for the OAU to achieve the political buy-in of its Member States for the Charter, it was one concession too many.

It is not entirely clear what the rationale is for basing asylum application on the receiving States' laws, as provided for by Article 12(3) of the African Human Rights Charter is. It is possible that the idea came from the 1969 Refugee Convention which entitles the receiving State, in Article I(6), to determine whether an applicant is a 'refugee'. This is certainly another way of saying that the

31 Forty-one States have signed and ratified, 9 have signed but not yet ratified and 4 States have neither signed nor ratified.

32 Art 12(3) States 'Every individual shall have the right, when persecuted, to seek and obtain asylum in other countries in accordance with laws of those countries and international conventions'.

receiving State shall make such a determination under and in accordance with its laws. But that provision is, in itself, out of sync with the evident collective spirit of the 1969 Convention and should, accordingly, be viewed with serious suspicion. It is therefore unfortunate that the Banjul Charter, adopted a dozen years after the Convention, had perpetuated this oddity instead of correcting the anomaly and setting African legal regime for asylum protection in the direction of a viable and strong regional system.

In the absence of domestic mechanisms to process asylum applications in the majority of AU Member States, there is greater chance of many of these States denying individuals the Charter rights. Also, given the plethora of conflicts in Africa and the interconnectedness of some of these conflicts, it is quite easy for States to invoke the ground of national security to oust the operation of the African Human Rights Charter. For instance, the conflicts in the Democratic Republic of Congo (DRC) engulfs all the countries in the Great Lakes region, making it potentially attractive for any of those countries to deny asylum application on the basis that intakes of people from countries affected by the DRC conflicts may pose threats to its own stability.[33]

Another provision subject to the law of a State is the expulsion of individuals from a receiving State.[34] Due to the already-noted absence of domestic legal protection of asylum in most African States, coupled with the practice common amongst these States to expel individuals or whole groups in what is arguably in violation of international law standards, it appears the Banjul Charter offers little succour. Consequently, while attempts have been made to prohibit mass expulsions of non-nationals,[35] these have not prevented mass expulsions taking place with little or no consequences.[36]

However, in light of the fact that the OAU did not originally include the protection of human rights as part of its primary goal,[37] its later developing a remarkably inclusive human rights Charter, which incorporate rights for refugees

---

33 See ZA Lomo, 'The Struggle for Protection of the Rights of Refugees and IDPs in Africa: Making the Existing International Legal Regime Work' (2000) 18 Berkeley Journal of International Law 268, 269 where he argues that 'many States have failed to enact laws necessary or to create the institutional frameworks to give effect to the international human rights protection regime'.

34 Art 12(4) 'A non-national legally admitted in a territory of a State Party to the present Charter, may only be expelled from it by virtue of a decision taken in accordance with the law'.

35 Art 12(5) 'The mass expulsion of non-nationals shall be prohibited. Mass expulsion shall be that which is aimed at national, racial, ethnic or religious groups'.

36 See the Tanzanian example where Rwandans and Burundian refugees were sent back to their country of origin en masse, 'Tanzania: Expulsions Put Vulnerable People at Risk', Human Rights Watch, 6 May 2007, available at http://www.hrw.org/news/2007/05/08/tanzania-expulsions-put-vulnerable-people-risk.

37 AM Abebe, 'Legal and Institutional Dimensions of Protecting and Assisting Internally Displaced Persons in Africa' (2009) Journal of Refugee Studies 154, 160.

and asylum seekers, is a plus to the organization. The Banjul Charter appears to have reinforced many of the OAU Convention's provisions, transforming them into rights and duties under the human rights framework of the African system. The net effect of this is the opening of a new forum for refugee rights to be heard in, namely the African Court of Human and Peoples' Rights and Justice.[38]

Protocol to the African Charter on Human and Peoples' Rights on the Rights of Women in Africa[39] *and the African Charter on the Rights and Welfare of the Child*[40]

The African legal framework affords women and children asylum seekers and refugees additional protection, or from a more pessimistic viewpoint, these groups are, at the very least, specifically identified as being eligible for certain rights. Under the Protocol to the African Charter on Human and Peoples' Rights on the Rights of Women in Africa, Member States are called upon to ensure that women and men are granted the same access to refugee status and determination procedures as well as the full protection and benefits afforded by international law.[41] In recognition of the particular problems faced by many asylum seekers and refugee women, the Protocol relating to women specifically addresses the issues of sexual and non-sexual violence and exploitation, calling upon both the receiving States and States of origin to prevent these, while also ensuring legal provisions are available under their national law for bringing perpetrators to justice.[42]

The African Charter on the Rights and Welfare of the Child (the Child Charter) includes a specific provision for refugee children (Article 23).[43] States are to grant

38 For the evolution of this court and the other African Union regional courts, see Ademola Abass, 'The Proposed International Criminal Jurisdiction for the African Court: Some Problematical Aspects' (2013) LX, Netherlands International Law Review 27; Ademola Abass, Prosecuting 'International Crimes in Africa: Rationale, Prospects and Challenges' 24(3) European Journal of International Law (2013 forthcoming).

39 Twenty-eight States have signed and ratified, 18 have signed but not yet ratified and eight States have neither signed nor ratified.

40 Forty-one States have signed and ratified, nine have signed but not yet ratified and four States have not signed nor ratified.

41 See Art 4(k) that States are to 'ensure that women and men enjoy equal rights in terms of access to refugee status determination procedures and that women refugees are accorded the full protection and benefits guaranteed under international refugee law, including their own identity and other documents'.

42 See Art 11(3) 'States Parties undertake to protect asylum seeking women, refugees, returnees and internally displaced persons, against all forms of violence, rape and other forms of sexual exploitation, and to ensure that such acts are considered war crimes, genocide and/or crimes against humanity and that their perpetrators are brought to justice before a competent criminal jurisdiction'.

43 The African Charter on the Rights and Welfare of the Child CAB/LEG/24.9/49 (1990) (adopted 11 July 1999 and entered into force 29 November 1999).

children, whether they are accompanied or not, the full protection afforded to them under international and national law while helping to ensure that they are able to enjoy the other rights contained in the Child Charter.[44] States are to cooperate with international organizations involved in the protection of refugee children and help to trace parents and relatives for the purpose of reunification.[45] In cases where reunification or identification of a guardian is not possible, States are to ensure the children are granted the same protection as granted to 'any other child permanently or temporarily deprived of his family environment for any reason'.[46] The ability to link a refugee or asylum-seeking child's rights to those of children in general increases the level of protection at the basic level in terms of not excluding any children. However in order to secure children's rights there do need to be specific provisions made and adhered to in order to brighten the chances of a child asylum seeker under international law.

The African Union and the Protection of Asylum Seekers

In principle it is inaccurate to seek a demarcation between the OAU and AU when discussing their legal frameworks on asylum protection, or on any other subject for that matter. Though different timelines apply to the legal instruments adopted under the OAU (1963–99) and the AU (2000–onward), the AU succeeded the OAU upon the latter's dissolution and assimilated all of the treaties adopted and ratified under the OAU so that they are now regarded as AU instruments.

Be that as it may, there is a remarkable distinction in the temperaments and approaches of the two organizations, and in their framing of the problems faced by Africa. This attitudinal disparity underscores the palpable variation in the two organizations' appreciation of the required solutions to the problems. While the prevalent culture in the OAU's approach to multilateral solutions is characterized more by gradualism and tepidity, the AU appears more radical and robust, at least as far as the contents of, and the objectives sought by its multilateral treaties are concerned. Whilst it has thus become customary to refer to 'OAU/AU' instruments or simply 'AU' legal instruments (which automatically subsumes those instruments concluded under the OAU's auspices), it is necessary to consider the specific approach of the AU to legal frameworks in order to better understand how the organization's general attitude to continental issues reflects its treatment of the asylum crisis.

44 Art 23(1).

45 Art 23(2).

46 Art 23(3) and further assistance as to what happens in such circumstances is provided for in Art 25 which deals with separation from parents.

The Constitutive Act and the Protocol Establishing the Peace and Security Council of the African Union

The Constitutive Act of the African Union (AU Act) founded an organization with huge ambitions to arrest political and social instability and the continent's determined drift into utter chaos. The constituent instrument embodies principles that are as groundbreaking as they are iconoclastic, not only in the received wisdom about Africa's ways of conducting intergovernmental organizations, but in the lexicon of international organizations in general.

Although the AU Act speaks of the need to tackle the causes of Africa's problems, it does not directly speak to the plight of refugees or asylum seekers. However, in Principle 4(d) the Act envisions 'the establishment of a common defence policy for the African Continent'. This provision is significant not only because it is cast in terms of a principle in accordance with which the Union will function – therefore implying that its implementation is mandatory – but also because it serves as a reference point for later normative development specifically in the area of asylum seekers and refugees.

The Protocol relating to the Establishment of the Peace and Security Council of the African Union (PSC Protocol) entered into force on 26 December 2003 to replace the OAU Mechanism for the Prevention, Management and Regulation of Conflicts in Africa.[47] Part of the functions of the PSC is the management of catastrophes and humanitarian actions that encompass situations where refugees, asylum seekers and IDPs will be present.

Unlike the Act, the PSC Protocol acknowledges the plight of refugees and IDPs, recording the concern of African States with 'the fact that conflicts have forced millions of our people, including women and children, into a drifting life as refugees and internally displaced persons, deprived of their means of livelihood, human dignity and hope'.[48] The PSC promises, in Article 14(3)(d), to assist Member States that have been adversely affected by violent conflicts by undertaking activities including 'resettlement and reintegration of refugees and internally displaced persons'. Much as the PSC's pledge to AU Member States is a welcome development, the fact the PSC Protocol only empowers the PSC to provide resettlement and reintegration support for affected Member States after cessation of hostilities completely ignores the problems and threats to peace and security that refugees and IDPs pose during conflicts and other crisis situations. The majority of those who will seek asylum in other African States and, as such, will require the assistance of the PSC under this provision should be expected

47 Also known as the Cairo Mechanism, see the Declaration of the Assembly of Heads of State and Government on the Establishment within the OAU of a Mechanism for Conflict Prevention, Management and Resolution AHG/DECL.3 (XXIX) (adopted June 1993 during the Twenty-Ninth Ordinary Session of the Assembly of Heads of State and Government, Cairo Egypt).

48 Preambular para 11.

to be fleeing or have fled conflicts while crisis ensues. It is highly unlikely that those who ride out the conflict inside their country will seek refuge in foreign lands, implying therefore that only IDPs will really benefit from such assistance as promised by the PSC under Article 14(3)(d) of its Protocol.

Solemn Declaration on a Common African Defence and Security Policy (CADSP)

The establishment of a common African defence and security policy was first contemplated in the AU Constitutive Act,[49] which the PSC was to develop.[50] The motivation behind CADSP was 'to strengthen our collective efforts to contribute to peace, security, stability, justice and development in Africa, as well as to intensify cooperation and integration in our continent in the best interest of our peoples'[51] and this is further reflected in the principles, goals and objectives of the CADSP.[52]

African States recognize the importance of a common defence and security policy,[53] and attempt to address many insecurity issues through this policy. The AU has continued to take a proactive role in formally recognizing that the refugee crisis presents insecurity issues in the form of common internal threats for the continent as a whole and is not just a concern for the host State.[54]

The CADSP lists the plight of African refugees as one of the 'principles and values forming the basis of the Common African defence and security policy'[55] and explicitly prescribes as an objective and goal of CADSP the provision of 'a framework for addressing the problems of refugees and internally displaced persons at the continental, regional and national levels'.[56] The combined effect of making refugee issues a principle and a goal of the CASDP is to attract maximum coverage and ensure a mandatory implementation of the obligations relating to them. The frameworks envisioned include the Assembly of the African Union and

49 See AU Constitutive Act Art 4(d).

50 See AU Constitutive Act Art 3.

51 Solemn Declaration on a Common African Defence and Security Policy, preamble para 2.

52 See Section III para 12 and para 13 of the Solemn Declaration on a Common African Defence and Security Policy.

53 See Section III para 13 of the Solemn Declaration on a Common African Defence and Security Policy which States 'a Common Defence and Security Policy tends to be a common feature of advanced co-operative frameworks, or of regions where integration is highly advanced, and taking into account the common historical, political, economic and international experiences which bind AU Member States together, a Common African Defence Policy is established in pursuit of a number of objectives and goals …'

54 See para 8(iv)(n) Solemn Declaration on a Common African Defence and Security Policy.

55 See para 12(v).

56 See para 13(v) Solemn Declaration on a Common African Defence and Security Policy.

the PSC, reiterating the PSC's role in 'the settlement and reintegration of refugees and internally displaced persons'.[57]

The African Charter on Democracy, Elections and Governance (ACDEG)

ACDEG entered into force on 15 February 2012, just five years after its adoption in 2007. It is the only international legal instrument of its kind to deal directly with the issue of democracy, a sensitive subject that comparable international organizations' instruments usually address within generic human rights frameworks. ACDEG regulates democratic governance through a prohibition of unconstitutional changes of governments in Africa and contains robust enforcement provisions.

ACDEG very briefly considers refugees and IDPs: Article 8(2) calls upon States to 'adopt legislative and administrative measures to guarantee the rights of … refugees and displaced persons and other marginalized and vulnerable social groups'. This provision is different from those contained in AU's previous instruments in principal respects. First, it is the first provision to directly require AU Member States to take direct responsibility for enacting laws and setting up institutions for the protection of asylum seekers. Prior to ACDEG, the AU's emphasis has always been on providing support for Member States towards resettling refugees, which implies that such measures are regional and non-specific. Secondly, by calling on its Member States to take legislative and administrative measures, the AU seems, through ACDEG, to recognize the inevitability of its Member States dealing with protecting asylum seekers' right at the point when they seek asylum, and not *only* after hostilities would have ended as some of its earlier instruments require. While Article 8(2) of ACDEG neither categorically States this fact as such nor goes into detail about what measures States should adopt in fulfilment of this provision, it will be extraordinary to imagine that the AU is here calling on its Member States to treat asylum seekers, after they might have become refugees, differently, or afford them different protection than it accords its own nationals. Therefore, it is more plausible to regard this provision as relating to the protection of asylum seekers' rights prior to their integration with the local populations.

The question can be raised whether, by not constitutively superimposing a regional structure on such national measures to be taken by AU member States in guaranteeing asylum seekers' rights, the AU is conceding too much to its Member States and leaving a great deal of responsibility to them. Thus, the provision of Article 8(2) of ACDEG should be interpreted in the context of: (a) the nature of that instrument itself; and (b) the overall direction of AU legal regime on the protection of asylum seekers. On the first point, Article 8(2) could not have taken a different approach given that ACDEG is based upon 'the respect for, and the supremacy

57 See para 22(v) Solemn Declaration on a Common African Defence and Security Policy.

of, the Constitution and constitutional order in the political arrangements of the State Parties'.[58] As an instrument adapted specifically to issues of democracy and governance – issues that are zealously guarded by States as belonging exclusively to the national province – it would have been unthinkable for the AU to include a regional guarantee of asylum seekers' rights within that instrument. On the second point, the overall direction of AU's legal regime for protecting asylum seekers up to and inclusive of ACDEG consists largely in recommending general measures rather than spelling out what measures are required by Member States to take nationally for this purpose. Consequently, while one hopes that the AU Member States can take concrete and specific legislative and administrative measures as recommended by Article 8(2), not doing so will in fact not violate that provision or depart from any regional regulation of asylum seekers by the AU.

Be that as it may, the AU misses a great opportunity in not *obligating* its Member States to take national and administrative measures towards the protection of asylum seekers under ACDEG. By simply *calling* on its member States (a call that many may never heed) the AU leaves it to the discretion of its Members whether to bother with this provision or not. ACDEG is a serious instrument and considering the already multiple applications of its sanctions regime to States that violate its norms, the AU could have used this medium to pressure its members into hard-core obligations towards asylum seekers. Certainly it would be much easier to expect African States to adopt a treaty which obligates them to provide for and protect those who seek asylum on their territories than endorse a treaty which outlaws coup d'état and other unconstitutional means of taking over governmental powers in the continent. One hope here is the fact that one of the ACDEG objectives is to promote 'sustainable development and human security'[59] while promoting adherence 'to the universal values and principles of democracy and respect for human rights'.[60] Given that refugees come under the scope of human rights and security there is thus potential scope for expanding ACDEG's framework on asylum seekers in the future.

The Coordinating Committee on Assistance and Protection to Refugees, Returnees and Internally Displaced Persons in Africa (CCAR) and The Humanitarian Affairs, Refugee and Displaced Persons Division (HARDP)

The standing committee and the consultative board of the OAU, which advised the Bureau for the Placement and Education of Refugees (BPEAR),[61] merged in 1970 to become the Coordinating Committee which, in 1981, was renamed the Coordinating Committee on Assistance and Protection to Refugees, Returnees

58 Art 2(2) African Charter on Democracy, Elections and Governance.

59 Art 2(8) African Charter on Democracy, Elections and Governance.

60 Art 2(1) African Charter on Democracy, Elections and Governance.

61 PE Chartrand, 'The organization of African Unity and African Refugees: A Progress Report', (1975) 137 World Affairs 265, 280.

and Internally Displaced Persons in Africa (CCAR).[62] CCAR was primarily mandated to help the OAU, acting in conjunction with the UNHCR, to organize the International Conference on the Assistance to Refugees in Africa (ICARA), an initiative meant to shore the weaknesses of OAU's regime on refugee protection and assistance. However, CCAR's broader mandate was to address the gaps of the OAU Commission on Refugees, and to coordinate the OAU's activities with UNHCR and NGOs.[63]

The CCAR is made up of AU Member States, NGOs and UNHCR, and it is HARDP which acts as secretariat.[64] The AU however expanded upon the mandate of the CCAR's by establishing new terms of reference and procedures, thus the CCAR's scope now includes refugees, IDPs and returnees.[65] This stems from CCAR's position as advisory body to the Permanent Representatives Committee's (PRC) Sub-Committee on Refugees, Returnees and IDPs. Through the AU's expansion of the CCAR mandate, the plight of refugees and IDPs has an increased forum in which to be heard, as well as a designated regional body to coordinate such matters. HARDP's role is to 'seek lasting solutions to the problem of refugees and IDPs; help the harmonization of policies and activities regarding refugees and IDPs; and provide assistance to refugees and victims of displacement'.[66]

The AU Permanent Representatives Committee's (PRC) Sub-Committee on Refugees, Returnees and Internally Displaced Persons

The last of the AU's 'regime for dealing with asylum is the Permanent Representatives Committee's Sub-Committee on Refugees, Returnees and Internally Displaced Persons' (hereafter PRC Sub-Comm). The PRC is an organ of the Union[67] and is tasked with responsibilities that do not form part of this chapter's remit. What is significant is the Sub-Comm of this organ concerned with the question of refugees and, by necessary implications, asylum seekers. By Article 21(2) of the AU Act, the PRC could create sub-committees and working groups to help the AU executive council with its work. It was in exercise of that provision that it created the Sub-Committee on Refugees, Returnees and Internally Displaced Persons.

While the Sub-Comm attracts attention to itself by adopting a title that seemingly puts it squarely in charge of asylum seekers' problems – after all, the PRC assists the executive council's works through its sub-committees – the

62 See M Sharpe, 'Organization of African Unity and African Union Engagement with Refugee Protection: 1963–2011' (2013) 21(1) African Journal of International and Comparative Law 50, 73.

63 Abebe, 'Legal and Institutional Dimensions' 154, 161.

64 HARDP is part of the AU Commission's Political Affairs Department.

65 Abebe, 'Legal and Institutional Dimensions' 154, 161.

66 Abebe, 'Legal and Institutional Dimensions' 154, 161.

67 Art 5 (1)(f) Constitutive Act of the Africa Union.

Sub-Committee on Refugees has not really impacted on the subject matter. It is clear that as a more or less handmaid of the executive council, the PRC's sub-committees can hardly exact serious influence on its activities and the most the Sub-Comm can come up with will be recommendations that the PRC may bring to the attention of the executive council.

The real players in the AU system are the Peace and Security Council (PSC), whose Protocol does not really deal with the asylum issue, and the Assembly of Heads of States and Government, which is most times hopelessly divided over such sensitive issues as asylum. The executive council, being the AU Council of Ministers, is an executory body and is most times beholden to the wishes of the Assembly of Heads of State and Government of the Union. The overall effect of all these dynamics on the PRC Sub-Comm concerned herewith is that it approaches its mandate on a more general rather than specific basis. That way, it is able to avoid dealing with the sensitive, specific issues that are inevitably raised by asylum, such as the protection of asylum seekers' rights and the question of how to ensure that AU Member States implement the Union's legal regimes on the subject matter.

Soft Law Approaches

Aside from the various multilateral instruments adopted by the OAU for the purpose of governing asylum in Africa, the organization adopted several soft law instruments in the hope of gently nudging its Member States towards assuming hard-core responsibilities towards asylum seekers and refugees. The OAU convened countless meetings and conferences related to dealing with asylum seekers and refugees and it is pointless to discuss all these here. As one commentator has rightly noted:

> There is no shortage of declaration, recommendations, or plans of action to solve the refugee and displacement crisis in Africa. If even half of these were to be implemented, there would be virtually no refugees or displaced persons in Africa today and none for the whole of the twenty-first century.[68]

Be that as it may, a brief overview of some of the most important of these meetings and the resulting declarations and decisions is appropriate in order to show what impact these have on Member States' attitude to asylum, on the one hand, and

68 G Okoth-Obbo, 'The OAU/UNHCR Symposium on Refugees and Forced Population Displacement in Africa – A Review Article', Special Summer Issue, International Journal of Refugee Law 279, 297; cited also in M Sharpe, 'Organization of African Unity and African Union Engagement with refuges Protection: 1963–2011' (2013) 20(1) African Journal of International and Comparative Law 50, 79.

how these soft instruments presaged the African Union's approach to the issue, on the other.

Grand Bay (Mauritius) Declaration and Action Plan 1999

The Grand Bay Declaration was the outcome of the very first OAU Ministerial Conference on Human Rights, held from 12 to 16 April 1999 at Grand Bay, Mauritius, where consideration was given to the human rights protection mechanisms and to the development of human rights in general in Africa.[69] In a remarkable departure from the OAU's previous attitude of regarding refugees in terms mainly of posing threats of destabilization and subversion to its affected Member States, the organization acknowledged, in the Grand Bay Declaration, that 'the high number of refugees, displaced persons and returnees in Africa constitutes an impediment to development … [and recognizes] the link between human rights violations and populations displacements and calls for redoubled and concerted efforts by States and the OAU to address the problem'.[70]

The placing of refugee issues within the human framework at Grand Bay implies that cases concerning refugees' protection and allied matters can potentially be adjudicated within a generic human rights framework even if there is an absence of asylum-specific regimes. This development is extremely useful considering that the Protocol for the ACHPR had been adopted in 1998 with high hopes that the Court would soon begin adjudicating human rights issues originating either from the African Charter on Human and Peoples' Rights or from any other such treaties that OAU/AU Member States are party to. As will be seen in other chapters in this volume, especially the one by Colin Harvey, the absence of asylum-specific legislation in the European Union legal regimes or in the regime of individual EU Member States has not proved fatal to the protection of asylum seekers before the community courts. The creative ability of the European Union's legal regime in regard to the protection of asylum rights is a beacon of hope. This is more so because the European Court of Human Rights continues to apply generic human rights provisions contained in the ECHR despite the absence of asylum-specific provisions in this instrument. It is unduly optimistic, no doubt, to expect the African Human Rights court to function with the same vision or robustness of its European counterpart. The lesson of the Grand Bay's decision lies rather in its opening a window of opportunity for the African Court to assert itself in the face of what will certainly be stiff resistance by AU Member States to any attempts to subsume asylum and refugee issues under general human rights frameworks.

The Ministerial Conference at Grand Bay was also supportive of the Protocols to the African Charter, which were to address women's and children's rights and recommended 'that States adopt measures to eradicate violence against

69 This was my own observation.

70 MIN/CONF/HRA/Dec 1 para 9, Organization of African Unity, Grand Bay (Mauritius) Declaration and Plan of Action' (OAU) Grand Bay 12–16 April 1999.

women and children … and to protect children in conflict with the law as well as refugee children'.[71]

Overall, while the Grand Bay Declaration has no legally binding authority on African States, it does show the desire and encouragement given to States to address the protection of such vulnerable groups within their own legislation and efforts by the regional organization itself.

The Kigali Declaration 2003

In 2003, a year after the Constitutive Act of the African Union entered into force, the Union convened its first AU Ministerial Conference on Human Rights in Kigali, Rwanda. The Kigali Declaration, adopted at the conference, arguably reflected Africa's new understanding of the plight of asylum seekers especially with regard to the causes of refugee outflows. Whereas colonial repression lay at the foundation of the pre-1969 OAU refugee Convention, refugee outflows, the ravaging of Africa by brutal civil wars and riveting authoritarian governments in the aftermath of the Cold War constitutes the single most enduring cause of humanitarian disasters and the flight of Africans from their homestead. Hosting the first AU Ministerial Conference on Human Rights in Rwanda, a country that is no stranger to massive uprooting of peoples from their homesteads by extreme violence, was a blunt reminder to African leaders that dealing with asylum seekers, refugees and internally displaced people in Africa in the 21st century should attract a sense of purpose not present before.

Thus, with the Kigali Declaration, the African Union calls 'upon all Member States to recognize forced displacement as a grave violation of human rights to peace, security and dignity, and to take all necessary means to address the problem'.[72] This clarion call, so to speak, entrenched the trail blazed by the Grand Bay Declaration with regard to how the continental organization, the African Union, regarded refugee and asylum issues. Thus, in the Kigali Declaration the AU recalled the Grand Bay Declaration and Action Plan, reaffirmed the 'commitment to the purposes and principles therein',[73] but noted its concern about the ongoing conflicts, human rights and humanitarian law violations which were directly causing 'movements of refugee populations and internally displaced persons'.[74] The Kigali Declaration emphasizes the importance of regional and international Conventions and calls upon AU Member States to implement the instruments, ratify them where necessary and to discharge their obligations stemming from the OAU Convention.[75]

71 Grand Bay Declaration and Action Plan para 6.

72 Kigali Declaration 2003, para 11.

73 Kigali Declaration 2003, preambular para 2.

74 Preambular para 7.

75 Kigali Declaration 2003, paras 12 and 13.

The fact that the Kigali Declaration specifically mentions the 1969 OAU Convention reaffirms its importance and primacy to the question of refugee and asylum protection, despite human rights instruments covering aspects of refugee rights. The tendency is often that the 1969 Convention is relegated to the background even in matters concerning refugees and asylum seekers. For instance, the African Commission seems to prefer the African Charter, as opposed to the OAU Convention, when dealing with cases involving violation of refugee and asylum rights.[76] Simultaneously with the Kigali Declaration, the Report of the Meeting of Experts of the First AU Ministerial Conference on Human Rights in Africa stipulated that the African Commission was to be the oversight body for the 1969 OAU Convention.[77] It was with this acknowledgment that the 1969 OAU Convention was given some sort of enforcement mechanism, which had the potential to enhance the protection and rights it provides for.

Special Rapporteur on Refugees, Asylum Seekers, Migrants and Internally Displaced Persons

To date the African Commission has created five special rapporteurs. Initially there were only three and none dealt directly with asylum. In fact despite the fact that the Special Rapporteur on Prisons and Conditions of Detention could in principle cover asylum seekers within their mandate, there was hardly any activity in this direction.[78] It was only in 2004 that the Special Rapporteur on Refugees, Asylum Seekers, Migrants and Internally Displaced Persons (Special Rapporteur) was created, replacing the newly established Focal Person on Refugees and Displaced Persons in Africa.[79]

The Special Rapporteur was established during the 35th Session of the African Commission in June 2004, with the mandate finalized during the 36th Session in December 2004 with Resolution 72. The mandate grants broad opportunities for the Special Rapporteur to address the problems: there is the ability to 'seek, receive, examine and act upon situations', undertake studies, research and other activities which will help identify methods in which to enhance protection; fact-finding missions, investigations and visits to refugee camps; assist with the development of policies, regulations and law of the Member States, along with dialogue, engagement and cooperation with Member States, National Human

---

76 See p. 21, et seq.

77 Report of the Meeting of Experts of the First AU Ministerial Conference on Human Rights in Africa para 40(2).

78 JD Mujuzi, 'The African Commission on Human and Peoples' Rights and the promotion and protection of refugees' rights' (2009) 9 African Human Rights Law Journal 160, 168.

79 The Focal Person on Refugees and Internally Displaced Persons had not long been in existence before it was replaced, having been established during the African Commission's 34th Session in November 2003.

Rights Institutions and NGOs and regional and international mechanisms; development of protection strategies; raising awareness and promotion of the 1951 UN Convention and the 1969 OAU Convention implementation; and finally the Special Rapporteur is to submit a report for every session of the African Commission.[80]

From the outset it is apparent that the Special Rapporteur was envisioned as having a proactive and effective role in the protection of refugees, however in reality this has not always been the case.[81] While there have been numerous efforts by the Special Rapporteur in terms of publications within journals, conferences and other promotional endeavours, the job is not without its challenges. The lack of finances available impedes the ability of the Special Rapporteur to undertake all elements of its mandate and undermines its protectional and promotional aspects. Furthermore, as the Special Rapporteur has noted, 'the Commission and Special Rapporteur do not have institution capacity to respond materially or physically to these requests [for specific assistance from refugees]', as the role which was given was to 'remind governments to adhere to their obligations under the Charter and other human rights instruments, and remedy the violations complained against by these individuals'.[82]

As a result the Special Rapporteur has more of an awareness-raising and engagement role than actual powers to address protection issues. While it is always useful to have a regional body or focal person undertaking work to identify, recognize and bring attention to the plight of refugees and asylum, the lack of any enforcement mechanisms or power to influence State practice limits the effect of the Special Rapporteur. It comes as no surprise therefore that there have been calls to rethink the role of the Special Rapporteur and to include greater collaboration between the UNHCR and the African Commission.[83]

The United Nations High Commissioner for Refugees (UNHCR)

As the 1969 OAU Convention is considered to be a complement to the 1951 UN Convention, it would only be logical to have some form of institutional cooperation between the AU and UN bodies concerned with refugees and asylum.

---

80 Resolution 72 paras 1(1)–(8), ACHPR/Res 72(XXXV)04.

81 For a discussion on what the former Special Rapporteur Tom Nyanduga achieved while in office see Mujuzi, 'The African Commission' 160, 168–71.

82 Report of the Special Rapporteur on Refugees and Internally Displaced Persons in Africa to the 36th Session of the African Commission, Dakar, Senegal, as cited by R Murray, 'The Special Rapporteur in the African System' in M Evans and R Murray (eds), *The African Charter on Human and Peoples' Rights: The System in Practice, 1986–2006* (2nd edn, Cambridge University Press, 2008) 368 footnote 119.

83 See R Murray 'The Special Rapporteur in the African System' in Evans and Murray '*The African Charter on Human and Peoples' Rights*' and Mujuzi, 'The African Commission' 160.

It was under this rubric that the Memorandum of Understanding between the African Commission on Human and Peoples' Rights and the United Nations Commissioner for Refugees (Memorandum of Understanding) was concluded with the aim of 'more effectively promoting and protecting the human rights of refugees, asylum seekers …'[84]

The Memorandum of Understanding envisions areas of cooperation which range from the sharing of information,[85] joint promotion through dissemination of information raising awareness and training,[86] joint research and publications promoting best practices,[87] supporting and promoting different procedures and mechanisms available within the African Commission,[88] joint actions with the aim to promote implementation of decisions and resolutions,[89] with regular communication between the organizations, and encouragement of closer cooperation with complementarity between their respective mandates.[90] On paper the cooperative relationship between the two looks like it goes a long way in helping to promote and protect asylum seekers and refugees, however there has been little cooperation between the two and a lack of undertaking in the areas of cooperation. Once again this lack of implementation and carrying out of the agreed roles is actually undermining protection and weakening the credibility of the two institutions' abilities to address refugee concerns.

Conclusion

There is no questioning the existence of a potentially revolutionary legal framework which seeks to protect asylum seekers in Africa, as well as recognizing the right to asylum albeit in a limited form. There are ample instruments to ensure asylum seekers and refugees are protected in both the receiving State and the State of origin. The inclusion of specific rights for asylum seekers and refugees in the African Charter and subsequent legal instruments have gone a long way to ensure the incorporation of these groups into the human rights framework and discourse within the region, something which opens up new avenues for addressing violations of protected rights. The AU has continued much of the OAU's innovative work, for example through the continuous application of the OAU Refugee Convention and adoption of new declarations, Conventions and Protocols on the subject matter.

84 See Art 1 and the preamble to the Memorandum of Understanding between the African Commission on Human and Peoples' Rights and the United Nations Commissioner for Refugees.

85 Memorandum of Understanding Art 2(1).

86 Art 2(2).

87 Art 2(3).

88 Art 2(4).

89 Art 2(5).

90 See Arts 2(8) and (7) respectively.

The AU has also managed to adopt instruments which seek to protect asylum seekers not merely after conflicts have ended, but while they are are ongoing.

Nonetheless, the protection of asylum seekers under the AU system is yet bedevilled with myriad shortcomings. The AU has not gone far enough in strengthening the OAU initiatives and developing new ones to address the ever-changing humanitarian environment in Africa. The 1969 OAU Refugee Convention was adopted in the shadows of Africa's struggle against colonialism and foreign domination. This was a historical incident that was so vehemently detested across Africa that it made it easier for African States to exuberantly accept asylum without creating legal and institutional structures to ground the practice. However, the humanitarian environment of post-colonial Africa has largely been characterized by civil wars and other autochthonous malaises, all of which have tilted the scale against rapproachment to asylum. The nascent humanitarian environment thus necessitates the establishment of strong regional regulatory and institutional mechanisms for the protection of asylum seekers against absent or draconian domestic systems. The African system has so far been spectacularly found wanting in this area.

The concessions that were made to secure African States' agreement to the largely morally abjuratory instruments that govern asylum, while understandable from a pragmatic and political point of view, have fundamentally undermined the efficacy of the system. Not only has this costly political price helped in freezing the problems the instruments are meant to address, it has also made it virtually impossible for more efficacious processes to be instituted. For instance, it has proved disastrously impossible for Africa to establish an effective enforcement mechanism either for the protection of asylum seekers in particular or for the protection of human rights in general.

The greatest challenge to protecting asylum and refugees in Africa is often stated to be the lack of political will, on the part of African leaders, to see through the initiatives undertaken by them and to adhere to the regional legal frameworks. The lack of political will certainly manifests in various ways, but, in context, one instance that is hardly acknowledged in discourse regards the seeming unreadiness of Africa's political leadership to actually determine, with clarity, what Africa really needs in order to confront its asylum crisis. African States confuse the proliferation of treaties with an effective tackling of the problems they govern.

The AU is remarkably prolific in adopting path-defining treaties, yet the organization has one of the worst records of implementation. With the requisite political will, it should be fairly clear to the African Union that if 50 years of adopting myriad admirable treaties and tons of forward-looking Conventions have produced nothing more than more disasters, incoherent agenda, confused actions and reactions to the continent's problems, then it is high time African leaders began serious soul-searching. It may not be a bad thing, after all, for the African Union to apply the brakes to its treaty adoption pace and increase the speed on its implementation drive. Until such a time when African leaders recognize and accept the futility of priming the quantity of treaties they adopt over the quality of implementation they bring to obligations assumed by their States, the future of the legal regulation of asylum seekers in Africa, as indeed with the future of human rights protection in the continent, will be nothing more than a whistle in the wind.

Bibliography

Abebe AM, 'Legal and Institutional Dimensions of Protecting and Assisting Internally Displaced Persons in Africa' (2009) Journal of Refugee Studies 154.

Abuya EO, 'Past Reflections, Future Insights: African Asylum Law and Policy in Historical Perspective' (2007) 19 International Journal of Refugee Law 51.

Aiboni SA, *Protection of Refugees in Africa* (Volume 3 of Studies in International Law, Svenska institutet för internationell rätt 1978).

Awuku EO, 'Refugee Movements in Africa and the OAU Convention on Refugees' (1995) 39 J Africa L 79.

Biegon J and Killander M, 'Human rights developments in the African Union during 2009' (2010) African Human Rights Law Journal 212.

Celebrating the African Charter at 30: A Guide to the African Human Rights System (Pretoria University Law Press 2011).

Essien U, 'The African Commission on Human and Peoples' Rights: Eleven Years After' (2000) 6 Buff Human Rights Law Review 93.

Evans M and Murray R (eds), *The African Charter on Human and Peoples' Rights: The System in Practice, 1986–2006* (2nd edn, Cambridge University Press, 2008).

Gil-Bazo MT and Nogueira MB, 'Asylum in the practice of Latin American and African States' UNHCR Policy Development and Evaluation Service Research Paper No. 249, available at http://www.unhcr.org/cgi-bin/texis/vtx/home/open docPDFViewer.html?docid=50e6d9a69&query=Asylum%20in%20the%20 practice%20of%20Latin%20American%20and%20African%20states.

Hathaway J, *The Rights of Refugees Under International Law* (Cambridge University Press, 2005).

Heyns C (ed), *Human Rights Law in Africa* (Vol 1, Martinus Nijhoff, 2004).

Kidane W, 'Managing Forced Displacement by Law in Africa: The Role of the New African Union IDPs Convention' (2011) 44 Vanderbilt Journal of International Law 1.

Lomo ZA, 'The Struggle for Protection of the Rights of Refugees and IDPs in Africa: Making the Existing International Legal Regime Work' (2000) 18 Berkley Journal of International Law 268.

Mujuzi JD, 'The African Commission on Human and Peoples' Rights and the promotion and protection of refugees' rights' (2009) 9 African Human Rights Law Journal 160.

Murray R, *Human Rights in Africa: From the OAU to the African Union* (Cambridge University Press, 2004).

Okoth-Obbo G, 'Thirty Years On: a Legal Review of the 1969 OAU Refugee Convention Governing the Specific Aspects of Refugee Problems in Africa' (2001) 20(1) Refugee Survey Quarterly 79.

Rwelamira MR, 'Two Decades of the 1969 OAU Convention Governing the Specific Aspects of the Refugee Problem in Africa' (1989) 1 International Journal of Refugee Law 557.

Udombana NJ, 'So Far, So Fair: The Local Remedies Rule in the Jurisprudence of the African Commission on Human and Peoples' Rights' (2003) 97 American Journal of International Law 1.

van Hövell tot Westerflier WJEM, 'Africa and Refugees; The OAU Refugee Convention in Theory and Practice' (1989) 7 Netherlands Quarterly Human Rights 172.

Viljoen F. and Louw L, 'State Compliance with the Recommendations of the African Commission on Human and Peoples' Rights, 1994–2004' (2007) 101 American Journal of International Law 1.

Chapter 3

The Role of the African Human Rights System with Reference to Asylum Seekers

Gino J. Naldi and Cristiano d'Orsi

Introduction

The plight of Africa's refugees and displaced persons remains an enduring legacy of its myriad problems, the conflicts, political unrest, human rights abuses,[1] impoverishment, natural disasters and environmental degradation[2] that have plagued the continent over many decades, contributing to the displacement of millions of people.[3] Most recently the conflict in the Darfur region of Sudan,[4] drought, crop failure and famine in east Africa[5] and the political revolution known

---

1 The United Nations (UN) has established links between human rights violations and population displacements, see, for example, Vienna Declaration and Programme of Action, UN Doc A/CONF.157/23 (1993), reprinted in (1993) 32(6) ILM 1661, Part I, para 23(2); *Report of the Group of Government Experts on International Co-operation to Avert New Flows of Refugees*, UN Doc A/41/324 (1986); *Report of the UN Secretary-General on Human Rights and Mass Exoduses*, UN Doc E/CN.4/1996/42, 4-12, 25. The Organization of African Unity (OAU), the predecessor of the African Union (AU), which was formally dissolved in 2002, also acknowledged this nexus, see *Grand Bay (Mauritius) Declaration and Plan of Action 1999*, para 9, reprinted in *Compendium of Key Human Rights Documents of the African Union* (Pretoria University Law Press 2005) 69.

2 See Progress Achieved Towards Meeting Objectives of the Earth Summit, UN General Assembly Resolution A/RES/S-19/2.

3 *Report of the UN Secretary-General on the Causes of Conflict and the Promotion of Durable Peace and Sustainable Development in Africa*, UN Doc A/52/871-S/1998/318 (1998) paras 7–15.

4 Over two million people have been displaced as a result, UN Doc E/CN.4/2006/71/Add.6, paras 6, 9. According to UN Security Council Resolution 1556 (2004) 200,000 refugees fled to neighbouring Chad. More recent estimates put the figure at around a quarter of a million, *Foreign & Commonwealth Office Annual Report on Human Rights 2009*: 149. See also, *Sudan Human Rights Organization and Sudan Centre for Housing Rights and Evictions v Sudan*, African Commission on Human and Peoples' Rights, Communication Nos 279/03, 296/05, (2010) 49(6) ILM 1573. The decisions of the African Commission on Human and Peoples' Rights on communications are available at http://www.achpr.org.

5 Over a quarter of a million people are reported to have died in a famine in Somalia between October 2010 and April 2012 according to a UN report, available at http://www.un.org/apps/news/story.asp?NewsID=44811&Cr=somalia&Cr1= [accessed 8 May 2013].

as the 'Arab Spring' that swept much of North Africa in 2011 have all added to the large-scale flow of those seeking asylum. A broad consensus exists to the effect that asylum seekers are members of a particularly underprivileged and vulnerable population group who are in need of special protection.[6] It is therefore important to draw attention to the fact that African States have contributed significantly to the progressive development of international refugee law and policy. More generally, the Organization of African Unity (OAU)/African Union (AU) have put in place mechanisms for the protection and enforcement of rights at a continental level that impact on the rights of refugees and asylum, or refuge, seekers. This chapter focuses on this specific topic.

The African Human Rights System

The African Commission on Human Rights

Any discussion of the rights of refugees, humanitarian or other, must take into consideration the relevance of human rights. As will be discussed subsequently, human rights are applicable in principle to refugees and asylum seekers.[7] The protection of human rights in Africa is based principally on the African Charter on Human and Peoples' Rights (African Charter, also known as the Banjul Charter) adopted by the OAU in 1981.[8] The African Charter is distinctive for enshrining in

6 *MSS v Belgium and Greece*, European Court of Human Rights (App no 30696/09), judgment of 21 January 2011, para 251, available at http://www.echr.coe.int [accessed 16 December 2011].

7 The European Court of Human Rights has stated that refuge seekers must not be deprived of the protection afforded by the UN Convention Relating to the Status of Refugees 1951, 189 UNTS 137, (Geneva Convention) and the European Convention on Human Rights, *MSS v Belgium and Greece*, above n 6, para 216; *Amuur v France* (1996) 22 EHRR 533, para 43. See further, *Hirsi Jamaa and Others v Italy*, European Court of Human Rights (App no 27765/09), judgment of 23 February 2012, available at http://www.echr.coe.int [accessed 24 February 2012]; *Saadi v United Kingdom*, European Court of Human Rights (App no 13229/03), 29 January 2008, available at http://www.echr.coe.int [accessed 15 December 2011]; *A v Australia*, Human Rights Committee, Communication No 560/1993, UN Doc CCPR/C/59/D/560/1993. The applicability of human rights follows inexorably from the concept of jurisdiction as laid out in for example Art 1 European Convention on Human Rights. See generally, DJ Harris, M O'Boyle and C Warbrick, *Law of the European Convention on Human Rights* (2nd edn, Oxford University Press, 2009) 804–7. It should be observed that the AU Convention on the Protection and Assistance to Internally Displaced Persons in Africa, reprinted in (2010) 49(1) ILM 83, in force 6 December 2012, (Kampala Convention) expressly affirms that IDPs enjoy human rights, see, for example, Arts 3(1)(d), 20(2).

8 African Charter on Human and Peoples' Rights, 1520 UNTS 217, (1982) 21(1) ILM 58, in force 21 October 1986. It has been ratified by all the Member States of the AU with the exception of South Sudan.

a sole binding legal document all three generations of human rights, that is, civil and political rights, economic, social and cultural rights and peoples' or group rights.[9] Responsibility for promoting and ensuring the protection of human and peoples' rights rests primarily with the African Commission on Human and Peoples' Rights (ACHPR) (Commission), a quasi-judicial body.[10] As part of its protective mandate the Commission is competent to entertain applications, or communications, from individuals and NGOs alleging violations of the African Charter.[11] The *locus standi* requirements before the Commission are comparatively broad since individuals and organizations other than the victim can submit a complaint.[12] In fact, the Commission has stated that it has adopted an *actio popularis* approach.[13]

---

9 *Centre for Minority Rights Development (Kenya) and Minority Rights Groups International on behalf of Endorois Welfare Council v Kenya Communication* No 276/2003, 27th Activity Report 2009, para 149. See generally, KD Magliveras and GJ Naldi, *The African Union* (Kluwer Law International, 2009) 161–63, Umozurike UO, *The African Charter on Human and Peoples' Rights* (Martinus Nijhoff, 1997).

10 African Charter, Arts 30, 45. Rule 3 of the Rules of Procedure of the African Commission on Human and Peoples' Rights (Rule of Commission), adopted in May 2010, describes it as 'an autonomous treaty body working within the framework of the African Union to promote human and peoples' rights and ensure their protection in Africa' available at http://www.achpr.org/files/instruments/rules-of-procedure-2010/rules_of_procedure_2010_en.pdf [accessed 15 January 2013]. See generally, Magliveras and Naldi, *The African Union* 199–203, EA Ankumah, *The African Commission on Human and Peoples' Rights* (Martinus Nijhoff 1996).

11 These so-called 'Other' communications are governed by the African Charter, Arts 55–9, Rule of Commission 93. In *Bissangou v Republic of Congo* Communication No 253/2002, 21st Activity Report 2005–06, para 47, the Commission described this aspect of its promotional and protective function, that 'in seizing the Commission, the complainant does not have any other intention than to request the latter to play its role by controlling the conformity to ... the Charter of an action ... of a State party'. See Magliveras and Naldi, *The African Union* 205–17.

12 Rule of Commission 93(1) refers to 'any natural or legal person'. See *Zitha & Zitha v Mozambique* Communication No 361/08, 29th Activity Report 2010, para 106. In *Malawi African Association et al. v Mauritania*, Communication Nos 54/91, 61/91, 98/93, 164/97–196/97, 210/98, 13th Activity Report 1999–2000, para 78, the Commission justified the position thus, 'This characteristic of the African Charter reflects sensitivity to the practical difficulties that individuals can face in countries where human rights are violated. The national or international channels of remedy may not be accessible to the victims themselves or may be dangerous to pursue'. See further, F Viljoen, 'Communications under the African Charter: Procedure and Admissibility' in MD Evans and R Murray (eds), *The African Charter on Human and Peoples' Rights: The System in Practice, 1986–2006* (Cambridge University Press, 2008) 76–138.

13 *Article 19 v Eritrea* Communication No 275/2003, 22nd Activity Report 2006–07, para 65. In *The Law Office of Ghazi Suleiman v Sudan* Communication Nos 222/98 and 229/99, 16th Activity Report 2002–03, para 39, the Commission stated that States' obligations were of an *erga omnes* nature not dependent on individuals, an apparent reference to the special character of human rights treaties.

A number of procedural hurdles have to be overcome initially under Articles 50 and 56 before the Commission will consider the substance of a communication.[14] Its decisions on communications do not formally have the binding force of a ruling of a court of law but rather have a persuasive authority,[15] but an expectation of compliance has developed.[16] Accordingly, under Rule of Commission 112(2), a State Party has 180 days in which to inform the Commission of the measures being taken, if any, to implement the Commission's decision. Where a State fails to comply with a Commission decision in an inter-State or individual communication, Rule of Commission 118(1) authorizes the Commission to submit this communication to the African Court on Human and Peoples' Rights (Court). Any situation of non-compliance will be reported to the AU in accordance with Rule of Commission 112(8).

Article 58 of the African Charter provides for exceptional cases where communications reveal 'the existence of a series of serious or massive violations of human and peoples' rights'. Specific, isolated violations, however serious, lie outside the scope of this provision; instead it refers to a pattern of large-scale violations.[17] Widespread allegations of human rights violations lead the Commission to presume a series of serious or massive violations as established.[18] The Commission must act promptly in such cases.[19] Alternatively, the Commission could choose to refer such cases to the Court.[20]

14 The seven admissibility requirements under Art 56 are cumulative, or 'conjunctive, meaning that if any one of them is absent, the communication will be declared inadmissible', *Article 19 v Eritrea*, above n 13, para 43; *Zimbabwe Lawyers for Human Rights & Associated Newspapers of Zimbabwe v Zimbabwe* Communication No 284/2003, 26th Activity Report 2008–09, para 81. Consequently, all the conditions must generally be fulfilled, *Zimbabwe Human Rights NGO Forum v Zimbabwe* Communication No 245/2002, 21st Activity Report 2005–06, para 36. See further, Viljoen 'Communications under the African Charter' 88–128.

15 African Charter, Art 59.

16 This approach would appear to be required under the African Charter, Art 1, *Civil Liberties Organization v Nigeria* Communication No 129/94, 9th Activity Report 1995–96. See further, *International Pen, Constitutional Rights Project, Interights on behalf of Ken Saro-Wiwa Jr and Civil Liberties Organisation v Nigeria* Communication Nos 137/94, 139/94, 154/96 and 161/97, 12th Activity Report 1998–99, paras 113–16.

17 *Amnesty International et al. v Sudan* Communication Nos 48/90, 50/91, 52/91, 89/93 13th Activity Report 1999–2000, para 32, *Anuak Justice Council v Ethiopia* Communication No 299/05, 20th Activity Report 2005–06, para 61.

18 *Anuak Justice Council v Ethiopia*, above n 17, para 60.

19 *Free Legal Assistance Group, Lawyers Committee for Human Rights, Union Interafricaine des Droits de l'Homme, and Les Temoins Jehoves v Zaïre*, Communication Nos 25/89, 47/90, 59/91, 100/93, Ninth Activity Report 1995–96.

20 Rules of Commission 84(2) and 118(3).

Another important protective power is the Commission's capacity to adopt provisional measures of protection, on its own motion[21] or at the request of a party,[22] to 'prevent irreparable harm to the victim … as urgently as the situation demands'.[23] Although there is nothing in the African Charter or the Rules of Procedure to assert that provisional measures are binding as such on the Parties, the fact that Nigeria ignored the provisional measures led the Commission to condemn Nigeria in the strongest possible terms in *International Pen v Nigeria*.[24] Under the current Rules of Commission an expectation of compliance exists, specifically Rule 118(2) authorizes the Commission to refer a communication to the Court where the State does not comply with the measures requested.[25] A corresponding responsibility is the expectation on States to report on the implementation of the measures within 15 days.[26]

The African Court of Human Rights

According to the Protocol on an African Court on Human and Peoples' Rights (Protocol) the Commission shares its protective mandate with the Court.[27] The contentious jurisdiction of the Court embraces all cases and disputes submitted to it concerning the interpretation and application of, *inter alia*, the African Charter, and any other relevant human rights instrument which a State has ratified.[28] This innovative clause is extremely broad in scope and has been described as conferring upon the Court an 'almost unlimited substantive jurisdiction'.[29] It cannot seriously

21 *Constitutional Rights Project, Civil Liberties Organisation and Media Rights Agenda v Nigeria* Communication Nos 140/94, 141/94 and 145/95, 13th Activity 1999–2000, para 17.

22 *International Pen v Nigeria*, above n 16, para 30.

23 Rule of Commission 98(1).

24 *International Pen v Nigeria*, above n 16, paras 103, 115, 285. See generally GJ Naldi, 'Interim measures of protection in the African system for the protection of human and peoples' rights' (2002) African Human Rights Law Journal 2(1) 1.

25 *In the Matter of the African Commission on Human and Peoples' Rights v Libya* (App no 002/2013), Provisional Measures of 15 March 2013.

26 Rule of Commission 98(4).

27 Protocol to the African Charter on Human and Peoples' Rights on the Establishment of an African Court on Human and Peoples' Rights 1998, Art 2. The Protocol entered into force on 25 January 2004, and at the time of writing has been ratified by 26 AU Member States. See GJ Naldi and KD Magliveras, 'Reinforcing the African System of Human Rights: The Protocol on the Establishment of a Regional Court on Human and Peoples' Rights' (1998) Netherlands Quarterly on Human Rights 16(4) 431. All of the Court's decisions, judgments and orders are available at http://www.african-court.org.

28 Protocol, Art 3(1), Rule of Court 26(1)(a), in force 2 June 2010, available at http://www.african-court.org [accessed 12 August 2011]. See *Femi Falana v African Union*, African Court of Human and Peoples' Rights (App no 001/2011), 26 June 2012, para 63.

29 J Harrington, 'The African Court on Human and Peoples' Rights' in MD Evans and R Murray (eds), *The African Charter on Human and Peoples' Rights: The System in Practice, 1986–2006* (Cambridge University Press, 2002) 305, 318.

be doubted that the Court's substantive jurisdiction clearly extends not only over the OAU Convention on Refugees[30] but also over the Geneva Convention.

Article 5 of the Protocol governs the contentious jurisdiction of the Court. According to Article 5(1) the following are entitled to submit contentious cases: (a) the Commission;[31] (b) a State Party which has lodged a complaint to the Commission; (c) a State Party against which a complaint has been lodged at the Commission; (d) a State Party whose citizen is a victim of a human rights violation; and (e) African Intergovernmental Organizations. These applicants, in contrast to those under Article 5(3), could be described as privileged applicants since access is automatic upon ratification of the Protocol and is not dependent on further declarations by State parties. The standing of other applicants is governed by Article 5(3). Thus, the Court *may* allow individuals and NGOs with observer status before the Commission to bring cases directly before it. Clearly the Court possesses discretion as to whether to accept an application, jurisdiction is optional in such instances.[32] Moreover, the competence of the Court to entertain an application against a particular State is dependent on that State's prior acceptance of the Court's jurisdiction in accordance with Article 34(6) of the Protocol. Under this provision States must make a separate declaration accepting the competence of the Court to receive petitions from these complainants.[33] This position, which compares unfavourably with that before the Commission, is regrettable since it is likely that some of the worst perpetrators of serious human rights abuses will not be brought to account given that it is improbable that they will accept the Court's exceptional jurisdiction under Article 5(3). These questions were at issue in the Court's first case, *Michelot Yogogombaye v Senegal*. For the Court to exercise jurisdiction it was necessary that the respondent State Party, Senegal, have deposited said declaration. However, in the absence of such declaration the Court was unable to entertain the case.[34] In *Association Juriste d'Afrique pour*

30 Convention Governing the Specific Aspects of Refugee Problems in Africa 1969, 1001 UNTS 45, in force 20 January 1974; ratified by 45 AU Member States. See *African Institute for Human Rights and Development (on behalf of Sierra Leonean refugees in Guinea) v Republic of Guinea* Communication No 249/2002, 20th Activity Report 2005–06, para 69.

31 See also, Rule of Commission 118(1). In March 2011 the Commission instituted proceedings against Libya alleging serious and massive violations of human rights guaranteed under the African Charter, *In the Matter of the African Commission on Human and Peoples' Rights v Libyan Arab Jamahiriya*, African Court of Human and Peoples' Rights (App no 004/2011), 4 March 2011. See also *African Commission on Human and Peoples' Rights v Libya*, above n 25, para 2.

32 NJ Udombana, 'Toward the African Court on Human and Peoples' Rights: Better Late than Never' (2000) Yale Human Rights & Development Law Journal 3(1) 87.

33 *Falana v African Union*, above n 28, para 73. As of April 2013 6 States had deposited the required declarations, Burkina Faso, Ghana, Malawi, Mali, Rwanda and Tanzania.

34 *Michelot Yogogombaye v Senegal,* African Court of Human and Peoples' Rights (App no 001/2008), 15 December 2009, paras 35–7. See also, for example, *Delta*

la Bonne Gouvernance v Ivory Coast the insurmountable difficulty was that the applicant NGO did not have observer status with the Commission as required by Article 5(3).[35] However, another possible avenue may exist for an applicant found not to have standing, *forum prorogatum*.[36]

The Court must obviously satisfy itself that it has jurisdiction and that the application is admissible.[37] In addition to establishing that the applicants have *locus standi* it needs to ensure that the complaint impleads a State Party,[38] that it possesses jurisdiction *ratione materiae*,[39] or that domestic remedies have been exhausted. Article 6(2) of the Protocol and Rule of Court 39(1) therefore state that the Court shall rule on the admissibility of cases taking account of Articles 50 and 56 of the African Charter, which, as has been seen, govern communications submitted by individuals and NGOs to the Commission. Rule of Court 40 makes it clear that applications *must* satisfy the hurdles of admissibility, which in every material respect are identical to those listed in Article 56 of the African Charter. Rule of Court 29(6), applying the *lis pendens* principle, provides that a communication before the Commission must be withdrawn if the case submitted to the Court relates to issues in said communication. In addition, any case submitted to the Court must satisfy the terms of Rule of Court 40(7) on conditions of admissibility which states, *inter alia*, that the application to the Court must 'not raise any matter or issues settled by the parties in accordance with … the provisions of the [African] Charter'. Commission decisions would therefore appear to come within the scope of this sub-rule as a result of the *res judicata* principle. This conclusion is reinforced by the fact that the Protocol and the Rules are silent on a right of appeal by States against Commission decisions. The Court

---

International Investments SA, Mr AGL de Lange and Mrs M. de Lange v Republic of South Africa, African Court of Human and Peoples' Rights (App no 002/2012), 30 March 2012; *Amir Adam Timan v Republic of Sudan*, African Court of Human and Peoples' Rights (App no 005/2012), 30 March 2012.

35 *Association Juriste d'Afrique pour la Bonne Gouvernance v Ivory Coast,* African Court of Human and Peoples' Rights (App no. 006/2011), 16 June 2011, paras 7–9. See also, *National Convention of Teachers Trade Union v Republic of Gabon*, African Court of Human and Peoples' Rights (App no 012/2011), 15 December 2011.

36 Separate Opinion of Judge Ouguergouz, *Yogogombaye v Senegal*, above n 34, paras 31–9.

37 Rule 39(1) of the Court. See *Yogogombaye v Senegal*, above n 34, para 40.

38 In *Youseff Ababou v Kingdom of Morocco*, African Court of Human and Peoples' Rights (App no 007/2011), 2 September 2011, para 12, the Court found it lacked jurisdiction because Morocco was not a member of the AU and thus not a party to the Protocol. See also, *Falana v African Union*, above n 28, where the applicant sought to implead, unsuccessfully, the AU itself. And only States may be respondents, Separate Opinion of Judge Mutsinzi, ibid.

39 See *Efoua Mbozo'o Samuel v Pan African Parliament*, African Court of Human and Peoples' Rights (App no 010/2011), 30 September 2011, para 6, where the Court found it lacked jurisdiction on the ground that the application was based exclusively upon breach of an employment contract.

will dismiss applications without merit (manifestly ill-founded) giving reasons for its decision.[40]

Individuals and NGOs may be confronted by another obstacle in that under Article 6(3) of the Protocol the Court is not compelled to entertain an admissible case but has the discretion of referring it to the Commission.[41] The Court has transferred cases to the Commission in instances of serious claims where it has found that it does not possess jurisdiction because a complainant under Article 5(3) of the Protocol lacks standing, either because a State Party has not made a declaration under Article 34(6) of the Protocol or an NGO does not have observer status with the Commission.[42] The Court appears to be guided by an equitable desire to avoid a denial of justice on a technicality. However, such emergent practice has attracted strong disapproval from Judge Ouguergouz who has argued convincingly that the Court's policy 'is not founded in law' and that the Court has 'deviated from the original purpose of that provision'.[43] Implicit in his criticism is the opinion that the issues of jurisdiction and admissibility have been incorrectly determined.[44] In his view, this procedure 'applies primarily to the consideration of the admissibility of a case over which the jurisdiction of the Court has already been established'.[45] He additionally contends that the principle of legal certainty demands that clear reasoned objective criteria should guide the Court in its practice of referrals to the Commission since the current policy was haphazard and unpredictable and was in danger of becoming 'systematic'.[46] In his view the Court could play 'the role of an "early warning mechanism" for the Commission' and that the procedure in question should be reserved for those cases displaying 'exceptional circumstances', such as those envisaged by Article 58 of the African Charter, where the former lacks jurisdiction.[47] He sees no reason why the Court

40 Rule of Court 38. See *Amare v Republic of Mozambique and Mozambique Airlines*, African Court of Human and Peoples' Rights (App no 005/2011), 16 June 2011, para 8. Judge Ouguergouz has argued that in such circumstances the application should not be 'considered judicially by the Court' but should be 'dismissed *de plano* by a simple letter from the Registry' on grounds of time and resources, see, for example, his Separate Opinion in *Yogogombaye v Senegal*, above n 34.

41 See also, Rule of Court 29(5)(a).

42 *Amare v Mozambique and Mozambique Airlines*, above n 40, para 9; *Association Juriste d'Afrique v Ivory Coast*, above n 35, para 10; *Ekollo Moundi Alexandre v Republic of Cameroon and Federal Republic of Nigeria*, African Court of Human and Peoples' Rights (App no 008/2011), 23 September 2011, para 11.

43 Dissenting Opinion of Judge Ouguergouz, *Alexandre v Cameroon and Nigeria*, above n 42, paras 12, 20.

44 Ibid., paras 14–19.

45 Ibid., para 13.

46 Ibid., paras 21–6.

47 Ibid., paras 22–9.

should not use its discretion to transfer cases over which it has jurisdiction to the Commission to rule on the merits.[48]

The Court is empowered to adopt such provisional measures of protection as it deems necessary in cases of 'extreme gravity and urgency', and 'to avoid irreparable harm to persons'.[49] They are also designed to preserve the *status quo ante* pending the determination of the case.[50] Stringent requirements must therefore be met. The Court found that 'circumstances ... of great urgency' relating especially to the rights to life and physical integrity during the revolution in Libya in early 2011 compelled it to adopt such measures ordering Libya to refrain from activities resulting in the violation of such rights under, *inter alia*, the African Charter.[51] In *African Commission on Human and Peoples' Rights v Kenya (Provisional Measures)* the Court took notice of prejudice to the substantive matter before it.[52]

Interim measures can be given at the request of a party to the case, the Commission[53] or the Court on its own accord.[54] The fact that the Court can order any measures 'it deems necessary' suggests that they could be 'in whole or in part other than those requested'. The Court need not satisfy itself that it has jurisdiction on the merits but simply that *prima facie* jurisdiction exists.[55] This it can do by establishing that the applicant is an entity entitled to submit a case to the Court and that the Respondent has ratified the African Charter and the Protocol.[56] The Court has stated that the indication of interim measures does not prejudge the question

---

48 Ibid., paras 31–3.

49 Protocol, Art 27(2). This capacity is supplemented by Rule of Court 51(1) which refers to 'the interest of the parties', no doubt corresponding to the preservation of their respective rights, or 'of justice', thus conferring upon the Court a sweeping discretion. See *African Commission on Human and Peoples' Rights v Libya*, above n 25, para 17. The Court has described provisional measures as 'a consequence of the right to protection under the [African] Charter', *African Commission on Human and Peoples' Rights v Libya*, above n 25, para 13.

50 *African Commission on Human and Peoples' Rights v Republic of Kenya*, African Court of Human and Peoples' Rights (App no. 006/2012), Provisional Measures of 15 March 2013, para 23.

51 *In the Matter of the African Commission on Human and Peoples' Rights v Libyan Arab People's Jamahiriya*, African Court of Human and Peoples' Rights (App no 004/2011), Provisional Measures of 25 March 2011. See also *African Commission on Human and Peoples' Rights v Libya*, above n 25.

52 *African Commission on Human and Peoples' Rights v Kenya*, above n 50, para 22.

53 *African Commission on Human and Peoples' Rights v Kenya*, above n 50.

54 In March 2011 the Court ordered provisional measures *proprio motu*, *African Commission on Human and Peoples' Rights v Libya*, above n 51.

55 *African Commission on Human and Peoples' Rights v Kenya*, above n 50, para 16; *African Commission on Human and Peoples' Rights v Libya*, above n 51, para 15.

56 *African Commission on Human and Peoples' Rights v Libya*, above n 51, paras 17–18.

of jurisdiction, the admissibility or merits of the case.[57] Both the Protocol and the Rules of Court are silent on whether interim measures have binding effect but the use of the verb 'prescribe' in Rule of Court 51(1) is capable of being interpreted as an order or a recommendation. And favouring the sense of a legal duty is the fact that the Court itself has issued 'orders' to the respondents.[58] However, to the contrary is the Court's obligation to 'make all such recommendations as it deems appropriate' in instances of non-compliance by States in its Annual Report to the Assembly under Article 31 of the Protocol and Rule of Court 51(4) which suggests that the final decision on such matters rests with the Assembly. The judgments of the Court are, however, binding on the parties.[59]

The 'New' African Court of Justice and Human Rights

The African Court may have a limited existence, as it is due to be replaced at some future stage by the African Court of Justice and Human Rights.[60] However, the 2008 Protocol does not seem to make any material changes to the substantive jurisdiction of the latter Court in terms of human rights. The African Court of Justice and Human Rights is composed of two sections, one of which is the Human Rights Section with jurisdiction over alleged violations of human rights.[61] Under Article 28(c) of the Statute the Human Rights Section has jurisdiction relating to the interpretation and application of the African Charter, the African Charter on the Rights of the Child,[62] the Protocol on the Rights of Women in Africa[63] or of any other legal instrument pertaining to human rights. Again the sweeping nature of the latter clause is noteworthy. The Human Rights Section appears to have jurisdiction to pronounce on multilateral instruments such as the Geneva Convention. The Human Rights Section could interpret and apply the

57 *African Commission on Human and Peoples' Rights v Kenya*, above n 50, para 24; *African Commission on Human and Peoples' Rights v Libya*, above n 25, para 19.

58 *African Commission on Human and Peoples' Rights v Libya*, above n 51.

59 Protocol, Arts 28(2), 30, Rule of Court 61(5).

60 Protocol on the Statute of the African Court of Justice and Human Rights 2008, reprinted in (2009) 48(2) ILM 337, Art 2 (2008 Protocol). The Protocol requires 15 ratifications to enter into force and as of March 2013 had been ratified by 5 States. See generally, GJ Naldi and KD Magliveras, 'The African Court of Justice and Human Rights: A Judicial Curate's Egg' (2012) International Organizations Law Review 9(2) 387.

61 Statute of the African Court of Justice and Human Rights (Statute), Art 17(2). See GJ Naldi, 'The Role of the Human Rights Section of the African Court of Justice and Human and Rights' in A Abass (ed.), *Protecting Human Security in Africa* (Oxford University Press, 2010) 284.

62 African Charter on the Rights and Welfare of the Child 1990, reprinted in (1989) 28(6) ILM 1456. in force 29 October 1999.

63 Protocol to the African Charter on Human and Peoples' Rights on the Rights of Women in Africa 2003, in force 25 November 2005, available at: http://au.int/treaties.

OAU Convention on Refugees either under this provision or paragraph (b) thereof as it is expressly granted jurisdiction over OAU/AU treaties.

The following entities possess standing according to Article 30 of the Statute to submit cases to the Human Rights Section: (a) States Parties to the 2008 Protocol; (b) the Commission; (c) the African Committee of Experts on the Rights of the Child; (d) African Intergovernmental Organizations; (e) African national human rights institutions; and (f) individuals and NGOs accredited to the AU or to its organs. Under the Statute a complainant is not required to be the victim of the alleged violation. Although not explicitly set out in the Statute it is likely that inter-State cases are permissible. Whether States will be allowed to appeal adverse opinions issued by the Commission and by the Committee of Experts on the Rights of the Child is by no means certain; it will be recalled that it was submitted earlier that Commission decisions cannot be appealed to the Court, but the language of the Statute suggests that it is likely to be so. That African intergovernmental organizations, such as The Economic Community of West African States (ECOWAS), and national human rights institutions have been listed as applicants is especially interesting. National human rights institutions could play a significant role if sufficiently independent. The fact that, in principle, the standing of duly accredited individuals and NGOs has been recognized is encouraging, although the requirement of accreditation may have a restrictive effect.[64] The standing of NGOs and individuals is still contingent on States making a separate optional declaration accepting the competence of the Court under Article 8(3) of the 2008 Protocol. It could be considered unfortunate that the opportunity was not taken to relax access to the Human Rights Section so that standing was made automatic upon ratification[65] but the African system is not unique in restricting access.[66] The Statute is silent on the issue of hurdles of admissibility. It must be assumed that detailed conditions governing admissibility will be laid down in the Rules of Court.

Under Article 35(1) of the Statute, the Human Rights Section can, *proprio motu*, or at the request of a party to the case, indicate such provisional measures to preserve the respective rights of the parties 'if it considers that circumstances so require'. This provision appears to depart from the more stringent language of Article 27(2) of the Protocol.

---

64 S Sceats, 'Africa's New Human Rights Court: Whistling in the Wind?' (2009) [online: Chatham House Briefing Paper IL BP 09/01], available at http://www.chathamhouse.org.uk/research/international_law/papers [accessed 16 January 2013]. And see *Association Juriste d'Afrique pour la Bonne Gouvernance v Ivory Coast*, above n 35. In July 2005 the Executive Council updated the criteria for accreditation for NGOs, Executive Council, *Criteria for Granting Observer Status and for a System of Accreditation within the AU* (EX.CL/Dec.195 (VII)).

65 Cf. European Convention on Human Rights, Art 34.

66 Cf. ACHR, Art 62.

The Application of Rights in the African Charter to Asylum Seekers

It is important to note that the rights guaranteed by the African Charter are applicable to asylum seekers and refugees.[67] This fact is especially significant because the protection afforded by international human rights law is more generous than that of international refugee law which has had to adapt to comply with these, often, superior norms. By virtue of Article 1 of the African Charter, States Parties have assumed a binding legal obligation to recognize and uphold the rights, duties and freedoms therein,[68] and, in accordance with Article 2 of the African Charter, they are additionally obliged to secure the rights protected by the African Charter to all persons within their jurisdiction, nationals and non-nationals alike.[69] Charter rights that the Commission has applied to refugees include the right to life,[70] the right to human dignity,[71] the right to liberty and

---

67 *Institute for Human Rights and Development in Africa v Angola* Communication No 292/2004, 24th Activity Report 2007–08, para 84. See generally R Murray, *Human Rights in Africa: From the OAU to the African Union* (Cambridge University Press, 2004) 185–234. The rights and freedoms enshrined in the African Charter are similarly relevant to the internally displaced, *Sudan Human Rights Organization and Sudan Centre for Housing Rights and Evictions v Sudan*, above n 4, paras 186–90. In *Doebbler v Sudan*, Communication No. 235/2000, 27th Activity Report 2009, para 126 the Commission expressed the view that the provisions of the Geneva Convention, the OAU Convention on Refugees and the African Charter complemented each other.

68 *International Pen v Nigeria*, above n 16, para 116, *Sir Dawda K Jawara v The Gambia* Communication Nos 147/95 and 149/96, 13th Activity Report 1999–2000, para 46, *Purohit and Moore v The Gambia* Communication No 241/2001, 16th Annual Report 2002–03, para 43.

69 *Rencontre Africaine pour la Defense des Droits de l'Homme v Zambia* Communication No 71/92, Tenth Activity Report 1996–97, para 22, *African Institute for Human Rights and Development v Guinea*, above n 30, para 68, *Institute for Human Rights and Development in Africa v Angola*, above n 67, para 84.

70 African Charter, Art 4, *Organisation Mondiale Contre La Torture and the Association Internationale des Juristes Democrates and Others v Rwanda*, Communication Nos 27/89, 46/91, 49/91, 99/93, Tenth Activity Report 1993–94, *African Institute for Human Rights and Development v Guinea*, above n 30.

71 African Charter, Art 5, *Organisation Mondiale Contre La Torture v Rwanda*, above n 70, *African Institute for Human Rights and Development v Guinea*, above n 30. The European Court of Human Rights has held in a number of cases that detention conditions for refuge seekers must be compatible with Art 3 European Convention on Human Rights, see *S D v Greece* (App no 53541/07), judgment of 11 June 2009, paras 49–54, available at http://www.echr.coe.int [accessed 16 December 2011], *Tabesh v Greece* (App no 8256/07), judgment of 26 November 2009, paras 38–44, available at http://www.echr.coe.int [accessed 16 December 2011], *AA v Greece* (App no 12186/08), judgment of 22 July 2010, paras 57–65, available at http://www.echr.coe.int [accessed 16 December 2011], *MSS v Belgium and Greece*, above n 6, paras 223–34. In *MSS v Belgium and Greece*, above n 6, paras 235–63, the European Court of Human Rights found a further breach of the European

security of the person,[72] the 'right of access to judicial protection'[73] and the right to property.[74]

The violation of the human rights of refugees on a massive scale in recent years engaged the attention of the international community which responded to the conflict in the Darfur region of Sudan that broke out in 2001, with atrocities perpetrated on civilian populations that led to forced displacement, in a collectively forceful manner.[75] The Commission also expressed its concern at the situation in Darfur,[76] and found that Sudan had committed widespread and gross violations of the African Charter in Darfur.[77]

There are other Charter rights that have a special significance for refugees. The principle of non-discrimination enshrined in Article 2 of the African Charter which guarantees every individual the rights pledged therein without distinction on a wide number of specified grounds, including sex, race, ethnic or national origin, political opinion or religion, supplements the guarantees contained in the UN and OAU Conventions on Refugees which are to be applied to all refugees without discrimination on specified grounds.[78] The fundamental point is that the principle of non-discrimination can be invoked by refugees, usually in association with other rights. In *Organisation Mondiale Contre La Torture v Rwanda* the Commission found that the expulsion from Rwanda of Burundi refugees was motivated by

---

Convention on Human Rights, Art 3, due to the squalid living conditions in which the applicant was forced to live.

72 *Organisation Mondiale Contre La Torture v Rwanda*, above n 70. See *Amuur v France*, above n 7 *18*, para 43, where the European Court of Human Rights stated that under Art 5 European Convention on Human Rights, the confinement of, *in casu*, refuge seekers could only be brief and was acceptable only in order to enable States to prevent unlawful immigration.

73 African Charter, Art 7(1), *Organisation Mondiale Contre La Torture v Rwanda*, above n 70, para 34. The European Court of Human Rights has found that an effective remedy against the rejection of an asylum application is required under Art 13 European Convention on Human Rights, *Chahal v United Kingdom* (1997) 23 EHRR 413, para 153.

74 African Charter, Art 14, *African Institute for Human Rights and Development v Guinea*, above n 30.

75 The UN Security Council categorized this conflict as a threat to international peace and security, Resolution 1556 (2004), adopted pursuant to Chapter VII UN Charter, which imposed sanctions on Sudan. See also, for example, Resolution 1784 (2007). Under Resolution 1593 (2005) the UN Security Council referred the situation in Darfur to the Prosecutor of the International Criminal Court. A warrant for the arrest of the President of Sudan, Omar Al Bashir, was reissued in July 2010, *Second Warrant of Arrest for Omar Hassan Ahmed Al Bashir*, ICC Pre-Trial Chamber I, ICC-02/05-01/09-95, available at http://www.icc-cpi.int [accessed 27 June 2012].

76 See, for example, Resolution on the Situation of Human Rights in the Darfur Region in Sudan, 20th Activity Report 2006.

77 *Sudan Human Rights Organization v Sudan*, above n 4.

78 Geneva Convention, Art 3, OAU Convention on Refugees, Art 4. The Kampala Convention contains a general non-discrimination clause, Art 3(1)(d).

their nationality or membership of a particular ethnic group and thus constituted a clear violation of Article 2 of the African Charter.[79] In *African Institute for Human Rights and Development v Guinea* the Commission held that mass expulsion of refugees amounted to discriminatory action contrary to Article 2 of the African Charter and Article 4 of the OAU Convention on Refugees.[80]

The principle of *non-refoulement* is given a measure of support by Article 12(3)–(4) of the African Charter. The latter clause states that an alien lawfully in the territory of a State may be expelled only in accordance with the due process of law.[81] The Commission has held that the provision must be interpreted so as to prevent arbitrary expulsions.[82] Furthermore, if the procedure for expulsion entails arrest and detention, the safeguards relating to deprivation of liberty are applicable, as is the right to have the case reviewed. Thus in *Organisation Mondiale Contre La Torture v Rwanda* the Commission found that by expelling Burundian refugees without giving them the opportunity to be heard by a competent court, Rwanda was in breach of Article 7(1) of the African Charter.[83] Consequently, Rwanda had additionally violated Article 12(4) of the African Charter prohibiting the arbitrary expulsion of such persons from the country of asylum.[84]

Opinion is divided as to whether the principle of *non-refoulement* must be observed in cases of mass influx of displaced persons, or whether States may

---

79 *Organisation Mondiale Contre La Torture v Rwanda*, above n 70, para 22. See also *African Institute for Human Rights and Development v Guinea*, above n 30, para 69.

80 *African Institute for Human Rights and Development v Guinea*, above n 30, para 69.

81 *Organisation Mondiale Contre La Torture v Rwanda*, above n 70, para 30, *Institute for Human Rights and Development in Africa v Angola*, above n 67, paras 63–5, *Union Interafricaine des Droits de l'Homme et al. v Angola* Communication No 159/96, 11th Activity Report 1997–98, paras 19–20. Cf. Seventh Protocol European Convention on Human Rights, Art 1. It is regrettable for the interests of refugees that Art 6 European Convention on Human Rights on the right to a fair trial has been found not applicable to asylum procedures, *Katani v Germany* (App no 67679/01), Decision of 31 May 2001.

82 The Commission has further stated that while the African Charter does not prohibit deportations as such, the State's right to expel individuals does not justify the manner in which it does so, *Rencontre Africaine pour la Defense des Droits de l'Homme v Zambia*, above n 69, para 23; *Union Interafricaine des Droits de l'Homme v Angola*, above n 81, paras 19–20; *Institute for Human Rights and Development in Africa v Angola*, above n 67, para 63. The European Court of Human Rights has stated that a principal concern is whether effective guarantees exist that protect the applicant against arbitrary *refoulement*, be it direct or indirect, to the country from which s/he has fled, *Müslim v Turkey* (App no 53566/99), judgment of 26 April 2005, paras 72–6, *MSS v Belgium and Greece*, above n 6, para 286, *Hirsi Jamaa v Italy*, above n 7, paras 153–6. The European Court of Human Rights has held additionally that a refuge seeker should not be removed to their country of origin without having had the opportunity to make an effective asylum claim to the domestic authorities or, should the need arise, an application to the Court for interim measures of protection, *KRS v United Kingdom* (App no 32733/08), decision of 2 December 2008.

83 *Organisation Mondiale contre la Torture v Rwanda*, above n 70, para 34.

84 *Organisation Mondiale contre la Torture v Rwanda*, above n 70, para 30.

legitimately invoke the national security exception in such situations, absent as such from the OAU Convention on Refugees.[85] The Commission will take note of the legitimate national security concerns of States,[86] which is not unlimited however.[87] Nevertheless, the practice of the Commission establishes that the principle of *non-refoulement* is applicable in cases of mass influx of refugees.[88]

A State's ability to *refoule* a person may be constrained by the operation of other human rights commitments.[89] The *non-refoulement* obligation can become operative as a result of a breach or the risk of a breach of the spirit of any guaranteed right. The degree of the obligation extant on the State is a graded one, dependent on the nature of the right at stake. When there is a risk of a violation of an absolute right in the receiving State the obligation of *non-refoulement* assumes a categorical aspect. When there is a risk of a violation of any other, qualified, right which allows for derogation the returning State is required to assess the proportionality of the competing principles at issue, except when the risk of a right's violation in the receiving State is 'flagrant' and the very essence of that right is in jeopardy. Consequently, if *refoulement* were to result in a person facing the death penalty the returning State would be prevented by the operation of Article 4 of the African Charter, which guarantees the right to life, from doing so. Whereas an individual's separation from one's family could be deemed a breach of Article 5 of the African Charter which protects human dignity,[90] it could be justifiable if the threat posed outweighed the rights secured to the individual.[91] The same standard applies to universal human rights law, which may be binding on African States. Article 3(1) of the UN Convention Against Torture 1984 expressly prohibits *refoulement*

---

85 EU Council Directive 2001/55 of 20 July 2001 on minimum standards for giving temporary protection in the case of a mass influx of displaced persons and on measures promoting a balance of efforts between Member States in receiving such persons and bearing the consequences thereof, OJ L 212/12, 7 August 2008 (Temporary Protection Directive), designed to provide a coordinated response to large influxes of displaced peoples as a result of armed conflict, endemic violence or serious human rights violations, explicitly applies the principle of *non-refoulement* to cases of mass influx of displaced persons, Art3(2). Judge Pinto de Albuquerque was clearly of this view, Concurring Opinion of Judge Pinto de Albuquerque, *Hirsi Jamaa v Italy*, above n 7.

86 *Rencontre Africaine pour la Defense des Droits de l'Homme v Zambia*, above n 69, para 71.

87 *DR Congo v Burundi, Rwanda and Uganda* Communication No 227/99, 20th Annual Activity Report 2005–06, para 76.

88 In *Doebbler v Sudan*, above n 67, para 146, the question whether the principle of *non-refoulement* applied to 14,000 Ethiopian refugees residing in Sudan was central to the case.

89 JC Hathaway, *The Rights of Refugees under International Law* (Cambridge University Press, 2005) 305.

90 *Amnesty International v Sudan*, above n 17, para 54, *The Law Office of Ghazi Suleiman v Sudan*, above n 13, para 44.

91 Harris, O'Boyle and Warbrick, *Law of the European Convention on Human Rights* 418–22.

where 'substantial grounds' exist for believing that the person would be in danger of being tortured.[92] While the European Convention on Human Rights contains no explicit prohibition the principle has been acknowledged by the European Court on Human Rights as extending beyond the similar guarantee under international refugee law, and its jurisprudence clearly establishes that expulsions will breach Article 3 European Convention on Human Rights if the individual in question faces a real risk of ill-treatment in the receiving State.[93] This also holds true for the International Covenant on Civil and Political Rights 1966.[94]

Other essential general principles applicable to the exceptions to *non-refoulement* are firstly, they must be interpreted restrictively or proportionately,[95] and, secondly, applied only to the particular circumstances of the case and based on the personal conduct of the individual concerned.[96] *Refoulement* must therefore be compatible with human rights.

An important consideration in this context is Article 12(5) of the African Charter, which prohibits the mass expulsion of aliens, described by the Commission as 'a special threat to human rights'.[97] This provision also applies

---

92 1465 UNTS 85, *Elmi v Australia*, Committee Against Torture, Communication No 120/1998, UN Doc CAT/C/22/D/120/1998, *Tahir Hussain Khan v Canada*, Committee Against Torture, Communication No 15/1994, UN Doc A/50/44. See also, UN International Convention for the Protection of All Persons from Enforced Disappearance 2006, UN Doc A/61/1488, Art 16(1).

93 'Under the European Convention, a refugee cannot be subjected to refoulement to his or her country of origin or any other country where he or she risks incurring serious harm caused by any identified or unidentified person or public or private entity', Concurring Opinion of Judge Pinto de Albuquerque, *Hirsi Jamaa v Italy*, above n 7. See, for example, *Chahal v United Kingdom*, above n 73, *Saadi v Italy*, European Court of Human Rights (2008) 47(4) ILM 545, *Ismoilov and Others v Russia*, European Court of Human Rights (App no 2947/06), 24 April 2008, available at http://www.echr.coe.int [accessed 15 August 2011]. See generally, H Lambert, 'Protection Against refoulement in Europe: Human Rights Comes to the Rescue' (1999) International and Comparative Law Quarterly 48(3) 515–44 515.

94 999 UNTS 171, *ARJ v Australia*, UN Human Rights Committee, Communication No 692/1996, UN Doc CCPR/C/60/D/692/1996, para 6.9.

95 Harris, O'Boyle and Warbrick, *Law of the European Convention on Human Rights* 10–11.

96 The test to be applied concerns the profound seriousness of the acts committed by the individual and of that individual's individual responsibility for them, Cases C-57/09 and C-101/09 *Federal Republic of Germany v B & D* [2010] ECR I-10979, paras 108–9.

97 *Rencontre Africaine pour la Defense des Droits de l'Homme v Zambia*, above n 69, para 20, *African Institute for Human Rights and Development v Guinea*, above n 30, para 69. The conditions for mass expulsion are satisfied where arrests occur over a period of several months at different places and deportation orders are served at different dates, *Institute for Human Rights and Development in Africa v Angola*, above n 67, para 69. The mass expulsion of aliens is prohibited by other treaties, such as the Fourth Protocol European Convention on Human Rights, Art 4.

to refugees and refuge seekers.[98] In *Organisation Mondiale contre la Torture v Rwanda* the Commission found that the expulsion of Burundian refugees on the basis of their nationality violated Article 12(5) of the African Charter.[99] While the Commission has taken cognisance of the economic and other challenges faced by many African States hosting large numbers of refugees and that States may sometimes resort to extreme measures to protect their citizens and economies, nevertheless, 'such measures should not be taken to the detriment of the enjoyment of human rights' and the mass expulsion of persons, whether on the basis of nationality, race, ethnicity or religion, 'is generally qualified as discriminatory in this sense as it has no legal basis'.[100] The Commission has therefore stressed that such expulsions must comply with the human rights obligations in the African Charter,[101] including due process requirements.[102]

Article 5 of the OAU Convention on Refugees contains another distinctive right in making provision for voluntary repatriation. While voluntary repatriation may offer one of the best solutions to the refugee crisis[103] it can only be made effective if human rights are protected, the rule of law is respected, property restitution is addressed and the safety of returnees can be assured.[104] But voluntary repatriation would be meaningless if a refugee was prevented from returning to their country of origin. International human rights norms dictate that a person cannot be arbitrarily deprived of the right to return to their own country. The OAU Convention on Refugees does not address this issue but under general international law a national cannot be denied entry to his or her country of origin.[105] According

98 See *Hirsi Jamaa v Italy*, above n 7, paras 166–86.

99 *Organisation Mondiale contre la Torture v Rwanda*, above n 70, para 32.

100 *African Institute for Human Rights and Development v Guinea*, above n 30, paras 67–9. See also, *Union Interafricaine des Droits de l'Homme v Angola*, above n 81, para 16, *Institute for Human Rights and Development in Africa v Angola*, above n 67, para 68.

101 *Institute for Human Rights and Development in Africa v Angola*, above n 67, para 69.

102 Persons are thus 'entitled to submit reasons against the expulsion, have the case reviewed and be represented for these purposes before a competent authority', *Institute for Human Rights and Development in Africa v Angola*, above n 67, para 70.

103 EO Awuku, 'Refugee Movements in Africa and the OAU Convention on Refugees' (1995) Journal of African Law 39(1) 85. In resolution 2003/52 the UN Commission on Human Rights makes the point that return is not and should not be perceived as the only solution to forcible displacement but that resettlement and local integration are policies that should also be considered.

104 See the *Kigali Declaration 2003*, para 14, reprinted in *Compendium of Key Human Rights Documents* above n 1, 80. In this respect the AU's Peace and Security Council has a role to play, see Protocol relating to the Establishment of the Peace and Security Council of the African Union 2002, in force 26 December 2003, Art 14(1)(d) available at: http://au.int/treaties.

105 Universal Declaration of Human Rights 1948, UN General Assembly Resolution 217(III) Art 13(2), ICCPR, Art 12(2).

to Article 12(2) of the African Charter, an individual has the right to return to his or her country subject to the law of public order and security.[106]

A development of 'real and practical importance' is the inclusion of a right of asylum in Article 12(3) of the African Charter.[107] According to the Commission this provision includes 'a general protection of all those who are subject to persecution, that they may seek refuge in another state'.[108] The definition of 'persecution' assumes a critical importance.[109] The wording of the provision, 'when persecuted', is capable of a restrictive interpretation in that refugees are required to have suffered actual persecution rather than simply demonstrating the more generous standard of a well-founded fear of persecution as required by refugee law.[110] The Commission's use of the phrase 'those who are subject to persecution'[111] suggests that this may well be the case.

Conclusion

The OAU Convention on Refugees constituted an advance on existing international refugee law, setting a more generous legal standard, and has been described as creating 'an impressive normative framework'.[112] These were welcome humanitarian developments that sought to address in some way Africa's considerable refugee problems. But human rights was not then the priority that it was later to become. In light of subsequent developments elsewhere, particularly the EU, it seems fair comment to suggest that the African response, once pioneering, now lags behind the times.[113] Unlike the EU, there exists no uniform set of procedures for determination of refugee status and appeals.[114] There

106 *Alhassan Abubakar v Ghana*, Communication No 103/93, 10th Activity Report 1996–97.

107 Ankumah *The African Commission on Human and Peoples' Rights* 139.

108 *Organisation Mondiale Contre La Torture v Rwanda*, above n 70, para 30.

109 Ankumah *The African Commission on Human and Peoples' Rights* 140. The definition of 'acts of persecution' contained in EU Council Directive 2004/83 of 29 April 2004 on minimum standards for the qualification and status of third country nationals or stateless persons as refugees or as persons who otherwise need international protection and the content of the protection granted, OJ L 304/12, 30 September 2004 (Qualification Directive), Art 9, is useful. While such acts must be 'sufficiently serious' or 'sufficiently severe' the definition is not exhaustive.

110 A well-founded fear of persecution is a core factor in the determination of refugee status, see Geneva Convention, Art 1A(2), Qualification Directive, Art 2(c).

111 *Organisation Mondiale Contre La Torture v Rwanda*, above n 70, para 30.

112 F Viljoen *International Human Rights Law in Africa* (Oxford University Press, 2007) 258.

113 Although it seems worth reiterating that with the Kampala Convention Africa is again setting the pace.

114 *Doebbler v Sudan*, above n 67, para 165.

should therefore be a uniform process, fair and effective, so that all refugees receive identical treatment.[115] Detention of refugees should be avoided unless there is no suitable alternative and should be monitored by judicial authorities.[116] Procedural safeguards must be applied. All asylum seekers should have a right of appeal if their application is rejected by the receiving State in accordance with Article 7(1)(a) of the African Charter.[117] Applications for asylum should be processed promptly and delays in reaching decisions should be kept to a minimum.[118] And it is not unimportant that African States that have not yet done so accede to the Geneva and/or OAU Conventions.[119] The Commission is, however, having a considerable influence on the progressive development of the law in this area. The fact that the African Charter, in addition to other human rights standards, is deemed applicable to asylum seekers is highly significant because it means at the very least that asylum seekers and refugees are entitled to basic rights and must be treated with dignity.[120] It is clear that the African Court of Human and Peoples' Rights is competent to hear cases relating to the rights of refugees. A comprehensive, pan-African protective system is thus available to protect and enforce the rights of refugees. But unless the root causes of mass displacement are effectively addressed, and ending a culture of impunity for human rights and humanitarian law violations is a crucial consideration, to be replaced by peace, security and stability, the international community is dealing in palliatives and the sorry plight of Africa's refugees will continue to be a stain on the conscience of humankind.

---

115 See the minimum refugee status determination procedures suggested by Judge Pinto de Albuquerque, Concurring Opinion of Judge Pinto de Albuquerque, *Hirsi Jamaa and Others v Italy*, above n 7.

116 The right to liberty and security of the person is guaranteed by the African Charter, Art 6 and applies to all deprivations of liberty, *Purohit and Moore v The Gambia*, above n 68, para 64.

117 *Organisation Mondiale Contre La Torture v Rwanda*, above n 70, para 34. Although the Commission has expressed the view that it is not always reasonable to expect refugees to apply to the courts 'given their extreme vulnerability and state of deprivation, their fear of being deported and their lack of adequate means to seek legal representation', *Doebbler v Sudan*, above n 67, para 116.

118 African Charter, Art 7(1)(d).

119 In *Hirsi Jamaa v Italy*, above n 7, paras 153, 156, the European Court of Human Rights was critical of Libya, observing that it had not ratified the Geneva Convention, that any asylum procedure was lacking and that the Libyan authorities refused to recognize refugee status granted by the UNHCR.

120 *African Institute for Human Rights and Development v Guinea*, above n 30.

References

Ankumah EA, *The African Commission on Human and Peoples' Rights* (Martinus Nijhoff 1996).

Awuku EO, 'Refugee Movements in Africa and the OAU Convention on Refugees' (1995) Journal of African Law 39(1) 79–86.

Compendium of Key Human Rights Documents of the African Union (Pretoria University Law Press 2005).

Harrington J, 'The African Court on Human and Peoples' Rights' in MD Evans and R Murray (eds), *The African Charter on Human and Peoples' Rights: The System in Practice, 1986–2006* (Cambridge University Press, 2002) 305.

Harris DJ, O'Boyle M and Warbrick C, *Law of the European Convention on Human Rights* (2nd edn, Oxford University Press, 2009).

Hathaway JC, *The Rights of Refugees under International Law* (Cambridge University Press, 2005).

Lambert H, 'Protection Against refoulement in Europe: Human Rights Comes to the Rescue' (1999) International and Comparative Law Quarterly 48(3) 515–44.

Magliveras KD and Naldi GJ, *The African Union* (Kluwer Law International, 2009).

Murray R, *Human Rights in Africa: From the OAU to the African Union* (Cambridge University Press, 2004).

Naldi GJ, 'Interim measures of protection in the African system for the protection of human and peoples' rights' (2002) African Human Rights Law Journal 2(1) 1–10.

Naldi GJ, 'The Role of the Human Rights Section of the African Court of Justice and Human and Rights' in A Abass (ed.), *Protecting Human Security in Africa* (Oxford University Press, 2010) 284–312.

Naldi GJ and Magliveras KD, 'Reinforcing the African System of Human Rights: The Protocol on the Establishment of a Regional Court on Human and Peoples' Rights' (1998) Netherlands Quarterly on Human Rights 16(4) 431–56.

Naldi GJ and Magliveras KD, 'The African Court of Justice and Human Rights: A Judicial Curate's Egg' (2012) International Organizations Law Review 9(2) 387–453.

Sceats S, 'Africa's New Human Rights Court: Whistling in the Wind?' (2009) [online: Chatham House Briefing Paper IL BP 09/01] available at: http://www.chathamhouse.org.uk/research/international_law/papers [accessed 16 January 2013].

Udombana NJ, 'Toward the African Court on Human and Peoples' Rights: Better Late than Never' (2000) Yale Human Rights & Development Law Journal 3(1) 45–111.

Umozurike UO, *The African Charter on Human and Peoples' Rights* (Martinus Nijhoff, 1997).

United Kingdom Foreign & Commonwealth Office 'Annual Report on Human Rights 2009' (2010) [online: Foreign & Commonwealth Office] available at: http://www.fco.gov.uk/humanrights [accessed 6 July 2012].

Viljoen F, *International Human Rights Law in Africa* (Oxford University Press, 2007).

Viljoen F, 'Communications under the African Charter: Procedure and Admissibility' in MD Evans and R Murray (eds), *The African Charter on Human and Peoples' Rights: The System in Practice, 1986–2006* (Cambridge University Press, 2008) 76–138.

Chapter 4

Sub-regional Frameworks for the Protection of Asylum Seekers and Refugees in Africa: Bringing Relief Closer to Trouble Zones

Solomon T. Ebobrah

Introduction

Owing to several historical factors, not the least of which was the colonization of most of what is now known as the African continent, the territories of Africa have become infamous as some of the major sources of 'large-scale dislocation' and mass 'movement of people across borders'.[1] The combination of violent conflicts, natural and man-made disasters as well as massive disregard for and abuse of human rights has created serious refugee problems in different parts of Africa. Naturally, the refugee problem has attracted the attention of the international community, especially agencies involved in the management of refugees, but it also became a concern for the governments of African States. Originally, following the trend of response, in academic circles as well as in policy discourse, a state-centric approach was adopted to the refugee problems in Africa.[2] Subsequently, these trends were partly captured in the literature from a continental view point, thereby prompting a continent-wide response in the form of the adoption by the Organisation of African Unity (OAU) of the 1969 OAU Convention governing the specific aspects of refugee problems in Africa (OAU Refugee Convention).[3] Thus, the OAU and its Refugee Convention became Africa's regional international platform and regime for refugee management.

Notwithstanding the initial continental approach spearheaded by the regional body, the OAU, sub-regional organizations are becoming important fora for

1 F Viljoen, *Human Rights Law in Africa* (Oxford University Press, 2007).

2 J Levitt, 'Conflict prevention, management, and resolution: Africa-regional strategies for the prevention of displacement and protection of displaced persons: the cases of the OAU, ECOWAS, SADC, and IGAD' (2001) 11 Duke Journal of International and Comparative Law 39.

3 The 1969 OAU Convention governing the specific aspects of refugee problems in Africa was adopted in 1969 and entered into force in 1974. The Convention is reproduced in C Heyns and M Killander *Compendium of key Human Rights Documents of the African Union* (PULP, 2010).

addressing refugee issues. For instance, some commentators have begun to conceptualize the refugee issues in sub-regional rather than continental terms. Hence, Crisp writes that 'two principal sub-regions of displacement have emerged in the course of the 1990s', effectively reducing the issues to smaller loci than the entire continent.[4] An important dimension to this emerging shift is the fact it increases the potential for the root causes and solutions to the refugee problems to be investigated and addressed as close as possible to the source of displacement.

As the analysis of the refugee questions gets closer to the sources of dislocation and displacement, the search for solutions to the asylum seekers' problem has also begun to take on sub-regional characters. Hence, for instance, the United Nations (UN) agency responsible for coordinating global protection of refugees, the office of the United Nations High Commissioner for Refugees (UNCHR), has begun to seek partnerships with sub-regional organizations in order to improve the protection available to asylum seekers and refugees. Despite the foregoing, sub-regional responses to the refugee challenge are, strictly speaking, underdeveloped and have remained largely unknown and unexplained.

Although, within the framework of their human rights activities, African sub-regional organizations may have some structures for protecting the human rights of refugees and asylum seekers, these human rights structures themselves are still in their infancy. Hence, while sub-regional structures for the protection of refugees are the closest to the conflict zones and therefore more likely to be most effective, they have remained relatively under-utilized. This chapter aims to outline the quantum of protection available for refugees and asylum seekers within the framework of African sub-regional organizations.

Refugee Protection in the Framework of Regional Integration

Regional integration in Africa is commonly pursued under the auspices of regional economic communities (RECs).[5] Generally, regional integration refers to cooperation between States that share, among other attributes, geographical proximity. However, it is not unusual for integration to take place among States that are not geographically proximate. Although integration can either be politically or economically motivated, early incidents of integration were mostly economic. Accordingly, some of the more popular theorists of integration were economists who perceived regional integration as a natural response to demands

4 J Crisp, 'Africa's Refugees: Patterns, Problems and Policy Challenges' (2000) 18 Journal of Contemporary African Studies 157–78.

5 There are over 14 RECs in Africa. Of this number, the African Union (AU) officially recognizes eight RECs as building blocs for the AU and its programmes. See Viljoen, *Human Rights Law in Africa* 488.

for the liberalization of markets.[6] In this largely economic framework, regional integration involves the adoption of economic and trade treaties aimed at enhancing the harmonization of national trade policies and the adoption of uniform trade liberalization frameworks.[7]

Traditionally, regionalism has been analysed as operating in a continuum between 'shallow' and 'deep' integration, wherein 'shallow' integration involved a reduction of trade barriers while 'deep' integration required policy harmonization and enhancement of internal mobility.[8] These were the views that prevailed between the 1950s and 1960s when 'the first wave of regionalism' was experienced.[9] In that era of regionalism, in strict compliance with the law of institutions, the focus of most integration organizations remained economic.

In contradistinction to the so-called first wave of regionalism, the literature records the emergence of a new wave of regional integration dubbed 'new regionalism'. In simplistic terms, new regionalism refers to a new trend of integration that is characterized by 'increased depth' in certain areas of cooperation that were traditionally considered to be within the competence of national governments.[10] An important question is whether the 'new regionalism' empowers integration agencies to engage in the protection of refugees and asylum seekers.

If there were doubts as to the possibility of protecting refugees on the platform of regional integration, in theoretical terms the 'new regionalism' opens up the space for such activities. To the extent that regional integration schemes such as the African RECs are empowered to engage in activities outside the traditional economic circumference including issue-areas such as the realization of human rights, room is created for the protection of refugees and asylum seekers with the framework of the RECs.[11] Accordingly, 'new regionalism' accounts for or justifies the entry of RECs into the politically volatile field of human rights, by extension warranting the protection of vulnerable groups such as refugees and asylum seekers on the platform of such international organizations.

From a more practical point of view, there appears to be a growing recognition by the drivers of regional integration in Africa that the objective of integration can

6 E Ngongang, 'New regionalism in sub-Saharan Africa: A means to attract foreign direct investment (FDI) and to legitimate democratic governments' (2009) 3 African Journal of Political Science and International Relations 15

7 Ibid. Also see A Waldkirch, 'The "new regionalism": Integration as commitment device for developing countries' (2004), available at SSRN: http://ssrn.com/abstract=470 163 or http://dx.doi.org/10.2139/ssrn.470163 [last accessed 24 August 2012].

8 ME Burfisher, S Robinson and K Thierfelder, 'Regionalism: old and new, theory and practice' (2003) paper presented at the International Agricultural Trade Research Consortium (IATRC) Conference Capri (Italy), 23–26 June 2003.

9 Waldkirch, 'The "new regionalism"' 1.

10 Burfisher et al., 'Regionalism: old and new, theory and practice'.

11 A very good example of state challenge to the competence of a sub-regional international organization's human rights work is the protest mounted by Zimbabwe against the assumption of human rights jurisdiction by the SADC Tribunal in 2010/2011.

only be realized in an atmosphere of peace and security and respect for human rights. As is recorded in the founding treaties and other relevant documents of African RECs, representatives of Member States adopted instruments in which principles of 'good neighbourliness' and 'respect for human rights' featured strongly as pre-conditions for successful integration.

Effectively, there are at least two strong bases for the involvement of African RECs in the business of protecting refugees and asylum seekers. First, as some stakeholders have observed, refugee protection is essentially a human rights question and therefore forms or should form part of any serious human rights regime.[12] Hence, to the extent that the pursuit of integration is hinged upon the principle of respect for human rights, refugee protection by RECs cannot be excluded. Second, the potentially disruptive effect that humanitarian crises in a neighbouring State can cause to the economic agenda of integration of a group of States is something integrating States can ill afford. This latter point accounts for the presence of 'collective defence regimes' in the institutional frameworks of African RECs.[13] Together, they complement the theory of new regionalism as the justification for introducing issues of refugee protection into the arena of economic integration discourse.[14]

Sub-regional Standards for the Protection of Asylum Seekers and Refugees

As already indicated above, sub-regional international organizations in Africa are mostly economic oriented. Thus, these organizations claim very little, if any express competence in relation to refugee protection. Consequently, it is almost impossible to find legal instruments expressly and specifically dedicated to refugee and asylum seekers' protection.

However, a perusal of relevant instruments indicates there are provisions within the legal frameworks of some RECs that have bearing on the protection of refugees and asylum seekers.[15] Such provisions have become the standards for refugee protection in the sub-regions. Sub-regional standards relevant for refugee protection can generally be classified into two broad categories of direct standards

12 E Feller, 'Asylum, Migration and Refugee Protection: Realities, Myths and the Promise of Things to Come' (2006) 10 IJRL 514.

13 See for instance Art 5 of the 1999 EAC Treaty, Art 5 of the ICGLR Pact on Security, Stability and Development and the ECOWAS Protocol on Mutual Assistance in Defence.

14 The point must be made that not all sub-regional organizations share the economic history and focus that is common in Africa. At least one organization, the International Conference on the Great Lakes Region (ICGLR), was founded with objectives that are more security based than economic based. Such an organization does not require motivation to justify or legitimize its operations within the field of refugee protection specifically and the promotion and protection of human rights generally.

15 See for example Levitt, 'Conflict prevention, management, and resolution' 61 for a similar argument.

and indirect standards. The term 'direct standards' is loosely applied in this chapter to cover all instruments and documents adopted within the legal framework of sub-regional organizations, which include provisions that expressly mention 'refugees' and 'asylum seekers'. Conversely, the term 'indirect standards' as used in this chapter refers to documents and instruments adopted on the platform of regional and global organizations but made directly applicable in the framework of sub-regional organizations.

Direct Provisions and Standards

Provisions in the founding treaties of sub-regional organizations constitute one form of direct standards for the protection of refugees and asylum seekers. Founding treaties are especially significant in the legal framework of international organizations as they occupy positions comparable to national constitutions. Thus, provisions in the founding treaties of African sub-regional organizations that mention or acknowledge the need for the protection of refugees ought to stand out as some of the most important direct sub-regional standards for the protection of refugees and asylum seekers. The East African Community (EAC)[16] and the Inter-Governmental Authority for Development (IGAD)[17] are the only RECs with pro-refugee provisions in their founding treaties. Article 124(4) of the 1999 revised Treaty of EAC enjoins States Parties to 'establish common mechanisms for the management of refugees'. Article 13(s) of the founding Instrument of IGAD identifies the facilitation of 'repatriation and reintegration of refugees' as IGAD areas of cooperation. While these two provisions may not contain comprehensive guarantees for the protection of refugees and asylum seekers, they are important acknowledgments of the existence of issues of mass displacement and can be built upon for the adoption of more robust specific standards.

The only other sub-regional organization that mentions the term 'refugees' in its founding document is the International Conference on the Great Lakes Region (ICGLR).[18] In the preamble to its Dar-es-Salaam Declaration on Peace, Security,

16 The EAC was initially founded by Kenya, Tanzania and Uganda in 1967 but became dissolved in 1977 following disputes between the partner states. With the new wave of regionalism partly prompted by reactions to globalization, the EAC was revived with the adoption of a new founding Treaty in 1999. This Treaty was first amended in 2006 and later in 2007. With the accession of Burundi and Rwanda to the Treaty of the EAC, the Community now has five partner states. The Treaty of the EAC (as amended) is reproduced in S Ebobrah and A Tanoh, *Compendium of African Sub-regional Human Rights Documents* (PULP, 2010) 37.

17 IGAD was established in 1996 to replace the defunct Intergovernmental Authority on Drought and Development (IGADD). The Member States of IGAD include Djibouti, Eritrea, Ethiopia, Kenya, Somalia, Sudan and Uganda. The Agreement establishing IGAD is reproduced in Ebobrah and Tanoh (2010): 305.

18 The ICGLR was founded in 2004 by heads of state of Angola, Burundi, the Central African Republic, Congo, the Democratic Republic of Congo, Kenya, Rwanda, Sudan,

Democracy and Development in the Great Lakes Region,[19] the ICGLR expresses concern about 'the effect of refugees and internally displaced persons on the degradation of the ecosystem of the Congo River Basin …' and 'the lack of full application of essential legal instruments … concerning refugees and displaced persons'.[20] These concerns are given fuller expressions in at least some nine other provisions in the Dar-es-Salaam Declaration. In those provisions,[21] ICGLR Member States make undertakings ranging from commitments to comply with regional and global instruments to commitments that promise the creation of regional mechanisms for the protection of refugees and asylum seekers.

Arguably, despite their location in the founding documents of the relevant organizations, the argument could be made that the references to 'refugee' in the founding documents of the EAC and IGAD do not carry significant legal weight. First, the references do not fall within the statement of objectives of these organizations. In the context of the law of international institutions, this potentially creates room for recalcitrant States to argue that there is no legal foundation for refugee protection within the framework of the organizations. Second, the references do not convey any significant statement of obligation to protect refugees and asylum seekers. In the absence of a clear formulation of rights in favour of refugees and a concomitant statement of State obligation, it is difficult to see Member States of these organizations acting on these provisions to provide any form of concrete protection for refugees. The challenges that refugees and asylum seekers in East Africa currently face in spite of the provisions of Article 124 of the EAC Treaty is indicative of this concern.[22] However, from a more optimistic point of view, the acknowledgement of the refugee problem in the constitutive document of an international organization can be positively explored when it is read together with the omnibus provisions commonly included in the treaties to authorize ancillary but relevant activities in pursuit of integration.[23]

As far as the EAC is concerned, the statement of intention to seek 'common mechanisms for the management of refugees' has remained mere written words because the EAC member states have neither moved, nor have they been prompted, to actualize the declared intention. Hence, while the simple statement in the founding Treaty could be a legal basis for building a robust collective platform

---

Uganda, Tanzania and Zambia meeting under the auspices of the United Nations and the African Union to 'discuss matters touching on the conflicts and persistent insecurity in the Great Lakes Region'.

19 This Declaration which was adopted in 2004 is the document on which the ICGLR is founded. See S Ebobrah and A Tanoh, *Compendium of African Sub-regional Human Rights Documents* 93 for a reproduction of the Declaration.

20 See paras 7 and 8 of the Dar-es-Salaam Declaration.

21 See especially, Arts 27, 57, 61, 62, 63, 64, 65, 68 and 69 of the Dar-es-Salaam Declaration.

22 L Carter, 'Refugee Refoulement in the East African Community' (2009) available at http://www.pambazuka.org/en/category/features/60018/print (last accessed 18 October 2013).

23 See for example Art 5(3)(h) of the 1999 EAC Treaty.

for the five EAC States to manage refugee challenges in the East African region, the potential is yet to be explored.

The picture is slightly more encouraging in the IGAD framework. While they are not specific on refugees, the IGAD Strategy Framework (1996), the IGAD Program on Conflict Prevention, Resolution and Management (1998) and the Proposal for the Enhancement of IGAD's Emergency Preparedness and Response Capacity for Humanitarian Emergencies within the IGAD Sub-Region (1999) are extensions of the commitment contained in the IGAD founding instrument to protect displaced person.

Perhaps the attention given to refugee issues within the founding Declaration of the ICGLR could be explained by the fact that the ICGLR is technically not a regional economic integration scheme. With its focus on peace and security, the numerous provisions promising protection or at least attention to refugee issues cannot be the subject of any challenge by States. This fact positions the ICGLR as a viable complement to the African regional and the global regimes for refugee protection. The complementary value of the ICGLR refugee protection regime is enhanced by the fact that the Dar-es-Salaam Declaration commits Member States to comply and arguably implement the relevant United Nations (UN) and African Union (AU) instruments. This is a promise that can be consolidated in favour of refugees and asylum seekers. As will be shown later in this chapter, the ICGLR has taken some relatively concrete steps to set standards regarding its 'concerns' about refugees through the adoption of more elaborate pro-refugee instruments.

A second class of direct standards with potential for refugee protection on the platform of sub-regional organizations are standards contained in the documents and instruments adopted in accordance with the relevant legislative processes of the given organization. Two kinds of such provisions are identifiable. One set empowers sub-regional organizations to set up collective mechanisms for the management of refugees. The other set of provisions deal directly with core refugee issues. The ICGLR arguably has gone the farthest in this latter regard with provisions in three different instruments relating to the promise of protection for refugees and asylum seekers. This is somewhat significant considering the origin of the ICGLR and the sustained conflicts in the Great Lakes Region.[24]

In the Pact on Security, Stability and Development,[25] the Protocol on the Property Rights of Returning Persons[26] and the Protocol on Democracy and

24 It would be recalled that the ICGLR was convened to tackle the issues and consequences of conflict in the region. Conflicts have persisted in the region and the sustained flow of refugees and asylum seekers has forced the region to become infamous for hosting the largest refugee camp in the world.

25 Adopted in 2006 and entered into force in 2008. Reproduced in Ebobrah and Tanoh, *Compendium of African Sub-regional Human Rights Documents* 96.

26 Adopted in 2006 and entered into force in 2008. Reproduced in Ebobrah and Tanoh, *Compendium of African Sub-regional Human Rights Documents*.

Good Governance,[27] States converging on the platform of the ICGLR make clear undertakings in favour of refugee protection. An outstanding feature of the ICGLR instruments is that no attempt is made to 'reinvent the wheel' in relation to the definition of refugees. Rather than adopt their own definition of the term 'refugee', ICGLR Member States define the term by reference to both the 1951 UN Convention relating to the Status of Refugees (as amended by the 1967 Protocol Relating to the Status of Refugees) (UN Refugee Convention)[28] and the AU Refugee Convention.[29] Accordingly, the criteria for recognizing asylum seekers for refugee status under the main UN and AU documents are covered in the ICGLR framework. This ensures that asylum seekers who meet either the UN or AU standards can easily fall within the protective bracket of the ICGLR.

Another outstanding feature of the ICGLR regime is that it pays so much attention to the protection of the property rights of returning refugees. Clearly, this shifts the focus of protection from would-be refugees or asylum seekers to acknowledged refugees. Considering that the existing AU regional and (UN) global regimes contain provisions that guarantee protection for asylum seekers, the ICGLR regime is an important complement that reduces the risk of unnecessary duplication of effort. It is also important to point out the value of the ICGLR provisions against the background of the subtle emergence of voluntary repatriation as a preferred form of 'durable solution' to the refugee challenge.[30] In the context of access to land and other supplies that returning refugees need to re-enter life in their countries of origin, the ICGLR Protocol on the Property of Returning Persons goes beyond the protection offered by the older and better known regimes.

The Economic Community of Central African States (ECCAS),[31] the Economic Community of West African States (ECOWAS)[32] and the Southern Africa Development Community (SADC)[33] are other sub-regional organizations

27 Adopted in 2006 and entered into force in 2008. Reproduced in Ebobrah and Tanoh, *Compendium of African Sub-regional Human Rights Documents*.

28 See Art 1(6) of the ICGLR Protocol on the Property Rights of Returning Persons.

29 Art 1(7) of the ICGLR Protocol on the Property Rights of Returning Persons.

30 R Da Costa, 'Rights of refugees in the context of integration: Legal standards and recommendations' (2006) UNCHR Legal and protection policy research series 10.

31 ECCAS was established in 1983 with the adoption of its founding Treaty. The current Member States of ECCAS include Angola, Burundi, Cameroon, Central African Republic, Chad, Congo-Brazzaville, DR Congo, Equatorial Guinea, Gabon and Sao Tome.

32 The original Treaty establishing ECOWAS was adopted in 1975. In 1993, a revised Treaty was adopted by ECOWAS Member States to replace the original 1975 Treaty. The original Member States of ECOWAS were Benin, Burkina Faso, Côte d'Ivoire, The Gambia, Ghana, Guinea, Guinea Bissau, Liberia, Mali, Mauritania, Niger, Nigeria, Sierra Leone and Togo. With the accession of Cape Verde to the 1975 ECOWAS Treaty, membership of the Community grew to 16. In 2000, Mauritania withdrew its membership of the Community.

33 SADC came into existence in 1992, following the dissolution of the Southern African Development Co-ordination Conference (SADCC). The SADC Treaty was amended

with provisions touching on refugee issues. The provisions in the instruments of ECCAS, ECOWAS and SADC are formulated in ways that authorize these sub-regional organizations to take steps towards collective management of refugee challenges.[34] While these provisions do not always create rights in favour of asylum seekers and refugees, they hold the potential for Member States of these organizations to develop functional regimes that will facilitate burden-sharing of responsibility for asylum seekers and refugees. This is important for at least two reasons. First, as some commentators have noted, the need for asylum generally occurs as a result of the failure or inability of the original State to offer the protection that displaced persons require. In such situations, allowing a single State to bear the responsibility of accommodating the mass of displaced persons is so huge that it has the potential to discourage any State. The fatigue that Kenya and Uganda experience in relation to Somali refugees and the unilateral actions taken by Burundi, Tanzania and Uganda to repatriate Rwandan refugees are examples of the consequences of unshared refugee-hosting-responsibilities.[35] Collective action by a group of neighbouring States would thus disperse the burden and make it lighter. Second, the proximity of the integrating States to the source of dislocation makes it easier for asylum seekers to run to such neighbouring States or pass through such States in search of more convenient asylum States. The risk of application of stringent immigration rules would arguably be lower once a collective scheme for refugee management is put in place.

Perhaps as a result of the recurring conflicts in West Africa, in addition to the more general provisions in some of its instruments, ECOWAS has also increasingly advanced in strengthening its regime for refugee protection. For instance, in August 2007 a Memorandum on the Equality of treatment for refugees with other citizens of Member States of ECOWAS in the exercise of Free Movement, Right of Residence and Establishment was adopted in the ECOWAS framework to encourage ECOWAS Member States to ensure that refugees from other ECOWAS Members continue to enjoy their freedoms under the relevant ECOWAS Protocols on Free Movement and Establishment in addition to any other rights they enjoy as refugees under international law. In March 2012, ECOWAS Heads of State and Government also approved a Common Humanitarian Policy for the organization which specially recognizes the vulnerability of refugees and makes it a policy of the organization to facilitate their integration into their host States.

---

in 2001. Current Member States of SADC are Angola, Botswana, DR Congo, Lesotho, Madagascar, Malawi, Mauritius, Mozambique, Namibia, South Africa, Swaziland, Tanzania, Zambia and Zimbabwe.

34 See Art 4(l) of the ECCWAS Protocol Relating to the Council for Peace and Security in Central Africa (COPAX) and Art 44(e) of the ECOWAS Protocol Relating to the Mechanism for Conflict Prevention, Management, Resolution, Peacekeeping and Security. Also see Art 28 of the SADC Protocol on the Facilitation of Movement of Persons.

35 Carter, 'Refugee Refoulement in the East African Community'.

A third class of direct standards applicable for refugee protection in African sub-regional organizations is the refugee-specific instruments adopted on the platform of international organizations such as the AU and the UN. With the practice of adopting instruments by reference, African sub-regional organizations commonly make instruments applicable in their legal framework even though such instruments have been adopted on the platform of other international bodies to which the majority of their Member States belong. In this regard, the UN Refugee Convention and the AU Refugee Convention are generally applicable in the frameworks of the ECCAS,[36] the ICGLR,[37] and IGAD.[38] Increasingly, the UN Refugee Convention is also being applied on the platform of ECOWAS on the basis of policy documents adopted in that platform. From an international law perspective, it is possible and legitimate for States that are Parties along with other States to an international treaty to commit themselves to implement such a treaty in a subsequent treaty insofar as that the earlier treaty does not conflict with the subsequent treaty.[39]

Generally, on the basis of reception or adoption clauses in sub-regional instruments, the regional and global instruments that guarantee protection for asylum seekers and refugees are directly applicable within the legal frameworks of these African sub-regional organizations. Although the UN and AU instruments are already applicable in the individual States and (in the case of the UN Convention) being administered by the UNCHR, the provision of sub-regional platforms ensures that some form of peer pressure is brought to bear on States to live up to their obligations in those instruments. In cases where some States have not signed up to those global or regional instruments, pressure is brought to bear on those States to ensure that they sign up. These practices enhance the enjoyment of the rights in those instruments by those most in need.

Indirect Instruments

In terms of instruments that indirectly protect the rights of asylum seekers and refugees within the frameworks of sub-regional organizations in Africa, there are at least two kinds that are applicable. The first kind of indirect instruments or standards are the general human rights laws applicable in these organizations. The second kind of instruments that indirectly protect asylum seekers and refugees are

36 Art 4(l) of COPAX states that the management of refugees should be 'in accordance with the provisions of international legal instruments in force'.

37 Art 57 of the Dar-es-Salaam Declaration of the ICGLR records the commitment of ICGLR Member States to comply with the obligations and principles of the UN and AU Refugee Conventions.

38 Art 15(s) envisages facilitation of repatriation and reintegration of refugees 'in accordance with existing … regional and international instruments'.

39 See Arts 30 and 59 of the Vienna Convention on the Law of Treaties.

the treaties adopted to facilitate free movement of persons recognized as citizens of the relevant sub-regional organizations.

As already mentioned, the traditional RECs in Africa are economic-oriented organizations. As such, the promotion and protection of human rights is usually a peripheral rather than a core or central objective of those organizations. Consequently, it is only on the rare occasion that African RECs have adopted human rights catalogues strictly for the purposes of enhancing the realization of human rights.[40] Instead, a common practice in these organizations is to adopt international human rights instruments by reference. In this regard, the Universal Declaration on Human Rights and the African Charter on Human and Peoples' Rights are commonly adopted by African RECs.[41] Other regional and global human rights instruments have also been occasionally adopted and applied by African sub-regional organizations. Thus, notwithstanding the fact that human rights are not a core business of African sub-regional organizations, the increasing involvement of these organizations in the promotion and protection of human rights is now widely acknowledged. As one commentator has noted, '… in some instances, the values and the legal norms advanced by sub-regional organizations are more progressive and have gained importance for the promotion of human rights and to this extent can also support refugee rights'.[42]

To some extent, the refugee question is considered to be essentially a human rights question.[43] Hence Levitt for instance includes human rights law as one of the three recognized regimes for the protection of displaced persons.[44] Insofar as this position is correct, the budding human rights regimes in the sub-regional organizations hold some potential for refugee protection. In fact Da Costa has correctly observed that in Africa, 'international and regional human rights instruments … are establishing new standards with regards to rights to basic needs … and other rights central to the successful integration of refugees'.[45]

An important aspect in the applicability of general human rights instruments is the fact that even in cases where specific mention is not made of asylum seekers and refugees, these sets of vulnerable people are entitled to enjoyment of the rights guaranteed in these instruments simply on the grounds that they are human beings. Thus, a layer of protection is available for asylum seekers and refugees to claim even where refugee-specific instruments are unavailable in the stables of a given sub-regional organization. However, the practice does not indicate that the potential that is presented by the applicability of these general human rights

40 See for instance the SADC Protocol on Gender and Development.

41 The case law of sub-regional courts and tribunals indicate that regional and global human rights instruments confer benefits that citizens of Member States of sub-regional organizations can claim before the organs and institutions of these sub-regional bodies.

42 R Da Costa, 'Rights of refugees in the context of integration' 15.

43 E Feller, 'Asylum, migration and refugee protection' 514.

44 Levitt, 'Conflict prevention, management, and resolution' 49.

45 R Da Costa, 'Rights of refugees in the context of integration' 12.

instruments is currently being fully explored for the benefit of asylum seekers and refugees.[46]

To a large extent, the human rights regimes in sub-regional organizations have tilted heavily towards judicial protection before the judicial organs of these organizations. This creates some difficulty for asylum seekers and refugees as the refugee problem does not lend itself too much to adjudication. Thus, it is non-judicial options for human rights protection that holds the best promise for these sets of vulnerable people. Where assistance has been made available to refugees under the framework of sub-regional organizations, it has usually occurred on humanitarian and compassionate grounds rather as part of a firm, coordinated and obligatory manner.[47]

Apart from the general international human rights instruments, the treaties on free movement, adopted by sub-regional organizations, are other laws that indirectly guarantee rights for asylum seekers and refugees. In this regard, ECOWAS and SADC currently hold the most promise even though the ECOWAS free movement regime is by far the most advanced in Africa.[48]

It is generally accepted that free movement Protocols are not adopted with refugees and asylum seekers in mind. However, there appears to some consensus among certain stakeholders[49] and certain commentators[50] (at least in the case of ECOWAS) that 'legal provisions governing residence and naturalisation, offer a range of possibilities for refugees … claim rights and access durable solutions … in addition to rights already granted by the refugee conventions'.[51] Even in a case like the SADC framework where the legal regime is yet to develop to the level of residency and establishment, the possibility of unrestricted mobility and the attendant guarantees that citizens ought to enjoy ensures that asylum seekers are able to travel with ease at short notice so far as they have the basic travel

46 ECOWAS may be seen as a rare exception in the sense that the ECOWAS Commission (in partnership with institutions such as the UNHCR) has been actively involved in the rehabilitation and reintegration of West African refugees.

47 See for instance, 'ECOWAS supports Ivorian refugees in Liberia with humanitarian assistance', (available at http://reliefweb.int/report/liberia/ecowas-supports-ivorian-refugees-liberia-humanitarian-assistance, last accessed 13 January 2013).

48 The ECOWAS Protocol Relating to Free Movement of Persons, Residence and Establishment was adopted in 1979 and entered into force in 1980. Since then, Supplementary Protocols have been adopted to operationalize the three phases of free movement; residence and establishment. See general Ebobrah and Tanoh (2010) for these Protocols. For its part, SADC has only recently come with a Protocol to facilitate the free movement of people within the SADC region.

49 ECOWAS and the UNCHR have been cited as being in agreement that free movement Protocols hold very good potentials for the protection of refugee rights.

50 See A Adepoju, A Boulton and M Levin, 'Promoting integration through mobility' (2007) UNCHR Research Paper 150.

51 IOM/UNCHR 'Protecting refugees and other persons on the move in the ECOWAS space' (2011).

documents required in the Protocols. Such ease of travel could make a crucial difference of survival for some asylum seekers.

In situations of protracted conflicts or disasters, which lead to protracted refugee situations, the possibilities offered by free movement arrangements in sub-regional integration schemes cannot be overemphasized. In terms of local settlement and local integration, proximity of States generally presupposes that there would be very little difference in cultures and values between the State of origin and the transit or destination State if such a State is within the same REC. Arguably, it is bound to be easier for integration to occur in such an environment. In the ECOWAS framework, the free movement, residence and establishment Protocols oblige ECOWAS Member States to respect the human rights of 'migrants' and to allow for the transfer of legitimate earnings and savings in the event that it becomes absolutely necessary to repatriate such a migrant.[52]

While the asylum seeker and refugee is not exactly a migrant, there appears to be some acknowledgment that in this era of mixed migration, the line between 'migrants' and 'refugees' is increasingly becoming blurred.[53] Thus, the protection that avails migrants under regimes such as the ECOWAS regime can very easily be enjoyed by a refugee who has managed to be self-reliant within the Community environment. Overall, the evidence is that asylum seekers and refugees have been able to take advantage of free movement Protocols to obtain protection and enhance their living standards while still outside the protection of their State of origin. Accordingly, these instruments are indirect but viable tools for the protection of asylum seekers and refugees. Even more positive is the fact that ECOWAS Policy documents recognize the special needs of refugees and asylum seekers and therefore encourage States to facilitate the integration of this category of ECOWAS citizens.[54] In some cases, reports indicate that on the basis of ECOWAS Protocols, refugees from other ECOWAS Member States have recently been integrated into their host communities and given citizenship status in the receiving ECOWAS States.[55]

Institutions, Institutional Relations and Refugee Protection

The potential for protection of asylum seekers and refugees within the framework of African sub-regional organizations can only be realized if the organs and

52 Art 17 of the 1986 Supplementary Protocol on the Second Phase (Right of Residence) of the Protocol on Free Movement of Persons, the Right of Residence and Establishment .

53 Feller, 'Asylum, Migration and Refugee Protection' 515.

54 For instance, the ECOWAS Memorandum on Equality of Treatment for Refugees encourages ECOWAS Member States to facilitate the issuance of travel documents and residence permits to refugees.

55 See 'West Africa: 395 Ex-Liberian Refugees Get ECOWAS Passports' available at http://allafrica.com/stories/201305091121.html (last accessed 18 October 2013).

institutions of sub-regional organizations are actively involved in the management of refugee situations. Accordingly, this part of the chapter peeks at the practice to show whether the rhetoric in the legal framework is matched by actual practice.

Notwithstanding the provisions that authorize the initiation of mechanisms within the legal frameworks of sub-regional organizations to engage in joint management of refugees, there are no identifiable dedicated refugee-protection mechanisms in any of the known sub-regional organizations in Africa. In the view of some commentators, among other reasons, the existence of a UN office for the management of refugees was considered sufficient and more convenient considering the enormous resources that are required for refugee management.[56] Thus, even where it is operationalized, the management of refugees within the framework of African sub-regional organizations is commonly delegated to offices in the secretariat of the given organization. Generally, the responsibility for refugee management in the African sub-regional organizations is lumped together with the office dealing with peace and security within the secretariat of the organization. Thus, the refugee question is considered more from a security angle than a human rights angle. However, as the UNCHR increasingly engages sub-regional organizations in collaborative work for the protection of refugees and asylum seekers, the human rights angle to the refugee question is becoming more central in the work of the sub-regional organizations.

In East Africa, there are at least three active sub-regional organizations that can impact on the protection of refugees and asylum seekers. These are the EAC, ICGLR and IGAD. The EAC currently does not boast of vibrant institutional involvement in refugee management. Although the promise in its 1999 Treaty and the potential for adapting the Common Market Protocol[57] for the benefit of refugees of East African origin creates expectation for an active EAC refugee protection unit, there is no evidence that such a unit is currently operational. Despite this absence of a dedicated unit, the EAC is not completely inactive in the protection of refugees and asylum seekers as the UNCHR maintains engagement with the organization. For instance, the UNCHR has prompted EAC action in the area of refugee protection by entering into a Memorandum of Understanding with the EAC with the aim of 'establishing a frame work for cooperation in the area of protecting refugees'.[58] In view of the ongoing conflicts in East African Region, the volume of displaced persons and the refugee camps in the region, involving the EAC in protective action is vital.

Unlike the EAC, both the ICGLR and IGAD have fairly promising units working in the field of refuge protection. Within the secretariat of the ICGLR,

56 A Alao, 'The role of African regional and sub-regional organizations in conflict prevention and resolution', available at http://www.unhcr.org/cgi-bin/texis/vtx/home/opendocPDFViewer.html?docid=3ae6a0c88&query=SADC.

57 The Common Market Protocol was adopted in 2010.

58 'UNCHR nominates representative to EAC', available at news.eac.int/index.php?option=com_content&view=article (accessed 23 August 2011).

the unit responsible for humanitarian and social issues coordinates a cluster of activities including aspects relating to the protection of refugees and asylum seekers. In a 2006 Regional Plan of Action for Humanitarian and Social Issues, the unit released a proposed Development Assistance for Refugees (DAR) programme with an overall objective to 'establish a regional framework for the protection, assistance and search for durable solutions for refugees'.[59] Some of the strategies envisaged by the unit include ensuring that refugee camps in Member States are located in accordance with standards approved in the 1969 OAU Refugee Convention; facilitating access and integration of refugees in the local structures of asylum host countries and the special treatment of female refugees.[60] Although the extent to which the DAR has been taken since 2006 leaves much to be desired, the existence of those structures is an important indication that the protection of refugees and asylum seekers is taken seriously in the ICGLR framework.

The Humanitarian Affairs Section of the Peace and Security Division is the office dedicated to refugee protection and related matters in the IGAD framework. One of the two main components of the Humanitarian Affairs Section is Alleviation and Mitigation of Humanitarian Crises, which in turn deals with refugees, returnees, and Internally Displaced Persons (IDPs). While it appears that the Disaster Risk Management Component has attracted more of IGAD's attention in the past, there is some evidence that refugee protection is gaining some attention. For instance, at a conference on refugees initiated by the IGAD Council of Ministers, the idea of a separate unit within the IGAD Secretariat dedicated to humanitarian issues, especially refugee protections, was mooted and adopted.[61] As a short-term measure, the same conference took a decision to authorize the IGAD Secretariat to amend and expand the 'mandate, members and Terms of Reference of the existing mechanism of the Disaster Risk Management Programme', including the protection of refugees and returnees.[62] A critical aspect of the IGAD Humanitarian Affairs Section's approach to the refugee question is the insistence on addressing the 'root causes of conflicts and natural hazards' as a sustainable basis for refugee protection. With the possibility of engaging Member States through organizational peace and security frameworks, sub-organizations stand a good chance of helping to address the root causes of displacement and therefore reduce the outflow of asylum seekers.

Responsibility for refugee management within the ECOWAS framework lies with the Humanitarian and Social Affairs Department of the ECOWAS Commission. However, the organization's work with refugees cuts across different

---

59 See the Regional Programme of Action for Humanitarian and Social Issues, available at http://www.icglr.org/IMG/pdf/Protection_Assitance_and_Search_for_durable_solutions.pdf.

60 Ibid.

61 Report Of The Ministerial Conference On Refugees, Returnees And Internally Displaced Persons (IDPS) In The IGAD Region, 20–21 February 2006, Nairobi, Kenya.

62 Ibid.

departments in the ECOWAS Commission. The Peacekeeping and Security Department and the Free Movement of Persons Department are usually involved in work that directly or indirectly impacts on refugee protection. The advantage in such a multi-faceted approach to refugee protection is that in cases of mixed migration where the difference between refugees and other forms of migrant is blurred, the risk of unintended denial of protection is limited.

Although the determination of refugee status in West Africa currently rests with individual States, the ECOWAS Commission provides an important 'political platform for dialogue' on migration issues which includes the protection of refugees.[63] The involvement of ECOWAS in peacekeeping and humanitarian work in the West African sub-region has resulted in the ECOWAS Commission playing a significant role in addressing issues of forced displacement. Accordingly, the most visible contribution of the ECOWAS institutions to the protection of refugees is the positive application of the Community's free movement Protocols for the benefit of refugees from Member States. In the aftermath of the civil wars in Liberia and Sierra Leone, the movement and settlement of refugees in neighbouring West African countries was partly facilitated by the ECOWAS institutions. The ECOWAS approach is to facilitate or enhance the local integration of displaced persons in the asylum State, not in their characters as refugees but as Community citizens from another Member State. The ECOWAS Commission encourages the sending State to process travel documents such as international passports to the displaced persons in order to enhance the grant of resident permits by the asylum or host State.

From a durable solution perspective, the encouragement of local integration is a crucial contribution to refugee protection. Although voluntary repatriation is still generally considered as the preferred mode for terminating refugee status, the fragile nature of post-conflict societies and the attendant risks of relapse discourage refugees from 'rushing' back to their home countries. Bearing this in mind, local integration as encouraged by the ECOWAS institutions represent a viable alternative durable solution.

While response to conflict-triggered displacement stands out in its refugee-related work, the ECOWAS Community involvement in refugee issues transcends the fallout of armed conflict. The ECOWAS Community institutions adopt a blend of unilateral and collaborative approaches to the protection of refugees. Examples of such unilateral and multilateral activities date back to the period following the end of the civil conflicts in the West African region. In relation to its post-conflict work, the ECOWAS Community entered into a multipartite agreement with the UNCHR and the governments of Liberia, Nigeria and Sierra Leone in 2007 to facilitate local integration of Liberian and Sierra Leonean refugees in Nigeria. In this regard, the ECOWAS Memorandum on 'Equality of treatment for refugees with other citizens of ECOWAS Member States in the exercise of Free Movement,

63 IOM-UNCHR 20.

Right of residence and Establishment' serves to promote a common understanding of the potentials that exist for refugee protection in the ECOWAS legal framework.[64]

In 2008, the ECOWAS Community adopted the ECOWAS Common Approach on Migration as the West African sub-regional Plan of Action on migration. While the Plan of Action is targeted at migration generally, it is on record that it has prompted a policy direction in ECOWAS that addresses 'mixed migration issues from a regional perspective, recognising the specificity of asylum seeker, refugees ...'[65] Although ECOWAS currently has no instrument or document totally dedicated to the protection of refugees and asylum seekers, the overall effect of the policy documents, memoranda and other relevant documents is to position the ECOWAS Community institutions for the important role of coordinating protection at a trans-boundary level.

Towards Improved Asylum Seeker Protection at the Sub-regions

Although African sub-regional organizations do not compare to the UNCHR in terms of contributions to the protection of asylum seekers, these organizations are not completely irrelevant in this area. A common feature of sub-regional protection regimes for asylum seekers is the preference for the application of regional and global standards rather than the introduction of new standards. One clear advantage in this practice is that it allows for consistency and coherence in standard setting.

However, as demonstrated by the additional protection introduced by the ICGLR instruments, the adoption of region-specific standards could add value to the protection of refugees and asylum seekers by addressing region-specific concerns not covered in the global and regional instruments. With the advantage of proximity to the locus of displacement, sub-regional organizations are better positioned to identify and address challenges peculiar to refugees emerging from their different sub-regions. Thus, it may be desirable for these organizations to develop region-specific standards for the protection of refugees and asylum seekers.

Another feature of sub-regional regimes is that peace and security structures are commonly adapted to cater for refugees and asylum seekers. While there may be advantages to this approach, there is also the risk that the protection of refugees and asylum seekers would play second fiddle to security issues. The absence of dedicated units for refugee protection within the sub-regional organizations reduces the potential impact that could have been made. In this regard, the intention to create such dedicated units with some organizations is encouraging and one that should be recommended to other organizations.

64 IOM-UNCHR 25.

65 Ibid. 17.

Conclusion

Over the last decade, sub-regional human rights regimes have developed out of various sub-regional international organizations in Africa. Since the protection of refugees and asylum seekers is an important aspect of any human rights protection regime, to different degrees, these sub-regional bodies have also been involved in the protection of these sets of vulnerable persons. Similar to their practices in relation to other aspects of human rights, African sub-regional organizations have relied largely on instruments adopted on the platform of the AU and the UN to pursue their protection activities. On the rare occasion, some have adopted or developed region-specific standards to enhance the scope of protection that they offer. However, it is the absence of dedicated refugee units that pose the biggest challenge to the quality of protection offered by these organizations.

Although the work of organizations such as the UNCHR has been very impressive, the prolongation of conflicts and the outbreak of new conflicts in different parts of Africa will definitely stretch the resources of those organizations. More importantly, the resettlement and integration of refugees would be easier in the regions of conflict than anywhere else. Thus, the involvement of sub-regional organizations, which are closer to the actual conflict zones, needs to be encouraged.

References

Adepoju A, Boulton A and Levin M, Promoting integration through mobility (2007) *UNCHR Research Paper* 150.

Alao A, The role of African regional and sub-regional organizations in conflict prevention and resolution, working paper 23 (2000) available at http://www.unhcr.org/cgi-bin/texis/vtx/home/opendocPDFViewer.html?docid=3ae6a0c88&query=SADC [last accessed 24 August 2012].

Burfisher ME, Robinson S and Thierfelder K, *Regionalism: Old and New, Theory and Practice in Agricultural Policy Reform and the WTO: Where are we Heading?* Edited by G Anania et al. (Edward Elgar Publishing, 2004) 539.

Crisp J, 'Africa's Refugees: Patterns, Problems and Policy Challenges' (2000) 18 *Journal of Contemporary African Studies*.

Da Costa R, 'Rights of refugees in the context of integration: Legal standards and recommendations' (2006) *UNCHR Legal and Protection Policy Research Series*.

Ebobrah S and Tanoh A, *Compendium of African Sub-regional Human Rights Documents* (PULP, 2010).

Feller E, 'Asylum, Migration and Refugee Protection: Realities, Myths and the Promise of Things to Come' (2006) 10 *International Journal of Refugee Law*.

Heyns C and Killander M, *Compendium of Key Human Rights Documents of the African Union* (PULP, 2010).

Levitt J, 'Conflict prevention, management, and resolution: Africa – regional strategies for the prevention of displacement and protection of displaced persons: the cases of the OAU, ECOWAS, SADC, and IGAD' (2001) 11 *Duke Journal of International and Comparative Law*.

Ngongang E, 'New regionalism in sub-Saharan Africa: A means to attract foreign direct investment (FDI) and to legitimate democratic governments' (2009) 3 *African Journal of Political Science and International Relations*.

Viljoen F, *Human rights law in Africa* (Oxford University Press, 2007).

Waldkirch A, 'The "new regionalism": Integration as commitment device for developing countries' available at SSRN: http://ssrn.com/abstract=470163 or http://dx.doi.org/10.2139/ssrn.470163 [last accessed 24 August 2012].

Chapter 5

The African National Human Rights Institutions and the Protection of Asylum Seekers: Existing Practices and Opportunities Through the Optional Protocol to the UN Convention Against Torture[1]

Elina Steinerte

Introduction

Recent years have witnessed a considerable proliferation of human rights institutions created by national governments around the world. These are traditionally anchored in either the constitutional instrument or regular legislation of the country and, having wide remit over the promotion and protection of human rights within the country, are to be totally independent of the government in question. These institutions take many shapes and forms, ranging from single-headed Ombudsperson institutions to more collegial bodies like Human Rights Commissions (HRCs), composed of a number of Commissioners. Collectively and especially since the adoption of the so-called Paris Principles,[2] these institutions are referred to as National Human Rights Institutions (NHRIs) and with their numbers around the world increasing, NHRIs are not only new actors on their national scenes, but have also become new actors on the international and regional

1 The author would like to express sincere thanks to Ms Lilian Ayete-Nyampong and Ms Josephine Akaba from the Commission on Human Rights and Administrative Justice, Ghana, and Ms Moniach Kareithi of the Human Rights Implementation Centre for the invaluable assistance with research materials for this chapter. Sincere thanks are also due to Ms Debra Long and Prof Rachel Murray from the Human Rights Implementation Centre, University of Bristol, for invaluable comments on the earlier drafts of this chapter. Any inaccuracies are the sole responsibility of the author.

2 UNGA, 'National Institutions for the Promotion and Protection of Human Rights', UN Doc A/RES/48/134 (20 December 1993).

planes[3] and are recognized as important partners of UN[4] and regional[5] human rights mechanisms.

The aim of this chapter is to highlight the various ways in which the NHRIs of the African region have engaged in the promotion and protection of asylum seekers' rights, as well as to allude to recent developments at the international level that may provide new ways for these entities to engage with the issue of the rights of asylum seekers further. The chapter will start by briefly examining the concept of NHRIs and then describe the specifics of African NHRIs. It will then move on to explore in more detail how the NHRIs of the region have engaged with the issues surrounding asylum seekers' rights through their work on legislation, policy shaping, examining conditions of detention and strategic litigation. It will then explore the potential that the coming into force of the Optional Protocol to the United Nations Convention against Torture (OPCAT) holds in strengthening the engagement of African NHRIs with asylum seekers' issues.

What is a National Human Rights Institution?

While the Paris Principles undeniably represent a benchmark for the assessment of NHRIs around the world,[6] the instrument actually does not contain a definition of what constitutes an NHRI. This of course is not surprising and is entirely pragmatic given the variety of shapes and forms that these bodies take around the world. Thus this term encompasses traditional Ombudsman offices, usually headed by one person, with powers to ensure that public authorities and their

3 R Carver, 'A New Answer to an Old Question: National Human Rights Institutions and the Domestication of International Law' (2010) 10(1) Human Rights Law Review 1–32; B Dickson, 'The contribution of human rights commissions to the protection of human rights' (2003) Public Law 272–85.

4 'The High Commissioner reiterated that national human rights institutions are critical partners for OHCHR due to the central place they have in the national human rights protection system, particularly in addressing the most critical human rights issues at the national level' National institutions for the promotion and protection of human rights. UNGA, 'Report by the Secretary-General on National institutions for the promotion and protection of human rights', UN Doc A/66/274 (8 August 2011), para 4.

5 For example, the African Commission on Human and Peoples' Rights recognizes NHRIs as partners through granting them affiliate status with the Commission. In 2010 there were 22 such NHRIs in the African continent. See ACHPR, Executive Council, *Report of the African Commission on Human and Peoples' Rights* (19–23 July 2010) EX.CL/600(XVII), para 34.

6 Even though some authors have challenged the usefulness of the instrument, arguing that the Paris Principles pay more attention to the formal requirements and fail to examine the actual effectiveness of NHRIs on the ground. See OC Okafor and SC Agbakwa, 'On Legalism, Popular Agency and "Voices of Suffering": the Nigerian National Human Rights Commission in Context' (2002) 24 Human Rights Quarterly 662–720.

staff comply with the laws that govern their actions, which is normally achieved through inspections and the consideration of complaints by individuals. The Parliamentary Commissioner for Civil and Military Administration in Denmark (Danish Ombudsman) is an example of such a traditional Ombudsman office.[7] The mandate of this institution is to oversee the proper administration of public authorities, which brings human rights issues into the Ombudsman's remit, and one of the central modes of operation is the consideration of complaints submitted by individuals.

The Ombudsman offices can be contrasted by the Human Rights Commissions (HRCs), which are usually collegial bodies, concerned with the broader aspects of protection and promotion of human rights. Thus, returning to the example of Denmark, the Danish Institute for Human Rights represents such an institution. Just like the Ombudsman, it is also an independent institution dealing with human rights issues in Denmark and established by the State through legislation,[8] but has research, education and implementation of various national and international human rights programmes as its main focus.[9] The Institute has no investigatory or complaints handling mandate and is headed by a director, supported by a management group and reports to the board.[10]

Somewhere in between these two illustrations there is a variety of NHRIs who combine different aspects of these contrasting Danish examples in a variety of ways. For example, the Kenya National Human Rights Commission (KNCHR), in addition to a human rights research and education mandate, also has the powers to issue a summons to require attendance of a person before the Commission, to carry out investigations and even, for example, to order the release of an unlawfully detained person.[11]

Similarly to this, the Commission on Human Rights and Administrative Justice in Ghana (CHRAJ) is a kind of hybrid institution, which combines the human rights research and education mandate with complaints-handling functions. However it also has a specific mandate to deal with anti-corruption issues stipulated directly in the legislation and thus the CHRAJ is also in fact an Anti-Corruption Agency[12] which makes its mandate strikingly different from mandates of more traditional HRCs.

---

7 See The Ombudsman Act, Act No 473 (12 June 1996).

8 Act governing the Establishment of the Danish Centre for International Studies and Human Rights, Act No 41 (6 June 2002).

9 Ibid. section 1.

10 Ibid. chap 2.

11 See http://www.knchr.org/index.php?option=com_content&task=view&id=2&Itemid=34.

12 See 1992 Ghana Constitution Art 218 (a)(e), 284–88; Section 7 (1)(a), (e) and (f); and See Act on the Commission on Human Rights and Administrative Justice, Act No 456 (1993).

Thus, as the above examples make clear, the variety of forms of NHRIs is great and their powers vary considerably, which may explain the lack of a strict definition in the Paris Principles. There is however a commonly accepted 'working definition' of an NHRI that has been adopted by the United Nations (UN), which states that an NHRI is 'a body which is established by a government under the constitution, or by a law or decree, the functions of which are specifically defined in terms of the promotion and protection of human rights'.[13]

At this juncture it should be emphasized that a distinction is often being made between the so-called Paris Principles 'compliant' and 'non-compliant' NHRIs. This distinction refers to the accreditation process adopted by the International Coordinating Committee of National Institutions for the promotion and protection of human rights (ICCom);[14] its Sub-Committee on Accreditation (ICCom Subcommittee),[15] to be precise. This accreditation process is a peer-review process, which until very recently relied on the information submitted by the applicant in question.[16] The outcome of the review process may mean that the NHRI in question is accorded either A-status as fully Paris Principles compliant, B-status as not fully compliant or C-status as non-compliant.[17] Additionally,

13 United Nations, National Human Rights Institutions, *A Handbook in the Establishment and Strengthening of National Institutions for the Promotion and Protection of Human Rights* (United Nations: Professional Training Series No 4, 1995) para 39.

14 The ICCom is an international association of NHRIs which promotes and strengthens NHRIs to be in accordance with the Paris Principles and provides leadership in the promotion and protection of human rights. See 'Rome Statute of the International Criminal Court', UN Doc A/CONF.183/9 (17 July 1998) Art 5.

15 See International Coordinating Committee, Statute of Association International Coordinating Committee of National Institutions for the Promotion and Protection of Human Rights (14 September 2004) Arts 10–14. It was amended by the member of the ICCom at its 20th session (15 April 2008).

16 In 2006 the ICCom initiated a revision of its accreditation process which, according to the ICCom, has resulted in a more transparent and rigorous process. See UNGA, *Report of the Secretary-General. Process currently utilized by the International Coordinating Committee of National Institutions for the Promotion and Protection of Human Rights to accredit national institutions in compliance with the Paris Principles*, UN Doc A/HRC/16/77 (3 February 2011) para 6. Arguably the most welcome innovation of this reform has been the possibility, since 2008, for the civil society and other stakeholders to submit alternative reports on NHRIs that are being considered: for example, more than 38 NGOs from Sri Lanka submitted reports criticizing the Sri Lankan Human Rights Commission and the ICCom called on the respective Commission to respond to the criticism raised. It appears that the NGO reports influenced significantly the decision of the ICCom to downgrade the Sri Lankan Human Rights Commission from status A to status B in 2009. See ANNI, *Report on the Performance and Establishment of National Human Rights Institutions in Asia* (Bangkok, Thailand, 2008) 176.

17 Until April 2008 there was also a category of A(R) meaning accreditation with reserve which is granted in cases when insufficient documentation was submitted to confer A-status.

accredited NHRIs undergo re-accreditation every five years, while C-status NHRIs may reapply for reaccreditation at any time.[18] Equally, the Chair of the ICCom or the ICCom Subcommittee may invite a review of an accredited NHRI at any time if it appears that the circumstances of the NHRI in question may have changed in a way that affects its compliance with the Paris Principles.[19] Crucially, the ICCom operates under the auspices of the Office of the High Commissioner for Human Rights (OHCHR), which has a designated National Institutions Unit[20] that serves as a Secretariat for the ICCom. This, coupled with the fact that the Paris Principles were endorsed by a UN General Assembly resolution in 1993, clearly indicate that the international community perceive the Paris Principles as representing a benchmark for the measurement of an effective NHRI.[21]

Interestingly, however, the roles and mandates of even those NHRIs that have undergone the accreditation process by the ICCom Subcommittee remain diverse, and the collective reference to 'NHRIs' still encompasses a great variety of bodies that are markedly different in terms of their mode of establishment, composition and competencies. The diversity of these bodies is also great if a comparison between the regions is made which in fact reveals certain patterns. For example the Americas region is characterized by more Ombudsman-type institutions,[22] while in Africa the Namibian Office of the Ombudsman stands alone among the other 23 HRCs that have undergone accreditation by the ICCom.[23] Thus Africa is typified by HRCs with quasi-judicial, complaints-handling mandates.

Moreover, it should be noted that in addition to the ICCom that unites NHRIs at the international level, there are also regional arrangements such as the: Network of African NHRIs,[24] Ibero-American Federation of the Ombudsman,[25] Network of National Institutions for the Promotion and Protection of Human Rights of the American Continent,[26] Asia Pacific Forum of National Human Rights Institutions[27]

18 *Guidelines for Accreditation and Re-Accreditation of National Human Rights Institutions to the International Coordinating Committee of National Human Rights Institutions*, version 4 June 2009, 4.

19 ICCom Sub-Committee on Accreditation, *General Observations*, June 2009, para 6.3.

20 See http://www.ohchr.org/en/countries/nhri/pages/nhrimain.aspx.

21 'Compliance with the Paris Principles is a key requirement for ensuring the effectiveness, independence, autonomy and pluralism of national human rights institutions', see UNGA, *Report by the Secretary-General on the National Institutions for the Promotion and Protection of Human Rights*, UN Doc A/66/274 (8 August 2011), para 90.

22 Of 25 institutions that have undergone ICCom accreditation from the Americas region, 20 are Ombudsman offices, see http://nhri.ohchr.org/EN/National/DirectoryOfInstitutions/Pages/Americas.aspx.

23 See http://nhri.ohchr.org/EN/National/DirectoryOfInstitutions/Pages/Africa.aspx.

24 See http://www.nanhri.org/.

25 See http://www.iidh.ed.cr/Comunidades/Ombudsnet/.

26 See http://www.rindhca.org.ve/.

27 See http://www.asiapacificforum.net/.

and the European Group of NHRIs.[28] Crucially, as will be examined later, the NHRIs are also recognized by and play an important role within the various regional human rights mechanisms.

Consequently, the affirmation by the General Assembly of the Paris Principles and the recognition of NHRIs at the regional levels clearly signal the acknowledgement by the international community as a whole that NHRIs are important partners in the implementation of international and regional human rights standards domestically and thus NHRIs nowadays are claiming a recognition of their status as fully-fledged members of the international community.

NHRIs in the African Region

Since the adoption of the Paris Principles, the number of NHRIs around the world has grown rapidly and the African region has not been an exception. The numbers have grown from just a single entity in 1989[29] to some 34 institutions in February 2012 and these are only those NHRIs who are members of the Network of African National Human Rights Institutions (African Network of NHRIs).[30]

The African Network of NHRIs, established in 1996, is a body uniting NHRIs of the region by providing a framework for these institutions to work together and cooperate on a regional basis through a variety of services such as training, capacity-building, networking and staff exchanges. It should be noted that the membership of the African Network of NHRIs includes not only those NHRIs that have been established in accordance with the Paris Principles and undergone the accreditation process by the ICCom Subcommittee, but also those who have not been accredited by the ICCom at all[31] and two have been accorded C-status.[32]

Issues surrounding the protection of asylum seekers' rights have been at the centre of the attention of the African Network of NHRIs, which is perhaps unsurprising given the scale of the problem in the African continent, as evidenced by other chapters of this book. The African Network of NHRIs holds bi-annual

28 See http://nhri.ohchr.org/EN/Regional/Europe/Pages/default.aspx.

29 Human Rights Watch, *Protectors or Pretenders? Government Human Rights Commissions in Africa* (Human Rights Watch, 2001).

30 See http://nhri.ohchr.org/EN/National/DirectoryOfInstitutions/Pages/Africa.aspx. Côte d'Ivoire appears to be a somewhat exception as its National Human Rights Commission is neither a member of the African Network of NHRIs nor has it undergone the ICCom accreditation.

31 There are 16 such NHRIs of the 40 members: National Human Rights Commissions of Angola, Burundi, Cape Verde, Congo-Brazzaville, Djibouti, Ethiopia, Gabon, Guinea Bissau, Guinea Conakry, Liberia, Mali, Niger, Sierra Leone, Southern Sudan, Swaziland, Tunisia and Zimbabwe. See http://www.nanhri.org/index.php?option=com_content&task=view&id=13&Itemid=7.

32 Benin Human Rights Commission and National Human Rights Commission of Madagascar.

conferences, and the 6th conference, which took place on 8–10 October 2007 in Kigali, Rwanda, was dedicated to the issues of protection of refugees, internally displaced and stateless persons. The overall aim of the conference was twofold: to raise awareness within the African NHRIs of their potential role in addressing the human rights of refugees, internally displaced and stateless persons, and to strengthen the capacity of African NHRIs to engage effectively on the protection of these vulnerable groups.[33] In his address to the conference, Dr Walter Kälin, the Representative of the UN Secretary-General on the Human Rights of Internally Displaced Persons, noted that the NHRIs in Africa can play an active role in protecting the rights of the internally displaced thorough, *inter alia*, monitoring conditions of displacement, following up on early warnings, educating, training and building capacity of civil society and working with governments on the development of laws and policies on internal displacement.[34]

The concluding document of this conference, the Kigali Declaration,[35] also reflects this statement by firstly noting that the rights of refugees, internally displaced and stateless persons remain a concern in the African region and that the African NHRIs have a critical role in protecting and promoting the rights of these vulnerable groups. The Declaration goes on to outline three sets of recommendations, addressing the specifics of each of the vulnerable groups and aiming to assist with the strategic engagement of African NHRIs with the protection and promotion of their rights. In respect of refugees, the Kigali Declaration provides more detail by setting out separate measures aimed at prevention, where such points as the need to enhance the mediatory role of the NHRIs in promoting pacific cooperation at the regional and sub-regional level in addressing refugee issues is underlined, and measures aimed at protection.[36]

The focus of the 6th bi-annual conference of African NHRIs thus has illuminated two interrelated points: firstly that issues surrounding the protection and promotion of the rights of refugees, internally displaced and stateless persons were of concern to the African region and secondly, the African NHRIs were recognized as important interlocutors in assisting with the protection and promotion of the rights of these vulnerable groups.

However, as the earlier sections identified, NHRIs are traditionally charged with rather wide mandates that encompass a whole range of human rights issues, so before embarking upon the examination of the practical ways in which NHRIs have engaged with the issues of the protection and promotion of the rights of

33 See http://nhri.ohchr.org/EN/Regional/Africa/Pages/6th-Conference-of-African-NHRI.aspx.

34 Statement of the Representative of the UN Secretary-General on the Human Rights of Internally Displaced Persons, Dr Walter Kälin, on the occasion of the 6th Conference of African National Human Rights Institutions; 8 October 2007, Kigali, Rwanda, p. 2.

35 Sixth Conference of African National Human Rights Institutions, Kigali Declaration, 8–10 October 2007.

36 Ibid. Section B.

these vulnerable groups, the scope of the mandates of NHRIs will be briefly analysed, in order to highlight the peculiar place that NHRIs occupy on the scene of international human rights law and the implication this has for the effectiveness of their work.

The Scope and Challenges of the Mandates of the NHRIs

The scope of NHRIs' mandates is as wide ranging as the NHRIs themselves. According to the Paris Principles, the NHRIs are to be charged with 'as broad a mandate as possible' and in particular they are to have the powers to submit opinions, recommendations, proposals and reports on any matters concerning the promotion and protection of human rights to any government, parliament or any competent body, especially concerning existing or draft legislation or any situation of violation of human rights.[37] The Paris Principles also endow NHRIs with wide-ranging powers to investigate any situation of human rights violation the institution decides to take up, to prepare reports on the national situation with regard to human rights in general and on more specific matters and to assist in the formulation of programmes for the teaching of and research into human rights, as well as to cooperate with relevant UN and regional human rights institutions.[38] Thus, the NHRIs have a great potential to support the protection and promotion of a variety of human rights at their respective national levels and indeed the UN High Commissioner for Human Rights has recognized NHRIs as 'critical partners for OHCHR due to the central place they have in the national human rights protection system, particularly in addressing the most critical human rights issues at the national level'.[39]

Within the African region, this potential was also recognized by the Organization of African Unity (OAU) which urged States 'to establish national human rights institutions and to provide them with adequate resources and ensure their independence'.[40] This was followed by a similar statement by the successor of the OAU, the African Union (AU).[41]

However, the NHRIs do not sit comfortably in the traditional dichotomy of international law, which draws a distinction between State and non-State actors. From a perspective of international law, it is the government of each individual country that bears the prime responsibility over the human rights record of its

37 See above, National Institutions for the Promotion and Protection of Human Rights n 1, principle A.

38 Ibid.

39 See above *Report by the Secretary-General on the National Institutions for the Promotion and Protection of Human Rights*, n 20, para 4.

40 Grand Bay (Mauritius) Declaration and Plan of Action, 16 April 1999, para 15.

41 The first AU Ministerial Conference on Human Rights, 'Kigali Declaration', MIN/CONF/HRA/Decl.1 (I) (8 May 2003) para 2.

country and has the key responsibility over the promotion and protection of human rights. Traditional means of fulfilling this obligation is through the enactment of legislation, the existence of an independent judiciary and also through establishment of national institutions. Therefore, the *raison d'être* of NHRIs is to provide a counter-balance to such efforts of the governments so as to ensure that these are carried out in good faith and are truly aimed at the fulfilment of governments' obligations in respect of human rights. The mere establishment of an NHRI in a country is not equal to the fulfillment of governments' human rights obligations: on the contrary, through the creation of an NHRI, a country in question is in effect creating a watchdog of its own activities.[42]

Equally the establishment of an NHRI requires an official commitment and action from a State, not least the provision of adequate funding.[43] Such a degree of involvement of a State in the establishment of a NHRI as well as in supporting, at least financially, its operation, firmly elevates these entities into a position beyond a non-governmental organization (NGO). Having said that, the legitimacy, credibility and therefore effectiveness of any NHRI rests on its ability to operate independently of the government, being perceived as independent and remaining free of any control by the government so as to not be or perceived as being a part of the State structure.[44] Moreover, in order to be effective, NHRIs need to be perceived as valid and independent partners by both the State and NGOs, which puts them in difficult waters to navigate. The study of an international NGO, Human Rights Watch, of the African NHRIs in 2001[45] revealed that NHRIs of the region struggle to juggle this complicated role and asks a very challenging question: are NHRIs in Africa State-sponsored 'pretenders' of human rights protection or true watchdogs over the human rights record of their respective countries?

To this overall picture of difficulties with the actual and perceived independence of NHRIs, one should add the impact of the rather wide mandates of the NHRIs who, being charged with such all-encompassing mandates covering the whole variety of human rights, often struggle to engage sufficiently with a variety of rights. Rarely do the NHRIs have sufficient human and financial resources to adequately respond to all human rights issues that arise at the national level and thus NHRIs must prioritize their involvement with various issues. The abovementioned Human Rights Watch report on African NHRIs makes a specific recommendation relating to the resources available to the NHRIs, arguing that necessary financial and

42 See for instance, Linda C Rief, 'Building Democratic Institutions: The Role of National Human Rights Institutions in Good Governance and Human Rights Protection' (2000) 13 HARV.HUM. RTS J. 1.

43 See Dickson 'The contribution of human rights commissions to the protection of human rights' 272.

44 S Livingstone and R Murray, *Evaluating the Effectiveness of National Human Rights Institutions: The Northern Ireland Human Rights Commission with Comparisons from South Africa* (University of Bristol and Queen's University Belfast Publication, 2005) 26.

45 See Human Rights Watch above n 28.

material resources that would allow human rights commissions to undertake their functions effectively must be provided as a priority and that it is the responsibility of the government to provide a substantial part of this funding.[46]

Against this backdrop of struggles over independence, the need to juggle broad mandates, to prioritize issues and insufficient human and financial resources, we now turn our attention to the specifics of the role of NHRIs in the protection of the rights of asylum seekers in Africa.

African NHRIs and Protection and Promotion of the Rights of Asylum Seekers: Examples from Practice

The aim of this section is to give an insight into the practical examples of how NHRIs in Africa have engaged with the issues of asylum seekers. By drawing on the experience of the HRCs of Uganda, Ghana, Kenya and South Africa, examples of working with legislation, engagement at the policy levels, the examination of the conditions of detention of refugees and asylum seekers and strategic litigation will be explored.

Work at the Policy Level and with the Legislation

The approach in terms of the government's policy towards refugees and asylum seekers, and the corresponding legislative framework, undeniably constitute the very basis for engagement with these vulnerable groups and serves as the main point of reference for the promotion and protection of their rights. The Ugandan Human Rights Commission, for example, has been advocating the adoption of the necessary legislation to regulate the procedures applicable to asylum seekers and refugees and thus in its 11th Annual Report the Commission commends the governments' full compliance with its earlier recommendations to adopt a Refugee Law and the Dual Citizenship Act.[47]

The KNCHR in 2007 carried out an extensive investigation into the procedures applicable to the issuance of national identification cards in Kenya,[48] which had significant ramifications for some groups of refugees in the country. The investigation was promoted by a large number of individual complaints about irregularities with the process of obtaining national identification cards as well as allegations that many Somali refugees in the Dadaab Refugee Camp had been

46 Ibid. see Recommendation 21.

47 Uganda Human Rights Commission, *The 11th Annual Report to the Parliament of Uganda of the Uganda Human Rights Commission* (2008) 134, 146, available at http://www.uhrc.ug/index.php?option=com_docman&Itemid=111.

48 Kenya National Commission on Human Rights, *An Identity in Crisis? A Study on the Issuance of National Identity Cards in Kenya* (2007), available at http://www.knchr.org/index.php?option=com_content&task=view&id=73&Itemid=85.

issued with Kenyan national identification cards.[49] In respect to refugees and asylum seekers, the report notes the significant gaps in legislation relating to these groups.[50] Moreover, the examination of the situation on the ground with respect to these groups showed that across the districts visited, there were negative perceptions noted in relation to people of Somali origin, who were viewed with suspicion by the Provincial Administration and registrars.[51] The investigation revealed cases of fraud when Kenyan national identification cards were obtained by refugees of Somali origin, the apparent xenophobic attitudes displayed by the provincial administration against Somalis in general and the negative outcomes that such a situation has brought as a result of those who have legal entitlement to reside in Kenya feeling alienated.[52]

The outcomes of this investigation appear to be far reaching. The KNCHR entered into discussions with the Ministry of Foreign Affairs, which established a department of registration within its structure. This new entity started work on the strategic implementation of the recommendations made in the report, one of the most important ones being a computerized central registration system that would allow accurate records of Kenyan citizens and ways in which citizenship has been obtained to be kept. Certainly this new body and these measures will strengthen the level of protection afforded to asylum seekers and refugees in Kenya by eliminating possibilities for arbitrary decisions to be made on citizenship and enabling the proper functioning of systems that will hopefully alleviate negative feelings within and towards these groups. Moreover, this investigation has also led the KNCHR to embark upon much a bigger research into the situation of statelessness in Kenya.[53] This project is being carried out in collaboration with the UN High Commissioner for Refugees and the draft results are currently under consideration.

Visiting Places of Deprivation of Liberty Where Asylum Seekers and Refugees Are Held

Given the widespread policies of governments around the world to detain asylum seekers,[54] one of the most effective means of ensuring the protection of their rights is carrying out independent visits to such places with the aim of examining both the

49 Ibid. 1–2.

50 Ibid. 5.

51 Ibid. 9.

52 Ibid.

53 Kenya National Commission on Human Rights, *Strategic Plan 2009–2013* (2009) 51, available at http://www.knchr.org/index.php?option=com_content&task=view&id=73&Itemid=85.

54 A Edwards, *Back to Basics: The Right to Liberty and Security of Person and 'Alternatives to Detention' of Refugees, Asylum-Seekers, Stateless Persons and Other Migrants* (UNHCR Legal and Protection Policy Research Series, Division of International Protection PPLA/2011/01 Rev.1 April 2011) 1.

treatment of people held in such places and the conditions in which these people are held. The CHRAJ in Ghana, for example, commenced such visits two years after its inception in 1993 through a broad interpretation of its mandate to promote respect for human rights. Thus, despite the absence of an explicit mandate that would grant it unrestricted access to places of deprivation of liberty, the CHRAJ has been carrying out such visits and in practice has not been denied access.[55]

Over the past few years, visits to refugee camps have been among the CHRAJ's priorities and the Commission has expressed a willingness to visit other immigration facilities, although it has been unable to do so due to resource constraints.[56] Visits to refugee camps however remained a part of the Commissions activities in 2006 and 2007[57] and in addition to visiting such places the Commission has also tried to focus on monitoring specific rights of refugees. Thus in 2006, for example, the special focus of the Commission was the implementation of the right to education in refugee camps and the CHRAJ noted the positive development in the Budumburam camp where the refugees, in particular young people, have been trained in areas such as technology, masonry, carpentry, joinery and road construction.[58]

In 2006 the Commission also examined the implementation of the right to health, noting with concern reported complaints of discrimination in favour of Ghanaians in the hospitals but commending the support of the UNHCR in the Volta Region in their effort to ensure that refugees enjoy the right to education and health.[59] These engagements have allowed the CHRAJ not only to have its own accurate data about the number of refugees and asylum seekers in the country but also provided it with a first-hand account of the problems faced by these groups, which the Commission has been able to use to make targeted and specific recommendations for the government authorities concerned.

Arguably the most well-known engagement in monitoring immigration facilities in Africa is the report on the assessment of conditions of detention in the Lindela Repatriation Centre in South Africa, which was carried out by the South African Human Rights Commission (SAHRC).[60] This highly influential report,

---

55 Association for Prevention of Torture, OPCAT Database, available at: http://apt.ch/opcat.

56 Ibid.

57 L Ayete-Nyampong, *Challenges facing the OPCAT in the Implementation of the OPCAT in the African Region. Visiting places of detention-Methods*, Paper to the Conference 'OPCAT in the African Region: Challenges of Implementation' (3–4 April 2008), available at http://www.bristol.ac.uk/law/research/centres-themes/opcat/docs.html#OPCATAfricanConference2008.

58 Commission on Human Rights and Administrative Justice, *State of Human Rights Report* (2006), section 8.2

59 Ibid. section 8.3.

60 South African Human Rights Commission, Lindela. *At the Crossroads for Detention and Repatriation. An Assessment of the Conditions of Detention by the South African Human Rights Commission* (2000), available at http://www.queensu.ca/samp/migrationresources/xenophobia/reports/sahrc1.pdf.

which followed an earlier report issued a year before,[61] starts with a staggering appraisal of the state of immigration detention in South Africa:

> The arbitrary and indiscriminate detention of undocumented migrants has become a commonplace, everyday occurrence. This practice flies in the face of the many universally recognised human rights that migrants are entitled to, whether they are documented or not. When asylum seekers are affected, such detention becomes a serious violation of their special right to international protection.[62]

The report goes on to uncover, in detail, the gaps in the legislative framework, lack of independent oversight over the detention, appalling conditions of detention and deep-rooted corruption in Lindela. In relation to asylum seekers and refugees specifically, the report notes, as a major concern, the process for identifying persons belonging to such groups thus, in effect, preventing such people from applying for asylum.[63] The crucial aspect of this issue was the finding of a failure to comply with the so-called '30-day rule' according to which a person, whose removal from the country is pending, may not be held for longer than 30 days unless his or her detention is reviewed by a judge of the High Court.[64] SAHRC therefore recommended that immigration officers advise people who claim to be asylum applicants of their right to apply for asylum in a language they understand and that the Department of Home Affairs ensures reasonable opportunities for persons detained at Lindela to apply for asylum by introducing refugee officers who are permanently stationed at the facility.[65]

The whole of the report concludes with a list of targeted recommendations that deal with all aspects of detention of the variety of groups held at Lindela, and certainly has added a significant boost to the voices of the NGOs in the country expressing grave concern over the situation in Lindela.[66] Accordingly, the attention of the authorities have been galvanized and a major review of the immigration policies has been undertaken. What is especially commendable is that this review appears to have been carried out in a transparent and inclusive manner whereby views of civil society were solicited.[67] Most importantly, this initiative

61 South African Human Rights Commission, *Illegal? Report on the arrest and detention of persons in terms of the Aliens Control Act* (1999), available at http://www.sahrc.org.za/home/21/files/Reports/Report%20into%20the%20Arrest%20and%20Detention%20of%20suspected%20migrants19.pdf.

62 South African Human Rights Commission, above n 58, 2.

63 Ibid. 48–50.

64 Ibid. 13; see also Aliens Control Act, No 96 (1991), section 55 (5).

65 Ibid. 51.

66 See, for example, Lawyers For Human Rights, *Monitoring Immigration Detention in South Africa* (2008), available at http://www.lhr.org.za/publications/monitoring-immigration-detention-south-africa-2008.

67 See, for example, Institute for Security Studies, *The Response of the Institute for Security Studies to the call by the Department of Home Affairs for interested parties*

of the SAHRC appears to have broken the back of the long-standing problem of independent access to the Lindela centre,[68] which is a major step in the right direction for the protection of the rights of those detained there.

Strategic Litigation

The example of the work of SAHRC in respect to the Lindela Repatriation Centre also provides an insight of the way this NHRI has used strategic litigation to advance the protection of the rights of asylum seekers. In 1999, the SAHRC, together with the Law Clinic of the University of Witwatersrand, obtained an important court decision[69] requiring the management of the Lindela Repatriation Centre to report the names of detainees to SAHRC every month in order to check the compliance with the so-called '30-day rule', mentioned above. The crucial aspect of this case was that the judgement provided for the release of 40 persons who had been detained in Lindela in breach of the '30-day rule' for up to five months.[70]

The longer-term outcome of this litigation is that the SAHRC and the Lawyers For Human Rights, a South African NGO, now have a joint monitoring project for Lindela and by a court order they are supposed to be given the names of all detainees who are detained for over 25 days even though in reality the lawyers must go and physically collect the list, which is not always accurate.[71] A crucial aspect to be mentioned in relation to the SAHRC and this case is the fact that it was the initiative of the SAHRC to approach the Law Clinic of the University of Witwatersrand directly to act on its behalf in the litigation process,[72] which demonstrates the real commitment of this NHRI to the issue.

An as yet unexplored,[73] but very useful strategic litigation tool to advance the rights of refugees and asylum seekers, which is at the disposal of African NHRIs, is the possibility of litigation before the African Court of Human and Peoples' Rights. Equally, the African Commission of Human and Peoples' Rights could be used by the NHRIs of the region. While it has happened in relation to the

---

to comment on the new Immigration Regulations by the Crime and Justice Programme (2 March 2005), available at http://www.iss.co.za/uploads/DHASUB020305.PDF.

68 O Fields and A Edwards, *Alternatives to Detention of Asylum Seekers and Refugees* (UNHCR Legal and Protection Policy Research Series A. POLAS/2006/03, 2006) 178.

69 *SAHRC and Forty Others v Minister of Home Affairs and Dyambu (Pty) Ltd*, Case No 28367/99, Witwatersrand High Court, November 1999.

70 Lindela, *At the Crossroads for Detention and Repatriation* 9.

71 Fields and Edwards, *Alternatives to Detention of Asylum Seekers and Refugees* 178–9.

72 See http://www.wits.ac.za/academic/clm/law/centresclinicsresearch/witslawclinic/11039/past.html.

73 A Edwards, *Back to Basics* 36.

protection of other rights,[74] there is a lack of any refugee-specific case law before the Commission, initiated by the NHRIs of the region.

In order to promote the possibility for the African NHRIs to use these regional human rights mechanisms, the African Network of NHRIs in November 2011 held 'Sensitization and Consultative Seminar for National Human Rights Institutions in Africa'.[75] Entitled 'The Relationship between the African Court on Human and Peoples' Rights and African National Human Rights Institutions', the seminar aimed to familiarize the African NHRIs with the litigation processes and procedures of the Court as well as to establish a relationship between the Court and NHRIs.

Potential for the Future: the Optional Protocol to the United Nations Convention Against Torture and NHRIs in Africa

The coming into force of the OPCAT on 22 June 2006[76] has presented NHRIs around the world with yet another opportunity to further strengthen their role in the domestic implementation of international human rights standards. The implementation mechanism of this international human rights treaty is markedly different since the traditional modes for supervision of State compliance, such as reporting obligations or individual communications, are absent. Instead, the OPCAT sets out a two-tier supervision system whereby another treaty body has been created at the international level, the Subcommittee on Prevention of Torture (SPT),[77] whilst one of the core obligations for States parties to the OPCAT is the creation of their own National Preventive Mechanisms (NPMs) to function at the domestic level.[78] These two tiers of institutions are charged with a preventive mandate, one of the core elements of it being the conduct of a system of regular visits to all places of deprivation of liberty.[79]

What is of special interest is that the OPCAT contains no blueprint as to how these NPMs ought to be. The instrument does not provide any more detail other than requirements for independence, including functional independence and

74 See, for example, *Interights, Institute for Human Rights and Development in Africa, and Association Mauritanienne des Droits de l'Homme v Islamic Republic of Mauritania* Communication No 373/2009 (formerly 242/2001).

75 The seminar took place in Arusha, Tanzania 16–18 November 2011. See http://www.nanhri.org/index.php?option=com_content&task=view&id=234&Itemid=7.

76 UNGA, 'Res. 57/199 on the Optional Protocol to the Convention against Torture and Other Cruel, Inhuman or Degrading Treatment or Punishmen', UN Doc A/RES/57/199 (18 December 2003). It was adopted by 127 votes to 4, with 42 abstentions.

77 Initially there were 10 members on the SPT, but in 2009 the number increased to 25: Art 5(1) stipulates that with 50th ratification of OPCAT the membership of the SPT is to expand to 25 members. The SPT now has become the largest UN treaty body.

78 See UNGA, 'Optional Protocol to the Convention against Torture and other Cruel, Inhuman or Degrading Treatment or Punishment (OPCAT)', UN Doc A/RES/57/199 (18 December 2002) Art 3.

79 See OPCAT above n 76, Art 4.

independence of NPMs' personnel, the necessary diversity of expertise and gender balance and representation of ethnic and minority groups in the country, as well as an obligation for States Parties to provide the necessary resources for the functioning of an NPM.[80] Crucially for the NHRIs however, Article 18(4) requires States to give due consideration to the Paris Principles when establishing NPMs, thus clearly indicating that the drafters of the instrument saw NHRIs as potential institutions that could carry out the NPM functions. Indeed, Article 17 of OPCAT makes it clear that States Parties are free to either establish entirely new institutions for the purposes of an NPM or to adopt and/or combine the mandates of existing ones; the main obligation is that an NPM is designated within one year of the ratification of the instrument.[81]

Within the emerging State practice in respect of the designation of NPMs four trends can be distinguished: designation of existing Ombudsman offices,[82] existing Human Rights Commissions,[83] designating a number of institutions that all together are to execute the NPM mandate[84] and the creation of entirely new institutions.[85] As these trends evidence, the role of NHRIs in the functioning of NPMs around the world is rather prominent: NHRIs are either designated to perform the NPM functions on their own in addition to their Ombudsman office or Human Rights Commissions' mandates[86] or to act as an NPM together with other existing statutory bodies or civil society.[87] It thus clear that the reference

80 See OPCAT above n 76, Art 18.

81 For detailed analysis of what is an NPM and various challenges surrounding the establishment of NPMs, see: R Murray, 'National Preventive Mechanisms under the Optional Protocol to the Torture Convention: One Size Does Not Fit All' (2008) 26(4) Netherlands Quarterly of Human Rights 485–516.

82 For example in Armenia it is the Office of Public Defender of Armenia that has been designated as the NPM while in Costa Rica it is the Ombudsman's Office (La Defensoría de los Habitantes).

83 For example in Mexico it is the Mexican National Human Rights Commission that has been designated as the only institution to carry out the mandate of the NPM, while in Mali it is the National Human Rights Commission (Commission Nationale des Droits de l'homme).

84 For example in the United Kingdom, 18 existing institutions have been designated to form an NPM for the country, with Her Majesty's Inspectorate for Prisons being charged with the coordinating function.

85 For example in France the institution of General Inspector of Places of Deprivation of Liberty (*Contrôleur général des lieux de privation de liberté*) has been created for the purposes of country's NPM while in Senegal it is the National Observer for Places of Deprivation of Liberty (*Observateur National des Lieux de Privation de Liberté*).

86 For example in Estonia it is the Office of the Chancellor of Justice who has been given the function of the NPM with an insertion to that effect in the Chancellor of Justice Act. See Chancellor of Justice Act (25 February 1999) Art 27.

87 For example in New Zealand, five institutions have been designated to carry out the mandate of the NPM: the Human Rights Commission (as a central body), Office of the Ombudsman, the Independent Police Conduct Authority, Office of the Children's Commissioner and the Inspector of Service Penal Establishments of the Office of the Judge

in Article 18(4) to the Paris Principles has certainly played an important role in guiding the choice of the States Parties for their respective NPMs.[88]

The significance of the potential role that NHRIs may be accorded as per OPCAT in relation specifically to the protection and promotion of the rights of asylum seekers lies in Article 4 of the OPCAT. This provision contains a very broad definition of 'place of deprivation of liberty' to which States Parties are to allow visits by their NPMs and the SPT. Thus any place under the jurisdiction and control of the State Party where a person is or may be deprived of liberty either by virtue of an order given by a public authority, at its instigation or with its consent or acquiescence, whether that is a public or private custodial setting, which a person is not permitted to leave at will by order of any judicial, administrative or other authority, fall within the 'jurisdiction' of the NPM and SPT visiting mandates. It therefore follows that not only are 'traditional' places of deprivation of liberty such as prisons and police cells included in the mandates of NPMs and SPT, but also 'less traditional' ones, like psychiatric institutions, care homes for elderly, transit points at international airports and of course places where migrants can be held, including refugee camps and detention centres for asylum seekers.[89]

Moreover, the NPMs are not just to carry our regular visits to such a wide variety of places of deprivation of liberty. As Article 1 of the OPCAT stipulates, such visits are to be carried out with the aim of preventing torture and other ill-treatment[90] and thus to achieve this aim NPMs are mandated to have full access to all places of deprivation of liberty, including unannounced visits; absolute freedom of movement within these places; access to information and the right to have private interviews with whomever the NPM deems it necessary; as well as

---

Advocate General of the Armed Forces; in Slovenia, on the other hand, it is the Ombudsman and, in agreement with him/her, the NGOs who are to carry out the tasks of the NPM.

88 For a detailed account on the OPCAT drafting process see R Murray, E Steinerte, MD Evans and A Hallo De Wolf, *The Optional Protocol to the UN Convention against Torture* (Oxford University Press, 2011), chapters 1–3; MD Evans and C Haenni-Dale, 'Preventing Torture? The Development of the Optional Protocol to the UN Convention Against Torture' (2004) 4(1) Human Rights Law Review 19–55.

89 For detailed analysis of the concept of 'deprivation of liberty' in OPCAT see Human Rights Implementation Centre, *Deprivation of liberty as per Article 4 of OPCAT: the scope* (Policy Paper by the Human Rights Implementation Centre: University of Bristol, 2011), available at http://www.bristol.ac.uk/law/research/centres-themes/hric/. On the scope of visiting mandates of the NPMs as well as associated challenges see R Murray, E Steinerte, MD Evans and A Hallo De Wolf, *The Optional Protocol to the UN Convention against Torture* chapter 4; A Hallo de Wolf, 'Visits to Less Traditional Places of Detention: Challenges under the OPCAT' (2009) 6(1) Essex Human Rights Review 103–37.

90 On what this entails, see The approach of the Subcommittee on Prevention of Torture to the concept of prevention of torture and other cruel, inhuman or degrading treatment or punishment under the 'Optional Protocol to the Convention against Torture and Other Cruel, Inhuman or Degrading Treatment or Punishment', UN Doc CAT/OP/12/6 (30 December 2010).

the right to issue recommendations to the respective authorities with the aim of improving the treatment and conditions of those deprived of their liberty as well as to prevent torture and other ill-treatment.[91] Crucially, the OPCAT specifically prescribes that the relevant authorities are to examine the recommendations of the NPMs and enter into dialogue with the NPM on the possible implementation measures.[92] Furthermore, NPMs are also empowered to submit proposals and observations concerning existing or draft legislation,[93] as well as to engage in other activities aimed at the prevention of torture and other ill-treatment.[94]

Clearly such an extensive mandate holds great potential to make a significant contribution to the protection and promotion of the rights of those deprived of their liberty, and given the widespread practice of many countries to detain asylum seekers, the potential of the NPMs' contribution to the protection and promotion of the rights of this vulnerable group is significant.[95]

African NHRIs and OPCAT

There are 63 States Parties to OPCAT[96] and of those 11[97] are from the African region, with a further 9 African States[98] having signed but not yet ratified the instrument. Among the 11 African countries that have ratified OPCAT, only four have actually designated their NPMs: Mali and Mauritius have chosen to designate their respective Human Rights Commissions[99] while Nigeria[100] and Senegal[101] have established new institutions to carry out the NPM mandate.

---

91 See OPCAT above n 76, Arts 19–20.

92 See OPCAT above n 76, Art 22.

93 Art 19(c).

94 See OPCAT above n 76, para 5 of the Preamble

95 For detailed analysis of opportunities and challenges that OPCAT presents in the protection of refugee rights see A Edwards, 'The Optional Protocol to the Convention Against Torture and the Detention of Refugees' (2008) 57 International and Comparative Law Quarterly 789–825.

96 Correct at 4 July 2012. For the list of ratifications see http://treaties.un.org/Pages/ViewDetails.aspx?src=TREATY&mtdsg_no=IV-9-b&chapter=4&lang=en.

97 These are Benin, Burkina Faso, Democratic Republic of Congo, Gabon, Liberia, Mali, Mauritius, Nigeria, Senegal, Togo and Tunisia. See ibid.

98 These are Cameroon, Cape Verde, the Republic of Congo, Ghana, Guinea, Madagascar, Sierra Leone, South African and Zambia. See ibid.

99 See APT, List of Designated National Preventive Mechanisms, available at http://www.apt.ch/index.php?option=com_k2&view=item&layout=item&id=767&Itemid=267&lang=en.

100 Penal Reform International. Nigerian government approves National Committee on Torture. See http://www.penalreform.org/news/nigerian-government-approves-national-committee-torture.

101 See List of Designated National Preventive Mechanisms above n 99.

However that is not an indication of the role that the African NHRIs have played and continue to play in OPCAT-related processes in the continent. Many NHRIs are the driving forces behind the OPCAT ratification campaigns in their respective countries. For example, the Ugandan Human Rights Commission has been including the ratification of OPCAT among its recommendations in its Annual Report for years now.[102] In Ghana the CHRAJ held a round-table conference on the ratification and implementation of OPCAT prior to Ghana's signature to OPCAT in November 2006, which was the first formal forum on the OPCAT in the country, gathering all the relevant State and civil society stakeholders. The Commission remains the driving force behind the OPCAT process in the country today.[103]

The NHRIs of the region have also been the leading institutions in promoting a proper implementation process, most notably a transparent and inclusive NPM designation process,[104] and many of them have done so in the absence of the OPCAT ratification. Thus the South African Human Rights Commission (SAHRC) has been very active on the OPCAT since the country's signature of the instrument. The decision of the SAHRC was very pragmatic – to assist with the thorough examination of the existing situation in South Africa so as to allow for a proper evaluation of the best options for the implementation of OPCAT and designation of an NPM. Thus, in 2006, the SAHRC together with the Centre for the Study of Violence and Reconciliation carried out an inventory of the existing monitoring mechanisms in South Africa,[105] which allowed for the analysis of the existing monitoring mechanisms in South Africa and their compliance with the OPCAT requirements. Following this, the so-called Section 5 Committee[106] was established, which has since led the work on torture prevention and OPCAT-

102 For example Uganda Human Rights Commission, The 13th Annual Report to the Parliament of Uganda of the Uganda Human Rights Commission (2011) 142; Uganda Human Rights Commission, *The 12th Annual Report to the Parliament of Uganda of the Uganda Human Rights Commission* (2010) 180; Uganda Human Rights Commission, *The 11th Annual Report to the Parliament of Uganda of the Uganda Human Rights Commission* (2008) 144 and Uganda Human Rights Commission, The 10th Annual Report to the Parliament of Uganda of the Uganda Human Rights Commission, 'Recommendation 12.13' (2007) 115–16, 118. At p. 118 the Commission notes earlier failure of the government to comply with the same recommendation previously, all available at http://www.uhrc.ug/index.php?option=com_docman&Itemid=111.

103 See OPCAT Database above n 55.

104 This is one of the key recommendations of SPT. See *Guidelines on national preventive mechanisms*, CAT/OP/12/5 (9 December 2010) para 16.

105 O Streater, 'Review of Existing Mechanisms for the Prevention and Investigation of Torture and Cruel, Inhuman or Degrading Treatment or Punishment in South Africa' Centre for the Study of Violence and Reconciliation' (2008), available at http://www.csvr.org.za/docs/torturereview1208.pdf.

106 According to Section 5 of the South African Human Rights Commission Act, the Commission may establish committees for the purposes it determines: No 54 of 1994: Human Rights Commission Act, 1994; section 5.

related issues in South Africa.[107] The proposals for various NPM models in South Africa currently also include a role for the SAHRC, mostly that of coordinating the work of other monitoring mechanisms.[108]

The Ugandan Human Rights Commission has been equally active and in 2008 was a co-organizer of a national workshop on the effective strategies for torture prevention in Uganda, where the ratification of OPCAT by Uganda was assessed as well as implementation options discussed.[109] The outcome of the event was the establishment of a working group on torture prevention in which the members of the Uganda Human Rights Commission were included.[110]

The HRCs of those African countries that have already designated their NPMs have also played a significant role in bringing about compliance with the OPCAT's obligation within their respective countries. For example, the Senegalese Human Rights Commission was part of the Follow-Up Committee on the implementation of OPCAT, established in December 2007, that decided to promote the establishment of an entirely new institution in Senegal for the purposes of the NPM. This finally led to the adoption of new legislation by the Senate, creating a new institution as NPM: the National Observer of Places of Deprivation of Liberty.[111]

The recent Africa regional conference on the prevention of torture and ill-treatment[112] has also recognized the role for the African NHRIs in the promotion and implementation of the OPCAT, as well as in the broader torture prevention agenda. Thus the so-called Dakar Plan of Action: points for Prevention of Torture and other Cruel, Inhuman or Degrading Treatment or Punishment in Africa, the concluding document of the conference, is addressed not only to States, governments and the African Commission on Human and People's Rights, but also to the NHRIs of the region, and specifically highlights the role of the NHRIs in inclusive and transparent dialogue on the implementation of OPCAT.[113] This very much echoes the acknowledgement of the role of African NHRIs in the prevention of torture and other ill-treatment in the region expressed in the Robben Island

107 See OPCAT Database above n 55.

108 Ibid.

109 See *The 11th Annual Report to the Parliament of Uganda of the Uganda Human Rights Commission* above n 45, 144; the recommendation to the government to ratify OPCAT 'as soon as possible' as in previous years was repeated: see 144, 147.

110 Ibid, 144.

111 See OPCAT Database above n 55.

112 The conference took place from 27 to 28 April 2010 in Dakar, Senegal, and was organized by the Association for the Prevention of Torture and Amnesty International Senegal, in collaboration with the African Commission on Human and Peoples' Rights; see http://www.apt.ch/index.php?option=com_k2&view=item&id=945:africa-torture-prevention-conference&Itemid=224&lang=en.

113 Africa Torture Prevention Conference, The Dakar Plan of Action: 8 points for Prevention of Torture and other Cruel, Inhuman or Degrading Treatment or Punishment in Africa (27–28 April 2010), preamble and point 3(a).

Guidelines,[114] which is the most detailed and authoritative soft law instrument of the region relating to the prevention of torture and other ill-treatment.

The role of the African NHRIs in the promotion of the ratification of the OPCAT and its proper implementation has been and continues to be a significant one and the few examples mentioned above are clear evidence of this. However a word of caution should be noted: HRC and Ombudsman institutions do not represent a perfect match to the requirements of OPCAT in relation to NPMs and the choices made by the four African countries that have designated their NPMs so far is clear evidence to this fact – only two HRCs are designated as NPMs. Thus for example, the Senegalese HRC has acquired a sound reputation and has received A-status accreditation with the ICCom since 2000,[115] yet it was not been chosen to become the NPM for the country, which goes to show that NHRIs are not 'a perfect match' for the NPM mandate.

There are a number of challenges facing HRCs if they are to become NPMs, for instance the need to ensure that the NPM work is not 'lost' in the wide human rights mandate of the HRCs; the need for the necessary variety of expertise; the need to ensure a system of regular visits to all places of deprivation of liberty and so on.[116] It is evident that many African NHRIs who are involved or even leading their national OPCAT ratification and/or implementation processes are acutely aware of these tensions and thus do not automatically propose themselves as institutions ready for the NPM mandate but rather engage in thorough and objective exploration of the options available for the country, which of course goes to the credit of these NHRIs.

Concluding Remarks

The aim of this chapter was to highlight the ways in which African NHRIs have engaged with the promotion and protection of asylum seekers' rights both collectively through the Network of African NHRIs and individually. Through individual examples of the HRCs of Ghana, Kenya, South Africa and Uganda, the aspects of their work at the policy level, work with legislation, visits to places of detention and strategic litigation have been examined, and it is evident that NHRIs

114 African Commission on Human and Peoples' Rights, Resolution on the Guidelines and Measures for the Prohibition and Prevention of Torture, Cruel, Inhuman or Degrading Treatment or Punishment in Africa (Robben Island Guidelines) (23 October 2002), para 41.

115 See http://nhri.ohchr.org/EN/National/DirectoryOfInstitutions/Pages/Africa.aspx.

116 For detailed analysis of designating Human Rights Commissions and Ombudsman Offices as NPMs under the OPCAT see E Steinerte and R Murray, 'Same but Different? National Human Rights Commissions and Ombudsman Institutions as National Preventive Mechanisms under the Optional Protocol to the UN Convention against Torture' (2009) 6(1) Essex Human Rights Review 77–101.

in these countries have made a significant contribution towards the protection and promotion of the rights of asylum seekers in their respective countries.

The difficult question that legitimately can be asked is if these NHRIs could do more and the inevitable truth is that they probably could. The obstacles to NHRIs doing more lies at the heart of the many challenges that NHRIs face in their day-to-day work. These are human rights bodies charged with wide mandates to protect and promote human rights in general where rights of asylum seekers constitute only one aspect of this extensive mandate. This has direct implications for the resources of NHRIs, both human and financial. As argued earlier, NHRIs within the African region suffer as a result of chronic under-resourcing and in such a situation the NHRIs naturally have to prioritize the issues they engage with, which may mean that the rights of asylum seekers are overlooked. The example of the Commission on Human Rights and Administrative Justice in Ghana (CHRAJ) was mentioned earlier is illustrative of this as the Commission had to cut its visits to places of deprivation of liberty due to concerns over resources.[117]

Equally, most of the NHRIs of the region are new institutions, with insufficient resources, working in a very complex and often turbulent political, social and economic situation and burdened with enormous, often quite unrealistic, expectations from society. This certainly has implications for the effectiveness of their work.

Nevertheless and despite this challenging environment, the NHRIs in Africa examined here have made their mark in the protection of the rights of asylum seekers. With the coming into force of the OPCAT and as more African countries become Parties to this unique international human rights treaty, the NHRIs may be in a position to further strengthen their role. The NHRIs of the region have played a leading part in their respective countries during ratification and implementation campaigns on the OPCAT and it is fair to say that they will continue to play a crucial part in the implementation of the OPCAT, either as part of their country's respective NPM or watchdogs of these NPMs, thus further strengthening the protection of asylum seekers' rights in Africa.

References

Documents

The Dakar Plan of Action: 8 points for Prevention of Torture and other Cruel, Inhuman or Degrading Treatment or Punishment in Africa.

Grand Bay (Mauritius) Declaration and Plan of Action, 12–16 April 1999.

Guidelines for Accreditation and Re-Accreditation of National Human Rights Institutions to the International Coordinating Committee of National Human Rights Institutions. Version 4 June 2009.

---

117 See above OPCAT Database n 55

ICCom Sub-Committee on Accreditation. General Observations (June 2009).
Kigali Declaration from the first AU Ministerial Conference on Human Rights, MIN/CONF/HRA/Decl.1 (I) of 8 May 2003.
Optional Protocol to the Convention against Torture and Other Cruel, Inhuman or Degrading Treatment or Punishment. UN Doc A/RES/57/199, 18 December 2003.
Principles Relating to the Status and Functioning of National Institutions for the Protection and Promotion of Human Rights (The Paris Principles), Resolution 1992/54, endorsed by the UN General Assembly Resolution 48/134, 20 December 1993.
Resolution on the Guidelines and Measures for the Prohibition and Prevention of Torture, Cruel, Inhuman or Degrading Treatment or Punishment in Africa (Robben Island Guidelines), 32nd Session, Banjul, The Gambia, October 2002.
The Statute of Association International Coordinating Committee of National Institutions for the Promotion and Protection of Human Rights (ICCom Statute).
Subcommittee on Prevention of Torture. The approach of the Subcommittee on Prevention of Torture to the concept of prevention of torture and other cruel, inhuman or degrading treatment or punishment under the Optional Protocol to the Convention against Torture and Other Cruel, Inhuman or Degrading Treatment or Punishment. UN Doc CAT/OP/12/6 of 30 December 2010.
Subcommittee on Prevention of Torture. Guidelines on national preventive mechanisms. CAT/OP/12/5 of 9 December 2010.

Presentations, Books and Articles

A Handbook in the Establishment and Strengthening of National Institutions for the Promotion and Protection of Human Rights. United Nations: Professional Training Series No 4.
Ayete-Nyampong L, *Challenges facing the OPCAT in the Implementation of the OPCAT in the African Region. Visiting places of detention-Methods.* (2008) Paper to the Conference 'OPCAT in the African Region: Challenges of Implementation' held 3–4 April 2008, Cape Town South Africa, available at http://www.bristol.ac.uk/law/research/centres-themes/opcat/docs.html#OPCATAfricanConference2008 [accessed on 4 July 2012].
Carver R, 'A New Answer to an Old Question: National Human Rights Institutions and the Domestication of International Law' (2010) 10(1) Human Rights Law Review 1–32.
Carver R and Korotaev A, *Assessing the Effectiveness of National Human Rights Institutions* (2008) Report on behalf of the UNDP Regional Centre in Bratislava.
Dickson B, 'The contribution of human rights commissions to the protection of human rights' (2003) Public Law 272–85.

Edwards A, 'The Optional Protocol to the Convention Against Torture and the Detention of Refugees' (2008) 57 International and Comparative Law Quarterly 789–825.

Edwards A, *Back to Basics: The Right to Liberty and Security of Person and 'Alternatives to Detention' of Refugees, Asylum-Seekers, Stateless Persons and Other Migrants* (2011) UNHCR Legal and Protection Policy Research Series. Division of International Protection PPLA/2011/01.Rev. 1 April 2011.

Evans MD and Haenni-Dale C, 'Preventing Torture? The Development of the Optional Protocol to the UN Convention Against Torture' (2004) 4(1) Human Rights Law Review 19–55.

Fields O and Edwards A, *Alternatives to Detention of Asylum Seekers and Refugees* (2006) UNHCR Legal and Protection Policy Research Series POLAS/2006/03.

Hallo de Wolf A, 'Visits to Less Traditional Places of Detention: Challenges under the OPCAT' (2009) 6(1) Essex Human Rights Review 103–37.

Human Rights Implementation Centre *'Deprivation of liberty' as per Article 4 of OPCAT: the scope.* (2011) Policy Paper by the Human Rights Implementation Centre, University of Bristol. [Online], available at http://www.bristol.ac.uk/law/research/centres-themes/hric/ [accessed on 4 July 2012].

Human Rights Watch *Protectors or Pretenders? Government Human Rights Commissions in Africa* (Human Rights Watch, 2001).

Livingstone S and Murray R, Evaluating the Effectiveness of National Human Rights Institutions: The Northern Ireland Human Rights Commission with Comparisons from South Africa. University of Bristol and Queen's University Belfast Publication (2005).

Murray R, 'National Preventive Mechanisms under the Optional Protocol to the Torture Convention: One Size Does Not Fit All' (2008) 26(4) Netherlands Quarterly of Human Rights 485–516.

Murray R, Steinerte E, Evans MD and Hallo de Wolf A, *The Optional Protocol to the UN Convention against Torture* (Oxford University Press, 2011).

Okafor OC and Agbakwa SC, 'On Legalism, Popular Agency and "Voices of Suffering": the Nigerian National Human Rights Commission in Context' (2002) 24 Human Rights Quarterly662–720.

Statement of the Representative of the UN Secretary-General on the Human Rights of Internally Displaced Persons, Dr Walter Kälin, on the occasion of the 6th Conference of African National Human Rights Institutions 8 October 2007, Kigali, Rwanda.

Steinerte E and Murray R, 'Same but Different? National Human Rights Commissions and Ombudsman Institutions as National Preventive Mechanisms under the Optional Protocol to the UN Convention against Torture' (2009) 6(1) Essex Human Rights Review 77–101.

Streater O, *Review of Existing Mechanisms for the Prevention and Investigation of Torture and Cruel, Inhuman or Degrading Treatment or Punishment in South Africa' Centre for the Study of Violence and Reconciliation* (2008), available at http://www.csvr.org.za/docs/torturereview1208.pdf [accessed on 4 July 2012].

Reports and Other Materials

ANNI, *Report on the Performance and Establishment of National Human Rights Institutions in Asia Bangkok, Thailand* (2008).

Association for Prevention of Torture. OPCAT Database available at: http://apt.ch/opcat [accessed on 4 July 2012].

Commission on Human Rights and Administrative Justice, *State of Human Rights Report* (2006).

Kenya National Commission on Human Rights, An Identity in Crisis? A Study on the Issuance of National Identity Cards in Kenya' (2007) [Online] available at http://www.knchr.org/index.php?option=com_content&task=view&id=73&Itemid=85 [accessed on 4 July 2012].

Kenya National Commission on Human Rights, Strategic Plan 2009–13 (2009) at p. 51; [Online], available at http://www.knchr.org/index.php?option=com_content&task=view&id=73&Itemid=85 [accessed on 4 July 2012].

Lawyers For Human Rights, Monitoring Immigration Detention in South Africa (2008) [Online] available at http://www.lhr.org.za/publications/monitoring-immigration-detention-south-africa-2008 [accessed on 4 July 2012].

National institutions for the promotion and protection of human rights. Report by the Secretary-General. UN Doc A/66/274 of 8 August 2011.

Process currently utilized by the International Coordinating Committee of National Institutions for the Promotion and Protection of Human Rights to accredit national institutions in compliance with the Paris Principles. Report of the Secretary-General. UN Doc A/HRC/16/77 of 3 February 2011.

Report of the African Commission on Human and Peoples' Rights (ACHPR). Executive Council. Seventeenth Ordinary Session. 19–23 July 2010. Kampala, Uganda; EX.CL/600(XVII).

The Response of the Institute for Security Studies to the call by the Department of Home Affairs for interested parties to comment on the new Immigration Regulations by the Crime and Justice Programme (2 March 2005), available at http://www.iss.co.za/uploads/DHASUB020305.PDF [accessed on 4 July 2012].

South African Human Rights Commission, Illegal? Report on the arrest and detention of persons in terms of the Aliens Control Act (1999), available at http://www.sahrc.org.za/home/21/files/Reports/Report%20into%20the%20Arrest%20and%20Detention%20of%20suspected%20migrants19.pdf.

South African Human Rights Commission, Lindela. At the Crossroads for Detention and Repatriation. An Assessment of the Conditions of Detention by the South African Human Rights Commission. Johannesburg (2000), available at http://www.queensu.ca/samp/migrationresources/xenophobia/reports/sahrc1.pdf [accessed on 4 July 2012].

Uganda Human Rights Commission, 2007, *The 10th Annual Report to the Parliament of Uganda of the Uganda Human Rights Commission* http://www.uhrc.ug/?p=1830.

Uganda Human Rights Commission, 2008, *The 11th Annual Report to the Parliament of Uganda of the Uganda Human Rights Commission* http://www.uhrc.ug/?p=1830.
Uganda Human Rights Commission, 2009, *The 12th Annual Report to the Parliament of Uganda of the Uganda Human Rights Commission* http://www.uhrc.ug/?p=1830.
Uganda Human Rights Commission, 2010, *The 13th Annual Report to the Parliament of Uganda of the Uganda Human Rights Commission* http://www.uhrc.ug/?p=1830.

Case Law and Legislation

Act 456 on the Commission on Human Rights and Administrative Justice of Ghana.
The Act on the Establishment of the Danish Centre for International Studies and Human Rights of 6 June 2002.
Aliens Control Act 96 of 1991 (South Africa).
Communication 373/2009 (formerly 242/2001) – *Interights, Institute for Human Rights and Development in Africa, and Association Mauritanienne des Droits de l'Homme v Islamic Republic of Mauritania.*
Constitution of Ghana 1992.
No 54 of 1994: Human Rights Commission Act, 1994 (South Africa).
The Ombudsman Act (Denmark), Act No 473 of 12 June 1996.
SAHRC and Forty Others v Minister of Home Affairs and Dyambu (Pty) Ltd, Case No 28367/99, Witwatersrand High Court, November 1999.

Chapter 6
Establishing the Common European Asylum System: 'it's a long long way to Tipperary'

Francesca Ippolito

Introduction

Since the entry into force of the Amsterdam Treaty the European Union has shared legislative competences with its Member States in the field of asylum. The Union's main goal is 'the adoption of a Common European Asylum System (CEAS)' based on the 'full and inclusive application' of the 1951 Convention and other relevant treaties. The CEAS aims to achieve a uniform and effective asylum procedure, joint guarantees for protection and guaranteed access to safe and uniform regimes across all Member States.[1]

The Union's legislative acts in the first period (1999–2005) of the establishment of the CEAS include three Directives and the Dublin II Regulation aimed at a minimum harmonization of national legislations in order to prevent an influx of asylum seekers in countries with better infrastructures and reception procedures.[2] Nonetheless, the evaluation of these instruments conducted by the European Commission,[3] and supplemented by the UNHCR and several NGOs' research reports issued between 2006 and 2010, have highlighted significant discrepancies between Member States' asylum laws and policies and their compliance with the international human rights standards.

---

1 Presidency Conclusions – Tampere European Council, 15–16 October 1999, SN 200/99, 3, Conclusion n 13.

2 Council Directive 2004/83/EC of 29 April 2004 on minimum standards for the qualification and status of third-country nationals or stateless persons as refugees or as persons who otherwise need international protection and the content of the protection granted, OJ L304/12, 30 September 2004; Council Directive 2005/85/EC of 1 December 2005 on minimum standards on procedures in Member States for granting and withdrawing refugee status, OJ L326/, 13 December 2005; Council Regulation No 343/2003 of 18 February 2003 establishing the criteria and mechanisms for determining the Member State responsible for examining an asylum application lodged in one of the Member States by a third-country national, OJ L50/1, 25 February 2003.

3 Communication from the Commission to the European Parliament, the Council, the European Economic and Social Committee and the Committee of Regions, Policy Plan on Asylum – an Integrated approach to protection across the EU, COM (2008) 360 final.

Due to the fact that such divergences cannot be overcome without the more harmonized and coherent application of the instruments, practical cooperation has been improved. In particular, the Council of the European Union and the European Parliament decided to create the European Asylum Support Office (EASO), which began functioning on 19 June 2011.[4] The EASO aims to improve information collection and quality, monitoring and quality control, and to develop practical cooperation between asylum systems and bodies in charge of asylum in Member States in order to allow the greater alignment of their practices.

Whilst the desire to maintain and develop the quality of asylum procedures in the EU is particularly welcomed, on their own practical cooperation measures are insufficient to adequately and comprehensively address the current problem. Considering that such measures derive mainly from States' extensive discretion or from the ambiguity of many of the existing legislation, there is a need for a 'comprehensive reconsideration of the existing European legal regime'.[5] The second phase of legislation has been agreed last June 2013[6] according to the new procedural rules introduced by the entry into force of the Lisbon Treaty: an exclusive right of initiative of the European Commission, the qualified majority voting procedure in the Council of the European Union and the co-decision of the European Parliament. This second phase aims to introduce a significant shift in the nature of the legislation by way of introducing mandatory obligations for

---

4 See EU Regulation 439/2010 of the European Parliament and of the Council of 19 May 2010 establishing a European Asylum Support Office, OJ L132/11, 29 May 2010.

5 ECtHR, 21 January 2011, *M.S.S. v Belgium and Greece* (App no 30696/09), para 350.

6 The first package of proposals includes the Proposal for a Regulation of the European Parliament and of the Council establishing the criteria and mechanisms for determining the Member State responsible for examining an application for international protection lodged in one of the Member States by a third-country national or a stateless person, COM (2008) 820; the Proposal for a Regulation of the European Parliament and of the Council concerning the establishment of 'Eurodac' for the comparison of fingerprints for the effective application of Regulation (EC) No 343/2003, COM (2008) 825); and the Proposal for a Directive of the European Parliament and of the Council laying down minimum standards for the reception of asylum seekers, COM (2008) 815. The second package includes the Directive of the European Parliament and of the Council 2011/95/EU on minimum standards for the qualification and status of third-country nationals or stateless persons as beneficiaries of international protection and the content of the protection granted [2011] OJ L337/9; and the Proposal for a Directive of the European Parliament and of the Council on minimum standards on procedures in Member States for granting and withdrawing international protection, COM (2009) 554/4. The United Kingdom has informed the European Commission of its intention to opt-in the proposal amending the Dublin Regulation but that it would not opt-in the Commission's proposal to amend the Qualification and Procedures Directive (letter of 22 January 2010) and the proposal to amend the Reception Conditions Directive (6 March 2009). See the Report on 'Asylum Directives: scrutiny of the opt-in decision' drawn up by the European Union Committee of the House of Lords, COM (2009) 551–4.

the Member States together with the abolition of opt-out clauses and the 'full' harmonization of both procedures and standards.

These standards appear to have been progressively enhanced by the European Court of Justice (ECJ), although unfortunately there are broad exceptions. Ten years after the decision to establish the Area of Freedom, Security and Justice, the European Court of Justice has had the opportunity to contribute to the development of EU asylum law only through a limited number of cases. Since the Lisbon Treaty's entry into force at the end of 2009 ex Article 267 of the Treaty on the Functioning of the European Union (TFEU), now not only the highest national courts, but also other courts and tribunals have the possibility to pose a prejudicial question.[7] So as the basis for review has expanded,[8] the scope and impact of the Court's activities in the field are likely to increase significantly. At present it is not only the number of rulings that have been requested which has increased, but also the range and subject matter of questions that have been put to the Court have been extended. This is the case for instance with regard to Dublin II cases that had not previously been heard in the ECJ because of the short time frames and narrow appeal rights under most States' Dublin II procedures, which may have prevented them reaching the highest level of domestic judicial structures. Rather on the contrary, since the entry into force of the Lisbon Treaty five cases concerning the Dublin II Regulation have been decided[9] and four other cases are pending at the time of writing.[10] Furthermore, since March 2010 when the first preliminary ruling request relating to the Asylum Procedures Directive came from a lower court to the Court dealing with accelerated procedures and effective remedies,[11] other issues of great procedural[12] and substantial[13] importance for the operation of lower-level judicial bodies have followed.

7 This limitation of preliminary reference power to final courts was seen as a means of ensuring that asylum cases would not flood the Court, given their prevalence in many judicial bodies at the national level.

8 A Hurwitz, *The Collective Responsibility of States to Protect Refugees* (Oxford University Press, 2009) 247–9.

9 CJEU, 29 January 2009, Case C-19/08, *Petrosian* [2009], ECR I-495; 3 May 2012, Case C-620/10, *Kastrati*, not yet reported; Joined cases C-411/10 e C-493/10, *N.S. and M.E.*, judgment of 21 December 2011, not yet reported; Case C-245/11, *K*, not yet reported.

10 CJEU, Case C-394/12, *Abdullahi*; Case C-666/11, *M.*; Case C-648/11, *M.A.* (opinion 21 February 2013); Case C-528/11, *Halaf*; and Case C-4/11, *Puid* (opinion 18 April 2013).

11 CJEU, 28 July 2011, Case C-69/10 *Samba Diouf*, not yet reported.

12 Concerning the Asylum Procedure Direcive see CJEU, Case C-175/11, *H.I.D.*, not yet reported, and as regards Reception Condition Directive see CJEU, Case C-179/11, *Cimade and Gisti*, not yet reported.

13 Concerning the Qualification Directive see CJEU, Joined case C-71/11 and C-99/11, *Y. and Z.*, not yet reported; Joined cases C-57/09 and C-101/09, *B. and D.* [2010] I-10979; Case C-31/09, *Bolbol* [2010] I-5537; Case C-175/08, *Abdullah a. o.* [2010] I-1493; Case C-465/07, *Elgafaji* [2009] I-921. There are actually pending Case C-285/12, *Diakite*; Case

The explicit obligation to ensure that asylum measures would conform to the 1951 Convention[14] and 'other relevant treaties' was introduced in the Amsterdam Treaty,[15] and it is hoped that the extended scope for preliminary reference requests will contribute beneficially to a more accurate and consistent application of basic asylum *acquis* rules at a practical level. Hence, a connection between EU law on asylum and the international protection system has been forged. It has been able to ensure that the European Court of Justice assumed jurisdiction over EU asylum law against a background of important and well-established international and regional principles of refugee law. In particular, the extensive case law of the European Court of Human Rights (ECtHR) addresses many aspects of Member States' treatment of asylum seekers and other persons who may be at risk of persecution or serious harm if removed to other countries.[16] A certain alignment of some ECJ standards to those of the European Court of Human Rights (ECtHR) case law[17] has already developed (also at a legislative level in the recast) in light of avoiding conflicting interpretations of human rights between the two European Courts. On the other side, a rights-based approach has been strengthened by the 'constitutionalization'[18] of the material scope of the right to asylum in the EU by Article 18 of the EU Charter of Fundamental Rights (EUCFR) and the binding legal effect of the Charter of Fundamental Rights imposed by the Treaty of Lisbon. Nevertheless, also before the EUCFR acquired binding status the European Court of Justice (ECJ) referred to the EUCFR as a key human rights instrument for the interpretation of EU asylum *acquis*. This had happened first in the *European Parliament v the Council*,[19] when the ECJ stated that EU legislation should be interpreted in the light of the provisions of the Charter the legislator referred to in the motivation of the legislation.[20] Then it was

C-201/12, *X v The Netherlands*; Case C-364/11, *El Kott a.o.* (opinion 13 September 2012); and Case C-277/11, *M.M.*

14 UN General Assembly, Convention Relating to the Status of Refugees, 28 July 1951.

15 Art 63 TEC reinforced by the Declaration of the Amsterdam Treaty, providing that 'consultations shall be established with the United Nations High Commissioner for Refugees and other relevant international organizations on matters relating to asylum policy'.

16 The Common European Asylum System and the European Court of Justice: New jurisdiction and new challenges *Madeline v Garlick, Brussels 2010.*

17 See more in detail at that regard F Ippolito, 'The contribution of the European Courts to the Common European Asylum System and its on-going recast process' (2013) 4 MJECL (forthcoming).

18 Study for the European Parliament, *Setting up a Common European Asylum System, Report on the Application of Existing Instruments and Proposals for the New System*, 2010, 430.

19 CJEU, *European Parliament v Council*, Case C-540/03, E.C.R. [2006] I-5769.

20 ECJ, 27 June 2006, Case C-540/03 *European Parliament against the Council*, [2006] ECR I-5769, para 38.

reaffirmed in *Salahadin Abdulla and Others*[21] concerning the revocation by the German authorities of the refugee status of Iraqi nationals as a result of the change in the circumstances in Iraq:[22] according to this case the Qualification Directive provisions 'must … be interpreted in a manner which respects the fundamental rights and the principles recognised in particular by the Charter'.[23]

This chapter intends to examine the EU Asylum Package aiming to highlight the progressive improvements and the deficiencies that still remain halfway through to the Stockholm goals because of some compromises made during the negotiations and because of the missed opportunities to clarify overly broad, complex and problematic provisions.

The Qualification Directive

The Qualification Directive,[24] issued in 2004, addressed three main issues, namely: the common standards for the recognition of refugee status, the content of refugee status and the approximation of rules. In addition, the Directive highlighted the grounds for qualification for subsidiary protection, thus becoming the first supranational instrument to apply a distinct status to extra-Convention refugees.[25] However, since the transposition of the Directive into the domestic laws of Member States it has emerged that the concept of subsidiary protection did not cover all persons who are in need of protection because of the wording of Article 15 of the Directive. Moreover, the Directive's provisions did not secure full compatibility with the evolving case law on human rights of the ECtHR, of the ECJ or of refugee law standards.

On the basis of a thorough evaluation of the implementation of the Directive the European Commission recognized that 'the objective of creating a level playing field with respect to the qualification and status of beneficiaries of international

---

21 ECJ, Joined cases C-175/08, C-176/08, C-178/08 and C-179/08, *Salahadin Abdulla and Others* [2009] ECR I-1493.

22 ECJ, Joined cases C-175/08, C-176/08, C-178/08 and C-179/08, *Salahadin Abdulla and Others*, qt [2010].

23 ECJ, Joined cases C-175/08, C-176/08, C-178/08 and C-179/08, *Salahadin Abdulla and Others*, qt [2010] para 54. And Opinion at para 49.

24 Council Document 8043/04 on Minimum Standards for the Qualification and Status of Third-country Nationals or Stateless Persons as Refugees or as Persons who Otherwise Need International Protection and the Content of the Protection Granted, 27 April 2004; Qualification Directive, Council Directive 2004/83/EC of 29 April 2004 on minimum standards for the qualification and status of third-country nationals or stateless persons as refugees or as persons who otherwise need international protection and the content of the protection granted.

25 J McAdam, 'The Qualification Directive: An Overview' in K Zwann (ed.), *The Qualification Directive: Central Themes, Problem Issues, and Implementation in Selected Member States* (Wolf Legal Publishers, 2007).

protection and to the content of the protection granted has not been fully achieved during the first phase of harmonization'.[26] As the Commission itself recognized that the divergences identified among national practices were due to the vagueness and the ambiguity of the standards themselves, they 'could only be addressed by the legislative amendment of the relevant provisions'.[27] Hence, on 21 October 2009 the European Commission presented its Recast Proposal for the Qualification Directive:[28] it was approved and it entered into force in January 2012.[29]

The purposes of this proposal were: (a) to reduce legal uncertainty by clarifying legal concepts, thus simplifying their application; (b) to streamline procedures and reduce the administrative burden and costs associated with maintaining two protection statuses; and (c) to ensure full compatibility between the standards of the *acquis* of the European Union and those that have been established since the adoption of the Directive by the European Court of Justice of the European Union and the European Court of Human Rights.

In concrete terms, the new provisions harmonizing the *content of protection* better facilitate access to education, vocational training, employment and accommodation, as well as to language training and other targeted integration activities. Furthermore, they take due account of the situation and needs also of beneficiaries of international protection, including particularly vulnerable persons. The European Commission's decision to move towards an alignment of the rights granted by both international protection statuses was justified by the fact that 'when subsidiary protection was introduced, it was assumed that this status was of a temporary nature. Accordingly, the Directive allows Member States to grant beneficiaries of subsidiary protection a lower level of rights in certain respects. However, practical experience so far has shown the inaccuracy of this assumption. It is therefore necessary to remove restrictions on the rights of beneficiaries of subsidiary protection which are no longer considered necessary and objectively justified'.[30] However, such 'approximation of the rights' of refugees and beneficiaries of subsidiary protection which *de facto* would have resulted in a uniform status for all those granted international protection has been only partially achieved.[31] Disparities

26 Report from the Commission to the European Parliament and the Council on the Application of Directive 2004/83/EC of 29 April 2004 on Minimum Standards for the Qualification and Status of Third-country Nationals or Stateless Persons as Refugees or as Persons who otherwise need International Protection and the content of the protection, COM (2010) 314 final, 6 June 2010.

27 Ibid.

28 Commission Recast Proposal for a Directive of the European Parliament and of the Council on minimum standards for the qualification and status of third-country nationals or stateless persons as beneficiaries of subsidiary protection and the content of the protection granted, 21 October 2009.

29 The United Kingdom still remains bound by 2004 Directive and Denmark is still not bound at all by the measure.

30 COM (2009) 551 final, 21 October 2009, 9.

31 Art 20 et ss Directive 2011/95/EU.

concern the rights to residence permits for beneficiaries of international protection and their families (for 'less than 3 years' for beneficiaries of subsidiary protection and for 'at least 3 years' for refugees)[32] and social welfare (limited to core benefits for beneficiaries of subsidiary protection).[33]

Moving on to the *eligibility criteria* for international protection, the Directive did broaden the notion of 'family members' but unfortunately it did not do so in the same way as the original proposal prepared by the Commission. In particular the new definition of 'family members' according to Article 2 (j) includes, in so far as the family already existed in the country of origin, the following members of the family of the beneficiary of international protection who are present in the same Member State in relation to the application for international protection:

> (1) the spouse of the beneficiary of international protection or his or her unmarried partner in a stable relationship, where the law or practice of the Member State concerned treats unmarried couples in a way comparable to married couples under its law relating to third-country nationals; (2) the minor children of the couples referred to above, on condition that they are unmarried and regardless of whether they were born in or out of wedlock or adopted as defined under national law and (3) the father, mother or another adult responsible for the beneficiary of international protection whether by law or by the practice of the Member State concerned, when that beneficiary is a minor and unmarried.

Except for this latter inclusion Directive 2011/95 does not take into any account the further categories the original proposal of the European Commission provided for: thus, married minor children, when it is in their best interest to reside in the same country as the beneficiary; the parents or another adult relative responsible for the beneficiary when he/she is a minor, including when he/she is married if it is in his/her best interest to reside in the same country as his/her parents or another responsible adult; and the minor siblings of the beneficiary, including when they are married if it is in their best interest to reside in the same country. But such a broadened definition of family would have better ensured consistency with the definition of family members in the recast proposals of the Reception Conditions Directive and the Dublin Regulation. Moreover, it would have also adequately reflected ECHR jurisprudence relating to family life under Article 8 ECHR where siblings also fall within the meaning of family[34] and which has refrained from giving a definition of family but takes a pragmatic approach in examining the existence of family life on the facts of each case.[35]

---

32 Art 24.

33 Art 29.

34 See for instance EctHR, 24 March 1988, *Olsson v Sweden* (App no 00013441/87).

35 For example in EctHR, 13 June 1975, *Marckx v Belgium* (App no 6833/74), the Court ruled that 'family life' within the meaning of Art 8 includes at least the ties between near relatives.

Furthermore, regrettably the notion of family members still remains conditioned by the fact that the family ties have to have already existed in the country of origin, with the consequent exclusion of all the ties that have been formed during the applicant's travels or in the host State. On the other hand, the fact that only family members who are present in the same Member State in relation to the application for international protection are covered by the Directive is hardly conciliable with the recent European Court of Human Rights (ECtHR)'s case law *Hode and Abdi v United Kingdom* (not yet finalized).[36] Indeed in *Hode and Abdi* the Court has confirmed that refugees who married after fleeing their country have the right to be joined by their spouses, otherwise a violation of Articles 14 and 8 ECHR would occur. In this specific case the Court found that the difference in treatment between the applicants and other categories of immigrants – such as refugees who had married before fleeing their country, students or workers – had not been objectively and reasonably justified.

As regards the provision defining the criteria of eligibility for subsidiary protection, the recasting does not lead to significant changes, while back in 2008 the European Commission had planned amending the criteria for qualifying for international protection.[37] In particular, the European Commission recognized the substantial divergences in the interpretation and the application of the concept across Member States, resulting in some national authorities only accepting applicants who have been personally targeted or applicants who face greater risk of harm than the rest of the population, or sections of it, in their country of origin. However, instead of addressing the wording of the current relevant provisions – such as Article 15 combined with Recital 35[38] – the European Commission excluded the necessity of a legislative recast of Article 15 because of a new development in ECJ case law (*Elgafaji*).[39] In 2006 Mr and Mrs Elgafaji submitted applications for temporary residence in The Netherlands, along with evidence seeking to prove the real risk which they would face if they were expelled back to their country of origin (in this case, Iraq). The responsible minister refused their application, and ruled that they had not proved satisfactorily the circumstances on which they were relying and, therefore, had not established the real risk of serious and individual threat to which they claimed to be exposed in their country of origin. Mr and Mrs Elgafaji brought an appeal before a higher court. This Court referred a question to the ECJ concerning Article 15(c) of the Qualification Directive. In particular

36 ECtHR, 6 November 2012, *Hode and Abdi v United Kingdom* (App no 22341/09).

37 Commission of the European Communities, Communication from the Commission to the European Parliament, the Council, the European Economic and Social Committee and the Committee of Regions 'Policy Plan on Asylum. An Integrated Approach to Protection across the EU', SEC (2008) 2029, 17.6.2008, 3 (Policy Plan on Asylum), 5.

38 'Risks to which a population of a country or a section of the population is generally exposed do normally not create, in themselves, an individual threat which would qualify as serious harm'.

39 CJEU, Case C-465/07, *Elgafaji c. Staatssecretaris van Justitie*, [2009] ECR I-921.

the Court was asked whether the relevant provisions of the directive must be interpreted as meaning that the existence of a serious and individual threat to the life or person of the applicant for subsidiary protection is subject to the condition that that applicant adduces evidence that he is specifically targeted by reason of factors particular to his circumstances. According to the ECJ:

> [T]he existence of such a threat can exceptionally be considered to be established where the degree of indiscriminate violence characterizing the armed conflict taking place – assessed by the competent national authorities before which an application for subsidiary protection is made, or by the courts of a Member State to which a decision refusing such an application is referred – reaches such a high level that substantial grounds are shown for believing that a civilian, returned to the relevant country or, as the case may be, to the relevant region, would, solely on account of his presence on the territory of that country or region, face a real risk of being subject to that threat.[40]

So the more the applicant could show that he was specifically affected by factors particular to his personal circumstances, the lower the level of indiscriminate violence required for him to be eligible for subsidiary protection.[41]

Unfortunately, contrary to the European Commission's assessment, the *Elgafaji* decision has not improved the protection system, thus preventing national jurisdictions from interpreting the requirement imposed by Article 15 in different ways. Nor has the decision removed doubts as to the interpretation of the term 'individual' threat, specifically in relation to whether Article 15 (c) requires a higher level of proof than Article 15 (a) and (b), and whether the provision's scope is broader than that of Article 3 ECHR. In particular, although the scope of Article 15 (c) is apparently broader than Article 3 ECHR, this is not so in practice.[42] The interpretation and protection provided by the Strasbourg judges is very similar.

In *NA v United Kingdom*[43] – to which the ECJ referred in an *obiter dictum* of the *Elgafaji* case – the ECtHR expressly considered its previous decision in *Vilvarajah* and stated that Article 3 ECHR should not be interpreted so as to require an applicant to show the existence of special distinguishing features if he could otherwise show that the general situation of violence in the country of destination

---

40 Ibid.: para 43.

41 Ibid.: para 39. Such an interpretation is in line with Recital 26 which stipulates that widely shared risks do not normally create an individual threat, while it leaves open the possibility that in certain exceptional circumstances they may abnormally create such a risk.

42 See in the same sense P. Tiedemann, *Subsidiary Protection and the Function of Article 15 (c) of the Qualification Directive* (2012) 31(1) Refugee Survey Quarterly 123–38, at 138, according to whom 'Article 15(c) is completely covered by Article 15(b). Thus, Article 15(c) is ultimately superfluous'.

43 ECtHR, *NA v the United Kingdom* (App no 25904/07) para 115.

was of a sufficient level of intensity to create a real risk that any removal to that country would violate Article 3 ECHR. More recently, according to *Sufi and Elmi v United Kingdom*,[44] Article 3 of the Convention as interpreted in *NA v United Kingdom*[45] offers comparable protection to that afforded under the Directive as 'the threshold set by both provisions may, in exceptional circumstances, be attained in consequence of a situation of general violence of such intensity that any person being returned to the region in question would be at risk simply on account of their presence there'. Furthermore, although the decision was based on arguments specific to the personal situation of the applicants not so easily transposable to the other asylum seekers from Somalia,[46] the ECtHR identified there some specific (albeit not exhaustive) criteria for assessing the level of severity of a situation of general violence that must be met in order to reach the threshold of a 'real risk'. Therefore, in the future the ECtHR might provide guidance for the assessment of applications for subsidiary protection as well as the impact on the application of the *Elgafaji* principle by domestic courts.

If all these considerations illustrate the remaining vagueness of one of the most important issues of the Directive, the recast improves other provisions that – like Article 15(c) – clearly go beyond the international refugee law standards. This is valid for the criterion adopted by the Qualification Directive according to which 'persecution' *can stem from non-state actors* where the State is unable or unwilling to provide protection. The same can be said as regards the inclusion of child-specific and gender-specific forms of persecution as well. With regard to gender-related aspects, it should be noted that the recast Recital 24 of the Directive specifies that 'for the purposes of defining a particular social group, issues arising from an applicant's gender should be given due consideration'. According to the Qualification Directive, membership of a particular social group means members who share an innate characteristic, or a common background that cannot be changed or share a characteristic or belief that is so fundamental to identity or conscience that a person should not be forced to renounce it. Moreover, that group should have a distinct identity in the relevant country, because it is perceived as being different by the surrounding society. The insertion of Recital 24 together with the amendment of Article 10 which removes the part of the provision which states that gender-related matters cannot create 'by themselves alone', a presumption of a particular social group may ensure that the Directive is more in line with relevant UNHCR Guidelines.[47] However, it may be argued that better compliance would

44 ECtHR, *Sufi and Elmi v United Kingdom* (App nos 8319/07 and 11449/07).

45 ECtHR, *NA v the United Kingdom* (Appl no 25904/07), para 115.

46 For a comment on the decision see M Bossuyt, *Strasbourg et les demandeurs d'asile (M.S.S. c. Belgique et Grèce et Sufi and Elmi c. le Royaume-Uni)*, in *Annuaire International des droits de l'homme*, VI-2011, 663–76.

47 See UNHCR, Guidelines on 'Membership of a Particular Social Group', UN Doc HCR/GIP/02/02, 7 May 2002; and Guidelines on Gender-Related Persecution, UN Doc HCR/GIP/02/01, 7 May 2002. Concerns about the denial of protection for the applicants in

have been achieved by explicitly providing that the criteria in Article 10(1)(d) for determining the concept of 'membership of a particular social group' have to be considered as alternative and not cumulative requirements. However, the denial of status to particular groups that are defined by an innate characteristic but that are not seen as set apart from society, or vice versa, might be overturned by the ECJ according to the UNHCR recommendation that the Directive should permit the alternative, rather than cumulative, application of the two concepts.[48] On 1 December 2010 the Highest Court of Nordrhein-Westfalen in Germany called for clarification on Article 10(1)(d) of the Qualification Directive asking, first, whether homosexuals should be considered as members of a group that 'share an innate characteristic, or a common background that cannot be changed, or share a characteristic or belief that is so fundamental to identity or conscience that a person should not be forced to renounce it', and if there are any 'specific prohibitions for the protection of public order and morals relevant when interpreting and applying Art. 10(1)(d)'.

The case (C-563/10) concerns an Iranian asylum seeker, Mr Khavand, who arrived in Germany from Turkey in November 2000 and applied for asylum, claiming to have fled from persecution on account of his homosexuality. His application was rejected in April 2001 and he has since challenged the negative decision on several occasions, the latest with the claim that since his arrival in the Netherlands he has espoused the Christian faith. The new grounds for asylum were also rejected with the argument that 'converts' in Iran are only persecuted if they carry out 'missionary' activities. As for his homosexuality, the German authorities argued that he should not face any persecution as long as the Iranian authorities did not know about it. They also dismissed his fears about being flogged or subject to the death penalty, insisting that he should have no problems in his home country as long as his homosexuality experiences were not shown openly. While the preliminary ruling was repealed in 2011 because the asylum applicant had been granted refugee status, the issue concerning the 'discretion requirement' (the possibility for asylum authorities to expect applicants to conceal their sexual orientation after their return to their country of origin) and whether criminalization of consensual same-sex sexual activity constitutes an act of persecution came again to the attention of the ECJ. The Dutch Council of State in three separate cases of gay asylum seekers from three different countries of origin (Senegal, Sierra Leone and Uganda) asked the ECJ whether homosexuals can be considered as 'a social

---

these situations has been expressed by ECRE in its Information Note on the Qualification Directive, Brussels, ECRE, 2004, 10, available at http://www.ecre.org/ files/qualpro.pdf (last visited 25 March 2011).

48 UNHCR comments on the European Commission's proposal for a Directive of the European Parliament and of the Council on minimum standards for the qualification and status of third-country nationals or stateless persons as beneficiaries of international protection and the content of the protection granted, COM (2009) 551, 21 October 2009, at 8.

group' in the sense of the Directive[49] and thus to what extent, if any, a person can be expected to exercise restraint in expressing their sexual orientation and whether national authorities can expect applicants to conceal their sexual orientation after their return to their country of origin.[50] Expecting a lesbian, gay, bisexual or transsexual person to be compelled to forsake or conceal their sexual orientation and gender identity would mean to conceal aspects fundamental to his/her identity. It will be interesting to see whether the ECJ will follow its reasoning concerning two Pakistani nationals who were members of the Ahmadiyya community and who applied in Germany for asylum and protection as refugees claiming that they were forced to leave Pakistan because of their membership of that religious community. On that occasion the ECJ has already clarified that in assessing an application for refugee status on an individual basis, authorities cannot reasonably expect the applicant to abstain from certain religious practices.[51]

The Dublin Regulation

Council Regulation (EC) No 343/2003 of 18 February 2003 'Dublin II', (hereinafter the Dublin Regulation) established a system for identifying the State responsible for examining an asylum application lodged in one of the Member States by a third-country national. The main goal of this Regulation was to ensure that every asylum application is only examined by one Member State, thus preventing the phenomenon of 'refugees in orbit'. It established clear criteria for identifying the State responsible for processing a specific application for protection. More precisely, Article 3(1) of the Regulation provided for asylum applications to be examined by a single Member State, according to the criteria set out in Chapter III. The criterion for determining which Member State is responsible consists of the identification of the Member State the asylum seeker first irregularly entered on his arrival from a third country (Article 10). Once responsibility is designated on the basis of the criteria listed in Chapter III, Article 11 provides that the first Member State the application for asylum was lodged with shall be responsible for examining it.

49 Available at http://www.raadvanstate.nl/uitspraken/zoeken_in_uitspraken/zoekresultaat/?verdict_id=NmVO3LaE2Ac%3D – in Dutch. 10 / ISSUE 110 / April–May 2012.

50 Note that on 1 December 2010 the Highest Court of Nordrhein-Westfalen in Germany had already called for clarification on Art 10(1)(d) of the Qualification Directive asking, first, whether homosexuals should be considered as members of a group that 'share an innate characteristic, or a common background that cannot be changed, or share a characteristic or belief that is so fundamental to identity or conscience that a person should not be forced to renounce it', and if there are any 'specific prohibitions for the protection of public order and morals relevant when interpreting and applying Art 10(1)(d)'. But it was repealed in 2011.

51 CJEU, Joined cases C-71 and C-99/11, *Y and Z*, judgment of 5 September 2012, not yet reported, para 80.

In order to enable the Dublin II Regulation to function on the premise that asylum seekers may rely on equal access to protection and justice in each Member State, the minimum Directives (Procedure Directive and the Reception Condition Directive) were adopted.[52] Whereas in the case of *T.I. v United Kingdom*,[53] and later in the case of *K.R.S. v United Kingdom*,[54] the ECtHR has recognized that the system created by the Dublin Regulation alongside the Member States' additional obligations under Council Directive 2005/85/EC and Council Directive 2003/9/EC 'protects fundamental rights, as regards both the substantive guarantees offered and the mechanisms controlling their observance', in the milestone case *M.S.S. v Belgium and Greece* the core and the necessary premise of the sharing of responsibility mechanism provided for by the EU law that all EU Member States respect fundamental rights[55] – and therefore an asylum seeker's chances of finding protection are the same in all Dublin participating States – was reversed.

The *M.S.S.* case concerns an interpreter who had fled Afghanistan in early 2008 after, as he claimed, an attempt was made on his life by the Taliban. He lodged an asylum application in Belgium. Based on the Dublin II Regulation Belgium sent him back to Greece, the country through which he had irregularly entered the EU. He complained to the ECtHR about his treatment by both Greece and Belgium. Against Greece he alleged breaches of Article 3 of the ECHR by reason of his conditions of detention, his conditions of living and a breach of Article 13 of the ECHR because of the deficiencies in the asylum procedure and the risk of his expulsion to Afghanistan without any serious examination of the merits of his asylum application or access to an effective remedy. His complaint against Belgium was that Belgium had breached Articles 3 and 13 by sending him to Greece as the Belgian authorities 'knew or ought to have known' that he had no guarantees that his claim for asylum would be properly examined by the Greek authorities. The Court ruled that both States violated their obligations under Articles 3 and 13 ECHR.[56]

The European Commission, in line with the Strasbourg judgement, proposed to recast the Dublin II Regulation *inter alia* having a formal procedure for suspending transfers.[57] But the emphasis of the discussion in the Council of

---

52 Amended Proposal for a Directive of the European Parliament and of the Council on minimum standards of procedures in Member States for the granting and withdrawing of international protection, Brussels, 1 June 2011, COM (2011) 319, in its Explanatory Memorandum, 8.

53 ECtHR, 7 March 2000, *T.I. v United Kingdom* (App no 43844/98).

54 ECtHR, 2 December 2008, *K.R.S v United Kingdom* (App no 32733/08).

55 Paragraph 2 of the Preamble states: 'Member States, all respecting the principle of *non-refoulement*, are considered as safe countries for third-country nationals'.

56 Para 358. The Court arrived at this conclusion considering the very small number of Rule 39 requests for interim measures against Greece lodged by asylum seekers in that country compared with the number lodged by asylum seekers in the other States.

57 COM (2008) 820 final. Art 31 provided that where a Member State was concerned that another Member State was not providing claimants with the protection to which they

the European Union shifted from addressing crisis situations after they have developed to addressing the root causes of such crises (stemming from particular pressures on a Member State as well as from dysfunctions in national asylum systems). Thus a clause was included in the compromise text agreed recasting Dublin II Regulation by the COREPER (from the French Comité des représentants permanents) on November 2012 which set out the structure of a process for early warning, preparedness and management of asylum crisis as an alternative to the emergency mechanism.[58]

Things partially changed when in a subsequent judgment – Joined Cases *N.E.* and *N.S.*[59] – the ECJ acknowledged the same interpretative result of the ECtHR. N.S. was an Afghan national who claimed asylum in the UK, after travelling through other EU Member States, including Greece where he was arrested and expelled to Turkey. The Secretary of State requested Greece to take charge of the asylum application, pursuant to Article 17 of the Dublin II Regulation. But N.S. requested the Secretary of State to exercise his discretion under Article 3(2) of Dublin II to accept responsibility for his asylum application on the ground that 'there was a risk that his fundamental rights under European Union law, the ECHR and/or the Geneva Convention would be breached if he was returned to Greece'.[60] The proceedings in N.S. were joined with the case of M.E. and Others concerning the proposed transfer of five asylum seekers to Greece from the Republic of Ireland. Arguing that the CEAS was based on the presumption of compliance by EU Member States with EU law and fundamental rights, the Court held that:

> … it would not be compatible with the aims of Regulation No 343/2003 were the slightest infringement of Directives 2003/9, 2004/83 or 2005/85 to be sufficient to prevent the transfer of an asylum seeker'. By contrast, if there are 'substantial

are entitled under EU law (the Procedure Directive and the Reception Conditions Directive are cited specifically), it can request the Commission to order a suspension of the transfer. Alternatively, the Commission would *motu proprio* base a decision to suspend transfers on 'an examination of all the relevant circumstances prevailing in the Member State'. In this respect, the Commission will use any relevant information at its disposal regarding the reception capacity or the asylum procedures in the concerned Member State. See Comments of the European Commission on opinions of National Parliaments concerning COM (2008) 820, Reply of 7th October 2009 to Czech Senate COM20080815_0820_EN.pdf.

58 See amended version of Art 31. Moreover, as a complement to the mechanism for early warning, preparedness and crisis management in the amended Dublin Regulation, in March 2012 the Council adopted conclusions on a common framework for genuine and practical solidarity towards Member States facing particular pressures on their asylum systems, including through mixed migration flows. These conclusions are intended to constitute a toolbox for EU-wide solidarity towards those Member States most affected by such pressures and/or encountering problems in their asylum systems.

59 CJEU, Joined cases C-411/10 e C-493/10, *N.S. and M.E.*, judgment of 21 December 2011, not yet reported.

60 Ibid.: para 40.

> grounds for believing that there are systemic flaws in the asylum procedure and reception conditions for asylum applicants … resulting in inhuman or degrading treatment, within the meaning of Article 4 of the Charter … the transfer would be incompatible with that provision.[61]

Dublin III Regulation reflects the Court's ruling in order to uphold the sending State's responsibility for determining the claim.[62] Nonetheless, the practical effect is not so revolutionary if the practice cited in the Commission Staff Working Document accompanying the recast proposal of the Dublin Regulation is considered.[63] Indeed it appears that the circumstances under which the sovereignty clause had been (reluctantly) used before that judgment range from purely practical reasons to humanitarian ones when a risk of violation of Article 3 (but also Article 8 ECHR) was ascertained; where asylum legislation and practice does not offer sufficient safeguards to ensure that persons in need of protection have access to a fair and efficient asylum procedure; where inadequate reception conditions constitute inhuman treatment; where access to healthcare is lacking; where procedural guarantees under the Dublin Regulation were not respected; and where procedural guarantees of the right to asylum were violated. Moreover, the sovereignty clause has been used for humanitarian reasons when the application was lodged by particularly vulnerable asylum seekers such as unaccompanied or separated child asylum seekers, single women, the elderly and families with minors or persons with serious health concerns. The same can be said for cases where countries do not ensure reception standards in line with the UN Convention on the Rights of the Child and the EU Reception Directive; similar situations would contravene the principle of the best interest of the child.

Unfortunately the legislator has not taken the opportunity to better clarify under which circumstances there are 'systemic deficiencies in the asylum procedure and reception conditions for asylum applicants'. Nor does the law go any further in affirming the existence of a veritable 'duty/obligation' for Member States to prevent transfers by applying the so-called 'sovereignty clause' as the ECJ established for

61 Ibid.: paras 86 and 94.

62 According to Article 3 (2) Regulation (EU) 604/2013 of 26 June 2013 of the European Parliament and of the Council establishing the criteria and mechanisms for determining the Member State responsible for examining an application for international protection lodged in one of the Member States by a third-country national or a stateless person (recast), OJ L 180/31, 29 July 2013, 'where it is impossible to transfer an applicant to the Member State primarily designated as responsible because there are substantial grounds for believing that there are systemic flaws in the asylum procedure and in the reception conditions for applicants in that Member State, resulting in a risk of inhuman or degrading treatment within the meaning of Article 4 of the Charter of Fundamental Rights of the European Union, the determining Member State shall continue to examine the criteria set out in Chapter III in order to establish whether another Member State can be designated as responsible'.

63 SEC (2008) 2962.

the 'humanitarian clause' in *K*.[64] In particular, in that case, the ECJ recognized that where the conditions of dependency (including both situations where the asylum seeker is dependent on the family and situations where a family member present in that State is dependent on the assistance of the asylum seeker[65]) were satisfied the Member State has the obligation to take charge of an asylum seeker.

However, the ECJ would have the chance to definitively clarify if the asylum seeker has a right, enforceable by him in the courts, to require a Member State to examine the assumption of responsibility under Article 3(2) and to inform him about the grounds for its decision;[66] and whether an enlarged hypothetical duty of the Member States to exercise the sovereignty clause can also be inferred from reasons not directly associated with the asylum-seeker himself/herself or other particularities of an individual case, but which result from a legal or administrative situation in the Member State assuming responsibility that poses a threat to the fundamental rights of asylum-seekers under the EUCFR or a failure to apply the minimum standards.[67] In *M.S.S.*, the ECtHR, in assessing the risk of ill-treatment in the Member State responsible according to the criteria set out in the Dublin Regulation, found as mostly significant the country's general situation rather than the individual circumstances of the asylum seeker.

Recently – in the exceptional situations as defined in the *N.S. and M.E.* judgment – AG Jääskinen in *Puid* denied that asylum seekers have an enforceable claim, based on Regulation No 343/2003, to compel an identified Member State to examine their application for asylum. However, according to the Advocate General, the national court which might review the decision not to examine the application and to transfer the applicant 'as a consequence of its duties to provide effective legal protection under Article 19(1) TEU, is bound to consider whether the exceptional circumstances of the *N.S. and M.E.* case have arisen and are applicable in any given case, and alter the obligations of the Member State in which asylum is being sought … A national court that cannot be unaware that systemic deficiencies in the asylum procedure, and in the reception conditions of asylum seekers in the Member State responsible under Article 3(1) of Regulation No 343/2003, amount to substantial grounds for believing that the asylum seeker would face a real risk of being subjected to inhuman or degrading treatment within the meaning of Article 4

---

64 CJEU, Case C-245/11, K qt.

65 On the same line of reasoning, the notion of 'family' for the purposes of Art 15 has been read by the ECJ as necessarily having a wider meaning than the definition of 'family members' under Art 2(i) of the Regulation. However, the new operational clause allocating responsibility on a humanitarian basis introduced by Art 16 A(2) of the Dublin III does not seem compliant with *K* jurisprudence. The reason is that the humanitarian clause would only apply specifically to children, siblings and parents who are legally resident as family members the Member State is normally obliged to keep together (on condition that the family ties existed in the country of origin).

66 CJEU, Case C-666/11, *M*, pending.

67 CJEU, *Federal Republic of Germany v Kaveh Puid*, Case C-4/11, pending.

of the Charter, is obliged to suspend transfer of asylum seekers to such a Member State, and if necessary, to set aside any national provision that would exclude such a decision'.[68]

Indeed in the wake of ECJ and ECtHR case law, procedural safeguards have already been introduced in other parts of the recast. For instance, the notification of the transfer decision, including the grounds on which it is based, has been ensured by new Article 26. This notification will also inform the asylum seeker on the available legal remedies (including the right to apply for suspending the implementation of the transfer decision pending the outcome of his/her appeal or review), time limits and where to find available legal assistance and/or representation. According to the new Article 27 the appeal or review will not suspend the implementation of the transfer decision unless a competent body so decides and if it is allowed under the national law of the Member State. At least the ECJ clarified in the *Petrosian* judgment[69] that if there was provision for an appeal under the domestic law of the sending State, the time period within which that State has to effect the transfer to the receiving State should begin not from the date of the decision suspending transfer following appeal, but from the date of the decision in the appeal, so that the merits of the proposed transfer could be exhausted.

Moving on to the interview and the right to information introduced in the Dublin III Regulation, these are based on the presumption of understanding (ex new Article 5 that information and decisions must be provided in a language the applicant is merely 'reasonably supposed to understand'). But the abovementioned presumption, together with the limited guarantee of the services of an interpreter only 'whenever necessary', contrast with Article 47 EU Charter and the *Hatami* case law according to which the language of communications has to be effectively understood by the applicant and that an interpreter is required in order to make the interviewer and the applicant able to understand each other.[70]

The Dublin II Regulation was accompanied by an electronic database storing asylum seekers' fingerprints – EURODAC – established by Regulation (EC) No 2725/2000. The database allows the identification of the first State where the application was lodged and enables the identification of the State responsible for the examination. In practice, the State responsible is predominantly the one through which the asylum seeker has entered the EU. Alongside the Dublin II Regulation, negotiations have also touched upon the modification of the EURODAC system. One of the major elements that have been introduced is the possibility for law enforcement agencies and Europol to have access (under certain circumstances) to the EURODAC database in order to prevent, detect or investigate the most serious crimes, such as murder, and terrorism, under a strict

68 Opinion of AG Jääskinen in *Puid*, Case C-4/11 delivered on 18 April 2013, not yet reported, paras 77 and 79.

69 CJEU, 29 January 2009, Case C-19/08, *Petrosian* qt [2009] ECR I-495.

70 ECHR, 23 April 1998, *Hatami v Sweden*, 32448/96, paras 96–109.

data protection regime.[71] Unfortunately this broader scope of utilization of the database does not seem to have been adequately assessed in the motivation the European institutions have to provide in terms of subsidiarity and proportionality of action. Recital 12 of the new Regulation 603/2013[72] makes reference to the possibility offered to the designated authorities of the Member States to compare a suspect's fingerprints with the fingerprint data which is stored in EURODAC in terms of a 'fundamental facility' in the field of police cooperation. This may sufficiently explain why the enlargement of its use might be appropriate in order to achieve the given aim proposed by using the chosen measure (the so-called suitability test). However, the *necessity test* – which implies that the assessment of whether the chosen measure is necessary to achieve the proposed goal, in the meaning that the measure to be chosen is the one that is the least restrictive on the given norm – does not seem adequately satisfactory. Nor does the third test, where the measure's proportionality is assessed *stricto sensu*, appear to be adequately fulfilled: here although a measure may be suitable and necessary, if it nevertheless imposes an excessive burden on the individual it may be considered disproportionate. Why are the existing legal instruments which allow one Member State to consult fingerprints and other law enforcement data held by another Member State not sufficient? What other substantive reasons are necessary for accessing data on asylum seekers? It would have been better to address these aspects, as the new scope of the database raises important questions relating to the possible stigmatization of an already vulnerable group, as well as concerns regarding the possible risk for refugees and their families if information is shared with law enforcement agencies in the countries they are fleeing from.

The Procedure Directive

The harmonization of asylum procedures is of vital importance for a common asylum system together with the reception conditions directive. Firstly, it contributes to the prevention of secondary movements of asylum seekers. Secondly, it is vital for the asylum seekers themselves as they are no longer able to

71 See COM (2012) 254 final.

72 Regulation (EU) No 603/2013 of the European Parliament and of the Council of 26 June 2013 on the establishment of 'Eurodac' for the comparison of fingerprints for the effective application of Regulation (EU) No 604/2013 establishing the criteria and mechanisms for determining the Member State responsible for examining an application for international protection lodged in one of the Member States by a third-country national or a stateless person and on requests for the comparison with Eurodac data by Member States' law enforcement authorities and Europol for law enforcement purposes, and amending Regulation (EU) No 1077/2011 establishing a European Agency for the operational management of large-scale IT systems in the area of freedom, security and justice (recast), OJ L180, 1 (29 June 2013).

freely choose their country of application under the Dublin Regulations. Thirdly, since asylum seekers cannot choose their country any more, it is vital to harmonize procedures in order to maintain fairness towards people in need of protection.

The Asylum Procedures Directive defines minimum standards for procedures, which include: (1) access to the asylum process; (2) the right to interview; (3) access to interpretation and legal assistance; (4) detention circumstances; and (5) the appeals procedure. Following severe criticisms that the Council Directive 2005/85[73] fails to secure a fair and efficient system of procedural guarantees, and falls short of respecting international human rights standards, it was recast in 2009 with the aim of ensuring a higher (albeit not maximum[74]) degree of harmonization in the EU Member States.[75] This proposal was renewed on 1 June 2011 by the publication of the Amended Recast Proposal on which a final political agreement was reached on 27 March 2013[76] and then approved by the European Parliament in June 2013.[77]

On the positive side, the scope of the proposed second generation Procedures Directive has been widened both on territorial aspects[78] and on applications for subsidiary protection, which according to the *Abdulla* judgment would have to be examined only after it has been determined that the applicant does not qualify as a refugee.[79] Furthermore, the limitations concerning procedures with national security considerations, subsequent applications, certain border procedures or expulsion towards a safe third country and transfer procedures ex Dublin Regulations[80] have been removed. Standards with regard to safe country concepts

---

73 Council Directive 2005/85/EC of 1 December 2005 on minimum standards on procedures in Member States for granting and withdrawing refugee status [2005] OJ L326/13.

74 Art 5 Amended Recast Proposal still allows Member States to provide more favourable standards.

75 See European Commission, Proposal for a Directive of the European Parliament and of the Council on minimum standards on procedures in Member States for granting and withdrawing international protection, COM (2009) 554/4.

76 Amended proposal for a Directive of the European Parliament and of the Council on common procedures for granting and withdrawing international protection status (Recast) [First reading] – Analysis of final compromise text with a view to agreement, 22 March 2013, 7695/13.

77 Directive 2013/32/EU of the European Parliament and of the Council of 26 June 2013 on common procedures for granting and withdrawing international protection (recast), OJ L 180/60 (29 June 2013).

78 See S Peers, 'Chapter 14: Asylum Procedures' in S Peers and N Rogers (eds), *EU Immigration and Asylum Law, Text and Commentary* (Martinus Nijhoff Publishers, 2006) 386; UNHCR, Improving Asylum Procedures, Comparative Analysis and Recommendations for Law and Practice, March 2010, 16; and the interpretation of the concept of 'jurisdiction' in ECtHR, 23 February 2012, *Hirshi Jamaa v Italy* (App no 27765/09).

79 CJEU, Joined cases C-175/08, 176/08, 178/08 and 179/08, *Salahadin Abdulla and Others*, qt [2010] paras 77–80.

80 While Art 4 Amended Proposal for a Directive of the European Parliament and of the Council on minimum standards of procedures in Member States for the granting and withdrawing of international protection, Brussels, 1 June 2011, COM (2011) 319, did not

have been slightly improved by more explicitly requiring that asylum seekers must be able to challenge the presumption of safety in their individual cases. However, EU legislation will still allow the use of widely diverging national lists of safe countries.

Improvements are also evident in regard to access to justice and procedural guarantees at the first instance level. For instance, all asylum seekers will now, in principle, have the right to be heard in an interview and to submit comments and clarifications after the interview and before a decision is taken on their claim. The reporting of the personal interview was considerably improved in the 2009 Recast Proposal. However, it seems to have been downgraded in the 2011 Proposal by the Council of the European Union. Contrary to the European Parliament and the European Commission which proposed a transcript of the interview, the Council of the European Union opted first for a 'thorough report containing all substantial elements'. Instead, new Article 17 provides at para 3 that:

> Member States shall ensure that the applicant has the opportunity to make comments and/or provide clarifications with regard to any mistranslations or misconceptions appearing in the report or the transcript, at the end of the personal interview or within a specified time limit before the determining authority takes a decision.

Analogously, concerning the time limit, the recast has positively provided that national authorities would have 72 hours from the moment a person has expressed his/her wish to apply for international protection. But whilst it has the merit of reducing legal uncertainty and gives asylum seekers quicker access to those benefits provided for in the Reception Conditions Directive, more flexibility (up to 10 days) is built in for Member States when they are confronted with large numbers of asylum applications, in order to derogate from these procedural standards. However, some contention remains over whether States should be allowed to delay decisions in a range of situations based on such a vague assessment that the situation in the country of origin is uncertain and expected to be temporarily able to undermine the needed protection of asylum seekers.

The same criterion of a large number of third-country nationals or stateless persons simultaneously requesting international protection which makes it impossible in practice to conclude the procedure within the six-month time limit has been introduced in order to allow Member States to extend the time limit for a period not exceeding a further 9 months. At least Article 31(7) improved the situation for the issue of time frames for accelerated procedures and/or procedures conducted at the border in accordance with Article 43 providing that Member

modify the scope of the Directive to the Dublin procedures, new Recital 54 – introduced into the compromise text submitted to the COREPER of December 2012 – provides that: 'This Directive should apply to applicants to whom Regulation (EU) No 604/2013 applies, in addition and without prejudice to the provisions of that Regulation'.

States shall lay down 'reasonable time limits' for the adoption of a decision in the procedure at first instance. In addition, asylum seekers in an accelerated procedure must now at least be given the opportunity to request in court to stay in the territory while they appeal against a negative decision on their case.[81]

On the other hand, the amended recast remains silent on the issue of time frames for prioritized procedure which may be applied to process certain categories of cases, such as well-founded cases or cases of applicants with special needs, and 'in other cases'. The recast just intervenes to limit the discretion left to Member States, namely as: (i) such a prioritized examination must not be based on considerations that the case in question may be unfounded; and (ii) the basic principles and guarantees as well as the requirement of an adequate and complete examination must be fully respected. This raises 'fairness' concerns in relation to ECtHR case law which emphasizes that: 'time limits should not be so short or applied so inflexibly, as to deny an applicant … a realistic opportunity to prove his or her claim'.[82]

Other aspects of Directive 2013/32/EU are disappointing. First of all the grounds for detention of asylum seekers are so broadly defined that they risk encouraging the systematic detention of asylum seekers instead of making the practice truly exceptional. Then, with regard to the procedural guarantees for vulnerable groups such as unaccompanied children and victims of torture, the definitive compromise text agreed departs completely from the 2011 amended European Commission proposal: neither of the two categories will be exempt from detention, nor from accelerated and border procedures,[83] and national authorities may consider the asylum applications of unaccompanied children inadmissible for those children transiting so-called 'safe third countries' provided that to do so is in the minor's best interests.. At least, the new text does no more provide the possibility of the application of accelerated procedures even to any other 'exceptional case' without any useful clarification. In addition, unaccompanied children's asylum can be refused free legal assistance for the purpose of appeal procedures in the case that their appeal is considered to have 'no tangible prospect of success'.

As concerns the access to legal assistance, contrary to Article 15 of the Directive 2005/85/EC which did not restrict the provision of a legal aid system restricted to the appeals procedure, new Directive 2013/32/EU at Article 20(2)

81 The same suspensive effect on deportation has been positively introduced by Art 46(5) while the asylum seeker has his/her appeal examined, though para 6 of this article considerably limits the scope of the right by enumerating certain exceptions.

82 See ECtHR, 19 February 2008, *Bahaddar v The Netherlands* (App no 25894/94).

83 Art 25(6) (a) allows Member States to apply accelerated procedures and/or conducted at the border or in transit zone to an unaccompanied minor when: (a) the applicant comes from a country which satisfies the criteria to be considered a safe country of origin within the meaning of this Directive; or (b) the applicant has introduced a subsequent application for international protection that is not inadmissible in accordance with Article 40(5); or (c) the applicant may for serious reasons be considered a danger to the national security or public order of the Member State, or the applicant has been forcibly expelled for serious reasons of public security or public order under national law.

merely provides that Member States '*may*' provide free legal assistance (preparation of documents) and representation (participation in the hearing) in procedures at first instance combined with the possibility that Member States allow NGOs to provide such legal assistance and representation. Beyond these, an asylum seeker in first instance procedures can only rely on the right to contact a lawyer at the applicant's own cost as well as on the national obligation of 'information on the procedure in the light of the applicant's particular circumstances and explanations of reasons in fact and in law in the event of a negative decision'.

However, this information provision is subject to the conditions and limitations of Article 21: lack of sufficient resources, monetary and/or time limits and the rules on filing and processing modalities provided by national law. These new requirements meet the conditions required by the latter ECtHR jurisprudence regarding asylum seekers built upon the *Airey* jurisprudence according to which the contracting States are obligated to provide legal aid to all asylum seekers but not necessarily free legal aid.[84] Nevertheless, the national margin of appreciation in granting the legal aid would still be constrained by another ECtHR judgment – *I.M. v France*[85] – which found that a lawyer being available only shortly before the hearing in an appeals procedure was not sufficient for France to comply with the right to an effective remedy.

Concerning the guarantee of legal assistance in the appeals procedures, new Article 20(3) has regrettably reintroduced the possibility of refusing free legal assistance for the purpose of appeal procedures in the case that their appeal is considered – by a court or tribunal (but not by the determining authority) to have a 'no tangible prospect of success'. Furthermore, Member States may undertake to grant free legal assistance and representation 'only for appeals procedures in accordance with Chapter V before a court or tribunal of first instance and not for any onward appeals or reviews provided for under national law including rehearings or reviews of appeals' and to not grant them to applicants who are no longer present on the territory in application of Article 41(2)(c).[86]

This overview makes it clear that some improvements are evident, as well as many failures, and considerable margin for manoeuvre is left to Member States. These features, combined with the fact that many provisions seem to be extremely vague, risk making monitoring by the Commission and interpretation by the Courts extremely difficult.

The Reception Conditions Directive

The substantial differences in reception conditions in the various EU Member States can be a factor for the migratory movement of refugees within the EU. According

84 ECtHR, 9 October 1979, *Airey v Ireland* (App no 6289/73).

85 ECtHR, 2 February 2012, *I.M. v France* (App no 9152/09).

86 Art 21(2).

to the Dublin III Regulation, as asylum seekers can only apply for asylum once in the EU, the conditions in which they are being received matter significantly in their choice.

The first Directive was adopted in 2003 (Directive 2003/9/EC)[87] with the aim of setting out minimum rules regarding the reception conditions to be guaranteed to asylum seekers. These conditions comprise *inter alia* material reception conditions (housing, food and clothing), access to health, schooling and access to employment. Unfortunately, the standards in the existing Reception Conditions Directive are not applied properly in practice.[88] The first recast of the Directive was proposed in 2008. While it progressed before the European Parliament, which on 7 May 2009 adopted its position on the Commission proposal that approves the great majority of the proposed amendments,[89] the discussions in the Council mainly under the Czech and the Swedish Presidencies were difficult and no position was reached on the text. Hence there was the necessity for the Commission to table amended proposals by June 2011 in order to restart and facilitate the negotiations between the two co-legislators and enable progress on this instrument of the CEAS.[90]

The main objective of this modified proposal (on which a political agreement between the Council and European Parliament was reached in October 2012,[91] then formally approved in June 2013[92]) is to further clarify and provide more flexibility to the proposed reception standards so that they can more easily be built into the national legal systems, while at the same time keeping the appropriate ambition on fundamental rights. As improvements it is sufficient to recall here: a broader personal (including subsidiary protection status) and territorial (transit zone and territorial water) scope; the provision of information in a language that (differently from the Procedures Directive) applicants are no longer merely supposed to understand but instead to effectively understand – Article 5 (2); as a rule, that

87 See Council Directive 2003/9/EC of 27 January 2003 [2003] OJ L31/186.

88 Lastly, according to the ECtHR in the leading case *M.S.S.*, quoted above, Greece failed to respect the positive obligation contained in the Directive to provide accommodation and decent material conditions to asylum seekers. Therefore, a violation of Art 3 ECHR was detected as the State did not ensure that detention conditions are compatible with respect for human *dignity*.

89 Proposal for a Directive of the European Parliament and of the Council laying down minimum standards for the reception of asylum seekers, COM (2008) 815.

90 Amended proposal for a Directive of the European Parliament and of the Council laying down standards for the reception of asylum seekers, 1 June 2011, COM (2011) 320 final.

91 See doc 14112/1/12.

92 Directive 2013/33/EU of the European Parliament and of the Council of 26 June 2013, laying down standards for the reception of applicants for international protection (recast), OJ L 180/96, 29 June 2013.

applicants for international protection must be detained in special reception facilities[93] and a mandatory review of detention measures should be undertaken.[94]

Detention of asylum seekers and access to the labour market were amongst the most sensitive issues discussed during the negotiations. Unlike in the 2003 Directive, Directive 2013/33/EU sets out rules regarding the detention of asylum seekers, as long as they are not detained for seeking asylum but for other reasons. In particular, an extensive set of rules governing detention makes it clear that detention cannot extend to a determination of the merits of the asylum claim (thus removing any possible ambiguity in the formulation of the rule, which might otherwise risk violating Article 5 ECHR). Moreover, detention will only be possible on the basis of an individual assessment which has to show that detention of asylum seekers should only occur as a measure of last resort 'if other less coercive alternative measures cannot be applied effectively'. Though this provision is in line with the more recent ECtHR jurisprudence,[95] it appears to be a less strict version of the recast than the previous version according to which detention should only occur after other non-custodial alternatives have proven to be or have been deemed to be insufficient in relation to the individual.[96] Analogously, the amendments to the original recast provide less detail concerning time limits for detention (in particular there is still no maximum time limit to detention, unlike the time limits for detaining other immigration detainees set out in the EU's Returns Directive).

93 If this is not possible, prison accommodation is allowed, but only under the condition that the applicant is kept separate from criminals.

94 However, in order to be compliant with recent case law, such as ECtHR 19 January 2012, *Popov v France* (App no 39472/07 and 39474/07), para 124, it should have provided that also the children who are accompanying his/her family in detention must have access to speedy judicial review of the detention measure.

95 See ECtHR, 12 October 2006, *Mubilanzila Mayeka and Kaniki Mitunga c. Belgium* (App no 13178/03), para 83; ECtHR, 5 April 2011, *Rahimi v Greece* (App no 8687/08), para 107–10. The same line of reasoning appeared subsequently in *Popov v France* (App no 39472/07 and 39474/07) where the Court stressed that detention of (asylum-seeking) minors can only be justified insofar as it can be considered to be a 'measure of last resort which could not be replaced by any alternative'; ECtHR 20 December 2011, *Yoh-Ekale Mwanje v Belgium* (App no 10486/10), concerned an HIV-positive Cameroonian woman who had been irregularly staying in Belgium since the rejection of her request for family reunification with her Dutch partner living in Belgium. In that case, according to the Court, in the absence of a consideration of 'less severe measures', detention cannot be considered to be closely connected to the detention ground and is therefore arbitrary.

96 This would be in line with ECtHR, *Saadi*, § 70 and the judgments cited as well with the interpretation of art 31 (2) of the Geneva Convention as proposed by Carlier and Hathaway according to which it imposes a test of necessity in the sense of an obligation 'to rely on less intrusive restrictions on freedom of movement, unless detention is clearly required'. See J-Y Carlier, 'L'accès au territoire et à la détention de l'étranger demandeur d'asile', Revue trimestrielle des droits de l'homme, Juillet 2009, 806; JC Hathaway, *The Right of Refugees Under International Law* (Cambridge University Press, 2005) 429.

There is also the absence of any requirement to inform asylum-seekers of the maximum period of detention.

Regarding access to the labour market, it must now be opened to asylum seekers no later than nine months (instead of the original 12 months) after the application was lodged. Whereas the Commission and the European Parliament proposed a six-month period, this provision of the Directive improves access to the labour market compared to the 2003 Directive. However, this remains conditioned on the fact that there is no first-instance decision on the claim by the competent authority in one year and this delay cannot be attributed to the applicant. Moreover, the previous concession granted to Member States to give priority of access to the labour market to EU citizens and nationals of States Parties to the Agreement on the European Economic Area has been reinserted.

Compared to the 2008 and 2009 initiatives – and also to the 2003 Directive – Directive 2013/33/EU goes instead in the direction of lowering standards as regards the issue of vulnerable people. Indeed Article 22 does not produce a real conceptual improvement on the definition of vulnerable people. It merely requires Member States to assess whether vulnerable persons have special reception needs, without first ascertaining whether the applicant for international protection fits among the examples of vulnerable people ex Article 21, and then whether he/she would also have 'special needs' as defined in their national legislation. However, it is often not self-evident whether a person is vulnerable. The only tangible improvement is therefore limited to the procedural side of the assessment. But contrary to the 2008 recast proposal, which provided that it should be initiated 'as soon as the application was lodged', a less protective time frame has been preferred which shall be initiated 'within a reasonable time after an application for international protection is made'. On the other hand, Member States are now requested to address these special reception needs 'if they become apparent at a later stage in the asylum procedure',[97] and they must also ensure support for such persons and shall provide for appropriate monitoring of their situation.

With regard to the additional safeguards established in relation to the detention of vulnerable persons and persons with special reception needs, the amended provision for unaccompanied minors – according to which they might be detained only in 'exceptional circumstances' and never in prison accommodation[98] – seems too vague in the absence of any specification about what this means. If its implementation can lead to potential discrepancies between Member States, the final text agreed at least has aligned the standard with the one laid down in the Return Directive requiring also that as far as possible unaccompanied minors should be granted accommodation in institutions provided with personnel and facilities which take into account the needs of persons of their age.

The amendments of the proposal also fail to achieve the result of a more advanced guarantee of the human dignity of asylum seekers as regards their 'direct support',

97 See new Art 22(1).

98 Art 11(3).

namely the rules on material reception conditions – that is, asylum-seekers' access to healthcare and social welfare. In particular, Directive 2013/32 eliminates the principle of equal treatment ('under the *same* conditions as nationals') regarding access to healthcare, taking note of the position of the European Parliament and strong reservations in the Council.[99] As regards social welfare assistance, the new Directive no more provides that the amount of assistance to be granted to asylum seekers has to be 'equivalent to the amount of social assistance granted to nationals requiring such assistance'. It provides instead that the amount thereof 'shall be *determined on the basis* of the level(s) established by the Member State concerned either by law or by the practice to ensure adequate standards of living for nationals'.[100] Despite the new formulation, the concept of equivalence has not been discarded. Article 17(5) which refers to 'less favourable treatment to applicants compared with nationals' indirectly confirms such an interpretation. Therefore, the new provisions are still in conflict with the aim of the Directive, that is, the guarantee of identical conditions in all Member States.[101] In fact such a purpose could only be attained with the adoption of minimum common standards which can overcome the existing differentiation among national systems that would have run the risk of increasing secondary flows of asylum seekers rather than reducing them as intended by the Directive. The lowering of the standard required by the new proposal continues if it is considered that it will now be possible to withdraw reception conditions entirely, and in a greater number of cases.[102] Moreover, there will no longer be an obligation to ensure the basic subsistence of asylum seekers in all such cases.

Lastly, as regards the possibility for granting, reducing and withdrawing material reception conditions for applicants for international protection, in exceptional and duly justified cases, the new text allows Member States to provide such migrants with low levels of benefits. While according to Article 20(1) the withdrawal of benefits is allowed in 'exceptional and duly justified cases', Article 20(2) provides for reduced benefits for late applicants when a Member State must demonstrate that the asylum seeker had not applied as soon as

99 Art 19 provides that Member States shall ensure that applicants receive the necessary health care which shall include, at least, emergency care and essential treatment of illness or post traumatic disorders as well as that Member States shall provide necessary medical or other assistance to applicants who have special need, including appropriate mental health care where needed.

100 See Art 17(5). Unfortunately, as ECRE pointed out in its Comment to the Amended Commission Proposal to Recast the Reception Condition Directive (September 2011), 'this may potentially lead to Member States granting unacceptably low levels of material reception conditions that may be well below what is an adequate standard of living as required under amended recast Article 17(1)'.

101 Briefing Note on the proposal of the Directive 2003/9/EC recast requested by the European Parliament to Kay Hailbronner, March 2009, available at http://www.ulb.ac.be/assoc/odysseus/CEAS/PE410.675.pdf.

102 Article 20.

'reasonably practicable' for asylum, 'for no justifiable reason'. However, in the event of the withdrawal of benefits, the core benefits that must be ensured have been enhanced: the new compromised recast provides that all healthcare and a dignified standard of living shall be granted.

At least the judicial activism of the ECJ in *CIMADE and Gisti*[103] brought about the result that a Member State in receipt of an application for asylum is obliged to grant the minimum conditions for the reception of asylum seekers laid down in Directive 2003/9, even to an asylum seeker in respect of whom it decides, under Dublin II, to call upon another Member State – as the State responsible for examining his application for asylum – to take charge of or take back that applicant. While the Court avoided any reference to the EUCFR, it would have been preferable to expressly hold that failure to make social assistance (and the rights enshrined in the Reception Directive) available to the so-called 'Dublinés' – asylum seekers awaiting transfer to another State to have their asylum application examined – may risk undermining the principle enshrined in Article 18 of the Charter that the right to asylum is to be protected in accordance with the provisions of the treaties.[104]

Concluding Remarks

There is still a long way to go before the EU could claim to offer a common standard of protection across its territory. To date, EU Member States have conceptualized the management of asylum and implemented EU asylum law in significantly different ways. In turn, this has led to a situation whereby there are huge disparities between Member States as regards the level and standard of protection, negatively impacting upon both asylum seekers and individual Member States. The recasting of key legislative EU instruments concerning the treatment, status and rights of those seeking international protection – as well as other initiatives concerning the external dimension of EU asylum policy such as the proposed EU resettlement scheme – aims to redress the gaps and weaknesses in the existing legislation. In particular, the recast intends to ensure a higher standard of protection of basic human rights in accordance with international and European human rights law while eliminating the wide scope of discretion, either explicitly afforded to Member States or implicitly derived from the lack of clarity of many provisions of the current legislation.

As shown in this paper, while the recasting process has introduced certain improvements, the resulting legislation provides an imperfect legal framework for a Common European Asylum System that still today only exists on paper. Translating this legal framework into humane asylum policies and further

---

103 CJEU, 27 September 2012, *Cimade* and Gisti, Case C-179/11.

104 See on the contrary AG Sharpston para 56 Opinion in *Cimade and Gisti* 15 May 2012.

strengthening fundamental rights for those seeking international protection in the European Union becomes now a task for Member States, the European Commission and the European Court of Justice. The still considerable margin for manoeuvre left to Member States in their implementation process might risk complicating the effective realization of a truly 'common' and 'fair' asylum system across Europe. But the de facto 'judicial European asylum policy' established by the constant recent dialogue between the Court of Justice of the European Union and the European Court of Human rights might redress the gap. The jurisprudence of both the European refugee law courts has already demonstrated an extremely positive impact on a stronger level of legal protection for those who are seeking asylum in Europe.[105] The influence of that jurisprudence on the implementation stage of the new legislative instruments of the second phase of the CEAS will be even more important because of the EU's possible accession to the Geneva Convention and the attached 1967 Protocol promoted by the Stockholm Programme,[106] and mostly because of the EU's accession to the ECHR[107] and the 'constitutionalization'[108] of the material scope of the right to asylum in the EU by Article 18 of the Charter of Fundamental Rights (CFREU) which implies a consistent interpretation of all the EU asylum legislation. 'We can't direct the wind, but we can adjust the sails'.

References

Bossuyt M, *Strasbourg et les demandeurs d'asile. (M.S.S. c. Belgique et Grèce et Sufi and Elmi c. le Royaume-Uni)* in *Annuaire International des droits de l'homme*, VI-2011, 663–76.

Briefing Note on the proposal of the Directive 2003/9/EC recast requested by the European Parliament to Kay Hailbronner, March 2009, available at http://www.ulb.ac.be/assoc/odysseus/CEAS/PE410.675.pdf.

Carlier J-Y, 'L'accès au territoire et à la détention de l'étranger demandeur d'asile', Revue trimestrielle des droits de l'homme, Juillet 2009, 806.

105 See for a recent detailed analysis F. Ippolito, 'The contribution of the European Courts to the Common European Asylum System and its on-going recast process' (2013) 2 MJECL 261–81.

106 The European Council has endorsed the view that the EU 'should seek accession to the 1951 Geneva Convention and its 1967 Protocol', see Presidency of the European Council, 'The Stockholm Programme – An open and secure Europe serving and protecting the citizen', Doc. No. 17024/09, available online: http://register.consilium.europa.eu/pdf/en/09/st17/st17024.en09.pdf (last visited 16 April 2013), p. 69, para. 6.2.1.

107 See Article 6(2) TEU.

108 Study for the European Parliament, 'Setting up a Common European Asylum System, Report on the Application of existing instruments and proposals for the new system', 2010, p. 430.

Comments of the European Commission on opinions of National Parliaments concerning COM (2008) 820, Reply of 7th October 2009 to Czech Senate COM20080815_0820_EN.pdf.

Commission Staff Working Document accompanying the Proposal for a Regulation of the European Parliament and of the Council establishing the criteria and mechanisms for determining the Member State responsible for examining an application for international protection lodged in one of the Member States by a third-country national or a stateless person (recast) Impact Assessment SEC (2008) 2962.

Communication from the Commission to the European Parliament, the Council, the European Economic and Social Committee and the Committee of Regions, Policy Plan on Asylum – an Integrated approach to protection across the EU, COM(2008) 360 final.

Council Directive 2004/83/EC of 29 April 2004 on minimum standards for the qualification and status of third-country nationals or stateless persons as refugees or as persons who otherwise need international protection and the content of the protection granted [2004] OJ L304/12.

Council Directive 2005/85/EC of 1 December 2005 on minimum standards on procedures in Member States for granting and withdrawing refugee status [2005] OJ L326/.

Council Regulation No 343/2003 of 18 February 2003 establishing the criteria and mechanisms for determining the Member State responsible for examining an asylum application lodged in one of the Member States by a third-country national [2003] OJ L50/1.

Directive of the European Parliament and of the Council 2011/95/EU on minimum standards for the qualification and status of third-country nationals or stateless persons as beneficiaries of international protection and the content of the protection granted [2011] OJ L337/9.

Directive 2013/32/EU of the European Parliament and of the Council of 26 June 2013 on common procedures for granting and withdrawing international protection (recast), [2013] OJ L 180/60.

Directive 2013/33/EU of the European Parliament and of the Council of 26 June 2013, laying down standards for the reception of applicants for international protection (recast), [2013] OJ L 180/96.

ECRE Comment to the Amended Commission Proposal to Recast the Reception Condition Directive, September 2011.

ECRE Information Note on the Qualification Directive, Brussels, 2004, available at: http://www.ecre.org/ files/qualpro.pdf [last accessed 25 March 2011].

EU Regulation 439/2010 of the European Parliament and of the Council of 19 May 2010 establishing a European Asylum Support Office [2010] OJ L132/11.

Garlick M, *The Common European Asylum System and the European Court of Justice: New jurisdiction and new challenges* (Bruylant, 2010).

Guild E, *Security and Migration in the 21st Century* (Polity Press, 2009).

Guild E, EU Immigration and the New EU Treaty Framework, in Satvinder S Juss, *The Ashgate Companion to Migration Law, Theory and Policy* (Ashgate, 2013), 43–59.

Hathaway JC, *The Right of Refugees under International Law* (Cambridge University Press, 2005).

Hurwitz A, *The Collective Responsibility of States to Protect Refugees* (Oxford University Press, 2009).

Ippolito, F, 'The contribution of the European Courts to the Common European Asylum System and its on-going recast process' (2013) 2 Maastricht Journal of European and Comparative Law, 61–81.

Ippolito F and Velluti S, 'The recast process of the EU asylum system: a balancing act between efficiency and fairness' (2011) 30 Refugee Survey Quarterly, 24–62.

Juss, Satvinder S, *The Ashgate Companian to Migration Law, Theory and Policy*, Ashgate, 2013.

McAdam J, 'The Qualification Directive: An Overview' in K. Zwaan (ed.), *The Qualification Directive: Central Themes, Problem Issues, and Implementation in Selected Member States* (Wolf Legal Publishers, 2007).

Peers S, 'Chapter 14: Asylum Procedures' in S Peers and N Rogers (eds), *EU Immigration and Asylum Law, Text and Commentary* (Martinus Nijhoff Publishers, 2006).

Peers S, *EU Justice and Home Affairs*, 3rd edition (Oxford University Press, 2011).

Peers S, Guild E, Acosta D, Groenendijk K and Moreno Lax V (eds), *EU Immigration and Asylum Law (Text and Commentary): Second Revised Edition, Volume 2: EU Immigration Law* (Martnuus Nijoff, 2012).

Presidency Conclusions Tampere European Council, 15–16 October 1999, SN 200/99, Conclusion n 13.

Presidency of the European Council, 'The Stockholm Programme – An open and secure Europe serving and protecting the citizen' Doc No 17024/09, available online: http://register.consilium.europa.eu/pdf/en/09/st17/st17024.en09.pdf.

Proposal for a Directive of the European Parliament and of the Council laying down minimum standards for the reception of asylum seekers, COM (2008) 815.

Proposal for a Directive of the European Parliament and of the Council on minimum standards on procedures in Member States for granting and withdrawing international protection COM (2009) 554/4.

Proposal for a Regulation of the European Parliament and of the Council establishing the criteria and mechanisms for determining the Member State responsible for examining an application for international protection lodged in one of the Member States by a third-country national or a stateless person COM (2008) 820.

Proposal for a Regulation of the European Parliament and of the Council concerning the establishment of 'Eurodac' for the comparison of fingerprints for the effective application of Regulation (EC) No 343/2003 COM (2008) 825.

Proposal for a Regulation of the European Parliament and of the Council establishing the criteria and mechanisms for determining the Member State responsible for examining an application for international protection lodged in one of the Member States by a third-country national or a stateless person [First reading], Political Agreement Council document 16332/12 [21 November 2012].

Regulation (EU) No 603/2013 of the European Parliament and of the Council of 26 June 2013 on the establishment of 'Eurodac' for the comparison of fingerprints for the effective application of Regulation (EU) No 604/2013 establishing the criteria and mechanisms for determining the Member State responsible for examining an application for international protection lodged in one of the Member States by a third-country national or a stateless person and on requests for the comparison with Eurodac data by Member States' law enforcement authorities and Europol for law enforcement purposes, and amending Regulation (EU) No 1077/2011 establishing a European Agency for the operational management of large-scale IT systems in the area of freedom, security and justice (recast), [2013] OJ L180/1.

Regulation (EU) No 604/2013 of 26 June 2013 of the European Parliament and of the Council establishing the criteria and mechanisms for determining the Member State responsible for examining an application for international protection lodged in one of the Member States by a third-country national or a stateless person (recast), [2013] OJ L 180/31

Report on 'Asylum Directives: scrutiny of the opt-in decision' by the European Union Committee of the House of Lords COM (2009) 551–4.

Report from the Commission to the European Parliament and the Council on the Application of Directive 2004/83/EC of 29 April 2004 on Minimum Standards for the Qualification and Status of Third-country Nationals or Stateless Persons as Refugees or as persons who otherwise need International Protection and the content of the protection, COM (2010) 314 fin [16 June 2010].

Sidorenko OF, *The common European asylum system: background, current state of affairs, future direction* (Asser Press, 2007).

Study for the European Parliament, *Setting up a Common European Asylum System, Report on the Application of existing instruments and proposals for the new system*, 2010.

Thielemann E, 'The Common European Asylum System: in Need of a More Comprehensive Burden-sharing Approach' in A Luedtke (ed.), *Migrants and Minorities: the European Response* (Cambridge Scholars Publishing, 2010), 82–97.

Tiendemans P, 'Subsidiary Protection and the function of Article 15 (c) of the Qualification Directive' (2012) 31(1) Refugee Survey Quarterly 123–38.

UNHCR, Guidelines on Gender-Related Persecution, UN Doc HCR/GIP/02/01, 7 May 2002.

UNHCR, Guidelines on 'Membership of a Particular Social Group', UN Doc HCR/GIP/02/02, 7 May 2002.

UNHCR, Improving Asylum Procedures, Comparative Analysis and Recommendations for Law and Practice, March 2010.

UNHCR comments on the European Commission's proposal for a Directive of the European Parliament and of the Council on minimum standards for the qualification and status of third-country nationals or stateless persons as beneficiaries of international protection and the content of the protection granted COM (2009) 551, 21 October 2009.

Van Hövell W, 'The Goals of the Common European Asylum System' in FANJ Goudappel and HS Raulus (eds), *The Future of Asylum in the European Union: Problems, Proposals and Human Rights* (T.M.C. Asser Press, 2011), 65–71.

Chapter 7
External Aspects of EU Asylum Law and Policy – 'New' Ways to Address 'Old' Woes

Samantha Velluti

Introduction

EU asylum and migration policy is traditionally viewed as having both an internal and an external dimension.[1] The internal dimension concerns the organization of asylum and migration within the European Union (EU) as well as at its borders. The external dimension includes measures aimed at managing asylum and migration through cooperation with third countries of origin and transit. However, due to the intrinsically cross-border nature of migration and asylum and the growing interaction between the international, European and domestic levels of policy-making, increasingly internal EU asylum and migration law has had significant effects on third countries and its nationals.[2] Terms such as 'external governance',[3] 'externalization'[4] or 'extra-territorialization'[5] all refer to the idea of the EU's regulatory influence in the field of migration beyond its territorial borders either

1 M Maes, D Vanheule, J Wouters and MC Foblets, 'The International Dimension of EU Asylum and Migration Policy: Framing the Issues' in M Maes, M Foblets and C De Bruycker (eds), *External Dimensions of EU Migration and Asylum Law and Policy* (Bruylant, 2011) 11.

2 See ibid.; Migration Policy Institute (MPI), *Study on The Feasibility of setting up resettlement schemes in EU Member States or at EU Le Lavenex and Ucarer 2002el, against the background of the Common European Asylum system and the goal of a Common Asylum Procedure* (European Commission, 2003), available at http://www.migrationpolicy.org/pubs/resettlement-study-full_2003_en.pdf.

3 S Lavenex, 'EU external governance in "wider Europe"' (2004) 11(4) Journal of European Public Policy 680–700.

4 C Boswell, 'The "external dimension" of EU immigration and asylum policy' (2003) 79(3) International Affairs 619–38; C Rodier, 'Analysis of the external dimension of the EU's asylum and immigration policies – summary and recommendations for the European Parliament', DT\619330EN.doc (8 June 2006); S Morgades, 'The Externalisation of the Asylum Function in the European Union' (2010) 4 Spring GRITIM Working Papers University of Pompeu Fabra, available at www.upf.edu/gritim.

5 JJ Rijpma and M Cremona, *The extra-territorialisation of EU migration policies* (EUI Working Papers LAW 2007/01).

through a relocation of the EU borders, or a transfer of responsibility to third countries or even private parties.

Hence, it may be questioned whether the above dichotomy may still be of any relevance for understanding problems and for developing meaningful solutions.[6] An example of what is being said is provided by the concepts of *safe third countries* and *first country of asylum* as defined in Articles 26 and 27 of the Asylum Procedures Directive (APD; Council of the European Union 2005),[7] which allows Member States to refuse asylum applications from persons who either stayed in or originated from these countries. Hence, the burden of giving asylum to or readmitting these persons is implicitly transferred to those countries.[8] However, for the purposes of the present chapter, we will follow the foregoing scholarly distinction between the internal and external dimensions as it facilitates the analysis of certain external aspects of EU asylum and migration policy.

Since the early 1990s both the EU and individual Member States have increasingly attempted to address the growing migration and refugee flows through cooperation programmes with migrant-sending countries and transit countries due to the incapacity of national asylum and migration structures and procedures to cope with the demands made upon them by irregular migration.[9] At EU level this 'new' approach has been advocated more forcefully since the entry into force of the Treaty of Amsterdam (ToA) and the 'communitarization' of immigration and asylum policies and, in particular, with the 1999 Tampere Programme and the subsequent adoption by the European Council of important programmatic documents calling for the development of the 'external dimension' of EU migration and asylum law and policy.

This alternative approach to migration management focusing on cooperation with sending and transit countries encompasses two different approaches:[10] on the one hand, one which attempts to restrict access to asylum systems by externalizing traditional domestic or EU migration control measures and, on the other hand, one which aims at addressing the root causes of migration and refugee flows thus providing refugees with access to protection in regions of refugee origin. The former is based on the idea of involving sending and transit countries in combating illegal entry, the smuggling and trafficking of migrants, the focus being mainly on strengthening border controls and readmitting illegal migrants. The latter is based on preventive measures that attempt to identify and tackle the reasons that explain refugee and migration flows.

---

6 See Maes et al. above n 1, 11.

7 These concepts, including recast proposals of the APD, are examined further below, see the section on Readmission Agreements.

8 See Maes et al. above n 1, 14.

9 G Loescher and J Milner, 'The Missing Link: the Need for Comprehensive Engagement in Regions of Refugee Origin' (2003) 79(3) International Affairs 595–617.

10 See Boswell above n 4, 619.

The external dimension of EU asylum law and policy is still in the making and the aforementioned cooperation is constantly evolving in search of identifying workable, sustainable and durable solutions to address mixed flows of asylum seekers and refugees. To date – even though cooperation comprises both the externalization of the asylum function and prevention – the control element seems to prevail in the adoption of the EU's external asylum measures.

The central argument put forward is that – given the unbalanced combination of the two main forms of cooperation with sending and transit countries – in order to address both the needs and concerns of Member States and the rights of refugees there has to be a shift in focus both in law and fact, namely one centered around a human rights discourse and on countries or regions of refugee origin. In particular, a much stronger comprehensive approach should be implemented in the EU in coordination with the involvement of other international actors such as the United Nations High Commissioner for Refugees (UNHCR), which is based on the combined deployment of development and assistance policies, trade and foreign direct investment as well as foreign policy instruments that aim at improving the capacity-building and good governance of countries or regions of refugee origin, *in primis* by supporting conflict resolution, restoring stability, promoting reconstruction and respect for human rights.

The chapter will proceed to examine the development of the external dimension of the EU's asylum law and policies from an historical perspective, following which it will analyse some of its key aspects, namely Resettlement, Regional Protection Programmes and Readmission Agreements.

EU Competence in Developing the External Dimension of EU Asylum Measures: an Historical Overview

It was in the Treaty of Amsterdam (ToA) that then European Community (EC) first enshrined provisions for the creation of an Area of Freedom Security and Justice (AFSJ) and provided the legal basis, as well as the drive for developing the Common European Asylum System (CEAS), giving competence to the European Community (EC) (now EU) in this field and adopting common rules on asylum with the insertion of Title IV TEC (now Title V TFEU) containing provisions for the creation of an AFSJ.[11]

While the ToA did not explicitly include the question of cooperation with third countries, the action plan for implementing the ToA,[12] which was subsequently

11 The AFSJ was originally mentioned in Arts 2 and 29 of the Treaty on European Union but was amended and given much greater prominence with the ToA.

12 Council of the European Union, *Action Plan of the Council and the Commission on how to best implement the provisions of the Treaty of Amsterdam on an Area of Freedom, Security and Justice* (3 December 1998), OJ 1999/C 19/01. Text adopted by the Justice and Home Affairs Council.

adopted at the Vienna European Council in December 1998, included some important points in relation to the 'external aspect' of Justice and Home Affairs (JHA). In particular, it emphasized a stronger international role for the EU, further to its expanded competence in the area of JHA giving the European Commission a more prominent role both in proposing new measures in the field as well as in negotiating agreements with third countries on immigration and asylum issues. In addition, as part of a list of measures to be taken within two years the action plan included assessment of countries of origin in order to formulate a country-specific integrated approach and setting up information campaigns in transit countries and in the countries of origin as a way of deterring illegal migration.

The Austrian Presidency of the Council of Ministers had drafted a strategy paper on immigration and asylum policy in July 1998, which emphasized that the EU had a crucial role in the 'reduction of migratory pressure in the main countries of origin of immigrants', through means including intervention in conflict regions, extended development aid and economic cooperation and the promotion of human rights.[13] This strategy was based on the 1992 Edinburgh Presidency Conclusions, which stated that 'coordination in the fields of foreign policy, economic cooperation and immigration and asylum policy' should 'contribute substantially to addressing the question of migratory movements'.[14] Already in 1991, the European Commission was calling for the integration of migration issues into the EU's external policy.

The strategy was not limited to proposals on prevention. It also called for increased measures to combat illegal migration through cooperation with transit countries – both future Member States (the so-called 'first circle') and transit countries neighbouring actual and prospective Member States (the 'second circle', including some of the former Soviet states and countries in the Mediterranean region). Cooperation included, for the most part, measures aimed at externalizing control. It was only for the 'third circle' – the major sending countries – that preventive approaches were deemed appropriate. For these countries, progress on addressing the causes of migration would be an important criterion in relation to development aid.

In December 1998 a High-Level Working Group (HLWG) in the Council of Ministers was set up with the task of preparing cross-pillar action plans for selected countries of origin and transit of asylum seekers and migrants.[15] The General Affairs Council then agreed to prepare action plans concerning six countries: Afghanistan, Albania, Morocco, Somalia, Sri Lanka and Iraq. Cooperation with third countries included both control and prevention measures.

The first five-year period (1999–2004) for the implementation of the EU's AFSJ was laid out by the so-called 'Tampere Programme' adopted by the Tampere

13 Council of the European Union, Presidency, *Strategy paper on immigration and asylum policy*, Doc No 9809/98 (OR. d) (1 July 1998), available at http://www.proasyl.de/texte/europe/eu-a-o.htm.

14 Council of the European Union, Presidency, *Conclusions* (12 December, 1992).

15 High-Level Working Group on Asylum and Migrants, *Final report of the High-Level Working Group on Asylum and Migration* (4 December 1999) 11281/99 (Presse 288-G).

European Council in 1999, which provided the first political mandate for the EU to combine EU migration and asylum with external relations policy. This was a Special European Council on Justice and Home Affairs, which committed the EU to create and further develop a CEAS and to cooperate with countries of origin. Under the heading on 'A common EU asylum and migration policy', the conclusions addressed the question of relations with countries of origin, which was one of four priorities.[16] They also clearly illustrated the reference to linking EU refugee policy with external relations, which stated:

> The European Union needs a comprehensive approach to migration addressing political, human rights and development issues in countries and regions of origin and transit. This requires combating poverty, improving living conditions and job opportunities, preventing conflicts and consolidating democratic states and ensuring respect for human rights, in particular rights of minorities, women and children. To that end, the Union as well as Member States are invited to contribute, within their respective competence under the Treaties, to a greater coherence of internal and external policies of the Union.

The importance of addressing the root causes of migration in countries of origin was therefore underlined, while the conclusions also called for full commitment to the obligations of the 1951 Refugee Convention and other relevant human rights instruments. In addition, the European Council stated that all EU competences and instruments and, in particular, in external relations must be used in an integrated and consistent way to build the AFSJ and that JHA concerns must be integrated in the definition and implementation of other Union policies and activities.

The Council and Commission were requested to draw up specific recommendations on policy objectives and measures for the Union's external action in JHA, including questions of working structure, prior to the European Council in Feira in June 2000, which were then presented to the Feira European Council, which specified that the mid-term review of Tampere planned for December 2001 should contain a chapter on progress in implementing the external dimension.[17]

The impetus for developing further the external dimension of the EU's asylum and immigration policies continued with the 2001 Laeken European Council, which called for 'the integration of the policy on migratory flows into the European Union's foreign policy', and also referred to the protection of refugees and the 1951 Convention.[18]

By the same token, the Seville European Council in June 2002 underlined the importance of the external dimension of asylum and migration, stating that an integrated, comprehensive and balanced approach to tackling the root

16 European Council, Presidency, *Conclusions* (15–16 October 1999).

17 European Council, Presidency, *Conclusions* (19–20 June 2000).

18 European Council, Presidency, *Conclusions* (14–15 December 2001).

causes of illegal immigration must remain the European Union's constant long-term objective.[19]

In the 2002 Communication on *Integrating Migration Issues in the European Union's Relations with Third Countries*[20] the Commission promoted a strategy aimed at using external relations tools to address the root causes of migration and forced migration, with particular attention given to prevention and protection measures and linking them to development programmes. The Communication devoted attention to outlining the different Community actions in favour of refugees, including humanitarian assistance being provided to refugee populations. A further Communication entitled *Towards More Accessible, Equitable and Managed Asylum Systems* focused on the importance of identifying new approaches looking outside the EU within a framework of genuine burden and responsibility sharing.[21]

Specifically, preparatory actions were to be adopted in order to see what could be done concretely in regions of origin also with the involvement of the United Nations High Commissioner for Refugees (UNHCR). However, at the same time, the focus was also on external border control and indeed the notion of Integrated Border Management (IBM) was first introduced by the European Commission[22] on the basis of the Laeken European Council in 2001. This system aims at ensuring an efficient management of external borders of the Member States through common operational coordination, integrated risk analysis, inter-operational equipment and burden-sharing[23] in order to fight against terrorism, prevent cross-border crime, manage migration flows and ensure internal security within the EU.

The Global Approach to Migration (GAM) was also adopted during the second period of the AFSJ (Council of the European Union 2005; European Commission 2006). The focus was on developing a holistic approach to reduce illegal migration ensuring the safe return of illegal migrants, identifying durable solutions and strengthening capacity-building to better manage migration. The

---

19 European Council, Presidency, *Conclusions* (21–22 June 2002).

20 European Commission, 'Communication on Integrating Migration Issues in the European Union's Relations with Third Countries', (2002) COM (2002) 703 final.

21 European Commission, 'Communication on Towards More Accessible, Equitable and Managed Asylum Systems' (2003) COM (2003) 315 final.

22 European Commission, 'Communication on Towards integrated management of the external borders of the Member States of the European Union' (2002) COM (2002) 233 final.

23 V Moreno-Lax, 'Searching Responsibilities and Rescuing Rights: Frontex, the Draft Guidelines for Joint Maritime Operations and Asylum Seeking in the Mediterranean' (2009) REFGOV Working Paper, REFGOV-FR-28, 3; J Monar, 'The External Shield of the Area of Freedom, Security and Justice: Progress and Deficits of the Integrated Management of External EU Borders' in JW de Zwaan and F Goudappel (eds), *Freedom, Security and Justice in the EU – Implementation of The Hague Programme* (TMC Asser Press, 2006), 73–88; P Hobbing, *Integrated Border Management at the EU Level* (CEPS, 2005), Working Document No 227.

GAM initially focused on Africa and the Mediterranean area but it has subsequently been extended to other regions (European Commission 2007).

In particular, actions under the GAM have aimed at developing operational cooperation between Member States on migratory roots and safety at sea with the coordination of FRONTEX, the European Agency for the Management of Operational Cooperation at the External Borders of the Member States of the European Union. This EU agency was established in 2004 as a 'first-pillar' agency with the aim of coordinating and assisting Member States' actions – specifically joint operations – in the surveillance and control of the external borders of the EU (Council of the European Union 2004; European Parliament and Council of the European Union 2007; European Parliament and Council of the European Union 2011).[24] The GAM was extended to include eastern and south-eastern neighbouring regions of the EU and strengthened by including policies on legal migration and integration. Consequently, it was renamed the 'Comprehensive Approach to Migration'. Moreover, following a risk analysis study of illegal immigration from Africa, regional networks of immigration liaison officers were set up along key migration routes through Africa, Rapid Border Intervention Teams (RABIT) were established[25] and a European Patrols Network was created and became operational in 2007.[26]

The IBM and the GAM models of management of asylum and irregular migration flows have become the main strategies of the EU's immigration and asylum policies as they combine both territorial and extraterritorial forms of control. They have come to 'legitimise the practice and promotion of a paradigm of control and surveillance, and whose implementation through systems like

24 More information is available on the agency's website http://www.frontex.europa.eu/ for commentary, see E Guild, et al., *Implementation of the EU Charter of Fundamental Rights and its Impact on EU Home Affairs Agencies Frontex, Europol and the European Asylum Support Office* (2011) study for the DG of Internal Policies, Committee on Civil Liberties, Justice and Home Affairs (LIBE) European Parliament, PE 453.196; V Moreno-Lax above n 23; V Moreno-Lax, *Frontex as a Global Actor: External Relations with Third Countries and International Organisations, in The External Dimension of the Area of Freedom, Security and Justice* in M Dony (ed), (Bruylant, 2013 forthcoming); J O'Dowd, 'Mutual Recognition in European Immigration Policy: Harmonised Protection or Coordinated Exclusion?' in F Goudappel and H Raulus (eds), *The Future of Asylum in the European Union. Problems, Proposals and Human Rights* (TMC Asser Press, 2011), 73–110; S Carrera 2007, *The EU Border Management Strategy: FRONTEX and the Challenges of Irregular Immigration in the Canary Islands* (CEPS, 2007), Working Paper No 261.

25 European Parliament and Council of the European Union, 'Regulation (EC) No 863/2007 of the European Parliament and of the Council of establishing a mechanism for the creation of Rapid Border Intervention Teams and amending Council Regulation (EC) No 2007/2004 as regards that mechanism and regulating the tasks and powers of guest officers', (11 July 2007) OJ L199/30.

26 For further information, visit http://www.frontex.europa.eu/news/european-patrols-network--3bKZex.

operational cooperation, risk analysis and exchange of information opens a series of concerns regarding the principle of legality, transparency and accountability as well as the compliance with human rights and European Community Law on borders'.[27]

Following a mandate from the Thessaloniki European Council in June 2003, the Commission published a Communication on the Managed Entry in the EU of Persons in Need of International Protection and the Enhancement of the Protection Capacity of the Regions of Origin – 'Improving Access to Durable Solutions' – in which it placed the focus on protection and respecting the rights of refugees.[28] It suggested that a system of international burden or responsibility-sharing is implicit in international relations between states and, consequently, the international refugee regime creates obligations on sovereign states. In the Communication the Commission committed itself to the creation of Regional Protection Programmes (RPPs), examined further below, focusing in particular on good governance, judiciary reform, institution-building, democratization and human rights.

After Tampere, The Hague Programme,[29] covering the second period of the AFSJ (2005–09), launched the external dimension of asylum.[30] The key idea in The Hague Programme was that improving the CEAS had to go hand in hand with the development of the external dimension of asylum and migration. The Hague Programme emphasized the need for a first stage during which it would be necessary to

> … assist third countries, in full partnership, using existing Community funds where appropriate, in their efforts to improve their capacity for migration management and refugee protection, prevent and combat illegal immigration, inform on legal channels for migration, resolve refugee situations by providing better access to durable solutions, build border-control capacity, enhance document security and tackle the problem of return.

27 See Carrera above n 24, 8. For a critical analysis on the legal problems posed by extraterritorial control of immigration, see B Ryan and V Mitsilegas, *Extraterritorial Immigration Control. Legal Challenges* (Martinus Nijhoff, 2010).

28 European Commission, 'Communication on the Managed Entry in the EU of Persons in Need of International Protection and Enhancement of the Protection Capacity of the Regions of Origin: Improving Access to Durable Solutions', (2004) COM (2004) 410 final.

29 European Council, The Hague Programme: Strengthening Freedom, Security and Justice in the European Union (2005) (2005/C 53/01) OJ 3.3.2005 N. C 53/1-14 para 1.6.

30 V Moreno-Lax, 'The External Dimension of the Common European Asylum System after Stockholm' in C Gortazar et al. (eds), *European Migration and Asylum Policies: Coherence or Contradiction?* (Bruylant, 2012); A Baldaccini, 'The External Dimension of the EU's Asylum and Immigration Policies: Old Concerns and New Approaches' in A Baldaccini, E Guild and H Toner (eds), *Whose Freedom, Security and Justice? EU Immigration and Asylum Law and Policy* (Hart Publishing, 2007).

With a 'spirit of shared responsibility' the emphasis was placed on cooperation with third countries and countries in the regions of origin, in order 'to provide access to protection and durable solutions at the earliest possible stage'.[31] The priority of The Hague Programme has been the adoption of measures to combat illegal immigration and to prevent the abuse of the asylum system. The main instruments adopted since have focused on increasing the level of protection in the regions of origin and transit, namely EU RPPs,[32] the establishment of an EU Joint Resettlement Programme[33] and Protected Entry Procedures (PEPs).[34]

The objectives of The Hague Programme have been further developed by the Stockholm Programme,[35] which covers the third period of the AFSJ (2010–14). The Stockholm Programme has been influenced by the 2008 European Pact on Immigration and Asylum,[36] which is intended 'to form the basis of a genuine common European policy on immigration and asylum, given the challenges of the coming years and the need for solidarity and cooperation in the management of migration flows'.[37] In practice, the Pact is heavily embedded with control mechanisms to reduce the flows of illegal migrants and improve efficient management of borders thus relying on mutual recognition in relation to return or expulsion decisions made by the Member States. The key priorities of the Stockholm Programme are centered around the instruments of the GAM focusing on Mobility Partnerships to develop comprehensive and long-term cooperation with third countries.

The Stockholm Programme also put forward a proposal that could positively influence the development of the EU's asylum law, including through the courts. The European Council in Stockholm stated that the EU 'should seek accession to the 1951 Geneva Convention and its 1967 Protocol'. EU accession would have the benefit of establishing a direct link between the Union institutions and the

31 Council of the European Union, 'Council Directive 2005/85/EC of 1 Dec. 2005 on minimum standards on procedures in Member States for granting and withdrawing refugee status', (13 December, 2005) OJ L326/.

32 European Commission, 'Communication from the Commission to the Council and the European Parliament on Regional Protection Programmes' (2005) COM (2005) 388 final.

33 European Commission, 'Communication from the Commission to the European Parliament and the Council on the establishment of a Joint EU Resettlement Programme' (2009) COM (2009) 447.

34 European Commission, 'Communication from the Commission to the European Parliament, the Council, the European Economic and Social Committee and the Committee of Regions Policy Plan on Asylum an Integrated Approach to protection across the EU' (2008) COM (2008) 360 final.

35 European Council, *The Stockholm Programme – An Open and Secure Europe Serving and Protecting Citizens* (2010) (2010/C 115/01), OJ 4.5.2010 N. C 115/1 para 6.

36 European Council, Presidency, *Conclusions* (16 October 2008) EU Doc 14368/08 CONCL 4.

37 Council of the European Union, *Justice and Home Affairs*, Press Release 12923/08 (Press 250), (25 September 2008).

international refugee protection system, as well as strengthening institutional ties between the UNHCR and the EU ensuring compliance with the Convention at all levels of EU action on asylum. Moreover, Article 80 TFEU provides that 'the policies of the Union set out in this Chapter and their implementation shall be governed by the principle of solidarity and fair sharing of responsibility, including its financial implications, between the Member States'. However, Member States remain reluctant to carry out this duty of cooperation and solidarity as evidenced also by the situation of deadlock in which the aforementioned process of creating a fully fledged CEAS by 2012 is at the time of writing.[38]

As posited by O'Dowd[39] 'the Stockholm Programme ... reflects the well-established formal symmetry in the European Union's approach to asylum and immigration – on the one hand, intensified cooperation to ensure the effectiveness of national decisions to exclude migrants and, on the other, a harmonisation of the standards which those national authorities apply in making decisions on asylum and other forms of international protection'.

By way of concluding this section it seems in order to briefly examine the external competence of the EU as regards asylum and immigration. While the ToA provided the legal basis for developing an AFSJ it did not provide for an explicit external competence in this area. The then EC Treaty referred to measures or rules but it did not specify which legal instruments should be employed.[40] However, because of the policy field itself and the need to develop it further outside the EU to ensure its effectiveness, international agreements seemed the proper legal instruments to be used and that the external competences of the EU could be implied from the then Title IV TEC. This has been the case of readmission agreements.[41] Under the EC Treaty, their legal basis were Articles 63(3)(b) and 300 EC. In particular, the former provision enabled the Council to adopt measures on immigration policy within the area of illegal immigration and illegal residence as well as the repatriation of illegal residents. With the entry into force of the Treaty of Lisbon (ToL) this implies that external competence has been made explicit with Article 79(3) TFEU which provides that the Union may sign agreements with third countries for the readmission to the countries of origin of third-country nationals who do not or who no longer fulfill the conditions for entry, presence or residence in the territory of one of the Member States.

38 S Peers, 'The revised 'Dublin' rules on responsibility for asylum-seekers: The Council's failure to fix a broken system' (2012) Statewatch Analysis 1–6, available at http://www.statewatch.org/analyses/no-173-dublin-III.pdf.

39 See O'Dowd, 'Mutual Recognition in European Immigration Policy' 82.

40 G De Baere, 'The Framework of EU External Competences for Developing the External Dimensions of EU Asylum and Migration Policy, Leuven Centre for Global Governance Studies' (May 2010) Working Paper No 50.

41 S Peers and N Rogers, *EU Immigration and Asylum Law. Text and Commentary* (Martinus Nijhoff, 2006) 881–98.

Other international agreements in the field of asylum and immigration are still concluded on the basis of implied external competences. This is the case, for example, of those concerning partnership and cooperation with third countries for the purpose of managing inflows of people applying for asylum or subsidiary protection under Article 78(2)(g) TFEU. Moreover, Article 4(2)(j) TFEU lists the Union's competences in the AFSJ – which includes visas, asylum and immigration – as shared competence. This provision should be read together with Articles 2(2) TFEU and 3(2) TFEU, the implication being for the Member States that they can only exercise their competence insofar as the Union has not exercised its competence or has ceased to do so, as well as that Member States cannot sign international agreements which would affect any acts adopted under Title V TFEU. With regard to external borders, Protocol 23 on External Relations of the Member States on the Crossing of External Borders provides that the provisions on the measures included in Article 77(2)(b) TFEU are without prejudice to the competence of the Member States to negotiate or sign agreements with third countries as long as they respect the Union laws and other relevant international agreements. This would seem to suggest that the Union does not have an exclusive competence in this area.

Developing Durable Solutions for Protracted Refugee Situations

The EU Joint Resettlement Programme

Resettlement involves the selection and transfer of refugees from a State in which they have sought protection to a third State which has agreed to admit them as refugees with permanent residence status.[42] Being a resettled refugee ensures protection against *refoulement*, guarantees a set of basic rights similar to the citizens of the host country as well as the possibility of acquiring citizenship of the resettlement country.[43] Resettlement is considered as a long-term solution for situations where refugees can neither return to their country of origin, nor receive effective protection or be integrated into the country of first asylum. There are three main goals of resettlement: protection, provision of durable solutions and burden-sharing with host countries. Hence, resettlement has the same humanitarian protection purpose as asylum. However, there are also significant differences.[44] Resettlement is a programme through which States decide in advance who they can help and select individuals whose protection they can guarantee upon arrival.

42 United Nations High Commissioner for Refugees (UNHCR), *UNHCR Resettlement Handbook* (July 2011), available at http://www.unhcr.org/4a2ccf4c6.html 3.

43 See *UNHCR Resettlement Handbook* above n 42.

44 See *Study on The Feasibility of setting up resettlement schemes in EU Member States or at EU Le Lavenex and Ucarer 2002el, against the background of the Common European Asylum system and the goal of a Common Asylum Procedure* above n 2.

Resettlement offers a durable solution in protracted refugee situations and it is a tool for the managed arrival of refugees whose status is determined in advance of their travel. In particular, resettlement is an administrative tool, while asylum is guaranteed by a set of rights and duties. The decision to resettle a refugee from another country is taken by the government of the resettlement country.[45]

The procedure, in the case of resettlement, is fundamentally different from the regular asylum procedure,[46] in the sense that, for a resettled refugee, the legal determination that the person in question is a refugee, that he/she deserves protection and that he/she qualifies for resettlement takes place before the refugee is effectively transferred. In contrast, the normal procedure for determining refugee status starts with the request of the asylum seeker, after the arrival of the asylum seeker in a Member State. Moreover, in comparison to asylum seekers, resettled refugees have different needs because they arrive with their refugee protection claim already considered and with a residence permit. Their needs are therefore different, even if the longer-term goal in their reception and integration plans may be the same.

Resettlement is generally carried out with the UNHCR acting as the key intermediary. UNHCR has a mandate with regard to international protection and is in a position to recognize refugees and to identify suitable cases for resettlement. UNHCR usually has an important role in this process and submits only cases for resettlement if the person in question has been recognized as a person in need of protection under the UNHCR mandate and after it has been established that the person is in need of resettlement.

As noted by the UNHCR Working Group on Resettlement,[47] the making available of resettlement opportunities in the first asylum country may assist in deterring further secondary movements by providing the prospect of a durable solution. In addition, entering into agreements with countries of first asylum for the provision of resettlement in conjunction with readmission would act as a significant deterrent to those who might consider irregular movement while at the same time acting to relieve the country of first asylum of some of the burden incurred. The use of resettlement in this manner would be 'strategic' in that it would deter irregular movements, provide an orderly durable solution for other refugees as well as relieve some of the burden on the country of first asylum.

In March 2012 the EU adopted an EU-wide resettlement scheme[48] as part of the GAM and on the basis of the European Commission's (2009) proposal.

---

45 Ibid.

46 Ibid.

47 United Nations High Commissioner for Refugees (UNHCR) Working Group on Resettlement, Executive Committee of the High Commissioner's Programme, Standing Committee, *The Strategic use of Resettlement (A Discussion Paper Prepared by the Working Group on Resettlement)* (3 June 2003) WGR/03/04/Rev3 2.

48 European Parliament and Council of the European Union, 'Decision No 281/2012/EU' (30 March 2012) OJ L92/1.

There are at present 11 Member States which participate annually in resettlement, on a voluntary basis, through national resettlement programmes: Bulgaria, the Czech Republic, Denmark, Finland, France, Ireland, Portugal, the Netherlands, Romania, Sweden and the United Kingdom. Other Member States have provided resettlement on an *ad hoc* basis such as Germany, Luxembourg, Italy and Belgium, which have made specific commitments to resettle Iraqi refugees from Syria and Jordan, following discussions in November 2008 by the EU Council of JHA Ministers, which called upon Member States to take resettled Iraqi refugees from Syria and Jordan. The priorities will be put forward by the Resettlement Expert Group made up of representatives of the Member States, the Commission as well as other stakeholders, and then adopted through a decision of the Commission as one of the implementing measures of the decision establishing the European Refugee Fund (ERF III).[49]

It is proposed that the European Asylum Support Office (EASO)[50] will be involved in the practical coordination of the programme by providing, in particular, the structural framework for joint activities which can be carried out by Member States, such as selection and fact-finding missions, pre-departure orientation programmes, medical screenings, travel or visa arrangements. Different stakeholders, both governmental and non-governmental, will be involved in these activities. Other forms of cooperation will include exchange of information and specific know-how and joint training. Some concerns about the scheme have been voiced over its funding and most importantly for the exclusion from consultation of those countries from which refugees will be resettled as well as the emphasis given to political considerations over humanitarian needs.[51]

Regional Protection Programmes (RPPs)

In 2005, following the adoption of The Hague Programme (2004–09) which stressed the partnership element with third countries, and in line with Article 78(2)(g) TFEU, which includes, among the measures that must be adopted to achieve the CEAS 'partnership and cooperation with third countries for the purpose of managing inflows of people applying for asylum ...', the European Commission (2005) issued a Communication on the creation and implementation of RPP with the aim

---

49 European Parliament and Council of the European Union, 'Decision No 573/2007/EC establishing the European Refugee Fund for the period 2008 to 2013 as part of the General programme 'Solidarity and Management of Migration Flows' and repealing Council Decision 2004/904/EC' (6 June 2007a) OJ L144/1.

50 European Parliament and Council of the European Union, 'Regulation (EU) No 439/2010 of the European Parliament and of the Council of 19 May 2010 establishing a European Asylum Support Office' (29 May 2010) OJ L132/11.

51 V Moreno-Lax, 'The External Dimension of the CEAS after Stockholm. In Need of a Comprehensive Approach to Access International Protection in the EU' (2010) REFGOV Working Paper, REFGOV-FR-30 8–10.

of improving access to protection and durable solutions for refugees outside the EU.[52] The idea, which found the support and cooperation of the UNHCR, was to establish links between aid projects and resettlement commitments of Member States on a voluntary basis, to enhance the asylum capacity-building of non-EU countries in the regions from which many refugees originate, or through which they pass in transit.[53]

Resources for strengthening cooperation with third countries were ensured through pre-existing financial and technical assistance programmes such as Poland and Hungary: Assistance for Restructuring their Economies (PHARE) (pre-accession countries), Technical Assistance to the Commonwealth of Independent States (TACIS) and MEsures D'Accompagnement (MEDA) (the Balkans, Mediterranean, Eastern Europe and Central Asia) as well as the AENEAS programme created in 2004 and specifically aimed at helping third countries in the field of migration and asylum. The AENEAS programme was replaced by the migration and asylum thematic programme for 2007–13, which focuses on capacity-building in countries of origin, transit countries and encourages cooperation initiatives to develop working methods and best practices.[54]

The European Commission put forward two RPP pilot projects: one in the Western Newly Independent States (Western NIS: Ukraine, Moldova, Belarus), and the other in sub-Saharan Africa (Great Lakes region of Africa), namely in Tanzania.[55] With regard to the latter, activities included training and capacity-building on asylum for officials and institutions, fostering voluntary return to Burundi and resettlement for Congolese, registering refugees and improving security in refugee camps in Tanzania, working with the civil society on refugee support and legal counselling and facilitating local integration. Results in terms of progress were modest which are explained in part by the fact that effective coordination with other EU actions proved to be difficult. Resettlement figures were disappointing which seemed to indicate the little understanding of resettlement schemes by Member States, particularly their use in the context of the RPP. In addition, the RPP was unable to play an important role for Africa's refugee population who received humanitarian and development aid mostly from other assistance programmes and sources indicating the lack of visibility of the RPP.

With regard to the Western NIS, capacity-building activities involved border monitoring, training and technical assistance, refugee counselling and resettlement. Other activities concerned local integration such as support to authorities, language

52 See http://europa.eu/legislation_summaries/justice_freedom_security/free_movement_of_persons_asylum_immigration/l33222_en.htm.

53 M Garlick, 'EU "regional protection programmes": development and prospects' in M Maes, M Foblets and C De Bruycker (eds), *External Dimensions of EU Migration and Asylum Law and Policy* (Bruylant, 2011) 371–86.

54 For further information visit http://ec.europa.eu/europeaid/how/finance/dci/migration_en.htm.

55 For detailed analysis, see Garlick, 'EU "regional protection programmes"' 379–83.

training, reception facilities and also awareness-raising to facilitate the acceptance of refugees in society. Progress was limited due in part to the lack of political will caused by the frequent changes in governmental partners. As for resettlement, similar problems encountered in Tanzania were observed which again illustrated a lack of coordination among EU resettlement countries and little understanding of how to use resettlement in the context of RPP.

Some key points may be made on the basis of the two pilot projects. First, for the success of RPPs it is pivotal to ensure the full involvement, support and commitment of the host countries. Second, it is necessary to increase availability of resources to ensure more visibility of RPPs. It should also be acknowledged that increased coordination with other actions, programmes and institutions would ensure a better impact of RPPs. Linked to the latter, they should not be a stand-alone displacement solution but rather they should be linked to other development aid and humanitarian tools. Indeed, a key limitation to the RPPs is the risk of considering the countries involved as safe countries and allowing Member States not to process asylum claims lodged by individuals who have transited through those countries.

Member States have reiterated their commitment to further developing and implementing RPPs in the Stockholm Programme (2010–14). In the future, RPPs should be applied as part of wider EU and international efforts to address international protection of refugees.

Readmission Agreements as a Form of Orderly Return of Irregular Migrants to Safe Third Countries

The ToA gave external powers to the then EC to sign and ratify readmission agreements in its own name with third countries.[56] Under the Third Pillar of the Maastricht Treaty, the Council agreed a standard clause to be considered for inclusion into 'mixed' agreements, namely agreements that have to be ratified by the Union and the Member States. In addition, it had agreed a Recommendation on a standard readmission agreement between a Member State and a third country,[57] a Recommendation on a standard Protocol on means of proof to be attached to such agreements[58] as well as a Recommendation on a standard travel document

56 Art 63(3)(b) EC (now Art 79 TFEU).

57 Council of the European Union, Council Directive 2005/85/EC of 1 December 2005 on minimum standards on procedures in Member States for granting and withdrawing refugee status (13 December 2005) OJ L326/.

58 Council of the European Union, Council Recommendation of 24 July 1995 on the guiding principles to be followed in drawing up protocols on the implementation of readmission agreements [1995a] (19 September 1996) OJ C274/25.

to be used for expulsion proceedings.[59] It may be argued that since the ToA and, in particular, since the Tampere Programme, which endorsed the Community's involvement in readmission, the purpose of the EU's readmission strategy is to expand and generalize readmission agreements and readmission clauses.[60]

Readmission agreements guarantee the return of illegal immigrants to their country of origin and, in some instances, to transit countries.[61] In particular, those immigrants who do not meet the Schengen Borders Code[62] entry requirements are returned according to the provisions of the Return Directive[63] and on the basis of readmission agreements with third countries.

What is problematic about bilateral readmission agreements is that rather than being an expression of an emerging pan-European system of cooperation and burden-sharing in which Member States cooperate on an equal basis, in practice they constitute an attempt to relieve their domestic asylum procedures by transferring their legal and humanitarian responsibilities to safe third countries, which are usually less wealthier states[64] and also suffer from political instability. Moreover, the readmission agreements signed so far do not distinguish between the readmission of economic migrants in an irregular situation in the requesting country and asylum seekers whose applications have been rejected in the admissibility procedure on the grounds of the *third safe country* concept, the meaning of which is rather ambiguous. Member States may justify the inadmissibility of asylum applications made by individuals who, before arriving,

59 Council of the European Union, Council Recommendation of 30 November 1994 concerning the adoption of a standard travel document for the expulsion of third-country nationals [1995b] (19 September 1996) OJ C274/18.

60 Council of the European Union, Action Plan of the Council and the Commission on how to best implement the provisions of the Treaty of Amsterdam on an Area of Freedom, Security and Justice – Text adopted by the Justice and Home Affairs Council of 3 December 1998 (23 January 1999) OJ 1999/C 19/01.

61 N Albuquerque Abell, 'The Compatibility of Readmission Agreements with the 1951 Convention relating to the Status of Refugees' (1999) 11(1) International Journal of Refugee Law 60–83; D Bouteillet-Paquet, 'Passing the Buck: A Critical Analysis of the Readmission Policy Implemented by the European Union and its Member States' (2003) 5(3) European Journal of Migration and Law 359–77; M Schieffer, 'Community Readmission Agreements with Third Countries–Objectives, Substance and Current State of Negotiations' (2003) 5(3) European Journal of Migration and Law 343–57.

62 European Parliament and Council of the European Union, Regulation (EC) No 562/2006 of the European Parliament and of the Council of 15 March 2006 establishing a Community Code on the rules governing the movement of persons across borders (Schengen Borders Code) (13 April 2006) OJ L105/1 art. 7(3).

63 European Parliament and Council of the European Union, Directive 2008/115/EC of the European Parliament and of the Council of 16 December 2008 on common standards and procedures in member states for returning illegally staying third-country nationals (24 December 2008) OJ L348/98.

64 S Lavenex, 'Passing the Buck: European Union Refugee Policies towards Central and Eastern Europe' (1998) 11(2) Journal of Refugee Studies 126–45.

have passed through countries considered safe especially if made at the border. The 1951 Geneva Convention, and in particular, the *non-refoulement* clause in Article 33, does not forbid them from doing so. Specifically, Member States may reject an application when asylum seekers are deemed protected – either in fact or by law – or could have obtained protection in those countries.

Directive 2005/85/EC – on minimum standards on procedures in Member States for granting and withdrawing refugee status[65] – provides a notion of *first countries of asylum* and *safe third countries*.[66] As posited by Morgades,[67] returning asylum seekers who apply for asylum in a Member State, but who have not arrived there directly from the country where persecution is feared, creates the 'externalization of the asylum function', on the basis of which the responsibility for asylum for people who have not arrived directly in a Member State is transferred to other countries where the asylum seekers have not applied for protection. The legitimacy of these decisions is questionable considering the strong differences that exist in the standard of protection between the EU and third countries, both of origin and transit.

Moreover, there is no uniform guarantee for asylum seekers in relation to admissibility, accelerated and border procedures and thus no certainty that the *safe*

65 Council of the European Union, Council Directive 2005/85/EC of 1 December 2005 on minimum standards on procedures in Member States for granting and withdrawing refugee status (13 December 2005) OJ L326/.

66 Art 26 provides that: 'A country can be considered to be a first country of asylum for a particular applicant for asylum if: (a) he/she has been recognised in that country as a refugee and he/she can still avail himself/herself of that protection; or (b) he/she otherwise enjoys sufficient protection in that country, including benefiting from the principle of *non-refoulement*; provided that he/she will be re-admitted to that country. In applying the concept of first country of asylum to the particular circumstances of an applicant for asylum Member States may take into account Art. 27(1)'. Art 27(1) provides that: '1. Member States may apply the safe third country concept only where the competent authorities are satisfied that a person seeking asylum will be treated in accordance with the following principles in the third country concerned: (a) life and liberty are not threatened on account of race, religion, nationality, membership of a particular social group or political opinion; (b) the principle of *non-refoulement* in accordance with the Geneva Convention is respected; (c) the prohibition of removal, in violation of the right to freedom from torture and cruel, inhuman or degrading treatment as laid down in international law, is respected; and (d) the possibility exists to request refugee status and, if found to be a refugee, to receive protection in accordance with the Geneva Convention'. Art 31(1) provides that '1. A third country designated as a safe country of origin in accordance with either art. 29 or 30 may, after an individual examination of the application, be considered as a safe country of origin for a particular applicant for asylum only if: (a) he/she has the nationality of that country; or (b) he/she is a stateless person and was formerly habitually resident in that country; and he/she has not submitted any serious grounds for considering the country not to be a safe country of origin in his/her particular circumstances and in terms of his/her qualification as a refugee in accordance with Directive 2004/83/EC'.

67 See Morgades above n 4, 8–10.

third country concept will be applied to them according to the same standard of safety across the EU as per Article 27(2) of Directive 2005/85/EC.[68] The European Commission's recast proposal[69] does not remove the above controversial concepts but only revisits them and a national definition is still permitted. Compliance with international human rights standards as well as Article 18 of the EU Charter of Fundamental Rights is thus debatable.[70] In 2011, the European Commission adopted an Amended Recast Proposal[71] to further take into account the criticisms made to the Asylum Procedures Directive *vis-à-vis* its conformity to international human rights obligations. The UNHCR[72] welcomed the changes as signalling an improvement with regard to the quality and efficiency of the asylum systems in the EU and further harmonization of protection standards in line with the objective of the CEAS.

A number of important proposed amendments have been introduced to bring the Directive more closely in line with human rights and refugee legal standards as expressed in recent case law from the Court of Justice of the EU (ECJ) and the European Court of Human Rights (ECtHR). Other amendments have been made to reflect the requirements introduced by Article 78(2)d TFEU. In particular, new Article 35 provides the applicant with the possibility of challenging the presumption of safety in cases where the *first country of asylum* concept is applied. However, the Amended Recast Proposal still has quite a few discretionary and optional provisions and although some changes have been introduced, the *safe country of origin* (Article 36) and national designation of third countries as *safe countries of origin* (Article 37) remain as well as the *safe third country* concept (Article 38). It may be argued, therefore, that the EU gives primacy to the objective of efficacy to the detriment of the protection of vulnerable people (CFR-CDF 2004: 25–38).

To date the EU has signed readmission agreements with Hong Kong, Macao, Albania, Sri Lanka, Russia, Ukraine, Macedonia, Montenegro, Serbia, Bosnia-

---

68 UN High Commissioner for Refugees (UNHCR), *Improving Asylum Procedures: Comparative Analysis and Recommendations for Law and Practice – Key Findings and Recommendations* (March 2010), available at http://www.unhcr.org/refworld/docid/4bab55752.html.

69 European Commission, Proposal for a Directive of the European Parliament and of the Council on Minimum Standards on Procedures in Member States for Granting and Withdrawing International Protection (Recast) (2009a) COM (2009) 554 final.

70 F Ippolito and S Velluti, 'The Recast Process of the EU Asylum System: A Balancing Act Between Efficiency and Fairness' (2011) 30(3) Refugee Survey Quarterly 54–6.

71 European Commission, Amended Proposal for a Directive of the European Parliament and the Council on common procedures for granting and withdrawing international protection status (Recast) (2011) COM (2011) 319 final.

72 United Nations High Commissioner for Refugees (UNHCR), UNHCR comments on the European Commission's Amended Proposal for a Directive of the European Parliament and of the Council on common procedures for granting and withdrawing international protection status (Recast) (2012) COM (2011) 319 final, available at http://www.unhcr.org/4f35256c9.pdf.

Herzegovina, Moldova, Pakistan and Georgia.[73] The Commission has been authorized to negotiate readmission agreements with Morocco, Algeria, Turkey and China and has recommended the conclusion of readmission agreements with Libya and Cape Verde. A readmission committee is established by each agreement to perform specified technical tasks.

Readmission agreements, apart from a few minor differences, are all essentially identical. They establish the obligation of parties to readmit their own and former own nationals, people from another jurisdiction (in the case of Macao and Hong Kong), third-country nationals (TCNs) or stateless people. The Preamble to the eight readmission agreements concluded with European countries emphasizing that the agreements are 'without prejudice to the rights, obligations and responsibilities of the Community, the Member States of the European Union' and the country concerned 'arising from International law, in particular from the European Convention of 4 November 1950 for the Protection of Human Rights, the Convention of 28 July 1951 and the Protocol of 31 January 1967 on the Status of Refugees' (in some readmission agreements other instruments are also mentioned). There is no specific reference to human rights or refugee law in the readmission agreement with Hong Kong, Macao, Sri Lanka, Ukraine and Pakistan.

In addition, contracting parties have the obligation to permit transit of persons back to a non-contracting party if necessary. There are detailed rules on the procedure for handing back persons, including the types of documents which constitute proof or *prima facie* evidence that a person is national or was on the territory (Peers 2011: 588). The agreements also require use of the EU's standard travel document in certain circumstances. Each agreement provides that Member States can draw up special implementing protocols with the non-EC party, but conversely that the agreement takes precedence over any incompatible bilateral agreement between a Member State and the other contracting party.

Conclusion – plus ça change, plus c'est la même chose

The chapter showed throughout that both the EU and its Member States have recognized the strict relationship between the internal and external dimension of EU asylum law and policy as well as the need to develop a comprehensive approach to migration which also requires the involvement of third countries, chiefly regions or countries of origin. At the same time, it also illustrated how the two key elements of these measures – securitization/control v prevention/protection – are not *pares inter partes*, or better-said, part of a level playing field in which refugees and asylum seekers are ensured a genuine and effective protection of their rights. As the chapter explained, conditions for the access to the protection of human rights differs across the EU as Member States may still rely on optional

73 Further information about readmission agreements is available at http://www.statewatch.org/news/2010/jul/04eu-readmission-agreements.htm.

or discretionary clauses in relation to many aspects concerning asylum and reforms of extant EU legislation leave these clauses untouched, largely explained by the lack of political will among most Member States to change the *status quo*. The readmission agreements implemented thus far also seem to indicate a preference for efficiency over the guarantee of refugees' human rights. However, the chapter also showed that even where there is the commitment on the part of the Member States such as, for example, in the case of RPPs, there are objective difficulties and practical or logistical problems which hinder progress. Moreover, when seeking cooperation with third countries there is no certainty that the EU can ensure that its third-country partners will respect human rights, indirect *refoulement* being a case in point.

As noted by Maes et al.,[74] cooperation with third countries in asylum and migration seems to be operating at three levels: an EU approach, a mixed approach and a purely bilateral approach. The coexistence of these three approaches is politically necessary but leads to fragmentation and lack of consistency in an area which is *per se* highly complex and a challenging task to regulate given the delicate and fragile balance between crisis management or control measures and the protection of human rights.

Hence, overall what we are presented with is a rather mixed picture which leaves us disappointingly with the puzzle of whether the bottle is half empty or half full: much remains to be done and while there has been some progress in many instances – either because of individual Member States' interests prevailing (hindering real change) or because of political instability in certain third countries – identifying and implementing those measures which ensure an equal balance between asylum and migration management and the effective protection of refugees' human rights will still remain challenging in the years to come.

Postscript

Please note that the chapter was written before the adoption of the Recast Asylum Package in June 2013. The chapter does incorporate, therefore, the changes introduced by the Recast measures.

References

Albuquerque AN, 'The Compatibility of Readmission Agreements with the 1951 Convention relating to the Status of Refugees' (1999) 11(1) International Journal of Refugee Law 60–83.

Baldaccini, A, 'The External Dimension of the EU's Asylum and Immigration Policies: Old Concerns and New Approaches' in A. Baldaccini, E. Guild and

74 See Maes et al. above n 1, 47.

H. Toner (eds), *Whose Freedom, Security and Justice? EU Immigration and Asylum Law and Policy* (Hart Publishing, 2007).

Boswell C, 'The 'external dimension' of EU immigration and asylum policy' (2003) 79(3) International Affairs 619–38.

Bouteillet-Paquet D, 'Passing the Buck: A Critical Analysis of the Readmission Policy Implemented by the European Union and its Member States' (2003) 5(3) European Journal of Migration and Law 359–77.

Carrera S, The EU Border Management Strategy: FRONTEX and the Challenges of Irregular Immigration in the Canary Islands (2007) CEPS Working Paper No 261, CEPS, Brussels.

Council of the European Communities and European Commission, Action Plan of the Council and the Commission on how best to implement the provisions of the Treaty of Amsterdam on an area of freedom, security and justice, text adopted by the Justice and Home Affairs Council of 3 December 1998 (1999) 1999/C 10/01.

Council of the European Union, Presidency. Conclusions. Edinburgh, December 12, 1992.

Council of the European Union, Council Recommendation of 30 November 1994 concerning a specimen bilateral readmission agreement between a Member State and a third country (1995) OJ C274/20, of 19 September 1996.

Council of the European Union, Council Recommendation of 24 July 1995 on the guiding principles to be followed in drawing up protocols on the implementation of readmission agreements (1995a) OJ C274/25, of 19 September 1996.

Council of the European Union, Council Recommendation of 30 November 1994 concerning the adoption of a standard travel document for the expulsion of third-country nationals (1995b) OJ C274/18, of 19 September 1996.

Council of the European Union, Presidency, 1998. Strategy paper on immigration and asylum policy, Brussels, 1 July 1998 (13.07), Doc No 9809/98 (OR. d), available at http://www.proasyl.de/texte/europe/eu-a-o.htm.

Council of the European Union, Action Plan of the Council and the Commission on how to best implement the provisions of the Treaty of Amsterdam on an Area of Freedom, Security and Justice – Text adopted by the Justice and Home Affairs Council of 3 December 1998 (1999) OJ (1999/C 19/01), 23 January 1999.

Council of the European Union, Council Regulation No 2007/2004 of 26 October 2004 establishing a European Agency for the Management of Operational Cooperation at the External Borders of the Member States of the European Union (2004) OJ L349/1, 25 November 2004.

Council of the European Union, Council Directive 2005/85/EC of 1 December 2005 on minimum standards on procedures in Member States for granting and withdrawing refugee status (2005) OJ L326/, 13 December 2005.

Council of the European Union, Presidency 2005a. Global approach to migration: Priority actions focusing on Africa and the Mediterranean. Council doc 15744/05, 13 December 2005.

Council of the European Union, Justice and Home Affairs. Press Release 12923/08 (Press 250) 2890th Council Meeting (2008) Brussels, 25 September 2008.

De Baere G, The Framework of EU External Competences for Developing the External Dimensions of EU Asylum and Migration Policy, Leuven Centre for Global Governance Studies (2010) Working Paper No 50 May 2010.

EU Network of Independent Experts on Fundamental Rights (CFR-CDF), Thematic Comment No 2: Fundamental Rights in the External Activities of the European Union in the Fields of Justice and Asylum and Immigration in 2003 (2004) CFR-CDF.Them.Com.2003.en. 4 February 2004.

European Commission, Communication on Integrating Migration Issues in the European Union's Relations with Third Countries (2002) COM (2002) 703 final.

European Commission, Communication on Towards integrated management of the external borders of the Member States of the European Union (2002a) COM (2002) 233 final.

European Commission, Communication on Towards More Accessible, Equitable and Managed Asylum Systems (2003) COM (2003) 315 final.

European Commission, Communication on the Managed Entry in the EU of Persons in Need of International Protection and Enhancement of the Protection Capacity of the Regions of Origin: Improving Access to Durable Solutions (2004) COM (2004) 410 final.

European Commission, Communication from the Commission to the Council and the European Parliament on Regional Protection Programmes (2005) COM (2005) 388 final.

European Commission, The Global Approach to Migration One Year On: Towards a Comprehensive European Migration Policy (2006) COM (2006) 735 final.

European Commission, Applying the Global Approach to Migration to the Eastern and South-Eastern Regions Neighbouring the European Union (2007) COM (2007) 247 final.

European Commission, Communication from the Commission to the European Parliament, the Council, the European Economic and Social Committee and the Committee of Regions Policy Plan on Asylum an Integrated Approach to protection across the EU (2008) COM (2008) 360 final.

European Commission, Communication from the Commission to the European Parliament and the Council on the establishment of a Joint EU Resettlement Programme (2009) COM (2009) 447.

European Commission, Proposal for a Directive of the European Parliament and of the Council on Minimum Standards on Procedures in Member States for Granting and Withdrawing International Protection (Recast) (2009a) COM (2009) 554 final.

European Commission, Amended Proposal for a Directive of the European Parliament and the Council on common procedures for granting and withdrawing international protection status (Recast) (2011) 1 June 2011, COM (2011) 319 final.

European Council, Presidency Conclusions (1999) Tampere 15–16 October 1999.
European Council, Presidency Conclusions (2000) Santa Maria da Feira 19–20 June 2000.
European Council, Presidency Conclusions (2001) Laeken 14–15 December 2001.
European Council, Presidency Conclusions (2000) Seville 21–22 June 2002.
European Council, The Hague Programme: Strengthening Freedom, Security and Justice in the European Union (2005) (2005/C 53/01), OJ 3.3.2005 N. C 53/ 1-14 §1.6.
European Council, Presidency Conclusions (2008) Brussels 15–16 October 2008 (16 October 2008), EU Doc. 14368/08 CONCL 4.
European Council, The Stockholm Programme – An Open and Secure Europe Serving and Protecting Citizens (2010) (2010/C 115/01), OJ 4.5.2010 N. C 115/1 §6.
European Parliament and Council of the European Union, Regulation (EC) No 562/2006 of the European Parliament and of the Council of 15 March 2006 establishing a Community Code on the rules governing the movement of persons across borders (Schengen Borders Code) (2006) OJ L105/1 of 13.04.2006, Art 7(3).
European Parliament and Council of the European Union, Regulation (EC) No 863/2007 of the European Parliament and of the Council of 11 July 2007 establishing a mechanism for the creation of Rapid Border Intervention Teams and amending Council Regulation (EC) No 2007/2004 as regards that mechanism and regulating the tasks and powers of guest officers (2007) OJ L199/30, 31 July 2007.
European Parliament and Council of the European Union, Decision No 573/2007/ EC establishing the European Refugee Fund for the period 2008 to 2013 as part of the General programme 'Solidarity and Management of Migration Flows' and repealing Council Decision (2007a) 2004/904/EC. OJ L144/1, 6 June 2007.
European Parliament and Council of the European Union, Regulation (EC) No 863/2007 of the European Parliament and of the Council of 11 July 2007 establishing a mechanism for the creation of Rapid Border Intervention Teams and amending Council Regulation (EC) No 2007/2004 as regards that mechanism and regulating the tasks and powers of guest officers (2007b) [2007] OJ L199/30.
European Parliament and Council of the European Union, Directive 2008/115/ EC of the European Parliament and of the Council of 16 December 2008 on common standards and procedures in Member States for returning illegally staying third-country nationals (2008) OJ L348/98 of 24 December 2008.
European Parliament and Council of the European Union, Regulation (EU) No 439/2010 of the European Parliament and of the Council of 19 May 2010 establishing a European Asylum Support Office (2010) OJ L132/11, 29 May 2010.

European Parliament and Council of the European Union, Regulation (EU) No 1168/2011 of the European Parliament and of the Council of 25 October 2011 amending Council Regulation (EC) No 2007/2004 establishing a European Agency for the Management of Operational Cooperation at the External Borders of the Member States of the European Union (2011) OJ L304/1, 22 November 2011.

European Parliament and Council of the European Union, Decision No 281/2012/EU of the European Parliament and of the Council of 29 March 2012 (2012) OJ L92/1, 30 March 2012.

Garlick M, EU 'regional protection programmes': development and prospects, in M Maes, M Foblets and C De Bruycker (eds), *External Dimensions of EU Migration and Asylum Law and Policy*(Bruylant, 2011) 371–86.

Guild E, et al. 'Implementation of the EU Charter of Fundamental Rights and its Impact on EU Home Affairs Agencies Frontex, Europol and the European Asylum Support Office'. Study for the DG of Internal Policies, Committee on Civil Liberties, Justice and Home Affairs (LIBE) European Parliament, PE 453.196.

HLWG, High-Level Working Group on Asylum and Migrants. Final report of the High-Level Working Group on Asylum and Migration, 11281/99 (1999) (Presse 288-G), 4 December 1999.

Hobbing P, Integrated Border Management at the EU level. Centre for European Policy Studies (2005) CEPS Working Document N. 227/August 2005.

Ippolito F and Velluti S, 'The Recast Process of the EU Asylum System: A Balancing Act Between Efficiency and Fairness' (2011) 30(3) Refugee Survey Quarterly 24–62.

Lavenex S, Passing the Buck: European Union Refugee Policies towards Central and Eastern Europe (1998) 11(2) Journal of Refugee Studies 126–45.

Lavenex S, 'EU external governance in "wider Europe"' (2004) 11(4) Journal of European Public Policy 680–700.

Lavenex S and Ucarer EM, 'The emergent EU migration regime and its external impact' in Lavenex and Ucarer (eds), *Migration and the externalities of European integration* (Lexington Books, 2002) 1–13.

Loescher G and Milner J, 'The Missing Link: the Need for Comprehensive Engagement in Regions of Refugee Origin' (2003) 79(3) International Affairs 595–617.

Maes M, Vanheule D, Wouters J and Foblets MC, 'The International Dimension of EU Asylum and Migration Policy: Framing the Issues' in M Maes, MC Foblets and Ph De Bruycker (eds), *External Dimensions of EU Migration and Asylum Law and Policy* (Bruylant, 2011) 9–60.

Migration Policy Institute (MPI, Study on The Feasibility of setting up resettlement schemes in EU Member States or at EU Level, against the background of the Common European Asylum system and the goal of a Common Asylum Procedure. Brussels: European Commission (2003), available at http://www.migrationpolicy.org/pubs/resettlement-study-full_2003_en.pdf.

Monar J, 'The External Shield of the Area of Freedom, Security and Justice: Progress and Deficits of the Integrated Management of External EU Borders' in JW de Zwaan and F Goudappel (eds), *Freedom, Security and Justice in the EU – Implementation of The Hague Programme* (TMC Asser Press, 2006) 73–88.

Moreno-Lax V, Searching Responsibilities and Rescuing Rights: Frontex, the Draft Guidelines for Joint Maritime Operations and Asylum Seeking in the Mediterranean (2009) REFGOV Working Paper, REFGOV-FR-28.

Moreno-Lax V, The External Dimension of the CEAS after Stockholm. In Need of a Comprehensive Approach to Access International Protection in the EU (2010) REFGOV Working Paper, REFGOV-FR-30,

Moreno-Lax V, The External Dimension of the Common European Asylum System after Stockholm, in European Migration and Asylum Policies: Coherence or Contradiction?edited by C Gortazar et al. (Bruylant, 2012).

Moreno-Lax V, 'Frontex as a Global Actor: External Relations with Third Countries and International Organisations' in M Dony (ed.), *The External Dimension of the Area of Freedom, Security and Justice* (Bruylant, 2013).

Morgades S, The Externalisation of the Asylum Function in the European Union (2010) No 4 Spring, GRITIM Working Papers, University of Pompeu Fabra, available at www.upf.edu/gritim.

O'Dowd J, Mutual Recognition in European Immigration Policy: Harmonised Protection or Coordinated Exclusion? in F. Goudappel and H. Raulus (eds), *The Future of Asylum in the European Union. Problems, Proposals and Human Rights* (TMC Asser Press, 2011) 73–110.

Peers S, *EU Justice and Home Affairs Law* (Oxford University Press, 2011).

Peers S, The revised 'Dublin' rules on responsibility for asylum-seekers: The Council's failure to fix a broken system. Statewatch Analysis (2012) http://www.statewatch.org/analyses/no-173-dublin-III.pdf 1–6.

Peers S and Rogers N, *EU Immigration and Asylum Law. Text and Commentary* (Martinus Nijhoff, 2006).

Rijpma JJ and Cremona M, *The extra-territorialisation of EU migration policies*. EUI Working Papers (2007) LAW 2007/01.

Rodier C, Analysis of the external dimension of the EU's asylum and immigration policies – summary and recommendations for the European Parliament (2006) 8 June 2006, DT\619330EN.doc.

Ryan B and Mitsilegas V, *Extraterritorial Immigration Control. Legal Challenges* (Martinus Nijhoff, 2010).

Schieffer M, Community Readmission Agreements with Third Countries–Objectives, Substance and Current State of Negotiations (2003) 5(3) European Journal of Migration and Law 343–57.

United Nations High Commissioner for Refugees (UNHCR) Working Group on Resettlement, Executive Committee of the High Commissioner's Programme, Standing Committee, The Strategic use of Resettlement (A Discussion Paper Prepared by the Working Group on Resettlement) (2003) WGR/03/04/Rev3, 3 June 2003 2.

UN High Commissioner for Refugees (UNHCR), Improving Asylum Procedures: Comparative Analysis and Recommendations for Law and Practice – Key Findings and Recommendations, March 2010, available at: http://www.unhcr.org/refworld/docid/4bab55752.html.

United Nations High Commissioner for Refugees (UNHCR), UNHCR Resettlement Handbook, July 2011, available at http://www.unhcr.org/4a2ccf4c6.html.

United Nations High Commissioner for Refugees (UNHCR), UNHCR comments on the European Commission's Amended Proposal for a Directive of the European Parliament and of the Council on common procedures for granting and withdrawing international protection status (Recast) (2012) COM (2011) 319 final, available at http://www.unhcr.org/4f35256c9.pdf.

Chapter 8

The International Protection of Refugees and Asylum Seekers: the Role of Article 3 of the European Convention on Human Rights

Colin Harvey

Introduction

International refugee law aligns protection with a defined status. The law does not extend to all those who suffer human rights abuses; it is specific and limited. The 1951 Convention relating to the Status of Refugees[1] and its 1967 Protocol[2] offer guarantees to 'refugees', as provided for in these instruments. The clear suggestion is that status matters, with the logical result that there will be some who will fall outside the legal definition. International human rights law – as its name indicates – tends to focus on 'everyone' and the priority is the fact of 'personhood'. It is a legal order oriented towards humanity and respect for human dignity. This might mean that refugee law could be characterized as outdated and exclusive. One of the aims of this chapter is to argue that this would be too simplistic. Even the seemingly inclusive normative order of human rights contains constructed limitations and embedded interpretative exclusions. There are interpretative boundaries in place in human rights law, and the most intriguing encounters are often to be located in discovering them.

Article 3 has generated much interest, and informed a wider international debate about the scope of the *non-refoulement* obligation; as it seems to be a potentially robust source of rights protection. It also raises the question of the status of those who might benefit from it. If such persons are not 'refugees' how are they to be categorized and what rights do they have? Should we welcome the formalization of new categories? Are subsidiary forms of international protection to be precisely that – do we have a 'hierarchy of victimhood'? There is little doubt that in seeking to make the provision practical and effective the European Court of Human Rights has done useful work. However, it is apparent from the case law that many of the major tensions that underpin migration management are lurking there still, often buried in the reasoning constructed; they are fought out within the interpretative horizons of the Convention and in the ongoing engagements with the

1 1951 Convention relating to the Status of Refugees, 28 July 1951, 189 UNTS 2545.

2 1967 Protocol relating to the Status of the Refugees, 606 UNTS 150.

Strasbourg Court. The assertion that Article 3 gives 'absolute' protection against return faces a carefully crafted body of jurisprudence that delimits the scale of the obligation. It therefore becomes necessary to understand the parameters in order to gain an insight into the opportunities and challenges offered by this provision of the European Convention on Human Rights.

Article 3, Asylum and *Non-Refoulement*

Article 3 provides:

> No one shall be subjected to torture or to inhuman or degrading treatment or punishment.

No exceptions are permitted, and it is a non-derogable legal guarantee. It reflects language that can be found in a range of international human rights instruments and has gained a powerful normative hold.[3] However, it is not immediately obvious that this provision has much to say about *non-refoulement*. The focus is on protecting a person (any person who is 'jurisdictionally present') against torture or inhuman and degrading treatment. The European Court of Human Rights, however (following the earlier approach adopted by the European Commission on Human Rights), interprets Article 3 to include a prohibition on return in prescribed circumstances.[4] The evolution of this interpretation is worth noting, before considering the substantive protection it offers.

3 Universal Declaration of Human Rights 1948, Art 5; International Covenant on Civil and Political Rights 1966, Art 7; UN Convention against Torture and Other Cruel, Inhuman or Degrading Treatment or Punishment 1984 Preamble and Art 3; Charter of Rights of the European Union 2000, Art 4; European Convention for the Prevention of Torture and Inhuman or Degrading Treatment or Punishment 1987, preamble; American Convention on Human Rights 1969, Art 5; Inter-American Convention to Prevent and Punish Torture 1985, preamble; African Charter on Human and Peoples' Rights 1981, Art 5; Arab Charter on Human Rights 1994, Art 13. In EU context, see also Council Directive 2004/83/EC on Minimum Standards for the Qualification and Status of Third-country Nationals or Stateless Persons as Refugees or as Persons Who Otherwise Need International Protection and the Content of the Protection Granted, 29 April 2004, OJ L304, 30/09/2004, 12–23 (Qualification Directive); 'Council Directive 2011/95/EU on Standards for the Qualification of Third-Country Nationals or Stateless Persons as Beneficiaries of International Protection, for a Uniform Status for Refugees or for Persons Eligible for Subsidiary Protection, and for the Content of the Protection Granted of 13 December 2011', O J L 337, 20/12/2011, 9–7 (Qualification Directive recast).

4 For comment, see GS Goodwin-Gill and J McAdam, *The Refugee in International Law* (3rd edn, Oxford University Press, 2007), 310–16; H Battjes, 'The *Soering* Threshold: Why Only Fundamental Values Prohibit *Refoulement* in ECHR Case Law' (2009) 11 European Journal of Migration and Law 205; M Den Heijer, 'Whose Rights and Which

In the extradition/expulsion case of *Soering v UK* the Court first set out the approach it would eventually apply more broadly.[5] The applicant was being extradited to the US to face charges of murder and argued that this would be in breach of Article 3. The argument was that he would be exposed to 'death row phenomenon' as a consequence of the extradition. The Court noted its general view of jurisdiction:

> Article 1 (art. 1) of the Convention, which provides that 'the High Contracting Parties shall secure to everyone within their jurisdiction the rights and freedoms defined in Section I', sets a limit, notably territorial, on the reach of the Convention. In particular, the engagement undertaken by a Contracting State is confined to 'securing' ('reconnoitre' in the French text) the listed rights and freedoms to persons within its own 'jurisdiction'. Further, the Convention does not govern the actions of States not Parties to it, nor does it purport to be a means of requiring the Contracting States to impose Convention standards on other States. Article 1 (art. 1) cannot be read as justifying a general principle to the effect that, notwithstanding its extradition obligations, a Contracting State may not surrender an individual unless satisfied that the conditions awaiting him in the country of destination are in full accord with each of the safeguards of the Convention. Indeed, as the United Kingdom Government stressed, the beneficial purpose of extradition in preventing fugitive offenders from evading justice cannot be ignored in determining the scope of application of the Convention and of Article 3 (art. 3) in particular.[6]

The Court was prepared to allocate responsibility on the basis of the *foreseeable consequences* of extradition.[7] What elements influenced the Court? The 'special character', 'general spirit' and its object and purpose were stressed, as the way of ensuring this human rights instrument is 'practical and effective'.[8] The role of Article 3 in enshrining one of the 'fundamental values of the democratic societies making up the Council of Europe' was underlined, as was the inclusion of an express provision in the UN Convention against Torture.[9] As the Court stated:

> It would hardly be compatible with the underlying values of the Convention, that 'common heritage of political traditions, ideals, freedom and the rule of law' to

Rights? The Continuing Story of *Non-Refoulement* under the European Convention on Human Rights' (2008) 10 European Journal of Migration and Law 277.

5 *Soering v UK* (App no 14038/88), 7 July 1989.

6 Ibid. para 86.

7 Ibid.: 'These considerations cannot, however, absolve the Contracting Parties from responsibility under Art 3 (Art 3) for all and any foreseeable consequences of extradition suffered outside their jurisdiction'.

8 Ibid. para 87.

9 Ibid. para 88.

> which the Preamble refers, were a Contracting State knowingly to surrender a fugitive to another State where there were substantial grounds for believing that he would be in danger of being subjected to torture, however heinous the crime allegedly committed. Extradition in such circumstances, while not explicitly referred to in the brief and general wording of Article 3 (art. 3), would plainly be contrary to the spirit and intendment of the Article, and in the Court's view this inherent obligation not to extradite also extends to cases in which the fugitive would be faced in the receiving State by a real risk of exposure to inhuman or degrading treatment or punishment proscribed by that Article. (art. 3).[10]

While the Court acknowledged the 'fair balance between the demands of the general interest of the community and the requirements of the protection of the individual's fundamental rights' that is at the heart of the Convention,[11] it was willing to hold that a potential violation of Article 3 could be adjudicated upon, and that responsibility could be ascribed to the State. Although the assessment did include an examination of the situation in the receiving State – with reference to Convention standards – this in no way implied the attribution of international legal liability for Convention purposes. The Court concluded that there was a real risk of being sentenced to death, and thus exposed to 'death row phenomenon'. The question then turned to whether this would cross the minimum threshold established in Article 3. In concluding that it would, the Court took account of: the length of detention prior to execution; conditions on death row; the applicant's age and mental state; and the possibility of extradition to Germany.[12] Taking all these elements together the Court held that extradition would breach Article 3.

In cases such as *Cruz Varas and others v Sweden*[13] and *Vilvarajah and others v UK* the Court made clear that the *Soering* approach would be applied to the general removal, expulsion and return process.[14] In *Cruz Varas* the applicant was deported to Chile – a country in which he feared being tortured (based in part on his alleged past experiences as a left-wing political activist) and expulsion was proposed for the other applicants. This presented the opportunity to apply *Soering* to asylum cases; and the Court took it:

10 Ibid. para 88.

11 Ibid. para 89. Cf *Babar Ahmad and others v UK* (App nos 24027/07, 11949/08, 36742/08, 66911/09 and 67354/09), 24 September 2012 final para: 'Indeed in the twenty-two years since the *Soering* judgment, in an Article 3 case the Court has never undertaken an examination of the proportionality of a proposed extradition or other form of removal from a Contracting State. To this extent, the Court must be taken to have departed from the approach contemplated by paragraphs 89 and 110 of the *Soering* judgment'.

12 Ibid. paras 106–10.

13 *Cruz Varas v Sweden* (App no 15576/89), 20 March 1991.

14 *Vilvarajah and others v UK* (App nos 13163/87, 13164/87, 13165/87, 13447/87, 13448/87), 30th October 1991. For an example of more recent developments (and the evolution of the assessment made by the Court) involving Sri Lanka, see *E.G. v UK* (App no 41178/08), 28th November 2011 final.

> Although the present case concerns expulsion as opposed to a decision to extradite, the Court considers that the above principle also applies to expulsion decisions and a fortiori to cases of actual expulsion.[15]

The Court expressed concern about the applicant's credibility in this case, noting how his allegations had changed in different police interviews, and observed the changing political situation in Chile and the experience of the Swedish government in these cases. The Court was thus not persuaded that substantial grounds had been shown that there was a real risk and found no breach of Article 3.

The applicants in *Vilvarajah* were Tamil asylum seekers who were returned by the UK to Sri Lanka, and some of the applicants had then been ill-treated. In holding that there had been no breach the Court noted: the general improvement in the country situation (evidenced by a UNHCR voluntary repatriation scheme); the applicants' personal position did not appear any worse than the generality of the population (there was a 'mere possibility' of ill-treatment); even if some of the applicants were mistreated or returned without the relevant identity documents, the focus was on the foreseeable consequences at the time of return and they were in no greater danger as a result; and the Court once again noted the experience of the UK and the careful consideration that had been given to the cases.

What we witness in these early cases (*Soering*, *Cruz Varas* and *Vilvarajah*[16]) is the establishment of a zone of Article 3 protection. The constitutive elements in making these assessments include the following steps. First, responsibility is prescribed in line with the foreseeable consequences of return (if it has already taken place the precise date of return is relevant). The Convention State is held accountable on the basis of assumed knowledge of what might happen. Second, the relevant point in time is the present, in the sense that the assessment rests on the consequences of return *now* or when return in fact took place. Third, there must be substantial grounds for believing that there is a real risk. The 'risk' must be capable of objective verification with reference to evidence, and the grounds for

15 *Cruz Varas* para 70.

16 To understand some of the continuing challenges raised by cases such as *Vilvarajah* see: *H. and B. v UK* (App nos 70073/10 and 44539/11), 9 April 2013; *S.H.H. v UK* (App no 60367/10) 29 January 2013; *Sufi and Elmi v UK* (App nos 8319/07 and 11449/07), 28 November 2011, final and *N.A. v UK* (App no 25904/07), 17 July 2008. The Court is grappling with situations of generalized and indiscriminate violence that are claimed to be so severe as to constitute a real risk for Article 3 purposes. The interpretative struggles that emerge (contrast *H. and B.* with *Sufi and Elmi*) reflect the tensions between an individualized approach and recognition of the appalling human rights situation in certain states. Note also the following from the Court in *H. and B.* para 91: 'The Court has never excluded the possibility that a general situation of violence in a country of destination will be of a sufficient level of intensity as to entail that any removal to it would necessarily breach Article 3 of the Convention. Nevertheless, the Court would adopt such an approach only in the most extreme cases of general violence, where there was a real risk of ill-treatment simply by virtue of an individual being exposed to such violence on return'.

holding this view must be 'substantial'; much thus rests on reliable and detailed country-specific information. Fourth, the treatment feared on return must be above the minimum level of severity necessary for general inclusion in Article 3. And finally, in making an Article 3 assessment only, the behaviour of the applicant is not a relevant consideration; the applicant may have been prosecuted for criminal offences in the host State or she may be a suspected terrorist; in reaching a conclusion about the 'risk', this is of no concern to the Court. This aspect of the approach has generated considerable governmental anxiety and comment, yet in no sense does it prescribe a general disregard of the applicant's past and present behavior or actions. The Court is honing in on the question of *real risk* only for the express purposes of the Article 3 test and the foreseeable consequences of return.

What has always been apparent is the boost this has given to the development of the international norm of *non-refoulement*. Along with other international instruments, it underlines and confirms the centrality of that established and inclusive legal principle. The focus on 'everyone' also merits comment; the Convention system is not wedded to intricate inclusion and exclusion clauses attached to a defined status. Yet, it is too simplistic to view this as a radical break – the steps to protection are steep, and as the figures on lack of success demonstrate, it is not straightforward to secure Article 3 protection. Grasping what it means substantively only flows from an analysis of the Convention cases in which it has been used. The tensions which surround its application are not hard to contextualize. When States wish to ensure the removal of particular persons from their territory they can find the constraints of Article 3 especially frustrating. Equally, however, it should be stressed that Article 3 rules out only particular ways of tackling suspected terrorism. The UK discussions in particular can lend weight to a distorted view that sees expulsion as the only genuine policy tool available.

Rights and National Security

The next step in this chapter is to select examples of the Court's evolving approach as illustrative of how Article 3 is applied in practice. Refugee, asylum and migration law can become part of a broader discussion about national security. This is particularly the case when a counter-terrorism frame emerges, and where deportation is then sought for national security reasons. In attempts to secure deportation – in contexts where there might be a real risk of ill-treatment on return – States have sought to negotiate assurances. This both acknowledges the difficulty of removal and raises distinct questions about national security-based expulsions (it is also an acceptance by States that deploy such assurances that risks *are* present – why else seek an assurance?).

Chahal v UK captures much of this, and remains a source of contention among States; it is worth reflecting on here.[17] The applicants were members of

17 *Chahal v UK* (App no 22414/93), 15 November 1996.

the same Sikh family who were living in the UK, having left India. Mr Chahal was a prominent political activist who had been alleged to be involved in terrorist/criminal activity – but who was never successfully prosecuted in relation to any of the allegations. However, a decision was taken by the Home Secretary to detain him with a view to seeking deportation as conducive to the public good for reasons of national security. His asylum application was refused (the UK government making clear that even if there was a well-founded fear of persecution, Articles 32 and 33 of the 1951 Refugee Convention would be applicable) and his only appeal against the order rested with the then-existing Advisory Panel procedure. It was evident that the government believed he had a long history of involvement in 'Sikh terrorism' relating to Punjab.[18] The argument thus unleashed in this case – over Article 3 and national security – continues. The UK suggested that there was an 'implied limitation to Article 3'[19] and that:

> ... in such cases, which required an uncertain prediction of future events in the receiving State, various factors should be taken into account, including the danger posed by the person in question to the security of the host nation. Thus, there was an implied limitation to Article 3 ... entitling a Contracting State to expel an individual to a receiving State even where a real risk of ill-treatment existed, if such removal was required on national security grounds.[20]

The UK noted that *Soering* had referred to a 'fair balance', and limitations were recognized in international refugee law.[21] If this was not acceptable, the government suggested that the Court should balance the threat to national security against any risk of ill-treatment.[22] The position was rejected, and has been consistently rejected by the Court: the prohibition 'is equally absolute in expulsion cases'.[23] To underline the point – and to reject explicitly the UK's suggestion – the Court stated:

> In these circumstances, the activities of the individual in question, however undesirable or dangerous, cannot be a material consideration. The protection afforded by Article 3 (art. 3) is thus wider than that provided by Articles 32 and 33 of the United Nations 1951 Convention on the Status of Refugees ...[24]

---

18 *Chahal* paras 30–31.

19 *Chahal* para 76.

20 *Chahal* para 76.

21 *Chahal* para 76.

22 *Chahal* para 76.

23 *Chahal* para 80.

24 *Chahal* para 80. It is worth noting what this practically also means, para 82: 'It follows from the above that it is not necessary for the Court to enter into a consideration of the Government's untested, but no doubt bona fide, allegations about the first applicant's terrorist activities and the threat posed by him to national security'.

The applicant argued here that the relevant point of time should be when the decision to deport him was finalized (1992); but this was rejected. The applicant had not as yet been deported, so the material time was the date of the Court proceedings.[25] The case revealed differences of view on the human rights situation in India and Punjab. The UK government stressed throughout that there had been a general improvement, and it was willing to return him to an airport of his choice in India; with the applicant arguing that Sikh activists still faced ill-treatment even outside their home State (as the Punjab police had demonstrated a capacity to act elsewhere).[26] The question of being a high-profile political activist was argued both ways: the governmental view that this would make the Indian government more careful and the applicant's belief that this would make ill-treatment more likely.[27] The Court placed weight on the body of evidence suggesting a 'police force completely beyond the control of lawful authority' that could operate beyond its home State and had done so; the fact that Mr Chahal was such a prominent activist was also relevant here.[28]

> The Court is persuaded by this evidence, which has been corroborated by material from a number of different objective sources, that, until mid-1994 at least, elements in the Punjab police were accustomed to acting without regard to the human rights of suspected Sikh militants and were fully capable of pursuing their targets into areas of India far away from Punjab.[29]

The Court did not doubt that improvements were happening and progress was being made but it attached significance to the absence of fundamental reorganization of the police force, and reports of continuing problems throughout India.[30] The good faith governmental assurances were therefore insufficient and the profile of Mr Chahal was only likely to increase the risk of harm.[31] In finding a breach of Article 3 – in the event of return – the Court underlined the evidence available about police and security force actions.[32]

Governmental concern about the *Chahal* judgment has persisted, and this was clear in *Saadi v Italy* where the UK exercised its right to intervene.[33] The applicant was subject to a deportation order to Tunisia (where he had been sentenced in his absence for terrorist offences), had been arrested on suspicion of participating in international terrorism, and convicted by the Italian court for involvement in a

25 *Chahal* paras 83–6.
26 *Chahal* paras 87–91.
27 *Chahal* paras 92–4.
28 *Chahal* para 99.
29 *Chahal* para 100.
30 *Chahal* para 102–5.
31 *Chahal* paras 105–6.
32 *Chahal* para 107.
33 *Saadi v Italy* (App no 37201/06), 28 February 2012 (GC).

criminal conspiracy. The Italian government sought diplomatic assurances from Tunisia (for the first time) that he would not be subjected to Article 3 ill-treatment.[34] His claim to asylum was rejected on national security grounds and the applicant argued that as a terror suspect he would be tortured on his return. The UK's intervention included further elaboration of the case for rethinking *Chahal*. The steps are worth spelling out. It argued that *Chahal* had caused problems for States and the option of criminal prosecution was not enough, it 'did not provide sufficient protection for the community'.[35] States should be permitted to use immigration law to 'protect themselves from external threats to their national security'.[36] The European Convention did not include reference to asylum and the coverage in international refugee law indicated that national security concerns could and should be accommodated.[37] Although Article 3 was an absolute protection it was relevant to note that the ill-treatment would be inflicted in another State, and thus this made the Court's jurisprudence on positive obligations relevant.[38] The protection applied not only to 'torture' but also to 'degrading treatment' and given that the threat level varied there was scope for some balancing to occur.[39] This 'balancing' would include weighing the risk of ill-treatment against the threat, altering the standard of proof to require stronger evidence if a threat to national security existed (the person should demonstrate it was 'more likely than not').[40]

The Court was not persuaded, once again, by the UK's argument and preceded to follow and rehearse its well-established case law and 'reaffirm' *Chahal*.[41]

> The Court notes first of all that States face immense difficulties in modern times in protecting their communities from terrorist violence. It cannot therefore underestimate the scale of the danger of terrorism today and the threat it presents to the community. That must not, however, call into question the absolute nature of Article 3. Accordingly, the Court cannot accept the argument of the United Kingdom government, supported by the respondent government, that a distinction must be drawn under Article 3 between treatment inflicted directly by a signatory State and treatment that might be inflicted by the authorities of another State, and that protection against this latter form of ill-treatment should be weighed against the interests of the community as a whole.[42]

34 *Saadi* para 53.
35 *Saadi* para 117.
36 *Saadi* para 119.
37 *Saadi* para 119.
38 *Saadi* para 120.
39 *Saadi* para 121.
40 *Saadi* para 122.
41 *Saadi* para 138.
42 *Saadi* paras 137–8.

The Court found the balancing argument 'misconceived' and underlined that the assessment of risk was independent of any analysis of the danger posed by non-return.[43] This also followed with the standard of proof and the 'more likely than not' test was rejected.[44]

> Even if, as the Italian and United Kingdom governments asserted, the terrorist threat has increased since that time, that circumstance would not call into question the conclusions of the *Chahal* judgment concerning the consequences of the absolute nature of Article 3.[45]

By way of reassurance to States the Court did also stress just how 'very cautious' it has been 'examining carefully the material placed before it in the light of the requisite standard of proof' and how rarely it has ever found States in breach.[46] The Court thus affirms its settled approach to Article 3 while also noting just how demanding it remains. In finding a breach if the removal was enforced the Court was influenced by: consistent reports from Amnesty International and Human Rights Watch on the torture and ill-treatment of suspected terrorists; and assurances were only reluctantly provided and in general terms (and even if the Italian government had received the assurances it wanted this would not end the Court's role).

What about non-State bodies? What if the ill-treatment is not feared from the State, but from its general inability or unwillingness to provide protection from non-State actors, including from terrorist violence in other States? In the early case of *Ahmed v Austria* the applicant had lost his refugee status (because of a criminal conviction) and faced expulsion to Somalia.[47] His fear of ill-treatment was from 'rival clans' in a context where the State was effectively 'absent'. In finding a potential breach of Article 3 the Court was particularly struck by the original grant of refugee status, and that the only reason for return now was the commission of the listed criminal offences – the human rights situation did not appear to have improved in Somalia and had not been properly taken into account. *Ahmed* thus confirmed that the ill-treatment need not emanate from the State.

The case of *Othman (Abu Qatada) v UK* is useful as another case study of the relationship between counter-terrorism policy, deportation and human rights protection.[48] The applicant (who had been recognized as a refugee in the UK) argued that deportation to Jordan would breach Article 3 of the Convention. The Court provided clarification on its approach to the use of diplomatic assurances

43 *Saadi* para 139.
44 *Saadi* para 140.
45 *Saadi* para 141.
46 *Saadi* para 141.
47 *Ahmed v Austria* (App no 25964/94), 17 December 1996.
48 *Othman (Abu Qatada) v UK* (App no 8139/09), 9 May 2012 final.

to attempt to secure Convention-compliant deportations.[49] Here the Court re-emphasized its understanding of the dilemmas faced by States: '... the Court considers it legitimate for Contracting States to take a firm stand against those who contribute to terrorist acts, which it cannot condone in any circumstances'.[50] It went on to note that:

> ... as part of the fight against terrorism, States must be allowed to deport non-nationals who they consider to be threats to national security. It is no part of this Court's function to review whether an individual is in fact such a threat; its only task is to consider whether that individual's deportation would be compatible with his or her rights under the Convention.[51]

On diplomatic assurances, the Court observed that its role was not necessarily to question in general terms the appropriateness of their use but to assess 'whether the assurances obtained in a particular case are sufficient to remove any real risk of ill-treatment'.[52] There might be occasions when the general human rights situation in another State was so severe as to lend them no weight, but this would only be in 'rare cases'.[53] The attention will therefore fall on the quality of the assurances (not merely the fact of their existence) and whether they can be relied on in particular cases. Questions considered by the Court include: have the assurances been disclosed?; are they specific or general?; who has provided the assurance and what is their status?; will other authorities in the State comply with them?; is the treatment covered legal or illegal in the receiving State?; were they given by a Contracting State?; what is the extent of relations between both States and what has happened regarding assurances in the past?; is objective verification of compliance possible?; is there an effective mechanism against torture and does it cooperate with international bodies?; has the applicant been ill-treated in the past?; have other courts looked at the reliability of the assurances?[54] Adopting this approach, and these tests, the Court was prepared to accept that the assurances were sufficient

49 See also the reference in the judgment to the national and international material on assurances, paras 141–54.

50 Ibid. para 183.

51 Ibid. para 184.

52 Ibid. para 187.

53 Ibid. para 188. See, for example, *Ergashev v Russia* above n para 114: 'As to the Government's argument that assurances were obtained from the Uzbek authorities, the Court has already cautioned against reliance on diplomatic assurances against torture from States where torture is endemic or persistent ... Given that the practice of torture in Uzbekistan is described by reputable international sources as systematic, the Court is not persuaded that the assurances from the Uzbek authorities offered a reliable guarantee against the risk of ill-treatment'. See also *Umirov v Russia* (App no 17455/11), 18 September 2012.

54 Ibid. para 189.

to remove the real risk of ill-treatment.[55] While the Court openly acknowledged the continuing and serious problems in Jordan, it seemed particularly impressed by the nature of the MOU adopted, and the detailed consideration by the Special Immigration Appeals Commission at the national level.

As in many of these cases, although Articles 3 and 2 tend to dominate, other Convention rights – such as Articles 5, 6, and 13 – are often involved. The Article 6 argument deployed in this case is worth noting. Following on from principles established in earlier case law it was alleged that Othman (Abu Qatada) would face a 'flagrant denial of justice' in Jordan, given the trial process there and the use of torture evidence. He had been arrested in the UK in 2002, and was tried on a number of occasions in Jordan *in absentia*. In order to assist its policy objectives on deportation the UK signed a memorandum of understanding with Jordan in 2005, and the applicant's deportation was then sought – and challenged. A central question which emerged in this case – as it travelled through the UK's legal system to Strasbourg – was the risk of use being made in his retrial of statements obtained by torture. On this issue, the European Court was willing to depart from the road taken by the Special Immigration Appeals Commission and the House of Lords and concluded that 'the present applicant has met the burden of proof required to demonstrate a real risk of a flagrant denial of justice if he were deported to Jordan'.[56]

The national security context arises in much of the relevant case law. As the *Soering* case demonstrates, return in the context of extradition can raise Article 3 issues. The approach of the Court in the case of extradition of terrorist suspects is again evident in cases such as *Babar Ahmad and others v UK*.[57] The applicants faced detention at a US 'supermax' prison (ADX Florence) and would be subject to 'special administrative measures', and argued that if sentenced they would receive life imprisonment. The Court was also presented with the opportunity to clarify the relationship between *Soering* and *Chahal*, and whether extradition proceedings could be regarded as distinct from other forms of removal. The Court rejected the idea of the application of different tests, confirmed that no distinction was to be made regarding the forms of ill-treatment for the assessment of the risk, and acknowledged the departure that had taken place in its jurisprudence from

55 Cf. *Labsi v Slovakia* (App no 33809/08), 15 May 2012, where the Court identified deficiencies in the assurances provided by the Algerian government.

56 Ibid. para 285.

57 *Babar Ahmad and others v UK* (App nos 24027/07, 11949/08, 36742/08, 66911/09 and 67354/09), 24 September 2012 final. For critical comment on *Babar Ahmad* see Mavronicola, N and Messineo, F, 'Relatively Absolute? The Undermining of Article 3 ECHR in *Ahmad v UK*' (2013) 76 *Modern Law Review* 589–619. On extradition, and the principles applied by the Court, see *Ergashev v Russia* (App no 12106/09), 4 June 2012 final and *Iskandarov v Russia* (App no 17185/05), 21 February 2011 final. For the approach of the Court to extraordinary rendition see: *El Masri v The Former Yugoslav Republic of Macedonia* (App no 39630/09) 13 December 2012 (GC).

Soering.[58] The Court will use the same test in all return cases, which will be applied equally to Article 3 forms of ill-treatment (in this case the Court found there would be no breach if returned). The Court expressly linked its argument to emergent human rights trends, such as the approach of the UN Human Rights Committee to Article 7 ICCPR, and Article 19 of the EU Charter of Fundamental Rights.[59]

In *A v the Netherlands* the applicant argued that his expulsion to Libya (based on a governmental belief that he was a threat to national security) would violate Article 3 because of his involvement with opposition groups there, and his high-profile trial in the Netherlands (and again other governments intervened in the case to repeat concerns about the Court's approach).[60] This provided another opportunity for the Court to 'once more' underline its position on Article 3, and again acknowledge that 'it is acutely conscious of the difficulties faced by States in protecting their populations from terrorist violence'.[61] The applicant feared he would be detained and ill-treated on return because of his political activities. The Court here placed particular emphasis on the media attention his trial in the Netherlands had attracted, and the fact that his removal had been highlighted to the Libyan authorities.[62] On this basis it was prepared to conclude that it was 'sufficiently plausible … that the applicant would be identified and detained for questioning after his arrival in Libya' and thus a real risk existed.[63]

In *Al Hanchi v Bosnia and Herzegovina* the applicant was a foreign Mujahedin fighter from Tunisian who had travelled to Bosnia and Herzegovina during the conflict from 1992–95.[64] He remained there and was married with two children. However, his deportation was sought in 2009 and his return to Tunisia was sought. The applicant's argument was that those in his position were regarded as suspected terrorists in Tunisia and treated accordingly – he thus feared Article 3 ill-treatment. The case coincided with the democratic transition then taking place and the replacement of the former regime; thus the country of origin conditions were changing.[65] As a consequence of this, and the view that 'there is no indication, let alone proof, that Islamists, as a group, have been systematically targeted after the change of regime'. The Court concluded there would be no breach of Article 3 on return.[66] In *Al Husin v Bosnia and Herzegovina* again the applicant was a foreign Mujahedin fighter from Syria who now faced deportation.[67] He claimed that he

58 *Babar Ahmad* para 173.

59 *Babar Ahmad* para 175.

60 *A v the Netherlands* (App no 4900/06), 20th October 2012 final. The governments of Lithuania, Portugal, Slovakia and the UK were third party interveners and submitted joint comments.

61 *A v the Netherlands* para 143.

62 *A v the Netherlands* paras 148–9.

63 *A v the Netherlands* para 149.

64 *Al Hanchi v Bosnia and Herzegovina* (App no 48205/09), 4 June 2012 final.

65 *Al Hanchi* para 43.

66 *Al Hanchi* paras 44–5.

67 *Al Husin v Bosnia Herzegovina* (App no 3727/08), 9 July 2012 final.

would be ill-treated upon return as a member of the Muslim Brotherhood or as an Islamist.[68] In concluding that there was a real risk of Article 3 ill-treatment, the Court noted the deteriorating situation in Syria, that the domestic authorities had not paid sufficient attention to the nature of the Mujahedin organization he had belonged to, that he had a high profile (worsened by being wrongly identified as Abu Hamza in a US State Department report) and he had produced direct evidence that the Syrian security services were interested in speaking with him on return.[69]

In *Auad v Bulgaria* the applicant was born in a Palestinian refugee camp in Lebanon.[70] His deportation from Bulgaria was sought on national security grounds. The Court wished again here to reassure governments that it 'considers it legitimate for Contracting States to take a firm stand against those who contribute to terrorist acts, which it cannot condone in any circumstances'.[71] But it stressed that 'any considerations … to do with the question whether the applicant presents a risk to the national security of Bulgaria are irrelevant for the Court's examination'.[72] The Court was particularly critical of the Supreme Administrative Court in Bulgaria, which had not undertaken any assessment of the risk on return,[73] as well as being sceptical about aspects of the evidence provided by the Bulgarian government.[74] In finding a potential breach of Article 3, the Court accepted that the applicant might be safe in other parts of Lebanon. However, it noted that the applicant was a stateless Palestinian, who might well be returned to the refugee camp he had fled from, and the position there remained volatile.[75] The case is once again illustrative of the sort of domestic safeguards the Court expects to be in place in order to find Article 3 compliance. Even where national security is raised the Court will continue to insist on rigorous and independent assessment of the nature of the risk.

Return, Interception and Jurisdiction?

M.S.S. v Belgium and Greece offers a reminder of the importance of human rights protection even in the intra-European context of supranational EU law and policy.[76]

---

68 *Al Husin* para 23.

69 *Al Husin* paras 53–4.

70 *Auad v Bulgaria* (App no 46390/10), 11 January 2012 final.

71 *Auad* para 95.

72 *Auad* para 101. See also, *Labsi v Slovakia* (App no 33809/08), 15th May 2012.

73 *Auad* para 101. 'In light of the domestic court's failings, it falls to the Court to assess the question of risk …'

74 *Auad* para 104.

75 *Auad* para 103.

76 *M.S.S. v Greece and Belgium* (App no 30696/09), 21 January 2011 (GC). Cf. *N.S. and M.E.* above n 9. For comment see, V Morena-Lax, 'Dismantling the Dublin System: *M.S.S. v Belgium and Greece*' (2012) 14 European Journal of Migration and Law 1; M Bossuyt, 'Belgium Condemned for Inhuman or Degrading Treatment Due to Violations by Greece of EU Asylum Law' (2011) European Human Rights Law Review 582. For an

A central feature of the EU Common European Asylum System (CEAS) is the attempt to attribute and allocate State responsibility for the assessment of asylum applications ('Dublin Regulation').[77] The purpose is to prevent what is sometimes unhelpfully termed 'asylum shopping' and move to a system where one Member State will take responsibility for a claimant, on the basis of a prescribed list of objective criteria. In this case, the applicant travelled from Afghanistan to Belgium via Greece (where his fingerprints had been taken). Belgium opted to return him (to Greece) and it was this action, and his subsequent treatment, that formed the basis for the application. The Court's analysis of his detention and living conditions in Greece – and the decision to find violations of Article 3 (and of Article 3 taken with Article 13) – is replete with reflections on the dignified treatment of all human persons.[78] The Court was willing to conclude that his position of 'extreme poverty' rendered him 'unable to cater for his most basic needs: food, hygiene and a place to live' and thus amounted to be breach of Article 3.[79]

The other major question focused on the decision of Belgium to send the applicant to Greece. Given the problems identified with the Greek asylum system, did removal constitute a breach of Articles 2 and 3? In its earlier cases (*T.I. v UK*[80] and *K.R.S. v UK*[81]) the Court had stressed that States remained responsible for Convention compliance in such circumstances, even in the context of the new supranational 'Dublin system'; but in both earlier cases (return to Germany, and to Greece) it was held there was no violation of Convention rights. In this instance, however, the Court formed a different view, concluding that 'at the time of the applicant's expulsion the Belgian authorities knew or ought to have known that he had no guarantee that his asylum application would be seriously examined by the Greek authorities'.[82] Crucial here was the weight of evidence available about the situation in Greece, including UNHCR's call for the suspension of transfers, and the fact that the authorities entertained no opportunity for an exception to be

example of the Court's approach to return to another State party to the Convention (Russian Federation) see *Bajsultanov v Austria* (App no 54131/10), 12 June 2012.

77 European Council, 'Regulation No 343/2003 establishing the criteria and mechanisms for determining the Member State responsible for examining an asylum application lodged in one of the Member States by a third-country national', OJ L50/1 (18 February 2003). See now: *Dublin Regulation*: Regulation (EU) No 604/2013 of the European Parliament and of the Council of 26 June 2013 establishing the criteria and mechanisms for determining the Member State responsible for examining an application for international protection lodged in one of the Member States by a third-country national or a stateless person OJ L 180/31 (26 June 2013).

78 Above n 76 para 221, detention conditions must be 'compatible with human dignity', see also para 263, 'The Court considers that the applicant has been the victim of humiliating treatment showing lack of respect for his dignity …'

79 Above n 76 para 254.

80 *T.I. v UK* (App no 43844/98), 7 March 2000.

81 *K.R.S. v UK* (App no 32733/08), 2 December 2008.

82 Above n 76, para 358.

made. Thus there appeared to be ample evidence to suggest that any automatically generated presumption of compliance could be straightforwardly rebutted. In exposing the applicant to the conditions noted above in Greece, the Court found Belgium in breach of Article 3, and the deficiencies of the challenge mechanism also resulted in a negative finding on Article 13. The broad ambition of securing a common system will therefore not determine the outcome in particular cases; reliance on the discharge of obligations by others cannot be presumed in a blanket way.

Another practical example of the Article 3 approach is *Hirsi Jamaa and others v Italy*.[83] The case involved a challenge to Italy's 'push-back' policy of intercepting asylum seekers at sea and returning them to Libya. Interception or interdiction at sea is not new, but this case presented an opportunity for the Grand Chamber of the European Court to make an assessment of its Convention compliance.[84] The applicants were 11 Somali nationals and 13 Eritrean nationals, and the case involved alleged breaches of Article 3, Article 4 of Protocol No 4 and Article 13. Given the nature of the interception policy the question of jurisdiction under Article 1 arose, with the Court concluding that this was indeed an exercise of jurisdiction by Italy (events took place on board military ships that were within Italian jurisdiction). The Article 3 question related to return to Libya, as well as the risk of being arbitrarily repatriated to Eritrea and Somalia. On these questions the Court found breaches of Article 3; the Italian authorities knew, or should have known, that there was a real risk that the applicants would be returned to their country of origin. Italy was also held to have violated Article 4 of Protocol No 4 and Article 13.

Socio-economic Rights and Asylum

Does return of a person to appalling socio-economic conditions give rise to a breach of Article 3? As noted in *M.S.S.* the court held that return to 'extreme poverty' in another Member State of the EU could result in an Article 3 breach. The Court has indicated for some time that such conditions elsewhere may raise issues for signatory States to the Convention. In *D v UK* the issue was the impact of the loss of medical treatment in the UK if the applicant (whose removal was sought for drug offences) was returned to St Kitts.[85] The applicant argued that he had no

83 (App no 27765/09), 23 February 2012 (GC).

84 See T Gammeltoft-Hansen, *Access to Asylum: International Refugee Law and the Globalisation of Migration Control* (Cambridge University Press, 2011) for a comprehensive examination of the right to seek asylum in a context where responsibility is often 'outsourced' and control exercised extra-territorially. Also see GS Goodwin-Gill, 'The Right to Seek Asylum: Interception at Sea and the Principle of *Non-Refoulement*' (2011) 23 International Journal of Refugee Law 443.

85 *D v UK* (App no 30240/96), 20 May 1997.

support available in St Kitts and that his life expectancy would be considerably shortened, and this would occur in conditions which would themselves be inhuman and degrading.[86] In finding a breach of Article 3 the Court attached particular significance to the applicant's personal situation and his medical condition. It stressed that this was an exceptional case; the applicant was in the advanced stages of his illness and that the 'abrupt withdrawal of these facilities will entail the most dramatic consequences for him' and his would be subject to additional 'acute mental and physical suffering'.[87] Since this case the Court has further underlined the highly exceptional nature of the circumstances and how narrowly this principle is applied. In *N v UK* the Grand Chamber confirmed the particular basis of the earlier decision.[88] The case involved possible return to Uganda of a woman seriously ill with HIV/AIDS.[89] The Court set out the principles applied to these cases: an entitlement to remain did not exist 'to continue to benefit from medical, social or other forms of assistance and services';[90] a reduction in life expectancy would not be enough; removal to a country with inferior medical services will only raise an issue in 'a very exceptional case, where humanitarian grounds against the removal are compelling'.[91] The Court indicated that in *D*, 'the applicant was critically ill and appeared to be close to death, could not be guaranteed any nursing or medical care in his country of origin and had no family there willing or able to care for him or provide him with even a basic level of food, shelter or social support'.[92] The Court went on to conclude:

> The Court does not exclude that there may be other very exceptional cases where the humanitarian considerations are equally compelling. However, it considers that it should maintain the high threshold set in *D v. the United Kingdom* and applied in its subsequent case-law, which it regards as correct in principle, given that in such cases the alleged future harm would emanate not from the intentional acts or omissions of public authorities or non-State bodies, but instead from a naturally occurring illness and the lack of sufficient resources to deal with it in the receiving country.[93]

86 *D v UK* paras 40–41.

87 *D v UK* para 52.

88 *N v UK* (App no 26565/05), 27 May 2008 (GC).

89 *N v UK* para 45: '… the Court observes that, although the present application, in common with most of those referred to above, is concerned with the expulsion of a person with an HIV and AIDS-related condition, the same principles must apply in relation to the expulsion of any person afflicted with any serious, naturally occurring physical or mental illness which may cause suffering, pain and reduced life expectancy and require specialised medical treatment which may not be so readily available in the applicant's country of origin of which may be available only at substantial cost'.

90 *N v UK* para 42.

91 *N v UK* para 42.

92 *N v UK* para 42.

93 *N v UK* para 43.

In underlining further the exceptional nature of protection the Court reconfirmed that the 'Convention is essentially directed at the protection of civil and political rights'. Given the 'fair balance' of the system and the global disparities in healthcare:

> Article 3 does not place an obligation on the Contracting State to alleviate such disparities through the provision of free and unlimited health care to all aliens without a right to stay within its jurisdiction. A finding to the contrary would place too great a burden on the Contracting States.[94]

The case reveals once again a cautious cou rt that is acutely conscious of context. First, the Court is careful to note that the claim does not relate to a 'risk of deliberate, politically motivated, ill-treatment' and is 'based solely on her medical condition'.[95] The fact that she was not presently 'critically ill' was relevant and assessment of her plight in Uganda would be speculative.[96] The Court thus concluded that this was not an exceptional case and there would be no breach of Article 3.[97]

Detention

What about the conditions of detention of those facing expulsion? Article 5 addresses the right to liberty and security of the person, but Article 3 also speaks to detention. In *Ergashevv Russia*[98] the applicant argued that the conditions of his detention in a police station, in a remand centre and transportation to a court – pending his extradition to Uzbekistan – breached Article 3.[99] The Court reiterated its established approach:

> In accordance with Article 3 of the Convention, the State must ensure that a person is detained under conditions which are compatible with respect for his human dignity and that the manner and method of the execution of the measure do not subject him to distress or hardship exceeding the unavoidable level of suffering inherent in detention …

In finding a breach of Article 3 the Court (in relation to two specific instances at the police station and remand centre) attached weight to the following: the applicant was held for four days in a cell designed for short-term detention with inadequate facilities (for use for not more than three hours, and lacked a toilet or a sink); reliance was on relatives to provide food, and basic needs had not been taken care

94 *N v UK* para 44.
95 *N v UK* para 46.
96 *N v UK* para 50.
97 *N v UK* para 51.
98 *Ergashev* para 128.
99 See above n 57.

of; in the remand centre, the applicant was forced to share the same cell with a large number of others for over five months.[100] It is apparent that the conditions in which those facing removal are held may give rise to a breach of Article 3.

Conclusion

The aim of this chapter is to examine aspects of the relevance of Article 3 to the protection of refugees and asylum seekers. This human rights guarantee has evolved through interpretation to include cases of deportation and the foreseeable consequences of return. The suggestion in this chapter is that the general discussion of Article 3 can occasionally be misleading; it cannot credibly be argued that the Court has now opened the gates of Europe to the oppressed of the world or that it has been thoughtless or irresponsible in its approach. Yes, Article 3 is 'absolute' in the sense that no textual limitations are there and no derogations are permitted. The Court has nevertheless carefully and intentionally delimited the scope of protection; successfully establishing a 'real risk' is not straightforward, and the interpretative battles fought across Europe are evident in the recent jurisprudence of the Court.

Should we be surprised? This is what courts do, so the fact is of less interest than how the Court constructs the contours of Article 3. The principles are now there and well-established, but insight can only be gained by assessing some of the leading cases in depth, and thinking about how the Court has carved out the legal boundaries. This chapter includes practical examples from the Article 3 jurisprudence to give a flavour of the Court's evolving approach. The limitations of refugee law should be fully noted and acknowledged, but care must also be taken to appreciate the opportunities and constraints offered by Article 3. As new forms of protection emerge in a European context, anchored around existing human rights guarantees, the continuing significance of refugee status (even with its limitations) should not be underestimated. Article 3 of the European Convention will evolve but it will only ever be able to do what is possible within the legal and practical constraints of contestation.

References

Battjes H, 'The *Soering* Threshold: Why Only Fundamental Values Prohibit *Refoulement* in ECHR Case Law' (2009) 11 *European Journal of Migration and Law* 205.

Bossuyt M, 'Belgium Condemned for Inhuman or Degrading Treatment Due to Violations by Greece of EU Asylum Law' (2011) European Human Rights Law Review 582.

100 *Ergashev* paras 126–43.

Duffy A, 'Expulsion to Torture? *Non-refoulement* in International Law' (2008) 20 International Journal of Refugee Law 373.
Gammeltoft-Hansen T, *Access to Asylum: International Refugee Law and the Globalisation of Migration Control* (Cambridge University Press, 2011).
Goodwin-Gill G, 'The Right to Seek Asylum: Interception at Sea and the Principle of *Non-Refoulement*' (2011) 23 International Journal of Refugee Law 443.
Goodwin-Gill GS and McAdam J, *The Refugee in International Law* (3rd edn, Oxford University Press, 2007) 310–16.
den Heijer M, 'Whose Rights and Which Rights? The Continuing Story of *Non-Refoulement* in ECHR Case Law' (2008) 10 European Journal of Migration and Law 277.
Mavronicola N and Messineo F, 'Relatively Absolute? The Undermining of Article 3 ECHR in *Ahmad v UK*' (2013) 76 Modern Law Review 589–619.
Morena-Lax V, 'Dismantling the Dublin System: *M.S.S. v. Belgium and Greece*' (2012) 14 European Journal of Migration and Law 1.

Chapter 9
'The Right to have Rights': the European Convention on Human Rights and the Procedural Rights of Asylum Seekers

Gina Clayton

Introduction

In his concurring opinion in *Hirsi Jamaa and others v Italy*, Judge Pinto de Albuquerque said '[t]he ultimate question in this case is how Europe should recognize that refugees have "the right to have rights"'.[1] This is the question addressed in this chapter. As European states develop increasingly sophisticated procedures for deterring asylum claims, how does Convention law protect access to an asylum determination process, or the capacity of that process to deliver protection from serious harm? How far is the Strasbourg Court able to go in responding to risks and obstacles encountered in the asylum process, given that seeking asylum is not mentioned in the European Convention on Human Rights (ECHR)?

Asylum Seekers as Foreign Nationals within the Purpose and Jurisdiction of the ECHR

The ECHR is an international agreement between the Member States of the Council of Europe, now numbering 47. The Council was part of a European movement after the Second World War to secure peace and prevent recurrence of the war's atrocities. It was based upon the conviction that 'the pursuit of peace based upon justice and international co-operation is vital for the preservation of human society and civilisation'.[2] The Convention, opened for signature in late 1950, was one vehicle by which the Council sought to realize aspirations for stronger inter-State cooperation and the protection of individuals against oppression.

Treatment of the stranger was not uppermost in the minds of drafters. It was a 'European Bill of Rights' and 'the principal bulwark for safeguarding [the member states'] common heritage of political traditions, of ideals, of freedom

1 (App no 27765/09), judgment 23 February 2012.

2 Preamble to the Statute of the Council of Europe, ETS 1 (5 May 1949).

and of respect for the rule of law'.[3] The Convention provided for an inter-State mechanism, so that one Member State could challenge another before the Court. The individual right of petition and the creation of a Court to adjudicate on complaints of violations gave effect to the political impetus for the Convention by supporting the dignity of the individual, and giving means of redress against state oppression. The post-war states were concerned with bringing hidden oppressive practices to light and creating a culture of mutual accountability.[4] The nature of the *espace juridique* – the 'legal space' within which the Convention rights are assured[5] – was not in essence a large private space which excluded others. It was a large public space in which the actions of each State would be visible to all.

Although the treatment of the stranger who might present themselves at the gates of this new Europe was not high on the agenda, the *travaux preparatoires* show that the focus on Europe was not based on excluding others. Rather, the drafters took an inclusive approach based on the values and purpose of the Convention, not on membership. They emphasized the universality and enforceability of the rights, and concluded that nationality of Member States was not a requirement to benefit from the Convention. The qualification 'living in' or 'residing in' the contracting states was rejected in favour of the qualifier 'within the jurisdiction'. The aim was to 'widen as far as possible the categories of persons who are to benefit by the guarantee contained in the Convention'.[6] The wording adopted could include even those 'not considered as residing there in the legal sense of the word'.[7]

Although these principles suggest that asylum seekers are close to the original purpose of the Convention, and are protected by virtue of their humanity not their nationality, as foreign nationals seeking entry asylum seekers face two major hurdles. Firstly, if they are not yet physically within the border, States may argue that they are not within the jurisdiction. Secondly, States have repeatedly argued that their decisions on entry and expulsion of foreign nationals are an exercise of sovereign power, and as such out of reach of the Convention. Although this claim was conclusively rejected by the Court in the case of *Abdulaziz, Cabales and Balkandali v UK* (1985) 7 EHRR 471, it persists in various forms, governments explicitly or implicitly arguing that human rights do not apply to decisions

3 J Sharpe (ed.), *The Conscience of Europe: 50 Years of the European Court of Human Rights* (Third Millenium Publishing Ltd, Council of Europe Publishing, 2010) 25; quoting Sir Humphrey Waldock, an early President of the Court and of the Commission.

4 See for example Lord Layton UK at TP II, 46 or Rep 1949 IV, 1184, ECHR Travaux ART1-COUR (77) 9, 26.

5 *Bankovic v Belgium and others* (App no. 52207/99), judgment 19 December 2001 and *Al-Skeini v UK* (App no 55721/07), judgment 7 July 2011.

6 ECHR Travaux-ART1-COUR (77) 9, 34, Report of the Sub-Committee instructed to make a preliminary study of the amendments proposed by the members of the Committee of Experts (5 February 1950) (1).

7 ECHR Travaux-ART1-COUR (77) 9, 49.

on entry, or that if they do they are weak and advisory, taking second place to immigration restrictions.

In considering the procedures applicable to asylum seekers, the Strasbourg Court generally rejects this approach. The exception is in relation to detention where it is arguable that deference to immigration procedures has influenced the Court.[8] The ECtHR has accepted that asylum seekers enter the territory as 'unauthorized' because they are not yet authorized.[9] This means that their detention is lawful pursuant to Article 5.1(f). That detention is still subject to human rights supervision and, by virtue of its duration or the conditions of detention, it may still found an application to the ECtHR for breach of other articles, but the detention of asylum-seeking adults *per se* on arrival is lawful within the Convention.[10] Like other foreign nationals, an asylum seeker in detention does not obtain equality with nationals in delivery of Convention rights.[11]

However, detention *per se* does not create a risk of *refoulement*. This is the Court's main concern in examining asylum procedures. The Court:

> … does not itself examine the actual asylum applications or verify how the States honour their obligations under the Geneva Convention. Its main concern is whether effective guarantees exist that protect the applicant against arbitrary *refoulement*, be it direct or indirect, to the country from which he or she has fled (*MSS v Belgium and Greece* para 286).

The obligation of *non-refoulement*, that is, to not expel someone to persecution or inhuman treatment, is fundamental to both the Refugee Convention (Article 33) and the ECHR (Article 3), and the Strasbourg Court in its extensive jurisprudence on Article 13 has emphasized the connection between procedural failings and *refoulement*. The deference to immigration control seen in *Saadi v UK* is not repeated when the question is one of access to an asylum determination procedure, without which there can be no guarantee of *non-refoulement*.

International human rights law supports the application of human rights norms to decisions on entry and expulsion. The Universal Declaration of Human Rights Article 14 and the EU Charter of Fundamental Rights Article 18 give a right to seek asylum, though not a right of entry to the territory. But if the right to *seek* asylum is obstructed, these Articles are violated. Lambert considers that in cases before the International Court of Justice States' power to admit and remove

8 *Saadi v UK* (App no 13229/03), judgment 29 January 2008.

9 See above *Saadi v UK* n 8.

10 Since *Saadi v UK* the Court has taken a robust attitude to the detention of asylum-seeking children, arguably outlawing such detention completely: *Popov v France* (App no 39472/07 and 39474/07), judgment 19 January 2012.

11 See for restrictions on the rights of resident foreign nationals H Lambert, *The Position of Aliens in Relation to the European Convention on Human Rights* (Council of Europe Publishing, 2007).

foreign nationals must be exercised within the rule of law, 'i.e. it must be in conformity with basic standards such as fairness and non-discrimination, and it must not clash with other individuals' basic human rights, such as family reunion, *non-refoulement*, and prohibition of torture or degrading treatment'.[12] Although the Strasbourg Court cannot adjudicate on the fulfilment of other international obligations,[13] it must ensure that application of the Convention does not derogate from rights and freedoms enshrined in other agreements (Article 53). These treaty obligations also affirm that immigration control is subject to human rights, not the other way round.

The Growing Significance of Procedural Issues in Asylum Claims

A would-be asylum seeker in Europe now faces enormous procedural hurdles in attempting to make their claim.[14] These include sanctions against carriers who transport undocumented or clandestine passengers, compulsory visa requirements for entry, technology to detect hidden passengers, digitally produced and screened travel documents, the deployment of immigration liaison officers and pre-entry procedures such as juxtaposed controls or interception at sea. Since entry to a country of refuge may not be authorized in advance for the purpose of seeking asylum, asylum seekers are vulnerable to not reaching or crossing the border of their destination country by falling foul of these prevention mechanisms.

In addition to laws and practices which may deny access to the country of refuge, procedures within that country may also be inaccessible or inadequate, with a resulting risk of *refoulement*.[15] In-country practices which create these risks may include:

> ... accelerated procedures, with the attendant risk of inadequate time for proper consideration and representation;
> lack of information about how to claim asylum, including misleading information, lack of transparency and poor or no interpretation;
> application requirements which cannot in practice be fulfilled;

12 See Lambert, *The Position of Aliens in Relation to the European Convention on Human Rights* 12.

13 This has been reiterated in recent cases in which alleged breaches of EU Asylum Directives have formed part of the legal and factual background to a claim before the ECtHR. See for instance *MSS v Belgium and Greece* (App no 30696/09), judgment 21 January 2011.

14 As described in for example SA Lomba, *The Right to Seek Refugee Status in the European Union* (Intersentia, 2004), 106 et seq.

15 See for example *IM v France* (App no 9152/09), judgment 2 February 2012 in which the ECtHR held that the main question in the context of examining an alleged breach of Art 13 in respect of a claim for asylum is whether the procedure protects the refugee from *refoulement*.

returning a passenger to a third country which is automatically regarded as safe, without scrutiny of objections;
appeals that do not automatically suspend removal while they are being heard;
lack of opportunity to challenge the application of accelerated procedures or non-suspensive appeals.

The Council of Europe's Human Rights Commissioner has made recommendations to address these obstacles

1. Everyone has the right, on arrival at the border of a member state, to be treated with respect for his or her human dignity rather than automatically considered to be a criminal or guilty of fraud.
2. On arrival, everyone whose right of entry is disputed must be given a hearing, where necessary with the help of an interpreter whose fees must be met by the country of arrival, in order to be able, where appropriate, to lodge a request for asylum. This must entail the right to open a file after having being duly informed, in a language which he or she understands, about the procedure to be followed. The practice of *refoulement* 'at the arrival gate' thus becomes unacceptable.[16]

More recently, the Council of Europe Parliamentary Assembly resolution 1821 (2011) on the interception and rescue at sea of asylum seekers, refugees and irregular migrants called on member states to 'guarantee access to protection and assistance, including to asylum procedures'. Spijkerboer (2009) refers to 'the tendency of European States to try to sidestep the substance of asylum claims by means of procedural sophistication'.[17] He argues that the ECtHR must engage more fully with the detail of asylum claims in order to be able to step back to its proper role as a supervisory court, and not a court of first instance. This is not only because of the procedural sophistication of governments, but also because of the 'passivity of national courts'.[18] Spijkerboer argues that the Strasbourg Court must force national courts to take a more active role.

The ECtHR has been considering its own procedural reforms in order to contain its increasingly unmanageable workload. The increase in workload is exceptionally high in immigration and asylum cases: in February 2011 that there had been a 4,000% increase over four years in applications for interim measures

16 Comm DH (2001) 19, Recommendation of the Commissioner for Human Rights concerning the rights of aliens wishing to enter a Council of Europe Member State and the enforcement of expulsion orders (Council of Europe 2001) 19.

17 T Spijkerboer, '"Subsidiarity" and "Arguability": the European Court of Human Rights Case Law on Judicial Review in Asylum Claims' (2009) 21(1) International Journal of Refugee Law 49.

18 See Spijkerboer, '"Subsidiarity" and "Arguability"' 17.

under Rule 39 to suspend deportation, extradition or expulsion proceedings.[19] If Spijkerboer is right, this tide of applications cannot be stemmed unless the Strasbourg Court steps in to establish the more proactive stance that human rights law requires. The procedural manoeuvres of governments, including pre-entry deflection, on-entry deterrence and restrictive appeal rights, have taken the struggle for human rights protection into the procedural arena. The Court in its most recent judgments is increasingly interventionist, demonstrating that protection against human rights abuses entails, in the case of threatened expulsions, the right to an effective remedy.

Effective Remedies for Asylum Seekers

Article 13 of the ECHR is the article which expressly guarantees the right to an effective remedy for breaches of other Convention rights. In addition, procedural rights and access to a procedure for asylum seekers may be derived from Protocol 4 Article 4, which prohibits the collective expulsion of aliens, and Article 3 itself – the prohibition on torture and inhuman and degrading treatment or punishment – also has procedural implications.

Article 13 provides that:

> Everyone whose rights and freedoms as set forth in this Convention are violated shall have an effective remedy before a national authority notwithstanding that the violation has been committed by persons acting in an official capacity.

Case law has established a number of principles in applying Article 13. These are relevant also in obtaining access to the Strasbourg Court, as for an application to be treated as admissible the applicant must have exhausted all available remedies that would be effective.

The starting point for requiring an effective remedy is simply that there is an 'arguable complaint' under one of the other articles. This is not a demanding standard, in order to meet the obligation of *non-refoulement*. The responsibility to assess any risk is that of the receiving government, and the Court's primary concern 'is whether effective guarantees exist in the present case to protect the applicant against arbitrary removal directly or indirectly back to his country of origin' (*MSS v Belgium and Greece* para 298).

A key principle in a case of threatened removal is that the remedy must be capable of suspending removal pending consideration of the claim (*Gebremedhin [Gaberamadhien] v France*).[20] For instance in *Abdolkhani and Karimnia v Turkey*

19 Human Rights Europe, *Rule 39 ECHR immigration appeals rise by 4,000 per cent* (February 11 2011), available at http://www.humanrightseurope.org/2011/02/rule-39-echr-immigration-appeals-rise-by-4000-per-cent/.

20 (App no 25389/05), judgment 26 April 2007.

the Court held since an application to the administrative courts, pursuant to Article 125 of the Constitution, seeking the annulment of a deportation order did not have automatic suspensive effect, this was not a remedy the applicants were required to exhaust in order to apply to the ECtHR. In this case the applicants had not even been served with deportation orders and so there was no application they could make.

It is settled law that a remedy which satisfies Article 13 does not mean a remedy that is bound to succeed (*Salah Sheekh v Netherlands*[21] para 154). In this case the Court held that the applicant's removal to Somalia would breach Article 3, but that there was a judicial authority which had the capacity to suspend the removal pending consideration of his claim, and this was sufficient to satisfy Article 13. Accordingly there was no breach of Article 13. In the same case the Court held that if a remedy is bound to fail, the applicant is not required to exhaust it before applying to Strasbourg (*Salah Sheekh v Netherlands* para 121).

Article 6, the right to a fair trial in criminal matters and to a fair hearing in determination of civil rights and obligations, has been held by the Grand Chamber of the ECtHR not to apply in immigration and asylum matters.[22] Article 6 contains specific requirements of a fair hearing. Article 13 does not contain any such provisions, but its principle, of the requirement of an effective remedy, is flexible. Article 6 requires access to a court. Article 13 allows that the remedy can be of any kind within the domestic system, provided it gives the necessary protection against *refoulement*. The remedy can be administrative or judicial provided it is able to 'deal with the substance of the relevant Convention complaint and to grant appropriate relief'.[23]

Unlike Article 6, in jurisprudence on Article 13, the concept of 'fairness' is not pursued. The question that the Court is addressing is not whether there is even-handedness between the parties, but whether the procedure provides protection against *refoulement*. Protection against *refoulement* requires not only suspensive effect but also 'independent and rigorous scrutiny of a claim that there exist substantial grounds for believing that there was a real risk of treatment contrary to Article 3 in the event of the applicant's expulsion to the country of destination'.[24] This requirement enables the Strasbourg Court to examine the quality of the decision-making process in order to ascertain whether it can in fact deliver protection. The Court can examine not only judicial processes, but also the day-to-day decision-making of government agents at borders and in offices.

The cases discussed below also show how the Court has also been flexible in its use of Article 3 to address procedural failings which result in risk of *refoulement*. Protocol 4 Article 4, prohibiting a large-scale abuse, was for a long time a little

---

21 (App no 1948/04), judgment 11 January 2007.

22 *Maaouia v France* (App no 39652/98), judgment 5 October 2000.

23 *Abdolkhani and Karimnia v Turkey* (App no 30471/08), judgment 22 September 2009.

24 See *Abdolkhani and Karimnia* above n 23.

used Article. However, as discussed below, this essentially procedural provision has been invoked with great effect before the Grand Chamber.

Scope and Quality of Decision-making Process

In order for a judicial remedy to be effective, the judicial body must have jurisdiction to consider the substance of the case in sufficient detail that the risk of *refoulement* is avoided. A clear example is that of *Jabari v Turkey*[25] in which the Court found a breach of Article 13 because the powers of the Ankara Administrative Court were limited to judicial review of the formal legality of the order for Ms Jabari's expulsion from Turkey. It would not consider the substance of the applicant's fears, for which there was compelling evidence.

By comparison in *Vilvarajah v UK*[26] the Court held that judicial review was an effective remedy for two refused asylum seekers to argue their case against return to Sri Lanka. They had no right of appeal against the decision, but the Court held that, although the High Court in judicial review could not examine the merits of the case, it would subject their claim to 'anxious scrutiny', and this was sufficient to constitute an effective remedy. The effectiveness of judicial review in the UK, a procedure whereby the merits of the case are not considered, has continued to be challenged before the ECtHR.[27] To date *Vilvarajah* has not been overturned.

The Strasbourg Court considers the existence of formal jurisdiction but also whether in practical reality that jurisdiction will be exercised. In *MSS v Belgium and Greece* the quality of a judicial process was held to be ineffective because the system in Greece was dysfunctional. An application could be made for judicial review of the refusal of the asylum claim, but this did not prevent the applicant from being removed. An appeal could be lodged against an expulsion order which would follow the refusal, and this would automatically suspend his expulsion. However, the malfunctions in communication between the authorities and the applicant gave the Court no confidence that he would have heard of the rejection of his application in time to lodge any appeal. In addition he had received no information about organizations, offering legal advice, and there was a shortage of lawyers.

While a favourable outcome is not a requirement of an effective remedy, the Court has also held that if there is no prospect of redress this is relevant to the effectiveness of a remedy. *MSS v Belgium and Greece* concerned a challenge to the implementation of the EU's so-called Dublin regulation which provides for

25 (App no 40035/98), judgment 11 July 2000.

26 (App no 45/1990/236/302-306), judgment 26 September 1991.

27 UN High Commissioner for Refugees (UNHCR), Statement of the right to an effective remedy in relation to accelerated asylum procedures, issued in the context of the preliminary ruling reference to the Court of Justice of the EU from the Luxembourg Administrative Tribunal regarding the interpretation of Art 39, Asylum procedures Directive, and Arts 6 and 13 ECH (UN High Commissioner for Refugees, 2010).

which Member State of the EU should take responsibility for an asylum claim.[28] In this case the application of the regulation in Belgium required the asylum applicant to return to Greece, the country through which he first entered Europe. The Court found that the Belgian system did provide for a request to be made to suspend enforcement of MSS' removal under the 'extremely urgent procedure', but the burden of proof applied in these cases was raised to such a level that it operated in effect as a deterrent to the proper examination of the complaint (para 389 of the *MSS* judgment). In practice, the Aliens Appeal Board, to whom the applications were made, systematically found that there was no 'irreparable damage' in proceeding with a removal because it could be presumed that Greece, the destination country pursuant to the EU's Dublin regulation, would fulfil its international obligations. In *MSS*' case, the application was scheduled for hearing one hour after it was lodged. His lawyer was 130km away and could not possibly attend. There was a legal aid office but it was not within their remit to represent in such a situation. The Belgian government agreed with MSS that there was virtually no chance of success in an application to the Aliens Appeal Board to suspend the removal. The Strasbourg Court remarked that 'while the effectiveness of a remedy does not depend on the certainty of a favourable outcome for the applicant, the lack of any prospect of obtaining adequate redress raises an issue under Article 13 (see *Kudla*, cited above, § 157)' (para 394). The Court found that Article 13 had been violated (para 396).

The obligation of *non-refoulement* requires that, in the face of a claim for protection, the authorities of the receiving state must enquire into it. In *Abdolkhani and Karimnia*, discussed below, the Court was

> … struck by the fact that both the administrative and judicial authorities remained totally passive regarding the applicants' serious allegations of a risk of ill-treatment if returned to Iraq or Iran. It considers that the lack of any response by the national authorities regarding the applicants' allegations amounted to a lack of the 'rigorous scrutiny' that is required by Article 13 of the Convention (para 113).

This requirement of the Court for a proactive response to a claimed fear of ill-treatment is evident also in the recent groundbreaking case of *Hirsi Jamaa*, discussed below. An effective remedy is regarded by the Court as a positive responsibility, and a passive response is not sufficient.

Delay in judicial processes as evidenced in *MSS v Belgium and Greece* was held to contribute to a finding of violation of Article 13. The Court took into account evidence that proceedings to challenge expulsion could take anything

28 Council of the European Union, 'Council Regulation (EC) No 343/2003 of 18 February 2003 establishing the criteria and mechanisms for determining the Member State responsible for examining an asylum application lodged in one of the Member States by a third-country national', OJ L50, 25 (18 February 2003).

between 10 days and four years. In cases concerning ill treatment by State agents' swift action was important. Therefore the length of proceedings in itself caused them concern. In addition,

> ... such swift action is all the more necessary where, as in the present case, the person concerned has lodged a complaint under Article 3 in the event of his deportation, has no procedural guarantee that the merits of his complaint will be given serious consideration at first instance, statistically has virtually no chance of being offered any form of protection and lives in a state of precariousness that the Court has found to be contrary to Article 3 (para 320).

The Court's engagement with the quality of decision-making goes beyond scrutiny of formalities. To fulfil the obligation of *non-refoulement*, the Court may engage with the actual weight given to the evidence of the asylum seeker. This is a critical issue in refugee protection since the majority of asylum claims are turned down in national systems because the asylum seeker is not believed. The ECtHR's approach warrants separate treatment.

Credibility

The frequency of refusals of asylum in national systems on grounds of credibility is not simply a question of evidence but often derives from a culture of disbelief or of denial entrenched in the decision-making body. Decisions of the ECtHR in which that court engages with the national system's treatment of evidence and assessment of credibility are of critical importance since they have the potential to establish standards which could radically affect the lawfulness of national procedures.

In *Hilal v UK*,[29] the applicant had been tortured in Tanzania, but did not mention this in his initial interview which he was told was not for the purpose of giving detail, but just to lodge his claim. He gave full details at the second interview, but his credibility was then doubted because he had not mentioned torture at his first interview and because he had no corroborating evidence. He later produced a hospital report which verified precisely the injuries he claimed to have suffered and the plausibility of his account of how they happened, but his asylum claim was refused at all stages through the UK legal system on the basis that his credibility had been put in doubt, and the authenticity of the documents he produced was doubted apparently as a consequence. The ECtHR said:

> Though the Government have expressed doubts on the authenticity of the medical report, they have not provided any evidence to substantiate these doubts or to contradict the opinion provided by the applicant (para 63).

29 (App no 45276/99), judgment 6 March 2001.

The experience of Mr Hilal is not unusual in the asylum system in the UK and in other States that are parties to the Convention. A number of elements in the process can be identified. Firstly, Mr Hilal received information from officials which was misleading (that the initial interview was just to record the outline and basic details of his claim).

Secondly, Mr Hilal's personal account of atrocities was disbelieved. The government had nothing to set against his story other than the procedural issue that the account had not been given at the earlier interview. In Convention law, the question of whether expulsion would entail a breach of Article 3 is a question of whether there are substantial grounds for believing that there is a real risk of the feared consequences occurring.[30] Similarly to refugee law, while it is for the applicant to substantiate their claim, the government has an obligation to ensure protection of human rights. What is in effect a presumption of disbelief of an applicant's account of torture is inconsistent with that obligation of *non-refoulement*.

Thirdly, his medical evidence, which corroborated his account of torture, was dismissed because he had not produced it before, and because it did not prove that the torture would happen again. Where a burden and standard or proof of this kind is applied, there is little that a person can do to substantiate their fear of ill-treatment. The Court found a breach of Article 3, but not of Article 13, on the basis that judicial review was an effective remedy, following *Vilvarajah*. However, their finding under Article 3, that there were substantial reasons for considering that there was a real risk of treatment contrary to Article 3 in Tanzania, was in effect a critique of the UK's standard and burden of proof, and its unfounded scepticism towards his evidence.

In *MSS v Belgium and Greece*, MSS said that he did not receive an information brochure on arrival telling him how the asylum process worked. The government asserted that he did because that was the procedure. The Court found MSS' account more credible because it was 'corroborated by a very large number of accounts collected from other witnesses by the Commissioner, the UNHCR and various non-governmental organisations' (para 304). This included evidence that others also took the same action as MSS of not going to the police for the same reason (that they had no address to declare) and that several witnesses had reported to international NGOs that 'the police led them to believe that declaring an address was an absolute condition for the procedure to go ahead' (para 179).

On 2 October 2012 a Chamber of the Strasbourg Court made a decision in *Singh v Belgium*[31] which entails a critical reversal of the common domestic approach to credibility and documents. The applicants were a Sikh family from Afghanistan. They were refused asylum in Belgium since the authorities doubted that they were from Afghanistan. On appeal their evidence included copies of documents showing that they were registered as refugees with the UNHCR. These were rejected on the

30 *Soering v UK* (App no 14308/88), judgment 7 July 1989.

31 (App no 33210/1).

grounds that they were easy to falsify and the applicants were not able to produce the originals. The deciding authorities took no steps themselves to subject the documents to authentication. This response to documentary evidence was held by the Court to entail a breach of Article 13 with Article 3. The authorities could easily have contacted UNHCR, and the fact that they did not do so, but dismissed documents which were highly relevant to the claim for protection, meant that they had failed to ensure effective protection against treatment in breach of Article 3.

Onerous Procedural Requirements and Access to a Determination Procedure

Arguably, access to an asylum determination procedure is the most fundamental requirement for an asylum seeker. The Convention may be invoked when access is hindered by a range of practices which include, at the most extreme, simple denial. For example, in *Abdolkhani and Karimnia v Turkey*, the government objected that the applicants did not have victim status under Article 34 of the Convention, because, although the applicants had been removed to Iraq, there had been no deportation orders served on them. The government maintained their right to do this as the applicants were illegal entrants to Turkey. The Court was satisfied that the absence of deportation orders did not prevent their victim status. They had in fact suffered deportation. The absence of legal process only compounded their lack of access to a remedy (para 116).

The applicants had the right to register a request for temporary asylum on entry to Turkey. They said that the authorities had refused to register their request, whereas the government denied that any request had been made. The Court said:

> In the absence of a legal procedure governing the applicants' deportation and providing procedural safeguards, even if they had sought asylum when they entered Turkey, there are reasons to believe that their requests would not have been officially recorded (para 111).

Furthermore,

> … by failing to consider the applicants' requests for temporary asylum, to notify them of the reasons for not taking their asylum requests into consideration and to authorise them to have access to legal assistance while in Hasköy police headquarters, the national authorities prevented the applicants from raising their allegations under Article 3 within the framework of the temporary asylum procedure provided for by the 1994 Regulation and Circular no 57 (para 115).

In view of these and other breaches such as failing to give reasons for decisions, the Court found that Turkey was in breach of Article 13.

The Convention may be invoked where procedural requirements in practice make a remedy inaccessible or incapable of delivering protection against *refoulement*. For instance in *Jabari v Turkey* the applicant's asylum application had been rejected because she had not submitted it within the mandatory period of five days since arriving in Turkey. The ECtHR held that 'the automatic and mechanical application of such a short time-limit for submitting an asylum application must be considered at variance with the protection of the fundamental value embodied in article 3 of the Convention'. An impossibly short time for submitting the application was itself a breach of Article 3 because it would result in her return to Iran, where she faced stoning for adultery.

In *MSS v Belgium and Greece* the Greek procedure gave three days for the applicant to present themselves to the Attica police headquarters, but this was held to be too short in the circumstances. The Strasbourg Court accepted evidence from international organizations that:

> The offices concerned are practically inaccessible because of the number of people waiting and because asylum applications can be lodged only on one day in the week. In addition, the selection criteria at the entrance to the offices are arbitrary and there is no standard arrangement for giving priority to those wishing to enter the building to apply for asylum. There are occasions when thousands of people turn up on the appointed day and only 300 to 350 applications are registered for that week. At the present time about twenty applications are being registered per day, while up to 2,000 people are waiting outside to complete various formalities (para 180).

The applicant's opportunity to lodge his asylum claim and thus prevent his *refoulement* had been impeded by the deficiencies in the asylum procedures.

MSS was detained on arrival in Greece (in conditions which were held to breach Article 3), and on release was notified that he was required to report within two days to the Attica police station to declare his home address so that he could be informed of the progress of his asylum application. MSS understood from this that a home address was a condition of proceeding with his claim. Since he did not have an address, MSS did not report to the police station, and so his claim did not progress. The procedural issues at this point in *MSS* are not just that the procedures are onerous, but also, as referred to in discussion of *Hilal* above, they are obscure, and the lack of transparency and adequate interpretation made them inaccessible. Again the underlying issue is whether this procedure is capable of delivering protection against *refoulement*. MSS was given a registration card, which had to be renewed at intervals. On a renewal of the card he was given a written notice in Greek that referred to a forthcoming asylum interview. However, the interpreter made no mention of an interview date, and since he could not understand the Greek notice, he assumed it was related to the renewal of his card, and did not realize it was a substantive step in his claim. He therefore did not attend the interview and his claim was rejected without his knowledge.

The Court, in finding a breach of Article 13, held that the Greek asylum system was marred by

> … insufficient information for asylum seekers about the procedures to be followed, difficult access to the Attica police headquarters, no reliable system of communication between the authorities and the asylum seekers, shortage of interpreters and lack of training of the staff responsible for conducting the individual interviews, lack of legal aid effectively depriving the asylum seekers of legal counsel, and excessively lengthy delays in receiving a decision (para 301).

By this level of detailed engagement with the inadequacies of the asylum system the Court has in effect picked up the challenge issued by Spijkerboer and stepped into the arena to deal with the procedural obfuscation that impedes refugee claims.

Form and Substance

One of the key principles in the application and interpretation of Article 13, and of the procedural aspects of Article 3, is the principle that the rights offered by the Convention must be 'practical and effective', not 'theoretical and illusory'.[32] In *MSS v Belgium and Greece* evidence showed that, on paper, the Greek system offered the opportunity to make an asylum claim promptly on arrival, gave the right to be informed of the process in a language that the asylum seeker understood and a right of appeal against unfavourable decisions.

The reality was otherwise, as revealed by the evidence of human rights organizations which had monitored the situation in Greece. The Court said:

> The scope of the Contracting States' obligations under Article 13 varies depending on the nature of the applicant's complaint; however, the remedy required by Article 13 must be 'effective' in practice as well as in law (para 288).

And further

> … in order to be effective, the remedy required by Article 13 must be available in practice as well as in law, in particular in the sense that its exercise must not be unjustifiably hindered by the acts or omissions of the authorities of the respondent State (para 290).

After detailed consideration of what actually happened to asylum seekers in Greece, the Court said:

> … for a number of years the UNHCR and the European Commissioner for Human Rights as well as many international non-governmental organisations have revealed repeatedly and consistently that *Greece's legislation is not being applied in practice* and that the asylum procedure is marked by such major

32 *Artico v Italy* (App no 6694/74), judgment 13 May 1980.

structural deficiencies that asylum seekers have very little chance of having their applications and their complaints under the Convention seriously examined by the Greek authorities (para 300, emphasis added).

Accelerated Procedures

UNHCR in a statement issued in the context of the preliminary ruling reference to the Court of Justice of the EU from the Luxembourg Administrative Tribunal examined the right to an effective remedy in relation to accelerated asylum procedures, with reference to the EU Asylum Procedures Directive, and Articles 6 and 13 ECHR. They took the view that the right to an effective remedy under Article 13 did not require a right of appeal against the decision to allocate an asylum application to an accelerated procedure, but did require that basic safeguards against *refoulement* must be maintained in any accelerated procedure. These must include the opportunity for rigorous independent scrutiny of the first instance decision.

The ECtHR's judgment in *IM v France*[33] cast doubt on the lawfulness of fast-track procedures. The applicant was detained immediately on crossing the border into France. He was charged with an immigration offence and was not initially permitted to lodge his asylum application. He had no legal assistance in drafting his challenge to the order for removal, and only a few minutes with a duty lawyer before the hearing of that challenge. Once his application for asylum was lodged it was allocated to a fast-track procedure. Eight days later he had a half an hour interview, and was refused the following day. His case was a complex first claim for asylum. The ECtHR found breaches of Article 13 in the short timescale and inadequate facilities for preparing his case, especially given that he was in detention. The effect of *IM* may be to enable further challenges to fast-track procedures entailing inadequate time for preparation and representation.

Deterrent or 'Push Back' Practices

Article 1 guarantees the rights and freedoms of the Convention to 'everyone within its jurisdiction'. Seeking asylum may take place outside a Member State's territory, or inside, or at a port, in a border zone or international zone. Jurisprudence applying and interpreting Article 1 has established that the jurisdiction is primarily territorial, but in exceptional circumstances effective control exercised by a Member State outside its territory creates jurisdiction.[34] Most of the case law on this issue comes from situations of armed conflict, in relation to which the latest development is that in the case of *Al-Skeini v UK*[35] where the Court held that the

33 (App no 9152/09) 2 February 2012.

34 See *Loizidou v Turkey* (App no 40/1993/435/514), judgment 28 November 1996.

35 (App no 55721/07), judgment 7 July 2011.

use of force could 'bring the individual thereby brought under the control of the State's authorities into the State's Article 1 jurisdiction'.

Al-Skeini in principle suggests that decisions on entry taken outside the territory fall within the jurisdiction, although this point was not addressed explicitly. The so-called 'consular exception' to territorial jurisdiction, previously established, implied that they would or at least could.[36] The critical test of this in relation to asylum seekers was to challenge the 'push-back' practices which are one of the key strategies of Western governments to reduce asylum claims.

This test came in *Hirsi Jamaa v Italy*.[37] The applicants to the ECtHR were 20 of a group of 200 individuals who had set off from the coast of Libya in three boats, with the aim of reaching Italy. As part of an Italian government crackdown on illegal migration to Italy, the vessels were intercepted by ships from the Italian revenue police and coastguard. The occupants of the intercepted vessels were transferred onto Italian military ships and returned to Tripoli and to the Libyan authorities.

The Italian government argued that the applicants were not within Italy's jurisdiction because they were outside the territory, and in taking the applicants onto their vessel, Italy was only fulfilling its obligations under the United Nations Convention on the Law of the Sea (the Montego Bay Convention). This obligation was limited to assisting vessels in distress, and they accompanied the intercepted migrants back to Libya in accordance with their bi-lateral agreement with that country. This was not a maritime police operation and did not establish that the passengers came within Italy's jurisdiction for ECHR purposes.

Following *Al-Skeini*, the decisive question in determining jurisdiction for ECHR purposes is 'effective control'. The Strasbourg Court noted that the events took place on board ships that were flying the Italian flag, and that international law stipulated that a vessel sailing on the high seas is subject to the exclusive jurisdiction of the State whose flag it is flying. The Court accepted the arguments of the applicants and the third party interveners that while on board the ship the applicants were under the 'continuous and exclusive *de jure* and *de facto* control of the Italian authorities' (para 81). The nature and purpose of the Italian ship's intervention could not affect the Court's conclusion on that point. The Court said:

> Whenever the State through its agents operating outside its territory exercises control and authority over an individual, and thus jurisdiction, the State is under an obligation under Article 1 to secure to that individual the rights and freedoms under Section 1 of the Convention that are relevant to the situation of that individual. In this sense, therefore, the Court has now accepted that Convention

36 In *Bankovic v Belgium and Others* the Court held that '… consular officials'. Whether any particular extra-territorial act did in fact come within the State's jurisdiction for ECHR purposes 'must be determined with reference to the particular facts'.

37 (App no 2776509) 23 February 2012.

> rights can be 'divided and tailored' (see *Al-Skeini*, cited above, § 136 and 137; compare *Banković*, cited above, § 75) (para 74).

Italy could not circumvent jurisdiction by describing the events as rescue operations (para 79).

In *Al-Skeini* and *Hirsi Jamaa*, the Court's approach to the scope of Article 1 and thus of the jurisdiction of the ECHR is concerned with the exercise of power. The physical location of the individual cannot of itself take an act outside the jurisdiction of the Court, if the State's exercise of control over that person is such that they should be brought within it.

This decision is important in the present political context. The capacity to scrutinize the exercise of authority outside the territory is vital to maintain the Convention's original purpose as an instrument to combat oppression, and to bring hidden abuses to light. If there is no possibility of jurisdiction outside the territory, then the state can choose to export malpractice. The experience of the Second World War was strong in the minds of the drafters; they would have readily seen the perils of, for instance, extraordinary rendition.[38] Indeed the ECHR has now addressed exactly this practice in *Abdulkhakov v Russia* [2012] ECHR 1771, in which the applicant had been abducted by Russian officials and taken to Tajikistan where he was tortured. *Abdulkhakov* was not an asylum case, but is an example of the court developing the Convention to address modern forms of human rights abuse which entail the state itself by-passing proper border controls.

Deterring and outsourcing asylum decision-making are in a sense different, since interception and 'push back' at sea appear to entail no asylum decision-making process. Irregular migrants and asylum seekers are not differentiated, and all are returned without examination of their situation. Outsourcing entails moving asylum decision-making processes to places outside the territory. On the facts of *Hirsi Jamaa* however the two are not so different. The evidence of some of the passengers was that they had specifically informed the Italian officials that they wanted to claim protection, but these requests were ignored. This *is* an asylum procedure. As soon as the request is made, the State is on notice that they are required to deal with the claim since not to do so entails a risk of *refoulement*.

The Italian government argued that what they called 'a request not to be handed over to the Libyan authorities' could not be interpreted as a request for asylum (para 96). The Court took account of evidence of the situation in Libya, which included that there was no refugee protection procedure, and that passengers would be detained in appalling conditions without any process for examining

---

38 The Council of Europe has investigated and reported on secret detentions and unlawful inter-State transfers of detainees in Council of Europe Member States, 'Evidence was that detainees had been subjected to treatment which violated art. 3', Doc no 10957 (2006). Council of Europe Parliamentary Assembly, 'Resolution 1562 called on member states to play no part in these practices and to make full disclosure of relevant information held by them' (2007).

the reason for their journey, and held that 'it was for the national authorities, faced with a situation in which human rights were being systematically violated [in Libya] … to find out about the treatment to which the applicants would be exposed on their return' (para 133). These points were considered in the context of the Italian government's argument that the applicants did not have victim status under Article 34 of the Convention. The Court held that they did. The failure to take into account the situation in Libya and to respond to the claim for protection constituted a violation of Article 3.

The Grand Chamber found violations of Article 3, Article 13 and Protocol 4 Article 4.

Individual Decision on the Facts of the Case

Protocol 4 Article 4 says:

> Collective expulsion of aliens is prohibited.

The essence of the protection of this protocol is the right to individual consideration. This is apparent from the *travaux preparatoires* where the alternative wording considered for this article was 'decisions of expulsion shall only be taken in individual cases'.[39] The protocol had previously been held to be violated when asylum seekers were brought to a police station on the basis of misleading information, and then faced with detention and removal.[40]

Hirsi Jamaa was the first time that the ECtHR had considered whether Article 4 Protocol 4 applies to the transfer of applicants to a third State, carried out outside the territory of the contracting State. Could such an action be described as an expulsion?

The applicants argued that a functional and teleological interpretation of the provision suggested that the primary purpose of the Article was to prevent States from transferring groups of aliens to other States without an individual examination of their circumstances. A push back of migrants on the high seas could constitute a 'hidden expulsion' (para 162) and an interpretation which prevented that would entail protection that was practical and effective rather than theoretical and illusory. The Columbia Law School Human Rights Clinic submitted that the 'principle of *non-refoulement* required States to refrain from removing individuals without having assessed their circumstances on a case by case basis' (para 165).

The Court examined the question in the light of its definition of collective expulsion in *Henning Becker v Denmark*:[41] 'any measure of the competent

39 Council of Europe, 'Collected edition of the Travaux Preparatoires of Protocol 4 to the Convention, securing certain rights and freedoms other than those already included in the Convention and the first Protocol thereto' (Council of Europe 1976), 429.

40 *Conka v Belgium* (App no 51564/99), judgment 5 February 2002.

41 (App no 7011/75), judgment 3 October 1975.

authority compelling aliens as a group to leave the country, except where such a measure is taken after and on the basis of a reasonable and objective examination of the particular cases of each alien in the group' (*Hirsi Jamaa* para 166). In considering, for the first time, whether this provision could apply to removal of aliens carried out outside national territory, the Court held that the wording of Article 4 of Protocol 4 posed no obstacle to its extra-territorial application. The *travaux preparatoires* revealed that the purpose of Article 4 Protocol 4 was to prohibit 'collective expulsion of aliens of the kind which was a matter of recent history'. The Court noted that, according to the Committee of Experts, the Article refers to

> … all those who have no actual right to nationality in a State, whether they are passing through a country or reside or are domiciled in it, whether they are refugees or entered the country on their own initiative, or whether they are stateless or possess another nationality (para 174).

The Court continued:

> Lastly, according to the drafters of Protocol no. 4, the word 'expulsion' should be interpreted 'in the generic meaning, in current use (to drive away from a place)'.

It followed that the *travaux preparatoires* did not preclude extra-territorial application of Article 4 Protocol 4. In *Hirsi Jamaa* the Court developed the application of Article 4 Protocol 4 to meet the changing circumstances that 'the interception of migrants on the high seas and their removal to countries of transit or origin are now a means of migratory control' (para 177). Since it is 'firmly rooted in the Court's case law', that the Convention is a 'living instrument', and the established purpose of Article 4 Protocol 4 was to prevent States from being able to remove certain aliens without examining their personal circumstances, the Court held:

> If therefore Article 4 Protocol 4 were to apply only to collective expulsions from the national territory of the States parties to the Convention, a significant component of contemporary migratory patterns would not fall within the ambit of that provision, notwithstanding that the conduct it is intended to prohibit can occur outside the national territory … Article 4 would thus be ineffective in practice in regard to … situations which are … on the increase (para 177).

Where the Court had found that the State had exercised its jurisdiction outside national territory, Article 4 Protocol 4 applied. To conclude otherwise 'would result in a discrepancy between the application of the Convention as such and that of Article 4 Protocol 4, which would go against the principle that the Convention must be interpreted as a whole' (para 178).

In the present case, the transfer of the applicants to Libya was carried out 'without any form of examination of each applicant's individual situation' (para 185). There had been a breach of Article 4 Protocol 4.

One of the justifications that States have relied on for practices which restrict or prevent asylum claims is that their procedures are open to 'genuine' claimants. A practice such as that in issue in *Hirsi Jamaa* does not begin to give an opportunity to consider the substance of any claim. This absence of individual consideration was relevant to all the Articles under which claims were made and violations found: Articles 3 and 13, and Protocol 4 Article 4.

Conclusion

Although refugees are not mentioned in the Convention, their situation as people seeking protection from persecution comes within the spirit of both the intention behind Article 1 and its development. The open-textured nature of the rights in the Convention – simply worded and based on principle rather than detail – gives flexibility to meet its role as a 'living instrument'. In this respect the Strasbourg Court has the potential to respond to procedural gaps and systemic practices by which States may erode the right of asylum. Since States have sought to control and deter asylum applications by procedural means, both the flexibility and practicality of the Court are well suited to making findings that can address the human rights infringements which may occur. The Court's capacity to hear evidence from human rights organizations which is of sufficient scope and volume to address systemic problems means that it also has a unique role to play in addressing fundamental and systemic problems such as procedural manifestations of the culture of disbelief, and extra-territorial deterrence of asylum claims.

References

Council of Europe, 'Collected edition of the Travaux Preparatoires of Protocol 4 to the Convention, securing certain rights and freedoms other than those already included in the Convention and the first Protocol thereto' (1976) Strasbourg: Council of Europe.

Council of Europe, 'ECHR Travaux preparatoires' Article 1.

Da Lomba S, *The Right to Seek Refugee Status in the European Union* (Intersentia, 2004).

Human Rights Europe, 'Rule 39 ECHR immigration appeals rise by 4,000 per cent' (11 February 2011).

Lambert H, *The Position of Aliens in Relation to the European Convention on Human Rights* (Council of Europe Publishing, 2007).

Mole N and Meredith C, *Asylum and the European Convention on Human Rights* (Council of Europe Publishing, 2010).

Sharpe J (ed.), *The Conscience of Europe: 50 Years of the European Court of Human Rights' London* (Third Millenium Publishing Ltd, Council of Europe Publishing, 2010).

Spijkerboer T, 'Subsidiarity and "Arguability": the European Court of Human Rights Case Law on Judicial Review in Asylum Claims' (2009) 21(1) International Journal of Refugee Law 48–74 at 49.

Statute of the Council of Europe, ETS 1, London, 5 May 1949.

UNHCR, 'Statement of the right to an effective remedy in relation to accelerated asylum procedures, issued in the context of the preliminary ruling reference to the Court of Justice of the EU from the Luxembourg Administrative Tribunal regarding the interpretation of Article 39, Asylum procedures Directive, and Articles 6 and 13 ECHR' (UN High Commissioner for Refugees, 2010).

Chapter 10

The Protection of Asylum Seekers with Particular Reference to African Women: the Contribution to the Contemporary Jurisprudence[1]

Rebecca Wallace

Introduction

Contemporary international refugee law 'has developed within a male paradigm which reflects the factual circumstances of male applicants, but which does not respond to the particular protection needs of women'. To what extent does this assessment, made almost two decades ago, remain an accurate reflection of the contemporary position encountered by women within the refugee process?

Traditionally a number of barriers have confronted women within the asylum determination process, namely: the alleged persecution is not recognized as such; the perpetrators are non-State actors; and the gender neutrality of the 1951 Refugee Convention and the 1967 New York Protocol.[2]

Biological sex is not synonymous with gender: gender embraces the social and culturally constructed experience of being a woman or a man and a relationship between them in society. 'It affects both women and men's social identity, status,

1 Certain parts of this chapter were addressed in an article, 'Non-State Actors in the Context of Refugee Determination Process, with Particular Reference to the Position of Women' (2007) 32 South African Yearbook of International Law 179–207. C Romany 'State Responsibility Goes Private' in Rebecca J Cook (ed.), *Human Rights of Women: National and International Perspectives* (University of Pennsylvania Press, 1994) 65–115, at 90. The author is a fee paid Judge of the First-tier Tribunal (Immigration and Asylum Chamber), however the views expressed are her own and do not reflect those of the Tribunal. The research assistance of Ms Karen Wylie, Robert Gordon University, Aberdeen, is acknowledged.

2 Convention Relating to the Status of Refugees, 28 July 1951, 189 UNTS 150 (entered into force 22 April 1954). The Refugee Convention contained both a temporal and geographical constraint and was confined to events happening in Europe before 1951. Both limitations were removed by The 1967 Protocol Relating to the Status of Refugees Protocol relating to the Status of Refugees, 31 January 1967, 606 UNTS 267 (entered into force 4 October 1967), also known as the New York Protocol.

roles and responsibilities'.[3] What it means to be male or female will vary according to time and place, as well as involving other factors such as race, age, class and marital status.

Persecution in the conventional sense does not always correspond with the experiences of women asylum applicants, and this has often been to their disadvantage within the refugee determination process. In an effort to counter this, a variety of initiatives have been adopted including recognition that non-State actors may perpetrate persecutory conduct, the development and use of gender guidelines and the employment of gender in defining a particular social group.

This chapter will consider how women and women's experiences have been invoked so as to encompass women as members of a 'particular social group' (PSG). Does for instance the current application of the law constitute an 'artificial construct'?[4] Is the law being stretched beyond its original intention in order to accommodate the claims of female asylum seekers? Is the PSG approach logical, consistent and an example of 'best practice'?[5]

It should be emphasized that what is being sought is not that gender-specific forms of harm be evaluated by a standard different from that applied to other forms of alleged persecutory harm but rather that women should be guaranteed equality of treatment with men. This should not be by way of preferential treatment, but rather through cognisance being given to the relevant specific factors which are involved in gender-related violence asylum claims.

The 1951 UN Refugee Convention remains the starting point, as it contains the legal definition of a refugee as found in Article 1(A) (2) *viz* a person:

> [O]wing to a well founded fear of being persecuted for reasons of race, religion, nationality, membership of a particular social group or political opinion, is outside the country of his nationality and is unable or, owing to such fear, is unwilling to avail himself of the protection of that country; or who, not having a nationality and being outside the country of his former habitual residence as a result of such events, is unable or, owing to such fear, is unwilling to return to it.

---

3 UK Immigration Appellate Authority (IAA) Gender Guidelines, 1.12, Crown Copyright – November 2000. The Guidelines were not official policy but their contents have been reflected in for instance the UK Home Office Asylum Policy Instructions (APIs), Gender Issues in the Asylum Claim, October 2006.

4 Dissenting Opinion of Lord Millet in *R v Immigration Appeal Tribunal, Ex p Shah and Islam* [1999] 2 AC 629, 27. Membership of PSG is one of the five grounds listed in the1951 Convention as warranting refugee protection. For further discussion on PSG, see below.

5 'Best practice' *viz* that which brings all those who warrant refugee status within the protective ambit of the 1951 UN Convention Relating to the Status of Refugees (the Refugee Convention), while not distorting the relevant law.

However, the expectations of the Convention drafters that the refugee problem was short term were not realized.[6] The flow of refugees has only increased in number since the 1950s, and the geographical spread of refugee-producing countries has widened far beyond Europe.[7] The typical refugee of the 21st century is a person who has been displaced through war, particularly intra-State conflict, and environmental factors. There has also been a rise in the number of Internally Displaced Persons (IDPs) who, although unable to seek refugee status having not crossed an international border, face many of the same problems as refugees.

Non-discrimination on grounds of sex is a well established principle in international law, however gender was not included in Article 1A(2) as the basis for a well-founded fear of persecution.[8] Interestingly no woman was present amongst the plenipotentiaries when the drafters of the Refugee Convention met in Geneva.[9] However, notwithstanding this, the omission of gender from the 1951 Refugee Convention should not be regarded as a deliberate plan designed to preclude the recognition of women applicants as refugees. 'They [the drafters] did not deliberately omit persecution based on gender – it was not even considered'.[10] A proposal by the Yugoslav delegate that the ground of 'sex' should be added to the enumerated grounds was rejected because, in the words of the British delegate, 'the equality of the sexes was a matter for national legislation'[11] and the Chairman of the Conference expressed strong doubts as to whether there would be any cases of persecution on account of sex.[12] The reality is that the Refugee Convention was a product of its time: a time which was not conversant with the concepts of 'gender based persecution' and 'gender based violence'. However the absence of such concepts from the refugee vocabulary meant 'the drafters of the Convention bequeath to history a critical, male, intellectual political activist with a high profile

6 The United Nations High Commissioner for Refugees (UNHCR) was originally given a limited three-year mandate to help post-Second World War refugees; thereafter it was assumed there would be no need for the organization. M Achiron, 'A Timeless Treaty Under Attack', UNHCR Refugees Magazine Vol 2(123) Geneva, Switzerland.

7 For up-to-date information and statistics relating to refugees see www.unhcr.org/statistics.html. This resource provides data, trends and statistical reports on persons who are of concern to UNHCR.

8 G Goodwin-Gill and J McAdam, *The Refugee in International Law* (Oxford University Press, 2007) 473. The five grounds as enumerated are race, religion, nationality, membership of a PSG or political opinion.

9 O Sircar, Can the Women Flee? Gender-Based Persecution, Forced Migration and Asylum Law in South Asia, in NC Behera (ed.), *Gender, Conflict and Migration* (Sage Publications, 2006) 255–73, 255.

10 J Kumin, *Gender: Persecution in the Spotlight* (UNHCR, 2001).

11 T Spijkerboer, *Gender and Refugee Status* (Ashgate Publishing Group, 2000) 1.

12 Spijkerboer, 2000.

in the resistance movement, organised and ideologically motivated, as the classic example of the refugee'.[13]

Accordingly, it is widely acknowledged that refugees have been defined from a traditionally male perspective with reference to male experiences, which can be, and are, very different to those of women.[14] Nevertheless, women undoubtedly are exposed to the same types of persecution as men but they also experience forms of persecutory treatment which are unique to them as women.[15] As a consequence of their role and status in society generally, and more specifically within family and kinship systems, women may in fact be exposed to a wider range of human rights abuses than their male counterparts.[16] Notwithstanding the 'common knowledge' that women are 'doubly disadvantaged' as refugees and women,[17] the protection of women refugees did not feature on the agenda of the United Nations High Commissioner for Refugees (UNHCR) Executive Committee until 1985.

As previously mentioned, gender is neither static nor innate and gender-related claims may be brought by both men and women,[18] although the parameters of this chapter dictate it will be restricted to the latter. Consequently different jurisdictions employ a variety of methods of dealing with gender within the context of the refugee determination process. Doreen Indra argues that 'gender is instead a way of "seeing" a wide range of phenomena, and emphasises that gender is not simply the study of women and their beliefs, but rather a relational dimension of all activities'.[19] Viewed from a feminist perspective, the use of language and the application of socially constructed definitions relating to the status of women have had wide-reaching ramifications for the application of the Refugee Convention in gender-related claims. International refugee law is not so much an exact science but rather a regime that needs to be responsive to individual circumstances.[20]

13 Quoted by Pia Prutz Phiri, Representative UNHCR Branch Office for Ireland, 'Women and Law: Gender and Asylum in Ireland', University College Cork, 8 March 2003.

14 Guidelines on International Protection No 1: Gender-Related Persecution within the context of Art 1A(2) of the Refugee Convention and/or its 1967 New York Protocol (HCR/GIP/02/01) (2002) 2.

15 UNHCR, 'The Special Situation and Needs of Refugee Women, Report of the UN Expert Group Meeting on International Migration Policies and the Status of Female Migrants' (San Miniato, Italy, 27–30 March, 1990).

16 A Bloch, T Galvin and B Harrell-Bond, 'Refugee Women in Europe: Some Aspects of the Legal and Policy Dimensions' (2000) 38(2) International Migration 171.

17 Goodwin-Gill, *The Refugee in International Law* 473.

18 UNHCR, 2002, 1(3).

19 'Changing Agendas in the Study of Forced Migration: A Report on the Fifth International and Research and Advisory Panel Meeting April 1996' (1996) 9(4) Journal of Refugee Studies 353–66, 360.

20 E Feller, V Türk and F Nicholson, *Refugee Protection in International Law, UNHCR's Global Consultations on International Protection* (Cambridge University Press, 2003) 42.

The cultural construction of gender does not take place in a vacuum;[21] the impact of the cultural, social and physical implications of gender will vary from case to case and decision-makers must keep this in mind.

Gender Issues in International Law

Looking at women's rights through an international lens, initial focus naturally falls on the 1979 Convention on the Elimination of all forms of Discrimination against Women (CEDAW), which came into force in September 1981.[22] That Convention represents the principal international legal framework for any discussion of the international legal rights of women. The Committee on the Elimination of Discrimination against Women, the body that monitors States Parties' compliance with CEDAW, has issued periodic General Recommendations which essentially add flesh to the bones of the Convention. Of particular relevance in this chapter are the General Recommendations on violence against women (General Recommendation No 12, 1989 and No 19, 1992) and on Female Genital Mutilation (FGM) (General Recommendation No 14, 1990).[23]

The last two decades of the 20th century witnessed *inter alia* the UN decade for women, the 1985 Nairobi Conference and the 1995 Beijing Conference on Women, which emphasized the plight of refugee women and provided the impetus to alleviate the situation of refugee women. In 1985, the Executive Committee of the High Commissioner's Programme noted that 'women asylum seekers who face harsh or inhuman treatment due to their having transgressed the social mores of the society in which they live may be considered as a "particular social group" within the meaning of Article 1A (2)', although it was left to States' discretion 'in the exercise of their sovereignty' whether or not to do so.[24]

The year 1993 saw the first mention of providing skilled female interviewers in refugee status determination procedures as well as ensuring access by

21 J Benson, 'Reinterpreting Gender: Southeast Asian Refugees and American Society' in L Carnio and R Krufeld (eds), *Reconstructing Lives, Recapturing Meaning* (Routledge, 1994) 75.

22 UN Gen Ass Resn 34/180 GOAR, 34th Sess, Supp 46, 193. This has since been supplemented by the Optional Protocol which allows for the Committee on the Elimination of Discrimination against Women – the body that monitors States Parties' compliance with the Convention – to receive and consider complaints from individuals or groups within its jurisdiction. The Optional Protocol entered into force on 22 December 2000.

23 A full list of the General Recommendations made by the Committee on the Elimination of Discrimination against Women can be found at: http://www.un.org/womenwatch/daw/cedaw/recommendations/recomm.htm.

24 Executive Committee, Conclusion No 39 (XXXVI), On Refugee Women and International Protection, para k (1985).

women asylum seekers to such procedures, 'even when accompanied by male family members'.[25]

In the same year the UN General Assembly adopted the Declaration on the Elimination of Violence against Women,[26] recognizing such violence as an issue of international concern and requiring all States to work towards its eradication. Article 1 defines violence for the purpose of the Declaration as:

> [A]ny act of gender-based violence that results in, or is likely to result in, physical, sexual or psychological harm or suffering to women, including threats of such acts, coercion or arbitrary depravation of liberty, whether occurring in public or private life.

The Office of UN Special Rapporteur on Violence against Women, its Causes and Consequences was created in 1994.[27] In 2009 the Special Rapporteur published 15 years of the United Nations Special Rapporteur on Violence against Women, its causes and consequences (1994–2009) – A critical review,[28] an evaluation of the previous 15 years of work on the Special Rapporteur's mandate. As well as noting achievements and progress made, it considers the potential for the future development and possible directions of the mandate.

In addition since then, there has been an increasing realization of the difficulties gender produces for women in conflict and post-conflict situations. The ascendancy of women's human rights on the international agenda is reflected *inter alia* in this context in UN Security Council Resolution 1325.[29]

---

25 Executive Committee, Conclusion No 64 (xli) 1990, On Refugee Women and International Protection, para a (iii).

26 UNGA Res 48/104, 20 December 1993.

27 The first Special Rapporteur was Ms Radhika Coomaraswamy of Sri Lanka, who held the post from July 1994 –- July 2003. She was succeeded by Dr Yakin Ertürk of Turkey, appointed from August 2003 – July 2009. Since August 2009, the South African Ms Rashida Manjoo has been in post.

28 Available at http://www2.ohchr.org/english/issues/women/rapporteur/docs/15YearReviewofVAWMandate.pdf.

29 Security Council Resolution 1325 adopted unanimously. UN Doc S/RES/1325 (31 October 2000). S/RES/ 1325 recognizes that civilians, particularly women and children, account for the vast majority of those adversely affected by armed conflict, including as refugees and internally displaced persons, and are increasingly targeted by combatants and armed elements. This it acknowledges has consequent impacts on durable peace and reconciliation. Thus, S/RES/1325 reaffirms the important role of women in the prevention and resolution of conflicts and in peace-building, and stresses the importance of their equal participation and full involvement in all efforts for the maintenance and promotion of peace and security, including the need to increase their role in decision-making with regard to conflict prevention and resolution; ensure increased representation of women at all decision-making levels in national, regional and international institutions; and in mechanisms for the prevention, management and resolution of conflict.

The Statutes of the International Tribunals for Former Yugoslavia (ICTY)[30] and Rwanda (ICTR),[31] (Article 5(g) and Article 3(g) respectively) and the resulting jurisprudence has also proved significant.[32] In the *Akayesu* case rape was characterized as equivalent in magnitude and gravity to torture:

> Like torture, rape is used for such purposes as intimidation, degradation, humiliation, discrimination, punishment, control or destruction of a person. Like torture, rape is a violation of personal dignity, and rape in fact constitutes torture when it is inflicted by or at the instigation of or with the consent or acquiescence of a public official or other person acting in an official capacity.[33]

The jurisprudence of the *ad hoc* Tribunals also influenced the drafting of the Rome Statute which established the International Criminal Court (ICC) in The Hague. Those framing the Rome Statute took account of the jurisprudence developed by the ICTY and ICTR despite the concerns of some activists that the jurisprudence emanating from the *ad hoc* Tribunals would be sidelined, taken as being too specialist to have much bearing on the development of mainstream international law.[34] This proved not to be the case, largely due to the efforts of the Women's Caucus for Gender Justice. This expert body, comprised of individuals and groups campaigning for women's human rights, was involved at all levels of the Rome Statute negotiations, advocating for a gendered perspective to be brought into the substance and procedure of the ICC. As a result the ICC has jurisdiction over a wide range of gender-based crimes, and led to a feeling of optimism shared by many

30 33 ILM 484 (1994).

31 33 ILM 1600 (1994), see also the Yearbook of the United Nations, Vol 50, (1996), 1194–201.

32 See for example 'Celebici' *Prosecutor v Delacic, Mucic, Delic and Land* (IT-96-21-T), *Prosecutor v Furundzija* (IT-95-17/1-T); *Prosecutor v Kunarac, Kovac and Vulkovic* ICTY T. Ch 11 22 February 2001; *Prosecutor v Akayesu*, ICTR -96-4-T, ICTR T. September 1998; see also Statute of the International Criminal Court, Arts 7, 8(2) (b) (xxii) and Art 54(1)(b); see also the Fourth World Conference on Women held in Beijing, September 1995 and the Programme of Action, Strategic Objective D1-D3 and the appointment of a Special Rapporteur on Violence against Women, 1994.

33 *Prosecutor v Akayesu*, Case No ICTR-96-4-T, para 687–8. The decision set the international precedent for rape being used as an act of genocide and also was the first occasion an international court had punished sexual violence in a civil war. See also the 2007 decisions of the Committee against Torture in *V.L. v Switzerland,* Communication No 262/2005, 20 November 2006, UN Doc CAT/C/37/D/262/2005 (2007) and *C.T. and K.M v Sweden*, Communication No 279/2005, 17 November 2006, UN Doc CAT/C/37/D/279/2005 (2007). See also Katharine Fortin's Student Paper, 'Rape as torture: An evaluation of the Committee against Torture's attitude to sexual violence' (2008) 4(3) 145.

34 H Charlesworth and C Chinkin, *The Boundaries of International Law: A Feminist Analysis* (Manchester University Press, 2000) 83.

that its inception marked a new era for international justice and accountability for women.[35]

Other previous campaigns to highlight women's human rights have included the UNHCR's implementation of 'age, gender and diversity' mainstreaming policy in 2004. There is now widespread acceptance that gender can 'influence, or dictate, the type of persecution or harm suffered and the reasons for this treatment',[36] although the Executive Committee has continued to express its concern about the 'less than full application of international refugee instruments by some states Parties'.[37]

The European Union (EU) Qualification Directive[38] also recognizes that sexual violence and gender-specific abuse can be persecution for the purposes of asylum claims. The recast Directive[39] reiterates the need to introduce the common concept of the persecution ground 'membership of a PSG'. It notes that for the purposes of defining a PSG, relevant factors may be an applicant's gender, including gender identity and sexual orientation, that may be related to certain traditional practices, such as FGM, forced sterilization or forced abortion. Acts which are characterized as examples of persecution include 'acts of a gender-specific … nature'.[40]

Guidelines which are available to decision-makers in the form of soft law have appeared at both the international and national level and include *inter alia* the UNHCR Global Gender Related Guidelines of 2002[41] and the 1991 Guidelines drawn up by the Refugee Women's Legal Group,[42] the UK Immigration and Asylum Tribunal Guidelines 2000[43] and the Canadian Immigration and Refugee

35 See for example E Rehn and E Johnson Sirleaf, *Women, War & Peace: The Independent Experts' Assessment on the Impact of Armed Conflict on Women & Women's Role in Peace-Building* (The United Nations Development Fund for Women (UNIFEM, 2002) 92.

36 UNHCR, 2002, at II A 6.

37 Executive Committee, Conclusion No 89 (LI), 2000.

38 Council Directive 2004/83/EC of 29 April 2004 on Minimum Standards for the Qualification and Status of Third Country Nationals or Stateless Persons as Refugees or as Persons Who Otherwise Need International Protection and the Content of the Protection Granted, Arts 9–2 (a) and (f). OJ L304/12 of 30 September 2004.

39 Directive 2011/95/EU of the European Parliament and of the Council 13 December 2011, OJ L337/9, 20 December 2011.

40 Recast Qualification Directive, 2011, Art 9(f).

41 These 2002 Guidelines came out of the 2nd Track of the Global Consultations on International Protection Process, following examination of this subject at an expert meeting in San Remo in 2001. In the wake of the Global Consultations the UNHCR prepared an Agenda for Protection in which six principal goals were identified, one being the protection needs of women and children.

42 Approved by Lord Hoffman in *Shah and Islam* [1999].

43 These guidelines drew upon the work by the Refugee Women's Legal Group (RWLG), which in turn had also looked at the practice of other countries for example the Canadian Guidelines.

Board Guidelines.[44] UNHCR has updated its Handbook for the Protection of Women and Girls,[45] and issued in May 2009 a *Guidance Note on Refugee Claims Relating to Female Genital Mutilation*.[46] Also, on 2 July 2010 the UN General Assembly adopted a Resolution for the establishment of the UN Entity for Gender Equality and the Empowerment of Women, to be known as UN Women.[47]

The African Charter on Human and Peoples' Rights (the Banjul Charter),[48] which entered into force 21 October 1986, provides the African dimension. The Charter has since been supplemented by the Protocol on the Rights of Women in Africa, which entered into force on 25 November 2005, having received its 15th ratification. This marked a milestone in the protection and promotion of women's rights in Africa, creating new rights for women in terms of international standards, explicitly setting forth health and reproductive rights, including a prohibition on

---

44 Women Refugee Claimants Fearing Gender-Related Persecution, Guidelines issued 9 March 1993 by the Chairperson pursuant to Section 65(3) of the Immigration Act, Immigration and Refugee Board (IRB), Ottawa, Canada, updated 1996. The 1993 Guidelines were the first to be issued by the Chairperson; a subsequent six Guidelines have been issued on, for example, Civilian Non-Combatants Fearing Persecution in Civil War Situations and Child Refugee Claimants: Procedural and Evidentiary Issues. The general purpose of Guidelines issued by the Chairperson whose statutory authority is now provided for by Section 159 (1)(h) of the Immigration and Refugee Protection Act, S.C.2001, c. 27 is to promote consistency, coherence and fairness. See also RMMWallace, 'Making the Refugee Convention Gender Sensitive: the Canadian Guidelines' (1996) 45 ICLQ 702; and RMM Wallace and Mrs Anne Holliday, 'Application of Gender Guidelines within the Asylum Determination Process: Reflections on the UK and Canadian Experience' in *Canada-UK Perspectives on International Law* (Niemhoff, 2006) 169–80. For other examples of Guidelines see Australian Department for Immigration and Multicultural Affairs (1996) Guidelines on Gender Issues for Decision-Makers (Refugee and Humanitarian Visa applications). Currently being revised as of September 2003; see also Report of the Australian Law Reform Commission, Part IV Section 11: Violence and Women's Refugee Status; N. Valji and L.A. De la Hunt, *South African Gender Guidelines for Asylum Determination* (National Consortium on Refugee Affairs, 1999), EU Foundation for Human Rights; Swedish Migration Board (2001) *Gender-Based Persecution: Guidelines for Investigation and Evaluation of the Needs of Women for Protection Available*.

45 This revised edition replaces the UNHCR's 1991 Guidelines on the Protection of Refugee Women, available at UN High Commissioner for Refugees, *UNHCR Handbook for the Protection of Women and Girls*, January 2008, available at http://www.unhcr.org/refworld/docid/47cfc2962.html.

46 Available at http://www.unhcr.org/refworld/pdfid/4a0c28492.pdf.

47 General Assembly Resolution A/64/L.56. This new body merged four of the UN's agencies and offices: UN Development Fund for Women (UNIFEM), the Division for the Advancement of Women (DAW), the Office of the Special Adviser on Gender Issues and the UN International Research and Training Institute for the Advancement of Women (UN-INSTRAW).

48 Available at http://www.hrcr.org/docs/Banjul/afrhr.html.

FGM. This instrument, also known as the 'Maputo Protocol', further sets out a broad range of economic and social welfare rights for women.[49]

'A Man's Home is His Castle': Private v Public Harm

Refugee protection is surrogate protection and so before being afforded the protection of refugee status, it is necessary to show more than persecution, or a likely risk of persecution. A claimant must demonstrate an absence of protection from the government of his/her State of nationality or habitual residence. Lord Hoffmann in *Shah and Islam*[50] accepted what he phrased the succinct interpretation of persecution as '[P]ersecution = Serious Harm + The Failure of State Protection'.[51]

This arguably has posed the greatest hurdle for women to navigate.[52] The perpetrators of gender-based violence are typically non-State actors, such as family or community members. The degree of willingness to consider women's claims as falling within the Refugee Convention is arguably structured by the gendered dichotomy between the private and the public spheres of social interaction and the corresponding social roles attributed to men and women.[53] What is public in one context may be private in another and the content of these categories may also vary over time.[54] In Westernized liberal states, the law has traditionally regulated activities that occur in the public sphere, but not in the private, hence the well-known adage 'a man's home is his castle', demonstrating the liberal notion that intervention by the State in the private sphere of family life was to be avoided.[55] This division is problematic, as women have traditionally been confined to the private sphere unlike men who of course also occupy the public arena.[56]

---

49 While the ratification of both CEDAW and the Maputo Protocol represent positive steps for the protection of women's rights in international law, it must be noted that of course the provisions contained within them are often disregarded and states still fail to either uphold their obligations or offer adequate protection.

50 *Shah and Islam* [1999].

51 *Shah and Islam* [1999] 17. Lord Hoffmann here was quoting from *Gender Guidelines for the Determination of Asylum Claims in the UK* (published by the Refugee Women's Legal Group in July 1988) 5.

52 *Shah and Islam* [1999] 13.

53 R Bacon and K Booth 'Intersection of Refugee Law and Gender: Private Harm and Public Responsibility' (2000) 23(3) University of New South Wales Law Journal 135–63, 140.

54 H Charlesworth and C Chinkin, *The Boundaries of International Law: A Feminist Analysis* 56.

55 M Thornton (ed.), *Public and Private: Feminist Legal Debates* (Oxford University Press, 1995) 11.

56 A Roberts, 'Gender and Refugee Law' (2002) 22 Australian Yearbook of International Law 161.

The invisibility of domestic violence in the international public arena is a natural consequence of its characterization 'private' at the local level:

> [I]t is the very inattention and inaction by the state in relation to 'battering' that tacitly condones and sustains it as a systematic practice ... The fact the state does not adequately protect women from domestic (and sexual) violence 'is both an institutional manifestation of the degraded social status of women, and is a cause of its perpetration'.[57]

The UNHCR Handbook notes private acts of violence constitute persecution 'if they are knowingly tolerated by the authorities, or if the authorities refuse, or prove unable, to offer effective protection'.[58]

However, rather than overemphasizing the public/private distinction, the relationship between a woman and the state should be understood. A definition of persecution encompassing a human rights dimension, in addition to recognizing women as a PSG, has been identified as necessary.[59] Although persuasive, the flaw is that for gender-based persecution claims, which traditionally fall within the 'private' realm, an open-minded and progressive approach is required from the judiciary in all jurisdictions.[60] The extent to which a government does not make criminal or penalize gender-based violence, or take steps to rigorously enforce existing laws that prohibit such violence, demonstrates it has condoned the violence and in doing so must assume State responsibility for the offensive acts.[61]

---

57 A Macklin, 'Cross-Border Shopping for Ideas: A Critical Review of United States, Canadian and Australian Approaches to Gender-Related Asylum Claims' (1998) 12 Georgetown Immigration Law Journal 28.

58 UNHCR Handbook on Procedures and Criteria for Determining Refugee Status under the 1951 Convention and the 1967 Protocol relating to the Status of Refugees (1992) at para 65.

59 J Greatbatch, 'The Gender Difference: Feminist Critiques of Refugee Discourse' (1989) 1, International Journal of Refugee Law 518.

60 H Charlesworth, 'What Are Women's International Human Rights?' in RJ Cook (ed.), *Human Rights of Women: National and International Perspectives* (University of Pennsylvania Press, 1994) 58. See also the claim that 'when men use their liberties socially to deprive women of theirs, it does not look like a human rights violation. But when men are deprived of theirs by the government, it does'. C MacKinnon, 'Crimes of War, Crimes of Peace' (1993) 59 UCLA Women's Law Journal 69–70, 69.

61 A Bahl, 'Home is Where the Brute Lives: Asylum Law and Gender-Based Claims of Persecution' (1997–98) 4, Cardozo Women's Law Journal 33–73, 42; K Bower, 'Recognising Violence Against Women as Persecution on the Basis of Membership of a Particular Social Group' (1993) 7 Georgetown Immigration Law Journal 173–83 'where a government offers no protection from gender-based violence, a woman's home and country become her prison and the violence is persecution'. See also *Case Of Rantsev v Cyprus and Russia* (App no 25965/04), judgement 7 January 2010, final 10/05/2010; *Opuz v Turkey*

A PSG can be formed by making reference to gender. What is important is that the particular group suffers or fears severe discrimination or harsh or inhuman treatment distinguished from the rest of the general population or from other women. The members have got to constitute a group within the eyes of society, but the group must be formed independently of the act of persecution. In 1993 the Canadian Supreme Court handed down the seminal decision of *Ward* in which three possible categories of PSG were identified.[62] Important in this context is the category formed by an innate or unchangeable characteristic, such as gender.[63] In *Matter of Acosta* the United States Board of Immigration Appeals (BIA) held that membership of a particular social group was based on a 'common immutable characteristic' which might be innate, such as 'sex, colour or kinship ties'.[64] The BIA invoked *ejusdem generis* to make such a finding:

> Each of these grounds [race, nationality etc.] describes persecution aimed at an immutable characteristic: a characteristic that either is beyond the power of an individual to change or is so fundamental to individual identity or conscience that it ought not be required to be changed … Thus, the other four grounds of persecution enumerated in the Act and the Protocol restrict refugee status to individuals who are either unable by their own actions, or as a matter of conscience should not be required, to avoid persecution.[65]

Pursuant to the doctrine of State responsibility, States are responsible for violations and omissions of their international obligations, whether they originate in a binding document or through customary means, if those violations are attributable to the state itself.[66] Violations can be attributed to a State not only when a State official allows the violation to occur, but when the State permits one of its citizens to violate the obligation with impunity. States are expected to protect their citizens, be it in the public or private sphere.

Some States have been reticent to acknowledge non-State actors as perpetrators of persecution where the government cannot or will not control the actors, for example France and Germany.[67] What is the level of protection demanded?

(App no 33401/02), 9 June 2009; *Ms. A.T. v Hungary*, CEDAW Communication No 2/2003, UN Doc CEDAW/C/32/D/2/2003 (26 January 2005).

62 *Attorney-General of Canada v Ward* [1993] 2 SCR 689.

63 *Canada v Ward* [1993], at 739.

64 Matter of Acosta, 19 I. and N. Dec. 211 (B.I.A. 1985).

65 Matter of Acosta, [1985].

66 S Rosenne, The International Law Commission's Draft Articles on State Responsibility (Martinus Nijhoff, 1991; T Meron, *Human Rights and Humanitarian Norms as Customary Law* (Clarendon Press, 1989) 135–245.

67 Qualification Directive, 2004 (Recast, 2011) acknowledges non-State actors as perpetrators of persecution pursuant to Art 6(c). A Subhan, '*Asylum in the EU Member States 11–12*' European Parliament, Directorate General for Research, Working Paper No LIBE 108 EN 2000.

The answer came in *Horvarth*[68] in which the appellant, a member of the Roma community from Slovakia, alleged he and his family had been victims of racist violence at the hands of neo-Nazi skinheads which the authorities had failed to investigate or take any action against. Therein Lord Hope highlighted that although persecution is normally related to action by the authorities of a country, it may also emanate from sections of the population that do not respect the standards established by the laws of the country concerned.[69] In the context of an allegation of persecution by non-State agents, the word 'persecution' implies a failure by the State to make protection available against the ill-treatment or violence which the person suffers at the hands of his persecutors.[70]

Lord Hope continued:

> [T]he obligation to afford refugee status arises only if the person's own state is unable or unwilling to discharge its own duty to protect its own nationals. I think that it follows that, in order to satisfy the fear test in a non-state agent case, the applicant for refugee status must show that the persecution which he fears consist of acts of violence or ill-treatment against which the state is unable or unwilling to provide protection. The applicant may have a well-founded fear of threats to his life due to famine or civil war or of isolated acts of violence or ill-treatment for a Convention reason which may be perpetrated against him. But the risk, however severe, and the fear, however well-founded, do not entitle him to the status of a refugee. The Convention has a more limited objective, the limits of which are identified by the list of Convention reasons and by the principle of surrogacy.

In summation Lord Hope stated that:

> [W]here the allegation is of persecution by non-state agents, the sufficiency of state protection is relevant to a consideration whether each of the two tests – the 'fear' test and the 'protection' test – is satisfied. The proper starting point, once the tribunal is satisfied that the applicant has a genuine and well-founded fear of serious violence or ill-treatment for a Convention reason, is to consider whether what he fears is 'persecution' within the meaning of the Convention. At that stage the question whether the state is able and willing to afford protection is put directly in issue by a holistic approach to the definition which is based on the principle of surrogacy.[71]

---

68 *Horvath v The Secretary of State for the Home Department* [2001] 1 AC 489.

69 *Horvath* [2001], 6. Lord Hope here is quoting paragraph 65 of the UNHCR *Handbook on Procedures and Criteria for Determining Refugee Status*, 1992.

70 *Horvath* [2001], 7.

71 *Horvath* [2001], 8.

The Horvath principle has been confirmed as the correct legal test for protection as reflected in subsequent case law and the United Kingdom's implementation of the EU Qualification Directive:[72]

> 1) In deciding whether a person is a refugee or a person eligible for humanitarian protection, protection from persecution or serious harm can be provided by:
>
> (a) the State; or
>
> (b) any party or organisation, including any international organisation, controlling the State or a substantial part of the territory of the State.
>
> (2) Protection shall be regarded as generally provided when the actors mentioned in paragraph 1(a) and (b) take reasonable steps to prevent the persecution or suffering of serious harm by operating an effective legal system for the detection, prosecution and punishment of acts constituting persecution or serious harm, and the person mentioned in paragraph (1) has access to such protection.[73]

In *IM* the view was expressed that the

> [O]ne feature of reg. 4 which we consider the facts of this case highlight is that the wording of reg. 4(2) reinforces the same point which we take to have been made by post-*Horvath* case law. The wording of this subparagraph is unmistakeably defeasible: '[p]rotection shall be regarded as *generally* provided ...' (emphasis added). It is not stated that the taking of 'reasonable steps to prevent the persecution...by operating an effective legal system ...' will amount to provision of adequate protection in every case, although it is said that it will in the generality of cases.[74]

The Tribunal continued that 'if there be any doubt that post-*Horvath* case law sets out the correct legal test for protection, then what we can now say is that that doubt

72 Appeal No: *IM* (Sufficiency of protection) Malawi [2007] UKAIT 00071AIT Reported.

73 The Protection Regulations and the Immigration Rules (as amended by Cm 6918) which implement within the UK the EU the Qualification Directive, 2004 (Recast, 2011). The Protection Regulations set out actors of persecution or serious harm (reg 3) and actors of protection (reg 4). The wording of the Protection Regulations is substantially the same as the text of Art 7 of the Qualification Directive save that the wording of reg 4(2) omits the phrase '*inter alia*' immediately before 'by operating' (Art 7(2) states '[p]rotection is generally provided when the actors mentioned in paragraph 1 take reasonable steps to prevent the persecution or suffering of serious harm, *inter alia*, by operating an effective legal system for the detection, prosecution and punishment of acts constituting persecution or serious harm, and the applicant has access to such protection').

74 *IM* (Malawi) [2007], at para 50.

has been dispelled by reg 4(2) whose wording closely mirrors that of the test set out in *Horvath* as we have construed it'.[75]

There has been an ever-expanding, but paradoxically increasingly narrow set of categories for claimants. This endless particularization misses the very crucial point of the analysis that sexual violence is itself a form of gender persecution and that it is gender which is both the common denominator defining the social group and which makes women the target of this form of persecution in the first place.[76]

Goodwin-Gill similarly agrees that such narrowly constructed PSGs cloud the issue: 'the exaggerated focus on sub-groups and identifying characteristics [leads] to the essential identifying factor being ignored, namely, women in context, that is, women in social context'.[77]

Likewise Lord Hope cautioned against the danger of over-qualifying the definition of a PSG, as the more qualifications the definition contains the more grounds there may be may be for objection.[78] In *Jo (internal relocation-no risk of re-trafficking) Nigeria* [2004] the more expansive definition of a PSG was welcomed:

> In our view their Lordships made clear in that judgment that the PSG category should not be interpreted too narrowly … too little regard has been paid to the fact that all that was required in *Shah and Islam* (per Lord Hoffman) was the existence of legal and social conditions which were discriminatory against women. Possibly also there has been too much focus on rejecting PSG arguments by reference to sub-categories (e.g. women at risk of FGM, or at one point in this case, trafficked women). The more delimited the proposed category the greater the prospect of circularity in definition.[79]

The difficulty with these decisions lies in what use these judgments form in a wider legal context. However, what this method of adjudication can offer is the advantage of flexibility. By using specific sub-criteria, a multitude of situations can be accommodated under the ambit of the 1951 Convention.

---

75 *IM* (Malawi) [2007].

76 M Randall, 'Refugee Law and State Accountability for Violence Against Women: A Comparative Analysis of Legal Approaches to Recognizing Asylum Claims Based on Gender Persecution' (2002) 25 Harvard Women's Law Journal, 25th Anniversary Issue 281–318, 292.

77 G Goodwin-Gill, 'Judicial Reasoning and "Social Group" after Islam and Shah' (1999) 11 International Journal of Refugee Law 537.

78 Taken from the case of *Fornah*. This case is dealt with in detail later in the chapter, see footnote 93 below for the full citation.

79 *JO (internal relocation-no risk of re-trafficking) Nigeria* [2004] UKIAT 00251.

African Jurisprudence

So how have African cases that have come before the UK asylum and decision-makers[80] contributed to the evolution of the debates regarding PSG; risk vs state protection relating to internal relocation; and the role of non-state actors as perpetrators of abuse? The best illustrative examples of cases that have been dealt with in the UK refugee determination process are those claims relating to either domestic violence or FGM.

In the case of *'P' and 'M' v Secretary of State for the Home Department* [2004] EWCA Civ 1640,[81] Mrs P claimed she was entitled to asylum in the UK on the basis of a well-founded fear of persecution if she were to be returned to Kenya. Her fear stemmed from the violence she and her children had experienced at the hands of her husband. Mrs P was initially granted asylum by an adjudicator,[82] but this was appealed by the Secretary of State who maintained the ill treatment was not persecution and notwithstanding this Mrs P could relocate safely to another part of Kenya.

Mrs P, a Sikh of South Asian background, had lived in Nairobi with her husband, daughter and son. Her allegations of extreme domestic violence were supported by her 18-year-old daughter's evidence. The daughter gave testimony to the effect that on the occasions she had tried to intervene, so as to protect her mother, she had also sustained beatings from her father. Mrs P's husband was a police reservist who boasted a number of friends in the senior ranks of the Kenyan Police authorities. He was in possession of a gun which he kept at home. The police did apparently intervene eventually and remove the gun, not because he was threatening to use it against the family but because he had been seen with it in public. Mrs P for her part felt she could not report the case to the police because domestic violence was recognized as an accepted part of the 'patriarchal society in Kenya'[83] and the police would take no action on the basis of a woman complainant. Mrs P's case was further compounded by her husband's association with senior ranking police officers.

There was also evidence Mrs P had been denied hospital treatment as she could only be admitted to hospital with the consent of her husband. This he had refused. However there was also supporting corroborating evidence from a doctor who had previously seen the injuries Mrs P had sustained at the hands of her husband.

80 The decision-making body in the UK has undergone several name changes in the last few years. To avoid confusion this chapter refers simply to 'the Tribunal'.

81 The cases were heard together because they raised similar issues. The Court went into greater detail in Mrs P's case and noted the arguments were as applicable to Miss M. For this reason, the chapter focuses on Mrs P.

82 Mrs P's immigration history was that she had been granted asylum by an adjudicator. This was reversed by the Tribunal. It was against this refusal that Mrs P referred the matter to the Court of Appeal. Mrs P's appeal was on both asylum and human rights grounds.

83 *P and M v SSHD* [2004], para 19.

Her, and her children's, exit from Kenya and travel to the UK was secured by an uncle. The adjudicator's affirmative decision in according Mrs P refugee status was premised on background evidence highlighting that the police would not have afforded Mrs P assistance, and that she was a member of a particular social group, namely women who are disadvantaged in Kenyan society because of their position in that society. The adjudicator also characterized the ill-treatment that Mrs P had suffered as amounting to torture, and she would be at real risk if returned to Kenya. The adjudicator had also upheld the appeal on human rights grounds, namely if she were returned to Kenya Mrs P would not be able to maintain her moral integrity, as encompassed in her right life to private life under Article 8 of the European Convention on Human Rights and Fundamental Freedoms.

The Tribunal at this juncture in the appeal from the adjudicator's decision engaged in a comparison with the position of women in Pakistan and drew extensively on the case of *Shah and Islam*.[84] The Tribunal concluded that although women in Kenya were disadvantaged to an extent, they were not so badly disadvantaged as women in Pakistan. The Court of Appeal in the case of Mrs P was somewhat critical of the Tribunal.[85]

When considering the risk to which Mrs P would be exposed if she returned, the Tribunal countered the argument that there was as absence of protection afforded to her, invoking two cases to illustrate that 'Kenyan society does not condone that kind of conduct' (that is, domestic violence).[86] However, in the instances relied upon by the Tribunal where it deemed the police to have taken adequate action, the outcome was not one that suggested protection. In one case the police authorities had only intervened after the woman had been killed, whereas in the other, sulphuric acid had been poured onto the woman's face causing permanent disfigurement. The Court of Appeal took issue with the Tribunal and held the Tribunal had missed the point being made by Mrs P, *viz* that the police had in reality to be compelled to intervene. The Tribunal had also dismissed the human rights claim on the basis that the offending conduct did not achieve the high threshold required. It did so by maintaining that as Mrs P came from a relatively wealthy family she could internally relocate and could be afforded protection from the authorities.

The Appeal Court in a very brief conclusion decided there was no reason why Kenyan women could not be regarded as a PSG on the basis of *Shah* and *Islam*. The Court also made reference to the Australian case of *S v MIMA*[87] in which it was maintained the adjudicator had correctly identified the ill treatment complained of as persecution, giving rise to the claimant's membership of a PSG. Furthermore,

84 *Shah and Islam* [1999].

85 *P and M v SSHD* [2004], at para 25 in which it is commented the IAT did so, 'presumably to distinguish the case of Shah and Islam and to allow the conclusion that the position in Kenya "is nothing like as bad as it is in Pakistan"'.

86 Cited in Court of Appeal, para 26.

87 *Applicant S v MIMA* [2004] 8 CA 25.

because of her membership of that PSG she would not be afforded the protection of the police, and hence her fear of persecution was well founded.

At this juncture and in this context, the need for the availability of information regarding the country of origin (COI) or return can be highlighted. Why is COI important? It is essential because although in itself COI will never be definitive in deciding a case, it is against the landscape painted by COI that every application will be decided with an applicant's credibility being evaluated in the light of country of origin conditions. Pursuant to Article 4 of the Qualifications Directive, the facts and circumstances of each claim are to be established by reference to '(a) all relevant facts as they relate to the country of origin at the time of taking a decision on the application; including laws and regulations of the country of origin and the manner in which they are applied'.[88] Hence accurate COI is of central importance in asylum and human rights cases. This is particularly true when the geographical and social conditions are outside the knowledge or experience of the fact-finding tribunal. While there remains some debate on how COI can consistently meet a high standard, there does exist a general consensus on what constitutes good quality COI, *viz*, that it be objective, accurate, current and transparently referenced.[89]

Another case dealing with an African claimant, *MD (Women) Ivory Coast CG* [2010][90] UKUT 215 (IAC), identifies what is to be considered expert evidence by contrasting Operational Guidance Notes (OGNs) to other COI, noting:

> Operational Guidance Notes fall into a different category. They are, in essence, policy statements. On many occasions, the Operational Guidance Notes will be supported by references to background material and may have sought assistance from RDS, as well as Tribunal case law taken from reported decisions. Insofar

---

88 Qualification Directive 2004, (Recast 2011). See also UNHCR Handbook (1992) para 42 which states, 'As regards the objective element, it is necessary to evaluate the statements made by the applicant. The competent authorities that are called upon to determine refugee status are not required to pass judgement on conditions in the applicant's country of origin. The applicant's statements cannot, however, be considered in the abstract, and must be viewed in the context of the relevant background situation. A knowledge of conditions in the applicant's country of origin – while not a primary objective – is an important element in assessing the applicant's credibility. In general, the applicant's fear should be considered well-founded if he can establish, to a reasonable degree, that his continued stay in his country of origin has become intolerable to him for the reasons stated in the definition, or would for the same reasons be intolerable if he returned there'.

89 See for example The Hungarian Helsinki Committee, 2007. *Country Information in Asylum Procedures – Quality as a Legal Requirement in the EU*, available at http://www.unhcr.org/refworld/pdfid/479074032.pdf.

90 This case focused on the risks faced by women in the Ivory Coast of FGM: forced marriage, domestic violence, the effects of adultery and discrimination. The Tribunal noted the levels of risk, and the sufficiency of protection offered by the state, varied throughout the country.

> as they include background material, the background material is to be regarded like any other background information, subject to the fact that its selection may not have the same objectivity and is not independently scrutinised.[91]

This illustrates how OGNs may not conform to the criteria which have been flagged up as prerequisite for good quality COI.[92]

Another case which has significantly contributed to the PSG debate is that of a young Sierra Leonean woman, in *Fornah*.[93] The appeal had gone to the House of Lords from the Court of Appeal, the latter having held that Miss Fornah would not be discriminated against because, having undergone FGM she would have undergone a cultural rite of passage, and thereby become part of women in society. The Court of Appeal on this basis concluded that she would the form part of the majority of women and could no longer be allegedly discriminated against. The Court also decided that because FGM is only performed once on an individual, after the act had taken place discrimination could not be described as ongoing.

PSG, the definition and membership thereof were considered in the *Fornah* case, as it raised the issue whether the appellant's well-founded fear of being persecuted was 'for reason of ... a particular social group'. The Secretary of State and the Court of Appeal[94] had held that although the treatment complained of would be persecutory it was not because of the appellant's membership of a PSG.[95]

The appellant, Miss Fornah, had arrived in the UK when she was 15 years of age and claimed asylum on the grounds that if returned to Sierra Leone she would

91 *MD (Women) Ivory Coast* [2010], para 265.

92 The appeal in this case was dismissed on the grounds the appellant could return safely to the area she grew up in.

93 *Secretary of State for the Home Department (Respondent) v K (FC) (appellant) Fornah (FC) (appellant) v Secretary of State for the Home Department (Respondent) Appellate Committee* [2006] UKHL 46. The House of Lords heard two appeals together as they dealt with similar circumstances, however for the purposes of this chapter which is dealing with the impact of African cases, reference will not be made to the appellant *K*, who was Iranian.

94 [2004] EWCA Civ 986; [2004] EWCA Civ 680.

95 The appellant was granted leave to remain in the UK. The Secretary of State having accepted that to return her to Sierra Leone would be contrary to European Convention for the Protection of Human Rights and Fundamental Freedoms (ECHR) (213 UNTS 221) Art 3. This to some extent mitigated the impact of the Secretary of State's decision and that of the Court of Appeal. However the denial of the stronger protection which would have been otherwise afforded with refugee status was highlighted by the Court and in the words of Lord Hope '[t]he question whether or not the appellants have refugee status is not just of theoretical importance ... The uncertainty that attaches to their present lack of status will be replaced by the status which the Contracting States have undertaken to accord to a refugee and by all the rights that attach to it. This is a very substantial additional benefit which is well worth arguing for'. *Fornah* [2006], para 35.

be at risk of FGM.[96] The Secretary of State rejected the appellant's asylum claim on the grounds that girls who were at risk of FGM did not form a PSG within the terms of the Refugee Convention. Miss Fornah appealed, her credibility was not challenged, and the Immigration Adjudicator found that her fear was for a Convention reason, that is, because of her membership of a PSG, 'that of young single Sierra Leonean women, who are clearly at considerable risk of enforced FGM'. The Secretary of State successfully appealed the decision to the Tribunal, and the Tribunal's decision was upheld by the Court of Appeal.[97] The UNHCR was granted leave to intervene in respect of Miss Fornah's appeal to the Lords.

In the House of Lords, Lord Bingham, in delivering his opinion, initially placed the concept of PSG in its contextual background and highlighted in contrast to the other four grounds most commonly relied upon under the Convention the meaning of PSG had been the subject of much consideration and analysis notwithstanding its apparent simplicity and intelligibility.[98] Lord Bingham emphasized the Convention should be interpreted in accordance with its broad humanitarian objective, with regard to the principles, expressed in its preamble, that human beings should enjoy fundamental rights and freedoms without discrimination and that refugees should enjoy the widest possible exercise of these rights and freedoms.[99]

The Refugee Convention is exhaustive in that '[c]entral to the definition of refugee are the five specified grounds, the Convention reasons … on which alone a claim to recognition as a refugee may be founded under the Convention. Treatment, however persecutory or abhorrent, will not found such a claim unless

96 Twenty-eight countries in Africa practise FGM in one form or another. FGM is an integral part of certain communities' cultures, but is totally foreign to others. In Sierra Leone, for example, approximately 90 per cent of all women have undergone FGM as part of their initiation into womanhood. The appellant had overheard discussions proposing her undergoing FGM. This had precipitated her running away but she had been captured by rebels and repeatedly raped by the rebel leader by whom she became pregnant. An uncle arranged the appellant's departure from Sierra Leone. On her arrival in the UK Miss Fornah as a minor had been granted leave to remain in the UK until the eve of her 18th birthday. The appellant maintained she would be unable to relocate within Sierra Leone and she would have no alternative but to live in her father's village. It should be noted that FGM is illegal in the UK under Female Genital Mutilation Act 2003 (England, Wales and Northern Ireland) and the Prohibition of Female Genital Mutilation (Scotland) Act 2005 [S]. These Acts not only make the procedure of FGM illegal, but also make it an offence to send a girl abroad from the UK for the purpose of FGM. However, there have currently been no prosecutions in the UK and this has given rise to parliamentary questions as to the adequacy of the legislation (House of Commons Hansard Debates, Column 156, 8 January 2013).

97 [2005] EWCA Civ 688 [2005] 1 WLR 3773.

98 *Fornah* [2006], para 11. The UNHCR was granted leave to intervene in respect of Miss Fornah's appeal to the Lords. Lord Bingham noted that the House had derived great help from the submissions of counsel of the UNHCR which although properly directed to principle, was strongly supportive of the second appellant's appeal (para 9).

99 *Fornah* [2006], para 10.

inflicted (or to be inflicted) for one or other of these five Convention grounds'. Thus the core issue before the House of Lords was whether the persecution feared arose through membership of a PSG.[100]

Invoking what was termed the leading domestic authority,[101] Lord Bingham elicited a number of important principles.[102] First, the 1951 Refugee Convention is concerned only with persecution based on discrimination, that is, the making of distinctions which principles of fundamental human rights regard as inconsistent with the right of every human being. Secondly, prerequisite to identifying a PSG is identification of the society of which it forms a part. A PSG may be recognized as such in one country and not in another. Thirdly, a PSG does not require to be cohesive; and fourthly a PSG must exist independently of any persecution to which its members are subject.[103]

The line of argument adopted by the House of Lords was premised on a number of authorities from other jurisdictions relating to membership of PSGs.[104] In looking at the concept of PSG Lord Bingham invoked the UNHCR *Guidelines on International Protection*,[105] which he characterized as providing a very accurate and helpful distillation of the effect of the international authorities.[106] In particular Lord Bingham noted that having identified 'the protected characteristics' or 'immutability' and 'social perception' approaches the UNHCR had sought to reconcile and give cognisance to the two dominant approaches thereby providing the formulation for a PSG as 'a group of persons who share a common characteristic other than their risk of being persecuted, or who are perceived as a group by society. The characteristic will often be one which is innate, unchangeable, or

100 *Fornah* [2006], para 10.

101 *Shah and Islam* [1999].

102 1951 Refugee Convention, para 13.

103 This is based on an application of *Applicant A v Minister for Immigration and Ethnic Affairs* (1997) 190 CLR 225 at 263, *viz* '[P]ersons who seek to fall within the definition of "refugee" in Art 1A(2) of the Convention must demonstrate that the form of persecution that they fear is not a defining characteristic of the "particular social group" of which they claim membership. If it were otherwise, Art 1A(2) would be rendered illogical and nonsensical. It would mean that persons who had a well-founded fear of persecution were members of a particular social group because they feared persecution. The only persecution that is relevant is persecution for reasons of membership of a group which means that the group must exist independently of, and not be defined by, the persecution'. (J. McHugh).

104 Decisions referred to included *In re Acosta* (1985) 19 I&N 211; *Attorney-General of Canada v Ward* [1993] 2 SCR 689 and *Applicant A*, ibid. n 16. The latter was referred to for yielding 'valuable insights'.

105 UNHCR Guidelines on International Protection: 'Membership of a Particular Social Group' within the context of Art 1A(2) of the 1951 Convention and/or its 1967 Protocol Relating to the Status of Refugees, HCR/GIP/02/02, 7 May 2002.

106 *Fornah* [2006], para 15.

which is otherwise fundamental to identity, conscience or the exercise of one's human rights'.[107]

Lord Bingham endorsed the UNHCR's acceptance that PSG could not be defined exclusively by the persecution members suffer or fear, but also accepted that persecutory actions towards a group may be a relevant factor in determining the visibility of a group in a particular society.[108]

Lord Bingham also made reference to the EU Qualification Directive[109] and the call therein for minimum standards and common criteria in the refugee definition as well as for a common concept of a PSG as a persecution ground. Lord Bingham gave some due consideration to the Directive and the consequential obligation incumbent on Member States when seeking to establish the nexus between particular social group and the reason for persecution. He concluded that the Directive sets out PSG in a manner consistent with established international authority.

However he did acknowledge some difficulty with Article 10(d) sub-para (iii), but appears to have come down in favour of the UNHCR comments on this provision within the Directive,[110] namely there is authority to the effect that women can constitute a PSG within the meaning of Article 1A(2) and gender is an example of a social subset of persons who are defined by innate and immutable characteristics and who are frequently subject to differentiated treatment and standards.

It is apparent that the burden of proof remains with the claimant to demonstrate a well-founded fear of persecution for reasons of membership of a PSG, and the comments of UNHCR in *Fornah* made that unequivocally clear. The causal link has to be established and there has to be evidence of a nexus. Lord Bingham did not find the test of causation as problematic in principle and maintained that

---

107 UNHCR 2002, para 11.

108 *Fornah* [2006], para 15.

109 Qualification Directive 2004. The Directive was incorporated into UK legislation by The Refugee of Person in Need of International Protection (Qualification) Regulations 2006 and entered into force on 9 October 2006. The directive also introduces 'subsidiary protection' for a person who does not qualify as a refugee but in respect of whom there are substantial grounds to show the person would face a real risk of suffering serious harm as within the Directive, Art 15, *viz* death penalty or execution; torture or inhuman or degrading treatment or punishment; serious and individual threat to civilian life or person by reason of indiscriminate violence in situations or international or internal armed conflict. For a different approach on the Directive's interpretation on PSG, see SB *(PSG – Protection Regulations – Reg. 6) Moldova CG* [2008] UKAIT 00002. As mentioned, the Directive was recast in 2011.

110 UNHCR Annotated Comments on the EC Council Directive 2004/83/EC of 29 April 2004 on Minimum Standards for the Qualification and Status of Third Country Nationals or Stateless Persons as Refugees or as Persons who otherwise need International Protection and the Content of the Protection granted, OJ L304/12 of 30 September 2004. Lord Bingham did not engage in any analysis of either the relevant provisions of the Directive or the comments of the UNHCR. He merely stated he did not 'understand these propositions to be contentious', *Fornah*, [2006], para 18.

what matters is the real reason for the persecution and recognized persecutory treatment need not be motivated by enmity, malignity or animus on the part of the persecutor, whose professed or apparent motives may or may not be the real reason for the persecution.[111]

In deciding whether the causal link is established, a simple 'but for' test of causation Lord Bingham held is inappropriate: the Convention he maintained calls for a more sophisticated approach, appropriate to the context and taking account of all the facts and circumstances relevant to the particular case.[112]

In dealing with *Fornah* their Lordships considered how a PSG may be defined and further endorsed the approach towards PSG adopted by the UNHCR Guidelines. Their Lordships also refuted the circularity argument adopted by the Court of Appeal in respect of the second appellant. The House of Lords unequivocally dismissed the Court of Appeal's contention that Miss Fornah was not a member of the claimed PSG because the claimed persecutory group was defined exclusively by the persecutory act.[113]

Their Lordships were also critical of the Court of Appeal's finding the claimed PSG did not possess immutable characteristics. The argument ran that once women have been submitted to FGM there is no further risk as FGM is a one-off event which can neither be undone nor repeated. Further it was not discriminatory because the practice of FGM did not in any way set those who had undergone it apart from society and in the absence of discriminatory conduct there could be no resort to insufficiency of state protection.[114]

On the other hand Lady Justice Arden[115] had been of the view the persecutory treatment feared could be because of membership of a PSG, *viz* those prospectively adult women in Sierra Leone who had not yet undergone FGM and so remain intact.[116]

---

111 *Fornah* [2006], paras 17 and 18.

112 Lord Bingham stated this was supported by authorities such *as Shah and Islam*,1999; *R (Sivakumar) v Secretary of State for the Home Department* [2003] UKHL 14, [2003] 1 WLR 840, paras 41–2; *Sepet v Secretary of State for the Home Department* [2003] UKHL 15 [2003] 1 WLR 856, paras 21–3; *Suarez v Secretary of State for the Home Department* [2002] EWCA Civ 722 [2002] 1 WLR 2663, para 29; *Chen Shi Hai v Minister for Immigration and Multicultural Affairs* (2000) 201 CLR 293, paras 32–3, 67–71; *Minister for Immigration and Multicultural Affairs v Sarrazola* [2001] FCA 263, para 52; and *Thomas v Gonzales* 409 F 3d 1177 (9th Cir, 2005).

113 *Fornah* [2006], para 78.

114 [2004] EWCA Civ 680, para 44. Lord Justice Chadwick, at para 56, likewise denied the creation of a particular social group because the defining characteristic of the group was inseparable from the feared persecution.

115 Significantly, the one woman judge on the Court of Appeal bench for the case.

116 *Fornah* [2006], para 66. Lady Justice Arden however denied Sierra Leonean women in general could not be a particular social group as such a group would include those who no longer feared FGM as they had undergone it and might practise it on others, at para 61.

The fact that women performed the FGM was not accepted by any of their Lordships as a reason for defeating the appellant's asylum claim. Lord Bingham acknowledged that most vicious initiatory rituals are in fact perpetuated by those who were themselves subject to the ritual as initiates and see no reason why others should not share their experience. Nor was it seen as pertinent that a practice is widely practised and accepted.[117]

Lord Bingham rejected, in no uncertain terms, the Court of Appeal's conclusion that FGM as practised in Sierra Leon was not discriminatory. This he did when he characterized FGM as 'an extreme expression of the discrimination to which all women in Sierra Leone are subject, as much those who have already undergone the process as those who have not'.[118] On this basis he had no difficulty in recognizing women in Sierra Leone as a PSG for the purposes of Article 1A(2) of the 1951 Refugee Convention.[119]

Lord Bingham found evidence that women in Sierra Leone had an unchangeable common characteristic, namely a position of social inferiority as compared with men. Women within Sierra Leonean society are perceived as inferior. This is true of all women, irrespective of whether they accept or willingly acknowledge their inferior position. Defining the group in this way made no reference to the persecution alleged. The position of social inferiority would exist as a characteristic even if FGM were not practised.[120] However if that view did not find favour[121] Lord Bingham recognized as an alternative the PSG favoured by Lady Justice Arden, namely 'intact women in Sierra Leone'.[122] Such a group displayed a common characteristic of intactness and thus was defined independently of persecution.

Their Lordships were unanimous in recognizing Miss Fornah's membership of a PSG although they differed as to how that group might be constructed. Baroness Hale agreed with Lord Bingham and favoured the inclusion in the group of all Sierra Leonean women, even those who had undergone FGM, whereas Lord Hope and Lord Rodger favoured a narrower construction of PSG namely that of uninitiated, intact women.[123] Thus their Lordships quite readily found that Miss Fornah came within the protective ambit of the Refugee Convention. Indeed Baroness Hale was highly critical of the earlier decisions in *Fornah* and found it

---

117 *Fornah* [2006], paras 31, 109 and 110.

118 *Fornah* [2006], para 31.

119 *Fornah* [2006].

120 *Fornah* [2006]. Lord Bingham did acknowledge that FGM is an extreme and very cruel expression of male dominance.

121 Lord Bingham was of the view that the second appellant's case could be resolved within the context of the established jurisprudence.

122 *Fornah* [2006], para 31.

123 *Fornah* [2006], paras 58, 80 and 119. Lord Brown refrained from giving a fully reasoned speech as he did not think 'it would contribute anything of value to an understanding of this issue' thus he confined himself to four comments, this was one of the four points.

hard to explain why Miss Fornah had to appeal to the House of Lords given the decision was 'so blindingly obvious'.[124]

It is all the more inexplicable that *Fornah* had to end up in the House of Lords in the light of the Human Rights Committee's (HRC) practice in dealing with cases relating to FGM and a potential engagement of the principle of *non refoulement*. FGM has arisen most commonly within the context of Article 7 (prohibition of torture and inhumane treatment) of the International Covenant on Civil and Political Rights (ICCPR)[125] and the HRC has on a number of occasions declared that deporting women to countries where it is foreseeable that they are at risk of FGM as incompatible with Article 7 of the Covenant.[126] Moreover, independently of any removal threat, the HRC views the practice of FGM as one amounting to a breach of Article 7 *per se*.[127] It is quite clear from the ICCPR perspective that a state would be in breach of its obligations under the ICCPR should a woman be removed who can demonstrate a well-founded fear of being subjected to the practice of FGM.

This resonates with the approach adopted by the Committee on the Elimination of Discrimination against Women in the previously mentioned General Recommendation No 14 wherein it expressly invited the States Parties to take the *appropriate and effective measures* (emphasis added) with the view of eradicating the practice of female circumcision[128] thus clearly demonstrating its abhorrence to the practice.

The *Fornah* judgment is important in that it endorses the correct approach for defining PSG as that advocated for within the UNHCR Guidelines, an approach

124 *Fornah* [2006], para 83. Baroness Hale took the opportunity to highlight that although the 1951 Refugee Convention is gender neutral, the world community had 'recognised the special problems of refugee women', and 'woken up to the fact that women as a sex may be persecuted in ways that are different from the ways in which men are persecuted and that they may be persecuted because of the inferior status accorded to their gender in their home society'. 1951 Refugee Convention, paras 84 and 86. As evidence of this 'wakening' she cited the relevant UNHCR Executive Committee Conclusions on *Refugee Women and International Protection*, 18 October 1985, the UNHCR *Guidelines on Gender Related Persecution* (2002) as well as international human rights instruments which promote gender equality such as the International Covenant on Civil and Political Rights and the Convention on the Elimination of All Forms of Discrimination against Women (19 ILM 33).

125 UKTS 6 (1977), *viz* Prohibition on torture or cruel, inhuman or degrading treatment or punishment.

126 Concluding Observations on the Netherlands (2001). UN Doc CCPR/CO/72/NET; para 11.

127 See Concluding Observations on Lesotho (1999) UN Doc CCPR/C/79/Add 106, para 12; Concluding Observations on Cameroon (1999) UN Doc CCPR/C/79/Add 116; para 12; Concluding Observations on Egypt, (2002) UN Doc CCPR/CO/76, para 11; Concluding Observations on Sweden, (2002) UN Doc CCPR/CO/74/SWE, para 8.

128 General Recommendation No 14, 1990.

which is to be adopted when interpreting the EU Qualification Directive and any implementing regulations.[129] The decision from their Lordships underscores the need for a holistic approach to PSG and the need to avoid focusing too heavily on the persecutory act. It also highlights the risk of over-qualifying the definition of a PSG, as the more qualifications the definition contains the more grounds there may be for objection.[130] The decision in *Fornah* represents acknowledgement by the House of Lords of shortcomings in the law as it stood and represents their Lordships putting the record straight.[131]

FGM, and the alleged fear of FGM, has precipitated a number of the asylum claims which have appeared in the UK from women coming from Africa. However, although FGM has been recognized as persecution, that does not negate the need for the applicant to demonstrate not only membership of a PSG but the absence of protection or the non-viability of relocation. Here again the importance of COI mentioned above is illustrated. In a Country Guidance case[132] involving *Sudan, FM (CG)* [2007] UKAIT 00060, it was highlighted that significant action was being taken in Sudan by the government and NGOs to combat FGM in all its forms. However, it was acknowledged that legal sanctions are unlikely to be applied when the perpetrator is a member of the woman's family.[133] The importance of this case in the overall development of the law is to show that it is not sufficient to claim a fear of FGM but that other factors will operate to determine the credibility of that fear. Such factors will include the family's level of education, family social status and the age and vulnerability of a woman.

The need to consider the individual circumstances of a claimant was also highlighted in *VM (FGM-risks-Mungiki-Kikuyu/Gikuyu) Kenya CG* [2008] UKAIT 00049. Again this was a case involving FGM which considered membership of a

129 *Fornah* [2006], Lord Brown para 18.

130 *Fornah* [2006], Lord Hope paras 37 and 58.

131 The analysis adopted in *Fornah* was employed by the Tribunal in *SK* (FGM-ethnic groups) Liberia CG [2007] UKAIT 00001 and it was held that 'Women in Liberia belonging to those ethnic groups (or sub-groups) where FGM is practised are a particular social group for the purposes of the 1951 Geneva Convention', para 1. In *SK* it was held that internal relocation will be available in Liberia to a woman who is at real risk of FGM in her home area in certain circumstances including *inter alia*, for example, she is not reasonably likely to encounter anyone in the place of relocation who would be in a position of power and influence over her and who would use that power or influence to require her to undergo FGM. The appeal in *SK* was dismissed on the basis of the appellant's adverse credibility.

132 Country Guidance cases (CG) are those cases in which the decision is regarded as representative and useful as a guide to country conditions. CG cases are to be followed except where there is a different factual matrix facing the decision-maker and the CG decision can properly be held inapplicable for legally adequate reasons.

133 In this case the appeal of the appellant and her two minor daughters was allowed on asylum grounds and human rights grounds, whilst the appellant's two sons had their appeals granted on human rights grounds (Art 8). The first appellant was also granted on Art 8 grounds.

PSG and the possibility of internal relocation. The decision in this case regarding PSG was in line with *Fornah*. When it comes to the possibility of internal relocation *VM* is also instructive:

> A thorough examination of all the relevant factors must be undertaken in each case, given the position of women within Kenyan society and the usual need for kinship links in the place of relocation in order to sustain such movement successfully.[134]

In *HM (Somali Women – Particular Social Group) Somalia* [2005] UKIAT 00040, the Tribunal again emphasized the need to focus on case-specific facts within the context of the objective evidence. While *HM* was granted asylum having been deemed to be a member of a PSG on the basis of her vulnerability as a young, single woman, the Tribunal noted:

> Although we have found that the appellant succeeds in her asylum appeal in this case, we would emphasise that Adjudicators must not equate a finding that there exists a PSG with a finding that there exists persecution or with a further finding that there exists a causal nexus between such persecution and the PSG. For unusual reasons this appeal proceeded on the basis of an acceptance of persecution, and hence, PSG was the only real issue, but in most cases each of these issues, albeit overlapping, will have to be decided in discrete fashion on the basis of the overall evidence at large.[135]

The Tribunal here emphasized that it was not enough to be a woman *per se*, but rather because of what it described as a cumulative picture, that is:

> Women in Somalia form a PSG not just because they are women, but because they are extensively discriminated against. Second the measures of discrimination to which women in Somalia are exposed include legislative, judicial and police or militia discrimination in the way in which women can obtain and suffer from seeking protection from the (regionalised or local) clan-based authorities. Thirdly, the serious harms they face from male sources arise in the context of very limited ability by these authorities to protect them. Finally, the measures of discrimination they face are extensive, intense and sustained.[136]

---

134 *VM (Kenya)*, para 216.

135 *HM (Somalia)* para 38. See also *SK (FGM – ethnic groups) Liberia* CG [2007] UKAIT 00001 in which it was noted the '[i]ndividual credibility, as well as country information, will usually have an important part to play in determining whether a woman is at real risk of FGM. The subjective element remains relevant' (para 3 of intro).

136 *HM (Somalia)* [2005], para 35.

African experiences have also been influential in the development of how the Tribunal has dealt with cases of suspected human trafficking. These cases again raise the issue of addressing an appellant's credibility, as well as the viability of internal relocation and sufficiency of State protection. In 2004 in *JO*,[137] even fully accepting the appellant was credible, the appellant still had to show that if she was returned to Nigeria she faced a real danger of persecution through being re-trafficked. However, the Tribunal held it to be implausible that those who had trafficked her from her home village would expend the effort necessary to find her if she returned to Nigeria and was able to relocate to a different part of the country.[138]

Similarly, in the case of *PO (Trafficked Women) Nigeria CG* [2009] UKAIT 00046, notwithstanding the credibility of the appellant, the Tribunal held that:

> There is in general no real risk of a trafficking victim being re-trafficked on return to Nigeria unless it is established that those responsible for the victim's initial trafficking formed part of a gang whose members were to share in the victim's earnings or a proportion of the victim's target earnings in circumstances where the victim fails to earn those target earnings. It is essential that the circumstances surrounding the victim's initial trafficking are carefully examined.[139]

Trafficking of course is not a phenomenon confined to the African continent, and therefore it is not surprising that the findings in *PO* resonate with the more recent CG cases on China[140] and Thailand.[141]

The issue of relocation is currently attracting some debate and there is a school of thought that a divergence is appearing in the way it is approached by certain jurisdictions. One argument is that, while not coming from a distinct perspective, there is at least a different emphasis being placed on assessing the level of risk of persecution someone internally relocated would face, and on the other hand the sufficiency of State protection being offered. However this debate has only surfaced relatively recently, and is ongoing.[142]

---

137 *JO (Nigeria)* [2004].

138 *JO (Nigeria)* [2004] para 12.

139 *PO (Nigeria)* para 2 of the Introduction.

140 *HC & RC (Trafficked women)* China CG [2009] UKAIT 00027AIT Reported.

141 *AZ (Trafficked women)* Thailand CG [2010] UKUT 118 (IAC).

142 For more discussion see for example, Asylum Aid's Report, *Relocation, Relocation: The Impact of Internal Relocation on women Asylum Seekers*, November 2008, available at http://www.asylumaid.org.uk/data/files/publications/89/Relocation_Relocation_research_report.pdf. Although this report identifies this divergence the case law, even within the UK, it does not support such a definitive conclusion.

Conclusion

African cases have made a contribution to refugee status determination in the context of women's claims. What can be posited is that they have been instrumental in identifying certain practices, such as FGM, or abuses perpetrated by non-State actors, for example domestic violence, as persecutory. Furthermore, this recognition has allowed women claiming asylum on the grounds of such persecutory treatment to be characterized as belonging to a PSG and thus to be deserving of refugee status and the protection that it affords.

The African cases are not special *per se*, but best characterized as informing and reinforcing UK refugee law. The broad humanitarian purpose of any refugee determination process must be to ensure that all those who warrant it are afforded the surrogate protection of the 1951 Refugee Convention. This, for women, demands that the persecutory treatment and PSG as jurisprudentially interpreted reflect a gender sensitivity. This gender sensitivity however does not dilute the standard of proof demanded, nor diminish the need to meet the legal definition of a refugee.

As this chapter has demonstrated, the imaginative interpretation of PSG and willingness to accept non-State actors as agents of persecution are examples of approaches that have been employed successfully and which must continue to be employed for the effective determination of women's asylum applications.

References

Achiron M, *A Timeless Treaty under Attack* (UNHCR Refugees Magazine. Volume 2, No 123, 2001).

Bacon R and Booth K, 'Intersection of Refugee Law and Gender: Private Harm and Public Responsibility' (2000) 23(3) University of New South Wales Law Journal 135–63.

Bahl A, 'Home is Where the Brute Lives: Asylum Law and Gender-Based Claims of Persecution' (1997) 4 Cardozo Women's Law Journal 33–73.

Bennett C, *Relocation, Relocation: The Impact of Internal Relocation on Women Asylum Seekers* (Asylum Aid, 2008).

Benson J, 'Reinterpreting Gender: Southeast Asian Refugees and American Society' in L Carnio and R Krufeld (eds), *Reconstructing Lives, Recapturing Meaning: Refugee Identity, Gender and Culture Change* (Routledge, 1994).

Bloch A, Galvin T and Harrell-Bond B, 'Refugee Women in Europe: Some Aspects of the Legal and Policy Dimensions' (2000) 38(2) International Migration.

Bower K, 'Recognising Violence Against Women as Persecution on the Basis of Membership of a Particular Social Group' (1993) 7 Georgetown Immigration Law Journal 173–83.

Charlesworth H, 'What Are Women's International Human Rights?' in Rebecca J Cook (ed.), *Human Rights of Women: National and International Perspective* (University of Pennsylvania Press, 1994).

Charlesworth H and Chinkin C, *The Boundaries of International Law: A Feminist Analysis* (Manchester University Press, 2000).

Feller E, Türk V and Nicholson F, *Refugee Protection in International Law, UNHCR's Global Consultations on International Protection* (Cambridge University Press, 2003).

Goodwin-Gill G, 'Judicial Reasoning and "Social Group" after Islam and Shah' (1999) 11 International Journal of Refugee Law.

Goodwin-Gill G and McAdam J, *The Refugee in International Law* (Oxford University Press, 2007).

Greatbatch J, 'The Gender Difference: Feminist Critiques of Refugee Discourse' (1989) 1 International Journal of Refugee Law.

Hungarian Helsinki Committee, *Country Information in Asylum Procedures: Quality as a Legal Requirement in the EU*, 2011.

Kumin J, *Gender: Persecution in the Spotlight*, UNHCR, 2001.

MacKinnon C, 'Crimes of War, Crimes of Peace' (1993) 59 UCLA Women's Law Journal 69–70.

Macklin A, 'Cross-Border Shopping for Ideas: A Critical Review of United States, Canadian and Australian Approaches to Gender-Related Asylum Claims' (1998) 13 Georgetown Immigration Law Journal.

Meron T, *Human Rights and Humanitarian Norms as Customary Law* (Clarendon Press, 1991).

Randall M, 'Refugee Law and State Accountability for Violence Against Women: A Comparative Analysis of Legal Approaches to Recognizing Asylum Claims Based on Gender Persecution' (2002) 25 Harvard Women's Law Journal, 25th Anniversary Issue 281–318.

Rehn E and Johnson Sirleaf E, *Women, War & Peace: The Independent Experts' Assessment on the Impact of Armed Conflict on Women & Women's Role in Peace-Building* (United Nations Development Fund for Women, 2002).

Roberts A, 'Gender and Refugee Law' (2002) 22 Australian Yearbook of International Law.

Romany C, 'State Responsibility Goes Private' in Rebecca J Cook (ed.), *Human Rights of Women: National and International Perspectives* (University of Pennsylvania Press, 1994) 65–115.

Sircar O, 'Can the Women Flee? Gender-Based Persecution, Forced Migration and Asylum Law in South Asia' in Behera Navnita Chadha (ed.), *Gender, Conflict and Migration* (Sage Publications, 2006) 255–73.

Spijkerboer T, *Gender and Refugee Status* (Ashgate Publishing Group, 2000).

Thornton M (ed.), *Public and Private: Feminist Legal Debates* (Oxford University Press, 1995).

UNHCR, *The Special Situation and Needs of Refugee Women, Report of the UN Expert Group Meeting on International Migration Policies and the Status of Female Migrants*, 1990.

UNHCR, *Handbook on Procedures and Criteria for Determining Refugee Status under the 1951 Convention and the 1967 Protocol relating to the Status of Refugees*, 1992.

UNHCR, *UNHCR Handbook for the Protection of Women and Girls*, 2008.

Wallace RMM, 'Making the Refugee Convention Gender Sensitive: the Canadian Guidelines' (1996) 45(3) International & Comparative Law Quarterly 702–11.

Wallace RMM, 'Non-State Actors in the Context of Refugee Determination Process, with Particular Reference to the Position of Women' (2007) 32 South African Yearbook of International Law 179–207.

Wallace RMM and Holliday A, 'Application of Gender Guidelines within the Asylum Determination Process: Reflections on the UK and Canadian Experience' in CPM Waters (ed.), *British and Canadian Perspectives on International Law* (Niemhoff, 2006) 169–80.

Chapter 11
Fora and Programmes for Refugees in Latin America

Liliana Lyra Jubilut

Introduction

In a book concerning regional protection of asylum seekers, a contribution focusing on Latin America[1] could not be absent. This is due to the fact that (i) the region has been involved, since the 1980s[2], in the advancement of International Refugee Law and protection through collective efforts and agendas, and (ii) that said efforts have been praised[3] and the region came to be regarded as something of a model in the topic by the international community.[4]

The regional approach has proved to have reflexes in two different scenarios. First, it reflects on national practice and policies, as States seem to be inspired by

1 For the purposes of this paper the expression 'Latin America' will be employed broadly to encompass all American countries located below Mexico, excluding States in the Caribbean even if they have a Latin-based language or a Latin-based historical background. The States in Latin America, thus, are the States of Central and South America combined; as defined by the United Nations Statistical Division (data available at http://unstats.un.org/unsd/methods/m49/m49region.htm#americas). In light of this the term Latin America in this paper refers to: Argentina, Belize, Bolivia, Brazil, Chile, Colombia, Costa Rica, Ecuador, El Salvador, Guatemala, Guyana, Honduras, Mexico, Nicaragua, Panama, Paraguay, Peru, Suriname, Uruguay, and Venezuela.

2 With the Cartagena Declaration of 1984, Latin America can be said to have started its regional approach to refugee protection.

3 The region has been said to use a 'creative, innovative and pragmatic approach' to refugee protection as well as to providing 'an example of how political will, regional and international solidarity, and shared responsibility are essential principles for offering protection and reaching durable solutions'. See UNHCR, *The Refugee Situation in Latin America: Protection and Solutions Based on the Pragmatic Approach of the Cartagena Declaration on Refugees of 1984 – Discussion Document* (2006) 18 Int'l J. Refugee L. 255. It also has been said that 'Latin America has a generous, long-standing tradition of asylum and protection of refugees'. See P Lavanchi, 'The Mexico Declaration and Plan of Action: Reaffirming Latin America's Generous Tradition of Asylum and Innovative Solutions' (2006) 18 Int'l J. Refugee L. 450.

4 As was the case of pronouncements by UNHCR staff during the International Meeting on Refugee and Stateless Persons Protection and Mixed Migratory Movements in the Americas that took place in Brasilia in November 2010.

the collective initiatives adopted by the region and try to include the developments brought along by them into the national legal systems, which may lead to improved protection. Second, it reflects on the region as a whole as collective standards and actions enhance international solidarity and cooperation and aim to balance the interests and needs of States and of the refugee population, thus enabling a more humane approach to International Refugee Law and protection.[5]

In light of this, it is important to describe how Latin America has been creating regional approaches to the protection of asylum seekers and refugees, through the establishment of fora and programs, which is the aim of this contribution.

In order to present as comprehensive scenario as possible, this chapter will highlight the backdrop against which Latin America's regional approach is set and the main documents that have emerged from the region. It will also note the main national developments that originate from the regional approach to International Refugee Law, with the purpose of allowing for conclusions on whether or not the region can truly be seen as a model of protection of asylum seekers and refugees in a regional or even international perspective.

This contribution is thus divided into three main sections: first, there is an assessment of refugees' protection emerging from a regional approach. This is followed by a description of the right of asylum in Latin America. The last part focuses more extensively on refugees' protection in Latin America, highlighting three important regional documents on the matter: the Cartagena Declaration, the Mexico Declaration and Plan of Action and the Brasilia Declaration.

Refugees' Protection Through a Regional Approach

It can be said that regionalism lies at the foundation of refugee protection, given that the first initiatives on the topic 'were regional in the sense that they were directed at a perceived "European" problem'.[6] In this sense, the term seems to have a delimiting significance, even a negative one as it is limiting the scope of attention and of protection.

This negative connotation also appears when regionalism leads to protectionism or when it serves as an excuse to not develop international mechanism and documents on refuge protection, and hence may lead to the diminishing of the universal international standards. In all of these cases, it seems that the inadequacy of the concept arises from the imposition of limitations to refugee protection, though the adoption of excluding concepts and/or the adoption of collective practices that, in reality, limit and violate International Refugee Law.

---

5 LL Jubilut and WP Carneiro, 'Resettlement in Solidarity: a regional new approach towards a more humane durable solution' (2011) 30(3) Refugee Survey Quarterly.

6 S Kneebone and F Rawlings-Sanaei (eds), *New Regionalism and Asylum Seekers: Challenges Ahead* (Berghahn Books, 2007), 4.

Nowadays, however, when one speaks of regionalism it seems to have a different undertone, rather as a new approach to refugee protection that can enhance the international system by coexisting with it and tailoring initiatives and documents to a region's reality.[7]

Regionalism can be said to mean 'a collective or communal response within a region to a global issue where the parties share a common purpose or destiny'.[8] It is in this sense that the UNHCR seems to have embraced regionalism as a way forward in the aspect of refugee protection with a view to strengthening it,[9] and has declared regional documents to be a part of International Refugee Law.[10]

This positive facet of regionalism seems to be the one in place when a region comes together in trying to enhance International Refugee Law and protection, through the adoption of new concepts, new documents and new initiatives that build upon the international system's minimum criteria to develop refugee protection. This seems to be the case of Latin America's attitude toward refugee protection since the 1980s[11] with the adoption of the Cartagena Declaration.

The adoption of a regional approach to Refugee Law and protection is not exclusive to Latin America. It seems, actually, to be the current trend in refugee protection.[12]

The regional approach to the protection of asylum seekers and refugees can be said to have started with the Organization of African Unity's Convention Governing the Specific Aspects of Refugee Problems in Africa[13] in 1969, which enlarged the

---

7 On the different meanings of regionalism see for instance International Law Commission, 'Report of the work of the Study Group on the Fragmentation of International Law: Difficulties arising from the diversification and expansion of international law' UN Doc A/CN.4/L.682 (2006), paras 195–217, available at http://daccess-dds-ny.un.org/doc/UNDOC/LTD/G06/610/77/PDF/G0661077.pdf?OpenElement.

8 Kneebone and Rawlings-Sanaei, *New Regionalism and Asylum Seekers: Challenges Ahead* 2.

9 UNHCR. Executive Committee of the High Commissioner's Program, *Note on International Protection*, UN Doc A/AC.96/930 (7 July 2000), para 39, available at http://www.unhcr.org/cgi-bin/texis/vtx/home/opendocPDFViewer.html?docid=3ae68d6c4&query=note%20on%20international%20protection.

10 Ibid. para 32: 'The international refugee protection regime is a dynamic body of universal and regional refugee law and standards …'.

11 It is interesting to note that regionalism in general has seen a revival and change in the 1980s. See J Mittelman, 'Rethinking the "New Regionalism" in the Context of Globalization' (1996) 2 Global Governance 189–213.

12 In an issue dedicated to regional solutions in 1995 (issue 99), Refugees Magazine pointed to the fact that 'regional and comprehensive responses may be the only possible solution to the complexity and magnitude of today's refugee problems', available at http://www.unhcr.org/cgi-bin/texis/vtx/search?page=search&docid=3b5423494&query=regionalism.

13 Adopted by the Organization of African Unity on 10 September 1969, available at http://www.africa-union.org/Official_documents/Treaties_%20Conventions_%20Protocols/Refugee_Convention.pdf.

definition of refugees,[14] tailoring it to the realities of the African continent, and has been producing results since them.[15] The regional approach to asylum differs from situation to situation, and 'sometimes, as in Central America and South East Asia, regional organizations have led the effort in close partnership with UNHCR. In other cases, such as Cambodia, Liberia or Rwanda, regional organizations may cooperate with U.N. peacekeeping missions that include UNHCR'.[16]

In reality, in an age of closed borders and mixed migratory fluxes, with many States – including major players of the international arena – not willing or not prepared to advance refugee protection in universal documents and efforts,[17] regional developments appear sometimes to be the only viable way forward.[18] This type of regionalism, especially when paired with the continuous respect to and advancement of the international standards,[19] appears to have a positive outcome in general, which certainly seems to be the case of Latin America.

The Right of Asylum in Latin America

A regional approach has been in place in Latin America since the 1800s in relation to granting protection for people suffering or that may suffer persecution in the form of the right of asylum.[20] In fact the first regional normative on this right is said to have been the one in this region.[21]

14 Art 1(2), which states that 'The term "refugee" shall also apply to every person who, owing to external aggression, occupation, foreign domination or events seriously disturbing public order in either part or the whole of his country of origin or nationality, is compelled to leave his place of habitual residence in order to seek refuge in another place outside his country of origin or nationality'.

15 As will be seen throughout this book.

16 BN Stein, 'Regional solutions' (1995) 99 Refugees Magazine.

17 The Convention Plus initiative from UNHCR seems to be build upon this idea, proposing new approaches to International Refugee Law and protection but not sponsoring a new universal document or even a reform of the existing legal norms.

18 See for instance the conclusion of UNHCR that: 'The international system has been in a state of significant transformation since the end of the Cold War. There was hope that these changes would result in the strengthening of international law and multilateral approaches to address international problems. Developments have not, however, fully realized this hope'. See *Note on International Protection* above n 9, para 31.

19 This seems to be the position of UNHCR. See for instance UNHCR. Executive Committee of the High Commissioner's Program, *Note on International Protection*, EC/62/SC/CRP.12 (31 May 2011), paras 2, 6, 8 and 80, available at http://www.unhcr.org/cgi-bin/texis/vtx/home/opendocPDFViewer.html?docid=4de4f6fc9&query=note%20on%20international%20protection.

20 LL Jubilut, *O Direito Internacional dos Refugiados e sua aplicação no ordenamento jurídico brasileiro* (São Paulo: Método, 2007) 38.

21 JH Fichel De Andrade, *Direito internacional dos refugiados – Evolução Histórica (1921–1952)* (Renovar, 1996) 18.

The right of asylum began to be theorized by Hugo Grotius[22] and was first declared in a Constitution after the French Revolution in 1793.[23] In Latin America it first appeared in a regional document in 1889 with the Treaty of International Penal Law of Montevideo (*Tratado de Direito Penal de Montevideo*).[24] The Treaty dedicated its second title to the subject of asylum, and established in its articles 15 to 18 provisions to protect people who had committed non-political offenses who it regarded as political refugees.[25]

Even though the mixture of the concepts of asylum and refuge are not technically adequate, as will be explored below, the Treaty is an important instrument in highlighting a regional concern with people suffering or that may suffer persecution since the end of the nineteenth century, and can be said to have inaugurated the legislation on the right of asylum in the region.[26] Such a right has been stated contemporarily both in universal and regional documents, with the latter being more assertive than the former.

In the universal arena the right is stated in Article 14 of the Universal Declaration of Human Rights which establishes that:

> (1) Everyone has the right to seek and to enjoy in other countries asylum from persecution; (2) This right may not be invoked in the case of prosecutions genuinely arising from non-political crimes or from acts contrary to the purposes and principles of the United Nations.[27]

In the regional arena, the right of asylum appears both on (i) Article 27 of the American Declaration of the Rights and Duties of Man which states that: 'Every person has the right, in case of pursuit not resulting from ordinary crimes, to seek and receive asylum in foreign territory, in accordance with the laws of each country and with international agreements',[28] and on (ii) Article 22 (7) of the American Convention of Human Rights which establishes that 'Every person has the right to seek and be granted asylum in a foreign territory, in accordance with the legislation

22 E Reut-Nicolussi, 'Displaced Persons in International Law' (1948) 73 Recueil des Cours de la Academie de Droit International 27.

23 Ibid.: 16.

24 Available at http://www.unhcr.org/refworld/type,MULTILATERALTREATY,AMERICAS,,3ae6b3781c,0.html.

25 See especially Arts 16 and 17.

26 It is important to note that the Treaty was adopted in the South American Congress on Private International Law in Montevideo on 23 January 1889; and although it is not a document for the whole of Latin America it served as the first document with a regional approach to people suffering or that may suffer persecution.

27 Available at http://www.un.org/en/documents/udhr/index.shtml#a14.

28 Available at http://www.cidh.oas.org/Basicos/English/Basic2.American%20Declaration.htm.

of the state and international conventions, in the event he is being pursued for political offenses or related common crimes'.[29]

From the wording of the provisions, one sees that the regional norm grants not only the right to seek asylum but also to be granted asylum in face of persecution, therefore reinforcing the protective framework of asylum in the Americas.

However, the broader wording of the universal provision can be said to expand the possibility of protection as it does not limit the persecution to cases of political offenses or related common crimes, as the American provision seems to do. In fact the universal norm does not qualify persecution in its general provision, thus enabling the formation of a larger protection network.

Besides being based on both regional and universal frameworks and of being in place since the end of the 19th century, the protection of people suffering or that may suffer persecution in Latin America has yet another relevant aspect to be noted: the right of asylum in the region is upheld through two distinct, yet complementary, institutes.

One the one hand, the region implements the right of asylum by means of the institution of asylum[30] which can take two different forms: territorial asylum – when the protection is requested in the territory of the granting States – and diplomatic asylum – when the protection is sought in representations of the granting State (for example Embassies).[31] On the other hand, the region upholds the basic premises of the right of asylum through its commitment to the institution of refuge. It is possible to highlight the major differences[32] between asylum and refuge in a schematic way, so as to make them clear but not detour from the focus of this contribution. In this sense while asylum: (i) exists since Ancient Times; (ii) is a sovereign and discretionary decision by the granting State; (iii) does not have legal standards to be met for concession; (iv) can only be granted in face of actual political persecution; (v) can be diplomatic – when granted inside the state of origin or residency of the person fleeing persecution – or territorial – when granted in the territory of the granting State; (vi) the only obligation that stems from it is legal residency and (vii) only exists once the State decides to grant it, consequently being based on a constitutive decision by the granting state; the institute of refuge (i) appeared in the beginning of the twentieth century; (ii) has an international normative; (iii) has its implementation supervised by an international organ – since the 1950s the United Nations High Commissioner for Refugees (UNHCR); (iv) cannot be applied in certain cases (exclusion clauses); (v) applies to cases of well-founded fear of persecution based on race, religion, nationality, social group

29 Available at http://www.oas.org/juridico/english/treaties/b-32.html.

30 See Jubilut, *O Direito Internacional dos Refugiados e sua aplicação no ordenamento jurídico brasileiro* 37–8.

31 See Jubilut, *O Direito Internacional dos Refugiados e sua aplicação no ordenamento jurídico brasileiro* 38.

32 See also LPTF Barreto, *Das diferenças entre os institutos jurídicos, asilos e refúgio*, available at www.mj.gov.br/sns/artigo_refugiado.htm.

or political opinion; (vi) requires alienage to be applied (i.e. the person seeking to be recognized as a refugee has to be outside their state of origin or habitual residence; (vii) generates responsibilities to the granting State in relation to the refugee and (viii) is a right of the refugee to be recognized as such in the cases set down by the normative standards; being hence granted by a declaratory decision.[33]

Nonetheless, both institutes aim at protecting people from (existing or possible) persecution and have a humanitarian nature, being, consequently, complementary forms of protection.[34]

Given that refuge has a deeper sense of normativity and hence assists many more people, it can be said to have been the preferred method in the region for advancing protection for people suffering or that may suffer persecution. In this sense, the commitment of the States in the Americas to the Convention Relating to the Status of Refugees of 1951 (1951 Convention)[35] and the Protocol Relating to the Status of Refugees of 1967 (67 Protocol) is paramount.

As of October 2013, 27 States[36] in the Americas and Caribbean were a part of the Convention,[37] and 2 States[38] were a part only of the 67 Protocol. This means that within Latin America, with the exception of Guyana,[39] all States in the region are committed to the universal documents on International Refugee Law, and, therefore, have obligations in implementing refugees' protection and therefore protecting both refugees and asylum seekers.

---

33 Liliana L. Jubilut, 'International Refugee Law and Protection in Brazil: a model in South America?' (2006) 19(1) Journal of Refugee Studies 29.

34 Ibid. at 29. See also Flavia Piovesan and Liliana L. Jubilut, 'Regional Developments: Americas' in Andreas Zimmermann (ed.), *Commentary on the 1951 Convention Relating to the Status of Refugees and its 1967 Protocol*, 2011 at 213.

35 Available at http://www.unhcr.org/3b66c2aa10.html.

36 Such States are: Antigua and Barbuda; Argentina; Bahamas; Belize; Bolivia; Brazil; Canada; Chile; Colombia; Costa Rica; Dominica; Dominican Republic; Ecuador; El Salvador; Guatemala; Haiti; Honduras; Jamaica; Mexico; Nicaragua; Panama; Paraguay; Peru; Saint Vincent and the Grenadines; Suriname; Trinidad and Tobago and Uruguay (cf. data available at http://treaties.un.org/pages/ShowMTDSGDetails.aspx?src=UNTSONLINE&tabid=2&mtdsg_no=V-5&chapter=5&lang=en#Participants, and, http://treaties.un.org/pages/ViewDetailsII.aspx?&src=UNTSONLINE&mtdsg_no=V~2&chapter=5&Temp=mtdsg2&lang=en. Access on October 23, 2013).

37 Saint Kitts and Nevis is a part only to the 51 Convention (cf. data available at http://treaties.un.org/pages/ShowMTDSGDetails.aspx?src=UNTSONLINE&tabid=2&mtdsg_no=V-5&chapter=5&lang=en#Participants. Access on October 23, 2013).

38 Such States are the United States of America and Venezuela (cf. data available at http://treaties.un.org/pages/ViewDetailsII.aspx?&src=UNTSONLINE&mtdsg_no=V~2&chapter=5&Temp=mtdsg2&lang=en. Access on October 23, 2013).

39 It is important here to remember the definition of Latin America for this chapter (as seen in footnote 1 supra), which excludes States such as Cuba, which are also not a part of the international system of refugee protection.

The Asylum Seeker's Protection in Latin America

The regional commitment to refuge, however, goes farther than the adoption of the universal standards, given that, as in the case of the right of asylum, truly regional approaches have been developed.

In the 1980s the Latin American region was faced, on the one hand, with armed conflicts in Central America[40] which generated massive fluxes of refugees[41] and, on the other hand, with waves of re-democratization[42] that brought about renewed commitments to human rights. With this scenario as its background, a balance between the needs of States and of refugees in a response to the Central American refugee crisis was required.[43] As a response to this need, a mainly academic symposium that also congregated governments' representatives and members of civil society organizations was held in Cartagena de Indias in Colombia in 1984.[44] From this seminar emerged the Cartagena Declaration on Refugees (Cartagena Declaration) that changed, and continues to change, the regional approach to refugee protection in the region.[45]

The Cartagena Declaration

The Cartagena Declaration[46] was adopted on 22 November 1984 and contains four main parts.[47] The first part consists of the preamble divided into seven paragraphs.

---

40 R William I, *Transnational Conflicts: Central America, Social Changes and Globalization* (Verso, 2003).

41 See for instance A Suhrke, 'A crisis diminished: refugees in the developing world' (1992–93) 48 Int'l J. 218. In this paper the author points to 2 to 3 million people displaced due to the conflicts in Central America.

42 GA Lopez and M Stohl, *Liberalization and Redemocratization in Latin America* (Greenwood Press, 1987).

43 See *The Refugee Situation in Latin America: Protection and Solutions Based on the Pragmatic Approach of the Cartagena Declaration on Refugees of 1984 – Discussion Document* above n 3, 263.

44 The symposium was sponsored by UNHCR, the government of Colombia, the University of Cartagena de Indias and the Regional Center for Third World Studies, according to CO Miranda, 'Toward a Broader Definition of Refugee: 20th Century Development Trends' (1989–90) 20 Cal. W. Int'l L.J. 323.

45 See, for instance, F Piovesan and LL Jubilut, 'Regional Developments: Americas' in A Zimmermann (ed.), *Commentary on the 1951 Convention Relating to the Status of Refugees and its 1967 Protocol* (Oxford University Press, 2011) .and Jubilut and Carneiro, 'Resettlement in Solidarity: a regional new approach towards a more humane durable solution'.

46 Cartagena Declaration on Refugees, 22 November 1984. Available at www.unhcr.ch/refworld/refworld/legal/instrume/asylum/cart_eng.htm, http://www.unhcr.org/refworld/docid/3ae6b36ec.html or at http://www.unhcr.org/basics/BASICS/45dc19084.pdf.

47 In the version presented at http://www.asylumlaw.org/docs/international/Central America.PDF the Cartagena Declaration has only three parts.

The second part makes reference to the Contadora Act on Peace and Co-operation in Central America, a document related to the Central America conflict of the 1980s and which aims at ending it and dealing with its consequences that include over 2 million refugees.[48] This reference highlights the links between the Cartagena Declaration and the context of political strife in the region and helps explain the reasoning behind its adoption.

The Colloquium on the International Protection of Refugees in Central America, Mexico and Panama – Legal and Humanitarian Problems (*Colloquio sobre la Protección Internacional de los Refugiados en América Central, México y Panamá – Problemas Jurídicos y Humanitários*) from which the Cartagena Declaration stems 'acknowledges with appreciation the commitments with regard to refugees included in the Contadora Act … the basis of which the Colloquium fully shares'.[49] After presenting its context, the Cartagena Declaration establishes 17 conclusions that form the core of the prescriptive provisions of the document, and which are followed in the subsequent parts by five recommendations and two paragraphs containing acknowledgments.

The main provisions of the Declaration are, thus, contained in its conclusions which bring important changes (and improvements) to International Refugee Law and protection in Latin America, leading to the Cartagena Declaration being regarded as 'one of the most encompassing approaches to the refugee question'.[50]

The first change brought about by the Declaration relates to establishing a regional commitment to refugees and asylum seekers and their protection in a region comprised mainly by democracies that are, as a result, willing to keep faith with their human rights obligations, as well as human rights' recognition and defense. This is important since, even if there had been previous regional efforts in Latin America, they were mainly devoted to the right of asylum broadly, as mentioned above, and were produced in the context of a region with dictatorships and/or military regimes. The Declaration of Cartagena was the first landmark of a new regional approach to refugees and allows for the topic to be developed within the context of States that are willing to advance the rule of law and human rights.[51]

In light of the above, the Cartagena Declaration endeavours to take into account the needs of refugees and proposes new initiatives that were tailored to the region's need; being, thus, a document with both a practical and an aspirational side.

The commitment to a regional approach to refugee law can be seen, for instance, in the call for 'systematic harmonization of national legislation on refugees' which appears in the First Conclusion of the Cartagena Declaration.

---

48 W Spindler, 'The Mexico Plan of Action: protecting refugees through international solidarity' (2005) 24 Forced Migration Review 24.

49 Cartagena Declaration on Refugees, above n 46. 1st paragraph of the preamble.

50 GS Goodwin-Gill, *The Refugee in International Law* (2nd edn, Oxford University Press, 1996) 38.

51 See Piovesan and Jubilut, 'Regional Developments: Americas' 218.

On the other hand, the commitment to human rights is highlighted in the second change brought along by the Cartagena Declaration: the establishment of a broader definition for the recognition of refugees.

The Declaration proposes, in its Third Conclusion, an enlargement of the universal definition by adding to it the possibility of including among refugees the asylum seekers,

> … who have fled their country because their lives, safety or freedom have been threatened by generalized violence, foreign aggression, internal conflicts, massive violation of human rights or other circumstances which have seriously disturbed public order.

The Cartagena Declaration states that this new criterion is motivated by the Organization of African Unity Convention Governing the Specific Aspects of Refugee Problems in Africa[52] and also the reports of the InterAmerican Commission of Human Rights,[53] thus demonstrating that the region avails itself of the best practices on International Refugee Law and protection around the world.

It has been said that the Cartagena Declaration has established a new criterion of recognizing refugees, an expanded definition[54] or a more comprehensive criteria[55] but this seemingly

> falls short of explaining the concept of Cartagena. In fact it is not simply an extension, as it does not introduce new criteria within the ranks of an individualized perspective. It builds the refugee definition upon the objective situation and the social and political environment of the country of origin as the main definition criterion. The recognition as a refugee, therefore, occurs regardless of the individual attributes of the person in need of protection (as religion, or ethnicity) as in the traditional universal criteria.[56]

The possibility of recognizing people fleeing massive violation of human rights as refugees is an important advancement of International Refugee Law and protection in the region, and allows for the protection of people escaping from civil conflicts or strife, war and even dictatorships, given that all of these situations are in themselves or can lead to violations of human rights.

---

52 See Cartagena Declaration above n 46, 3rd Conclusion.

53 See Cartagena Declaration above n 46, 3rd Conclusion. See also *The Refugee Situation in Latin America: Protection and Solutions Based on the Pragmatic Approach of the Cartagena Declaration on Refugees of 1984 – Discussion Document*, (2006) above n 3, 264.

54 Carlos Ortiz Miranda. Op. cit. supra at 44 at 324.

55 JC Hathaway, *The Rights of Refugees under International Law*, 2005 at 67.

56 Liliana L Jubilut and Wellington P Carneiro. Op. cit., supra at 5 at 67.

It is important to highlight that the regional definition of refugees is to be used alongside the universal criteria, as it does not mean to replace but complement it.

In this sense: 'The Cartagena Declaration declares that aside from the refugees recognized under the 1951 Convention there exists other persons that require international protection'.[57]

The Cartagena Declaration itself highlights the importance for States to accede and/or to respect the universal standards of International Refugee Law and protection[58] and recalls some of its most relevant provisions such as: (i) 'the peaceful, non-political and exclusively humanitarian nature' of granting refugee status;[59] (ii) the imperative nature of the *non-refoulement* principle, which is a corner-stone of International Refugee Law and protection and which it declares to be a rule of *jus cogens*;[60] and (iii) the fact that the 1951 Convention and the 1967 Protocol establish a minimum standard of treatment for refugees.[61]

The Cartagena Declaration was approved by the General Assembly of the Organization of American States in 1985, 'which resolved to urge member states to extend support and, insofar as possible, to implement the conclusions and recommendations to the Cartagena Declaration on Refugees'.[62]

Given that the Declaration was inspired by the InterAmerican Human Rights System, as already mentioned, and that this system has approved the Declaration, one can see that the topic of International Refugee Law and protection in Latin American is, on the one hand, being treated in a holistic manner and in a context of human rights,[63] consequently allowing for a more integral protection and that, on the other hand, it has different fora in which it is to be dealt with, which can enable debates with different actors and against different backgrounds.

The Cartagena Declaration's definition of refugees has been adopted by 15 Latin American States[64] in their national legislation, which is relevant in so far as

57 See *The Refugee Situation in Latin America: Protection and Solutions Based on the Pragmatic Approach of the Cartagena Declaration on Refugees of 1984 – Discussion Document* above n 3, 262.

58 See Cartagena Declaration above n 46, 1st and 2nd Conclusions.

59 See Cartagena Declaration above n 46, 4th Conclusion.

60 See Cartagena Declaration above n 46, 5th Conclusion.

61 See Cartagena Declaration above n 46, 8th Conclusion.

62 Cf. data available at http://www.hrea.org/index.php?doc_id=413.

63 See Piovesan and Jubilut, 'Regional Developments: Americas' 218 and seq.

64 Such States are Argentina, Belize, Bolivia, Brazil, Chile, Colombia, Ecuador, El Salvador, Guatemala, Honduras, Mexico, Nicaragua, Paraguay, Peru and Uruguay (cf. data available at http://www.acnur.org/t3/que-hace/proteccion/declaracion-de-cartagena-sobre-los-refugiados/paises-que-incorporan-cartagena-en-la-legislacion-nacional/?L=gulnlxwoshxdx and on http://www.acnur.org/t3/fileadmin/scripts/doc.php?file=biblioteca/pdf/2541). (It is relevant to note that the data here is a combination of both sources as, for instance, Ecuador does not appear on the list present on the first webpage mentioned in this footnote but appears on the list presented by the second webpage mentioned in this footnote). Accessed on October 23, 2013. In 2012 Ecuador has changed its legislation and is

the Declaration itself is a soft law instrument. Some States have kept the original wording of the Declaration and others have changed it[65] but maintaining the so-called 'spirit of Cartagena' that has come to mean an approach to International Refugee Law and protection that is (i) broader in scope, (ii) more closely related to human rights and (iii) more beneficial in terms of people being protected given the added criterion for refugee status.

This relation to human rights is also present in the sense that,

> ... [t]he Declaration includes the protection and treatment that should be offered to refugees during the entire cycle of forced displacement. In fact, it deals with a summary of good practices, based on the 1951 Convention relating to the Status of Refugees and its 1967 Protocol, which brings together the generous tradition of asylum in Latin America and is complemented by the integration of the norms and standards of human rights protection, in particular the American Convention on Human Rights, and international humanitarian law.[66]

Also, 'the Cartagena Declaration makes a pioneering reference as much for the economic, social and cultural rights of the asylum seekers and refugees as for the problem of the internally displaced persons'.[67]

This close link between Refugee Law and protection to human rights is important given that 'nowadays the prevailing view is that refugee law and protection are a part of international human rights law in its broader sense (i.e. international law on the protection of human beings)'.[68] Besides this, refugees as human beings have to have their human rights respected in order for protection to be considered integral.[69]

Moreover, in relation to the Latin American context this link between human rights and International Refugee Law and protection shows a change in the politics of the region which have been marked by human rights abuse[70] in the past and seem nowadays to be more committed to international human rights and show, as

---

not currently using the criteria from the Cartagena Declaration, so only 14 States have now the Cartagena Declaration definition of refugees in their national legislation.

65 Piovesan and Jubilut, 'Regional Developments: Americas' 219–20.

66 See *The Refugee Situation in Latin America: Protection and Solutions Based on the Pragmatic Approach of the Cartagena Declaration on Refugees of 1984 – Discussion Document*, (2006) above n 3, 262.

67 Ibid. 263.

68 See Piovesan and Jubilut, 'Regional Developments: Americas' 208.

69 LL Jubilut and SMOS Apolinário, 'A necessidade de proteção internacional no âmbito da migração' (2010) 11(6)(1) Revista Direito GV 275 and seq.

70 D Harris, 'Regional Protection of Human Rights: The Inter-American Achievement' in HJ Steiner and P Alston (eds), *International Human Rights in Context* (2nd edn, Oxford University Press, 2000) 874–7.

a result, the protection of the rights stemming from human dignity; thus providing for a more holistic approach and protection of refugees.[71]

This more comprehensive attitude towards refugees has had some impact on national legislation, leading some Latin American countries to establish gender-based persecution or sexual violence as reasons for refugee status[72] and others to have specific provisions for refugee children in their national legislation.[73]

The third change produced by the Cartagena Declaration is the establishment of fora to debate International Refugee Law and protection with a view to continuing to improve it in the region. Such debates occur in periodical assessment meetings of the implementation of the Declaration, and from which new regional instruments have emerged.

The Regional Instrumental Consequences of the Cartagena Declaration

Since the adoption of the Cartagena Declaration, regular regional meetings, where debate fora were established, have been held. Generally the meetings that have had the most impact have occurred in commemoration and/or celebration of the most relevant anniversaries of the documents on International Refugee Law and protection. This was the case, for instance, of the San Jose Declaration on Refugees and Displaced Persons,[74] adopted in 1994, during the International Colloquium

71 See Piovesan and Jubilut, 'Regional Developments: Americas' 218.

72 See for instance as in the cases of Guatemala that have listed gender-based persecution and sexual violence as criteria for refugee status in art. 11(d) of Acuerdo Gubernativo No 383 del 14 de Septiembre de 2001 – Reglamento para la protección y determinación del estatuto de refugiado en el territorio del Estado de Guatemala, available at http://www.acnur.org/t3/fileadmin/scripts/doc.php?file=biblioteca/pdf/1410. And see of Honduras, in art. 42, 3, e of Decreto No 208 del 3 de marzo de 2003 – Ley de migración y extranjería, available at http://www.acnur.org/t3/fileadmin/scripts/doc.php?file=biblioteca/pdf/2528.

73 JCM González, 'La Protección Internacional de Refugiados en el Continente Americano: Nuevos Desarrollos' 2008, in Comité Jurídico Interamericano, Departamento de Derecho Internacional, Secretaría de Asuntos Jurídicos, Secretaría General (eds) (2008) *XXXV Curso de Derecho Internacional* 358.

74 See San José Declaration on Refugees and Displaced Persons, 7 December 1994, available at http://www.unhcr.org/refworld/docid/4a54bc3fd.html. There have been other regional documents adopted in the region. However they either had (i) a specific focus; or (ii) were developed by civil society and did not count with States' commitments; or (iii) are considered to be of lesser importance to the development of Refugee Law and protection in the region; or (iv) do not represent the most current perceptions on International Refugee Law. These documents are: Declaración de Quito, 2010 (a document from civil society); Declaración de Quito sobre migraciones, democracia, desarrollo y derechos humanos. Quito, Ecuador, 2002 (a document from civil society); Declaración de Río sobre la institución del refugio. Rio de Janeiro, Brasil, 2000 (a document by MERCOSUL, Bolivia and Chile); Declaración de Tlatelolco, México, 1999 (a document from the Seminario de Tlatelolco

in Commemoration of the 'Tenth Anniversary of the Cartagena Declaration on Refugees'. The San Jose Declaration[75] stressed the importance of the Cartagena Declaration and highlighted that

> pursuant to the adoption of the Cartagena Declaration a significant process in the search for durable solutions has been initiated, whereby such solutions have been integrated within the framework of convergence between respect for human rights, peace-building and linkage with economic and social development.[76]

In its conclusions, the San Jose Declaration mostly repeats and reinforces the provisions of the Cartagena Declaration, but states through an innovative proposition the 'complementary nature and convergence between the systems of protection to persons established in International Human Rights Law, International Humanitarian Law and International Refugee Law'.[77]

It also encourages 'governments to seek humanitarian solutions, within a coordinated framework'[78] which means that the San Jose Declaration not only continues with the idea of regional fora and the 'spirit of Cartagena' to tackle the issue of refugees but also sets the premises for further advancing International Refugee Law and protection in Latin America, which will be done in a profound way ten years later.

The Mexico Declaration and Plan of Action

A new significant regional program in dealing with refugee protection was achieved in the celebration of the Twentieth Anniversary of the Cartagena Declaration: the Mexico Declaration and Plan of Action (MPA).[79]

The MPA 'is a regional strategic and operational framework developed to address the complex humanitarian situation resulting from forced displacement

---

de 1989 sobre Acciones Prácticas en el Derecho de los Refugiados en América Latina y el Caribe, that presents refuge and asylum as synonyms); and Declaración y compromiso del Primer Foro Regional 'Enfoque de género en el trabajo con las mujeres refugiadas, repatriadas y desplazadas' (FOREFEM), Guatemala, 1992. (Cf. data available at http://www.acnur.org/t3/que-hace/proteccion/declaracion-de-cartagena-sobre-los-refugiados/antecedentes-juridicos-y-desarrollos-de-la-declaracion-de-cartagena-sobre-refugiados/ and http://www.cartamesoamericana.com/modules.php?name=News&file=article&sid=477 on the topic of the Declaration of Tlatelolco take on refuge and asylum).

75 See San José Declaration above n 74.

76 Ibid. Part I, para 4.

77 Ibid. 3rd Conclusion.

78 Ibid. 6th Conclusion.

79 ACNUR, Mexico Declaration and Plan of Action to Strengthen the International Protection of Refugees in Latin America, 16 November 2004, available at http://www.acnur.org/biblioteca/pdf/3453.pdf.

in Latin America'[80] which was adopted in 2004[81] by 20 States,[82] including 17 States from Latin America,[83] and has as its context not only the celebration of the Cartagena Declaration but also the Colombian refugee crisis.[84]

Once again, one sees that the region is compelled to deal with a significant refugee crisis – with numbers of refugees and internally displaced people sitting at over four million[85] – stemming from a conflict that has been in place for over 40 years[86] and choosing to do so in a regional framework.

More specifically, the MPA proposed a regional approach to the Colombian refugee crisis, building upon the 'spirit of Cartagena'. In this sense the MPA developed a two-pillar strategy. On the one hand, one finds the second chapter of the MPA which deals with the international protection of refugees, and, on

80 UNHCR, *Mexico Plan of Action: The impact of regional solidarity* (1st edn 2007), 11.

81 The MPA was adopted after meetings in San Jose, Brasilia, Cartagena and Bogota. See *The Refugee Situation in Latin America: Protection and Solutions Based on the Pragmatic Approach of the Cartagena Declaration on Refugees of 1984 – Discussion Document* above n 3, 252.

82 The MPA was adopted by Argentina, Bolivia, Brazil, Chile, Colombia, Costa Rica, Cuba, Dominican Republic, Ecuador, El Salvador, Guatemala, Haiti, Honduras, Mexico, Nicaragua, Panama, Paraguay, Peru, Uruguay and Venezuela. Cf. data obtained with Juan Carlos Murillo González – UNHCR Regional Legal Officer for the Americas, who the author would like to thank for this contribution and at UNHCR, *Memoir of the Twentieth Anniversary of the Cartagena Declaration on Refugees* (2005) 365–7, available at http://www.acnur.org/biblioteca/pdf/3868.pdf?view=1.

83 Only Belize, Guyana and Suriname are not a part of the MPA. It is interesting to note though that (i) Belize was a Observer State at the event in which the MPA was adopted (see UNHCR above n 82, 367); (ii) that in a document assessing Latin America and the MPA, UNHCR has included these three States (see data available at:www.unhcr.org/455443b30.html); and that (iii) the Dominican Republic and Haiti that were Observer States during the adoption of the MPA later became parts of it (see UNHCR above n 82, 368).

84 See *The Refugee Situation in Latin America: Protection and Solutions Based on the Pragmatic Approach of the Cartagena Declaration on Refugees of 1984 – Discussion Document* above n 3, 254.

85 The numbers of displacement caused by the Colombia refugee crisis are not consensual, especially giving the disputed data on internally displaced persons in the country. The number used in this paper builds upon the numbers used by United Nations High Commissioner for Refugees (UNHCR), *Global Trends 2010* (2011), available at http://www.unhcr.org/4dfa11499.html.

86 For more on the Colombian refugee crisis and on the background of the MPA see Jubilut and Carneiro (2011): 64 and seq. (64–6 on the Colombia refugee crisis, and 66–8 on the Cartagena Declaration as a background of the MPA). In 2010, the Colombian refugee crisis was the 6th major source of refugees in the world with 395,600 refugees and 3.6 million internally displaced persons. See UNHCR above n 85, 15.

the other hand, the third chapter of the MPA that deals with durable solutions.[87] Each chapter is being referred to as one component of the MPA – the protection component and the durable solutions component.[88]

This double focus can be justified by the fact that '[t]he primary aim in drafting the Mexico Plan of Action (MPA) was to move beyond empty rhetoric on the protection needs of refugees, internally displaced persons (IDPs), and others in Latin America. The fundamental goal was to produce concrete action …'.[89]

Focusing both on government and the civil society, the protection component aims to (i) strengthen research and doctrinal development and (ii) enhance training and institutional capacity-building.[90] It has obtained positive results, as the adoption or revision of national legislation on refugees in the region;[9192] and has fostered new forms of complementary protection.

Complementary protection has appeared in the region, for instance, through humanitarian visas, protection to victims of torture and new forms of legal residence, which have occurred in Mexico, Honduras, Panama and Costa Rica, Brazil and Argentina.[93]

The durable component presents three different programs: (1) borders of solidarity – focusing both on (i) security and access to secure areas at the borders and on (ii) the needs and structure of the receiving communities; (2) cities of solidarity – addressing local integration needs and self-reliance of refugees and (3) resettlement in solidarity – establishing a regional resettlement program for Colombian refugees.[94]

This component of the MPA has highlighted 'the importance of the diffusion of "best practices" in the region, allowing for a South-South cooperation, as

87 See Mexico Declaration and Plan of Action to Strengthen the International Protection of Refugees in Latin America above n 79.

88 See, for instance, *Mexico Plan of Action: The impact of regional solidarity* above n 80.

89 Ibid. 5.

90 See Mexico Declaration and Plan of Action to Strengthen the International Protection of Refugees in Latin America above n 79, chap 2.

91 As in the cases of Argentina which adopted in 2006 the *Ley No 26.165 – Ley General de Reconocimiento y protección de refugiados*, available at http://www.acnur.org/t3/fileadmin/scripts/doc.php?file=biblioteca/pdf/4658. And Mexico which adopted in 2011 the *Ley sobre Refugiados y Protección Complementaria*, available at http://www.acnur.org/t3/fileadmin/scripts/doc.php?file=biblioteca/pdf/8150.

92 See *Mexico Plan of Action: The impact of regional solidarity* above n 80, 16.

93 Information obtained during presentations at International Meeting on Refugee and Stateless Persons Protection and Mixed Migratory Movements in the Americas, which took place in Brasilia in November 2010.

94 See Mexico Declaration and Plan of Action to Strengthen the International Protection of Refugees in Latin America above n 79, chap 3. For more details on each program see *Mexico Plan of Action: The impact of regional solidarity* above n 80; Piovesan and Jubilut (2011): 223; Jubilut and Carneiro (2011).

well as the need of addressing two specific situations[95] with the aid of the international community'.[96]

Besides establishing specific programs, that can be evaluated through pragmatic tools and indexes,[97] the MPA enormously contributed to International Law and protection in Latin American by introducing, through a normative approach, the concept of solidarity into actions aimed at refugees. In this sense, the MPA brings about more humane and newer discourses in International Refugee Law in which one sees the use of the term responsibility-sharing *in lieu* of burden-sharing,[98][99] which is relevant in so far as,

> … this change represents much more than a simple shift in semantics but rather a transformation of how refugee protection and refugees are perceived: not as a problem and a situation of sharing refugees but as a responsibility for protecting the victims of violations of human rights.[100]

And thus, the MPA enables a more equitable balance between the needs of refugees and asylum seekers and the interests and needs of States.[101]

Based on this idea of solidarity, and despite being created as a regional instrument with a regional focus and allowing for the improvement of regional protection of refugees, the MPA has provided the basis for the protection of over 100 Palestinian refugees that have been resettled in Brazil and Chile,[102] in an example of international solidarity.[103] In this regard, the MPA is a major advancement in Refugee Law and protection in Latin American with both theoretical and practical consequences that help to foster more protective standards for the whole refugee population in the region.

95 The Colombia refugee crisis has affected Ecuador and Costa Rica as receiving States, as a result the MPA focused on resettling refugees from these two countries to other countries in the region.

96 González, 'La Protección Internacional de Refugiados en el Continente Americano: Nuevos Desarrollos' 363 (translation by the author).

97 See for instance http://www.pamacnur2010.com/.

98 See Jubilut and Carneiro, 'Regional Developments: Americas' 70.

99 On burden-sharing see, for instance, PH Schuck, 'Refugee Burden-Sharing: A Modest Proposal' (1997) 22 Yale J. Int'l L. 243.

100 See Jubilut and Carneiro, 'Regional Developments: Americas' 70.

101 Ibid. 84.

102 Ibid. 83.

103 See *The Refugee Situation in Latin America: Protection and Solutions Based on the Pragmatic Approach of the Cartagena Declaration on Refugees of 1984 – Discussion Document* above n 3, 255.

The Brasilia Declaration

The will to maintain the process of a continuing effort of regional approaches to International Refugee Law which started with the Cartagena Declaration and advanced with the MPA was demonstrated, once again, at the end of 2011, when 18 countries[104] adopted the Brasilia Declaration on the Protection of Refugees and Stateless Persons[105] in the Americas (Brasilia Declaration),[106] reaffirming their commitment to enhancing Refugee Law and protection in the region with a humane and humanitarian approach.

Differently from the MPA, the Brasilia Declaration was adopted not in the celebration of an anniversary of the Cartagena Declaration but rather in relation to the anniversaries of the Convention relating to Refugee Status of 1951, the Convention Relating to the Status of Stateless Persons of 1951[107] and the Convention on the Reduction of Statelessness of 1961,[108] which justified the focus not only on refugees but also on Stateless Persons.[109]

The Brasilia Declaration recalls and builds upon the mentioned regional documents, and tries to update them, mentioning the difficulties arising from mixed migration flows[110] and the need for the values of solidarity, respect, tolerance and multiculturalism to underscore the application of refuge.[111]

---

104 The Brasilia Declaration was signed by Argentina, Bolivia, Brazil, Chile, Colombia, Costa Rica, Cuba, Dominican Republic, Ecuador, El Salvador, Guatemala, Mexico, Nicaragua, Panama, Paraguay, Peru, Uruguay and Venezuela.

105 See the Brasilia Declaration on the Protection of Refugees and Stateless Persons in the Americas (Brasilia Declaration), 11 November 2010, available at http://www.unhcr.org/refworld/docid/4cdd44582.html. It is relevant to note that Stateless Persons are comprised in the 'persons of concern' category of UNHCR ever since its creation. In the beginning referring only to refugees that were stateless and since 1974 to stateless persons more generally. See H Massey, *UNHCR and De Facto Statelessness. Legal and Protection Policy* (Research Series, 2010), I, available at http://www.unhcr.org/4bc2ddeb9.pdf.

106 Available at http://www.unhcr.org/4cdd3fac6.html.

107 Convention Relating to the Status of Stateless Persons, 28 September 1954, United Nations, Treaty Series, Vol. 360, 117, available at http://www.unhcr.org/refworld/docid/3ae6b3840.html.

108 Convention on the Reduction of Statelessness, 30 August 1961, United Nations, Treaty Series, Vol. 989, 175, available at http://untreaty.un.org/ilc/texts/instruments/english/conventions/6_1_1961.pdf.

109 In relation to Stateless Persons it is interesting to note that besides from UNHCR's efforts to have States accede to the international documents on the matter, the American Convention on Human Rights establishes *ius solis* as a rule for nationality in order to avoid statelessness (Article 20(2)). The American Convention is, available at http://www.unhcr.org/refworld/docid/3ae6b36510.html.

110 See Brasilia Declaration above n 105, 3rd Resolution.

111 Ibid. 8th Resolution.

Besides this, the Brasilia Declaration is relevant as 'the number of persons affected by forced migration has not significantly decreased worldwide or in the Americas'[112] and that

> the existing legal framework for the protection of refugees and stateless persons still contains significant gaps that need to be addressed. Some of the particular sections in the Brasilia Declaration reference themes that are not addressed in the existing regional instruments.[113]

In this sense, the Brasilia Declaration demonstrate that Latin America still wants to improve its commitment to International Refugee Law and protection through a regional approach, hence continuing with the region's tradition encompassed in the 'spirit of Cartagena'.

Conclusion

In light of all the above, one sees that Latin America has a tradition of having regional fora and programs in relation to refugees. Some of them have emerged from practical needs in the face of conflicts, but even so they have allowed for the continuing advancement of International Refugee Law and protection in the region in general.

The regional approach to International Refugee Law and protection however does not replace the universal standards, but rather serves as a way to encourage States to accede to these documents and to complement them with regional tailored programs and actions, therefore aiming to enhance the protection of refugees.

From the regional Latin American approach, improvements have been noted in national practice and legislation, as norms more in keeping with the international standards, complementary protection and a broader definition of refugees have emerged from the Cartagena Declaration, the San Jose Declaration, the MPA and the Brasilia Declaration.

In this sense, the existence of regional fora and programs in Latin America can be regarded as positive tools in ascertaining the rights of refugees and asylum seekers and guaranteeing protection; especially when they aim to have a practical approach and to balance the interests and needs of States with the needs of the refugee population.[114]

The regional efforts in Latin America on International Refugee Law and protection are, consequently, constructive examples that may lead to a more humane

112 D Costa, 'Introductory note to the Brasilia Declaration on the Protection of Refugees and Stateless Persons in the Americas' (2011) 50 International Legal Materials 357.

113 Ibid. 358.

114 See Jubilut and Carneiro (2011): 5.

attitude towards refugees and asylum seekers and a better and more effective system of guaranteeing that the refugee population have integral protection, being in this sense a model in regionalism in International Refugee Law and protection.

References

Barreto LPTF, *Das diferenças entre os institutos jurídicos, asilos e refúgio.* Available at http://www.migrante.org.br/IMDH/ControlConteudo.aspx?area=001c1b0d-181f-450a-83fb-47915ce5f2eb.

Costa D, 'Introductory note to the Brasilia Declaration on the Protection of Refugees and Stateless Persons in the Americas' (2011) 50 International Legal Materials.

Fischel de Andrade JH, *Direito internacional dos refugiados – Evolução Histórica (1921–1952)* (Renovar, 1996).

González JCM, 'La Protección Internacional de Refugiados en el Continente Americano: Nuevos Desarrollos'. In *XXXV Curso de Derecho Internacional* (Comité Jurídico Interamericano, Departamento de Derecho Internacional, Secretaría de Asuntos Jurídicos, Secretaría General, 2008).

González JCM, 'El derecho de asilo y la protección de refugiados en el continente americano'. In ACNUR. *La protección internacional de refugiados en las Américas.* (ACNUR; Oficina del Alto Comisariado de las Naciones Unidas para Derechos Humanos, 2011).

Goodwin-Gill GS and McAdam J, *The Refugee in International Law* (3rd edn, Oxford University Press, 2007).

Harris D, 'Regional Protection of Human Rights: The Inter-American Achievement' in HJ Steiner and P Alston (eds), *International Human Rights in Context* (2nd edn, Oxford University Press, 2000).

Hathaway JC, *The Rights of Refugees under International Law* (Cambridge University Press, 2005).

International Law Commission, *Report of the work of the Study Group on the Fragmentation of International Law: Difficulties arising from the diversification and expansion of international law*, UN. A/CN.4/L.682, 2006.

Jubilut LL, 'International Refugee Law and Protection in Brazil: a model in South America?' (2006) 19(1) Journal of Refugee Studies

Jubilut LL, *O Direito Internacional dos Refugiados e sua aplicação no ordenamento jurídico brasileiro* (Método, 2007).

Jubilut LL and Apolinário SMOS, 'A necessidade de proteção internacional no âmbito da migração' (2010) 11(6)(1) Revista Direito GV.

Jubilut LL and Apolinario SMOS, 'O Direito Internacional dos Refugiados e seu Contexto Atual na América Latina'. In Carlos F. Dominguez Avila and Renata de Melo Rosa (eds), *América Latina no Labirinto Global – Economia, Política e Segurança* (2nd edn, CRV, 2012).

Jubilut LL and Carneiro WP, 'Resettlement in Solidarity: a regional new approach towards a more humane durable solution' (2011) 30(3) Refugee Survey Quarterly.

Kneebone S and Rawlings-Sanaei F (eds), *New regionalism and asylum seekers: challenges ahead* (Berghahn Books, 2007).

Lavanchi P, 'The Mexico Declaration and Plan of Action: Reaffirming Latin America's Generous Tradition of Asylum and Innovative Solutions' (2006) 18 Int'l J. Refugee L.

Lopez GA and Stohl M, *Liberalization and Redemocratization in Latin America* (Greenwood Press, 1987).

Massey H, *UNHCR and De Facto Statelessness*. Legal and Protection Policy Research Series, 2010.

Miranda CO, 'Toward a Broader Definition of Refugee: 20th Century Development Trends' (1989–90) 20 Cal. W. Int'l L.J.

Mittelman J, 'Rethinking the "New Regionalism" in the Context of Globalization' (1996) 2 Global Governance.

Piovesan F and Jubilut LL, 'Regional Developments: Americas' in A Zimmermann (ed.), *Commentary on the 1951 Convention Relating to the Status of Refugees and its 1967 Protocol* (Oxford University Press, 2011).

Reut-Nicolussi E, 'Displaced Persons in International Law' (1948) 73 (II) *Recueil des Cours de la Academie de Droit International.*

Schuck PH, 'Refugee Burden-Sharing: A Modest Proposal' (1997) 22 Yale J. Int'l L.

Spindler W, 'The Mexico Plan of Action: protecting refugees through international solidarity' (November 2005) 24 Forced Migration Review.

Stein BN, 'Regional solutions – Package deals' (1995) 99 Refugees Magazine.

Suhrke A, 'A crisis diminished: refugees in the developing world' (1992–93) 48 International Journal.

UNHCR. Executive Committee of the High Commissioner's Program, *Note on International Protection*, UN Doc A/AC.96/930, 2000.

UNHCR, *Mexico Declaration and Plan of Action to Strengthen the International Protection of Refugees in Latin America*, 2004.

UNHCR, *Memoir of the Twentieth Anniversary of the Cartagena Declaration on Refugees*. 1st edn, 2005.

UNHCR, 'The Refugee Situation in Latin America: Protection and Solutions Based on the Pragmatic Approach of the Cartagena Declaration on Refugees of 1984 – Discussion Document' (2006) 18 Int'l J. Refugee L.

UNHCR, *Mexico Plan of Action: The impact of regional solidarity*. 1st edn, 2007.

UNHCR, *Países de América Latina Que Han Incorporado la Definicion de Refugiado de la Declaración de Cartagena sobre los Refugiados en Su Legislación Nacional*, 2008.

UNHCR, *Definición Ampliada de Refugiados en América Latina: Incorporación de la Declaración de Cartagena sobre Refugiados en la Legislación de los Países de la Región*, 2009.

UNHCR. Executive Committee of the High Commissioner's Program, *Note on International Protection*, EC/62/SC/CRP.12 2011.
UNHCR, *Global Trends 2010*, 2011.
William RI, *Transnational Conflicts: Central America, Social Changes and Globalization* (Verso, 2003).

Chapter 12
Protection of Asylum Seekers under the Inter-American Human Rights System

David James Cantor and Stefania Barichello

> It is perhaps symptomatic of our days that one has to invoke the conquests of the past in order to stop or avoid even greater steps backwards in the present and in the future.[1]

The sentiments behind these concerns regarding the legal protection of asylum seekers and refugees expressed almost ten years ago by Judge Antônio A Cançado Trinidade, then President of the Inter-American Court, ring equally true in the American continents today. The Inter-American human rights system – that totality of human rights standards and institutions created by the Organization of American States (OAS)[2] – has recently found itself again the subject of critique by States that seek to curtail its influence on securing human rights in the region.[3]

---

1 *Advisory Opinion on Juridical Condition and Rights of Undocumented Migrants* (17 September 2003) Series A No 18, Concurring Opinion of Judge Antônio A Cançado Trinidade (President) para 40.

2 The general functioning of the system is relatively well documented. See, *inter alia*, DJ Harris and S Livingstone (eds), *The Inter-American System of Human Rights* (Clarendon Press, 1998); CM Quiroga, *The Battle of Human Rights: Gross, Systematic Violations and the Inter-American System* (Martinus Nijhoff, 1988); JM Pasqualucci, *The Practice and Procedure of the Inter-American Court of Human Rights* (Cambridge University Press, 2003); L Burgorgue-Larsen et al, *The Inter-American Court of Human Rights: Case Law and Commentary* (Oxford University Press, 2011).

3 The tense 2011–12 Special Working Group to Reflect on the Workings of the Inter-American Commission on Human Rights was characterized by attacks on the IASHR from States including Brazil, Venezuela, Colombia and Ecuador (see V Amato, 'Taking Stock of the Reflection on the Workings of the Commission' (2012) 16 Aportes 4). Certain States have also begun suggesting in recent months that States in the sub-regional organization (UNASUR) should withdraw from the IASHR (El Comercio, 'Ecuador apuesta po nueva instancia de derechos humanos para Suramérica', 3 May 2012). In reaction to IASHR decisions in particular cases, Colombia has also aired strong criticisms of the IASHR (El Tiempo, 'Decisión de la CIDH podría limitar operaciones militares', 29 July 2011, and 'Gobierno buscará milionarias indemnizaciones por Mapiripán', 26 October 2011) and Venezuela recently formally denounced the American Convention on Human Rights (OAS, 'Secretario General de la OEA comunica denuncia de la Convención Americana sobre Derechos Humanos de parte de Venezuela' (Press Release C-307/12, 10 September 2012)).

In this highly charged political context, a reflective assessment of the system's contribution to the promotion of human rights is most urgently required, not least in view of the estimated 800,000 refugees and asylum seekers who currently represent one of the most vulnerable sectors in the Americas.[4]

The present chapter rises to the challenge by providing a rigorous analysis of the new 'complementary' human rights framework for refugees and asylum seekers developed by the Inter-American human rights system. In particular, it will show how the recent distinctive and progressive 'jurisprudence' on point from the system's main institutions – the Inter-American Commission on Human Rights and the Court – advances the frontiers of international legal protection for such persons. The analysis thus vindicates predictions by earlier observers as to the potential for the Inter-American human rights system to provide complementary protection to asylum seekers and refugees.[5] The rapidity and scope of these jurisprudential developments is such that even relatively recent attempts to describe the contours of this framework appear to have been overtaken by events.[6]

The scope of the new legal framework and its implications for the legal protection of asylum seekers and refugees in the Americas require that the chapter limits itself to identifying and describing its contours. As such, other novel features of the Inter-American jurisprudence – such as protection for internally displaced persons or reparations for refugees – fall outside its scope.[7] Regional refugee law from Latin America is also not directly addressed.[8] Instead, after giving an overview of the Inter-American human rights system, the chapter will explore how the concept of asylum as a human right has been developed by the Inter-American system. It then turns to analyse how the broader range of human rights in Inter-American instruments have been applied to the situation of asylum seekers and refugees. It concludes by examining the Commission's attempt to frame the principle of burden-sharing in human rights terms and assessing the

4 Figure from United Nations High Commissioner for Refugees (UNHCR), *Global Trends 2011* (2012) 11–13.

5 KW Yundt, 'The Organization of American States and Legal Protection to Political Refugees in Central America' (1989) 23 International Migration Review 201; MC Pulido and M Blanchard, 'La Comisión Interamericana de Derechos Humanos y sus mecanismos de protección aplicados a la situación de los refugiados, apátridas y solicitantes de asilo' in L Franco (ed.), *El asilo y la protección internacional de los refugiados en América Latina* (Costa Rica: Editorama, 2004).

6 C Sandoval, 'A Critical View of the Protection of Refugees and IDPs by the Inter-American System of Human Rights: Re-assessing its Powers and Examining the Challenges for the Future' (2005) 17 International Journal of Refugee Law 43.

7 See, respectively, DJ Cantor, *The Return of Internally Displaced Persons under International Law* (Martinus Nijohff, forthcoming) and DJ Cantor, 'Restitution, Compensation, Satisfaction: Transnational Reparations and Colombia's Victims' Law' (2011). 215 UNHCR, New Issues in Refugee, Research 1.

8 For a study of the topic, see the chapter in the present volumes by LL Jubilut.

overall scope of protection offered by the Inter-American human rights system to asylum seekers and refugees.

IASHR Standards and Institutions

The Organization of American States (OAS) was created through the entry into force of the OAS Charter,[9] adopted as an outcome of the 9th International Conference of American States. All 35 independent States of the Americas are currently members. The principal OAS organs include its governing bodies – the General Assembly, Permanent Council, Inter-American Council for Integral Development and ad hoc Meetings of Consultation of Ministers of Foreign Affairs – as well as a General Secretariat, Inter-American Juridical Committee, Inter-American Commission on Human Rights and a range of specialized conferences and agencies. Amongst the governing bodies, the General Assembly – as supreme organ of the OAS – is noteworthy for having adopted an important series of resolutions concerning the protection of refugees and asylum seekers within the region.[10]

The present chapter focuses on the practice of those institutions created by the OAS specifically to watch over the observance of regional human rights standards in the Americas, namely the Inter-American Commission on Human Rights and the Inter-American Court of Human Rights. It will be shown that these bodies have carved out an important framework for the protection of asylum seekers and refugees through creative interpretation of the regional human rights framework developed by the OAS. However, before describing the main features of these two institutions, it is important to provide an overview of the main regional instruments that describe the Inter-American human rights standards that form the basis for their monitoring and compliance work.

Human Rights Standards

The OAS Charter – as the organization's constitutional document – limits itself to affirming the general principle of 'the fundamental rights of the individual'.[11] The specific human rights standards implicit in this principle were proclaimed by

---

9 Charter of the Organization of American States, Bogotá, Colombia, 30 April 1948, in force 13 December 1951, 1-C and 61 OAS Treaty Series 1.

10 Beginning with its 'Resolution AG/RES. 774 (XV-O/85) on Legal Situation of Asylum-Seekers, Refugees and Displaced Persons on the American Continent' (9 December 1985) the OAS General Assembly has since adopted resolutions on this theme on an almost annual basis, culminating most recently with its 'Resolution AG/RES. 2758 (XLII-O/12) on Protection of Asylum Seekers and Refugees in the Americas' (5 June 2012).

11 Art 3(l). This was Art 5(l) prior to the Charter's amendment by the Protocol of Amendment to the Charter of the Organization of American States, Buenos Aires, Argentina, 27 February 1967, in force 27 February 1970, 1-A OAS Treaty Series 1.

OAS Member States through the contemporary 1948 American Declaration on the Rights and Duties of Man (ADHR).[12] Predating the adoption of the Universal Declaration of Human Rights (UDHR) by several months, the ADHR lays out the first set of comprehensive international standards in relation to human rights and duties. These represent the fundamental common standards that speak to all OAS Member States. Moreover, although the ADHR takes the form of a declaration rather than a treaty, its provisions are treated as a legally binding specification of the more general human rights obligations imposed by the OAS Charter.[13]

The ADHR not only serves as the basic point of reference for human rights standards in the Americas, it also provided an important source of inspiration for the American Convention on Human Rights (ACHR), the foundational OAS human rights treaty.[14] Presently, 24 of the 35 OAS Member States are party to the treaty and thus bound as a matter of international law to observe its provisions, the Parties being mostly from Latin America rather than North America or the Caribbean. In addition to establishing the Inter-American Court of Human Rights and conferring ACHR competence upon the Commission, the ACHR sets out an extensive list of predominantly civil and political rights that States Parties are obligated to ensure for all persons subject to their jurisdiction. The ACHR standards are notable not only for their inclusion of a standalone right to judicial protection and the relatively narrow scope afforded for derogation from the treaty obligations,[15] but also for the provision requiring progressive development of OAS economic, social, educational, scientific and cultural standards.[16]

Crucially for the protection of refugees and asylum seekers, both core OAS human rights instruments protect a right of asylum; the ACHR also regulates expulsion and *refoulement* in human rights terms.[17] Yet these human rights standards are situated within a broader international law framework. Firstly, other Inter-American human rights treaties also tangentially address the issue of asylum, such as the Convention to Prevent and Punish Torture, which prohibits extradition tantamount to *refoulement* and explicitly preserves the 'right of asylum'.[18]

12 American Declaration on the Rights and Duties of Man, Bogotá, Colombia, adopted by Resolution XXX, Final Act of the Ninth International Conference of American States (Pan American Union), 30 March–2 May 1948, 1 Annals of the OAS 130 (1949).

13 See, for example, *Advisory Opinion on Interpretation of the American Declaration of the Rights and Duties of Man within the Framework of Article 64 of the American Convention on Human Rights* (14 July 1989) Series A No 10.

14 American Convention on Human Rights, San José, Costa Rica, 22 November 1969, in force 18 July 1978, 36 Treaty Series 1.

15 Arts 25 and 27 respectively.

16 Art 26. A treaty on economic, social and cultural rights was later concluded by the OAS in the form of the Additional Protocol to the American Convention on Human Rights in the Area of Economic, Social and Cultural Rights, San Salvador, El Salvador, 17 November 1988, in force 16 November 1999, 69 OAS Treaty Series 1.

17 See further below.

18 Arts 13 and 15 respectively.

Secondly, regional conventions – some of which predate the formation of the OAS – regulate the long-standing institution of political asylum in the Americas.[19] Finally, in more recent years, certain Latin American States have concluded regional refugee protection instruments, such as the Cartagena Declaration on Refugees,[20] which harmonize or extend their obligations under the UN refugee law treaties.[21] This chapter will demonstrate how the Inter-American Commission and Court have deployed these frameworks in developing human rights protection for refugees and asylum seekers under the ADHR and ACHR.

Institutions

Created in 1959, the Inter-American Commission on Human Rights (Commission) has been a principal organ of the OAS since 1967 with the mandate to 'promote the observance and protection of human rights' in all OAS Member States.[22] Based in Washington DC, USA, it is composed of seven independent experts, each elected for four-year terms, whose general functions include: making recommendations to States; preparing country and thematic reports on human rights, which may include on-site observations in a Member State; and submitting its Annual Report each year to the OAS General Assembly.[23] The Commission also has the power to examine petitions alleging a violation by an OAS State of the human rights standards expressed in the ACHR (for States Parties) or the ADHR (for States not party to the ACHR) and to make recommendations on the case.[24] The process in both cases is similar, except that in cases involving States Parties to the ACHR, the Commission or the State may elect to refer the case to the Court, subject to

---

19 See, for example, Treaty on Political Asylum and Refuge, Montevideo, Uruguay, 4 August 1939, reprinted in MO Hudson (ed), *International Legislation* (Carnegie Endowment for International Peace, 1949) Vol 8, 404; Convention on Territorial Asylum, Caracas, Venezuela, 28 March 1954, in force 29 December 1954, 19 OAS Treaty Series 1. The question of whether a regional custom of diplomatic asylum existed in the Americas was addressed by the International Court of Justice in *Colombian-Peruvian Asylum Case* (20 November 1950) ICJ Rep 266.

20 Cartagena Declaration on Refugees, Cartagena, Colombia, 22 November 1984, adopted by the Colloquium on the International Protection of Refugees in Central America, Mexico and Panama; reprinted in *Annual Report of the Inter-American Commission on Human Rights 1984–1985* (1 October 1985) OEA/Ser.L/V/II.66/doc.10, rev 1, 190–93.

21 Convention relating to the Status of Refugees, Geneva, 28 July 1951, in force 22 April 1954, 189 UNTS 137; Protocol relating to the Status of Refugees, New York, 31 January 1967, in force 4 October 1967, 606 UNTS 267.

22 OAS Charter, Art. 106. This provision was incorporated into the OAS Charter through the amendments introduced by the 1967 Buenos Aires Protocol.

23 See, Statute of the Inter-American Commission on Human Rights, approved by OAS General Assembly, 'Resolution No. 447 (IX-0/79) Statute of the Inter-American Commission on Human Rights' (31 October 1979).

24 Commission Statute, Arts 19–20; ACHR, Arts 44, 50–51.

certain steps having been completed within the Commission procedure.[25] In either process, admissibility criteria must be met before the substance of the petition can be examined.[26]

Unlike the Commission, which is a charter-based body with treaty functions, the Inter-American Court of Human Rights is a pure treaty body created by the ACHR. As a result, its competence extends only to those OAS States that are Parties to the treaty and which have also expressly declared their acceptance of its jurisdiction.[27] Based in San José, Costa Rica, the Court is composed of seven judges who are elected for six-year terms by the Parties to the ACHR.[28] The Court may offer advisory opinions to the Member States and organs of the OAS regarding interpretation of the ACHR or 'other treaties concerning the protection of human rights in the American States', as well as the compatibility of domestic laws with these instruments on the request of the State.[29] The Court may also hear and give final binding judgment on petitions under consideration by the Commission, but only if the case is properly referred by either the Commission or the impugned State.[30] Where it finds that a right protected by the ACHR has been violated, the Court will order reparations,[31] and its jurisprudence on this theme is extensive.[32]

Engagement by the Commission and Court with the theme of refugees and asylum seekers has been undertaken largely through the country and thematic reports that constitute the main focus of the Commission's work. Over the years, these have addressed the protection of refugees and asylum seekers in a range of contexts and served to develop its interpretation of the applicable human rights norms.[33] For instance, the first Commission report on 'political refugees' in the Americas appeared in 1965,[34] and led to an (ultimately aborted) attempt by the OAS Inter-American Juridical Committee to draft an Inter-American refugee convention.[35] By contrast, the Commission's country report on refugee protection

---

25 Commission Statute, Arts 19–20; ACHR, Arts 45–51, 61. See also Rules of Procedure of the Inter-American Commission on Human Rights, approved at its 109th Special Session, 4–8 December 2000, and amended at its 116th regular session, 7–25 October 2002.

26 Commission Statute, Arts 19(a) and 20(c); ACHR, Arts 46–7; Commission Regulations, Arts 26, 32–41.

27 ACHR, Art 62.

28 Regarding the organization of the Court, see ACHR, Arts 52–60.

29 ACHR, Art 64.

30 ACHR, Arts 61, 67, 68(1).

31 ACHR, Art 63(1).

32 See, for example, relevant chapters in Burgorgue-Larsen et al. above n 4.

33 See text below.

34 See 'La situación de los refugiados políticos en América', OEA/Ser.L/V/II.11, Doc 7, in *La Organización de los Estados Americanos y los Derechos Humanos: Actividades de la Comisión Americana de Derechos Humanos 1960–1967* (OAS 1972).

35 See *Informe anual de la Comisión Interamericana de Derechos Humanos 1981–1982* (OAS 1982) OEA/Ser.L/V/II.57/doc.6, rev1, chap. VI.B.

in Canada (2000) and the thematic report on Terrorism and Human Rights (2002) were central to the development of its legal thinking on the human rights framework for asylum, although asylum and refugee issues have also been addressed in its reports on Cuba (1962), the Dominican Republic (1966), Chile (1974), Argentina (1980), Nicaragua (1983), Haiti (1993), Guatemala (1993), Haiti (1995), Bolivia (2007) and the USA (2010).[36]

The jurisprudence on human rights protection for asylum seekers has also been increasingly developed through the consideration of petitions, thus far principally by the Commission in such famous cases as the *Haitian Interdictions*.[37] The majority of these cases involve North American States as respondents, likely reflecting the status of these countries as important asylum destinations, as well as the more pronounced emphasis on litigation of refugee claims as compared to other countries in the region. Alongside the development of this jurisprudence on the content of substantive human rights, the Commission has also dealt sympathetically with the admissibility of petitions involving refugees and asylum seekers. For instance, it has held that where asylum-seeking petitioners face inadequate procedures for conducting refugee status determination then the relevant exception to the requirement to exhaust domestic remedies is engaged.[38] Similarly, both the Commission and the Court have made use of their powers to order precautionary or provisional measures in order to prevent the imminent violation of human rights of asylum seekers and refugees, *inter alia*, through prohibiting their deportation or expulsion.[39]

Asylum as a Human Right

The Inter-American system not only regulates the granting of asylum as an act of States but also protects the institution as a human right. This right of asylum, expressed in both the ADHR and ACHR, constitutes the starting point for the protection of asylum seekers in the Americas. The present section analyses this right of asylum and its interpretation by the Commission as the foundation of its strong regional framework of human rights protection for asylum seekers and refugees.

---

36 Electronic copies of all these country reports can be found on the website of the Inter-American Commission on Human Rights at http://www.oas.org/en/iachr/reports/country.asp.

37 *Haitian Centre for Human Rights et al v USA* Case 10675 (Commission Report No 51/96, 13 March 1997). See text below for further discussion of this case.

38 *120 Cuban Nationals and 8 Haitian Nationals Detained in the Bahamas* Case 12071 (Commission Report No 6/02, 27 February 2002) para 50.

39 *Frank Ewonwu v USA* Case 87-08 (Commission Report No 60/09, 20 July 2009); *Haitian and Haitian-Origin Dominican Persons in the Dominican Republic* (Provisional Measures Order by the Court, 18 August 2000).

Regional Framework and Nexus with Asylum Law

Asylum was first consecrated as a human right by Article XXVII ADHR:[40]

> Every person has the right, in case of pursuit not resulting from ordinary crimes, to seek and receive asylum in foreign territory, in accordance with the laws of each country and with international agreements.

This language is reflected in the Inter-American expression of this human right in treaty form at Article 22(7) ACHR:

> Every person has the right to seek and be granted asylum in a foreign territory, in accordance with the legislation of the state and international conventions, in the event he is being pursued for political offenses or related common crimes.

Each provision offers an independent legal basis for the human right of asylum in the Americas. However, despite their similar construction, Article 22(7) ACHR appears narrower in scope since it codifies a right to asylum only in respect of 'political offences or related common crimes', and not other forms of 'pursuit not resulting from ordinary crimes' as per Article XXVII ADHR.

A crucial commonality is that both provisions define the interests protected by the right via reference to external sources, namely domestic and international law. Although the Court has yet to pronounce upon the issue, it is the subject of a rich seam of jurisprudence produced by the Commission. Initially, this interpreted Article XXVII ADHR in light of American treaties on political asylum, such as the Havana, Montevideo and Caracas Conventions.[41] Against such a backdrop, it is hardly surprising to see the Commission describe the act of granting asylum (to which the right to 'receive' asylum relates) as a right – rather than an obligation – of States:

> Any individual who considers himself the object of persecution may seek asylum, although asylum may be granted only by the state to which this *right* belongs.[42]

---

40 For a comparative analysis of the drafting of this provision with the asylum provision in the Universal Declaration of Human Rights, see M Manly, 'La consagración del asilo como un derecho humano: Análisis comparative de la Declaración Universal, la Declaración Americana y la Convención Americana sobre Derechos Humanos' in L Franco (ed.), *El asilo y la protección internacional de los refugiados en América Latina* (Editorama, 2004).

41 Inter-American Commission on Human Rights, *Informe sobre la situación de derechos humanos en la República de Cuba* (OAS 1962) OEA/Ser.L/V/II.4/doc.2.

42 Inter-American Commission on Human Rights, *Report on the Situation of Human Rights in Argentina* (OAS 1980) OEA/Ser.L/V/II.49/Doc 19, corr 1, chap IV.G.4.

A product of the time when political asylum had greater currency among OAS States than did refugee law, this interpretation arose in the context of scenarios such as the refusal by territorial States to allow beneficiaries of diplomatic asylum safe passage to leave their territories, rather than reception of refugees and asylum-seekers in foreign territory.

The Commission's jurisprudence on the right of asylum shifted dramatically from the mid-1990s, particularly with the *Haitian Interdictions* case, such that it now interprets the right of asylum almost exclusively by reference to refugee protection instruments. One important consequence of this shift is that the right to 'receive' asylum is now framed in terms of the State obligation to provide protection to any person who objectively fulfils the international law definition of a refugee,[43] rather than as a matter of State discretion. In the words of the Commission, asylum under this framework is 'recognized by the State rather than conferred by it'.[44] In line with this understanding, and given the 'interpretative interrelationships' that exist between refugee law and human rights law,[45] the Commission has also held that the right of asylum extends to persons claiming the non-*refoulement* protections offered by international human rights law as well as to those seeking asylum under refugee law.[46]

The Commission interprets the broader purpose of asylum as protection of the person from violation of her fundamental human rights. Thus, it is

> … an institution that provides for the protection of individuals whose life or liberty is threatened or endangered by acts of persecution or violence stemming from the acts or omissions of a State. One form, political asylum, has been especially well-developed in Latin America.[47]

This understanding is not confined to the jurisprudence construing the right of asylum in terms of international refugee and human rights law (which also implies that the Commission views protection from human rights violations in the home country as the ultimate purpose of refugee law).[48] It is equally apparent in the Commission's characterization of political asylum as a framework intended

43 Inter-American Commission on Human Rights, *Report on the Situation of Human Rights of Asylum-Seekers within the Canadian Refugee Determination System* (OAS 2000) OEA/Ser.L/V/II.106/Doc 40 rev, para 60. However, the Commission is clear that there is no guarantee that the right of asylum will be granted for persons who are not refugees.

44 Inter-American Commission on Human Rights, *Report on Terrorism and Human Rights* (OAS 2002) OEA/Ser.L/V/II.116/Doc 5 rev 1 corr, para 394.

45 Ibid.

46 Ibid. para 405.

47 Inter-American Commission on Human Rights, 'Recommendation on Asylum and International Crimes' (20 October 2000) in *Annual Report of the Inter-American Commission on Human Rights 2000* (OAS 2001) OEA/Ser.L/V/II.111/Doc 20 rev.

48 See, for example, *Michael Edwards et al v The Bahamas* Case 12067 (Commission Report No 48/01, 4 April 2001) paras 171–2.

to 'safeguard the freedom, safety and physical integrity of individuals'.[49] This purposive interpretation of asylum as a means of protecting other fundamental human rights is applied by the Commission to define the scope and content of the right of asylum.

Firstly, the Commission has adopted this understanding in order to rationalize certain limits to the right of asylum. This appears to be the basis for its recommendation that any person alleged to be the material or intellectual author of 'international crimes' not be granted asylum since:

> [Asylum] presupposes that the person seeking protection is persecuted in his or her state of origin, and is not supported by it in applying for asylum.[50]

The Court is even more explicit in its reasoning – albeit on the point of general principle rather than specifically in relation to the rights of 'those accused of crimes against human rights'.[51] Of course, these limits are broadly consistent with the textual scope of the right of asylum under the ADHR and ACHR, which does not benefit persons who are pursued for 'ordinary crimes'. It also implies that such 'international crimes' should always fall to be considered as 'ordinary' rather than 'political' crimes.

Secondly, the Commission has deployed its purposive interpretation in order to define the content of the right of asylum as comprising a set of procedural protections that serve 'to ensure that [refugee status] is recognized in every case where it is justified'.[52] It has elsewhere described this right as providing 'a *baseline of due process* for refugee claimants to seek asylum in foreign territory'.[53] These protections are founded in the Commission's important finding that international refugee law has

> … developed to a level at which there is recognition of a *right of a person seeking refuge to a hearing* in order to determine whether that person meets the criteria in the [Refugee] Convention.[54]

Since it implements 'the most fundamental element of the right to seek asylum',[55] this principle of 'hearing the person' is developed by the Commission into a range

---

49 See *Argentina Report* above n 42, chap IV.G.4.

50 See 'Recommendation on Asylum and International Crimes' above n 47.

51 *Goiburú et al v Paraguay* (22 September 2006) Series C No 153, para 132.

52 See *Report on Terrorism and Human Rights* above n 44, para 394. See further below.

53 *John Doe et al v Canada* Case 12586 (Commission Report No 78/11, 21 July 2011) para 92.

54 See *Haitian Interdictions* above n 37 para 155. The source for this affirmation, and the question of whether international custom (if such it is) constitutes an 'international agreement' in the terms of Art XXVII ADHR, are not explicitly addressed by the Commission.

55 See *John Doe* above n 53 para 92.

of component procedural guarantees.[56] The content of these standards is informed by refugee protection instruments, often in the form of UNHCR soft law guidance.[57] However, the Commission affirms that it is the nature of the rights that ultimately may be put in jeopardy through the *refoulement* of an asylum seeker – such as the right to life and freedom from torture – that requires the 'strictest adherence' to these procedural standards on the part of American States.[58]

Turning to domestic law as an external source for the right of asylum, we can identify a further shift in the Commission's views through time. In the *Haitian Interdictions* case,[59] the Commission suggested that the existence of relevant domestic law represented an additional (rather than an alternative) criterion for the existence of a right of asylum in respect of any particular State.[60] This statement was later rightly disowned by the Commission on the common-sense basis that it would enable States to avoid their obligations under Article XXVII simply by excluding 'broad classes of refugee claimants through domestic law'.[61] As a result, an OAS State must recognize the human right of asylum in respect of its own domestic legal provisions on asylum *and* in respect of any relevant international by which it is bound, regardless of whether the former (properly) implements the latter.

Consequent Procedural Guarantees

For the Commission,[62] the right of asylum implies the right of a person seeking refuge to a hearing from which a range of component protections follow. The present section analyses these procedural guarantees, which may broadly be categorized as encompassing (i) the right to apply to the authorities for asylum; (ii) the right to have the claim determined by a fully competent authority; (iii) the right to a fair process of hearing the claim; (iv) the right to receive a proper decision; and (v) the right not to be *refouled* pending determination of the claim for asylum (and following recognition).

Turning to the first of these guarantees, the jurisprudence clearly affirms the importance of the 'right of an individual to apply to the appropriate authorities for asylum'.[63] On the basis of this guarantee, the Commission has held that

---

56 See text below.

57 See, for example, the *Canada Report* above n 43 throughout.

58 See, for example, the *Report on Terrorism and Human Rights* above n 44 para 394.

59 Interestingly, the Commission's jurisprudence on political asylum gives little consideration to this criterion.

60 See above *Haitian Interdictions* n 37, paras 151–3. This required the Commission to add an unnecessary element of legal complexity in order to find that USA law recognized this right for intercepted Haitians (ibid. para 160).

61 Interestingly the Commission's jurisprudence on political asylum gives little consideration to this criterion.

62 See *John Doe* above n 53, para 92.

63 See *Michael Edwards* above n 50, para 171.

the summary repatriation of Haitians intercepted on the high seas by the USA prevented the victims from exercising their right to seek and receive asylum in the USA or some other regional State.[64] Similarly, Canada's operation of a 'direct-back' scheme, which sent asylum claimants arriving by land back to the USA until the date of their refugee eligibility interviews, was held by the Commission to breach the victims' right to seek asylum in a foreign territory.[65] An unusual early decision by the Commission implies that this right may even be breached where a country of origin refuses to allow a persecuted person to leave the country to seek asylum overseas.[66] We may thus infer that this guarantee directly implements the right to 'seek' asylum.

The second set of procedural guarantees concern the nature of the institution with responsibility for determining the asylum claim. In an early report, the Commission outlined the minimum requirement that the decision-making authority be 'competent to determine refugee status':[67]

> While applicable international law leaves the decision as to which procedural means are necessary to accomplish this to the national authorities, the Commission shares the view of UNHCR that eligibility determinations are best made by those tasked with interpreting and applying refugee law and policy.[68]

However, an apparently higher standard was adopted in a later report by the Commission that affirmed a right for asylum seekers to have their claims determined by a 'competent, independent and impartial decision-maker'.[69] This would suggest that any national system where the first instance decision is taken by the executive must offer the possibility of automatic appeal to an independent and impartial decision-maker in cases where asylum is refused.[70]

The third set of guarantees demands that the process of determining the asylum claim be both 'fair and transparent'.[71] In this respect, the need to ensure the participation of the asylum seeker in the hearing requires that they have the opportunity to 'effectively state their claim'[72] and 'make representations [to the decision-maker] in support of their application'.[73] Mechanisms are thus required to allow the asylum seeker to 'submit all the evidence he deems pertinent and

64 See *Haitian Interdictions* above n 37, para 163.

65 See *John Doe* above n 53, paras 94–5.

66 *Eduardo Alvarez v Cuba* Case 7898 (Commission Resolution No 11/82, 8 March 1982).

67 See *Canada Report* above n 43, para 60.

68 Ibid.

69 See above *Report on Terrorism and Human Rights* n 44, para 394.

70 See further below.

71 See *Report on Terrorism and Human Rights* above n 44, para 394.

72 See *Canada Report* above n 43, para 60.

73 See *Michael Edwards* above n 50, para 171.

present arguments in favour of recognition'.[74] The process must also be capable of admitting 'newly available material facts or evidence deemed to meet a reasonable threshold of relevance'.[75] It is essential that the effects of detention on these participation and due process rights be taken into account.[76]

The right of an asylum seeker to effectively state his/her claim, or otherwise engage with the administrative or judicial procedures surrounding his/her situation, gives rise to an additional important due process guarantee. This is the right of access to legal aid for those asylum claimants who require it in order to 'effectively vindicate their rights within the refugee system as a whole', that is, whether in status determination proceedings, review of detention, post-claim administrative review or post-claim judicial review. The Commission has characterized such access to legal aid as an 'important safeguard' not only for protection of the right of asylum but also for asylum-seekers' other due process rights.[77] Applying such reasoning, it has specifically held that all unaccompanied children should have legal representation during asylum or immigration proceedings.[78]

The fourth set of component guarantees concerns the integrity of the asylum decision itself. Of course, all asylum seekers possess the right to receive a decision on their claim.[79] However, the Commission has also specified that this decision must be the result of an individualized and adequate assessment of the situation of risk facing the person, even where removal is to a third State rather than to the State of origin.[80] A decision refusing asylum or revoking refugee status must evidence 'sufficient substantiation' of the reasons for refusal. Adequate notification and publicity mechanisms are also obligatory.[81] Moreover, administrative or judicial review mechanisms may be required in order to allow negative decisions to be challenged, given the fundamental nature of the rights that are in play.[82] Any appeal must be suspensive in effect in order to safeguard the underlying right of asylum.[83] In any event, as we will see below, such appeal procedures may also be required by other human rights provisions.[84]

The final set of guarantees involve the Commission reading into Article XXVII a right for the asylum seeker not to be *refouled* pending the determination of her

74 Inter-American Commission on Human Rights, *Access to Justice and Social Inclusion: The Road towards Strengthening Democracy in Bolivia* (OAS 2007) OEA/Ser.L/V/II.Doc 34, para 410.

75 See *Canada Report* above n 43, para 173.

76 Inter-American Commission on Human Rights, *Report on Immigration in the United States: Detention and Due Process* (OAS 2010) OEA/Ser.L/II.Doc. 78/10, para 63.

77 See *Canada Report* above n 43, para 174.

78 See *USA Report* above n 76, para 409.

79 See *Michael Edwards* above n 50, para 171.

80 See *John Doe* above n 53, para 94.

81 See *Bolivia Report* above n 74, para 410.

82 See ibid. para 101; *Canada Report* above n 43, paras 101 and 173.

83 See *Bolivia Report* above n 74, para 410.

84 See *Haitian Interdictions* above n 37, para 163.

refugee status,[85] or his/her eligibility for complementary protection under human rights law.[86] This is effectively a holding mechanism that allows the person to fully exercise his/her right to 'seek' asylum. However, the Commission has also read the substantive non-*refoulement* protections in these wider bodies of international law into the scope of the right of asylum.[87] As such, 'genuine refugees' have a 'right to non-return' under Article XXVII ADHR.[88] This aspect of the right to 'receive' asylum thus encompasses both recognized refugees (and other persons in need of international protection) as well as those awaiting recognition of their status.[89] As such, the right of asylum expresses as a rule of regional human rights law the principle of non-*refoulement* for asylum seekers, refugees and beneficiaries of complementary human rights protection.

Implications

The overall sweep of the Commission's jurisprudence is impressive. Nonetheless, three words of caution are appropriate. Firstly, the Commission's interpretation of the right of asylum is rooted in Article XXVII ADHR; it is less clear whether the narrower wording of Article 22(7) ACHR could sustain similar recourse to external sources not relating to political asylum. Secondly, the Commission's extension of the right of asylum to include non-*refoulement* under international human rights law implies that persons 'pursued for ordinary crimes' (including international crimes) may possess this right if their *refoulement* implies a violation of their fundamental rights. This is difficult to reconcile with the fact that the text of Article XXVII ADHR (and the Commission's own view on perpetrators of international crimes) implies that such persons should be excluded. Finally, it is not clear whether the range of substantive and procedural protections read from refugee protection instruments into the right of asylum are also applicable to individuals seeking asylum under the political asylum framework. How the Commission, or Court, will address such conflicts between textual and purposive interpretations remains to be seen.

Despite these outstanding questions, the Commission's jurisprudence gives real meaning to the right of asylum as a human rights safeguard for refugees and other persons seeking international protection. Moreover, by interpreting the right in the concept of preventing *refoulement* to human rights violations, the Commission ensures that there is parity in the human rights guarantees afforded to the person whether the asylum claim is to be determined under refugee law or international human rights law.

85 See ibid.

86 See *Report on Terrorism and Human Rights* above n 44, para 405.

87 See *Report on Terrorism and Human Rights* above n 44, para 385.

88 See *Canada Report* above n 43, para 173.

89 See *John Doe* above n 53, paras 99–103.

Broader Human Rights Protection

The framework of regional human rights protection for asylum seekers and refugees is not limited to the safeguards offered by the right of asylum. Rather, a wider set of Inter-American human rights provisions provide the basis for an alternative framework of protection for such persons. Whereas the right of asylum is available only to a specific class of migrants, this broader set of human rights standards is applicable to all aliens (and nationals) under the jurisdiction of a State. This is because – as affirmed by the preamble to the ADHR and reiterated by the Commission – these are 'essential rights of man ... not derived from the fact that he is a national of a certain state'.[90] Nonetheless, as the present section will show, these standards hold special relevance for asylum seekers since they relate to such modalities as *refoulement* and removal, due process, detention and employment.

Non-refoulement

The Commission has repeatedly observed that State discretion to control the entry of aliens onto its territory must be exercised in conformity with its obligations under international human rights law.[91] In this respect, it is important to appreciate that the ACHR is the only broad-based human rights treaty that expressly prohibits *refoulement* to a risk of human rights abuse. Article 22(8) provides that:

> In no case may an alien be deported or returned to a country, regardless of whether or not it is his country of origin, if in that country his right to life or personal freedom is in danger of being violated because of his race, nationality, religion, social status, or political opinions.

Clearly inspired by Article 33(1) CSR, this provision has the advantage that it is not qualified by a provision analogous to Article 33(2) CSR nor is it limited to refugees but rather applicable to all aliens. It does, however, protect only against *refoulement* to human rights violation carried out on certain discriminatory grounds. It has been suggested that the inclusion of this provision was inspired by contemporaneous developments in Europe.[92] By comparison, Article 13 of the IATC prohibits the *extradition* of torture suspects where 'there are grounds to believe' the person would face death, torture or cruel, inhuman and degrading treatment or trial by 'special or ad hoc courts' in the requesting State.

Neither the Commission nor the Court has yet had the opportunity to apply the treaty rules in Article 22(8) ACHR or Article 13 IATC. Nonetheless, the Commission has interpreted certain fundamental ADHR rights as offering inherent

90 *Rafael Ferrer-Mazorra et al v USA* Case 9903 (Commission Report No 51/01, 4 April 2001) para 178.

91 Ibid. para 177.

92 See Manly, 'La consagración del asilo como un derecho humano, 149.

protection against *refoulement*. In its jurisprudence, the Commission appears to follow international authority to hold that State responsibility is engaged where it removes a person to another jurisdiction where there exists a 'real risk' that his/her right to life or his/her right to security of person under Article I ADHR will be violated.[93] The prohibition of *refoulement* to torture also follows as a consequence,[94] not least given the Commission's view that the ADHR (and presumably ACHR) codifies this 'norm of *jus cogens*'.[95] Whether this protection may be derived from rights other than the right to life and security of person expressed in Article I ADHR is an open question. Nonetheless, in respect of these rights, the protection afforded is potentially broader than that offered by Article 22(8) since the feared human rights violation need not be carried out on a discriminatory basis. As such, the Commission has issued precautionary measures requiring States not to deport persons to situations where detention conditions or a lack of access to medical treatment may result in a breach of these fundamental rights.[96]

Other Bars to Removal

The Commission has also determined that the act of the removing an alien may interfere with rights enjoyed in the host State. One interesting example involves an AIDS-sufferer facing deportation to her home country following a criminal conviction.[97] The Commission found that the case engaged the prohibition on cruel, infamous or unusual punishment in Article XXVI ADHR either because deportation as a result of criminal proceedings could formally be considered a 'punishment',[98] or the severely detrimental change in his/her situation subjectively made deportation a 'punishment' for this petitioner.[99] To determine whether the punishment was sufficiently severe as to violate this provision, the Commission borrowed an 'exceptionality' test inspired by the European case law on point, although this was not nearly as strictly applied. The Commission concluded that the petitioner would indeed suffer 'extraordinary hardship' due to the 'sub-standard' medical care in the home country for a person in the 'advanced (albeit not terminal)' stages of this terminal illness combined with his/her lack of social support after 30 years outside the country.[100] The planned deportation

93 See *Haitian Interdictions* above n 37, paras 167–71. The Commission here defines the right to security of the person in Art I ADHR as covering 'a person's legal and uninterrupted enjoyment of his life, limbs, his body, his health, and his reputation'.

94 See *Canada Report* above n 43, para 174.2.

95 See *Report on Terrorism and Human Rights* above n 44, para 395.

96 See, respectively Inter-American Commission on Human Rights, *Gary Resil et al v United States* (PM 5/11, 2011) and Inter-American Commission on Human Rights, *Edwin A Márquez González v United States* (PM 171/11, 2011).

97 *Andrea Mortlock v USA* Case 12534 (Commission Report No 63/08, 25 July 2008).

98 Ibid. para 84.

99 Ibid. para 85.

100 Ibid. para 91.

thus amounted to 'a *de facto* sentence to protracted suffering and unnecessarily premature death' in violation of Article XXVI.[101]

Ostensibly lawful removal measures enforced against aliens may also violate the ADHR and/or ACHR through their indirect consequences for the enjoyment of family rights and the rights of affected children in the host country. Yet neither State rights to enforce immigration laws nor the rights to family life of aliens are absolute, such that a 'balancing test' must be applied.[102] Drawing upon the international jurisprudence, the Commission provides an illustrative list of factors that may be relevant to this test:

- Age at which the non-citizen immigrated to the host State;
- Non-citizen's length of residence in the host State;
- Non-citizen's family ties in the host State;
- Extent of hardship the non-citizen's deportation poses for the family in the host State;
- Extent of the non-citizen's links to the country of origin;
- Non-citizen's ability to speak the principal language(s) of the country of origin;
- Nature and severity of the non-citizen's criminal offense(s);
- Non-citizen's age at the time of the criminal offense(s) was/were committed;
- Time span of the non-citizen's criminal activity;
- Evidence of the non-citizen's rehabilitation from criminal activity;
- Non-citizen's efforts to gain citizenship in the host State.[103]

Whilst the determination must ultimately revolve around the facts of the individual case,[104] the best interests of a minor child are a weight factor and must be taken into account during a parent's removal proceeding.[105] The State must also not enforce immigration laws in the home unless other enforcement alternatives against the alien have been considered and the authorities have 'probable cause, based on reliable information' of the location of the individual and of 'great' risk to the community.[106]

Procedural Protections

The Commission has emphasized that one of the fundamental objectives behind formulating the ADHR was to assure 'equal protection of the law to nationals and

---

101 Ibid. para 94.

102 *Wayne Smith et al v USA* Case 12562 (Commission Report No 81/10, 12 July 2010) paras 48–51.

103 Ibid. para 54.

104 Ibid. para 55.

105 Ibid. para 56.

106 See *USA Report* above n 76, para 98.

aliens alike in respect of the rights set forth [therein]'.[107] In this respect, the positive emphasis placed on the existence of procedural protections by the Inter-American system of human rights is reflected in the specific context of procedural standards for the treatment of aliens, especially in the context of removal or expulsion. This is accomplished not only through the confirmation in the jurisprudence that the general provisions on due process apply to the asylum context but also through the language of certain specific provisions relating to aliens.

A core feature of the jurisprudence is the consistent view of the Commission that the right of resort to the courts and associated due process guarantees apply to claims for asylum.[108] Moreover, where the violation of fundamental rights through *refoulement* is in play, the Commission has held that legal aid must be provided when required to ensure effective exercise of the right to judicial protection.[109] Minimum due process standards normally applicable to criminal trials must also be observed in removal proceedings against aliens,[110] particularly in the asylum context,[111] including:

> [T]he right to be assisted by a lawyer if they wish or by a representative in whom they have confidence, sufficient time to ascertain the charge against them, a reasonable time in which to prepare and formalize a response, and to seek and adduce responding evidence. Hearings must be conducted in public to the extent required by due guarantees and fairness ...[112]

Representatives must have the ability to give legal advice and representation to the asylum seeker during removal proceedings, including on the availability of judicial remedies.[113] The Commission has also recently affirmed that criminal deportation proceedings may sometimes amount to a 'punishment' that directly attracts the full range of criminal trial protections in Article XXVI ADHR.[114]

This framework is reinforced by those ACHR provisions that regulate the expulsion of aliens. While the collective expulsion of aliens is prohibited by Article 22(9), Article 22(6) requires that:

---

107 See *Rafael Ferrer-Mazorra* n 90, para 239.

108 This right is protected – albeit in slightly different terms – in Art XXVIII and XXVI ADHR and Arts 8(1) and 25 ACHR.

109 See *Canada Report* above n 43, paras 127 and 174. Similar findings have been made by the Court in respect of the due process standards applicable to removal proceedings involving broader classes of migrants (see *Advisory Opinion OC-18/03* above n 1, paras 121–6).

110 Protected by Art XXVI ADHR and Art 8(2) ACHR.

111 See *Canada Report* above n 43, para 60.

112 See *Report on Terrorism and Human Rights* above n 44, para 403.

113 *Loren Rieve et al v Mexico* Case 11610 (Commission Report No 49/99, 13 April 1999) para 75.

114 See the development of this idea in *Andrea Mortlock* above n 97, paras 85–6; and its wider application in *Wayne Smith* above n 102, para 63.

> An alien lawfully in the territory of a State Party to this Convention may be expelled from it only pursuant to a decision reached in accordance with law.

The jurisprudence indicates that this provision will be violated, *inter alia*, where the decision to expel an alien does not respect the guarantees of due process and effective judicial counsel.[115] Moreover, the Commission has purported to read the protections provided by both Article 22(6) and 22(9) ACHR into the ADHR, although it is not clear under which provision. In so doing, it reformulated Article 22(6) as a broad right of foreign nationals (that is, not merely those lawfully present in the territory) 'not to be deported without a decision firmly supported by the law'.[116] In principle, these protections will be available to asylum seekers and refugees 'lawfully' present in the State.

The Commission has also interpreted the right to equality as a form of procedural protection for asylum seekers.[117] This is a standalone right that can be breached not only in the application of another substantive right but also by 'any unreasonable differentiation in respect of the actual treatment of persons belonging to the same category of class'.[118] Thus, in the *Haitian Interdictions* case, the USA was held to have breached this provision by interdicting Haitians but not migrants of other nationalities as well as by applying different procedures to Haitians intercepted on the high seas in contrast to others intercepted in this way.[119] In a case concerning the detention of Cubans, the Commission confirmed that making policy distinctions between groups – such as between different nationalities or between nationals and aliens – will be lawful only if shown to be reasonable and proportionate to the objectives sought in the circumstances.[120] Meanwhile, positive measures to ensure that family rights and the best interests of affected children are factored into any immigration decision are not only permissible under this provision but in fact are required to secure family and child rights.[121]

Finally, the Commission has held that, where the removal of asylum seekers or other aliens takes place in violation of these broader procedural standards, other rights that the person had enjoyed in the country of asylum may also be indirectly violated. Hence, in a case heard under the ACHR involving the summary expulsion of three foreign priests from Mexico back to their home countries, the Commission found that because the decision to expel was taken in violation of due process rights, the expulsion thereby also violated the petitioners' right to freedom of association under Article 16 ACHR 'since it radically and definitively

115 See *Loren Rieve* above n 113, para 107.

116 See *Andrea Mortlock* above n 97, para 78.

117 This right is expressed by Art II ADHR and Art 24 ACHR.

118 See *Haitian Interdictions* above n 37, para 178.

119 See ibid. para 177.

120 See *Rafael Ferrer-Mazorra* above n 90, para 239.

121 Art V-VII ADHR; Art 11, 17 and 19 ACHR. See *Wayne Smith* above n 102, paras 55–60; *USA Report* above n 76, para 98.

cut them off from contact with their parishioners in Chiapas'.[122] A similar rationale is implicit in a separate decision by the Commission suggesting that a parent's deportation under unfair procedures will violate not only due process guarantees but thereby also the enjoyment of family rights in the host country.[123]

Detention

The Commission has pronounced on the detention of asylum seekers and other migrants in a number of different scenarios. This jurisprudence confirms that the basic framework for assessing the legality of detention is derived from the right to liberty (Article I ADHR) and the right to protection against arbitrary arrest (Article XXV ADHR). Crucially, the Commission has held that the right to liberty in Article I ADHR may be engaged not only by the incarceration of a person but also where a State takes measures of control over the person, as happened with the interdiction of Haitians in vessels on the high seas.[124]

In general, the Commission treats the right to protection from arbitrary arrest in Article XXV as *lex specialis* in relation to the deprivation of liberty in Article I. As such, grounds for the detention of migrants may be justified against these criteria in some instances.[125] However, the Commission has firmly rejected the human rights compatibility of laws that attribute excessive discretion to the administration in its exercise of the power to detain aliens. One decision with important implications for asylum seekers is that of the *Mariel Cubans*, in which domestic courts had interpreted the discretion of the USA Attorney General to 'parole' aliens into the country as conceptually placing such aliens 'always at the border seeking admission and as never having entered the [USA]'.[126] Notwithstanding the aliens' physical presence in the State, this legal fiction purported to deny them fundamental constitutional protections including the right to liberty. The Commission characterized this as prescribing 'a presumption of detention rather than a presumption of liberty', which it described as 'fundamentally antithetical' to Articles I and XXV.[127] The jurisprudence makes clear that migrants, even undocumented, are not criminals, nor are they suspected of any crime – as such, they must not be held in regular prisons with criminals.[128]

Relevant procedural guarantees must also be fully observed in order for the detention of aliens to be lawful. Its findings in the *Mariel Cubans* case illustrate a particular example of procedures that fall foul of these standards as 'arbitrary':

122 See *Loren Rieve* above n 113, para 105.
123 See *Wayne Smith* above n 102, paras 55–60; *USA Report* above n 76, para 48.
124 See *Haitian Interdictions* above n 37, para 169.
125 See *Rafael Ferrer-Mazorra* above n 90, para 239.
126 Ibid. para 218.
127 Ibid. paras 218–19.
128 See *Report on Terrorism and Human Rights* above n 44, para 396.

> [The domestic laws] fail to define with sufficient particularity the grounds upon which the petitioners have been deprived of their liberty; they place the onus upon the detainee to justify his or her release; they are subject to a degree of discretion on the part of officials that exceeds reasonable limits; and they fail to provide for detention reviews at reasonable intervals.[129]

Detention must also be challengeable in court,[130] under the right to a fair trial and due process protections analysed in the preceding section. Legal aid must be provided to those detainees who require it in order to vindicate their rights in the context of detention reviews.[131] Finally, the right to family life under Article V ADHR means that 'under no circumstances' can the detention of an immigrant parent be used as a factor for losing the legal custody of his or her children.[132] This range of detention-related standards for aliens applies equally to asylum-seekers as a particular class of alien.

Specifically in relation to asylum-seekers, the Commission has developed an extra level of protections by reading Article 31 CSR – on the non-penalization of illegal entry – into Article XXVII ADHR as a general limitation on restrictions to the liberty of refugees and asylum seekers. The Commission also cites with approval from UNHCR guidance to the effect that detention of asylum-seekers should be resorted to only 'in cases of necessity' and 'after a full consideration of all possible alternatives'. UNHCR guidelines on 'Applicable Criteria and Standards relating to the Detention of Asylum-Seekers' are also cited in relation to the minimum procedural guarantees that must be available to detained asylum-seekers,[133] as well as for the specific rights of asylum seekers during detention.[134] Although these standards appear to be located under the right to seek asylum in Article XXVII ADHR, the Commission has also addressed the detention of asylum seekers as a deprivation of liberty under Articles I and XXV ADHR, observing that 'the longer detention [of asylum-seekers] as a preventative measure continues, the greater the resulting burden of the rights of the person deprived of liberty'.[135]

Employment

Access to employment is an important consideration for asylum seekers. Although the Commission has not addressed this question directly, consideration of the labour rights of migrants has been undertaken by the Court. Following the rationale of its advisory opinion on this topic, it would appear that asylum seekers, like

129 See *Rafael Ferrer-Mazorra* above n 90, para 221.
130 Ibid. para 235; See also *USA Report* above n 76, para 139.
131 See *Canada Report* above n 43, para 174.3.
132 See *USA Report* above n 76, para 98.
133 Ibid. para 47.
134 Ibid. para 91.
135 Ibid. para 48.

other migrants, acquire labour rights on assuming 'the employment relationship', regardless of their regular or irregular status in the relevant State.[136] According to the Court, the mere fact of being a worker entitles asylum seekers and other migrants to the 'same labor rights as those that correspond to other workers of the State of employment'. The State must take all necessary measures to ensure these rights are 'recognized and guaranteed in practice'.[137]

Implications

A robust regional framework specifically oriented towards the protection of the human rights of aliens has been created through the instruments and jurisprudence of the Inter-American system. Although not specific to asylum seekers and refugees, it provides these groups of migrants with an additional set of rights guarantees that reinforces and – in many aspects – overlaps with the protection framework based upon the right of asylum. Whereas the latter framework develops specific standards by reference to external sources such as refugee law, the regional framework described and analysed in the present section merely confirms and specifies the application of general human rights norms contained in the ADHR and ACHR to the particular situation of aliens.

Nonetheless, there is a marked tendency in the Commission's jurisprudence on this area to seek inspiration from doctrinal developments in other regional human rights systems, particularly Europe. In so doing, the Commission does not always apply the borrowed concepts in precisely the way that they were originally framed. One example is the Commission's apparently more sympathetic treatment of the 'exceptionality' test developed by Europe in relation to cases involving the removal of terminally ill aliens to a home country where access to life-prolonging medical treatment will be curtailed.[138] Overall, the end result is that the Inter-American system now contains a framework of 'complementary' human rights protection against *refoulement* that is as generous as those presently found under other human rights systems, if not more so.

Cooperation within the Region

The Commission has also sought to provide a human rights basis to the necessity of cooperation at the regional level in order to address the implications of massive flows of migrants and refugees in the Americas. Particularly in the context of crisis in Haiti, the Commission was moved to note the fact that some countries tend to absorb a 'proportionately larger share of the Haitian diaspora' with attendant

136 See *Advisory Opinion OC-18/03* above n 1, paras 133–4.

137 Ibid. para 160.

138 Ibid.

consequences for their budget and infrastructure.[139] Its response has been to cloak the idea that such States deserve to receive assistance from the international community in the language of human rights obligations:

> The Commission would like to observe that the member countries of the [OAS] have an obligation, whenever a major crisis such as the present one occurs in the hemipshery [sic.] to confront the resulting problems jointly. The refugee questions gave rise to grave human rights problems that demanded positive action from all States subject to the obligations enshrined in the Charter of the [OAS], the [ADHR] and the [ACHR].[140]

In a separate Opinion to a decision by the Court on precautionary measures for Haitians and persons of Haitian origin expelled from the Dominican Republic, Judge Cançado Trinidade reinforced the idea that the truly global dimensions of such 'uprootedness' make it a problem at the heart of the international community that no single State should be required to shoulder alone.[141]

Conclusion: a Model of 'Complementary' Human Rights Protection

Almost ten years have passed since Judge Cançado Trinidade adopted the Concurring Opinion with which this chapter opened. In this same Opinion, the Judge identified the potential of international human rights law to respond to the unfulfilled protection needs of asylum seekers by offering a form of asylum broader even than that provided by international refugee law and supporting the construction of 'a true individual right *to* asylum'.[142] The analysis carried out by this chapter suggests that this vision is presently close to reality in the regional human rights system in force in the Americas, where asylum seekers and refugees are now protected by two distinct frameworks rooted in the human rights standards expressed in the ADHR and ACHR.

It is important to appreciate that the first of these frameworks has been developed through the Commission's jurisprudence on the right of asylum protected under the ADHR, an instrument binding on all OAS Member States. Since asylum is treated as a mechanism to prevent *refoulement* to the violation of fundamental human rights, an expansive series of procedural standards have been developed

---

139 Inter-American Commission on Human Rights, *Report on the Situation of Human Rights in Haiti* (OAS 1995) OEA/Ser.L/V/II.88/Doc 10 rev para 31.

140 Ibid. para 239.

141 See *Haitian and Haitian-Origin Dominican Persons in the Dominican Republic* above n 41, Concurring Opinion of Judge Antônio A Cançado Trinidade (President), paras 2, 10.

142 See *Advisory Opinion OC-18/03* above n 1, Concurring Opinion of Judge Antônio A Cançado Trinidade (President), paras 38–9, emphasis added.

to ensure the right to 'seek and receive' asylum. As a result, the soft law from the refugee field that is the external source of these standards is recast as hard law human rights obligations upon States. Nonetheless, certain fault lines within this interpretation are already evident and require to be addressed by the authoritative institutions of the Inter-American human rights system.

By contrast, the second framework relies even less directly on recourse to external sources. It is based on the method of specifying how the general human rights standards expressed in the ADHR and ACHR relate to aliens in contexts such as *refoulement*, removal, judicial proceedings, detention and employment. The application of this framework is not dependent upon the person satisfying external criteria for asylum, although it certainly protects asylum seekers and refugees as well as other aliens. Certain key jurisprudential features are inspired by developments, particularly from Europe, although the resulting framework in the Americas is more generous in the protection that it offers.

Overall, therefore, the Inter-American system appears to provide the most expansive set of protections for asylum seekers and refugees of any human rights system. In the future, it will be important for the integrity of the framework – developed largely by the Commission – to see whether it is adopted also by the Court. We may not have to wait long for an answer, since the first petition by an asylum seeker is listed to be heard shortly before the Court.[143] More broadly, the ability of the two human rights bodies to provide international monitoring and enforcement of these standards will depend on the ultimate impact of the renewed antagonism by certain OAS States towards the Inter-American human rights system. At this moment 'of shadow rather than light' – to again invoke the words of Judge Cançado Trinidade – it is important to 'preserve the advances achieved by past generations'.[144] In the field of asylum, this is the goal of the framework created by the Inter-American human rights system.

Bibliography

International Instruments

Additional Protocol to the American Convention on Human Rights in the Area of Economic, Social and Cultural Rights, San Salvador, El Salvador, 17 November 1988, in force 16 November 1999, 69 OAS Treaty Series 1.

143 On 21 February 2012, the Commission filed an application with the Court in a case concerning *refoulement* of Peruvian refugees by Bolivia (Inter-American Commission on Human Rights, 'Press Release: IACHR Takes Case Involving Bolivia to the Inter-American Court' (Press Release No 22/12, 23 February 2012)).

144 See *Advisory Opinion OC-18/03* above n 1, Concurring Opinion of Judge Antônio A Cançado Trinidade (President), para 40.

American Convention on Human Rights, San José, Costa Rica, 22 November 1969, in force 18 July 1978, 36 Treaty Series 1.

American Declaration on the Rights and Duties of Man, Bogotá, Colombia, adopted by Resolution XXX, Final Act of the Ninth International Conference of American States (Pan American Union), 30 March–2 May 1948, 1 Annals of the OAS 130 (1949).

Cartagena Declaration on Refugees, Cartagena, Colombia, 22 November 1984, adopted by the Colloquium on the International Protection of Refugees in Central America, Mexico and Panama; reprinted in *Annual Report of the Inter-American Commission on Human Rights 1984–1985* (1 October 1985) OEA/Ser.L/V/II.66/doc.10, rev 1, 190–193.

Charter of the Organization of American States, Bogotá, Colombia, 30 April 1948, in force 13 December 1951, 1-C and 61 OAS Treaty Series 1.

Convention on Territorial Asylum, Caracas, Venezuela, 28 March 1954, in force 29 December 1954, 19 OAS Treaty Series 1.

Convention relating to the Status of Refugees, Geneva, 28 July 1951, in force 22 April 1954, 189 UNTS 137.

Protocol of Amendment to the Charter of the Organization of American States, Buenos Aires, Argentina, 27 February 1967, in force 27 February 1970, 1-A OAS Treaty Series 1.

Protocol relating to the Status of Refugees, New York, 31 January 1967, in force 4 October 1967, 606 UNTS 267.

Rules of Procedure of the Inter-American Commission on Human Rights, approved at its 109th Special Session, 4–8 December 2000, and amended at its 116th regular session, 7–25 October 2002.

Statute of the Inter-American Commission on Human Rights, approved by OAS General Assembly, 'Resolution No. 447 (IX-0/79) Statute of the Inter-American Commission on Human Rights' (31 October 1979).

Treaty on Political Asylum and Refuge, Montevideo, Uruguay, 4 August 1939, reprinted in MO Hudson (ed), *International Legislation* (Carnegie Endowment for International Peace, 1949) Vol 8, 404.

Cases

Inter-American Commission on Human Rights, *Eduardo Alvarez v Cuba* Case 7898 (Commission Resolution No. 11/82, 8 March 1982).

Inter-American Commission on Human Rights, *Haitian Centre for Human Rights et al v USA* Case 10675 (Commission Report No 51/96, 13 March 1997).

Inter-American Commission on Human Rights, *Loren Rieve et al v Mexico* Case 11610 (Commission Report No 49/99, 13 April 1999).

Inter-American Commission on Human Rights, *Michael Edwards et al v The Bahamas* Case 12067 (Commission Report No 48/01, 4 April 2001).

Inter-American Commission on Human Rights, *Rafael Ferrer-Mazorra et al. v USA* Case 9903 (Commission Report No 51/01, 4 April 2001).

Inter-American Commission on Human Rights, *120 Cuban Nationals and 8 Haitian Nationals Detained in the Bahamas* Case 12071 (Commission Report No 6/02, 27 February 2002).
Inter-American Commission on Human Rights, *Andrea Mortlock v USA* Case 12534 (Commission Report No 63/08, 25 July 2008).
Inter-American Commission on Human Rights, *Frank Ewonwu v USA* Case 87-08 (Commission Report No. 60/09, 20 July 2009).
Inter-American Commission on Human Rights, *Wayne Smith et al. v USA* Case 12562 (Commission Report No 81/10, 12 July 2010).
Inter-American Commission on Human Rights, *Edwin A Márquez González v United States* (PM 171/11, 2011).
Inter-American Commission on Human Rights, *Gary Resil et al v United States* (PM 5/11, 2011).
Inter-American Commission on Human Rights, *John Doe et al v Canada* Case 12586 (Commission Report No 78/11, 21 July 2011).
Inter-American Court of Human Rights, *Advisory Opinion on Interpretation of the American Declaration of the Rights and Duties of Man within the Framework of Article 64 of the American Convention on Human Rights* (14 July 1989) Series A No 10.
Inter-American Court of Human Rights, *Haitian and Haitian-Origin Dominican Persons in the Dominican Republic* (Provisional Measures Order by the Court, 18 August 2000).
Inter-American Court of Human Rights, *Advisory Opinion on Juridical Condition and Rights of Undocumented Migrants* (17 September 2003) Series A No 18.
Inter-American Court of Human Rights, *Goiburú et al v Paraguay* (22 September 2006) Series C No 153.
International Court of Justice, *Colombian-Peruvian Asylum Case* (20 November 1950) ICJ Rep 266.

Other Sources

Amato V, 'Taking Stock of the Reflection on the Workings of the Commission' (2012) 16 Aportes 4.
Burgorgue-Larsen L et al, *The Inter-American Court of Human Rights: Case Law and Commentary* (Oxford University Press, 2011).
Cantor DJ, 'Restitution, Compensation, Satisfaction: Transnational Reparations and Colombia's Victims' Law' (2011) 215 UNHCR New Issues in Refugee Research 1.
Cantor DJ, *The Return of Internally Displaced Persons under International Law* (Martinus Nijohff, forthcoming).
El Comercio (newspaper), 'Ecuador apuesta po nueva instancia de derechos humanos para Suramérica', 3 May 2012.

El Tiempo (newspaper), 'Decisión de la CIDH podría limitar operaciones militares', 29 July 2011.

El Tiempo (newspaper), 'Gobierno buscará milionarias indemnizaciones por Mapiripán', 26 October 2011.

Harris DJ and Livingstone S (eds), *The Inter-American System of Human Rights* (Clarendon, 1998).

Inter-American Commission on Human Rights, *Informe sobre la situación de derechos humanos en la República de Cuba* (OAS 1962) OEA/Ser.L/V/II.4/doc.2.

Inter-American Commission on Human Rights, 'La situación de los refugiados políticos en América', OEA/Ser.L/V/II.11, Doc. 7, in *La Organización de los Estados Americanos y los Derechos Humanos: Actividades de la Comisión Americana de Derechos Humanos 1960–1967* (OAS 1972).

Inter-American Commission on Human Rights, *Report on the Situation of Human Rights in Argentina* (OAS 1980) OEA/Ser.L/V/II.49/Doc.19, corr.1.

Inter-American Commission on Human Rights, *Informe anual de la Comisión Interamericana de Derechos Humanos 1981–1982* (OAS 1982) OEA/Ser.L/V/II.57/doc.6, rev.1.

Inter-American Commission on Human Rights, *Report on the Situation of Human Rights in Haiti* (OAS 1995) OEA/Ser.L/V/II.88/Doc.10 rev.

Inter-American Commission on Human Rights, *Report on the Situation of Human Rights of Asylum-Seekers within the Canadian Refugee Determination System* (OAS 2000) OEA/Ser.L/V/II.106/Doc.40 rev.

Inter-American Commission on Human Rights, 'Recommendation on Asylum and International Crimes' (20 October 2000) in Annual Report of the Inter-American Commission on Human Rights 2000 (OAS 2001) OEA/Ser.L/V/II.111/Doc.20 rev.

Inter-American Commission on Human Rights, *Report on Terrorism and Human Rights* (OAS 2002) OEA/Ser.L/V/II.116/Doc.5 rev.1 corr.

Inter-American Commission on Human Rights, *Access to Justice and Social Inclusion: The Road towards Strengthening Democracy in Bolivia* (OAS 2007) OEA/Ser.L/V/II.Doc 34.

Inter-American Commission on Human Rights, *Report on Immigration in the United States: Detention and Due Process* (OAS 2010) OEA/Ser.L/II.Doc. 78/10.

Inter-American Commission on Human Rights, 'Press Release: IACHR Takes Case Involving Bolivia to the Inter-American Court' (Press Release No 22/12, 23 February 2012).

Manly M, 'La consagración del asilo como un derecho humano: Análisis comparative de la Declaración Universal, la Declaración Americana y la Convención Americana sobre Derechos Humanos' in L Franco (ed), *El asilo y la protección internacional de los refugiados en América Latina* (Editorama, 2004).

Medina C, *The Battle of Human Rights: Gross, Systematic Violations and the Inter-American System* (Martinus Nijhoff, 1988).
Organization of American States, 'Secretario General de la OEA comunica denuncia de la Convención Americana sobre Derechos Humanos de parte de Venezuela' (Press Release C-307/12, 10 September 2012).
Organization of American States General Assembly, 'Resolution AG/RES. 774 (XV-O/85) on Legal Situation of Asylum-Seekers, Refugees and Displaced Persons on the American Continent' (9 December 1985).
Organization of American States General Assembly, 'Resolution AG/RES. 2758 (XLII-O/12) on Protection of Asylum Seekers and Refugees in the Americas' (5 June 2012).
Pasqualucci J, *The Practice and Procedure of the Inter-American Court of Human Rights* (Cambridge University Press. 2003).
Pulido MC and Blanchard M, 'La Comisión Interamericana de Derechos Humanos y sus mecanismos de protección aplicados a la situación de los refugiados, apátridas y solicitantes de asilo' in L Franco (ed), *El asilo y la protección internacional de los refugiados en América Latina* (Editorama, 2004).
Sandoval C, 'A Critical View of the Protection of Refugees and IDPs by the Inter-American System of Human Rights: Re-assessing its Powers and Examining the Challenges for the Future' (2005) 17 International Journal of Refugee Law 43.
United Nations High Commissioner for Refugees, *Global Trends 2011* (UNHCR 2012).
Yundt KW, 'The Organization of American States and Legal Protection to Political Refugees in Central America' (1989) 23 International Migration Review 201.

Chapter 13

ASEAN and the Conceptualization of Refugee Protection in Southeastern Asian States

Susan Kneebone

Introduction

The refugee 'problem' within the Asia-Pacific region is described in the 2012 Regional Update by the UNHCR as follows:

> The Asia-Pacific region is home to the world's largest and oldest refugee populations. The protection environment continues to be fragile with very few countries having signed the 1951 Convention relating to the Status of Refugees … The region is characterized by population movements, with asylum-seekers from Afghanistan, Myanmar and Sri Lanka representing the three largest groups moving irregularly. The majority of these individuals settle in urban areas.[1]

Indeed the Asia and the Pacific region is host to some 10.6 million people 'of concern' to UNHCR, representing almost 30 per cent of the global refugee population.[2] This includes internally displaced persons (IDPs) numbering approximately 4.3 million. The Asia-Pacific region includes several overlapping and diverse sub-regions, namely South Asia (including India, Sri Lanka and Bangladesh) and Southeast Asia, which covers the ASEAN[3] countries, and East

My thanks to Sayomi Ariyawansa, Reyvi Mariñas, Claerwen O'Hara and Fiona Ransom for invaluable research assistance in preparation of this chapter.

1 UNHCR, EXCOM, 'Regional update – Asia and the Pacific' (63rd session, Geneva, 1–5 October 2012) para A.

2 UNHCR, 'Asia and the Pacific – 2012 Regional Operations Profile', available at http://www.unhcr.org/pages/4a02d8ec6.html (accessed 27 November 2012).

3 ASEAN (Association of South East Asia Nations) founded in 1967 originally involved five states, Singapore, Malaysia, Thailand, Philippines and Indonesia, to promote 'common political interests as well as a forum for private business and community-level interactions'. See ASEAN, *The ASEAN Declaration ('Bangkok Declaration')*, Bangkok, Thailand, 8 August 1967, available at: http://www.asean.org/news/item/the-asean-declaration-bangkok-declaration (accessed 25 February 2013) Brunei was added in 1984, Vietnam in 1995, Lao PDR and Mynamar in 1997 and Cambodia in 1999.

Asia (South Korea and Japan). Thus as this chapter is focused on the ASEAN regional response to refugee protection, it will concentrate on the Southeast Asian region. Within Southeast Asia, the main 'hosting' countries of refugee populations are Thailand, Malaysia, and Indonesia.[4] Whilst the Southeast Asian region has a 'protracted refugee' problem, Indonesia and Malaysia are well-known transit countries for asylum seekers en route to Australia. Thus another process, which is relevant to the regional response, is the Bali Process (the Conference on People Smuggling, Trafficking in Persons and Related Transnational Crime) which is co-chaired by Australia and Indonesia, and which the ASEAN Secretariat sometimes attends as an observer.[5] Although ASEAN is not as such a party to the Bali Process, all the individual ASEAN countries participate in it. Australia is however part of a group known as ASEAN + 6.[6]

The conceptualization of refugee protection in Southeast Asian States and under the ASEAN process requires discussion of two main themes, namely the characterization ion of refugees as 'irregular migrants' and the recognition of human rights within the ASEAN process. As an organization, ASEAN is known for its preference for decision-making through consultation and consensus-formation and for its respect for the individual sovereignty of States, which translates into the principle of 'non-interference'. Its methods of governance and its approach to irregular migration mean that it is unlikely to insist that individual States conform to the paradigm of universal human rights which underlies the international refugee protection regime. The language of human rights is not generally well received by some Southeast Asian governments; rather the focus on refugees is upon their status as 'irregular migrants' under a traditional or 'border' security characterization. This characterization is also a feature of the Bali Process. However, there are recent indications of a change in approach led by ASEAN, which may be shifting the paradigms of security and human rights. But as I argue in this chapter, these shifts are not leading to improvements in refugee protection. Moreover, the recent adoption of an ASEAN Human Rights Declaration (AHRD)[7] has ambiguous consequences for the rights of refugees.

---

4 Details about individual country refugee issues and responses can be obtained from UNHCR websites – for example for Thailand see http://www.unhcr.org/pages/49e489646.html.

5 See Bali Process Senior Officials Meeting, Co-Chairs Statement, 10 March 2011; Third Bali Regional Ministerial Conference on People Smuggling, Trafficking in Persons and Related Transnational Crime. Co-Chairs Statement, 14–15 April 2009.

6 This refers to the Regional Comprehensive Economic Partnership (RCEP) Agreement between ASEAN and six trading partner countries, namely China, India, Japan, South Korea, Australia and New Zealand, concluded in November 2012 and slated to begin negotiations in May 2013. See The Jakarta News, http://www.thejakartapost.com/news/2013/01/31/talks-asean6-trade-bloc-kick-may.html (accessed 7 February 2013).

7 ASEAN Intergovernmental Commission on Human Rights, 'The Adoption of the ASEAN Human Rights Declaration (AHRD) at the 21st ASEAN Summit and the Special Meeting of the ASEAN Intergovernmental Commision on Human Rights (AICHR)'

In order to understand ASEAN and the conceptualization of refugee protection, it is necessary to explain the regional and ASEAN approach to irregular migration and security, and the recent development of a human rights dialogue within ASEAN, through the AHRD. The latter will be contrasted with another 'dialogue' that has developed within the Asian African Legal Consultative Organization (AACLO), which conceives refugee protection in terms more consistent with the international refugee protection regime.

Refugees, Irregular Migration and the Development of a Regional Security Discourse

Whilst countries within the Southeast Asian region have considerable experience with providing shelter to refugees, there is a persistent reluctance in some States to recognize their status.[8] As Vitit Muntarbhorn has explained in relation to Thailand, refugees are seen as a political embarrassment, and as a threat to State sovereignty and national security.[9] This perception portrays refugees as a political problem[10] and leads to the characterization of them as a threat to 'border' security within ASEAN.[11]

It is also the characteristic response of a region that lacks coherent migration policies. As one commentator on the region, Ronald Skeldon, has said, there is a fear of the 'outsider' and the desire to control borders in the region:

(Phnom Penh, 17–18 November 2012), available at http://aichr.org/press-release/the-adoption-of-the-asean-human-rights-declaration-ahrd-at-the-21st-asean-summit-and-the-special-meeting-of-the-asean-intergovernmental-commission-on-human-rights-aichr/ (accessed 25 February 2013).

8 For example A Alexander, 'Without refuge: Chin refugees in India and Malaysia' (2008) 30 Forced Migration Review 36.

9 V Muntarbhorn, 'Refugee Law and Practice in the Asia and Pacific Region: Thailand as a Case Study' (Research Paper: Thailand UNCHR, 2004), available at http://www.en.refugeelawreader.org/index.php?option=com_docman&task=doc_view&lang=en&gid=564&level=1&ml=5&mlt=system&tmpl=component (accessed 25 February 2013). This is despite the fact that the Thai government hosted the Asian-African Legal Consultative Organization's 8th session where the 1966 Bangkok Principles on Status and Treatment of Refugees were agreed upon (see Asian-African Legal Consultative Organisation, *Bangkok Principles on Status and Treatment of Refugees*, 8th session, Bangkok, Thailand, 8–17 August 1996) and actively supported the Comprehensive Plan of Action for Indo-Chinese refugees (CPA), which was agreed upon, at a Geneva Conference held 13–14 June 1989, by the UNHCR, the countries of first asylum and 50 resettlement countries in the West.

10 GS Goodwin-Gill, 'The Politics of Refugee Protection' (2008) 27(1) Refugee Survey Quarterly 8.

11 See also Sara E. Davies in this volume.

> There is the perpetual fear of the outsider and the fear that foreigners will create trouble within the borders of the state and, if present in sufficient numbers, lead to changing identities of the nation itself.[12]

As Caballero-Anthony has explained, within the region migration is 'elevated by the state above the course of normal politics' and is viewed through a 'security lens'.[13] For example, migrant workers are seen as a 'menace to society' to 'societal identity and security'.[14] Malaysia's current immigration laws and policies associate breach of its laws with criminality[15] and put the onus on immigrants to ensure that their status is 'regular'. In Malaysia refugees who have been recognized as such by the UNHCR are at risk of being sanctioned under the legislation.[16] Thus within the region, refugees have long been associated with threats to national sovereignty and identity, and with border or 'traditional' security rather than as victims of human rights abuse (although as discussed below, the 1993 *Bangkok Declaration*[17] recognized their rights). Predominantly, they are seen as 'irregular migrants'.

By the end of the 1990s, despite the persistent presence of refugees, another problem of 'irregular migration' became an important and visible issue in the Southeast Asian region. This arose from the related issues of human trafficking and irregular labour migrants. Although at this time there were large numbers of refugees in camps on the Thai-Myanmar border, who were fleeing from human rights abuses in Myanmar, and there was increasing displacement caused by

12 R Skeldon, 'Trafficking: A Perspective from Asia' (2000–01) 38(3) International Migration 7, 21.

13 M Caballero-Anthony, 'Reflections on managing migration in South East Asia: mitigating the unintended consequences of securitisation' in MG Curley and W Siu-lun, *Security and Migration in Asia: The Dynamics of Securitisation* (Routledge, 2008) 165.

14 Ibid. 166. See also Y Chalamwong, J Meepien and K Hongprayoon, 'Management of Cross-border Migration: Thailand as a Case of Net Migration' (2012) 40(4) Asian Journal of Social Science 447, 452.

15 A Nah, 'Struggling with (Il)Legality: The Indeterminate Functioning of Malaysia's Borders for Asylum Seekers, Refugees, and Stateless Persons' in PK Rajaram and C Grundy-Warr (eds), *Borderscapes: Hidden Geographies and Politics at Territory's Edge* (University of Minnesota Press, 2007) chaps 2, 37.

16 This is recognized in French CJ's judgment in *Plaintiffs M70/2011 and M106 of 2011 v Minister for Immigration and Citizenship* ('*the Malaysia-Swap Arrangement case*' – *Plaintiffs M70*) referring to the DFAT assessment tendered in evidence where it was stated that: 'Illegal immigrants in Malaysia are liable to imprisonment and/or a fine and caning of not more than six strokes'. See [2011] HCA 32, [28].

17 Final Declaration of the Regional Meeting for Asia of the World Conference on Human Rights, World Conference on Human Rights Bangkok, 29 March–2 April 1993, UN Doc A/CONF.157/PC/59 (7 April 1993) ('1993 Bangkok Declaration'). 1993 Bangkok Declaration, Art 11 emphasizes 'the importance of guaranteeing the human rights and fundamental freedoms of vulnerable groups such as ethnic, national, racial, religious and linguistic minorities, migrant workers, disabled persons, indigenous peoples, refugees and displaced persons'.

development and conflict in the region which particularly affected ethnic groups, the most visible irregular migration issue was that of labour migrants. However, little attention was paid at this time to either category of irregular migrant, namely refugee or labour migrant. Rather the attention was focused upon the problem of human trafficking, which was linked to a security paradigm.[18]

This security discourse was apparent in the 1999 *Bangkok Declaration on Irregular Migration*[19] which arose from a 1996 Regional Seminar on Irregular Migration and Migrant Trafficking in East and South Asia (the 'Manila Process').[20] The 1999 *Bangkok Declaration* refers to this and to another process,[21] namely the Inter-governmental Asia-Pacific Consultations on Refugees, Displaced Persons and Migrants (APC).[22]

The 1999 Declaration, from which the Bali Process arose, and to which Australia is a party, was made at an International Symposium on Migration, held on 21–23 April 1999, under the chairmanship of the Deputy Prime Minister of Thailand, 'to address the question of international migration, with particular attention to regional cooperation on irregular/undocumented migration'.[23] Paragraph 1 of the 1999 *Bangkok Declaration* provides that migration, and in particular irregular migration 'should be addressed in a comprehensive and balanced manner, considering its causes, manifestations and effects, both positive and negative, in the countries of origin, transit and destination'.[24] Throughout the Declaration, international migration is conceived as involving irregular migration and 'smuggling and trafficking in human beings'. There is no reference to refugees or human rights in this document.

---

18 S Kneebone and J Debeljak, *Transnational Crime and Human Rights: Responses to Human Trafficking in the Greater Mekong Subregion* (Routledge, 2012) 86–95.

19 Bangkok Declaration on Irregular Migration, International Symposium on Migration, Bangkok, Thailand, 21–23 April 1999, available at http://www.iom.int/jahia/webdav/site/myjahiasite/shared/shared/mainsite/policy_and_research/rcp/APC/BANGKOK_DECLARATION.pdf (accessed 25 February 2013) ('1999 Bangkok Declaration').

20 This was a 1996 Regional Seminar on Irregular Migration and Migrant Trafficking in East and South Asia which was organized by IOM. The purpose of this process in which IOM takes a lead role, is to hold intergovernmental meetings on trafficking and irregular migration in East and South East Asia. Notably the Bali Process arose out of this process; it was initiated at the First Bali Regional Ministerial Conference on People Smuggling, Trafficking in Persons and Related Transnational Crime, Bali, Indonesia, 26–28 February 2002; see Bali Process, 'About the Bali Process', available at http://www.baliprocess.net/index.asp?pageID=2145831401 (accessed 5 June 2011).

21 Above n 19. See preambular clause 12.

22 Asia Pacific Consultations on Refugees, Displaced Persons and Migrants (1 March 2010), available at http://www.apcprocess.net/.

23 Available at http://www.smc.org.ph/rights/bangkok.htm.

24 See 1999 Bangkok Declaration, above n 19.

The 1999 Declaration focuses strongly on regional cooperation for the orderly 'management of migration'. For example, paragraph 2 of the Declaration provides that:

> [T]he orderly management of migration and addressing of irregular migration and trafficking will require the concerted efforts of countries concerned, whether bilaterally, regionally or otherwise, based on sound principles of equality, mutual understanding and respect.

The language of the Declaration presages the 'securitized' concept of international irregular migration[25] which infuses both ASEAN and the Bali Process. Significantly, the Co-Chairs Statement from the 2002 Regional Ministerial Conference on People Smuggling, Trafficking in Persons and Related Transnational Crime held in Bali in February 2002,[26] which was the first formal meeting of the Bali Process, acknowledges the legacy of the 1999 Declaration, the work of the APC and of ASEAN.[27] It also welcomed the 'existing ASEAN mechanisms in combating people smuggling, trafficking in persons and related transnational crime'.[28]

In relation to human trafficking, ASEAN very quickly adopted the security characterization of the issue.[29] The first formal ASEAN response to human trafficking in the region arose out of a concern to combat transnational crime. This was the 1997 ASEAN Declaration on Transnational Crime[30] which was supplemented in 1999 by the ASEAN Plan of Action to Combat Transnational Crime, which established the basic institutional and normative framework for a regional criminal justice response to transnational issues.[31] Then, at the 10th ASEAN Summit on the 29 November 2004 the ASEAN Declaration Against Trafficking in Persons Particularly Women and Children ('2004 ASEAN Trafficking in Persons Declaration')[32] was created.

25 Kneebone and Debeljak, *Transnational Crime and Human Rights* 91–8.

26 See http://www.baliprocess.net/ accessed 8 November 2012.

27 Co-Chairs' Statement 2002 [7].

28 Ibid. [14].

29 See Kneebone and Debeljak, *Transnational Crime and Human Rights* chapter 2.

30 ASEAN, *ASEAN Declaration on Transnational Crime*, Manila, The Philippines, 20 December 1997, available at http://www.asean.org/communities/asean-political-security-community/item/asean-declaration-on-transnational-crime-manila-20-december-1997 (accessed 25 February 2013).

31 ASEAN, *ASEAN Plan of Action to Combat Transnational Crime*, endorsed by the 2nd ASEAN Ministerial Meeting on Transnational Crime (AMMTC), Yangon, Myanmar, 23 June 1999, available at http://www.asean.org/communities/asean-political-security-community/item/joint-communique-of-the-second-asean-ministerial-meeting-on-transnational-crime-ammtc-yangon-23-june-1999 (accessed 25 February 2013). See Kneebone and Debeljak, *Transnational Crime and Human Rights* 188–92.

32 ASEAN, *ASEAN Declaration Against Trafficking In Persons Particularly Women and Children ('ASEAN Trafficking Declaration')*, Vientiane, Lao PDR, 29 November 2004,

It is now necessary to explain the development of the concept of an ASEAN Community and the ASEAN concept of security, to determine whether refugees fit into the picture. We will see that there is an emerging convergence between 'human security' concerns and development, which encompasses some human rights. However, within this framework the rights of refugees are still conceived in ambiguous terms.

The ASEAN Community, Human Rights, Human Security and Development: Where do Refugees Fit?

ASEAN was founded in 1967 with the aim of building a 'prosperous and peaceful community of Southeast Asian Nations'.[33] One commentator has suggested that 'ASEAN started life at the height of the Vietnam War as a united front Cold War political association, fighting the communist threat'.[34] However, another has suggested that when ASEAN was established, intra-regional tensions were very high and almost on the brink of military hostilities.[35] For that reason, Tan Hsien-Li says that ASEAN 'had an implicit security and political function to prevent armed confrontation among its members'.[36] Its focus on security reflects the instability and mistrust which characterized Southeast Asia in the period leading up to the establishment of ASEAN.[37]

The current ASEAN is probably even less united in characteristics than the original. There are disparities in income which continue to grow between the older ASEAN members and the newer members, such as Cambodia, Laos, Myanmar and Vietnam. There are economic differentials among the older ASEAN members, with great differences between Singapore and Brunei and the Philippines, for example. There are also striking income disparities within each country, particularly between urban and rural areas, with the latter experiencing much more

---

available at http://www.asean.org/communities/asean-political-security-community/item/asean-declaration-against-trafficking-in-persons-particularly-women-and-children-3 (accessed 25 February 2013).

33 ASEAN, *The ASEAN Declaration ('Bangkok Declaration')*, Bangkok, Thailand, 8 August 1967, above n 3.

34 EKB Tan, 'The ASEAN Charter as "Legs To Go Places": Ideational Norms and Pragmatic Legalism in Community Building in South East Asia' (2008) 12 Singapore Year Book of International Law 197.

35 T Hsien-Li, *The ASEAN Intergovernmental Commission on Human Rights: Institutionalising Human Rights in Southeast Asia* (Cambridge University Press, 2011) 144.

36 Ibid., 144–5.

37 AJ Bellamy and C Drummond, 'The responsibility to protect in Southeast Asia: between non-interference and sovereignty as responsibility' (2011) 24(2) The Pacific Review 179–200.

poverty.[38] There are gaps in institutional capacity and resource limitations between ASEAN Member States, with particular difficulties for Cambodia, Laos, Myanmar and Vietnam, which all have agricultural-based economies and which are still in transition from centrally planned to market-orientated economic systems. There are also differences in styles of governance and accountability, with some ASEAN members claiming to have democratic systems (Cambodia, Indonesia, Malaysia, Philippines and Singapore), whilst others have strong monarchies (Brunei), socialist-oriented systems (Laos and Vietnam) and military regimes (Myanmar).[39]

In this context 40 years after its founding in 2007, the ASEAN Charter was signed,[40] and an ASEAN Community established comprising: the ASEAN Political-Security Community (APSC), the ASEAN Economic Community (AEC), and the ASEAN Socio-Cultural Community (ASCC). Article 35 of the ASEAN Charter provides that 'ASEAN shall promote its common ASEAN identity and a sense of belonging among its peoples in order to achieve its shared destiny, goals and values'. Another important institution, the ASEAN Intergovernmental Commission on Human Rights (AICHR) was created pursuant to Article 14 of the Charter.[41] The AICHR is intended to assist ASEAN to conform to the 'purposes and principles of the ASEAN Charter relating to the promotion and protection of human rights and fundamental freedoms'. The Preamble to the Charter refers to adherence to 'the principles of democracy, the rule of law and good governance, respect for and protection of' such rights and freedoms. Thus the ASEAN Charter expressly incorporates rights and freedoms into the concept of an ASEAN Community.

The obvious question is why human rights were incorporated into the ASEAN Charter and concept of a Community, and whether this affects the conceptualization of refugees. Famously, the 1993 *Bangkok Declaration*,[42] which was made by

---

38 M Caballero-Anthony, 'Bridging Development Gaps in Southeast Asia: Towards an ASEAN Community' (2006) 11 UNISCI Discussion Papers 37–48.

39 Ibid.

40 The Charter was signed by the 10 ASEAN Member States on 20 November 2007 during the 13th ASEAN Summit in Singapore and entered into force on 15 December 2008 – ASEAN, *ASEAN Charter*, opened for signature at the 13th ASEAN Summit, Singapore, 20 November 2008 (entered into force 15 December 2008), available at http://www.asean.org/archive/publications/ASEAN-Charter.pdf (accessed 25 February 2013).

41 Additionally the ASEAN Commission on the Promotion and Protection of the Rights of Women and Children (ACWC) was formally inaugurated on 7 April 2010.

42 *Final Declaration of the Regional Meeting for Asia of the World Conference on Human Rights*, World Conference on Human Rights Bangkok, 29 March–2 April 1993, UN Doc A/CONF.157/PC/59 (7 April 1993) ('1993 *Bangkok Declaration*'), available at http://www.unhchr.ch/Huridocda/Huridoca.nsf/TestFrame/9d23b88f115fb827802569030037ed44?Opendocument (accessed 25 February 2013). *1993 Bangkok Declaration*, Art 11 emphasizes 'the importance of guaranteeing the human rights and fundamental freedoms of vulnerable groups such as ethnic, national, racial, religious and linguistic minorities, migrant workers, disabled persons, indigenous peoples, refugees and displaced persons'.

Ministers and representatives of Asian States in preparation for the Vienna World Conference on Human Rights, made a specific reference to the rights of refugees and displaced persons, referring to them collectively as 'vulnerable' persons. In the 1993 Declaration the rights of such persons were linked to inequalities in development between the Global North and the Global South,[43] and to the need to create favourable conditions for effective enjoyment of human rights at both the national and international levels.[44]

Whilst some see the 1993 *Bangkok Declaration* as heralding the beginning of a shift to human rights,[45] it could also be interpreted as a strident and defensive declaration of 'Asian values' or Asian 'exceptionalism' on human rights questions.[46] Whichever interpretation is correct, it presents a view of how Asian States perceived human rights issues at the time; namely that improvement in human rights was understood to be the responsibility of the West, in the context of uneven development between the Global North and South regions.

In comparison to the 1993 Declaration, the 1999 *Bangkok Declaration on Irregular Migration* did not refer specifically to refugees and displaced persons. Rather it focuses upon inequalities *within the region* and the regionalized concept of security. It reflects the unevenness of development in the region. The 1999 Declaration recognizes that 'international migration, particularly irregular migration, has increasingly become a major economic, social, humanitarian, political and security concern for a number of countries in the Asia-Pacific region'.[47] It also recognizes that 'comprehensive, coherent and effective policies on irregular/undocumented migration have to be formulated within the context of a broader regional framework based on a spirit of partnership and common understanding' and the need for 'international cooperation to promote sustained economic growth and sustainable development in the countries of origin as a long-term strategy to address irregular migration'.[48] Importantly, it followed the 1997 Global Financial Crisis (GFC) which badly affected Asian economies as discussed below.

43 Ibid., Art 18.

44 Ibid., Art 2.

45 S Linton, 'ASEAN States, Their Reservations to Human Rights Treaties and the Proposed ASEAN Commission on Women and Children' (2008) 30 Human Rights Quarterly 436.

46 B Saul, J Mowbray and I Baghoomians, 'Resistance to regional human rights cooperation in the Asia-Pacific: demythologizing regional exceptionalism by learning from the Americas, Europe and Africa' in H Nasu and B Saul (eds), *Human Rights in the Asia Pacific Region* (Routledge, 2011) chapter 6.

47 1999 Bangkok Declaration preamble [4].

48 Ibid., preamble [8] [10].

Consistent with the 1999 Declaration, the ASEAN Hanoi Plan of Action 1998 (HPA)[49] targeted development and poverty.[50] It contained several measures related to immigration and trafficking, including accelerating the freer flow of skilled and professional labour in the region and the strengthening of ASEAN collaboration in combating the trafficking of, and violent crimes against women and children.[51] This latter focus was consistent with the 1993 Bangkok Declaration[52] and the 1993 ASEAN Plan of Action for Children.[53]

Tan Hsien-Li suggests that although the HPA made the ASEAN human rights agenda 'more explicit',[54] that the real turning point[55] was the Vientiane Action Programme (VAP) created in November 2004,[56] which spelt out the concept of an ASEAN Community. The VAP was fuelled by concern about:

> [T]he development gap among the Member Countries so that the benefit of ASEAN integration are shared and which will enable all Member Countries to move forward in a unified and cohesive manner.[57]

Although no reference was made in the VAP to the rights of refugees, there was reference to the need to 'promote education and public awareness on human rights', and specific reference to the rights of migrant workers, and women and children. However, advocates of human rights were disappointed by the fact that such rights were to be protected within an ASEAN 'Security Community' rather than in the 'Socio-Cultural Community'.[58]

The timing of the VAP is important. The Preamble to the VAP acknowledges 'that the global and regional economic environment has changed and is continuously challenged by new developments which impact upon trade and investment flows'. These external challenges included the 1997 Asian financial crisis following the

---

49 Hanoi Plan of Action (HPA) 1997, available at http://www.asean.org/asean/asean-summit/item/hanoi-plan-of-action (accessed 25 February 2013).

50 See preamble [2].

51 But see Linton, 'ASEAN States, Their Reservations to Human Rights Treaties and the Proposed ASEAN Commission on Women and Children' 436.

52 See above.

53 ASEAN Secretariat, 'Resolution on the ASEAN Plan of Action for Children', Manila, the Philippines, 2 December 2003, available at http://www.mwa.gov.kh/files/PDF/ASEAN/4.3_Resolution%20on%20ASEAN%20PoA%20for%20Children-1993.pdf (accessed 25 February 2013).

54 Tan, 'The ASEAN Charter as "Legs To Go Places"' 152.

55 Ibid. 154.

56 Vientiane Action Programme (VAP) 2004–10, Laos, 29 November 2004, available at http://cil.nus.edu.sg/rp/pdf/2004%20Vientiane%20Action%20Programme%202004-2010-pdf.pdf (accessed 25 February 2013).

57 Preamble.

58 Tan, 'The ASEAN Charter as "Legs To Go Places"' 154.

GFC, the 1999 East Timor crisis and natural disasters including health pandemics.[59] Significantly the Preamble to the VAP characterized those challenges as creating 'a new strategic context'. In the first decade of the 21st century those challenges increased. Thus it seems that ASEAN's focus on human rights arose out of concern for the consequences arising from 'development gaps' between individual ASEAN States. This has been expressed as an issue of 'human security'.

The next part of this discussion considers whether human rights are incorporated into a human security dialogue within ASEAN, and where refugees fit within the ASEAN Community.

Security, Human Security and Human Rights: the ASEAN Community

The ASEAN Security Community in the 2004 VAP was renamed the Political-Security Community (APSC) in the 2007 Charter. The issue of refugees falls within the APSC which also extends the idea of traditional or national State security to cover 'human security' issues.

The APSC Blueprint requires it to promote:

> [P]olitical development in adherence to the principles of democracy, the rule of law and good governance, respect for and promotion and protection of human rights and fundamental freedoms as inscribed in the ASEAN Charter … [And] a people-oriented ASEAN in which all sectors of society, regardless of gender, race, religion, language, or social and cultural background, are encouraged to participate in, and benefit from, the process of ASEAN integration and community building.[60]

It also envisages 'that the APSC will bring ASEAN's political and security cooperation to a higher plane'[61] It subscribes to 'a comprehensive approach to security, which acknowledges the interwoven relationships of political, economic, social-cultural and environmental dimensions of development'.[62] This principle of *comprehensive security* is explained as going 'beyond the requirements of traditional security but also takes into account *non-traditional* aspects vital to regional and national resilience, such as the economic, socio-cultural, and environmental dimensions of *development*'.[63] It is further explained that 'ASEAN

---

59 Ibid. 153.

60 ASEAN, APSC Blueprint para 7.

61 Ibid.

62 Ibid. para 9. Note that the principle of comprehensive security, to all forms of threats transnational crimes and transboundary challenges' is enshrined in the Purposes of the Charter (Article 1(8)).

63 ASEAN, APSC Blueprint para 17, emphasis added.

is *also* committed to conflict prevention/confidence building measures, preventive diplomacy, and post-conflict peace building'.[64]

Thus the APSC extends the idea of traditional security, which encompasses direct threats to the State as such from military action and the like, to non-traditional security risks, arising from gaps in development. In the APSC Blueprint at B.4, specific examples of 'non-traditional security issues' are given, including 'transnational crimes and transboundary challenges' such as human trafficking. As has been noted, the regional response 'securitizes' migration and especially labour migration issues as challenges to the State, termed as 'non-traditional security' risks.[65]

Refugees are mentioned within the ASEAN Community, only in the APSC Blueprint, and in the context of 'post-conflict peace building' (see B.3), and in particular under the heading at B.3.1., namely 'Strengthen ASEAN humanitarian assistance'. Thus refugees are conceived doubly narrowly, both within a security paradigm and as 'victims of conflict', for whom 'orderly repatriation' and resettlement (as internally displaced persons) is promoted. There is no reference to basic principles of *non-refoulement* or asylum. It is also significant that despite the reference in the APSC Blueprint to promoting non-discrimination on the basis of race, or religion, there is no evidence of any understanding that refugees within the region suffer from such discrimination.

It is also significant that refugees are absent from the ASEAN Socio-Cultural Community (ASCC) Blueprint, which is intended to realize an ASEAN Community that is 'people-centred and socially responsible'. The ASCC Blueprint has a strong emphasis on human rights protection and social welfare, including women and children, the elderly and persons with disabilities, and also deals in detail with the '[p]rotection and promotion of the rights of migrant workers', including operationalizing a Declaration on the Rights of Migrant Workers. But as I have explained elsewhere, the approach to migrant workers under the concept of an ASEAN Community is ambiguous.[66] On the one hand migrant workers are seen as a potential threat to social cohesion and associated with 'transnational crimes and transboundary challenges'; on the other they are portrayed as individuals with rights. By their inclusion in the APSC, refugees by implication are seen as a potential threat to social cohesion and as posing 'transboundary challenges'.

---

64 Ibid., emphasis added.

65 M Caballero-Anthony, 'Challenging Change: Nontraditional Security, Democracy and Regionalism' in DK Emmerson (ed), *Hard Choices: Security, Democracy, and Regionalism in Southeast Asia* (Institute of Southeast Asian Studies, 2008) 191.

66 Kneebone, 'ASEAN Norms and Setting The Agenda For The Rights of Migrant Workers' in H Nasu and B Saul (eds), *Human Rights in the Asia Pacific Region* (Routledge, 2011) 301–38.

This is confirmed by a rare reference to refugee issues, in the Chairman's Statement on the 14th ASEAN Summit in March 2009,[67] which celebrated the ASEAN Charter's entry into force on 15 December 2008 and the creation of an ASEAN Community. The Chairman referred to the problem of 'illegal migrants in the Indian Ocean' and encouraged cooperation among countries of origin, transit and destination, as well as addressing the issue through the Bali Process. The Chairman tasked the ASEAN Secretary-General to coordinate with the Myanmar government to obtain statistics related to the illegal migrants in the Indian Ocean. In the same Statement the Chairman suggested that the 'welfare and well-being of the Palestinian people in the Gaza was of paramount importance'. These statements refer to the problem of Rohingya refugees from Myanmar which was taxing refugee advocates at that time. The reference to Palestinian people may be an oblique reference to the fact that a large number of such are part of the refugee problem in Southeast Asia. The reference to the Bali Process is also significant, as that process does not focus upon the human rights of refugees, but rather upon management of irregular migration.

Another important feature of the ASEAN Community is the incorporation of a concept of 'human security', through the focus on non-traditional security risks, including gaps in development. In the ASEAN region where there is uneven acceptance of the language and concept of human rights,[68] the concept of human security[69] is promoted as an alternative. For example, Caballero-Anthony argues that the human security concept has developed under ASEAN into a 'people centred' discourse, and that it reflects the concept of human rights.[70] She suggests that there is 'tentative consensus on locating human rights at the core of a human security community' in Southeast Asia.[71] However, there are others who question the breadth of this assertion.

The term human security has different meanings. For example, the United Nations Development Programme (UNDP) has identified seven different but interrelated components of human security: economic, food, health, environmental, personal, communal and political.[72] UNDP summarized these as: first, safety

---

67 Chairman's Statement on the 14th ASEAN Summit, 'ASEAN Charter for ASEAN Peoples' (cha-am, 28 February–1 March 2009), available at http://www.asean.org/asean/asean-summit/item/chairman-s-statement-of-the-14th-asean-summit-asean-charter-for-asean-peoples (accessed 25 February 2013).

68 Tan, 'The ASEAN Charter as "Legs To Go Places"' 133–4.

69 A Edwards and C Ferstman, 'Humanising Non-Citizens: the Convergence of Human Rights and Human Security' in Edwards and Ferstman (eds), *Human Security and Non-Citizens: Law Policy and International Affairs* (Cambridge University Press, 2010) 3.

70 M Caballero-Anthony, 'The Responsibility to Protect in Southeast Asia: opening up spaces for advancing human security' (2012) 25(1) The Pacific Review 113–34.

71 Ibid., 127.

72 K Grayson, 'Human Security as Power/Knowledge: The Biopolitics of a Definitional Debate' (2008) 21(3) Cambridge Review of International Affairs 383, 389 citing UNDP 1995.

from 'chronic' threats such as 'hunger, disease and repression'; and, secondly, 'protection from sudden and hurtful disruptions in the patterns of daily life'.[73]

One way of testing the meaning and scope of human security in the region is to examine the circumstances in which ASEAN has chosen to relax its 'principle of non-interference' in recent years. For example, as Takeshi Terada points out,[74] there have been various crises since the late 1990s, including the 1997 Asian financial crisis, the 1999 East Timor crisis, the 2005 Indian Ocean Tsunami Crisis and the 2008 Cyclone Nargis Crisis, which have spurred ASEAN Member States into implementing collective action on human security issues. However, he explains that this has been predominantly with regard to 'freedom from want'-type security such as poverty, disease and natural disasters, rather than 'freedom from fear', human security which focuses on violent conflicts.[75]

Is 'human security' tied to the State-centred 'traditional' concept of security, in which the State is seen as the principal referent of security concerns, or has it developed under ASEAN into a 'people centred' discourse, which reflects the concept of human rights?[76] A qualification to a dichotomized view of human security is suggested by Lee Jones, who argues that the concept of non-traditional security threats is better addressed by reference to State-society relations (the 'social conflict' approach) rather than as threats to the State as such.[77] Under this approach, as explained by Jones, securitization of some social conflicts arises from power struggles; thus some issues are seen as security threats, whilst others are not.[78] For example, he argues that in the context of ASEAN's relationship with Myanmar (which is a major source of refugees in the region), State (and ASEAN) policy is highly influenced by the business interests of the ruling oligarchy in countries such as Thailand and Malaysia. Thus, refugees in Thailand and Malaysia are not necessarily seen as a security issue but as a source of cheap, exploitable

73 UNDP, *Human Development Report: New Dimensions of Human Security*, 1994, 23.

74 T Terada, *ASEAN and Human Security: Crisis-Driven Explanation* (Waseda University, Japan, February 2011), available at http://www.waseda-giari.jp/sysimg/imgs/wp2010_e5.pdf.

75 An aspect of this argument is that there is an emerging 'responsibility to protect' (R2P) or willingness to interfere in the region. See also Caballero-Anthony, 'The Responsibility to Protect in Southeast Asia'. A J Bellamy and C Drummond, 'The responsibility to protect in Southeast Asia: between non-interference and sovereignty as responsibility' (2011) 24(2) The Pacific Review 179–200.

76 Edwards and Ferstman, 'Humanising Non-Citizens'. It has been suggested that a 'realist' discourse rejects the idea of human rights; J Flynn, 'Habermas on Human Rights: Law, Morality, and Intercultural Discourse' (2003) 29(3) Social and Political Theory 455.

77 L Jones, 'Beyond securitization: explaining the scope of security policy in Southeast Asia' (2011) 11(3) International Relations of the Asia-Pacific 403–32.

78 See also M McDonald, 'Securitization and the Construction of Security' (2008) 14(4) European Journal of International Relations 563–87. These analyses stem from a Foucauldian analysis.

labour. There is, in other words, a degree of selectivity about how refugees are perceived, depending on the power relationships involved.

These developments and debate show that there is recent ASEAN recognition that some regional trans-boundary issues involving displaced persons, and labour migration, cannot merely be viewed as internal domestic affairs, and that regional cooperation may be necessary. There is also a suggestion that ASEAN may be moving towards an acceptance that some issues, even if they are not trans-boundary, may be so grave as to require attention from the region. However, as yet, this has not translated into cooperative action on refugees, which is sorely needed in the region, as a response to human security issues arising from both 'want' and 'fear'.[79] However, when we turn to the ASEAN human rights framework, we can see some incorporation of refugee rights.

The ASEAN Human Declaration and Refugee Rights

ASEAN States have been hesitant in adopting a regional human rights mechanism, because of potential interference with State interests and preferences.[80] Different States in the region have varying attitudes to human rights protection.[81] However, the 2007 Charter created the ASEAN Intergovernmental Commission on Human Rights (AICHR) which seems quite a remarkable achievement. Recently after much discussion behind closed doors, and speculative debate and outrage from civil society about its exclusion from the consultations, ASEAN members reached agreement and adopted the ASEAN Human Rights Declaration (AHRD).[82] Importantly in the preamble it reiterates the commitment of:

> ASEAN and its Member States … to the Charter of the United Nations, the Universal Declaration of Human Rights, the Vienna Declaration and Programme of Action, and other international human rights instruments, to which ASEAN Member States are parties as well as to relevant ASEAN declarations and instruments pertaining to human rights.

Article 6 of the AHDR is a key provision. It provides:

> The enjoyment of human rights and fundamental freedoms must be balanced with the performance of corresponding duties as every person has responsibilities to all other individuals, the community and the society where one lives. It is

79 R Tirtosudarmo, 'Critical Issues on Forced Migration Studies and the Refugee Crisis in Southeast Asia' (2008) 3(1) Journal Kependudukan Indonesia 1–20.

80 Tan, 'The ASEAN Charter as "Legs To Go Places"' 141.

81 Ibid., 137.

82 Source: http://jurist.org/paperchase/2012/11/asean-adopts-human-rights-declaration .php (accessed 25 February 2013).

> ultimately the primary responsibility of all ASEAN Member States to promote and protect all human rights and fundamental freedoms.

This provision has been criticized as misrepresenting the nature of individual, universal human rights, as possibly representing a return to Asian 'exceptionalism' and as a return to the principle of non-interference. The concept of individual human rights is problematic in the case of socialist countries such as Lao PDR and Vietnam. Singapore also maintains that the collective good outweighs individual freedoms on many issues. This provision appears to be an acknowledgment of these divergent approaches. Catherine Renshaw[83] has concluded in relation to Article 6, that on the best interpretation, it simply represents a restatement of the idea of rights and corresponding individual duties. Renshaw suggests that the final sentence is carefully crafted so as to assuage any concern that it might be interpreted negatively. Another comment is that it is consistent with respecting the sovereignty and responsibility of individual ASEAN states. It is also consistent with the thrust of the ASEAN Charter as summarized above, to promote a common ASEAN identity, and respect within that Community for rights and freedoms.

This observation is confirmed by Article 39 of the ADHR which is headed 'Cooperation in the Promotion and Protection of Human Rights'. It states:

> ASEAN Member States share a common interest in and commitment to the promotion and protection of human rights and fundamental freedoms which shall be achieved through, inter alia, cooperation with one another as well as with relevant national, regional and international institutions/organisations, in accordance with the ASEAN Charter.

Further, the ADHR needs to be read as a whole, and in the context of the development of an ASEAN Community and the concept of 'human security' outlined above. Importantly, Article 35 promotes the right to development which is an essential feature of current ASEAN initiatives. This article provides:

> The right to development is an inalienable human right by virtue of which every human person and the peoples of ASEAN are entitled to participate in, contribute to, enjoy and benefit equitably and sustainably from economic, social, cultural and political development. The right to development should be fulfilled so as to meet equitably the developmental and environmental needs of present and future generations. While development facilitates and is necessary for the enjoyment of all human rights, the lack of development may not be invoked to justify the violations of internationally recognised human rights.

---

83 CS Renshaw, 'The ASEAN Human Rights Declaration' (25 January 2013), available at http://cigj.wordpress.com/2013/01/25/the-asean-human-rights-declaration-cause-for-celebration/ (accessed 25 February 2013).

The last sentence of that article is very important in guiding the interpretation of Article 6 on the scope of individual ASEAN member state obligations. Notably, it imposes a much stronger obligation on developing states than the International Covenant on Economic, Social and Cultural Rights (ICESCR),[84] Article 2(3).

Although in commentary preceding the ADHR, Vitit Muntarbhorn urged that the rights of refugees be addressed,[85] they are referred to only in limited respect, and are included by implication. As Muntarbhorn said, 'some rights such as the right to life and freedom from torture, are absolute and cannot be constrained'. Therefore it is important to note that Article 14 of the ADHR states without qualification that 'No person shall be subject to torture or to cruel, inhuman or degrading treatment or punishment'.

Further the ADHR provides guarantees of the very freedoms which are at the base of refugee status in the region. Article 2 says:

> Every person is entitled to the rights and freedoms set forth herein, without distinction of any kind, such as race, gender, age, language, religion, political or other opinion, national or social origin, economic status, birth, disability or other status.

Moreover, Article 22 provides an unqualified right 'to freedom of thought, conscience and religion'. It provides that 'All forms of intolerance, discrimination and incitement of hatred based on religion and beliefs shall be eliminated'. However, when Article 4 refers to the rights of 'vulnerable and marginalised groups', it does not specifically include refugees and displaced persons, unlike the 1993 *Bangkok Declaration*. As Muntarbhorn had pointed out:

> [H]uman rights are based on non-discrimination; they are not only the rights of our nationals but of all persons on our territory, including stateless persons, refugees, displaced persons, migrant workers, minorities and indigenous peoples, bearing in mind gender sensibility.

There is thus some inconsistency in the ADHR in terms of recognition of refugees and asylum seekers as persons with human rights. This is more so as Articles 15 and 16 refer respectively to freedom of movement and the right to seek asylum as follows:

---

84 International Covenant on Economic, Social and Cultural Rights, New York, 16 December 1966, in force 3 January 1976, UN Doc A/ 6316 (1966), 99 UNTS 3 (ICESR).

85 'Towards an Asean declaration of human rights' 20 January 2012, available at http://www.bangkokpost.com/opinion/opinion/275923/towards-an-asean-declaration-of-human-rights (accessed 25 February 2013).

> 15. Every person has the right to freedom of movement and residence within the borders of each State. Every person has the right to leave any country including his or her own, and to return to his or her country.
>
> 16. Every person has the right to seek and receive asylum in another State *in accordance with the laws of such State* and applicable international agreements. (Emphasis added.)

Whilst this does not amount to full recognition of the rights of refugees, it can be claimed as a cautious beginning.

The right to freedom of movement in Article 15, which is an important aspect of the right to seek asylum, is in some respects broader than the right contained in the International Covenant on Civil and Political Rights (ICCPR)[86] (Article 12). The ICCPR restricts the right to 'everyone *lawfully* within the territory of a State', whereas the ADHR refers to 'every person … within the borders of each State'. In another respect Article 15 is at first sight broader as it does not contain the explicit public order exception (ICCPR, Article 12(3)). However Article 8 of the AHRD states:

> The human rights and fundamental freedoms of every person shall be exercised with due regard to the human rights and fundamental freedoms of others. The exercise of human rights and fundamental freedoms shall be subject only to such limitations as are determined by law solely for the purpose of securing due recognition for the human rights and fundamental freedoms of others, and to meet the just requirements of national security, public order, public health, public safety, public morality, as well as the general welfare of the peoples in a democratic society.

As Renshaw has pointed out, this provision applies to all rights in the ADHR. She suggests that it is an acknowledgement of the political nature of human rights within ASEAN (particularly through the reference to 'public morality'), of the security concerns outlined above.

Article 16 of the AHRD is particularly significant as it specifically recognizes the 'right to seek and receive asylum in another State in accordance with … applicable international agreements'. Such a right is missing from the Refugee Convention although it is contained in the Universal Declaration of Human Rights (UDHR)[87] (Article 14). It is also referred to in some regional instruments such as the 1969 Organization of African Unity Convention Governing the Specific

86 International Covenant on Civil and Political Rights, New York, 16 December 1966, in force 23 March 1976, UN Doc A/6316 (1966), 999 UNTS 171 ('ICCPR').

87 Universal Declaration of Human Rights, Paris, 10 December 1948, GA Res. 217 A (III), UN Doc A/810 ('UDHR').

Aspects of Refugee Problems in Africa (OAU Convention).[88] However, under the ADHR, the right to asylum is qualified by the emphasized words, namely that the right exists 'in accordance with the laws of such State'. This latter qualification is consistent with Article 7 of the ADHR which provides:

> All human rights are universal, indivisible, interdependent and interrelated. All human rights and fundamental freedoms in this Declaration must be treated in a fair and equal manner, on the same footing and with the same emphasis. At the same time, the realisation of human rights must be considered in the regional and national context bearing in mind different political, economic, legal, social, cultural, historical and religious backgrounds.

A number of other rights under the ADHR are similarly qualified (namely in accordance with the laws of the relevant State), including the right to nationality (Article 18), the right to marry (Article 19), the right to political participation (Article 25) and the right to join a trade union (Article 25(2)). These are rights which are particularly relevant to migrant workers in host countries, and these qualifications can be seen as consistent with the restrictive measures taken to prevent integration by 'foreigners' taken by states in the region.[89]

Thus it can be concluded that under the ADHR, recognition of the right of asylum seekers to freedom from persecution, or from *refoulement* which is the complement of this right, is incomplete, especially as there is no reference to the right not to be returned. Further, rights to integration are hedged with qualifications which could potentially preclude refugees from being granted a status in the host country. In comparison to the 2001 version of the AALCO Bangkok Principles (discussed below), the ADHR contains an incomplete statement of refugees rights. This suggests that refugees are not yet recognized within the ASEAN Community as rights-bearing individuals.

Asian African Legal Consultative Organisation (AALCO) and the Bangkok Principles[90]

In this final section I contrast another alternative forum through which refugee issues are promoted in Southeast Asia. This is the Asian African Legal Consultative Organization (AALCO), which in 1966 formulated an instrument for the protection

88 Entered into force on 20 June 1974.

89 See S Kneebone, 'Transnational labour migrants: whose responsibility?' in K Rubenstein (ed.), *Allegiance and Identity in a Globalised World* (Cambridge University Press, 2013 – in press).

90 This information was taken from the following sources: http://www.aalco.int/scripts/view-posting.asp?recordid=1 (accessed 25 February 2013).

of refugee rights, known as the Bangkok Principles.[91] There were reaffirmed in 2001 ('Final Text of the AALCO's 1966 Bangkok Principles on the Status and Treatment of Refugees' as Adopted on 24 June 2001 at the AALCO's 40th Session, New Delhi).[92] They constitute a progressive and respected set of principles on refugee protection. Importantly, the UNHCR is included in this process. Within the South\Southeast Asia region there is considerable pride in these lesser known principles, which are seen by UNHCR as recognition of its practice as 'a region with a good record of providing asylum to a large number of refugees'.[93]

AALCO was original known as the 'Asian Legal Consultative Committee' (ALCC). Its name changed in April 1958 to reflect the participation of countries from Africa. It was constituted on 15 November 1956 and is considered a tangible outcome of the Asian African or '1955 Bandung Conference' held in Indonesia, one of the formative meetings of the Non-Aligned Movement of less-developed States that sought to steer a neutral path during the Cold War between the United States and the Soviet Union.[94] The original members were Burma, Ceylon, India, Indonesia, Iraq, Japan and Syria. Subsequently, the United Arab Republic, formed by the merger of Syria and Egypt, became an original participating party. These historical facts are important as they suggest that AALCO reflected both a united response to colonialism, and an attempt to engage with pan-African nationalism.[95]

Another important feature of AALCO is that the process is one which operates as a South-South rather than North-South dialogue. Whilst it is difficult to judge its effectiveness without further research, its very existence and credibility suggests that principles of refugee protection have a regional normative basis, through the

91 Principles Concerning Treatment of Refugees as adopted by the Asian-African Legal Consultative Committee at its Eighth Session, Bangkok, August, 1966; reproduced in E Jahn, 'The Work of Asian-African Legal Consultative Committee on the Legal Status of Refugees' 1967 Max-Planck-Institut, available at http://www.zaoerv.de/27_1967/27_1967_1_2_b_122_138.pdf (accessed 25 February 2013).

92 Report of the 40th Session of the Asian-African Legal Consultative Organization, Fifth General Meeting, available at http://www.aalco.int/report40thsession/Fifth%20General%20Meeting%202001.pdf (accessed 25 February 2013); and Report of the 40th Session of the Asian-African Legal Consultative Organization, Seventh General Meeting, available at http://www.aalco.int/report40thsession/Seventh%20General%20Meeting%202001.pdf (accessed 25 February 2013).

93 UNHCR, Ex Co, 'Regional update – Asia and the Pacific' (63rd session, Geneva, 1–5 October 2012) para A. This is part of the statement cited at the beginning of this paper.

94 M Smith, 'The Bangkok Principles on the Status and Treatment of Refugees' (2011) 14 Fahuma Refugees Legal Aid Newsletter (December), available at http://frlan.tumblr.com/post/13676403836/the-bangkok-principles-on-the-status-and-treatment-of (accessed 25 February 2013).

95 Saul et al., 'Resistance to regional human rights cooperation in the Asia-Pacific' 116.

Bangkok Principles. Importantly, the UNHCR is a common factor in both the OAU and AALCO processes.

According to Article 3 of the Asian Legal Consultative Committee Statutes (now replaced by revised statutes), the main purposes of ALCC were:

> (a) to examine questions that are under consideration by the International Law Commission and to arrange for the views of the Committee to be placed before the said Commission;
>
> (b) to consider legal problems that may be referred to the Committee by any of the participating countries and to make such recommendations to Governments as may be thought fit;
>
> (c) to exchange views and information on legal matters of common concern.
>
> The original Committee was to function for an initial period of five years: Article 3. This period was extended on four occasions until 1981 when, at its Colombo Session, it was made permanent.

The Bangkok Principles were first formulated in 1966 after the 6th Annual Session, held in Cairo in 1964. The subject 'The Rights of Refugees' was referred to the Committee by the Government of the United Arab Republic under Article 3(b) of the Statutes. The UNHCR was invited to state its views on the subject of refugees and AALCO directed the Secretariat to collect further material, on, inter alia, the minimum standard of treatment of asylum-seekers. The Bangkok Principles were presented at the 8th Annual Session, in Bangkok 1966, when again 'The Rights of Refugees' was a priority item. At that meeting, the Legal Adviser of the UNHCR and the representative of the League of Arab States played a key role. AALCO concluded that the Bangkok Principles constituted an advisory document, and it was up to each government to decide how it should give effect to the recommendations therein.

It is unclear from the records whether the Bangkok Principles were inspired by the 1969 Organization of African Unity Convention Governing the Specific Aspects of Refugee Problems in Africa (OAU Convention)[96] and the process leading up to it, which was contemporaneous, or whether by converse AALCO influenced the OAU. The OAU Convention was a specific response to the massive displacements in Africa in this period and arguably was intended to fill the gaps in the Refugees Convention definition, with its temporal and geographical limits.[97] The importance of the OAU Convention is its attempt to tailor protection to the particular issues raised in the region, and to provide for regional solutions.

96 Entered into force on 20 June 1974.

97 S Kneebone and F Rawlings-Sanaei, eds, *New Regionalism and Asylum Seekers: Challenges Ahead* (Berghahn Books, 2007) 5–8.

According to Fontaine,[98] the Bangkok Principles foreshadowed the principal innovation of the OAU Convention (namely, the expanded definition of refugee). The 1966 draft contained an expanded version of the 1951 Convention definition, namely persons obliged to leave their State though 'illegal acts' or invasions. But according to Marina Sharpe, the OAU Convention aimed to make the African response consistent with the European-inspired Refugee Convention, and did not reach the final stages of drafting until 1969.[99] It is probable however that when the AALCO was considering how to define a 'refugee' it was with the knowledge that the OAU Convention definition was likely to be broader than that in the Refugees Convention. The understanding in the Asian region is that these principles 'aimed to provide a common normative framework of refugee protection for the Afro-Asian region'.[100]

At the 39th Annual Session, Cairo 2000, the UNHCR Representative stressed the need for a regional response on the basis that ad hoc responses are no longer sufficient, noting that this was the reason for the original Bangkok Principles. A Resolution urged Member States to finalize the revision of the consolidated text of the Bangkok Principles and place it for final adoption at the next session. It seems then, that the adoption of the Bangkok Principles in 2001 was the culmination of a long process of revision that was prompted by the 30th anniversary of the Bangkok Principles in 1996. It was not precipitated by any other particular event, although it was contemporaneous with the beginning of the Bali Process.

An important feature of the original Bangkok Principles (1966) was an acknowledgement of the principle of *non-refoulement* and the principle of 'provisional' or temporary asylum.[101] Article III (1) referred to the 'sovereign right to grant or refuse asylum in its territory', and Article III (2) to the fact that the grant of such asylum is not to be regarded as an 'unfriendly act' but 'shall be respected by all other States'. The 1966 Principles removed any reference to a date for their application, thus anticipating the 1967 Protocol.[102] They also contained a right of return to country of nationality and a right to compensation.

Article I (2) of the 1969 OAU Convention states:

98 P-M Fontaine, 'The Governance of the Refugee Problem in Africa: A Research Agenda' (2006) 25(4) Refugee Survey Quarterly 67, 70.

99 M Sharpe, 'The Impact of Regional Law on the Regional, Sub-Regional and National Planes in Africa' in Helene Lambert, Maryellen Fullerton and Jane McAdam (eds), *The Global Reach of European Refugee Law* (Cambridge University Press, forthcoming 2013).

100 P Oberei, 'Regional Initiatives on Refugee Protection in South Asia' (1999) 11(1) International Journal of Refugee Law 193, 195.

101 Jahn, 'The Work of Asian-African Legal Consultative Committee on the Legal Status of Refugees' 123.

102 Protocol relating to the Status of Refugees, New York, 31 January 1967, in force 4 October 1967, 19 UST 6223, 6257 ('Refugee Protocol').

> The term 'refugee' shall also apply to every person, who owing to external aggression, occupation, foreign domination or events seriously disturbing public order in either part or the whole of his country of origin or nationality, is compelled to leave his place of habitual residence in order to seek refuge in another place outside his country of origin or nationality.

Article II of the OAU Convention which is headed 'Asylum' deals specifically with asylum, *non-refoulement* and durable solutions. Article II(1) states that:

> Member States of the OAU shall use their best endeavours consistent with their respective legislations to receive refugees and to secure the settlement of those refugees who, for well-founded reasons, are unable or unwilling to return to their country of origin or nationality.

Unlike the 1951 Refugees Convention,[103] the right of asylum is specifically mentioned in the OAU Convention, although it is qualified by the requirement that the right be 'consistent with their [domestic] legislations'. To take the political 'sting' out of asylum, Article II(2) states that the grant of asylum is 'a peaceful and humanitarian act'. The *non-refoulement* obligation is contained in Article II(3) and is applicable to persons whose 'life, physical integrity or liberty' would be threatened for the reasons set out in both refugee definitions.

The current (2001) version of the Bangkok Principles contains the expanded definition of the OAU Convention (Article I (2)) although Singapore has placed a reservation on that provision. It also mirrors the OAU Convention's provision that the grant of asylum is a 'humanitarian, peaceful and non-political act' (Article II (3)). Article III contains a *non-refoulement* provision which applies to persons 'seeking asylum'. Importantly Thailand has sought to change the words to apply the protection 'after asylum is granted'. Article X is a provision about the need for international burden-sharing for a global problem to which Singapore has objected, maintaining that 'the responsibility of refugees rests ultimately on the countries which caused the refugees to flee and/or remain abroad'.

As Pia Oberei says: 'In a region where refugee flows are dealt with primarily as issues of state security', initiatives within which 'to construct refugee policy must be welcomed'.[104] Oberei explains that the Bangkok Principles have been used by countries in the region, for example to justify: 'in 1981 its policy towards refugees from Afghanistan, the Government of Pakistan referred to the refugee definition contained within the Bangkok Principles'.[105] Some individual states within the region, such as Indonesia, do refer to the Bangkok Principles as evidence of their respect for refugee rights. The questions which this discussion leaves unexplained

---

103 Convention relating to the Status of Refugees, Geneva, 28 July 1951, in force 22 April 1954, 1989 UNTS 137 ('Refugee Convention').

104 Oberei, 'Regional Initiatives on Refugee Protection in South Asia' 197.

105 Ibid. 195.

are, first, why some individual states within the region respect refugee rights under the AALCO principles, in contradistinction to the collective ASEAN approach outlined in this chapter; and, secondly, whether the role of the UNHCR is pivotal in advancing the Bangkok Principles. Clearly, some States such as Singapore, which has a consistently restrictive stance on refugees, have stronger 'voices' within ASEAN.

Conclusion

The first theme in this discussion of the conceptualization of refugee protection under the ASEAN process was their characterization as 'irregular migrants' and, within the ASEAN Community, as a 'security' concern. This characterization and approach is coincidentally consistent with the focus of the regional Bali Process.

Although there is some evidence that the security focus of the ASEAN Community is shifting to include 'human security' issues, arising from gaps in development which result inter alia from human rights issues, the placing of refugee issues in the ASEAN Political-Security Community (APSC) and the characterization of the refugee 'problem' as the outcome of conflict precludes their inclusion in this dialogue. Indeed consistent with the 'social conflict' approach suggested by Lee Jones, there appears to be a degree of conscious tolerance of the exploitation of refugees as 'migrant workers' in host countries by some ASEAN states. That is, within ASEAN refugees are doubly jeopardized as exploitable cheap labour on one hand, and on the other as a threat to State security.

The second theme in this discussion was the recognition of human rights in the ASEAN process. It was shown that under the recent ASEAN Human Rights Declaration (AHRD), there is a slight but incomplete focus on recognizing the rights of refugees. For example, whilst the right to seek asylum is respected, there is no corresponding right not to be *refouled*; freedom of movement is not equated to the grant of asylum; whilst breaches of human rights which lead to refugee status are recognized, these breaches are not linked to 'refugeehood'. A comparison of the AHRD with the AALCO's Bangkok Principles, which respects fully the rights of refugees, demonstrates that the AHRD paints a conflicting image of refugees. Indeed what the practical experience of refugees within the region demonstrates is that much needs to be done in order to protect their rights, a prospect that is not helped by ASEAN's unclear stance on the status of refugees in its community.

The practice of refugee protection in some individual states within the region (for example, Indonesia and India – which has not been the subject of this discussion) highlights the difference between the ASEAN collective characterization of refugees and that of individual Southeast Asian States. The ASEAN approach suggests that the rights of refugees are being sacrificed at the altar of the ASEAN Community.

References

Alexander A, 'Without refuge: Chin refugees in India and Malaysia' (2008) 30 Forced Migration Review 36–7.

ASEAN, 'The ASEAN Declaration ("Bangkok Declaration")' (1976), Bangkok, Thailand, 8 August 1967 available at http://www.asean.org/news/item/the-asean-declaration-bangkok-declaration [accessed 25 February 2013].

ASEAN, 'ASEAN Declaration on Transnational Crime' (1997) Manila, Philippines, 20 December 1997 available at: http://www.asean.org/communities/asean-political-security-community/item/asean-declaration-on-transnational-crime-manila-20-december-1997 [accessed 25 February 2013].

ASEAN, 'ASEAN Plan of Action to Combat Transnational Crime' (1999), endorsed by the 2nd ASEAN Ministerial Meeting on Transnational Crime ('AMMTC'), Yangon, Myanmar, 23 June 1999 available at http://www.asean.org/communities/asean-political-security-community/item/joint-communique-of-the-second-asean-ministerial-meeting-on-transnational-crime-ammtc-yangon-23-june-1999 [accessed 25 February 2013].

ASEAN, 'ASEAN Declaration Against Trafficking In Persons Particularly Women and Children ("ASEAN Trafficking Declaration")' (2004) Vientiane, Lao PDR, 29 November 2004 available at http://www.asean.org/communities/asean-political-security-community/item/asean-declaration-against-trafficking-in-persons-particularly-women-and-children-3 [accessed 25 February 2013].

ASEAN Intergovernmental Commission on Human Rights, 'The Adoption of the ASEAN Human Rights Declaration (AHRD) at the 21st ASEAN Summit and the Special Meeting of the ASEAN Intergovernmental Commission on Human Rights (AICHR)' (2012) Phnom Penh, 17–18 November 2012 available at http://aichr.org/press-release/the-adoption-of-the-asean-human-rights-declaration-ahrd-at-the-21st-asean-summit-and-the-special-meeting-of-the-asean-intergovernmental-commission-on-human-rights-aichr/ [accessed 25 February 2013].

ASEAN Secretariat, 'Resolution on the ASEAN Plan of Action for Children' (2003) Manila, the Philippines, 2 December 2003, available at http://www.mwa.gov.kh/files/PDF/ASEAN/4.3_Resolution%20on%20ASEAN%20PoA%20for%20Children-1993.pdf [accessed 25 February 2013].

Asian-African Legal Consultative Organization, Fifth General Meeting (2001), 23 June 2001 available at http://www.aalco.int/report40thsession/Fifth%20General%20Meeting%202001.pdf [accessed 25 February 2013].

Asian-African Legal Consultative Organization, 'Seventh General Meeting' (2001) available at: http://www.aalco.int/report40thsession/Seventh%20General%20Meeting%202001.pdf [accessed 25 February 2013].

Bangkok Declaration on Irregular Migration, International Symposium on Migration (1999) Bangkok, Thailand, 21–23 April 1999, available at Document2http://www.iom.int/jahia/webdav/site/myjahiasite/shared/shared/

mainsite/policy_and_research/rcp/APC/BANGKOK_DECLARATION.pdf [accessed 12 June 2013].

Bellamy AJ and Drummond C, 'The responsibility to protect in Southeast Asia: between non-interference and sovereignty as responsibility' (2001) 24(2) The Pacific Review 179–200.

Caballero-Anthony M, 'Bridging Development Gaps in Southeast Asia: Towards an ASEAN Community' (2006) 11 UNISCI Discussion Papers 7–48.

Caballero-Anthony M, 'Challenging Change: Nontraditional Security, Democracy and Regionalism' in DK Ememerson (ed.), *Hard Choices: Security, Democracy, and Regionalism in Southeast Asia* (Institute of Southeast Asian Studies, 2008a) 191–218.

Caballero-Anthony M, 'Reflections on managing migration in South East Asia: mitigating the unintended consequences of securitisation' in MG Curley and SI Wong (eds), *Security and Migration in Asia: The Dynamics of Securitisation* (Routledge, 2008b) 165–76.

Caballero-Anthony M, 'The Responsibility to Protect in Southeast Asia: opening up spaces for advancing human security' (2012) 25(1) The Pacific Review 113–34.

Chairman's Statement, ASEAN Charter for ASEAN Peoples (2009) 14th ASEAN Summit, Cha-am, Thailand. 28 February–1 March 2009, available at http://www.asean.org/asean/asean-summit/item/chairman-s-statement-of-the-14th-asean-summit-asean-charter-for-asean-peoples [accessed 25 February 2013].

Chalamwong Y, Meepien J and Hongprayoon K, 'Management of Cross-border Migration: Thailand as a Case of Net Migration' (2012) 40(4) Asian Journal of Social Science 447–63.

Co-Chair's Statement, Bali Ministerial Conference on People Smuggling, Trafficking in Persons and Related Transnational Crime (2002) Bali, Indonesia 26–28 February 2002 available at http://www.baliprocess.net/files/ConferenceDocumentation/BRMC1.pdf [accessed 12 June 2013].

Co-Chair's Statement, Third Bali Regional Ministerial Conference on People Smuggling, Trafficking in Persons and Related Transnational Crime (2009) Bali, Indonesia 14-15 April 2009 available at http://www.baliprocess.net/files/Co%20chairs%20statement%20BRMC%20III_FINAL.doc [accessed 20 June 2013].

Co-Chair's Statement, Bali Process Senior Officials Meeting (2011) Bali, Indonesia, 10 March 2011 available at: http://www.baliprocess.net/ministerial-conferences-and-senior-officials-meetings [accessed 20 June 2013].

Convention relating to the Status of Refugees, 1951. Geneva, 28 July 1951, in force 22 April 1954, 1989 UNTS 137.

Edwards A and Ferstman C, 'Humanising Non-Citizens: the Convergence of Human Rights and Human Security' in A Edwards and C Ferstman (eds), *Human Security and Non-Citizens: Law Policy and International Affairs* (Cambridge University Press, 2010) 3–46.

Final Declaration of the Regional Meeting for Asia of the World Conference on Human Rights ('1993 Bangkok Declaration'), (1993) World Conference on Human Rights Bangkok, 29 March–2 April 1993, UN Doc A/CONF.157/PC/59 (7 April 1993) available at http://www.unhchr.ch/Huridocda/Huridoca.nsf/TestFrame/9d23b88f115fb827802569030037ed44?Opendocument [accessed 25 February 2013].

Flynn J, 'Habermas on Human Rights: Law, Morality, and Intercultural Discourse' (2003) 29(3), Social Theory and Practices 431–57.

Fontaine PM, 'The Governance of the Refugee Problem in Africa: A Research Agenda' (2006) 25(4) Refugee Survey Quarterly 67–84.

Goodwin-Gill GS, 'The Politics of Refugee Protection' (2008) 27(1) Refugee Survey Quarterly 8–23.

Grayson K, 'Human Security as Power/Knowledge: The Biopolitics of a Definitional Debate' (2008) 21(3) Cambridge Review of International Affairs 383–401.

Hanoi Plan of Action, 1997 available at http://www.asean.org/asean/asean-summit/item/hanoi-plan-of-action [accessed 25 February 2013].

International Covenant on Civil and Political Rights, 1966. New York, 16 December 1966, in force 23 March 1976, UN Doc. A/6316 (1966), 999 UNTS 171.

International Covenant on Economic, Social and Cultural Rights, 1966. New York, 16 December 1966, in force 3 January 1976, UN Doc. A/ 6316 (1966), 99 UNTS 3.

Kneebone S, 'ASEAN Norms and Setting The Agenda For The Rights of Migrant Workers' in H Nasu and B Saul (eds), *Human Rights in the Asia Pacific Region* (Routledge, 2011) 301–38.

Kneebone S and Debeljak J, *Transnational Crime and Human Rights: Responses to Human Trafficking in the Greater Mekong Subregion* (Routledge, 2012).

Kneebone S and Rawlings-Sanaei F, *New Regionalism and Asylum Seekers: Challenges Ahead* (Berghahn Books, 2007).

Lee JL, 'Beyond securitization: explaining the scope of security policy in Southeast Asia' (2011) 11(3), International Relations of the Asia-Pacific 403–32.

Linton S, 'ASEAN States, Their Reservations to Human Rights Treaties and the Proposed ASEAN Commission on Women and Children' (2008) 30(2) Human Rights Quarterly 436–93.

McDonald M, 'Securitization and the Construction of Security' (2008) 14(4), European Journal of International Relations 563–87.

Muntarbhorn V, Refugee Law and Practice in the Asia and Pacific Region: Thailand as a Case Study (2005), in *Refugee Law Reader: Cases, Documents and Materials* [Online]. Hungarian Helsinki Committee, available at http://www.en.refugeelawreader.org/index.php?option=com_docman&task=doc_view&=&gid=564&ml=5&mlt=system&tmpl=component [accessed 20 June 2013].

Nah A, 'Struggling with (Il)Legality: The Indeterminate Functioning of Malaysia's Borders for Asylum Seekers, Refugees, and Stateless Persons' in PK. Rajaram and C Grundy-Warr (eds), *Borderscapes: Hidden Geographies and Politics at Territory's Edge* (University of Minnesota Press, 2007) 35–64.

Oberei P, 'Regional Initiatives on Refugee Protection in South Asia' (1999) 11(1) International Journal of Refugee Law 193–201.

Plaintiffs M70/2011 and M106 of 2011 v Minister for Immigration and Citizenship ('*the Malaysia-Swap Arrangement case*' – *Plaintiffs M70*) [2011] HCA 32.

Protocol relating to the Status of Refugees. 1967. New York, 31 January 1967, in force 4 October 1967, 19 UST 6223

Renshaw CS, The ASEAN Human Rights Declaration, in *Regarding Rights: Academic and activist perspectives on human rights* (2013) available at http://cigj.wordpress.com/2013/01/25/the-asean-human-rights-declaration-cause-for-celebration/ [accessed 25 February 2013].

Saul B, Mowbray J and Baghoomians I, 'Resistance to regional human rights cooperation in the Asia-Pacific: demythologizing regional exceptionalism by learning from the Americas, Europe and Africa' in H Nasu and B Saul (eds), *Human Rights in the Asia Pacific Region*, (Routledge, 2011) 107–26.

Sharpe M, 'The Impact of Regional Law on the Regional, Sub-Regional and National Planes in Africa' in H Lambert, M Fullerton and J McAdam (eds), *The Global Reach of European Refugee Law* (Cambridge University Press, 2013 forthcoming).

Skeldon R, 'Trafficking: A Perspective from Asia' (2000) 38(3) International Migration 7–30.

Smith M, The Bangkok Principles on the Status and Treatment of Refugees, *Fahuma Refugees Legal Aid Newsletter* (2011) 14, 3 December 2011 available at http://frlan.tumblr.com/post/13676403836/the-bangkok-principles-on-the-status-and-treatment-of [accessed 25 February 2013].

Tan EKB, 'The ASEAN Charter as "Legs To Go Places": Ideational Norms and Pragmatic Legalism in Community Building in South East Asia' (2008) *Singapore Year Book of International Law* [Online] 12, 171–98, available at http://law.nus.edu.sg/sybil/downloads/articles/SYBIL-2008/SYBIL-2008-171.pdf [accessed 20 June 2013].

Tan HL, *The ASEAN Intergovernmental Commission on Human Rights: Institutionalising Human Rights in Southeast Asia* (Cambridge University Press, 2011).

Terada T, *ASEAN and Human Security: Crisis-Driven Explanation* (2011) [Online] Waseda University, Japan, February 2011, available at http://www.waseda-giari.jp/sysimg/imgs/wp2010_e5.pdf [accessed 20 June 2013].

The Bangkok Post, Towards an Asean declaration of human rights (2012) *The Bangkok Post*, 20 January 2012, available at http://www.bangkokpost.com/opinion/opinion/275923/towards-an-asean-declaration-of-human-rights [accessed 25 February 2013].

Tirtosudarmo R, Critical Issues on Forced Migration Studies and the Refugee Crisis in Southeast Asia (2008) 3(1) Journal Kependudukan Indonesia 1–20.

UNDP, *Human Development Report: New Dimensions of Human Security* (Oxford University Press, 1994) available at: http://hdr.undp.org/en/reports/global/hdr1994/ [accessed 20 June 2013].

UNHCR, *Asia and the Pacific – 2012 Regional Operations Profile* (2012) [Online: United Nations High Commissioner for Refugees], available at http://www.unhcr.org/pages/4a02d8ec6.html [accessed 27 November 2012].

UNHCR, *Regional update – Asia and the Pacific* (2012) 63rd session, Geneva, 1–5 October 2012.

Universal Declaration of Human Rights, 1948. Paris, 10 December 1948, GA Res. 217 A (III), UN Doc. A/810.

Vientiane Action Programme (VAP) 2004–10, Laos, 29 November 2004, available at http://cil.nus.edu.sg/rp/pdf/2004%20Vientiane%20Action%20Programme%202004-2010-pdf.pdf [accessed 25 February 2013].

Yulisman L, Talks on ASEAN+6 trade bloc to kick off in May (2013) [Online, 7 February] available at http://www.thejakartapost.com/news/2013/01/31/talks-asean6-trade-bloc-kick-may.html [accessed 7 February 2013].

Chapter 14
The 1989 Comprehensive Plan of Action (CPA) and Refugee Policy in Southeast Asia: Twenty Years Forward What Has Changed?

Sara E. Davies

Introduction

In 2012, the only Southeast Asian countries that have ratified the 1951 Convention relating to the Status of Refugees and the 1967 Protocol Relating to the Status of Refugees (hereafter referred to as the 1951 Convention and the 1967 Protocol) are the Philippines (signed 1954), Cambodia (signed 1995) and Timor Leste (signed 2001). Countries such as Indonesia, Malaysia and Thailand have annual asylum-seeking populations from Myanmar, South Asia and Middle East, that are estimated to be at 15,000–20,000 per country.[1] The lack of a permanent and formal asylum process in these countries means that asylum-seeking populations in the region are reliant on the local offices of the United Nations High Commission for Refugees based in the region to process their claims. These offices rely upon the goodwill of these governments to have a presence near detention camps and in capital cities to process claims of those who manage to reach the UNHCR representative office. The only burden-sharing mechanism within the region primarily exists under the Bali Process on People Smuggling, Trafficking in Persons and Related Transnational Crime (the Bali Process), introduced in 2002. The Bali Process refers to an informal cooperative agreement amongst the States from the Asia-Pacific region, with Australia and Indonesia as the co-chairs, which discusses its namesake: primarily anti-people smuggling activities and migration protocols. There is no provision within this process to discuss the development of national asylum-seeking legislation, processes for domestic processing of asylum claims or burden-sharing in contrast to other regions such as Africa and South America (that is, the 2009 African Union Convention for the Protection and Assistance of the Internally Displaced, 1969 African Union Convention Governing the Specific

1 UNHCR. World Refuge Day: UNHCR report finds 80 per cent of the world's refugees in developing countries (20 June 2011), available at http://www.unhcr.org/4dfb66ef9.html.

Aspects of Refugee Problems in Africa and 1984 Cartagena Declaration on Refugees [Americas]).[2]

The UNHCR 2009 Global Trends revealed that more than half of the world's refugees (5.5 million) have been living in what is called a 'protracted situation' – they have lived for five years or more in refugee camps in host countries that cannot or will not provide permanent residency – nor can they return home for fear of being persecuted.[3] The majority of these protracted situations are in developing countries (over 80 per cent), and there are now cases where second generation refugees are living in the camps. The Southeast Asian region is the third largest host to such populations that exist under these conditions – primarily individuals from Afghanistan, Iran, Myanmar, North Korea and Sri Lanka.[4] Some of these individuals have been living 'illegally' in countries due to a lack of opportunity to seek refugee status from UNHCR: they may have failed to meet the UNHCR definition of a refugee but be considered requiring complementary protection due to possible torture or mistreatment upon return to their country of origin, and many are in transit hoping to secure passage to Australia to have their refugee claim processed (which has become far from a certainty in recent years, heightening the burden in the region).

As a Bangkok based civil society organization notes, there are 'hundreds of thousands of refugees, asylum seekers, and other forcibly displaced people in Southeast Asia falling through the cracks of national legal mechanisms inadequate to ensure their rights, it is time for ASEAN to include refugee rights protection in their formal agenda'.[5] The Association of Southeast Asian Nations (ASEAN) is the regional organization comprising nine States from the region, first created in 1967 based on the mutual recognition of Member States' sovereignty right to non-intervention and non-interference in domestic affairs. Within this membership, only Cambodia and the Philippines are signatories to the 1951 Convention and the 1967 Protocol. ASEAN's recognition of the responsibility of its Member States to respect international refugee law has been consistently lacking. Even with the adoption of the ASEAN Charter, which entered into force in 2008 and includes a Human Rights Body to promote and protect 'human rights and fundamental

---

2 See People's Empowerment Foundation, *Refugee Protection in ASEAN: National failures, regional responsibilities* (Bangkok: PEF, 2010), 19, available at http://www.peoplesempowerment.org/news/pef-report-refugee-protection-in-asean-national-failures-regional-responsibilities.

3 UNHCR, *2009 Global Trends: Refugees, Asylum-seekers, Returnees, Internally Displaced and Stateless Persons. Division of Programme Support and Management* (2010), 1, available at http://www.unhcr.org/4c11f0be9.html.

4 UNHCR, *2012 Regional Operations Profile – South East Asia* (2012), available at http://www.unhcr.org/pages/4b17be9b6.html.

5 See *Refugee Protection in ASEAN: National failures, regional responsibilities* above n 3.

freedoms', there is no mention of a regional strategy concerning the shared responsibility of asylum seekers and protracted refugee situations in the region.[6]

The high number of protracted refugee situations is rising, as is the figure of people being forcibly displaced from their homes – some 25 million people (10.5 million refugees and 15 million internally displaced).[7] This number has not been as high since the mid-1990s, which experienced a high number of territorial conflicts following the end of the Cold War. In addition to the protracted refugee situation and rising number of displaced persons, there are an increasing number of people refusing to return to their home countries. Since the end of the Cold War, voluntary repatriation – refugees agreeing to return home – has become the dominant practice for handling refugee populations. People are held in refugee camps or given temporary protection visas and then returned home once the war has ended or the regime commits to not persecuting the individuals in question. With this solution diminishing, there will be greater pressure on refugee camps and on States to take refugees as permanent residents. Southeast Asia has proven to be a popular transit and host region for people fleeing within Asia and the Middle East.[8]

There has been much debate about the best way to resolve the (rising) global imbalance in the refugee intake and resettlement numbers. The problem of how to develop an international solution that addresses this imbalance has led to lengthy debates in the literature on differing State definitions of persecution, differing humanitarian responses to protracted refugee situations, and how to reinvigorate Western States' responsibility to adopt their share of the 'refugee burden'.[9]

An early practical example of the course of this debate occurred in the late 1980s as the Cold War was coming to an end. The Comprehensive Plan of Action (CPA) was created by the ASEAN States, Hong Kong, Western States and the Office of the United Nations High Commissioner for Refugees (UNHCR) in a collaborative effort to solve the protracted Vietnamese and Laotian refugee problem in the late 1980s.[10] The CPA became the subject of both criticism and

---

6 ASEAN, *The ASEAN Charter* (2008).

7 See *2009 Global Trends: Refugees, Asylum-seekers, Returnees, Internally Displaced and Stateless Persons. Division of Programme Support and Management* above n 3 and *World Refuge Day: UNHCR report finds 80 percent of world's refugees in developing countries* above n 1.

8 See *2009 Global Trends: Refugees, Asylum-seekers, Returnees, Internally Displaced and Stateless Persons. Division of Programme Support and Management* above n 3.

9 ME Price, *Rethinking Asylum: History, Purpose and Limits* (Cambridge University Press, 2004); A Betts, *Protection by Persuasion: International Cooperation in the Refugee Regime* (Cornell University Press, 2009); T Gammeltoft-Hansen, *Access to Asylum: International Refugee Law and the Globalization of Migration Control* (Cambridge University Press, 2011).

10 A different response was formulated for Cambodians, who were not part of the CPA, due to their classification as 'displaced persons' and the nature of the political situation surrounding their displacement. See WC Robinson, *Terms of Refuge: The Indochinese Exodus and the International Response* (Zed Books, 1998), 239.

applause immediately after its creation.[11] However, over recent years the emerging consensus has been that the CPA was a sound example of genuine multi-actor cooperation that proved effective in responding to these broader debates that have characterized the recent protracted refugee situations, allaying State-legitimate fear over persecution and burden-sharing. The CPA, it has been noted, reduced the number of clandestine departures from Indochina and separated the genuine from non-genuine refugee claimants.[12] Furthermore, it has been recently argued that the CPA 'focused on providing protection within the context of an asylum-migration nexus situation' and achieved a comprehensive approach to protecting 'genuine' refugees and finding solutions for the 'non-genuine'.[13] This has resulted in discussions about the merits of applying CPA-based approaches to Somali, Iraqi and Afghan refugee populations.[14] But what of the States that hosted the original CPA? In this chapter, I argue that the CPA legitimized an already recalcitrant region when it came to recognizing and implementing international refugee law. The CPA legitimated an existing notion within the region that asylum seekers, for the most part, were a temporary burden to which States had to provide no more than a 'transit service'. This loose interpretation of State responsibility to asylum seekers has had great costs for asylum seekers and the region's reputation in terms of living up to its human rights obligation in this area.

This chapter is divided into three parts. The first part charts the introduction of the 1989 Comprehensive Plan of Action; the second part discusses the CPA

11 G Hugo and C Kwok-Bun, 'Conceptualizing and Defining Refugee and Forced Migrations in Asia' (1990) 18(1) Southeast Asian Journal of Social Science 19–42; AC Barcher, 'First Asylum in Southeast Asia: Customary Norm or Ephemeral Concept?' (1992) 24(3) New York Journal of International Law and Politics 1253–86; S Bari, 'Refugee Status Determination under the Comprehensive Plan of Action (CPA): A Personal Assessment' (1992) 4(4) International Journal of Refugee Law 487–513; A Helton, 'The Malaysian Policy to Redirect Vietnamese Boat People: Non-refoulement as a Human Rights Remedy' (1992) 24(3) New York University Journal of International Law and Politics 1203–18; C McDonald, 'The CPA and the Children: A Personal Perspective' (1993) 5(4) International Journal of Refugee Law 580–84.

12 E Feller, 'The Evolution of the International Refugee Protection Regime' (2001) 5 Washington University Journal of Law and Policy 129–43; G Loescher and J Milner, 'The Missing Link: the need for Comprehensive Engagement in regions of refugee origin' (2003) 79(3) International Affairs 583–617; WC Robinson, 'The Comprehensive Plan of Action for Indochinese Refugees, 1989–1997: Sharing the Burden and Passing the Buck' (2004) 17(3) International Journal of Refugee Law 319–33.

13 A Betts, 'Comprehensive Plans of Action: Insights from CIREFCA and the Indochinese CPA' (2006) Working Paper No 120 *New Issues in Refugee Research* (UNHCR) 62.

14 UNHCR, *UNHCR's Plan of Action for Afghanistan* (2001); UNHCR, *Strengthening Refugee Protection, Assistance and Support to Host Communities in Kenya and Comprehensive Plan of Action for Somali Refugees* (2005), available at http://www.unhcr.org/protect/PROTECTION/438d6fed2.pdf.

itself, focusing on what it aimed to achieve. The two central strategies of the CPA – screening and repatriation – were met with a variety of responses by implementing States. But one theme, I contend, remained consistent during and after the CPA: ASEAN States were never persuaded that they had to comply with international refugee law on a permanent basis. Their obligations were temporary and only subscribed to the CPA definition of refugees. This resulted in the CPA institutionalizing non-compliance and compromising asylum seekers' full access to seek refugee status. In the final part of the article, I argue that the failure to institutionalize State responsibility towards refugees within the region continues to affect asylum seekers in the region to this day, placing an inordinate burden on the UNHCR to find resettlement solutions for people that are simply not present in the region.

The Conditions that Led to the 1989 CPA

Between 1988 and 1989, the number of Vietnamese who sought asylum in Southeast Asia and Hong Kong increased by 84 per cent.[15] This was largely attributed to a temporary lapse in the Orderly Departure Program (ODP), as well as continued poverty and instability in the region. The ODP had been developed in 1979 through a Memorandum of Understanding between the UNHCR and Vietnamese government to permit the 'orderly departure' of family reunion cases and special humanitarian cases, while preventing 'illegal' departures. Lists would be prepared by the Vietnamese government and receiving countries – then the lists were compared and those who appeared on both were permitted leave.[16] However, for the ten years of its duration there were perpetual problems due to differences between the US and Vietnam governments about who could be given immediate refugee status and resettlement, leading to significant delays in the ODP.[17] As a result, the numbers prepared to pay people smugglers $1,500 for a place in a boat steadily rose by the mid-1980s.[18] At the same time as the number of asylum seekers increased, Southeast Asian States and Hong Kong became increasingly frustrated with the slow rates of persons within their detention camps being resettled to the West. Due to the failure of the ODP, a seemingly endless stream of arrivals was now joining long-stayers, who were repeatedly denied refugee status but refused repatriation.[19]

---

15 UNGA, Overview of UNHCR Activities, Report for 1988–1989, Executive Committee of the High Commissioner's Programme, 40th Session, UN Doc A/AC.96/729 (25 August 1989).

16 See Robinson 'The Comprehensive Plan of Action' 57.

17 Ibid. 195.

18 United States Committee for Refugees (USCR), Refugee Reports, Vol 8, No 3 (20 March 1987).

19 USCR, Refugee Reports, Vol 9, No 5 (20 May 1988).

From 1986 to 1987 there was a major increase in the number of Vietnamese boat people, from 19,527 to 28,056.[20] In December 1988, the UNHCR attempted to negotiate a new Memorandum of Understanding with Vietnam to restart the ODP. There was some success: the ODP expanded and accelerated departures, while the UNHCR was given access to those seeking resettlement. Still, these efforts failed to reduce the rate of those leaving independently. The problem with the majority of those leaving by boat was that they were not eligible for ODP departure.[21] In addition, Vietnam blocked many requests for people wishing to leave under the ODP to reunite with their families and those in re-education camps were particularly 'off-limits'. In addition, because the ODP waiting period was so long, many preferred to take their chances by boat and others were simply not aware of the ODP procedures and how they could use them to secure departure.[22]

As a result, there was a continued increase in the number of asylum seekers between 1988 and 1989. Several Southeast Asian States started to publicly decry the failure of the 1979 ODP agreement and call for new solutions. In 1988, ASEAN denounced the 1979 ODP agreement as inherently unable to produce a durable solution to the problem:

> The ASEAN Foreign Ministers are seriously concerned about the continued outflow of refugees, displaced persons and illegal immigrants from Indochina and the problems this poses for the ASEAN countries. The Foreign Ministers note with particular concern the large increase in the number of Vietnamese boat people coming into the ASEAN region over the past year. The Foreign Ministers are of the view that the structures, premises and assumptions of the past are no longer capable of dealing with the Vietnamese boat people problem. The Foreign Ministers agree that a new comprehensive programme of action is needed.[23]

At the 1988 UNHCR Executive Committee of the High Commissioner's Programme (hereafter referred to as the Executive Committee) meetings, the ASEAN States, with the support of Australia and Japan, further expressed their discontent with the system of response set up in 1979. ASEAN States drafted a proposal for the Executive Committee's consideration: an international conference to resolve the Indochinese refugee crisis. Australia was the first to support it, followed by

20 L Druke, *Preventative Action for Refugee Producing Situations* (Peter Lang, 1993) 80.

21 ODP required that the receiving state – primarily the United States – agreed with the listing of those on Vietnam's departure list and vice versa, making the process quite prolonged and susceptible to politics.

22 See *Refugee Reports* above n 18.

23 ASEAN, *Joint Statement by the ASEAN Foreign Ministers on the Indochinese Refugees* (4 July 1988) available at http://www.aseansec.org/907.html.

Japan.[24] Indonesia, Malaysia and Thailand repeatedly stressed the importance of a new conference.[25] Thailand, notably, argued that it was becoming 'increasingly apparent that the *norms and principles formulated at an earlier time in one part of the world and under a particular set of circumstances could not always be applied automatically to other regions or situations*'.[26] The new conference's purpose was to reach a 'new consensus ... on comprehensive and durable solutions to deal [with the situation] in a realistic yet humanitarian manner'.[27]

In the first five months of 1989, Malaysia also had 'near-record levels' of boat people arriving; Indonesia, Japan, the Philippines and Thailand recorded 'unusually high arrival figures'.[28] By the end of June 1989, the number of boat people registered at UNHCR camps in the region stood at 96,669 – representing an 82 per cent rise compared with the same period in 1988.[29]

In response to the ongoing arrivals, the ASEAN Foreign Ministers meeting in Bangkok on 4 July 1988 called for a 'new comprehensive plan of action' to be implemented across the region.[30] This in turn led to a decision by the UNHCR Executive Committee to host a new international conference on Indochinese refugees. The Malaysian government convened another meeting in Kuala Lumpur from 2–9 March 1989, to discuss the first draft of the Comprehensive Plan of Action (CPA).

The UNHCR drafted an agreement that introduced a cut-off date for asylum seekers' access to immediate refugee status, 14 March 1989. After this date all arrivals would be screened and the CPA provided a precise formula for how the

24 UNGA, Summary Record of the 426th Meeting on 3rd October 1988, Executive Committee of the High Commissioner's Programme, Thirty-Ninth Session, UN Doc A/AC.96/SR.426 (18 October 1988); UNGA, Summary Record of the 427th Meeting on 4th October 1988, Executive Committee of the High Commissioner's Programme, Thirty-Ninth Session, UN Doc A/AC.96/SR.427 (9 November 1988).

25 UNGA, Summary Record of the 428th Meeting on 4th October 1988, Executive Committee of the High Commissioner's Programme, Thirty-Ninth Session, UN Doc A/AC.96/SR.428 (10 October 1988) 12, 16.

26 UNGA, Summary Record of the 427th Meeting on 4th October 1988, Executive Committee of the High Commissioner's Programme, Thirty-Ninth Session, UN Doc A/AC.96/SR.427 (9 November 1988) 5 (emphasis added).

27 UNGA, Summary Record of the 432nd Meeting on 6th October 1988, Executive Committee of the High Commissioner's Programme, Thirty-Ninth Session, UN Doc A/AC.96/SR.432 (13 October 1988) 11.

28 UNGA, UNHCR Activities Financed by Voluntary Funds: Report for 1988–89 and Proposed Programmes and Budget for 1990, Part II: Asia and Oceania, Executive Committee of the High Commissioner's Programme, 40th Session, UN Doc A/AC.96/724 (28 August 1989) Part II, 2.

29 Ibid.

30 See *Joint Statement by the ASEAN Foreign Ministers on the Indochinese Refugees* above n 23.

asylum seekers would be met, treated and dealt with according to whether or not they received refugee status.

There were eight sections in the CPA. The first covered clandestine departure and the objective here was to enlist the Vietnamese and Laotian governments to prevent people leaving their country illegally. This is done partly through the central government directing local authorities on the need to prevent departures, by using the media to alert its listeners to the dangers of clandestine departures, and also through the introduction of status determination in asylum countries, and addressing the problems of resettlement, as well as dealing with the need to consider alternative, regular, means of departure. The second section covered the regular departure programme, through which the UNHCR and Intergovernmental Committee for Migration (ICM now International Organization of Migration) would assist in expediting and processing departures. The third section concerned the reception of new arrivals and that the UNHCR was to be given 'full and early access to arrivals' and 'full access to the refugee status-determination process'.[31] The fourth section covered refugee status and insisted that all asylum seekers, regardless of mode of arrival and whether they arrived before or after the cut-off date, should be given the opportunity to seek refugee status and must be considered refugees until proven otherwise. The status of an asylum seeker was to be determined by national authorities, according to the refugee criteria and procedures set out in the 1951 Convention and the 1967 Protocol. In addition, the UNHCR Handbook on Procedures and Criteria for Determining Refugee Status was to be 'an authoritative and interpretative guide in developing and applying the criteria'.[32] UNHCR was to train officials across the region in the determination process. However, it is significant to note that the status determination process was still a national exercise, carried out by government officials.

The fifth section of the CPA focused on resettlement and stated that a resettlement program should be formulated specifically for the 'long-stayers' present in camps prior to the cut-off date.[33] A resettlement programme for 'newly determined refugees' was also created with resettlement countries asked to accept all those screened in as genuine refugees within a 'prescribed period'.[34] The sixth section of the CPA covered repatriation/plan of repatriation. Those who had been determined not to be refugees were to 'return to their country of origin in accordance with international practices reflecting the responsibilities of States towards their own citizens', that is, not be forcibly repatriated.[35] But the document also noted:

31 UNGA, Draft Declaration and Comprehensive Plan of Action Approved by the Preparatory Meeting for the International Conference on Indochinese Refugees on 8 March 1989, UN Doc A/CONF.148/2 (26 April 1989) 4.

32 Ibid. 5.

33 Ibid. 6.

34 Ibid.

35 Ibid. 7.

> If, after the passage of reasonable time, it becomes clear that voluntary repatriation is not making sufficient progress towards the desired objective, alternatives recognized as being acceptable under international practices would be examined.[36]

The seventh section of the CPA addressed Laotian asylum seekers, the majority of whom had sought asylum in Thailand. A screening process had been in place for them since 1985. The only resettlement country accepting Laotians by 1989 was the United States. The CPA's purpose in this regard was to give all displaced Laotians safe access to the Lao screening process and the Laotian government was required to improve its compliance in permitting those deemed not to be refugees to return home safely.[37]

The eighth and final section of the CPA covered implementation and review procedures. This section created the Steering Committee, which was to be based in Southeast Asia and contained representatives from all governments making commitments to the CPA. It was to meet under UNHCR chairmanship to discuss the implementation of the CPA, provide for areas found to need improvement and deal with the implementation of status determination, repatriation and resettlement.[38] The CPA was also to be reviewed annually at the UNHCR Executive Committee sessions.

In the next section I will focus particularly on points four and six of the CPA – status determination and repatriation. I examine how implementation of these objectives question whether any obligation was ever placed on Southeast Asian States Parties to recognize and uphold the basic principles of the 1951 Convention and the 1967 Protocol.

CPA in Practice: Screening and Repatriation

The introduction of screening procedures, some argued, marked a new level of compliance and recognition by Southeast Asian States by conceding to the terms for determining the status of asylum seekers according to both the 1951 Convention and the 1967 Protocol.[39] The repatriation of 'non-genuine' asylum seekers to their country of origin and the prevention of the continual exodus of such people has also been cited as evidence of the CPA's success in dealing with

---

36 Ibid.

37 Ibid. 7.

38 Ibid.

39 V Muntarbhorn, *The Status of Refugees in Asia* (Clarendon Press, 1992); DA Martin, 'Refugees and Migration' in C Joyner (ed.), *The United Nations and International Law* (Cambridge University Press/The American Society of International Law, 1997).

complex, enduring refugee situations.[40] It must be kept in mind though that the primary purpose of the CPA was actually to be 'a deterrent measure to facilitate the return of those determined by the authorities not to be refugees'.[41] The CPA was the result of Southeast Asian States successfully arguing that the majority of asylum seekers from Indochina were *not* genuine refugees. Therefore, this section will look at how screening and repatriation developed in relation to that objective of the CPA – to end non-genuine refugees seeking asylum. I argue that Southeast Asian practices in screening procedures and repatriation did not reflect an affirmation of international refugee protection principles; the actions of Southeast Asian States were primarily geared towards ending what they saw as non-genuine refugees exploiting their charitable generosity. The effect of the CPA was that it served an immediate problem but possibly contributed to a long-term problem that remains to this day – poor regional compliance with the 1951 Convention and 1967 Protocol.

CPA Procedures in Practice

A number of changes were made to the CPA by the first asylum countries right after these procedures were agreed to in June 1989 at the International Conference on Indochinese Refugees. But first let us briefly look at the difference that the first year of screening made, keeping in mind that before March 1989, arrivals were given immediate refugee status on a *prima facie* basis. In the first five months of 1990, the number of boat people arrivals fell overall by 40 per cent.[42] There was an increase of arrivals in Indonesia and Thailand, but a shift away from the more popular arrival destinations of Malaysia and Hong Kong. The shift can largely be accounted for by increased awareness of the 'deplorable' conditions in Hong Kong camps and the pushback of boats by Malaysia.[43] The Malaysian authorities had been practising pushbacks since March 1989 and even after the 1989 Conference this activity continued, with most of the boats towed towards Indonesian waters.[44] The refusal by resettlement States to take any more *prima facie* refugees after March 1989 led Malaysia to 'cut its losses' and conduct its own first asylum policy irrespective of its commitments to the CPA.[45] These actions in Malaysia produced

40 See Feller 'The Evolution of the International Refugee Protection Regime' and Loescher and Milner 'The Missing Link'.

41 A Helton, 'Refugee Determination under the Comprehensive Plan of Action: Overview and Assessment' (1993) 5(4) International Journal of Refugee Law 556.

42 UNGA, *UNHCR Activities Financed by Voluntary Funds: Report for 1989–90 and Proposed Programmes and Budget for 1991, Part II: Asia and Oceania, Executive Committee of the High Commissioner's Programme, Forty-First Session*, UN Doc A/AC.96/751 (13 August 1990) Part II, 1–2.

43 USCR, Refugee Reports, Vol 11, No 1 (31 January 1990).

44 See Helton, 'The Malaysian Policy to Redirect Vietnamese Boat People'.

45 Ibid. 191.

a tenfold increase in arrivals in Indonesia in 1990, while Malaysia's arrivals for the same year numbered only 1,300 (in 1989 it had been 20,475 in Malaysia and 4,428 in Indonesia).[46]

Further changes to boat arrival figures during the CPA was due to the number of people that left via the ODP: in the first five months of 1990, 23,300 left via the ODP (15,123 in 1988, 43,177 in 1989) and during the six years of the CPA numbers leaving via ODP were higher than boat departures.[47] Meanwhile, over 60 per cent of those who arrived by boat before the cut-off date had been resettled by the beginning of 1990.[48]

In 1990 the UNHCR reported the refugee status determination procedures were 'functioning' in Southeast Asian States, but there was still a region-wide need for more 'expeditious decisions on refugee status'.[49] The single greatest concern was the inability to 'reach a consensus related to the future of those Vietnamese asylum-seekers determined not to be refugees, and, in particular, the question of their return, other than voluntary, to their country of origin'.[50] Repatriation will be discussed in more detail later, but suffice to say at this stage, the backlog of 'non-genuine' refugees in first asylum camps was affecting the refugee status determination procedures.

By 1992–93, it had become clear that there were problems with the way refugee status determination was being conducted under the CPA in Southeast Asia. Robinson's verdict of the region's screening process was that 'the most fundamental consistency across the region proved to be that each country did things differently, some better than others and none perfectly'.[51] There are two obvious reasons for this. The first is that, internally, UNHCR officers had difficulty with uniform refugee status determination procedures. In Hong Kong, a field officer argued that those Vietnamese who were seeking asylum because they had family members who had been persecuted were to be 'given full and due consideration' for the 'UNHCR is in a very dangerous position right now of losing all creditability with the Vietnamese asylum seekers'.[52] In contrast, Erika Feller, the UNHCR's Representative in Malaysia and Regional Coordinator of Status Determination, was quoted as saying that though the boat peoples' stories were not ones 'I should like to have for my children … these are not refugee stories'.[53]

---

46 See *UNHCR Activities Financed by Voluntary Funds: Report for 1989–90 and Proposed Programmes and Budget for 1991, Part II: Asia and Oceania, Executive Committee of the High Commissioner's Programme, Forty-First Session* above n 42, 13, 17.

47 See Robinson, *Terms of Refuge* 198.

48 See *UNHCR Activities Financed by Voluntary Funds: Report for 1989–90 and Proposed Programmes and Budget for 1991, Part II: Asia and Oceania, Executive Committee of the High Commissioner's Programme, Forty-First Session* above n 42, 1.

49 Ibid.

50 Ibid.

51 See Robinson, *Terms of Refuge* 202–3.

52 Ibid. 204.

53 Ibid. 205.

The second problem with the screening process was that it was conducted by States that believed they had no legal or moral obligation to the 1951 Convention and its 1967 Protocol. The screening process that these States engaged in was strictly perfunctory, in the sense that it was done as a deterrent exercise to future asylum seekers.[54] A humanitarian consideration of determining 'genuine' from 'non-genuine' refugees was not at the forefront of this practice. The region had a history of using its non-signatory status to extract more assistance from the international community while delivering very little in terms of protection for asylum seekers. In this case, due to the Cold War origins of the Indochinese refugee problem, ASEAN States disowned any responsibility to deal with the crisis.

Arthur Helton's 1993 analysis of the screening process in a number of ASEAN States demonstrated that non-signatory States disavowed the protection principle, as the screening officials' underlying assumption was that 'most of the boat people were not refugees'.[55] As Helton further notes, status determination was implemented 'in a way that fails to accord the benefit of the doubt to asylum seekers … due to the fact that the arrangement has been imbued with migration control considerations'.[56] The situation pertaining to voluntary repatriation appeared little better, in terms of adhering to the 1951 Convention, than the refugee status determination process.

The CPA stated that in the 'first instance, every effort will be made to encourage the voluntary return' of persons deemed not to be refugees.[57] However, if 'after the passage of reasonable time' voluntary repatriation was not efficiently expediting the return of asylum seekers who did not receive refugee status, then 'alternatives recognized as being acceptable under international practices would be examined'.[58] Educational and orientation programmes were also to be delivered to the failed asylum seekers aimed at encouraging their return. At the 1989 Conference, all but two States agreed with the possible necessity of forced repatriation.[59] Rather ironically, these two States were the United States and Vietnam. The United States argued that 'unless and until dramatic improvements occur in [Vietnam's] economic, social and political life, the United States will remain unalterably opposed to the forced repatriation of Vietnamese asylum seekers'.[60] Vietnam concurred with the need to avoid forced repatriation; it argued that such

54 SE Davies, *Legitimising Rejection: International Refugee Law in Southeast Asia* (Martinus Nijhoff, 2007).

55 See Helton, 'Refugee Determination under the Comprehensive Plan of Action' 556.

56 Ibid.

57 UNGA, Overview of UNHCR Activities: Report for 1988-1989, Executive Committee of the High Commissioner's Programme, 40th Session, UN Doc A/AC.96/729 (25 August 1989).

58 Ibid.

59 USCR, *Refugee Reports*, Vol 10, No 6 (16 June 1989).

60 USCR, *Refugee Reports*, Vol 10, No 7 (28 July 1989).

'coercion constitutes a violation of the Declaration of Human Rights and could only bring on unforeseeable consequences'.[61]

The progress of repatriation for those deemed 'non-genuine' refugees was to be reported in Steering Committee meetings of the CPA. The first of these was held in October 1989 and, as at the earlier Conference, it was agreed that if no progress had been made in convincing people to return, 'alternative measures including compulsory repatriation may have to be considered'.[62] At the same time, the United Kingdom was meeting with Vietnam to prepare the way for their acceptance of non-genuine refugees from camps in Hong Kong. However, Vietnam insisted returnees would not be accepted unless their return was voluntary. On 12 December 1989, Hong Kong began its first forcible repatriation of Vietnamese asylum seekers, after a repatriation agreement (involving a sizable aid program) had been signed between Vietnam and Britain earlier that month. It should be noted that Hong Kong, though at the time under United Kingdom administration, was excised from the UK's signatory status to the 1951 Convention and the 1967 Protocol.

At the Steering Committee Conference on Indochinese refugees in Geneva on 23 and 24 January 1990, the US and Vietnam reiterated their opposition to involuntary repatriation of asylum seekers until at least after July.[63] The United States had originally been 'unalterably opposed' to forced returns until after 1 July 1991, and Vietnam was opposed until after 1 October 1990. However, the remaining 27 countries at the Steering Committee Conference insisted on 1 July 1990 as the deadline.[64] United Kingdom said that it would continue permitting Hong Kong officials to return non-genuine refugees to Vietnam by force if necessary, while ASEAN States started to suggest the possibility of refusing first asylum until the situation improved and the backlog of non-genuine refugees refusing to return voluntarily to Vietnam were forcibly returned.[65]

In a Joint Declaration of the 8th ASEAN-EC Ministerial Meeting in Kuala Lumpur on 16–17 February 1990, ministers all agreed that 'there must be an early implementation of the CPA as regards the repatriation of those not qualifying for the status of refugees to the country of origin in a phased, orderly and safe manner' – but the term 'voluntary return' was not mentioned.[66] On the 16 May 1990, the ASEAN Foreign Ministers issued their first statement indicating that if the CPA continued to be undermined by 'selective representation of its provisions by states' (mainly US and Vietnam), countries of asylum had the 'right to take such unilateral action as they deem necessary to safeguard their national interests, including the

61 Ibid.

62 Ibid.

63 See *Refugee Reports* above n 43.

64 Ibid.

65 USCR, *Refugee Reports*, Vol 11, No 5 (18 May 1990).

66 Ibid. 7.

abandonment of temporary refuge'.[67] Furthermore, they insisted that any country which opposed involuntary repatriation had a direct obligation to offer a solution.[68]

In essence, the ASEAN States argued that as other participants in the CPA were only practising 'selective implementation' of the CPA, they were absolved of any 'responsibility to honor their own commitments'.[69] ASEAN States therefore did not see the CPA as the stepping stone to the acceptance of wider refugee principles, but rather as a means to end the refugee problem in which everyone involved had reciprocal obligations and if one member broke it ASEAN States were not under any moral or legal obligation to uphold their end of the deal. There were no 'rules' which they had to obey and obligation was only necessary if reciprocal. As Hathaway argued, the CPA was perhaps most damaging for the UNHCR as it had been 'co-opted into the legitimation of the tacit pact between first asylum and resettlement states to relegate the explicit human rights mandate to the realm of pure symbolism'.[70] In sum, the CPA legitimated the abrogation of regional responsibility when even signatory States such as Australia and the United Kingdom came to support forced repatriation when the *refuge* no longer met political objectives.[71]

CPA – the End Result

The actions taken to bring the CPA to a close and resolve the repatriation problem were numerous and troubling. In particular, three circumstances of concern arose when attempts were made to close the CPA. The first was the repeated threats by ASEAN States to stop providing first asylum when the rate of voluntary repatriation slowed. This galvanized non-governmental organizations such as the USCR to request that the United States change its policy against forcible repatriation, so that more could be sent back to their country of origin. The second was the UNHCR's own efforts to bring the CPA to a 'rapid close'. This involved not only speeding up the forcible return of non-refugees, but also agreeing to allow conditions in the camps to worsen so as to encourage departures. The final act was an agreement made between Vietnam and each of the Southeast Asian States concerning the forcible return of the Vietnamese still in camps. To this day, I argue, these events have shaped the region's view that asylum seekers should be treated as a transient

67 Ibid.

68 ASEAN, *Joint Statement by the ASEAN Foreign Ministers on the Problem of Vietnamese Boat People* (24 July 1990), available at http://www.aseansec.org/1205.html.

69 See *Refugee Reports* above n 65.

70 JC Hathaway, 'Labelling the "boat people": the failure of the human rights mandate of the Comprehensive Plan of Action for Indochinese Refugees' (1993) 15(4) Human Rights Quarterly 686–702.

71 E Haddad, *The Refugee in International Society* (Cambridge University Press, 2008), 210.

group with little recourse for demanding rights and protection from the States in which they 'illegally' reside.

In 1993, the Hong Kong UNHCR office drew up a paper to present at the CPA Steering Committee Meeting in Jakarta to discuss the progress of the CPA. At this stage, 44,000 Vietnamese had returned home, the screening process was nearly completed and the Vietnamese exodus had dramatically slowed down.[72] However, there were still tens of thousands of 'screened-out' Vietnamese refusing to leave the camps. The UNHCR report argued, 'time is and has been the worst enemy of those who still remain. There is an urgent need to act'.[73] The recommendations were that screening be quickly completed; new arrivals be 'summarily returned' unless an obvious basis for asylum was demonstrated; and that further agreements on the involuntary return of non-refugees should be 'promoted and implemented' between Vietnam and first asylum States. The final UNHCR recommendation was that conditions in camps be sharply reviewed so that 'expectations of permanence of life in detention should cease'.[74]

These acts were in marked contrast to the 1989 agreement that even if rejected asylum seekers refused to return to their country of origin there were not to be any steps taken to increase their 'social outcast mentality'.[75] In addition to the UNHCR's deterrence measures, ASEAN States began signing Orderly Return Programmes (ORP) agreements with the Vietnamese government. Indonesia signed the first on 2 October 1993, and the remaining ASEAN States followed suit soon after. By this stage, neither Vietnam nor the US opposed involuntary repatriation. The deadline for repatriation was set for 25 June 1996, and Malaysia was the first to send its remaining camp populations back by the due date. Singapore followed in the next two days, and on the 30 June, UNHCR ceased all funding for processing Vietnamese boat people. Indonesia and Thailand were not able to successfully repatriate all of their rejected cases by the deadline, but 'each moved aggressively on involuntary repatriations in the latter half of 1996'.[76] During these operations, the UNHCR was not allowed to access the camps and thus there has been little discussion of the extent to which force was used to repatriate the asylum seekers.

The seemingly endless arrival of boat people heightened Southeast Asia's resistance to boat people and increased resistance amongst resettlement States. Most crucially, the end of the Cold War meant that the political conditions had

72 See Helton, 'Refugee Determination under the Comprehensive Plan of Action'.

73 See Robinson, *Terms of Refuge* 218.

74 Ibid.

75 UNGA, Office of the United Nations High Commissioner for Refugees, *International Conference on Indo-Chinese Refugees, Report of the Secretary-Genera, Annex: Declaration and Comprehensive Plan of Action (CPA), Forty-Fourth Session Item 111 (c)*, UN Doc A/44/523 (22 September 1989), annex, section C – Reception of New Arrivals.

76 Ibid. 220.

changed for asylum seekers.[77] Even if individuals did not feel safe to return, resettlement States had increasingly started to agree with Southeast Asian States' characterization of arrivals as 'economic migrants' and 'non-genuine' refugees. With asylum States and resettlement States joining forces on the Indochinese refugee population, the UNHCR had little option but to agree to compulsory screening and, eventually, forcible repatriation.

After the CPA: Refugee Protection in the Region Today

Was the CPA course of events devastating for the credibility of international refugee law in the region? The fact that until March 1989 if an Indochinese arrived on any shore they were to be granted *prima facie* refugee status, and then a month later they were not, demonstrated the malleability of refugee protection. This malleability arguably impacted on ASEAN member States' perception of their duty to asylum seekers to this day. Essentially, the CPA created a mechanism that enabled the region to utilize elements of the 1951 Convention to justify the expulsion of asylum seekers. The 1951 Convention became a useful procedural tool for dividing 'genuine' refugees from 'non-genuine', rather than a protection document that all States were to be held to account for upholding. As Helton's analysis of status procedures in the region demonstrated, Southeast Asian States never embraced screening in the name of refugee protection but only as a deterrent measure to the Indochinese refugees.[78] Richard Towle, who takes a less critical view of the CPA, acknowledges that the presence of UNHCR was crucial during the screening process to ensure the protection refugees and the institution of asylum was upheld.[79] It was a credit to the UNHCR that the CPA was as successful as it was, but in the long term it has proved an unsettling precedent for promoting States' (lack of) responsibility to uphold international refugee law.

Then as now, Southeast Asian States' primary concern has not been how to provide refugee protection, but how to deter individuals from seeking their protection and transferring this responsibility to the UNHCR – to this day.[80] As Chang-Muy argued, the CPA screening procedures had no basis in refugee law and were 'formed in response to specific refugee caseloads', and as a result 'the regime

77 See Haddad, *The Refugee in International Society* 211.

78 See Helton, 'Refugee Determination under the Comprehensive Plan of Action'.

79 R Towle, 'Processes and Critiques of the Indo-Chinese Comprehensive Plan of Action: An Instrument of International Burden-Sharing?' (2006) 18(3–4) International Journal of Refugee Law 537–70.

80 JN Crisp, L Obi and L Umlas, *But when will our turn come? A review of the implementation of UNHCR's urban refugee policy in Malaysia*. United Nations High Commissioner for Refugees Policy Development and Evaluation Service, PDES/2012/02 (May 2012), available at http://www.unhcr.org/4faa1e6e9.html.

for the protection of refugees in Asia remains fragile'.[81] As such, we must have concerns about the effectiveness of the 1951 Convention being used as a 'tool' by non-signatory, and even signatory States when the stated priority is deterrence rather than protection. Most damning, none of the Southeast Asian States (with the exception of the Philippines and Cambodia) were compelled to ratify the 1951 Convention and the 1967 Protocol during this crisis or since (nor have those two signatory States introduced domestic refugee legislation).

As a consequence, the CPA failed to compel Member States to create their own refugee processing procedures and responsibility – the 1951 Convention has never been institutionalized in the region. Southeast Asian States were financially assisted in the screening processes, those accepted as refugees were resettled in another country, and those who were not were repatriated. To this day, the CPA in effect continues with large asylum receiving populations such as Malaysia, Indonesia and Thailand temporarily allowing individuals who have been processed and granted refugee status by UNHCR offices (in location) to stay until repatriated elsewhere. None of these individuals are able to seek refugee status from these States or be received for settlement by these States.[82] During the CPA, as now, these States continue to allow a screening process to occur in their territory to expedite a problem for which governments do want to bear responsibility. The desire to end an, admittedly extreme, protracted refugee problem possibly came at the cost of holding States to account for their responsibilities to provide asylum and refugee protection.

In the literature on Southeast Asian refugees today, a quick Google search reveals a clear division between those who study 'migrants' (legal or illegal) and those whose object of analysis is 'refugees'. A search of ASEAN and 'refugees' by the same search engine reveals little political or academic engagement with the region's continued failure to promote the rights of refugees into regional frameworks.[83] The reality is that in Southeast Asia, asylum seekers today have received little improvement to their rights from the 1989 situation. They do not have the opportunity to seek refugee status and this means that an individual is often forced to live in fear of being found to be an 'illegal migrant'.[84] Such status means detention or immediate deportation, which, depending on their reason for leaving their country of origin, could well be considered an act of *refoulement*. The Asian region accounts for the UNHCR's highest number of refugee status determination programmes largely because this region hosts 30 per cent of the world's global refugee population and has no 'local normative frameworks for

81 F Chang-Muy, 'International Refugee Law in Asia' 1992 24(3) New York University Journal of International Law and Politics 1177.

82 See Crisp et al., *But when will our turn come?*

83 See *Refugee Protection in ASEAN: National failures, regional responsibilities* above n 2.

84 Communication with Diego Rosero, (then) Senior Legal Officer, UNHCR Tokyo (27 August 2003).

refugee protection'.[85] On a day-to-day basis, when the literature refers to a group of people as 'refugees' in Southeast Asia, this does not signify that the host country sees these people in the same light; it does not guarantee them better treatment according to the 1951 Convention, nor does it mean that they have greater security. All it means is that if the UNHCR recognizes this individual as a refugee they may have a chance of being resettled, after a long wait, in a country that has a refugee humanitarian intake quota. Not surprisingly, individuals seek transit on their own accord to countries that are signatory to both the 1951 Convention and the 1967 Protocol. However, here, too, individuals increasingly encounter harsh detention and processing requirements if they arrive, for example, in Australia by boat. Australia's argument has partly been based on the proposition that until the region shares responsibility for the refugee burden, they do not wish to carry the sole burden. Whether or not a wealthy nation such as Australia should abrogate their responsibility to uphold international refugee law, the broader point is true: there is no mechanism in place in the region to share protection and resettlement obligations.

Conclusion

As this chapter has demonstrated, the CPA endorsed the Southeast Asian position that asylum seekers were illegal migrants until proven otherwise. This meant that non-signatory States were applying the 1951 Convention's refugee status determination procedures without the 'benefit of doubt'. Though the CPA did lead to more than 507,000 Indochinese being resettled (either out of first asylum countries or through direct departure) compared to 442,000 in the same period prior to the CPA – it also led to a large number of individuals being forcibly repatriated to their country of origin.[86] By the early 1990s, Southeast Asian States were signing individual agreements with Vietnam to forcibly remove those resisting repatriation. There is little doubt that the UNHCR was vulnerable to both budgetary and political attacks in relation to the Indochinese refugee crisis. But this vulnerability was the product of a political situation that saw Western States eager to agree with Southeast Asian States' position on the status of boat arrivals, despite prior years of resisting the 'non-genuine' refugee tag. The abrupt political turnaround by these resettlement States undermined the notion that States' responsibility to uphold international refugee law was enduring. The result was that Southeast Asian States' view of the 1951 Convention as an inappropriate instrument for their specific regional context was legitimated, and this view has remained unchallenged to this day.

---

85 See 2012 *Regional Operations Profile – South East Asia* above n 4.

86 See Towle, 'Processes and Critiques of the Indo-Chinese Comprehensive Plan of Action' 537–70.

The lack of a regional mechanism to collectively deal with asylum seekers will remain a source of periodic tension in Southeast Asia with ongoing political shifts in and around the region, not to mention the likelihood of increased natural disasters testing informal migratory paths. The lack of a legal framework to protect people and guide States on appropriate behaviour during these events is a sign of the political weakness of the region to progressively discuss their collective responsibilities in this area. The adoption of the 2008 ASEAN Charter, and lack of reference to a coordinated burden-sharing mechanism for asylum seekers, was a significant opportunity lost. The political and economic reliance on the UNHCR to fill the regional gap in processing asylum seekers needs to be examined in further detail. In addition, we need to acknowledge the fact that in some parts of the world, individuals do not have access to the rights and protection that elements of international law seek to offer. This means that we need to remain vigilant to the justifications that can be made to deny protection and also be wary of temporary mechanisms that do not demand long-term solutions, such as the CPA. The result is that the cost of Southeast Asian States' success in rejecting international refugee law has been, and will continue to be, paid by those most vulnerable.

References

ASEAN, *Joint Statement by the ASEAN Foreign Ministers on the Problem of Vietnamese Boat People* (1990) Jakarta, 24 July 1990 http://www.aseansec.org/1205.html.

ASEAN, *Joint Statement by the ASEAN Foreign Ministers on the Indochinese Refugees* (1998) Bangkok, Thailand, 4 July http://www.aseansec.org/907.html.

ASEAN, *The ASEAN Charter* (2008) Jakarta: ASEAN Secretariat.

Barcher AC, 'First Asylum in Southeast Asia: Customary Norm or Ephemeral Concept?' (1992) 24(3) New York Journal of International Law and Politics 1253–86.

Bari S, 'Refugee Status Determination under the Comprehensive Plan of Action (CPA): A Personal Assessment' (1992) 4(4) International Journal of Refugee Law 487–513.

Barnett M and Finnemore m, *Rules for the World: International Organization in Global Politics* (Cornell University Press, 2004).

Betts A, 'Comprehensive Plans of Action: Insights from CIREFCA and the Indochinese CPA' (2006) New Issues in Refugee Research, Working Paper No 120 Geneva: UNHCR.

Betts A, *Protection by Persuasion: International Cooperation in the Refugee Regime* (Cornell University Press, 2009).

Chang-Muy F, 'International Refugee Law in Asia' (1992) 24(3) New York University Journal of International Law and Politics 1171–80.

Crisp J Obi N and Umlas L, But when will our turn come? A review of the implementation of UNHCR's urban refugee policy in Malaysia. United Nations

High Commissioner for Refugees Policy Development and Evaluation Service (2012) May, PDES/2012/02 accessed at http://www.unhcr.org/4faa1e6e9.html Date accessed June 2012.
Druke L, *Preventative Action for Refugee Producing Situations* (Peter Lang, 1993),
Feller E 'The Evolution of the International Refugee Protection Regime' (2001) 5 Washington University Journal of Law and Policy 129–43.
Gammeltoft-Hansen T, *Access to Asylum: International Refugee Law and the Globalization of Migration Control* (Cambridge University Press, 2011).
Goodwin-Gill G, *The Refugee in International Law* (Clarendon Press, 1996).
Haddad E. *The Refugee in International Society* (Cambridge University Press, 2008).
Hathaway JC, 'Labelling the 'boat people': the failure of the human rights mandate of the Comprehensive Plan of Action for Indochinese Refugees' (1993) 15(4) Human Rights Quarterly 686–702.
Helton A, 'The Malaysian Policy to Redirect Vietnamese Boat People: Non-refoulement as a Human Rights Remedy' (1992) 24(3) New York University Journal of International Law and Politics 1203–18.
Helton A, 'Refugee Determination under the Comprehensive Plan of Action: Overview and Assessment' (1993) 5(4) International Journal of Refugee Law 544–58.
Hugo G and Chan Kwok B, 'Conceptualizing and Defining Refugee and Forced Migrations in Asia' (1990) 18)1) Southeast Asian Journal of Social Science 19–42.
Loescher G, *The UNHCR and World Politics: A Perilous Path* (Oxford University Press, 2001).
Loescher G and Milner J, 'The Missing Link: the need for Comprehensive Engagement in regions of refugee origin' (2003) 79(3) International Affairs 583–617.
McDonald C, 'The CPA and the Children: A Personal Perspective' (1993) 5(4) International Journal of Refugee Law 580–584.
Martin DA, 'Refugees and Migration' in C. Joyner (ed.), *The United Nations and International Law* (Cambridge University Press/The American Society of International Law, 1997).
Muntarbhorn V, *The Status of Refugees in Asia* (Clarendon Press, 1992).
Nichols A and White P, *Refugee Dilemmas: Reviewing the Comprehensive Plan of Action for Vietnamese Asylum Seekers* (1993) Manila: LAWASIA Human Rights Committee.
People's Empowerment Foundation, *Refugee Protection in ASEAN: National failures, regional responsibilities* (2010) Bangkok: PEF. Accessed online: http://www.peoplesempowerment.org/news/pef-report-refugee-protection-in-asean-national-failures-regional-responsibilities.
Price ME, *Rethinking Asylum: History, Purpose and Limits* (Cambridge University Press, 2004).

Robinson WC, *Terms of Refuge: The Indochinese Exodus and the International Response* (Zed Books. 1998).

Robinson WC, 'The Comprehensive Plan of Action for Indochinese Refugees, 1989-1997: Sharing the Burden and Passing the Buck' (2004) 17(3) International Journal of Refugee Law 319–33.

Towle R, 'Processes and Critiques of the Indo-Chinese Comprehensive Plan of Action: An Instrument of International Burden-Sharing?' (2006) 18(3–4) International Journal of Refugee Law 537–70.

UNGA, Summary Record of the 428th Meeting on 4th October 1988, Executive Committee of the High Commissioner's Programme (1988a) Thirty-Ninth Session, A/AC.96/SR.428, 10 October.

UNGA, Summary Record of the 432nd Meeting on 6th October 1988, Executive Committee of the High Commissioner's Programme (1988b) Thirty-Ninth Session, A/AC.96/SR.432, 13 October.

UNGA, Summary Record of the 426th Meeting on 3rd October 1988, Executive Committee of the High Commissioner's Programme (1988c) Thirty-Ninth Session, A/AC.96/SR.426, 18 October.

UNGA, Summary Record of the 427th Meeting on 4th October 1988, Executive Committee of the High Commissioner's Programme (1988d) Thirty-Ninth Session, A/AC.96/SR.427, 9 November 1988.

UNGA, Draft Declaration and Comprehensive Plan of Action Approved by the Preparatory Meeting for the International Conference on Indo-Chinese Refugees on 8 March 1989 (1989a) A/CONF.148/2, 26 April.

UNGA, Overview of UNHCR Activities: Report for 1988-1989, Executive Committee of the High Commissioner's Programme (1989b) 40th Session, A/AC.96/729, 25 August.

UNGA, UNHCR Activities Financed by Voluntary Funds: Report for 1988–89 and Proposed Programmes and Budget for 1990 (1989c) Part II: Asia and Oceania, Executive Committee of the High Commissioner's Programme, 40th Session, A/AC.96/724 (Part II) 28 August.

UNGA, Office of the United Nations High Commissioner for Refugees: International Conference on Indo-Chinese Refugees, Report of the Secretary-General, Annex: Declaration and Comprehensive Plan of Action (CPA) (1989d) Forty-Fourth Session Item 111 (c), 22 September, A/44/523/Annex, Section C – Reception of New Arrivals.

UNGA, UNHCR Activities Financed by Voluntary Funds: Report for 1989-1990 and Proposed Programmes and Budget for 1991, Part II: Asia and Oceania, Executive Committee of the High Commissioner's Programme (1990) Forty-First Session, A/AC.96/751 (Part II), 13 August.

UNGA, Summary Record of the 473rd Meeting on 5 October 1992 (1992) Executive Committee of the High Commissioner's Programme, A/AC.96/SR.473, 12 October.

UNHCR, Information Package on the Comprehensive Plan of Action on Indo-Chinese Refugees (CPA) (1995) Geneva: UNHCR.

UNHCR, 'UNHCR's Plan of Action for Afghanistan' (2001) UNHCR News Stories, 27 November.

UNHCR, Strengthening Refugee Protection, Assistance and Support to Host Communities in Kenya And Comprehensive Plan of Action for Somali Refugees (2005) Nairobi: UNHCR Branch Office. Accessed online: http://www.unhcr.org/protect/PROTECTION/438d6fed2.pdf. Date accessed: 8 March 2012.

UNHCR, 2009 Global Trends: Refugees, Asylum–seekers, Returnees, Internally Displaced and Stateless Persons. Division of Programme Support and Management (2010) Geneva: UNHCR. Accessed online: http://www.unhcr.org/4c11f0be9.html Date accessed: 8 March 2012.

UNHCR, 'World Refuge Day: UNHCR report finds 80 percent of world's refugees in developing countries' (2010) News Stories 20 June. Accessed online: http://www.unhcr.org/4dfb66ef9.html Date accessed: 8 March 2012.

UNHCR, '2012 Regional Operations Profile – South East Asia' (2012). Accessed online: http://www.unhcr.org/pages/4b17be9b6.html Date accessed: 8 March 2012.

United States Committee for Refugees (USCR), Volume 8, Number 3, 20 March (1987).

USCR, Refugee Reports, Volume 9, Number 5, 20 May (1988).

USCR, Refugee Reports, Volume 10, Number 6, 16 June (1989a).

USCR, Refugee Reports, Volume 10, Number 7, 28 July (1989b).

USCR, Refugee Reports, Volume 11, Number 1, 31 January (1990b).

USCR, Refugee Reports, Volume 11, Number 5, 18 May (1990b).

Zolberg A, Suhrke A and Aguayo S, *Escape From Political Violence: Conflict and the Refugee Crisis in the Developing World* (Oxford University Press, 1989).

Chapter 15
The Protection of Asylum Seekers in East Asian State Parties to the 1951 Convention Relating to the Status of Refugees and its 1967 Protocol

Kelley Loper[1]

Introduction

The majority of Asian States[2] are not party to the 1951 Convention Relating to the Status of Refugees (Refugee Convention)[3] or its 1967 Protocol[4] – the instruments that constitute the core of the international legal framework governing refugee protection. Scholars have dubbed this phenomenon the 'Asian rejection'[5] and one of the advocacy priorities of the United Nations High Commissioner for Refugees (UNHCR) in the region has been to emphasize the importance of accession to these treaties.[6] Nevertheless, a significant minority of Asian States[7] have acceded to either or both of these instruments and thus signalled their willingness to take

---

1 The author would like to thank Lea Raible for her excellent research assistance and Emma Daae Kim and Brian Barbour for their helpful comments on an earlier draft of this chapter. Portions of this chapter are based on research supported by a grant from the Research Grants Council of the Hong Kong Special Administrative Region (Project Code: HKU 7008-PPR-09).

2 References to Asian States in this chapter include the 30 States classified by the United Nations Statistical Division within four of the Asian sub-regional groupings: Central Asia, Eastern Asia, Southern Asia and South-Eastern Asia: http://unstats.un.org/unsd/methods/m49/m49regin.htm#asia accessed 30 April 2013.

3 Convention relating to the Status of Refugees (adopted 28 July 1951, entered into force 22 April 1954) 189 UNTS 137 (Refugee Convention).

4 Protocol relating to the Status of Refugees (adopted 31 January 1967, entered into force 4 October 1967) 606 UNTS 267 (Protocol).

5 S Davies, 'The Asian Rejection?: International Refugee Law in Asia' (2006) 52(4) Australian Journal of Politics and History 562.

6 UNHCR, 'Global Appeal 2012–13: Asia and the Pacific, Regional Summary' http://www.unhcr.org/4ec230f20.html accessed 30 April 2013.

7 Twelve out of 30 (4 of 5 States in Central Asia; 3 of 5 States in Eastern Asia; 2 of 9 States in Southern Asia, and 3 of 11 States in Southeastern Asia).

on international protection obligations. These State Parties represent a variety of economic, legal, political, social and cultural systems and have adopted a range of refugee policies that fall along a broad protection spectrum. One end of the spectrum includes States that have enacted full-fledged refugee laws, conduct State-run refugee status determination (RSD) subject to judicial review by independent courts and offer at least minimal reception conditions including the right to work for asylum seekers and recognized refugees. At the other end of the scale are States with few relevant legal provisions, a lack of State-run RSD, and inconsistent approaches toward refugee arrivals that may be influenced to a greater degree by political or foreign policy considerations.

Due to space constraints, this chapter cannot adequately examine the practice of all Asian State Parties to the Refugee Convention. It therefore focuses on the responses of States within one sub-region: East Asia.[8] Although the sub-region has a relatively small number of States overall, its total population amounts to more than 1.5 billion people. The majority of States (three out of five) are party to the international refugee instruments and their implementation policies fall at both ends of the protection spectrum described above. One State, China, is both a significant source of refugees who have sought protection elsewhere as well as a destination country. China also exhibits a variety of systems and approaches internally. The situation in East Asian State Parties therefore presents a diversity of experience allowing for a rich examination of practice at both ends of the protection spectrum.

The unique context of each State party has, of course, influenced these States' particularized response to their obligations. While this review describes a range of approaches, it also gives rise to a common observation that the Refugee Convention – to varying degrees – has played an important role and provided a framework for developing and shaping domestic law and policy toward refugees within these States.

The chapter's examination of these developments provides an opportunity to reflect on methods of domestic implementation of the Convention in the Asian context. It suggests that the Refugee Convention has influenced approaches toward protection, even in settings with greater or lesser degrees of respect for rule of law and democratic governance. While accession to the Convention does not necessarily guarantee a higher level of protection in practice (and certainly none of the State Parties under review have achieved full implementation or compliance), it has provided a basis for advocacy for more progressive law reform and policy change. Perhaps not surprisingly, the States with stronger rule of law institutions and those that allow greater space for civil society to engage in discussion about human rights have been more responsive to their obligations. Even in China, where civil society has been more constrained and the measures adopted less robust,

8 'Eastern Asia' or 'East Asia' comprises China (including the Hong Kong and Macau Special Administrative Regions), the Democratic People's Republic of Korea (North Korea), Japan, Mongolia, and the Republic of Korea (South Korea).

the UNHCR and international NGOs have leveraged the Refugee Convention to achieve limited advances.

The second part of this chapter summarizes the application of the Convention in the three East Asian State Parties: Japan, the Republic of Korea (South Korea) and China. These case studies represent a range of responses and some diversity of protection environments. Accession has triggered some form of domestic legislative reform in all three States and this analysis concludes with some initial observations. First, several common influences – in addition to the applicability of the international refugee protection instruments – have contributed to complex processes of implementation in these countries. These factors include, for example: 1) ratification of other international human rights treaties and State and civil society engagement with the UN human rights monitoring processes; 2) domestic civil society responses and growing awareness among lawyers, decision-makers and others working with refugees of the content and scope of the Refugee Convention's obligations; 3) UNHCR's role in negotiating greater State responsibility for refugee protection; and 4) domestic politics, security concerns and other foreign affairs priorities. Second, while all four jurisdictions have achieved varying degrees of progress, protection gaps remain and campaigns for law and policy reform to achieve full compliance continue. This review of East Asian State practice indicates that the Refugee Convention has continuing relevance for addressing current refugee flows, even in the Asian region, and for providing a framework to guide the development of protection initiatives.

The third part further illustrates the value of the international refugee protection instruments through a discussion of legal and policy developments in the Hong Kong Special Administrative Region of China (Hong Kong). Despite China's accession, the Refugee Convention and Protocol are not binding on Hong Kong.[9] However, the authorities generally respect the rule of law and civil society organizations freely and actively advocate on human rights issues, including the rights of refugees. As in Japan and South Korea, the UN human rights treaty monitoring processes, the UNHCR, the legal profession and other civil society advocates have played a role in strengthening protection for refugees in Hong Kong. However, in the absence of the applicability of specialized international refugee instruments or domestic refugee provisions, these efforts have been insufficient to achieve a broader protection framework encompassing the full range of refugee rights beyond *non-refoulement*. The Hong Kong experience suggests that even in an environment with relatively strong general human rights protections and rule of law, the absence of the Refugee Convention is an obstacle to achieving further reform. This comparison between a jurisdiction not bound by the Convention and States Parties within the same region emphasizes the continuing relevance of the Refugee Convention. It also indicates that refugee-specific norms coupled with and reinforced by general human rights duties can be more effective than either set of obligations on their own.

---

9 K Loper, 'Human rights, *non-refoulement* and the protection of refugees in Hong Kong' (2010) 22(3) IJRL 404.

The fourth part concludes that the Asian practice considered in this chapter demonstrates the impact of the Refugee Convention on the development of States' policies toward refugees, even in light of rapid developments in international human rights law since 1951. While international human rights treaties have supplemented and reinforced the more specialized protection offered by the refugee instruments, the human rights standards are not sufficient on their own to provide a strong foundation for a refugee protection regime.[10]

Overview of Selected States Parties

This section provides an overview of protection developments and activities in the three East Asian State Parties to the Refugee Convention and Protocol. The first two States considered here, Japan and South Korea, have more developed asylum systems than the third, China, and have implemented increasingly robust RSD procedures. The differences between these States may be attributed to the relative strength of their legal institutions, the degree of respect for rule of law and whether civil society is free to, or has chosen to, actively pursue advocacy to enhance protection for refugee rights. While an effective determination procedure is critical for ensuring protection from *refoulement* in compliance with Article 33 of the Refugee Convention and customary international law,[11] these States have also provided additional measures, including a legal status, at least minimal reception conditions and the right to work for recognized refugees. Both Japan and South Korea have also been innovators in Asia; Japan was the first State in Asia to accept a certain number of recognized refugees waiting in a third State for resettlement and South Korea has recently enacted a comprehensive, stand-alone refugee law that replaces the more limited protection that had previously been available.

China on the other hand has one of the weakest refugee protection systems in Asia and excludes large numbers of claimants from certain States such as the Democratic People's Republic of Korea (North Korea). The government allows the UNHCR to screen for refugee status of asylum seekers coming from other

10 For a discussion of the intersection of international human rights law, international refugee law and international humanitarian law see, for example, J McAdam, 'The Refugee Convention as a rights blueprint for persons in need of international protection' (UNHCR, Policy Development and Evaluation Service, July 2006). McAdam observes that although one might like 'to point to human rights law as offering a complementary and, in part, more generous set of rights than the Refugee Convention, the generality and vagueness of those rights, combined with a lack of implementing mechanisms at the domestic level, make them in practice comparatively weak' (McAdam 4).

11 See UNHCR, *Global Consultations on International Protection/Third Track: Asylum Processes (Fair and Efficient Asylum Procedures)* 31 May 2001, UN Doc EC/GC/01/12, http://www.refworld.org/docid/3b36f2fca.html accessed 30 April 2013.

countries but does not conduct status determination itself. China has also been criticized for serious human rights abuses and is a major source of refugees as well as a country of asylum.[12] Nevertheless recent, nascent developments indicate some potential for progress toward implementation of its refugee protection obligations that may not have been possible without the application of the Refugee Convention.

Japan

Since its accession to the Refugee Convention and Protocol, Japan has gradually developed a system for determining the validity of refugee claims, integrating recognized refugees into Japanese society, and even resettling a limited number of refugees coming from camps outside Japan. A number of factors have influenced this process of implementation and the nature of Japan's approach toward its refugee protection obligations. These include, for example, international pressure, domestic public opinion, patterns of regional refugee flows and local, regional and international advocacy by lawyers, UNHCR and NGOs. Despite important developments, however, advocates have identified a number of remaining protection gaps that could hinder Japan's full compliance with its duties under international refugee law.

Japan acceded to the Refugee Convention on 3 October 1981 and to the Protocol on 1 January 1982 in response to increasing numbers of asylum seekers arriving from Vietnam, Cambodia and Laos after the end of the Vietnam War. The Japanese government had previously resisted application of the Refugee Convention, fearing that accession might signal 'openness' toward refugees and encourage an influx of arrivals from neighbouring States.[13] However, a number of other countries, especially the United States, pressured Japan to increase its contribution to international burden-sharing efforts after the Indochinese refugee crisis began in the mid-1970s.[14] According to Arakaki, Japan had a strong interest in maintaining good relations with the United States and in demonstrating its 'commitment to humanitarian cooperation' before both domestic and international audiences.[15] Additional incentives, such as the need to normalize the legal status of asylum seekers who had already arrived, may have also influenced the eventual decision to accede.[16]

---

12 See Human Rights Watch, 'World Report 2012: China' http://www.hrw.org/world-report-2012/world-report-2012-china accessed 30 April 2013.

13 M Dean and M Nagashima, 'Sharing the Burden: The Role of Government and Ngos in Protecting and Providing for Asylum Seekers and Refugees in Japan' (2007) 20(3) Journal of Refugee Studies 481, 486.

14 See ibid. 482, 6 and 8.

15 O Arakaki, *Refugee Law and Practice in Japan* (Ashgate, 2008) 18.

16 Ibid.

Japan is a monist jurisdiction and international treaties in theory are directly applicable within the Japanese legal system.[17] The Refugee Convention and Protocol were also partially incorporated into domestic law in 1982 by way of amendment to the 1951 Immigration Control Order,[18] which governs various aspects of the admission, residence and departure of foreigners. The Act refers to the definition of 'refugee' as expressed in Article 1A(2) of the Refugee Convention and Article 1 of the Protocol.[19] It grants the Minister of Justice jurisdiction to consider refugee claims and grant refugee status and provides for conditions of residence and the circumstances under which recognition of refugee status could be revoked.[20]

The law was further amended in 2004 in response to criticism of some of its more stringent measures and more sympathetic public opinion toward refugees.[21] The 2004 amendments abolished the imposition of a 60-day time limit for submitting an application for refugee status,[22] introduced a more independent appeals procedure with decision-makers from outside the Ministry of Justice,[23] allowed for long-term residency rights for recognized refugees[24] and made asylum seekers eligible for provisional stay.[25] The Act was further amended in 2009 to establish an expert committee to enhance transparency and better manage immigration detention facilities.[26] The amendments also more clearly

---

17 The Japan Federation of Bar Associations (JFBA) has noted: 'In the spirit of Article 98.2 of the Constitution of Japan that provides the obligation of observing the treaties and established laws of nations, treaties ratified by Japan are incorporated into the domestic legal system and have the same force as domestic law'. However, according to the JFBA, '[c]ourts are disinclined to apply international human rights treaties as judicial norms …' Japan Federation of Bar Associations 'Written Information Submitted for the Summary of the Human Rights Situation in Japan to be Prepared by the United Nations Office of High Commissioner for Human Rights' (February 2008).

18 Cabinet Order No 319 of 1951.

19 Immigration Control and Refugee Recognition Act (Cabinet Order No 319 of 4 October 1951), Art 2(iii-2) (Japan Immigration Bureau, provisional and unofficial translation 2009) http://www.immi-moj.go.jp/english/newimmiact/pdf/RefugeeRecognitionAct02.pdf accessed 30 April 2013.

20 Chapter VII-2: Recognition of Refugee Status and Other Related Matters.

21 Arakaki, *Refugee Law and Practice in Japan* 35. Arakaki notes the public reaction to an incident in Shenyang, China, where the Chinese police arrested a family of North Korean asylum seekers that included a two-year-old girl, as they attempted to seek asylum at the Japanese consulate.

22 Ibid. 34, 60.

23 Ibid. 61–2 and Dean and Nagashima, 'Sharing the Burden' 498.

24 Dean and Nagashima, 'Sharing the Burden' 498.

25 Ibid.

26 Human Rights Council, 'Report of the Working Group on the Universal Periodic Review' (14 December 2012) UN Doc A/HRC/22/14, par 20; Japan Ministry of Justice, 'Changes to the Immigration Control Act!' (2009) www.immi-moj.go.jp/english/newimmiact/newimmiact_english.html accessed 30 April 2013.

prohibit deportations to destinations that would amount to violations of Japan's *non-refoulement* obligations under Article 3 of the Convention Against Torture and Other Cruel, Inhuman or Degrading Treatment or Punishment (CAT) and Article 16(1) of the International Convention for the Protection of All Persons from Enforced Disappearance.[27] According to the UNHCR, Japan's refugee status determination procedures have improved in recent years, including a decrease in the time it takes to process applications, but only at the first instance stage.[28]
In addition to these procedural and legislative reforms, Japan has taken other measures to enhance refugee protection and contribute to global burden-sharing arrangements. For example, Japan has contributed substantial financial resources to the UNHCR since 1979, after it was reproached for its rigid policy toward Indochinese refugees,[29] and was the second largest donor to the agency in 2012.[30] In 2008, Japan announced that it would establish a pilot scheme to resettle 90 refugees from Myanmar living in camps in Thailand over a three-year period beginning in 2010.[31] In March 2012, Japan agreed to extend the scheme for a further two years and by September 2012 had resettled 45 people.[32]

Despite apparent progress and active efforts at awareness raising, training and policy advocacy, scholars and advocates have raised a number of remaining concerns about Japan's treatment of asylum seekers and refugees and the fairness of its refugee status determination procedures. These issues include: lingering questions about procedural transparency and independence;[33] an extremely low refugee recognition rate (only .56 per cent of the 3,194 claims decided in 2012 were successful);[34] problems arising from the conflation of immigration law and

---

27 Ibid. However, the UN Committee Against Torture raised concerns about '[t]he lack of effective implementation of article 53(3) of the [Immigration Control and Refugee Recognition Act], which prohibits the removal of a person to any country where he or she may be subject to torture, as proscribed by article 3 of the Convention'. UN Committee Against Torture, 'Concluding Observations on the Second Periodic Report of Japan' (28 June 2013) UN Doc CAT/C/JPN/CO/2, para. 9(e).

28 UNHCR Japan, 'Fact Sheet' (September 2012) http://www.unhcr.org/5000196c13.pdf accessed 30 April 2013.

29 Dean and Nagashima 'Sharing the Burden' 488–9.

30 UNHCR Japan (n 28).

31 'Japan to Resettle Myanmar Refugees' (Asia Pacific Refugee Rights Network, 3 February 2010) http://www.aprrn.info/1/index.php/2-uncategorised/54-japan-to-resettle-myanmar-refugees accessed 30 April 2013.

32 UNHCR Japan (n 28). See also B Barbour, 'Japan Announces that 0 Refugees will be Resettled this Year', Fahamu Refugee Legal Aid Newsletter (December 2012).

33 Dean and Nagashima 'Sharing the Burden' 498–9.

34 Japanese Ministry of Justice: www.moj.go.jp/nyuukokukanri/kouhou/nyuukokukanri03_00094.html accessed 30 April 2013 as reported by Brian Barbour, Director, External Relations Unity, Japan Association for Refugees by email to the Asia Pacific Refugee Rights Network (20 March 2013) (on file with the author). At first instance, 5 out of 2,198 decisions were successful and on appeal 13 of 996 appeals were allowed. See also

border control with refugee protection;[35] inadequate interpretation and translation services for refugees;[36] a reactive policy that has developed in response to external pressures and national interests rather than protection priorities;[37] insufficient social welfare support for refugees and financial difficulties while waiting for the outcome of their claims;[38] routine detention of asylum seekers or potential asylum seekers without valid travel documents;[39] and difficulties accessing legal representation while in detention. Some have also suggested that Japan's generous approach to funding global refugee protection activities has actually been designed to avoid taking on resettlement responsibilities.[40] While Japan has been praised for eventually agreeing to resettle refugees from Myanmar by launching its pilot scheme in 2010, the numbers Japan has agreed to resettle are relatively small (only 30 per year) and it is not clear whether a sufficient number of refugees are interested in applying for the scheme.[41] In September 2012, 16 refugees from the Thai refugee camps apparently declined, at the last minute, to take up their resettlement places.[42]

Civil society organizations, including NGOs and networks of refugee lawyers, have played an active role in identifying issues, advocating for changes to the system and contributing towards enhanced protection of refugee rights.[43] Namba

---

Japan Lawyers Network for Refugees, 'Statement on Asylum Trends and Levels in 2012 in Japan' Fahamu Refugee Legal Aid Newsletter (June 2013).

35 Dean and Nagashima 'Sharing the Burden' 489.

36 Fourth Asia-Pacific Consultation on Refugee Rights in Seoul, Korea (Asia Pacific Refugee Rights Network 22–24 August 2012), Summary of remarks by Mizuno Makiko, 'Workshop 5 – Community Interpreter Training' 19.

37 Dean and Nagashima 'Sharing the Burden' 489.

38 Ibid. 499, 502–3.

39 The press reported that one asylum seeker from Myanmar who had filed an application for refugee status was arrested after overstaying his visa. S Knight, 'Asylum Seekers Find Little Refuge in Japan', *Japan Today*, 26 July 2009 www.japantoday.com/category/lifestyle/view/asylum-seekers-find-little-refuge-in-japan accessed 30 April 2013.

40 Dean and Nagashima 'Sharing the Burden' 489, 493–4, 505 (referring to Japan's 'chequebook assistance' response to international pressure to take on greater burden-sharing responsibilities toward refugees).

41 'Seeing refugees as regular members of Japanese society' (*The Mainichi* 1 December 2012) http://mainichi.jp/english/english/perspectives/news/20121201p2a00m0na002000c.html accessed 30 April 2013.

42 Ibid. The article cites a comment by Mika Hasebe, 'a specially appointed lecturer at the Tokyo University of Foreign Studies' that Japan lacks 'a perspective on "social integration" that considers how refugees can blend in to become members of society – not just with regard to the refugee resettlement system, but with respect to the nation's refugee policy as a whole'. See also Barbour (n 32).

43 See Dean and Nagashima's discussion of the role of NGOs in refugee protection in Japan, 'Sharing the Burden' 500–503. They note that 'NGOs are bearing an unequal burden in providing for the financial and social welfare needs of asylum seekers and refugees in Japan …'

and Sugimoto describe the development and activities of networks of lawyers advocating for refugee rights in Japan since the late 1970s.[44] These networks, such as the Japan Lawyers Network for Refugees and the Committee on Refugee Protection of the Japan Federation of Bar Associations, have shared information among their members about refugee cases and developments in international refugee law; advocated for procedural improvements with government officials; and provided legal assistance to individual refugee claimants.[45] These groups have also cooperated with UNCHR, NGOs and academics to campaign for amendments to the Immigration Control and Recognition of Refugees Act.[46] UNHCR has also played a role, providing training for decision-makers and working closely with NGOs on a number of aspects of refugee protection including advocacy.[47]

Republic of Korea

The Republic of Korea (South Korea) acceded to both the Refugee Convention and Protocol in December 1992. As a monist jurisdiction, international treaties are self-executing in South Korea and therefore automatically apply within the domestic legal order.[48] In theory, the authorities therefore have direct obligations under the Refugee Convention and Protocol but in practice, implementing legislation is necessary to actualize these duties.[49] The government amended the Immigration Control Act (ICA) in 1993 to include a number of provisions on refugee protection, including a reference to the definition of 'refugee' in the Convention and Protocol. The Ministry of Justice began operating an asylum system in 1994[50] and the ICA, most recently amended in 2010, continued to govern refugee protection until the introduction of a new, separate Law on the Status and Treatment of Refugees (Refugee Act) discussed below.

Since 1994, the numbers of civil society organizations and lawyers working with refugees have significantly increased. Advocates have built strong networks,

---

44 M Namba and D Sugimoto (Japan Lawyers Network for Refugees), 'Development and Challenges of Lawyers Networks for Refugee Protection in Japan' (Asia Pacific Refugee Rights Network, East Asia Symposium: Legislation and the Developing Asylum Policy in East Asia, Taipei, Taiwan, October 2012).

45 Ibid.

46 Ibid.

47 UNHCR Japan (n 28); 'UNHCR Global Report 2011: East Asia and the Pacific' (2011) 278. www.unhcr.org/4fc880b80.html accessed 30 April 2013.

48 C Kim, 'A Step Forward to Refugee Protection? South Korea's New Refugee Act' (June 2012) 2 Oxford Monitor of Forced Migration 8. UNHCR 'UNHCR's Comments on the 2009 Draft Bill on Refugee Status Determination and Treatment of Refugees and Others' 2.

49 Ibid.

50 UNHCR 'Submission by the United Nations High Commissioner for Refugees for the Office of the High Commissioner for Human Rights' Compilation Report – Universal Periodic Review' (April 2012) (UNHCR UPR Submission).

launched local campaigns and backed comprehensive field and comparative research to support these efforts.[51] These groups, along with international organizations and NGOs such as the UNHCR and UN human rights treaty monitoring bodies, have identified a number of protection gaps and procedural problems in the functioning of the Korean asylum system based on the ICA.[52] First, commentators have consistently criticized Korea's relatively low refugee recognition rate.[53] South Korea did not recognize its first refugee until 2001[54] and although the numbers of claimants and the rate of recognition subsequently increased, it remained low by global standards. By October 2012, the authorities had recognized 299 refugees out of a total of 4,748 asylum applicants and had granted humanitarian status to 151 individuals.[55] Most asylum seekers had come from Pakistan, Sri Lanka, Nepal, China, Myanmar, Nigeria, Uganda and Bangladesh. Other concerns related to the RSD procedures included delays in the decision-making process, the lack of alternate remedies for failed asylum seekers and that persons waiting for their decisions were generally not allowed to work.[56]

A 2009 joint NGO alternative report to the UN Committee on Economic, Social and Cultural Rights, the body tasked with monitoring States' obligations under the International Covenant on Economic, Social and Cultural Rights (ICESCR),[57] raises several issues including the low refugee recognition rate; long processing times; the requirement that refugee claims be made within one year of arrival; the ICA's weak requirement that the government must merely 'strive to' guarantee the rights in the Refugee Convention; and the level of professionalism, transparency, impartiality and fairness of the Refugee Recognition Council, the administrative

51 P Hwang (Korean Public Interest Lawyers Group, GONGGAM), 'Review of Refugee Law in Taiwan and South Korea' (Asia Pacific Refugee Rights Network, East Asia Symposium: Legislation and the Developing Asylum Policy in East Asia, Taipei, Taiwan, October 2012); H Lee (Refuge pNan), 'Practices in Korea' (Asia Pacific Refugee Rights Network, East Asia Symposium: Legislation and the Developing Asylum Policy in East Asia, Taipei, Taiwan, October 2012).

52 UNHCR UPR Submission (n 50).

53 B Adams, 'Korea Needs to Open Its Doors', JoongAng Daily, 22 August 2007 http://koreajoongangdaily.joinsmsn.com/news/article/article.aspx?aid=2879496 accessed 30 April 2013; B H Cho, 'Refugee Protection in Korean Judiciary' (International Association of Refugee Law Judges 9th World Conference, Bled, 8 September 2011) http://www.iarlj.org/general/images/stories/BLED_conference/papers/08._Cho_-Bled_2011.pdf accessed 30 April 2013.

54 Cho, 'Refugee Protection in Korean Judiciary'.

55 H Lee, 'Practices in Korea'. For numbers as of February 2012, see C Kim 'A Step Forward to Refugee Protection?' See also 'Asylum Seekers Expected to Hit Record Number', JoongAng Daily (17 August 2011) http://koreajoongangdaily.joinsmsn.com/news/article/article.aspx?aid=2940321 accessed 30 April 2013.

56 Adams, 'Korea Needs to Open Its Doors'.

57 International Covenant on Economic, Social and Cultural Rights (adopted 16 December 1966, entered into force 3 January 1976) 993 UNTS 3 (ICESCR).

body that considers appeals of negative decisions in first instance claims.[58] It also questioned whether immigration officials should be considering refugee claims since their 'main duty … is to regulate undocumented immigrants' and they may therefore 'have the general perception that non-Koreans with expired visas are abusing the refugee determination system to extend their stay'.[59] The National Human Rights Commission also identified the need to increase capacity, including the number of officers involved in RSD, in order to remedy long procedural delays.[60]

In its concluding comments on South Korea's State report in 2009, the CESCR noted many of these issues.[61] It expressed 'concern about the difficulties faced by applicants for refugee and asylum status because of the long waiting periods while their applications are processed'. It added that it remained 'concerned about the extremely low rate of recognition of refugees and asylum-seekers by the State party, and by the still lengthy status recognition process'.[62] It recommended 'that the State party make more efforts to shorten waiting periods for the recognition of refugee and asylum-seeker status' through various means including '(a) Providing adequate resources for the implementation of the revised [ICA] and relevant enforcement decree, including by increasing the number of immigration officers; (b) Standardizing asylum procedures; [and] (c) Systematically collecting data on refugees and asylum-seekers'.[63] It also asked the Korean authorities to 'include information on the measures taken in this regard, including statistics on the granting of refugee and asylum status, in its next periodic report'.[64]

These advocacy efforts by lawyers, local NGOs, members of the Asia Pacific Refugee Rights Network (APRRN)[65] the National Human Rights Commission, UN human rights bodies and the UNHCR office in Korea have played an important role in achieving legal reforms. Cho notes that 'strong demands for more generous acceptance of refugees', reflected in critical reports by the Korean media about the

58 'NGOs' Alternative Report to the UN Committee on Economic, Social and Cultural Rights on the Third Periodic Report submitted by the Republic of Korea Under Arts 16 &17 of the International Covenant on Economic, Social, and Cultural Rights' (September 2009) 15–17.

59 Ibid 17.

60 'Submission by National Human Rights Commission of the Republic of Korea to the forty third session of the Committee on the Economic, Social and Cultural Rights in connection with the consideration of the third periodic report of the Republic of Korea' (1 October 2009) 28.

61 UN Committee on Economic Social and Cultural Rights, 'Concluding Observations: Republic of Korea' (17 December 2009) UN Doc E/C.12/KOR/CO/3, para 10.

62 Ibid.

63 Ibid.

64 Ibid.

65 According to the APRRN website, the network 'is an open and growing network of over 140 members, consisting of civil society organisations and individuals committed to advancing the rights of refugees in the Asia Pacific Region'. See http://www.aprrn.info/1/ accessed 30 April 2013.

low refugee recognition rate, have driven the legislative process.[66] The reforms include amendments to the ICA in 2010 and, most significantly, the enactment of the Refugee Act on 29 December 2011 (scheduled to come into effect on 1 July 2013).[67] The changes in 2010 centralized the RSD procedures at the Seoul Immigration Office therefore facilitating further specialization and development of expertise among first instance decision-makers.[68] In 2010, the government also guaranteed, by presidential decree, access to free primary and secondary education for all children in Korea, regardless of status.

The new independent Refugee Act builds on these advances, setting out a more comprehensive legal framework for the protection of refugees, including safeguards to support fairer asylum procedures as well as better reception conditions.[69] Some have commented that the introduction of an independent refugee law that is distinct from immigration legislation is a significant, positive development with broader regional implications.[70]

The Act improves on the previous system in a number of ways. It provides access to: information about determination procedures at entry points such as airports, a right to legal assistance, interpretation services and records of interviews.[71] It also allows the claimant to be interviewed by an officer of the same gender, to request video and audio recording of the interview, to invite a trusted person to accompany him or her when attending the interview and to review and duplicate the interview records.[72] It also permits asylum applicants to remain in Korea while waiting for the outcome of their appeals of a negative decision after the second level administrative process. It allows humanitarian status-holders to work and reduces the time that asylum seekers must wait for permission to find employment from one year to six months.[73]

Although generally welcomed as a positive development toward more comprehensive refugee protection and fuller implementation of South Korea's duties under the Refugee Convention, some have criticized certain features of

---

66 Cho, 'Refugee Protection in Korean Judiciary'.

67 See 'Refugee Act in Korea Passed', on *Asia Pacific Refugee Rights Network* (16 January 2012) http://refugeerightsasiapacific.org/2012/01/16/refugee-act-in-korea-passed/; UNHCR UPR Submission (n 50) 2; C Kim, 'A Step Forward to Refugee Protection?'.

68 UNHCR UPR Submission (n 50).

69 Ibid.

70 J-C Kim, 'Enactment of Refugee Law and extended suggestions on its unsolved issues' (Advocates for Public Interest Law, translated by S-E Lee, 13 June 2012 http://www.apil.or.kr/1122 accessed 30 April 2013. Kim observes that this is the first autonomous refugee law enacted at the national level in East Asia. UNHCR UPR Submission (n 50).

71 UNHCR UPR Submission (n 50); J-C Kim, 'Enactment of Refugee Law and extended suggestions on its unsolved issues'; C Kim, 'A Step Forward to Refugee Protection?'.

72 Ibid.

73 UNHCR UPR Submission (n 50).

the new law.[74] In particular, the Act allows for a simplified, 'fast-track' procedure under certain circumstances. For example, some procedural steps may be skipped if an asylum seeker attempts to conceal facts or produces false documents.[75] Kim observes, however, that this provision does not account for circumstances when a claimant's memory may be affected due to past trauma or when he/she feels the need to conceal information for reasons of personal safety.[76] Other problems with the new Act and the relevant Draft Presidential Decree identified by NGOs relate to the procedures established to consider refugee applications at ports of entry; risks associated with the operation of a new refugee reception centre; procedures for local integration; rights of humanitarian status-holders; qualification of interpreters; and social support and work permits for refugees and asylum seekers.[77]

North Koreans seeking asylum in South Korea are treated differently than those arriving from other countries since they are not technically 'refugees' but are essentially citizens under the South Korean constitution.[78] Although they receive financial assistance, healthcare and professional training, some still experience economic and social difficulties. Many live on an income that is below average and language barriers created by differences in dialects often impede successful integration.[79]

China

China acceded to the Refugee Convention and Protocol on 24 September 1982.[80] While the status of international treaties in the Chinese legal system is not entirely clear, domestic incorporation is apparently necessary to give effect to China's

74 UNHCR UPR Submission (n 50); UNHCR (2009) (n 48); J-C Kim, 'Enactment of Refugee Law and extended suggestions on its unsolved issues'; C Kim, 'A Step Forward to Refugee Protection?'.

75 J-C Kim, 'Enactment of Refugee Law and extended suggestions on its unsolved issues'; C Kim, 'A Step Forward to Refugee Protection?'.

76 J-C Kim, 'Enactment of Refugee Law and extended suggestions on its unsolved issues'.

77 Email from Dongcheon Foundation, 'Korea's public hearing on the draft enforcement ordinance for the Refuge Act' to APRRN List (25 March 2013).

78 E Chan and A Schloenhardt, 'North Korean Refugees and International Refugee Law' (2007) 19 IJRL 215, 233. See also A Wolman, 'North Korean Asylum Seekers and Dual Nationality' (2013) 24 IJRL 793.

79 J-U Kim and D-J Jang, 'Aliens among Brothers? The Status and Perception of North Korean Refugees in South Korea' (2007) 31 Asian Perspective 5.

80 China acceded with reservations to portions of Arts 14 and 16(3) of the Refugee Convention (on the standard of treatment in relation to artistic rights and industrial property as well as access to the courts) and Art 4 of the Protocol (related to settlement of disputes before the International Court of Justice).

international obligations in practice.[81] In contrast to Japan and South Korea, however, China has yet to absorb these standards into domestic law and does not administer a RSD system, although it allows the UNHCR office in Beijing to consider some refugee claims. China has at times tolerated the presence of large numbers of refugees, including approximately 300,000 ethnically Chinese Vietnamese who arrived between 1978 and 1982 and who are now largely integrated into Chinese society, although discussion continues on how best to finalize their status.[82]

China has also taken tentative steps towards legislative reform to incorporate refugee protection norms although currently only a small number of legal provisions mention asylum seekers or refugees. These are brief and drafted in vague, permissive language; they do not create strong duties on the State to offer protection even from *refoulement*, and as such do not provide a solid basis for developing a more comprehensive domestic legal framework. For example, Article 32 of the Chinese Constitution provides that 'the [PRC] *may* grant asylum to foreigners who request it for political reasons'.[83] Article 15 of the 1985 Law of the PRC on the Control of the Exit and Entry of Foreigners similarly provides that 'Aliens who seek asylum for political reasons shall be permitted to reside in China upon approval by the competent authorities of the Chinese Government'.[84] A new Exit-Entry Administration Law promulgated on 30 June 2012 will replace the 1985 law on 1 July 2013. Article 46 of the new law will allow applicants for refugee status to remain in China during the RSD process with temporary identity cards issued by the public security organs. If granted refugee status, individuals may stay and reside in China and obtain a refugee identification certificate.[85] At the time of writing, it was unclear how this provision would be further elaborated and implemented although UNHCR and the Chinese authorities have engaged in ongoing discussions about legislation. In its report submitted to the Committee on Economic, Social and Cultural Rights in 2010, China noted that it has 'maintained good cooperative relations with UNHCR' and:

> In recent years, China and the UNHCR Representative in China have jointly launched a series of cooperative projects. Each year from 2005 to 2009,

---

81 See, for example, X Hanqin and J Qian, 'International Treaties in the Chinese Domestic Legal System' (2009) 8 CJIL 299.

82 UNHCR Regional Representation for China and Mongolia, 'Factsheet' (September 2012).

83 Constitution of the People's Republic of China (4 December 1982) http://english.people.com.cn/constitution/constitution.html accessed 30 April 2013 (emphasis added).

84 http://www.npc.gov.cn/englishnpc/Law/2007-12/13/content_1383957.htm accessed 30 April 2013.

85 Exit-Entry Administration Law of the People's Republic of China (30 June 2012), unofficial translation by Gary Chodorow: http://lawandborder.com/wp-content/uploads/2012/07/Exit-Entry-Administration-Law-2012-07-05.pdf viewed 30 April 2013.

> training workshops and seminars have been jointly organized, covering such issues as emergency aid in refugee crises, refugee legislation, and refugee screening procedures. China will continue to support international protection work for refugees, and is willing to enhance its cooperation with UNHCR and its representatives.[86]

Francis identified other 'signs of change' in domestic discussions on refugee issues such as increased interest in and awareness of international refugee law among Chinese scholars.[87] Some Chinese commentators have even called for enactment of domestic refugee legislation.[88]

Despite these developments, the ongoing efforts by the UNHCR, and the real possibility that the State will gradually introduce more detailed measures and take greater responsibility for refugee protection, political and diplomatic priorities often prevail over respect for international protection norms.

For example, the Chinese authorities have refused protection to certain groups of refugees arriving from particular countries and denied them access to the UNHCR apparently for political reasons. For example, China refuses to allow North Korean asylum seekers to remain in China pending determination of their status, forcibly removing them despite strong evidence of likely persecution upon return.[89] China has justified this practice by categorically denying they are refugees

86 'Implementation of the International Covenant on Economic, Social and Cultural Rights Second periodic reports submitted by States Parties under articles 16 and 17 of the Covenant, China' (6 July 2012) Un Doc E/C.12/CHN/2, p. 10.

87 A Francis, 'China's Refugee Policy: Pathways to Reform' (2011) 17 Australian Journal of Human Rights 29, 30. Song Lili speculates that 'although the refugee issue remains a sensitive one for the Chinese government, it is not taboo … If China becomes more confident in maintaining its domestic stability, it is conceivable that China will adopt a less conservative refugee policy'. S Lili, 'Who are Refugees in China? The Refugee Definition in a Chinese Context' (The Australian and New Zealand Society of International Law & the Asian Society of International Law Joint Conference on International Law and Justice, Sydney, Australia, 25–26 October 2012) (on file with the author).

88 G Kaipeng, 'The Lack of a Legal System of Refugee Protection and its Establishment in China' (2010) 28(1) Science Economy Society [Kexue, Kingji, Shehui] 151, as cited in ibid (both Francis and Song).

89 See, for example, Chan and Schloenhardt, 'North Korean Refugees and International Refugee Law', T. Kumar (International Advocacy Director, Amnesty International), 'China's Repatriation of North Korean Refugees Before the Congressional-Executive Commission on China' (5 March 2012) http://www.amnestyusa.org/news/news-item/china-s-repatriation-of-north-korean-refugees accessed 30 April 2013; Human Rights Watch, 'The International Coalition to Stop Crimes Against Humanity in North Korea Condemns China's Expulsion of North Korean Refugees (14 March 2012); P Robertson, 'The Problem of North Korean Refugees in China and Possible Solutions' 2nd KINU Chaillot Human Rights Forum 2012 on International Cooperation to Improve North Korean Human Rights Conditions under the Kim Jong-Un Regime, Seoul (Human Rights Watch,

and labelling them 'economic migrants'.[90] Some have suggested that China's desire to maintain its complex relationship with North Korea has influenced this position. Human Rights Watch has reported that Chinese authorities have also forcibly returned large numbers of Kachin asylum seekers who have fled fighting in Myanmar between the Burmese army and the Kachin Independence Army since June 2011.[91] State policies that deem entire categories of persons arriving from particular countries unworthy of protection and refuse them access to fair status determination procedures prior to deportation clearly fail to comply with the Refugee Convention's obligations to respect the principle of *non-refoulement*.[92]

China has also pressured other States to return Chinese asylum seekers in exchange for economic aid, a sign of China's growing influence in the region. For example in 2009 Cambodia deported 20 Uighur asylum seekers back to China, despite protests by the UN and a number of States.[93] Hours later, the Chinese vice-president arrived in the Cambodian capital, thanked the Cambodian government for returning the Uighurs and announced that China would provide Cambodia with a substantial amount of development aid.[94]

The UN human rights treaty bodies have raised these issues when considering China's periodic reports and called on the Chinese government to address its lack of compliance with international human rights and refugee protection standards. For example, in 2005 the Committee on Economic, Social and Cultural Rights expressed concern 'that non-citizens, including asylum-seekers, refugees and stateless persons, are excluded from the constitutional guarantees to the enjoyment of rights and freedoms enshrined in the Covenant extended to all citizens in the State party'.[95] It noted 'that some asylum-seekers are excluded by the refugee

19 July 2012) http://www.hrw.org/news/2012/07/19/problem-north-korean-refugees-china-and-possible-solutions accessed 30 April 2013.

90 See Human Rights Council, 'Report of the Working Group on Universal Periodic Review: China' (5 October 2009) UN Doc A/HRC/11/25, para 112 http://daccess-dds-ny.un.org/doc/UNDOC/GEN/G09/162/99/PDF/G0916299.pdf?OpenElement accessed 30 April 2013.

91 Human Rights Watch, 'China: Stop Expelling Refugees, Forced Return of Kachin Violates International Law' (6 September 2012) http://www.hrw.org/news/2012/09/06/china-stop-expelling-refugees accessed 30 April 2013.

92 JC Hathaway, *The Rights of Refugees in International Law* (Cambridge University Press, 2005) 284–5.

93 Human Rights Watch, 'China: Forcibly Returned Uighur Asylum Seekers at Risk, Cambodian Government Makes a Mockery of Its Refugee Commitments' (22 December 2009). www.hrw.org/news/2009/12/22/china-forcibly-returned-uighur-asylum-seekers-risk accessed 30 April 2013.

94 Ibid.

95 UN Committee on Economic, Social and Cultural Rights, 'Consideration of Reports Submitted by States Parties under Arts 16 and 17 of the Covenant, Concluding Observations, People's Republic of China (including Hong Kong and Macao)' (13 May 2005) UN Doc E/C.12/1/Add.107 (2005) para 14.

determination procedure of the State party, in particular those coming from [North] Korea, who are regarded by the State party as economic migrants and are thus compelled to return to their countries'.[96] They also suggested that China adopt 'subsidiary forms of protection to guarantee the right to remain for persons who are not formally recognized as refugees but are seeking asylum and nevertheless require protection during that period' and allow UNHCR and humanitarian organizations access to them.[97]

In 2009, the Committee on the Elimination of Racial Discrimination reiterated 'that asylum-seekers from [North] Korea continue to be systematically refused asylum and forcibly returned'.[98] It recommended that China 'adopt legislation relating to refugee status as soon as possible' and 'take all necessary legal and policy measures to ensure that all asylum-seekers have the merits of their individual cases considered by an independent and impartial authority'.[99] In 2006, the Committee on the Elimination of Discrimination Against Women commented on China's 'lack of laws or regulations for the protection of women refugees and asylum-seekers' and expressed particular concern 'at the situation of North Korean women, whose status remains precarious and who are particularly vulnerable to being or becoming victims of abuse, trafficking, forced marriage and virtual slavery'.[100]

The Central government's approach toward refugee protection differs substantially from the policies adopted in its special administrative regions (SARs) of Macau and Hong Kong which both enjoy a high degree of autonomy in a number of areas.[101] The constitutional documents of both SARs grant the regional governments the power to 'apply immigration controls on entry into, stay in and departure from the Region by persons from foreign States or regions'.[102] The positions in Macau and Hong Kong, however, also diverge. China extended the Refugee Convention to Macau, continuing Portugal's previous position before China resumed sovereignty in 1999. Macau has adopted refugee regulations and

96 Ibid.

97 Ibid. para 45.

98 UN Committee on the Elimination of Racial Discrimination, 'Consideration of Reports Submitted by States Parties under Art 9 of the Convention, Concluding Observations, China (including Hong Kong and Macau Special Administrative Regions) (15 September 2009) UN Doc CERD/C/CHN/CO/10-13, para 16.

99 Ibid.

100 UN Committee on the Elimination of Discrimination Against Women, 'Concluding Comments, China' (25 August 2006) UN Doc CEDAW/C/CHN/CO/6, para 33.

101 Art 2 of the Basic Laws of both the Hong Kong and Macau Special Administrative Regions, authorize the regional governments 'to exercise a high degree of autonomy and enjoy executive, legislative and independent judicial power, including that of final adjudication'.

102 The Basic Law of the Hong Kong Special Administrative Region Art 154 and the Basic Law of the Macau Special Administrative Region Art 139.

administers a RSD system. As mentioned above, China has not extended the Refugee Convention or Protocol to Hong Kong and the regional government does not acknowledge international protection obligations toward refugees. Hong Kong has allowed the UNHCR to maintain a presence in the territory and the agency has conducted RSD and arranged for resettlement of recognized refugees in third countries. This arrangement is expected to change, however, when the Hong Kong authorities introduce a new government-administered Unified Screening Mechanism, possibly by the end of 2013, that will include consideration of refugee claims.[103]

International Human Rights Law and the Hong Kong Example

As discussed above, a number of protection gaps remain even in States with the most developed refugee protection regimes in the East Asian region. In States that exhibit weaker judicial institutions and rule of law, such as China,[104] protection measures remain underdeveloped and political and foreign policy considerations may hold greater sway than international or domestic legal norms over decisions about the fate of refugees. In these States, the Refugee Convention and other international human rights treaties have served as less of a constraint on State action. For example, China's treatment of North Korean asylum seekers fails to ensure the procedural standards necessary to avoid violation of the principle of *non-refoulement*.

Even in States that are widely regarded as having democratic institutions, independent judiciaries and respect for the rule of law, such as Japan and South Korea,[105] protection issues remain; for example the exceedingly low refugee recognition rates in both countries raise a number of concerns about procedural fairness and how substantive provisions of the Refugee Convention, such as the refugee definition, have been interpreted in practice.

In other words, the Refugee Convention is not a panacea. Despite the gaps and remaining issues, however, the Asian States Parties considered in this chapter have all taken some steps – albeit to varying degrees – to at least partially implement their obligations under the Refugee Convention and Protocol. Government acknowledgement of State responsibility for refugee protection, evidenced by accession, is significant and generally serves as the starting point for the development of further protection measures. It also provides the framework from

103 Security Bureau, Hong Kong SAR Government, 'Panel on Security of the Legislative Council, Screening of *Non-refoulement* Claims' (June 2013).

104 See the rankings in MD Agrast, JC Botero, J Martinez, A Ponce and CS Pratt, 'World Justice Project, Rule of Law Index 2012–2013' (The World Justice Project, 2012–2013) 73, 77 http://worldjusticeproject.org/sites/default/files/WJP_Index_Report_2012.pdf accessed 30 April 2013.

105 Agrast et al., 'World Justice Project, Rule of Law Index 2012–2013' 103, 130.

which civil society, UNHCR and others can advocate for strengthened protection. This recognition of State responsibility toward refugees is an important factor that distinguishes the State and non-State Parties within the region.

Asian States that have not acceded to the Refugee Convention are all nevertheless bound by other international and domestic human rights provisions that apply generally and therefore require respect for the human rights of refugees (along with everyone else) regardless of citizenship or immigration status. As such these States are not devoid of responsibility and must ensure all refugees access to the economic, social, cultural, civil and political rights set out in the relevant human rights instruments. The human rights treaties also prohibit *refoulement*. Article 3 of the CAT prohibits *refoulement* to torture and Articles 6 and 7 of the International Covenant on Civil and Political Rights (ICCPR)[106] imply protection from removal due to a threat to life or cruel, inhuman or degrading treatment or punishment.[107] The Human Rights Committee has confirmed that State Parties must not 'extradite, deport, expel or otherwise remove a person from their territory, where there are substantial grounds for believing that there is a real risk of irreparable harm, such as that contemplated by articles 6 and 7 of the Covenant, either in the country to which removal is to be effected or in any country to which the person may subsequently be removed'.[108]

These general human rights norms, however, may have limited impact on refugee protection in practice. While international human rights law complements, enhances and supplements the refugee instruments, refugee-specific norms can address concerns of particular relevance to the refugee experience,[109] providing a more solid basis from which to advocate for reform. The *non-refoulement* provisions in the human rights instruments also fail to specify a legal status for protection claimants.

In order to further explore and highlight the relevance of the Refugee Convention within the Asian context and its impact on State Parties' approaches toward protection, it is useful to compare their experience to that of other Asian States that are not bound by the Convention. The following discussion contrasts the State practice discussed in the second part above with recent developments in Hong Kong, a jurisdiction not bound by the Refugee Convention but where

106 International Covenant on Civil and Political Rights (adopted 16 December 1966, entered into force 23 March 1976) 999 UNTS 171 (ICCPR).

107 UN Human Rights Committee, 'General Comment No 20 concerning prohibition of torture and cruel treatment or punishment (Art. 7)' (1992) para 9.

108 UN Human Rights Committee, 'General Comment 31' para 12.

109 For example, Art 31 of the Refugee Convention prohibits State Parties from imposing 'penalties, on account of their illegal entry or presence, on refugees who, coming directly from a territory where their life or freedom was threatened in the sense of article 1 [the refugee definition], enter or are present in their territory without authorization, provided they present themselves without delay to the authorities and show good cause for their illegal entry or presence'.

advocates have relied upon human rights standards to achieve greater protection for refugees. As discussed above, China is party to the Refugee Convention and Protocol and has applied these instruments to Macau but not Hong Kong. Municipal law, policy and practice related to *non-refoulement* and other elements of refugee protection falls squarely within the remit of Hong Kong's autonomy and does not require Central Chinese government involvement.

Hong Kong arguably serves as a 'best-case' scenario among Asian jurisdictions not bound by the Refugee Convention and therefore provides a particularly useful point of comparison. There is general respect for the rule of law and separation of powers.[110] Seven of the core international human rights treaties apply to Hong Kong and the courts have been willing to draw on international materials for guidance when interpreting local statutes.[111] The ICCPR and the ICESCR have been implemented through domestic laws and attained constitutional status.

In Hong Kong, advocates have effectively leveraged international human rights standards, constitutional guarantees and common law principles to secure significant advances for the protection of refugees.[112] These include a government-administered screening mechanism that considers *non-refoulement* claims under Article 3 of the CAT which prohibits States from sending individuals back to another State where there are substantial grounds for believing the person would be subjected to torture. In 2004, the Hong Kong Court of Final Appeal (CFA) considered whether Hong Kong could rely on the UNHCR's largely unexplained decisions in refugee claims when implementing its policy of *non-refoulement* under Article 3 of the CAT. Although the government did not accept that it had domestic legal obligations to respect Article 3, the authorities had reported to the UN Committee Against Torture in 1999 that, as a matter of policy, 'Should potential removees or deportees claim that they would be subjected to torture

---

110 See Agrast et al., 'World Justice Project, Rule of Law Index 2012–2013' 96.

111 CJ Petersen, 'Embracing Universal Standards? The Role of International Human Rights Treaties in Constitutional Jurisprudence' in HL Fu, Lison Harris and Simon NM Young (eds), *Interpreting Hong Kong's Basic Law: the Struggle for Coherence* (Palgrave Macmillan, 2007) 33; A Mason, 'The Place of Comparative Law in Developing the Jurisprudence on the Rule of Law and Human Rights in Hong Kong' (2007) 37 HKLJ 299; JMM Chan, 'Basic Law and Constitutional Review: The First Decade' (2007) 37 HKLJ 407, and 'Hong Kong's Bill of Rights: Its Reception of and Contribution to International and Comparative Jurisprudence' (1998) 47 ICLQ 306.

112 For further discussion of these developments in Hong Kong see: Loper (n 9); K Loper, 'Prospects for Refugee Rights in Hong Kong: Towards the Legalization and Expansion of Protection from *Refoulement*' in A Francis and Rowena Maguire (eds), *Protection of Refugees and Displaced Persons in the Asia Pacific Region* (Ashgate, 2013) 75–93; K Loper, 'Toward Comprehensive Refugee Legislation in Hong Kong? Reflections on Reform of the "Torture Screening" Procedures' (2009) 39 HKLJ 253; CS Kochhar-George, 'Recent Developments in Hong Kong's Torture Screening Process' (2012) 42 HKLJ 385; and O Jones, 'Customary *Non-refoulement* of Refugees and Automatic Incorporation into the Common Law: A Hong Kong Perspective' (2009) 58 ICLQ 443.

in the country to which they are to be returned, the claim would be carefully assessed … Where such a claim was considered to be well founded, the subject's return would not be ordered'.[113] The CFA decided that it did not need to decide whether Article 3 created binding duties as a matter of domestic law. Instead it held that because the Director of Immigration had a *policy* to respect Article 3, and in light of the fundamental human rights at stake, the policy must be implemented in accordance with 'high standards of fairness'.[114] In December 2008, the Hong Kong Court of First Instance decided that the authorities had failed to adhere to the requirements of the 2004 CFA decision.[115] In response, the government revised the system, enhanced a number of procedures, established an appeal body and began providing publicly funded legal assistance for the claimants.

In December 2012, the CFA held that Hong Kong has duties as a matter of domestic law to comply with Article 7 of the ICCPR – which prohibits torture, cruel, inhuman or degrading treatment or punishment, referred to by the court as 'CIDTP' – when deciding whether to remove or deport a person under Hong Kong's immigration legislation. The court held that Article 7[116] articulated absolute and non-derogable rights and therefore a reservation to the ICCPR[117] (that essentially limits human rights challenges of immigration legislation by individuals who do not have the right to remain in Hong Kong) should not apply to 'CIDTP' *non-refoulement* claims. The court therefore concluded that 'a sufficiently established threat of [Bill of Rights] Article 3 [ICCPR Article 7] being violated by the receiving country if the deportee should be sent there constitutes a ground for restraining the Hong Kong Government from proceeding with the deportation'.[118]

In early 2013, the CFA considered another important challenge to Hong Kong's refugee policy. In this case, *C v Director of Immigration*,[119] the appellants argued that Hong Kong has duties under customary international law, incorporated into domestic law through the common law, to respect the principle of 'persecution *non-refoulement*'. As such, the government cannot rely on the UNHCR's RSD procedures – which suffer from a number of shortcomings and cannot be reviewed by Hong Kong courts – when deciding whether or not to allow individuals to remain pending determination of their claims. Although in its judgement the CFA declined to decide whether Hong Kong has a legal duty to respect persecution *non-refoulement* under international custom and the common law, it noted Hong Kong's *de facto* 'policy' of allowing asylum seekers and refugees to remain

---

113 China's Periodic Report to the UN Committee Against Torture, CAT/C/39/Add.2, para 122.

114 *Secretary for Security v Sakthevel Prabakar* [2005] 1 HKLRD 289.

115 *FB v Director of Immigration* [2008] HKEC 2072.

116 Incorporated by Art 3 of Section 8 of the Hong Kong Bill of Rights Ordinance (1991).

117 Incorporated by Section 11 of the Hong Kong Bill of Rights Ordinance (1991).

118 *Ubamaka Edward Wilson v Secretary for Security* [2012] HKEC 1757, para 160.

119 FACV No 18, 19 and 20 of 2011 (Court of Final Appeal, 25 March 2013).

pending UNHCR status determination and resettlement. The court reasoned that such a policy or practice must conform to the high standards of fairness required by its earlier *Prabakar* judgement. Tang PJ explained that:

> … given it is the practice of the Director [of Immigration], when deciding whether or not to exercise his power … to remove a refugee claimant to the country of putative persecution, to have regard to humanitarian considerations, and that whether such claim is well-founded, is a relevant humanitarian consideration, the Director must determine whether the claim is well-founded. Moreover, any such determination must satisfy the high standards of fairness required having regard to the gravity of the consequence of the determination.[120]

Anthony Mason NPJ, concurring, added:

> … the [Government] asserts publicly that, although not bound by the [Refugee] Convention, it nonetheless voluntarily complies with its requirements. Having adopted that policy in these circumstances, no doubt by reason of the powerful humanitarian considerations which are involved in RSD determinations and the consequences they may entail, the requirement of fairness, arising from the adoption by the Director [of Immigration] of a policy under the authority of the statute, calls for him to make an independent assessment of the UNHCR determination, especially in those cases where the UNHCR determination is adverse to the claimant. In making that assessment, the Director must observe high standards of fairness.[121]

In July 2013, the Hong Kong government announced that it would incorporate 'CIDTP' and 'persecution' *non-refoulement* into the existing government CAT screening mechanism and that it aimed to commence operation of the new 'Unified Screening Mechanism' by the end of 2013.[122] The Hong Kong example affirms the value of human rights standards as well as legal principles associated with procedural fairness and the rule of law, their applicability to refugees and their capacity to contribute to progress even in the absence of refugee-specific norms. However, this case study also demonstrates the limits of such an approach.

Obligations on the Hong Kong authorities under the CAT and the ICCPR are limited to respect for the principle of *non-refoulement* in relation to individuals who may face serious human rights violations if returned to their countries of origin. The courts thus far have not recognized other duties similar, or parallel, to those found in the Refugee Convention. Indeed, advocates have been less successful in their attempts to secure other rights beyond *non-refoulement* for refugees in Hong Kong by relying on international human rights instruments,

120 Ibid. para 56.
121 Ibid. para 98.
122 Security Bureau (n 103).

including the ICCPR and the ICESCR. For example, the courts have thus far rejected challenges to legislative provisions that do not allow recognized refugees or CAT claimants to engage in employment – whether paid or unpaid – in Hong Kong, although at the time of writing, the CFA had yet to hear the final appeal.[123] Another case challenging the requirement that a CAT claimant must be 'illegally' in Hong Kong before she or he can make a CAT claim has also failed before the courts.[124] Indeed, even successful CAT claimants cannot obtain any legal status in Hong Kong,[125] cannot work except under exceptional circumstances and are stuck in limbo presumably waiting for conditions in their countries of origin to improve. The numbers of successful torture claimants remains exceedingly low. Although thousands of claims have been determined since the enhanced CAT screening began in December 2009, only four claimants had been successful as of April 2013.

In this environment, advocates have recognized that despite important achievements, improvements in refugee protection in Hong Kong may stall without access to the more comprehensive set of norms in the Refugee Convention and Protocol. Indeed, civil society organizations continue to advocate for extension of the Convention to Hong Kong as part of a broader strategy to secure better refugee protection measures. In addition, the UN human rights treaty bodies have maintained their criticism of Hong Kong's resistance to the application of the Refugee Convention and reinforced the relevance and importance of the Convention in conjunction with better implementation of general human rights standards.[126]

Conclusion

This chapter illustrates that in Asia – as in other regions – a number of factors contribute to the process of domestic internalization of refugee protection norms. State Parties to the Refugee Convention and Protocol have adopted a variety of approaches toward their duties, ranging from minimal measures to more robust law reform. Despite important progress in all of these States, none have embraced their obligations with enthusiasm or without the influence of internal and external pressure. The tension inherent in the concept of international refugee protection

123 *MA v Director of Immigration* [2012] HKCU 2413 (Court of Appeal).

124 *CH v Director of Immigration* [2011] HKCU 758.

125 Hong Kong Immigration (Amendment) Ordinance 2012.

126 The Human Rights Committee commented in its Concluding Observations on Hong Kong's report in March 2013 that it 'regrets that Hong Kong, China maintains a position not to seek the extension of the 1951 United Nations Convention relating to the Status of Refugees and its 1967 Protocol'. UN Human Rights Committee, Concluding observations on the third periodic report of Hong Kong, China (advanced unedited version March 2013), para 9.

and the sovereign rights of States to control their borders is evident in the often halting progress toward more fully developed asylum systems. The Refugee Convention is an important starting point but mere accession does not guarantee effective protection especially in light of potentially competing considerations, such as political, foreign policy and economic priorities.

Despite these observations about the economic and political realities of State responses to refugees, the diversity of the contexts considered and the continuing existence of significant protection gaps, accession to the Refugee Convention and Protocol has generally had a positive impact on States' policies toward refugees in East Asia. While these systems remain insufficient in several respects, the Refugee Convention has provided a key advocacy platform that has garnered momentum for reform in favour of State responsibility for refugee protection.

Indeed, a number of actors – such as civil society organizations, refugee claimants, lawyers, governments, the UNHCR and UN human rights treaty-monitoring bodies – have helped shape the discourse about what these norms require. These discussions have been translated into context-specific legal and policy responses at the national level. Other factors, such as those related to economic development, foreign policy and the nature of the political and legal systems of particular States, may facilitate or constrain the process. The manner in which these multiple influences combine, intersect and interact, as well as the eventual outcomes, may vary significantly from State to State. The conversation, however, begins with reference to the legal norms and thus underscores the critical value of the international standards.

References

Adams B, 'Korea Needs to Open Its Doors', *JoongAng Daily*, 22 August 2007 http://koreajoongangdaily.joinsmsn.com/news/article/article.aspx?aid=2879496 accessed 30 April 2013.

Agrast MD, Botero JC, Martinez J, Ponce A and Pratt CS, 'World Justice Project, Rule of Law Index 2012-2013' (The World Justice Project, 2012–13), http://worldjusticeproject.org/sites/default/files/WJP_Index_Report_2012.pdf accessed 30 April 2013.

Arakaki O, *Refugee Law and Practice in Japan* (Ashgate 2008).

Asia Pacific Refugee Rights Network, 'Japan to Resettle Myanmar Refugees' (3 February 2010) http://www.aprrn.info/1/index.php/2-uncategorised/54-japan-to-resettle-myanmar-refugees accessed 30 April 2013.

Asia Pacific Refugee Rights Network, 'Refugee Act in Korea Passed' (16 January 2012) http://refugeerightsasiapacific.org/2012/01/16/refugee-act-in-korea-passed/ accessed 30 April 2013.

'Asylum Seekers Expected to Hit Record Number' (*JoongAng Daily*, 17 August 2011) http://koreajoongangdaily.joinsmsn.com/news/article/article.aspx?aid=2940321 accessed 30 April 2013.

Barbour B, 'Japan Announces that 0 Refugees will be Resettled this Year' Fahamu Refugee Legal Aid Newsletter (December 2012) http://frlan.tumblr.com/post/36945934059/japan-announces-that-0-refugees-will-be-resettled accessed 25 October 2013.

The Basic Law of the Hong Kong Special Administrative Region.

The Basic Law of the Macau Special Administrative Region.

Chan E and Schloenhardt A, 'North Korean Refugees and International Refugee Law' (2007) 19 IJRL 215.

Chan JMM, 'Basic Law and Constitutional Review: The First Decade' (2007) 37 HKLJ 407, and 'Hong Kong's Bill of Rights: Its Reception of and Contribution to International and Comparative Jurisprudence' (1998) 47 ICLQ 306.

'China's second periodic report to the Committee on Economic, Social and Cultural Rights' (6 July 2012) UN Doc E/C.12/CHN/2.

'China's third periodic report to the UN Committee Against Torture' (5 January 2000) CAT/C/39/Add.2.

Cho BH, 'Refugee Protection in Korean Judiciary' (International Association of Refugee Law Judges 9th World Conference, Bled, 8 September 2011) http://www.iarlj.org/general/images/stories/BLED_conference/papers/08._Cho_-Bled_2011.pdf accessed 30 April 2013.

Constitution of the People's Republic of China (4 December 1982) http://english.people.com.cn/constitution/constitution.html accessed 30 April 2013.

Convention relating to the Status of Refugees (adopted 28 July 1951, entered into force 22 April 1954) 189 UNTS 137.

Davies S, 'The Asian Rejection?: International Refugee Law in Asia' (2006) 52(4) Australian Journal of Politics and History 562.

Dean M and Nagashima M, 'Sharing the Burden: The Role of Government and Ngos in Protecting and Providing for Asylum Seekers and Refugees in Japan' (2007) 20(3) Journal of Refugee Studies 481.

Dongcheon Foundation, 'Korea's public hearing on the draft enforcement ordinance for the Refugee Act', email to Asia Pacific Refugee Rights Network list (25 March 2013).

Exit-Entry Administration Law of the People's Republic of China (30 June 2012), unofficial translation by Chodorow G, http://lawandborder.com/wp-content/uploads/2012/07/Exit-Entry-Administration-Law-2012-07-05.pdf accessed 30 April 2013.

Fourth Asia-Pacific Consultation on Refugee Rights in Seoul, Korea (Asia Pacific Refugee Rights Network 22–24 August 2012).

Francis A, 'China's Refugee Policy: Pathways to Reform' (2011) 17 Australian Journal of Human Rights 29.

Gan K, 'The Lack of a Legal System of Refugee Protection and its Establishment in China' (2010) 28(1) Science Economy Society [Kexue, Kingji, Shehui] 151.

Hathaway JC, *The Rights of Refugees in International Law* (Cambridge University Press, 2005).

Hong Kong Bill of Rights Ordinance (1991).

Hong Kong Immigration (Amendment) Ordinance 2012.

Human Rights Watch, 'China: Forcibly Returned Uighur Asylum Seekers at Risk, Cambodian Government Makes a Mockery of Its Refugee Commitments' (22 December 2009) www.hrw.org/news/2009/12/22/china-forcibly-returned-uighur-asylum-seekers-risk accessed 30 April 2013.

Human Rights Watch, 'The International Coalition to Stop Crimes Against Humanity in North Korea Condemns China's Expulsion of North Korean Refugees' (14 March 2012).

Human Rights Watch, 'China: Stop Expelling Refugees, Forced Return of Kachin Violates International Law' (6 September 2012) http://www.hrw.org/news/2012/09/06/china-stop-expelling-refugees accessed 30 April 2013.

Human Rights Watch, 'World Report 2012: China' http://www.hrw.org/world-report-2012/world-report-2012-china accessed 30 April 2013.

Hwang P (Korean Public Interest Lawyers Group, GONGGAM), 'Review of Refugee Law in Taiwan and South Korea' (Asia Pacific Refugee Rights Network, East Asia Symposium: Legislation and the Developing Asylum Policy in East Asia, Taipei, Taiwan, October 2012).

Immigration Control and Refugee Recognition Act (Cabinet Order No 319 of 4 October 1951) (Japan Immigration Bureau, provisional and unofficial translation 2009) http://www.immi-moj.go.jp/english/newimmiact/pdf/RefugeeRecognitionAct02.pdf accessed 30 April 2013.

International Covenant on Civil and Political Rights (adopted 16 December 1966, entered into force 23 March 1976) 999 UNTS 171.

International Covenant on Economic, Social and Cultural Rights (adopted 16 December 1966, entered into force 3 January 1976) 993 UNTS 3.

Japan Federation of Bar Associations 'Written Information Submitted for the Summary of the Human Rights Situation in Japan to be Prepared by the United Nations Office of High Commissioner for Human Rights' (February 2008) http://lib.ohchr.org/HRBodies/UPR/Documents/Session2/JP/JFBA_JPN_UPR_S2_2008_JapanFederationofBarAssociations_uprsubmission.pdf accessed 25 October 2013.

Japan Lawyers Network for Refugees, 'Statement on Asylum Trends and Levels in 2012 in Japan' Fahamu Refugee Legal Aid Newsletter (June 2013) http://frlan.tumblr.com/post/51872023327/statement-on-asylum-trends-and-levels-in-2012-in-japan accessed 25 October 2013.

Japanese Ministry of Justice, www.moj.go.jp/nyuukokukanri/kouhou/nyuukokukanri03_00094.html accessed 30 April 2013 as reported by Brian Barbour, Director, External Relations Unity, Japan Association for Refugees by email to the Asia Pacific Refugee Rights Network (20 March 2013) (on file with the author).

Jones O, 'Customary *Non-refoulement* of Refugees and Automatic Incorporation into the Common Law: A Hong Kong Perspective' (2009) 58 ICLQ 443.

Kim C, 'A Step Forward to Refugee Protection? South Korea's New Refugee Act' (June 2012) 2 Oxford Monitor of Forced Migration 8.

Kim JC, 'Enactment of Refugee Law and extended suggestions on its unsolved issues', (Advocates for Public Interest Law, translated by Sung-Eun Lee, 13 June 2012) http://www.apil.or.kr/1122 accessed 30 April 2013.

Kim JU and Jang DJ, 'Aliens among Brothers? The Status and Perception of North Korean Refugees in South Korea' (2007) 31 Asian Perspective 5.

Knight S, 'Asylum Seekers Find Little Refuge in Japan', *Japan Today*, 26 July 2009 www.japantoday.com/category/lifestyle/view/asylum-seekers-find-little-refuge-in-japan accessed 30 April 2013.

Kumar T (International Advocacy Director, Amnesty International), 'China's Repatriation of North Korean Refugees Before the Congressional-Executive Commission on China' (5 March 2012) http://www.amnestyusa.org/news/news-item/china-s-repatriation-of-north-korean-refugees accessed 30 April 2013.

Law of the People's Republic of China on the Control of the Exit and Entry of Foreigners (1985) http://www.npc.gov.cn/englishnpc/Law/2007-12/13/content_1383957.htm accessed 30 April 2013.

Lee H (Refuge pNan), 'Practices in Korea' (Asia Pacific Refugee Rights Network, East Asia Symposium: Legislation and the Developing Asylum Policy in East Asia, Taipei, Taiwan, October 2012).

Loper K, 'Toward Comprehensive Refugee Legislation in Hong Kong? Reflections on Reform of the 'Torture Screening Procedures' (2009) 39 HKLJ 253.

Loper K, 'Human rights, *non-refoulement* and the protection of refugees in Hong Kong' (2010) 22(3) IJRL 404.

Loper K, 'Prospects for Refugee Rights in Hong Kong: Towards the Legalization and Expansion of Protection from *Refoulement*' in A Francis and R Maguire (eds), *Protection of Refugees and Displaced Persons in the Asia Pacific Region* (Ashgate, 2013).

McAdam J, 'The Refugee Convention as a rights blueprint for persons in need of international protection' (UNHCR, Policy Development and Evaluation Service, July 2006).

Mason A, 'The Place of Comparative Law in Developing the Jurisprudence on the Rule of Law and Human Rights in Hong Kong' (2007) 37 HKLJ 299.

Namba M and Sugimoto D (Japan Lawyers Network for Refugees), 'Development and Challenges of Lawyers Networks for Refugee Protection in Japan' (Asia Pacific Refugee Rights Network, East Asia Symposium: Legislation and the Developing Asylum Policy in East Asia, Taipei, Taiwan, October 2012).

National Human Rights Commission of the Republic of Korea, 'Submission to the forty third session of the Committee on the Economic, Social and Cultural Rights in connection with the consideration of the third periodic report of the Republic of Korea' (1 October 2009).

'NGOs' Alternative Report to the UN Committee on Economic, Social and Cultural Rights on the Third Periodic Report submitted by the Republic of Korea Under Article 16 and17 of the International Covenant on Economic, Social, and Cultural Rights' (September 2009).

Petersen CJ, 'Embracing Universal Standards? The Role of International Human Rights Treaties in Constitutional Jurisprudence' in HL Fu, L Harris and SNM Young (eds), *Interpreting Hong Kong's Basic Law: the Struggle for Coherence* (Palgrave Macmillan, 2007).

Protocol relating to the Status of Refugees (adopted 31 January 1967, entered into force 4 October 1967) 606 UNTS 267.

Robertson P, 'The Problem of North Korean Refugees in China and Possible Solutions' 2nd KINU Chaillot Human Rights Forum 2012 on International Cooperation to Improve North Korean Human Rights Conditions under the Kim -Un Regime, Seoul (Human Rights Watch, 19 July 2012) http://www.hrw.org/news/2012/07/19/problem-north-korean-refugees-china-and-possible-solutions accessed 30 April 2013.

Security Bureau, Hong Kong SAR Government, 'Panel on Security of the Legislative Council, Screening of *Non-refoulement* Claims' (June 2013) http://www.legco.gov.hk/yr12-13/english/panels/se/papers/se0702cb2-1465-1-e.pdf accessed 25 October 2013.

'Seeing refugees as regular members of Japanese society' (*The Mainichi* 1 December 2012) http://mainichi.jp/english/english/perspectives/news/20121201p2a00m0na002000c.html accessed 30 April 2013.

Singh Kochhar-George C, 'Recent Developments in Hong Kong's Torture Screening Process', (2012) 42 HKLJ 385.

Song L, 'Who are Refugees in China? The Refugee Definition in a Chinese Context' (The Australian and New Zealand Society of International Law & the Asian Society of International Law Joint Conference on International Law and Justice, Sydney, Australia, 25–26 October 2012).

UN Committee Against Torture, 'Concluding Observations on the Second Periodic Report of Japan' (28 June 2013) UN Doc CAT/C/JPN/CO/2.

UN Committee on Economic, Social and Cultural Rights, 'Consideration of Reports Submitted by States Parties under Articles 16 and 17 of the Covenant, Concluding Observations, People's Republic of China (including Hong Kong and Macao)' (13 May 2005) UN Doc E/C.12/1/Add.107 (2005).

UN Committee on Economic Social and Cultural Rights, 'Concluding Observations: Republic of Korea' (17 December 2009) UN Doc E/C.12/KOR/CO/3.

UN Committee on the Elimination of Discrimination Against Women, 'Concluding Comments, China' (25 August 2006) UN Doc. CEDAW/C/CHN/CO/6.

UN Committee on the Elimination of Racial Discrimination, 'Consideration of Reports Submitted by States Parties under Article 9 of the Convention, Concluding Observations, China (including Hong Kong and Macau Special Administrative Regions)' (15 September 2009) UN Doc CERD/C/CHN/CO/10-13.

UN Human Rights Committee, 'General Comment No. 20 concerning prohibition of torture and cruel treatment or punishment (Art 7)' (1992).

UN Human Rights Committee, 'General Comment 31: The Nature of the General Legal Obligation Imposed on States Parties to the Covenant' (2004) UN Doc CCPR/C/21/Rev.1/Add. 13.

UN Human Rights Committee, 'Concluding observations on the third periodic report of Hong Kong, China' (advanced unedited version March 2013).

UN Human Rights Council, 'Report of the Working Group on Universal Periodic Review: China' (5 October 2009) UN Doc A/HRC/11/25 para 112 http://daccess-dds-ny.un.org/doc/UNDOC/GEN/G09/162/99/PDF/G0916299.pdf?OpenElement accessed 30 April 2013.

UN Human Rights Council, 'Report of the Working Group on the Universal Periodic Review' (14 December 2012) UN Doc A/HRC/22/14 para 20; Japan Ministry of Justice, 'Changes to the Immigration Control Act' (2009) www.immi-moj.go.jp/english/newimmiact/newimmiact_english.html accessed 30 April 2013.

UNHCR, 'Global Appeal 2012–13: Asia and the Pacific, Regional Summary' http://www.unhcr.org/4ec230f20.html accessed 30 April 2013.

UNHCR, Global Consultations on International Protection/Third Track: Asylum Processes (Fair and Efficient Asylum Procedures), 31 May 2001, UN Doc EC/GC/01/12 http://www.refworld.org/docid/3b36f2fca.html accessed 30 April 2013.

UNHCR, 'UNHCR's Comments on the 2009 Draft Bill on Refugee Status Determination and Treatment of Refugees and Others' (2009).

UNHCR, 'Global Report 2011: East Asia and the Pacific' (2011) www.unhcr.org/4fc880b80.html accessed 30 April 2013.

UNHCR, 'Submission by the United Nations High Commissioner for Refugees for the Office of the High Commissioner for Human Rights' Compilation Report – Universal Periodic Review' (April 2012).

UNHCR Japan, 'Fact Sheet' (September 2012) http://www.unhcr.org/5000196c13.pdf accessed 30 April 2013.

UNHCR Regional Representative for China and Mongolia, 'Factsheet' (September 2012)

Wolman A, 'North Korean Asylum Seekers and Dual Nationality' (2013) 24 IJRL 793.

Xue H and Jin Q, 'International Treaties in the Chinese Domestic Legal System' (2009) 8 CJIL 299.

Cases

C v Director of Immigration, FACV No 18, 19 and 20 of 2011 (Court of Final Appeal, 25 March 2013).

CH v Director of Immigration [2011] HKCU 758.

FB v Director of Immigration [2008] HKEC 2072.

MA v Director of Immigration [2012] HKCU 2413.

Secretary for Security v Sakthevel Prabakar [2005] 1 HKLRD 289.
Ubamaka Edward Wilson v Secretary for Security [2012] HKEC 1757.

Chapter 16
Conclusions: the Future of the Regional Protection of Asylum Seekers

Ademola Abass and Francesca Ippolito

If this book has demonstrated anything, it is probably that the problem of the regional protection of asylum seekers is multi-faceted and defies easy solutions. There are as many general problems as there are region-specific ones besetting the protection of asylum seekers by regional systems, and it is nothing short of oversimplification to advocate the enactment of more laws or more regional enforcement machineries, such as courts and human rights courts, as a panacea. The existence of functioning regional systems in Europe undoubtedly justifies the need for such institutions, but the fact that Africa has more regional courts than any other region in the world, and is endowed with pivotal groundbreaking treaties, has had little or no impact on the implementation of an effective human rights agenda in general and the protection of asylum seekers in particular.

It is important not to confuse States' ready conclusion of treaties with their preparedness to fulfil the obligations contained therein. The African Union's adoption of the IDP Convention in 2012 has been hailed as a milestone, just as with many of the organization's multilateral endeavours. But the question will always arise: what is the value of adopting treaties that will never (or may never) be implemented? Is it not more pragmatic and sensible to adopt one modest treaty that will be implemented and achieve realistic objectives than pursue tons of ambitious conventions, the majority of which will be left to rot in the archives of unconcerned organizations soon after the fanfare of adoption ceremonies ends?

The lesson from the African example seems to be that if care is not taken then regional human rights systems are an end in themselves rather than being a means to an end. If the end of regional legal regimes and enforcement mechanisms is an effective protection of asylum seekers, then the absence of regional laws and enforcement institutions has not spelt doom for asylum seekers in Southeast Asia where some States with strong cultures of rule of law and democratic governance, such as Hong Kong, have been able to fill the regional void by resourceful national legislation. The point being made here is not that regional regimes and systems have no value – and this book has shown that they very much do – but that the issue is that regional systems should not be judged simply by virtue of their presence or existence, but by their ability to discharge an effective regime of asylum seekers' protection.

It is beyond doubt that States will always vie for control over the governance of asylum issues despite the existence of community or regional laws which aim to unify the treatment of asylum seekers and regional enforcement mechanisms and hold States accountable when they breach their international obligations towards asylum seekers. States' sensitivity over asylum matters is not a malady peculiar to the less progressive Global South or developing world but, as many cases involving the EU Member States before the European Court of Human Right discussed in this book demonstrate, the North has had its fair share of this reluctance syndrome. Protectionist behaviour in matters of asylum-seeking should be expected to worsen or, at the very least, not to ease while such global threats as terrorism are on the increase, and for as long as States' economic fortunes dwindle and collapse. To expect States which themselves rely on financial handouts (or bailouts) from others to survive – Greece, Spain, Italy, Portugal and Ireland are some recent examples – to happily embrace obligations that could only deepen their economic woes is grossly unrealistic. Certainly, if the conflicts in Africa continue unabated, if autocratic governments across the globe do not yield to democratic governance, it should be expected that even the most kind-hearted of States might soon start showing symptoms of 'receiving fatigue' towards asylum seekers.

The fact that each region comprises people that are uniquely different in terms of culture and cosmogony instructs that solutions to the global crisis in asylum protection must reflect diverse realities. It will be difficult to make laws that will enable receiving States to clinically separate genuine asylum seekers from those randomly shopping for nicer lives abroad. Yet, showing total disregard for cultural predilections of peoples who seek asylum or automatically treating every asylum seeker as a common criminal simply because they do not fit into predetermined admission criteria is hardly a good solution to what is truly a daunting problem.

We should not also expect the problem of voluntary repatriation to be determined solely by law so that as soon as the situations which necessitated asylum have ceased then refugees must voluntarily return to their countries of origin. While provisions that afford asylum seekers this opportunity are golden, they should not be used as a pretext to exact subtle pressure on asylum seekers to embark on hazardous journeys. The momentary termination of a malady, such as the collapse of an authoritarian government or end of a civil war, does not automatically presuppose safety. Africa is replete with examples where particular ethnic, religious or tribal groups are subjected to fierce persecution after formal cessation of hostilities. Thus, encouraging an asylum seeker to embark on a voluntary repatriation during what might yet turn out to be only an interlude may be too risky.

However, laws can ensure that no one is unjustifiably denied the protection and enjoyment of their rights just because a State or a regional organization fails to set up institutions that can help determine whether those rights have been violated, and where breaches have occurred, to make available the best forum where they can be vindicated. This standard should be the common denominator for an effective protection of the rights of asylum seekers across the board. It is highly commendable that States occasionally offer protection to asylum seekers where there are no effective regional systems or any regional system at all for the asylum purpose. South Asia urgently needs to develop a robust regional asylum protection system. A region home to almost a third of the world's population and some of its most advanced and developing economies deserves more than leaving the crucial issues of asylum protection to the wanton generosity of individual States.

Cooperation between individual States and regional organizations has begun in the areas of asylum protection. As we have seen in this book, the European Union especially has developed such relations with many States in Africa and in the Middle East. Such State/region relations is also strong between China and the Africa Union, and it may be that extending this relation to the area of asylum protection is desirable, especially given the increasing outflows of Africans to China.

However, interregional cooperation for asylum seekers' protection purposes is almost a rarity. The primordial version of this relation, which began between Asia and Africa in the 1960s as discussed in this book, has neither been refined nor enhanced to adapt to evolutionary trends in the field of asylum over the years. Yet incidences of collaboration between regions have increased in other endeavours, such as in trade and economy, politics and institutions-building. Trans-equatorial collaboration – North/South and South/South – is on the rise and it is hoped that these models could be brought to bear strongly on the protection of asylum seekers.

Areas of tension between asylum-generating and asylum-receiving countries need to be ironed out and more resources need to be invested by rich countries in order to help their developing counterparts to develop stronger economies and be able to deal with chronic shortages of much needed expertise in order to drive infrastructural developments in those countries. Without decisively identifying and tackling the causes of asylum from their roots – though such endeavours admittedly require a total rethinking of the approach – adopting more laws and setting up more institutions will only be treating the symptoms of asylum protection crisis and not the real ailment.

In the meantime, the various efforts being made across globe –the EU revisiting and recasting its legislation, Africa creating multiple institutions and adopting more treaties, Latin America using different fora to continue to advocate the issue – are all steps in the right direction. It may be that keeping the asylum theme visible in the public domain through small measures is the best means of ensuring that it does not disappear from the global radar or be swallowed by such big beasts as the fight against terrorism. Realistically, States cannot be expected to respond equally to threats posed by those who at worst they regard as constituting strains on their resources and those whose very presence on their territories threaten the life and limb of the State itself.

While this distinction may serve to explain why the protection of asylum seekers has not received the kind of attention both in terms of political will and the investment of huge resources that the global fight against terrorism has attracted, such a distinction is hardly tenable in the present day. What is beginning to emerge is that agents of terror are today mostly recruited from the disillusioned, the downtrodden and the frustrated segments of the society. One wonders if refugee camps where hundreds or even thousands of needy individuals, already traumatized and psychologically damaged in their own countries, are locked up often for as long as five years, ill-fed, poorly educated and routinely humiliated, all in the name of being processed into acceptable members of a foreign land, do not risk falling prey to dangerous purposes. Avoiding this unintended consequence requires prioritizing the welfare of human beings over long, laborious and often-tortuous asylum application processes. Achieving a better regime for the protection of asylum seekers requires putting people before politics, and putting the welfare of humans before consideration of State security. For the truth is if human beings do not feel secure, there can hardly be security for the State, and it is in the deft management of the two that a better future for asylum protection can be guaranteed.

Index

A v the Netherlands 183
Abdolkhani and Karimnia v Turkey 196–7, 199, 202
Abdulkhakov v Russia 207
accelerated procedures 205
Africa
- Asian African Legal Consultative Organization (AALCO) 313–18
- human rights
  - application of to asylum seekers 56–62
  - Charter on Human and Peoples' Rights 1981 27–9, 46–7, 48, 56–62, 221
  - Commission on Human and Peoples' Rights 39, 47–8
  - Court of Human Rights 49–54
  - Court of Justice and Human Rights 54–6
  - improvements needed 62–3
  - National Human Rights Institutions (NHRIs) 91–4, 96–101, 104–7
- and myths concerning asylum crisis 4
- post-colonial era 20
- sub-regional frameworks
  - beginnings of 67–8
  - direct provisions and standards 71–6
  - EAC 80
  - East African Community (EAC) 71, 72–3
  - ECCAS 74–5
  - economic focus of organizations 68–70
  - ECOWAS 74–5, 81–3
  - founding treaties 71–3
  - free movement Protocols 78–9
  - human rights instruments 77–8
  - institutions, role of 79–83
  - Intergovernmental Authority for Development (IGAD) 71, 73, 81
  - International Conference on the Great Lakes Region (ICGLR) 71–2, 73, 80–81
  - international instruments, use of by 76
  - legislative processes, documents related to 73–5
  - SADC 74–5
- women
  - Charter on Human and People's Rights 221
  - domestic violence cases 228–30
  - female genital mutilation (FGM) cases 231–9, 232n96
  - human trafficking cases 240
  - Particular Social Groups (PSGs) 224, 227, 231–9
  - Protocol on the Rights of Women in Africa 221–2

African Institute for Human Rights and Development v Guinea 58
African Union
- Charter on Democracy, Elections and Governance (ACDEG) 33–4
- Charter on Human and Peoples' Rights 1981 27–9
- Charter on the Rights and Welfare of the Child 29–30
- Common African Defense and Security Policy (CADSP) 32–3
- compared to OAU 30
- Constitutive Act 31
- Convention Governing the Specific Aspects of Refugee Problems in Africa 1969 21–7
- Coordinating Committee on Assistance and Protection to Refugees,

Returnees and Internally Displaced Persons in Africa (CCAR) 34–5
Grand Bay Declaration and Action Plan 1999 37–8
Humanitarian Affairs, Refugee and Displaced Persons Division (HARDP) 35
Kigali Declaration 2003 38–9
Permanent Representatives Committee's (PRC) Sub-Committee on Refugees, Returnees and Internally Displaced Persons 35–6
Protocol relating to the Establishment of the Peace and Security Council (PSC Protocol) 31–2
Protocol to the Charter on Human and Peoples' Rights on the Rights of Women in Africa 29
shortcomings of system 42–3
soft law approaches 36–41
Ahmed v Austria 180
Al Hanchi v Bosnia and Herzegovina 183–4
Al-Skeini v UK 205–6, 207
American Convention on Human Rights (ACHR) 270, 274, 281, 284–5
American Declaration on the Rights and Duties of Man (ADHR) 270, 274
Andrea Mortlock v USA 282–3
anti-terrorism, expulsions based on 176–84
Arakaki, O. 351
ASEAN *see* Association of Southeast Asian Nations (ASEAN)
Asia-Pacific region
and myths concerning asylum crisis 6
refugee problem in 295–6
see also Association of Southeast Asian Nations (ASEAN); East Asian, 1951 Convention parties in; Southeast Asian region
Asian African Legal Consultative Organization (AALCO) 313–18
Association of Southeast Asian Nations (ASEAN)
Bangkok Declaration 1993 302–3
Bangkok Declaration on Irregular Migration 1999 299–300
Chairman's statement Mar 2009 307
Charter and Community 302
differences between members 301–2
formation of 301
Hanoi Plan of Action (HPA) 1998 304
and human rights 302–9
Human Rights Declaration (AHRD) 309–13
human trafficking 298–300
irregular migration 297–300
national security and refugees 297–300
Political-Security Community (APSC) 305–6
security and human security 305–9
Socio-Cultural Community (ASCC) Blueprint 306
Vientiane Action Programme (VAP) 2004 304–5
see also Southeast Asian region
asylum compared to refuge 250–51
asylum crisis
causes of 3
myths concerning 4–6
wider definition of 3–4
asylum seekers
cat-and-mouse game with host states 3
definition of compared to refugees 15–16
Auad v Bulgaria 184

Babar Ahmad and others v UK 182–3
Bangkok Declaration 1993 302–3
Bangkok Declaration on Irregular Migration 1999 299–300, 303
Bangkok Principles 314–18
Banjul Charter 27–9, 46–7, 48
benefits, withdrawal of 138–9
Brasilia Declaration 262–3

Caballero-Anthony, M. 298, 307
Cartagena Declaration 252–7
Chahal v UK 176–8, 179
Chang-Muy, F. 340
Charter on Democracy, Elections and Governance (ACDEG) 33–4
Charter on Human and Peoples' Rights 1981 27–9, 46–7, 48
application to asylum seekers 56–62

discrimination, anti- 57–8
gender 221
non-refoulement principle 58–60
Charter on the Rights and Welfare of the Child 29–30
children
Charter on the Rights and Welfare of the Child 29–30
Grand Bay Declaration and Action Plan 1999 37–8
China 359–64
civil society
Japan 354–5
Republic of Korea 355–6
colonial era, end of and asylum-seeking in Africa 20
Commission on Human and Peoples' Rights
mandate 47–8
provisional measures, capacity for 49
Special Rapporteur on Refugees, Asylum Seekers, Migrants and Internally Displaced Persons 39–40
United Nations High Commissioner for Refugees (UNHCR) 40–41
Commission on Human Rights and Administrative Justice in Ghana (CHRAJ) 89, 98, 105
Common African Defense and Security Policy (CADSP) 32–3
Common European Asylum System (CEAS)
access to justice 132
aims of 113
detention of asylum seekers 133
Dublin Regulation 124–30
eligibility criteria 119–24
EURODAC system 129–30
gender 122–3
homosexuality 123–4
legal assistance, access to 133–4
Procedure Directive 130–34
Qualification Directive 117–24
Recast Proposal for Qualification Directive 118
Reception Conditions Directive 134–9
second phase of legislation 114–15, 114n6
subsidiary protection 117, 118–19, 120
time limits 132–3
Comprehensive Plan of Action (CPA), Southeast Asia
conditions leading to 329–33
end result of 338–40
Indochinese refugee crisis 329–31
Orderly Departure Program (ODP) 329–30
positive impact of 327–8
screening process 334–6
sections of 332–3
Vietnamese refugees 329–30, 338–40
Constitutive Act of the African Union (AU Act) 31
Convention Governing the Specific Aspects of Refugee Problems in Africa 1969 21–7
denouncement of provisions by states 26
discrimination, anti- 25
human rights 26
Kigali Declaration 39
limitations and exclusions 25–6
non-refoulement principle 24
right to asylum 23
subversive activities, provisions against 25
voluntary repatriation 24, 61–2
Convention on the Elimination of all forms of Discrimination against Women (CEDAW) 217
Coordinating Committee on Assistance and Protection to Refugees, Returnees and Internally Displaced Persons in Africa (CCAR) 34–5
country of origin, information on 230
Court of Justice and Human Rights (African) 54–6
credibility, refusal of asylum on grounds of 200–202, 240
Crisp, J. 68
Cruz Varas and others v Sweden 174–5

D v UK 186–8
Dakar Plan of Action 106–7
decision-making, scope and quality of 198–200

Declaration on the Elimination of Violence against Women 218
defence (Common African Defence and Security Policy (CADSP)) 32–3
democracy (Charter on Democracy, Elections and Governance (ACDEG)) 33–4
denial, culture of 200–202
denouncement of provisions by states 26
detention of asylum seekers
  European Convention on Human Rights 188–9, 193
  Inter-American human rights system 286–7
  Procedures Directive 133
  Reception Conditions Directive 136–7
  visits to centres by NHRIs 97–100
determination procedures
  access to 202
  Southeast Asia's Comprehensive Plan of Action (CPA) 334–6
deterrent/push-back practices 205–8
disbelief, culture of 200–202
discrimination, anti-
  Charter on Human and Peoples' Rights 1981 57–8
  Convention Governing the Specific Aspects of Refugee Problems in Africa 1969 25
domestic violence cases 228–30
Dublin Regulation 124–30

East African Community (EAC) 71, 72–3, 80
East Asian, 1951 Convention parties in
  China 359–64
  Japan 351–5
  Republic of Korea 355–9
Economic Community of Central African States (ECCAS) 74–5
Economic Community of West African States (ECOWAS) 74–5, 78–9, 81–3
effective control in determining jurisdiction 206–7
elections (Charter on Democracy, Elections and Governance (ACDEG)) 33–4
Elgafaji c. Staatsecretsris van Justitie 120–21
eligibility criteria in CEAS 119–24
employment
  access to and Reception Conditions Directive 137
  Inter-American human rights system 287–8
Ergashevv Russia 188–9
EURODAC system 129–30
European Asylum Support Office (EASO) 114, 157
European Convention on Human Rights
  accelerated procedures 205
  Article 3
    interception and return 184–6
    national-security based expulsions 176–84
    and *non-refoulement* 172–6
    socio-economic rights 186–8
  Article 6 182
  credibility, refusal of asylum on grounds of 200–202
  detention conditions 188–9, 193
  determination procedures, access to 202
  deterrent/push-back practices 205–8
  and foreign nationals 191–4
  form and substance of rights 204–5
  hurdles for asylum seekers 192–3
  individual case decisions 208–10
  non-refoulement 193–4, 197–8, 199
  procedural requirements 202–4
  remedies for asylum seekers 196–210
  scope and quality of decision-making 198–200
European Court of Justice (ECJ), extended scope and impact of 115
European Union
  Common European Asylum System (CEAS)
    access to justice 132
    aims of 113
    detention of asylum seekers 133
    Dublin Regulation 124–30
    eligibility criteria 119–24
    EURODAC system 129–30
    gender 122–3

homosexuality 123–4
improvements still needed 139–40
legal assistance, access to 133–4
Procedures Directive 130–34
Qualification Directive 117–24
Recast Proposal for Qualification Directive 118
Reception Conditions Directive 134–9
second phase of legislation 114–15, 114n6
state responsibility for application 124–30
subsidiary protection 117, 118–19, 120
time limits 132–3
European Asylum Support Office (EASO) 114
European Court of Justice (ECJ) 115
external aspects
cooperation with sending/transit countries 146–7
FRONTEX 151
Global Approach to Migration (GAM) 150–52
Hague Programme 152–3
history of 147–55
Integrated Border Management (IBM) 150, 151–2
Joint Resettlement Programme 155–7
Pact on Immigration and Asylum 153
Procedures Directive 161–2
protracted situations 155–9
readmission agreements 159–63
Regional Protection Programmes (RPPs) 157–9
resettlement 155–7
shift in focus needed 147
Stockholm Programme 153–4
Tampere European Council 149
Treaty of Amsterdam 147–8
Treaty on the Functioning of the European Union (TFEU) 154–5
internal/external dichotomy 145–6
and international protection system 116–17
and myths concerning asylum crisis 5
procedural issues for asylum seekers 194–6
Qualification Directive 220
see also European Convention on Human Rights

fast-track procedures 205
Feller, Erika 335
female genital mutilation (FGM) cases 231–9, 232n96
fingerprints, database of 129–30
Fontaine, P.-M. 316
Fornah 231–9, 232n96
founding treaties 71–3
Francis, A. 361
free movement Protocols 78–9
FRONTEX 151

gender
Common European Asylum System (CEAS) 122–3
country of origin, information on 230
domestic violence cases 228–30
female genital mutilation (FGM) cases 231–9
in international law 217–22
non-State actors, protection from 224–5
Particular Social Groups (PSGs) 224, 227
persecutory treatment unique to women 216
private v public harm 222–7
soft law 220–21
UN Refugee Convention 1951 214–16
Ghana, Commission on Human Rights and Administrative Justice (CHRAJ) 89, 98, 105
Global Approach to Migration (GAM) 150–52
Goodwin-Gill, G. 227
governance (Charter on Democracy, Elections and Governance (ACDEG)) 33–4
Grand Bay Declaration and Action Plan 1999 37–8

Hague Programme 152–3
Haiti 288–9
Haitian Interdictions cases 273, 275, 277, 285
Hanoi Plan of Action (HPA) 1998 304
healthcare
European Convention on Human Rights, Article 3 186–8
Reception Conditions Directive 138
Helton, Arthur 336, 340
Henning Becker v Denmark 208–9
Hilal v UK 200–201
Hirsi Jamaa and others v Italy 186, 191, 206–8, 208, 209–10
HM (Somali Women – Particular Social Group) Somalia 239
Hode and Abdi v United Kingdom 120
homosexuality 123–4
Hong Kong 366–9
Horvath 225–7
host states, cat-and-mouse game with asylum seekers 3
Hsien-li, Tan 301
human rights
Africa
application of rights to asylum seekers 56–62
Charter on Human and Peoples' Rights 1981 27–9, 46–7, 48, 221
Commission on Human and Peoples' Rights 47–8
Convention Governing the Specific Aspects of Refugee Problems in Africa 1969 26
Court of Human Rights 49–54
Court of Justice and Human Rights 54–6
Grand Bay Declaration and Action Plan 1999 37–8
improvements needed 62–3
Kigali Declaration 2003 38–9
NHRIs 91–4
voluntary repatriation 61–2
ASEAN Human Rights Declaration (AHRD) 309–13
Association of Southeast Asian Nations (ASEAN) 302–9
Cartagena Declaration 253–7
European Convention on Human Rights
accelerated procedures 205
credibility, refusal of asylum on grounds of 200–202
detention conditions 188–9, 193
determination procedures, access to 202
deterrent/push-back practices 205–8
and foreign nationals 191–4
form and substance of rights 204–5
individual case decisions 208–10
interception and return 184–6
national-security based expulsions 176–84
non-refoulement 172–6, 193–4, 197–8, 199
procedural requirements 202–4
remedies for asylum seekers 196–210
scope and quality of decision-making 198–200
socio-economic rights 186–8
and Hong Kong 364–9
Human Rights Commissions (HRCs) 89, 105–7
Inter-American human rights system
American Convention on Human Rights (ACHR) 270, 274, 281
American Declaration on the Rights and Duties of Man (ADHR) 270, 274
asylum as human right 273–80
bars to removal 282–3
cooperation in the region 288–9
detention of asylum seekers 286–7
employment 287–8
engagement with asylum seekers and refugees 272–3
inspiration from other regional systems 288
institutions 271–3
Inter-American Commission on Human Rights 271–2
Inter-American Court of Human Rights 272
non-refoulement 281–2

Organization of American States (OAS) 269
procedural guarantees 277–80
standards 269–71
National Human Rights Institutions (NHRIs)
African, and OPCAT 104–7
African examples 96–101
challenges faced by 108
definition 90
forms of 88–92
Human Rights Commissions (HRCs) 89, 96–7
increase in 87–8
legitimacy and credibility of 95
Ombudsman offices 88–9
Optional Protocol to the UN Convention Against Torture (OPCAT) 101–7
Paris Principles compliance 90–91
regional arrangements 91–2
scope and mandates of 94–6
strategic litigation, use of by 100–101
visits to detention centres 97–100
sub-regional frameworks 77–8
human security in Southeast Asian region 305–9
human trafficking
Africa 240
Southeast Asia 298–300
Humanitarian Affairs, Refugee and Displaced Persons Division (HARDP) 35

IM v France 205
individual case decisions 208–10, 279
Indochinese refugee crisis 329–31
Indra, Doreen 216
information, right to 129
Integrated Border Management (IBM) 150, 151–2
Inter-American human rights system
American Convention on Human Rights (ACHR) 270, 274, 281
American Declaration on the Rights and Duties of Man (ADHR) 270, 274
asylum as human right 273–80
bars to removal 282–3
detention of asylum seekers 286–7
employment 287–8
engagement with asylum seekers and refugees 272–3
equality 285
institutions 271–3
Inter-American Commission on Human Rights 271–2
non-refoulement 279–80, 281–2
Organization of American States (OAS) 269
procedural guarantees 277–80
standards 269–71
interception and return 277–8
European Convention on Human Rights, Article 3 184–6
Intergovernmental Authority for Development (IGAD) 71, 73, 81
internally displaced persons (IDPs)
Coordinating Committee on Assistance and Protection to Refugees, Returnees and Internally Displaced Persons in Africa (CCAR) 34–5
Permanent Representatives Committee's (PRC) Sub-Committee on Refugees, Returnees and Internally Displaced Persons 35–6
Special Rapporteur on Refugees, Asylum Seekers, Migrants and Internally Displaced Persons 39–40
International Conference on the Great Lakes Region (ICGLR) 71–2, 73–4
International Criminal Court (ICC) 219–20
international law
gender issues in 217–22
and Hong Kong 364–9
International Tribunals for Former Rwanda (ICTR) 219
International Tribunals for Former Yugoslavia (ICTY) 219
interpretation services 129

Jabari v Turkey 198, 202–3
Japan as 1951 Convention party 351–5
Joint Resettlement Programme (EU) 155–7

Jones, Lee 308
judicial processes, scope and quality of 198–200

Kenyan Human Rights Commission (KNCHR) 89, 96–7
Kigali Declaration 2003 38–9, 93
Korea
 North Koreans 359, 361–2, 363
 Republic of 355–9

labour market, access to
 Inter-American human rights system 287–8
 Reception Conditions Directive 137
Lambert, H. 193–4
Latin America
 Brasilia Declaration 262–3
 Cartagena Declaration 252–7
 Mexico Declaration and Plan of Action 258–61
 and myths concerning asylum crisis 5
 refuge compared to asylum 250–51
 regional approach 246–8
 right of asylum in 248–51
 San Jose Declaration on Refugees and Displaced Persons 257–8
legal assistance, access to 133–4, 279
Lindela Repatriation Centre 98–100
litigation, strategic, and NHRIs, use of by 100–101
Loren Rieve et al v Mexico 285–6

Macau 363–4
Malaysia 334–5
Mariel Cubans 286–7
MD (women) Ivory Coast CG 230–31
medical treatment and European Convention on Human Rights 186–8
Mexico Declaration and Plan of Action 258–61
minors, unaccompanied, and Reception Conditions Directive 137
M.S.S. v Belgium and Greece 125, 128, 184–6, 198–9, 199–200, 201, 203–5
Muntarbhorn, Vitit 297, 311

N v UK 187
NA v United Kingdom 121–2
Namba, M. 354–5
National Human Rights Institutions (NHRIs)
 Africa 91–4, 96–101
 challenges faced by 108
 definition 90
 forms of 88–92
 Human Rights Commissions (HRCs) 89, 96–7
 increase in 87–8
 legitimacy and credibility of 95
 Ombudsman offices 88–9
 Optional Protocol to the UN Convention Against Torture (OPCAT) 101–7
 Paris Principles compliance 90–91
 policy/legislative level work 96–7
 regional arrangements 91–2
 scope and mandates of 94–6
 strategic litigation, use of by 100–101
 visits to detention centres 97–100
National Preventative Mechanisms (NPTs) 101–4
national security
 expulsions based on 176–84
 Southeast Asia 297–8
non-refoulement
 Bangkok Principles 317
 Charter on Human and Peoples' Rights 1981 58–60
 China 361–2
 Convention Governing the Specific Aspects of Refugee Problems in Africa 1969 24
 European Convention on Human Rights 172–6, 193–4, 197–8, 199
 Hong Kong 366–8
 Inter-American human rights system 279–80, 281–2
non-State actors, protection from 180, 224–5
North Koreans 359, 361–2, 363
N.S. and M.E. 126–7, 128

Oberei, Pia 317
Ombudsman offices 88–9

Optional Protocol to the UN Convention Against Torture (OPCAT) 101–7
Orderly Departure Program (ODP) 329–30
Organisation Mondiale Contre La Torture v Rwanda 57–8, 61
Organization of African Unity (OAU)
  compared to AU 30
  Convention Governing the Specific Aspects of Refugee Problems in Africa 315–17
  Grand Bay Declaration and Action Plan 1999 37–8
  soft law approaches 36–41
Organization of American States (OAS) 269
Othman (Abu Qatada) v UK 180–82
outsourcing decision-making 207

'P' and 'M' v Secretary of State for the Home Department 228–30
Particular Social Groups (PSGs) 224, 227, 231–9
Peace and Security Council Protocol (PSC Protocol) 31–2, 36
Permanent Representatives Committee's (PRC) Sub-Committee on Refugees, Returnees and Internally Displaced Persons 35–6
PO (Trafficked Women) Nigeria CG 240
post-colonial era and asylum-seeking in Africa 20
PRC Sub-Comm *see* Permanent Representatives Committee's (PRC) Sub-Committee on Refugees, Returnees and Internally Displaced Persons
private v public harm 222–7
procedures
  accelerated 205
  Europe 194–6
  Inter-American human rights system 277–80
  onerous, and ECHR 202–4
Procedures Directive 130–34, 161–2
property rights of returnees 74
Protocol relating to the Establishment of the Peace and Security Council of the African Union (PSC Protocol) 31–2, 36
Protocol to the Charter on Human and Peoples' Rights on the Rights of Women in Africa 29
protracted situations
  European Union 155–9
  Southeast Asia 326–7
public v private harm 222–7
push-back practices 205–8, 277–8

Qualification Directive 117–24, 220, 226, 230, 234n109
quality of decision-making 198–200

Rafael Ferrer-Mazorra et al v USA 285
readmission agreements 159–63
Reception Conditions Directive 134–9
refoulement see non-refoulement
refuge compared to asylum 250–51
refugee camps, visits to by NHRIs 97–100
  see also detention of asylum seekers
Refugee Convention 1951 231–9
  East Asian parties to
    China 359–64
    Japan 351–5
    Republic of Korea 355–9
  and gender 214–16
refugees
  Cartagena Declaration 253–7
  Charter on Human and Peoples' Rights 1981 56–62
  defining 22–3
  definition of compared to asylum seekers 15–16
  Special Rapporteur on Refugees, Asylum Seekers, Migrants and Internally Displaced Persons 39–40
  use of term 16
regional economic committees (RECs) 68–70
regional integration
  defined 68–9
  new regionalism 69
  regional economic committees (RECs) 68–70
  shallow/deep 69
Regional Protection Programmes (RPPs) 157–9
Renshaw, Catherine 310

repatriation
  centres, visits to by NHRIs 97–100
  Comprehensive Plan of Action (CPA) 336–8
  Convention Governing the Specific Aspects of Refugee Problems in Africa 1969 24
Republic of Korea 355–9
resettlement 155–7
returnees
  Coordinating Committee on Assistance and Protection to Refugees, Returnees and Internally Displaced Persons in Africa (CCAR) 34–5
  Permanent Representatives Committee's (PRC) Sub-Committee on Refugees, Returnees and Internally Displaced Persons 35–6
  property rights 74
Robinson, W.C. 335

S v MIMA 229–30
Saadi v Italy 178–80
safe third country concept 161–2
Salah Sheekh v Netherlands 197
San Jose Declaration on Refugees and Displaced Persons 257–8
scope and quality of decision-making 198–200
screening under Southeast Asia's Comprehensive Plan of Action (CPA) 334–6
security
  Common African Defence and Security Policy (CADSP) 32–3
  expulsions based on 176–84
  Southeast Asia 297–8
  Southeast Asian region 305–9
Sharpe, Marina 316
Singh v Belgium 201–2
SK (FGM-ethnic groups) Liberia CG 238n131
Skeldon, Ronald 297–8
social welfare in Reception Conditions Directive 138
socio-economic rights and European Convention on Human Rights 186–8
Soering v UK 173–4, 177
soft law
  gender 220–21
  Organization of African Unity (OAU) 36–41
Solemn Declaration on a Common African Defence and Security Policy (CADSP) 32–3
South African Human Rights Commission (SAHRC) 98–100, 105
South Korea 355–9
Southeast Asian region
  Asian African Legal Consultative Organization (AALCO) 313–18
  Bangkok Declaration 1993 302–3
  Bangkok Declaration on Irregular Migration 1999 299–300, 303
  Bangkok Principles 314–18
  Comprehensive Plan of Action (CPA)
    1951 Convention as useful tool only 340–41
    conditions leading to 329–33
    disowning of responsibility 336, 338
    end result of 338–40
    Indochinese refugee crisis 329–31
    lack of protection mechanisms after 340–42
    Orderly Departure Program (ODP) 329–30
    positive impact of 327–8
    repatriation 336–8
    screening process 334–6
    sections of 332–3
    Vietnamese refugees 329–30, 338–40
  fear of outsiders 297–8
  Hanoi Plan of Action (HPA) 1998 304
  human trafficking 298–300
  irregular migration 297–300
  national security 297–8
  OAU Convention Governing the Specific Aspects of Refugee Problems in Africa 315–17
  political problem, refugees as 297
  protracted situations 326–7
  security and human security 305–9

Vientiane Action Programme (VAP) 2004 304–5
see also Association of Southeast Asian Nations (ASEAN)
Southern Africa Development Community (SADC) 74–5, 78
Special Rapporteur on Refugees, Asylum Seekers, Migrants and Internally Displaced Persons 39–40
Special Rapporteur on Violence against Women 218
Spijkerboer, T. 195
states
denouncement of provisions by
Convention Governing the Specific Aspects of Refugee Problems in Africa 1969 26
private v public harm 223–6
responsibility for asylum seekers 124–30
Stockholm Programme 153–4
strategic litigation, NHRIs' use of 100–101
sub-regional frameworks
beginnings of 67–8
direct provisions and standards 71–6
EAC 80
East African Community (EAC) 71, 72–3
ECCAS 74–5
economic focus of organizations 68–70
ECOWAS 74–5, 78–9, 81–3
founding treaties 71–3
free movement Protocols 78–9
human rights instruments 77–8
improving protection 83
indirect instruments 76–9
institutions, role of 79–83
Intergovernmental Authority for Development (IGAD) 71, 73, 81
International Conference on the Great Lakes Region (ICGLR) 71–2, 73–4, 80–81
international instruments, use of by 76
legislative processes, documents related to 73–5
SADC 74–5, 78
subsidiary protection 117, 118–19, 120
subversive activities, provisions against
Convention Governing the Specific Aspects of Refugee Problems in Africa 1969 25
lack of determination criteria 25
Sudan, FM (CG) 238
Sugimoto, D. 355

Tampere European Council 148–9
Terada, Takeshi 308
terrorism, anti-, expulsions based on 176–84
time limits 132–3
Towle, Richard 340
trafficking, human
African cases 240
Southeast Asia 298–300
Treaty of Amsterdam 147–8
Treaty on the Functioning of the European Union (TFEU) 154–5

Ugandan Human Rights Commission 96, 105, 106
United Nations
Convention on the Elimination of all forms of Discrimination against Women (CEDAW) 217
Declaration on the Elimination of Violence against Women 218
Refugee Convention 1951 231–9
East Asian parties to 351–64
and gender 214–16
Security Council Resolution 1325 218, 218n29
Special Rapporteur on Violence against Women 218
United Nations High Commissioner for Refugees (UNHCR)
African Commission on Human and Peoples' Rights 40–41
resettlement 156

Vientiane Action Programme (VAP) 2004 304–5
Vietnamese refugees 329–30, 338–40
Vilvarajah and others v UK 175, 198
VM (FGM-risks-Mungiki-Kikiyu-Gikuyu) Kenya CG 238–9

voluntary repatriation
  Convention Governing the Specific Aspects of Refugee Problems in Africa 1969 24
  human rights 61–2
vulnerable people in Reception Conditions Directive 137

Wayne Smith et al v USA 286
women
  Africa
    Charter on Human and People's Rights 221
    female genital mutilation (FGM) cases 231–9, 232n96
    human trafficking cases 240
    Particular Social Groups (PSGs) 231–9
    Protocol on the Rights of Women in Africa 221–2
  country of origin, information on 230
  domestic violence cases 228–30
  Grand Bay Declaration and Action Plan 1999 37–8
  international law, gender issues in 217–22
  non-State actors, protection from 224–5
  persecutory treatment unique to 216
  private v public harm 222–7
  Protocol to the Charter on Human and Peoples' Rights on the Rights of Women in Africa 29
  soft law 220–21
  UN Refugee Convention 1951 214–16
Women's Caucus for Gender Justice 219